"This is an insightful, helpful, and tactful presentation of Mormonism. It reflects extensive research, in-depth analysis, and valuable evaluation. It is a major contribution to the study of one of the largest and fastest growing religious groups in America."

—Dr. Norman Geisler
author,
President of Southern Evangelical Seminary

❊ ❊ ❊

"Richard Abanes is part of a generation of Christian writers who have come to recognize that responding to alternative religious movements...is not merely a matter of refuting a position. Rather, it requires a careful and thoughtful analysis.... No one, including believers in Mormonism, will question the charitable spirit in which he offers his case."

—Francis J. Beckwith
general editor of *The New Mormon Challenge;*
Associate Professor of Church-State Studies and
Associate Director of the J. M. Dawson Institute
of Church-State Studies, Baylor University

"Richard Abanes combines careful research with journalistic skill to give us insight to some of the major errors of Mormon doctrine, but does so in a respectful manner so that his words may be read, hopefully, by Mormons who are willing to reevaluate the teachings of their religion. Abanes provides numerous interesting tidbits in his sidebars, many that I had never considered or read before....I...believe that Christians will be greatly benefited by reading *Becoming Gods*."

—H. Wayne House
Distinguished Professor of Biblical and Theological Studies at Faith Seminary, Adjunct Professor of Law at Trinity Law School of Trinity International University

☖ ☖ ☖

"*Becoming Gods* takes evangelicals and Mormons into the next generation of amicable confrontation. Abanes' book is extensively researched and abounding in Web-site citations accessible to anyone interested in verifying source material....This volume will keep you informed on the most current responses to some of the latest and best defenses of the Mormon faith and will prepare you for that challenge and others to come."

—Shandon L. Guthrie
adjunct professor of philosophy at the University of Nevada, Las Vegas; writer and speaker on apologetics, comparative religions, and ethical issues

Becoming
Gods

Richard
Abanes

HARVEST HOUSE PUBLISHERS

EUGENE, OREGON

Unless otherwise indicated, all Scripture quotations are taken from the King James Version of the Bible.

Verses marked NASB are taken from the New American Standard Bible ®, © 1960, 1962, 1963, 1968, 1971, 1972, 1973, 1975, 1977, 1995 by The Lockman Foundation. Used by permission. (www.Lockman.org)

Verses marked NIV are taken from the HOLY BIBLE, NEW INTERNATIONAL VERSION®. NIV®. Copyright © 1973, 1978, 1984 by the International Bible Society. Used by permission of Zondervan. All rights reserved.

Verses marked ASV are taken from the American Standard Version of the Bible.

Verses marked NEB are taken from The New English Bible, copyright © Oxford University Press and Cambridge University Press 1961, 1970. All rights reserved.

Cover by Left Coast Design, Portland, Oregon

Cover photo of Salt Lake City Mormon steeples © Kevin Fleming/Corbis

Cover photo of Angel Moroni of Washington Mormon Temple © Paul A. Souders/Corbis

BECOMING GODS
Copyright © 2004 by Richard Abanes
Published by Harvest House Publishers
Eugene, Oregon 97402
www.harvesthousepublishers.com

Library of Congress Cataloging-in-Publication Data
Abanes, Richard.
  Becoming gods / Richard Abanes.
    p. cm.
  Includes bibliographical references and index.
  ISBN 0-7369-1355-6 (pbk.)
  1. Church of Jesus Christ of Latter-day Saints—Controversial literature. 2. Mormon Church—Controversial literature. I. Title.
  BX8645.A22 2004
  289.3—dc22   2004001424

All rights reserved. No part of this publication may be reproduced, stored in a retrieval system, or transmitted in any form or by any means—electronic, mechanical, digital, photocopy, recording, or any other—except for brief quotations in printed reviews, without the prior permission of the publisher.

Printed in the United States of America

04 05 06 07 08 09 10 11 / DP-MS / 10 9 8 7 6 5 4 3 2 1

To Bob Passantino—dear friend, wise teacher, and trusted advisor

*Thanks for everything. You ran the race well. The race has been won.
Enjoy your eternal reward. You will be missed beyond words.*

THANK YOU

Evangeline, my wife, for your patience and understanding. Mom and Dad, for your continuing love. Pastor Rick Muchow, for your friendship and counsel. Fellow servants of Christ, too numerous to mention, for your prayers. My Saddleback Church family, for your support and much-needed fellowship. My Mormon friends, for your willingness to share with me what you believe and why you believe it. My Mormon critics, for your words of correction and arguments, which have made me think about issues I may have otherwise overlooked. BYU professor Dan Peterson, for your kindheartedness toward me and your willingness to treat me with respect despite the doctrinal differences that separate us. Harvest House, for publishing this volume in hopes of further equipping the church and reaching out to Mormons in the spirit of Christ. Harvest House president, Bob Hawkins Jr.; acquisitions editor Terry Glaspey; and text editor Paul Gossard—for your hard work and dedication.

CONTENTS

"CAN'T WE ALL JUST GET ALONG?"

If we have the truth, [it] cannot be harmed by investigation.
If we have not the truth, it ought to be harmed. [1]
—J. Reuben Clark (1871–1961), Mormon apostle

I encountered the store's impressive display of Bibles just inside the main entrance. It was beautifully set up, so I stood there leafing through the Scriptures for about ten minutes. Then, it suddenly dawned on me that I was not only reading, but humming...humming along with dulcet tones being piped through the air. The vocalist, who sounded remarkably like Michael W. Smith, was singing a tender song about the sufferings Christ endured for us.

Out of curiosity I strolled over to the music section and, much to my surprise, found several CDs that looked as if they would blend quite nicely into my own collection. Before I could choose one, however, my eyes were drawn to some attractive stationery across the aisle. I also noticed a dozen or so shelves of what looked liked Christian fiction. I even found assorted calendars imprinted with daily Bible verses.

Everything was so familiar...so Christian. For a moment, I thought I might run into my pastor near the language and archaeology study guides. But such an encounter would have been quite unlikely since I was not in a Christian bookstore. The shop was owned by The Church of Jesus Christ of Latter-day Saints (LDS)—the Mormons.

Yet this same place had been labeled a "Christian" store by a friend of mine. That did not surprise me. The social, cultural, and theological lines dividing Mormonism and classic Christianity have been steadily blurring ever since 1890, when Mormons banned the earthly practice of polygamy. [2]

Today, this ongoing and increasing lack of delineation between the two faiths is largely because of

1. a willingness on the part of *some* Mormon leaders to be less than up-front with the public about the more controversial aspects of LDS history and theology

2. a trend among *some* Mormon scholars to make LDS beliefs sound quite mainstream

3. an evolution of thought within Mormonism that is moving *some* Latter-day Saints toward doctrinal opinions that are very close to evangelical views*

Added confusion over Mormonism's relationship to Christianity stems from the ethical–moral ground Latter-day Saints share with evangelicals.[3] Moreover, LDS Church members engage in typically evangelical activities (for example, listening to Christian radio programs, watching Christian TV shows, and reading Christian magazines).[4] Mormons also have joined with evangelicals "to counter destructive trends in the larger culture."[5]

Such a situation has given rise to several delicate questions:

• How can traditional Christians present and protect their faith, yet still honor Mormons as fellow theists (believers in a God) with whom they share many ethical–moral concerns?[6]

• What are the appropriate and accurate definitions of *Christian* and *Christianity?*

• Where is the dividing line between honest criticisms of Mormonism and ungodly verbal attacks?

Unfortunately, too many books not only fail to address these issues fairly, but they also tend to offer obsolete responses. Consider the standard Bible verses used by evangelicals against LDS beliefs—for example, Numbers 23:19; Psalm 90:2; John 4:24. All of these passages have been countered

---

* In general terms, an evangelical is a Christian who adheres to the traditional Protestant doctrines of God, salvation, and the authority and reliability of the Bible as outlined in the various creeds of Christendom and the writings of the Reformation era (about 1517–1560). Evangelicals also tend to stress one's personal relationship to God over mere attendance of a church. Evangelicalism should not be confused with Fundamentalism, which has become a term used derogatorily by the media and throughout the secular community for any Protestant Christians who appear to them to be anti-intellectual, overdogmatic, and excessively literal in their biblical interpretation.

by LDS scholars from Brigham Young University (BYU)—Robert L. Millet, Daniel C. Peterson, and Stephen E. Robinson, to name but a few.

Several of these same individuals now comprise a small cadre of Mormonism defenders who work under the auspices of BYU.[7] Their apologetic organization, known as the Foundation for Ancient Research and Mormon Studies (FARMS), produces highly technical material that seeks to defend LDS beliefs. FARMS "has become synonymous with encouraging and supporting 'faithful scholarship' on the Book of Mormon, the Book of Abraham, the Bible, other ancient scriptures and on related subjects."[8]

And along with their new defensive and offensive replies to Christians have come a flood of highly complex arguments. They defend Mormonism by using ancient Near East studies, by boldly changing classic LDS thinking, and by employing revisionism of Latter-day Saint history (much to the chagrin of non-Mormon historians). Also utilized are some rather novel interpretations of numerous biblical verses. Sadly, few Christians are equipped to discern which of these arguments have some merit, which are flawed, and which are patently false.

Up-to-Date Responses

Many evangelical books offer little help. Some are strident or mocking. Others repeat inaccuracies regarding LDS history. A few even contain errors relating to LDS beliefs and practices.[9] This is not to say that all materials generated by the "countercult" community, as it is called, are of no use. Literature produced by well-established and respected ministries to Latter-day Saints can be very helpful.[10] However, there is still a scarcity of widely available resources that deal head-on with the most recent and articulate arguments developed by LDS scholars, apologists, and leaders.

The lack of cutting-edge LDS-related work was highlighted in "Mormon Scholarship, Apologetics and Evangelical Neglect: Losing the Battle and Not Knowing It?" a 1998 *Trinity Journal* article by Christian scholars Paul Owen and Carl Mosser.[11] A review of this article published by the Latter-day Saint–owned *Meridian Magazine* cited the following "unprecedented and stunning admissions" made by Mosser and Owen:

- "There are, contrary to popular evangelical perceptions, legitimate Mormon scholars."

- "Mormon scholars and apologists...have, with varying degrees of success, answered most of the usual evangelical criticisms."

- "There are no books from an evangelical perspective that responsibly interact with contemporary LDS scholarly and apologetic writings."

- "The sophistication and erudition of LDS apologetics has risen considerably while evangelical responses have not."

- "Most involved in the counter-cult movement lack the skills and training necessary to answer Mormon scholarly apologetic."[12]

Such disclosures resulted in the 2002 release of *The New Mormon Challenge*, edited by Francis Beckwith, Carl Mosser, and Paul Owen, which was an attempt to fill the resource gap with scholarly Christian responses to LDS defenses of Mormonism. As the book's editors explained, "We have sought to evaluate Mormon theology in fresh ways and in areas that are rarely, if ever, discussed in other books on Mormonism."[13]

In a similar vein, I submit *Becoming Gods*. I, however, am not a scholar. So the following pages are not written according to rigid academic standards, but in a popular, journalistic style that is more like *Time* or *Newsweek* than anything else. (For those who wish to explore issues in greater depth, I have included additional examples, explanations, and responses in the notes, as well as many useful sources in the "Research Resources" section at the back of the book.)

Becoming Gods was born of my own discovery that there is indeed a lack of up-to-date, user-friendly material that

- compares twenty-first-century LDS belief with classic Christianity

- presents the most recent pro-Mormon arguments

- explains why evangelicals cannot accept these LDS arguments as valid

The need for resources like *Becoming Gods* was expressed long ago by the LDS Church's third president, John Taylor (1808–1887):

There is one of two things true. We are either labouring under one of the greatest delusions that ever afflicted the human race, or we

are under the direction of the great god. There is no half-way business about it.[14]

With a religion as theologically and historically vast as Mormonism
it is impossible to delve into every argument currently being used by
Latter-day Saints. Consequently, I have limited myself to the ones I have
heard most often repeated. My hope is that both evangelicals and Mormons will benefit from this volume by at least understanding how the
other camp sees things.

Discerning LDS Doctrine

I also should mention that Mormonism is currently experiencing some
interesting shifts of perspective. This is nothing new. Evolution in belief
has walked hand in hand with LDS doctrine since its earliest days.[15] But
now, thanks to the Internet, there seems to be more doctrinal drifting
among Mormons than ever before witnessed.

The Internet has provided innumerable pathways to controversial
information that most Mormons in the past could never have accessed.
Consequently, Mormons who are investigating this material have out of
necessity had to come up with radically new arguments to counter the
information they have found. But this has led to the adoption of many
nontraditional ideas.

Some onlookers have gone so far as to assert that there actually has
been a division of Mormons into two distinct groups: 1) those who adhere
to classic LDS thought (Chapel Mormons); and 2) those who have come
up with new twists on classic LDS teachings in order to counter Internet-
accessed information (Internet Mormons).[16] Consequently, one cannot
say that *all* Mormons believe this or *all* Mormons believe that. It would
be more accurate to recognize that there are at least three categories of
LDS doctrine:

(1) widespread and historically held positions; (2) widespread contemporary views; or (3) minority views permitted within contemporary Mormonism that seem to be the most plausible and
defensible of LDS options.[17]

Furthermore, one must be attentive to what constitutes *official* LDS doctrine and its *official* sources. Evangelicals have for many years made far too much of private speculations offered by LDS leaders, speculations that go beyond the teachings found in what Mormons acknowledge as their holy writings (the "Standard Works"): the Bible, the Book of Mormon, Doctrine and Covenants, and the Pearl of Great Price.

These works, except for the Bible, are equally authoritative. The Bible is God's Word only "as far as it is translated correctly."[18] This caveat means that the other texts take precedence over the Bible, which Mormons feel has been adulterated by "[i]gnorant translators, careless transcribers, or designing and corrupt priests."[19]

That opinion can be traced to Mormonism's founder, Joseph Smith (1805–1844). In a 1998 speech, Robert Millet noted that Smith "did not believe the Bible was complete or that religious difficulties could necessarily be handled by turning to the Old and New Testaments for help."[20] Millet also indicated that modern Mormons view the Bible in a similar way (see notes 19 and 21 for excerpts from Millet's speech).[21]

Latter-day Saints additionally accept as scripture "the inspired words of living prophets [LDS presidents]....Their words come to us through conferences, Church publications, and instructions to local priesthood leaders."[22] A living prophet's words are vital, as Mormonism's thirteenth president, Ezra Taft Benson (1899–1994), pointed out to Mormons in 1975: "[I]t is essential that you have access to and carefully read his words in Church periodicals."[23]

These "inspired" teachings, however, are open not only to future alteration by LDS authorities, but blatant refutation and open contradiction. LDS philosopher James E. Faulconer has observed, "One of the spin-offs of a belief in continuing revelation is an implicit refusal to allow theology to be set once and for all."[24] As LDS apologist Blake Ostler says, Mormonism is "open textured" because "God is still speaking."[25] This acceptance of evolving "truth" and doctrinal revision also dates back to Mormonism's founder, Joseph Smith.[26] It is but one reason why LDS president Benson warned, "Beware of those who would pit the dead prophets against the living prophets, for the living prophets always take precedence."[27]

Ultimately, the teachings of a deceased LDS leader mean little if those teachings and scriptural interpretations are no longer being sustained by current authorities of the church. Mormon doctrines, therefore, unlike mainstream Christian beliefs, are not "systematized or codified."[28] In fact, LDS philosopher David Paulsen has gone so far as to say that Latter-day Saints "have no official theology."[29]

> **Did You Know?** In raising their concerns about Mormon beliefs, many evangelicals have routinely cited the remarks made by nineteenth-century LDS leaders as they appear in the *Journal of Discourses*—an LDS Church–published compilation of the lectures and sermons given by Latter-day Saint authorities from around 1843 to 1886. Many of the statements found in this multivolume set are not only highly controversial, but also very damaging to some Mormon claims. In fact, a few of the comments made in it by LDS prophets and apostles are downright embarrassing to modern Mormons.
>
> In response, today's LDS apologists have begun arguing that the discourses were never meant to be taken as doctrine—and that they are merely the flawed transcripts of opinion-laden speeches and lectures made by Mormon leaders of the past. Thus, they certainly are not at all on par with any of the Standard Works of the Church.
>
> However, this is not how Mormons of the 1800s viewed the *Journal of Discourses,* as evidenced by the preface that appears in volume 8 (published in 1861, when Brigham Young was Mormonism's president). It reads, "The *Journal of Discourses* deservedly ranks as one of the standard works of the Church, and every right-minded Saint will certainly welcome with joy every Number as it comes forth from the press as an additional reflector of 'the light that shines from Zion's hill.'"

Contributing to the Confusion

Such flexibility has proven to be problematic—at least for non-Mormons, who have difficulty piecing together exactly what Mormons believe, especially when considering the many nonofficial books written by prominent Mormons (prophets, apostles, apologists, and others).[30]

Although these works have greatly influenced LDS beliefs, they are not *official.* They are *unofficial* interpretations of Standard Works and present *unofficial* views covering various issues. Technically speaking, they are personal opinion.

The list of official Standard Works may be constant, but the interpretations of them are open-ended, changeable, and subject to contradiction and revision. These re-interpretations might occur simply because a prophet dies (for example, Brigham Young), or a scientific discovery makes a certain belief untenable (for example, the belief that *all* Native American Indians are descended from Israelites), or some doctrine is no longer socially tolerated (for example, the doctrine that blacks cannot hold the LDS priesthood).

One also must not forget that the LDS Church even recommends resources created by rank-and-file Mormons (for example, BYU professors) designed to answer Latter-day Saints' questions about their faith. But at the same time the Church invariably adds some kind of disclaimer such as, "The following are not official Church positions or statements."[31]

Even more puzzling are similar words of warning that appear in works copyrighted or published by the LDS Church itself and distributed by the Mormon leaders as instructional literature...but not *officially.* Consider, for example, the influential and widely read *Gospel Principles.* It is sold in LDS bookstores, is contained in the LDS Missionary Reference Library, and is usually recommended to Latter-day Saints as a volume that contains most, if not all, of the main LDS tenets. The title page even reads, "Published by The Church of Jesus Christ of Latter-day Saints." And the copyright information states, "©1978 Corporation of the President, The Church of Jesus Christ of Latter-day Saints."

Yet immediately after these clear indications that the book has a high level of Mormon authority, there appears the following caution: "This work is not an official publication of The Church of Jesus Christ of Latter-day Saints. The views expressed herein are the responsibility of the author and do not necessarily represent the position of the Church." (And oddly, no author's name is given.)

Agreeing to Disagree Agreeably

Within Mormonism, then, one can find living prophets contradicting dead prophets, a current interpretation of a Standard Work differing from a past interpretation of that same work, LDS teachings that at one time were official or quasi-official but are no longer believed, and varying opinions among LDS leaders on many topics. Bluntly put, nailing down exactly what Mormonism *officially* teaches can be an untidy task.[32]

Further complicating this issue is how Mormons often seek to distance themselves and their church from a problematic past comment of an LDS leader by

- re-interpreting the comment in a way other than how it was understood by its original hearers[33]
- claiming that the remark is being taken out of context
- asserting that the words are being misquoted
- arguing that the statement is not a "doctrine," but merely a "belief" or a "practice"[34]
- narrowly splitting terms in order to focus on a minor issue while dismissing the broader point that is being made by a critic of the church[35]

I, therefore, have tried to focus on LDS doctrines, as well as LDS beliefs—ones that are *now* embraced by *most* Latter-day Saints—based on *the context* and the *original intent* of any Mormon leaders whose words I cite. Even this approach, however, may be inadequate when it comes to certain issues, since some LDS teachings are accepted as "true," but are still not looked upon as "part of the doctrine of the Church."[36] I believe that this LDS way of thinking continues to be the greatest obstacle to fruitful evangelical–LDS interaction.

To Mormon readers, I apologize in advance for anything you may find offensive in this approach. My intent has been not to offend, but to inform. I have sought to heed the wise words of your current prophet, Gordon B. Hinckley:

> We must work harder to build mutual respect, an attitude of forbearance, with tolerance one for another regardless of the doctrines

and philosophies which we may espouse. Concerning these you and I may disagree. But we can do so with respect and civility.[37]

Doctrinal disagreements, of course, are usually neither easy nor pleasant. And yet, like so many LDS leaders in the past who have felt it necessary to say some harsh things in the interest of "truth," I, too, must share what I see as "truth" (Ephesians 4:15). Admittedly, voicing one's perception of truth can sound abrasive, particularly when using words like "deception," "apostasy," and "heresy." But these terms are foreign to neither Christianity nor Mormonism, as LDS apostle Bruce McConkie (1915–1985) explained:

> The issue…is whether the doctrine is true or false. (2 Pet. 2:1.)… Heresy is false doctrine. Even members of the true Church are guilty of the crime of heresy to the extent that they accept false views which do not accord with the revealed word. "For there must be also heresies among you, that they which are approved may be made manifest among you" (1 Cor. 11:19; Gal. 5:20).[38]

Nevertheless, my sincere hope is that all of us will be able to live up to the admirable sentiments expressed in 2001 by Mormon apostle M. Russell Ballard. In seeking to express his own understanding of how best to handle religious conflict, he aptly summarized not only my views but those of countless other evangelicals:

> If there are issues of concern, let us talk about them. We want to be helpful. Please understand, however, that our doctrines and teachings are set by the Lord, so sometimes we will have to agree to disagree with you, but we can do so without being disagreeable.[39]

In 1986, LDS apostle Neal Maxwell articulated a similar understanding of the unfortunate, yet understandable and unavoidable, tension between persons who disagree theologically. It is a two-way street, so to speak, with everyone having the right to pose not only questions, but criticisms. The key to successful and peaceful interaction, as Maxwell rightly observed, is good will:

[Latter-day Saints] seek tolerance for our gospel views, not involuntary agreement with them. We fully expect such doctrines to be scrutinized and even criticized by others. We reserve the same freedom to engage in scrutiny of their beliefs. All in mutual good will, however.[40]

Evangelicals and Mormons can no longer view each other as foes. Neither group can afford to maintain animosity for the other. Scripture itself declares that "we wrestle not against flesh and blood, but against principalities, against powers, against the rulers of the darkness of this world, against spiritual wickedness in high places" (Ephesians 6:12).

So, with full confidence that Mormons and evangelicals can respectfully discuss the many important matters concerning all of us, I invite readers of both persuasions to consider this book's contents. As LDS apostle George A. Smith (1816–1875) said,

If a faith will not bear to be investigated; if its preachers and professors are afraid to have it examined, their foundation must be very weak.[41]

BECOMING
GODS

GOD'S LATTER-DAY PROPHET

*Joseph Smith was either a true prophet
or a conscious fraud or villain.*[1]
—B.H. Roberts (1907), Mormon apologist,
First Council of the Seventy

*Joseph Smith must be accepted either
as a prophet of God or else as a charlatan.*[2]
—Jeffrey R. Holland (1997), Mormon apostle

The validity of Mormonism rests on the claims of one man—Joseph Smith Jr.[3] I can still remember the first time I heard his name mentioned. I was a senior in high school, and my best friend told me she had met a guy who believed in something called the Book of Mormon by Joseph Smith. It claimed that Jesus had appeared to the American Indians centuries before Columbus. She then told me that Smith, when he was only 14 years old, also had experienced not only visions of angels, but even a visit from Christ himself. My initial thought was, *Cooooool, man.* (It was 1978.)

Then a few years later, while living in New York City, I went to the Mormon Visitor's Center. It offered a whole series of images depicting this same Joseph Smith. And sure enough, just as my friend had said, Smith had apparently been visited by Jesus Christ and some angel named Moroni. It was a fascinating display, especially the scenes that showed Smith finding the golden plates of the Book of Mormon and translating them. I also found out that there was something called "priesthood authority," which according to my courteous Mormon guide, had been lost by Christianity but restored through Smith.

"Smith's pretty important, huh?" I asked.

"Yes, very important," answered my new acquaintance. "Without Joseph we would not have God's church restored to the way it was in Jesus' day. And we would not know the truth about the kind of being God is. He is our Heavenly Father."

I continued, "Oh, I see. But how do you know what he said is true?"

"Because I have a witness of the Spirit. I bear you my testimony that Joseph Smith was a true prophet of God and that in answer to prayer he received a vision of Heavenly Father and Jesus Christ. I *know* it's true."

Forty-five minutes later I was still asking for proof—finally deciding to leave because there was simply nothing left to discuss. I understood at that point that whatever "proof" I was looking for was not going to be found in that Visitor's Center. Numerous questions remained in my mind: What was Smith really like? How do we know his story can be trusted? What documentation exists that might support his claims?

These questions were ultimately answered for me over the course of many years as I explored and studied numerous different religions, including Mormonism. They are still valid questions, not only for non-Mormons, but also for Latter-day Saints. And they deserve thoughtful responses.

辈 ⋇ 辈

Joseph Smith Jr. was born in 1805 to Joseph Smith and Lucy Mack, an impoverished but hard-working couple living in Vermont. It was a financially difficult life in New England for the Smiths. So in 1816 the family moved to the Manchester–Palmyra area of New York, where they hoped their battle against poverty could be won.[4]

But within ten years the family's best efforts to avoid destitution had failed.[5] So they entrusted their survival to money-digging (also known as treasure hunting by means of divination and folk magick*).[6] The activity enthralled young Joseph, who quickly gained a reputation among treasure seekers as a skilled digger adept at occult ritual.[7] Many neighbors, however, felt differently about "Joe."[8] To them he was "an imposter, hypocrite and liar."[9]

---

* Throughout this book I use the term *magick* to refer to those rituals, beliefs, and practices associated with occultism as opposed to stage illusions *(magic).*

Mormons, of course, see Smith as one of history's most honorable men. They believe he exemplified a host of praiseworthy traits: patience, kindness, humility, faithfulness, purity, godliness, righteousness, gentleness, honesty, and bravery.[10] He is depicted in LDS literature as nothing less than God's prophet for the latter-days—a prophet to whom the Christ himself appeared and spoke.

Mormon Point: Smith was never too involved with money-digging. It was not something he enjoyed. In fact, he only started money-digging under pressure from others.

Counterpoint:

One interpretation current among Mormon historians sees Joseph Smith, Jr., as a reluctant treasure-seeker egged on by his father and neighbors who ill-understood the spiritual purpose of his gifts and twisted them to material ends. This sets up a false distinction between what was inseparable in treasure-seeking (at least, in treasure-seeking as practiced by the Smith family): spirituality and materialism....Smith eagerly pursued treasure-seeking as a peculiarly tangible way to practice "experimental religion," as an opportunity to develop his spiritual gift through regular exercise in repeated contests with guardian spirits (history professor Alan Taylor, University of California, Davis).

Despite an attempt to minimize his early involvement in treasure searching, Smith was in reality an aggressive and ambitious leader among the competing treasure seers of Manchester, New York (Dan Vogel, award-winning author and researcher of Mormon history).[15]

Joseph's calling, as the *official* story goes, began in 1820 after some unusual religious "excitement" hit the Palmyra area. The revival allegedly converted "great multitudes," who were then solicited for membership by local churches. This moved young Joseph to ask, "Who of all these parties are right; or, are they all wrong?"[11] Once Smith decided that God alone could answer him, he supposedly went into a secluded grove to pray.

According to the *current* LDS version of what happened next, a pillar of light descended and two radiant "personages" appeared.[12] The first one pointed to the other and said, *"This is my beloved son. Hear him!"*[13]

Joseph asked these heavenly individuals which Christian sect was right and which one he should join. In response, the second personage said to "join none of them, for they were all wrong." Joseph also was told that all Christian creeds were "an abomination" in the Lord's sight and that all Christian teachers were "corrupt" because they taught commandments of men rather than doctrines of God.[14]

Smith's "First Vision" is vital to the doctrinal framework of the LDS faith. Mormon president Gordon B. Hinckley admitted as much in 1996.[16] Two years later, he reiterated his position, saying that the "entire case" of Mormonism "rests on the validity of this glorious First Vision."[17] In 2002, Hinckley added, "Upon that unique and wonderful experience stands the validity of this Church."[18]

Smith's First Vision is but one reason why Mormons compare their church's founder to biblical figures like Moses, Joseph (the son of Jacob), and the apostle Paul.[19] Untold numbers of Latter-day Saints actually believe that their salvation, to a limited degree, rests upon Smith.[20] As noted in *Doctrines of Salvation* by LDS president Joseph Fielding Smith (1876–1972), "FAITH IN CHRIST AND JOSEPH SMITH GO TOGETHER."[21]

──────── **MORMON QUOTES** ────────────────────

"Jesus Christ excepted, no better man [than Joseph Smith] ever lived or does live upon this earth" (Brigham Young, LDS president, 1862).[22]

"[A]ll men in the latter days—must turn to Joseph Smith to gain salvation. Why?…He alone can bring them the gospel; he alone can perform for them the ordinances of salvation and exaltation; he stands, as have all the prophets of all the ages in their times and seasons, in the place and stead of the Heavenly One in administering salvation to men on earth" (Bruce McConkie, LDS apostle, 1982).[23]

"Like other faithful Latter-day Saints, I have built my life on the testimony and mission of the Prophet Joseph Smith" (Dallin Oaks, LDS apostle, 1996).[24]

"Smith was the greatest prophet who ever lived upon the earth" (James E. Faust, First Presidency, 1997).[25]

"Joseph Smith, the Prophet and Seer of the Lord, has done more, save Jesus only, for the salvation of men in this world, than any other man that ever lived" (D&C* 135:3).[26]

A CLOSER LOOK

What was Joseph Smith really like?[27] This question is not easily answered. He exhibited two wholly opposite sides. Smith was kind and sensitive, but also harsh and violent.[28] To some he was humble. To others he was haughty.[29] He could forgive hostile enemies (as long as they repented), yet hold a hateful grudge toward anyone audacious enough to remain his foe.[30] He was both honest and deceptive (see sidebar, page 28).

His virtuous image probably developed in response to his many leadership qualities.[31] He possessed a keen wit, for example—and a good deal of charm, complemented by a liberal dose of charisma. Smith also was a natural speaker, as well as handsome and athletic.[32]

Moreover, Smith possessed an indomitable spirit, a highly active imagination, and uncanny intuition. He also was politically savvy and certainly had religious zeal. Smith's most valuable asset, however, may have been his facile mind, which could absorb, process, and utilize new information almost instantaneously.[33]

Did these qualities make Smith a prophet, a model Christian, or an admirable person? Not necessarily, say traditional Christians,† who see other aspects of Smith's life and character as proof that he was not divinely ordained. Some evangelicals have gone so far as to paint him as an utter scoundrel devoid of all goodness and integrity.

---

* D&C—standard abbreviation for the Doctrine and Covenants, one of the LDS Standard Works. See chapter 3 for a discussion of the Standard Works.

† I use the terms *orthodox, Christian, Christians, mainstream Christians, traditional Christians,* and *Christianity* to refer to any and all people, churches, and denominations that are either consistent with, or in essential agreement with, the three earliest Christian expressions of faith: the Apostles' Creed (A.D. 215–340), the Niceno–Constantinopolitan Creed (A.D. 381), and the Creed of Chalcedon (A.D. 451).

But there are other plausible portraits of the man. Researcher Dan Vogel, for instance, has posited that Smith may have been "a 'pious deceiver' or 'sincere fraud,' someone who deceives to achieve holy objectives."[34] He "may have engaged in fraudulent activities while at the same time believing that he had been called of God to preach repentance in the most effective way possible."[35]

> **Something to Consider:** Smith and other high-ranking LDS leaders often used deception to conceal their activities. Consider the initiation of polygamy. Smith took a second wife in 1832 or 1833. He took a third wife in 1838 or 1839 and three more wives in 1841. Smith then received a revelation on July 12, 1843, commanding his first wife, Emma, to accept polygamy. Yet, in public, Smith and other Mormons denied polygamy. An 1843 issue of his *Times and Seasons* periodical, for instance, declared, "We are charged with advocating a plurality of wives....[T]his is as false as the many other ridiculous charges which are brought against us. No sect has a greater reverence for the laws of matrimony or the rights of private property; and we do what others do not, practice what we preach."[36]

Mormons, of course, have always accepted Smith as a modern-day Moses above serious criticism.[37] This attitude held sway as far back as LDS president Wilford Woodruff (1807–1898), who noted in his diary that there was "not a greater man than Joseph."[38] Heber C. Kimball (1801–1868) predicted that this world would some day see Joseph "as a God."[39] Brigham Young (1801–1877) actually applied to Smith one of the most popular of all Bible verses about Jesus (1 John 4:3):

> Whosoever confesseth that Joseph Smith was sent of God...[A]nd every spirit that does not confess that God has sent Joseph Smith, and revealed the everlasting Gospel to and through him, is of Antichrist.[40]

This level of veneration has not diminished in the least among today's Mormons, who place Smith just below Jesus in religious importance.[41]

They even draw parallels between him and Christ: their lives, missions, experiences, persecutions, and deaths.[42]

But to evangelicals, such devotion is excessive and inappropriate because of a plethora of historical documents that cast Smith in a rather unflattering light. Traditional Christians find the evidence so overwhelming that they simply cannot accept even the possibility that Smith was, in any sense of the word, a prophet of God.

EVANGELICAL THOUGHTS

There are many reasons why Christians reject Joseph Smith. First, his religious teachings diverged from those beliefs that have long been accepted by Christians as biblically sound.[43] Second, his life was rife with behavior that impugns his character so severely that any claims about his being a prophet must be dismissed.[44] Third—which we will now examine in detail—historical data suggests that today's *official* First Vision story is fraudulent.

Which Vision?

LDS prophet David O. McKay (1873–1970) described Smith's First Vision as foundational to Mormonism.[45] His point was made even more cogently in 1961 by today's LDS president, Gordon B. Hinckley: "Either Joseph Smith talked with the Father and the Son or he did not. If he did not, we are engaged in a blasphemy."[46]

Given this admission, it is noteworthy that the First Vision is greatly lacking in verifiable facts and consistency of detail. The saga, in fact, evolved during Smith's life, which directly challenges the LDS claim that he "told but one" First Vision.[47] Today's *official* version of the story did not even exist when Mormonism was founded (1830).[48]

Evangelicals, therefore, cannot help but be troubled by comments like the one made in 1984 by LDS apostle James E. Faust:

> There are several other accounts of the magnificent vision near Palmyra recorded by the Prophet's associates or friends before the Prophet's death, who, at various times, heard the Prophet recount

the First Vision. These accounts corroborate the First Vision as written by Joseph Smith himself.[49]

But this is untrue. Although Smith and his first followers told many tales, none of them were about the Father and Son appearing in 1820. As for the account "written by" Smith in 1832, it bears little resemblance to the version espoused by today's Mormons.[50] According to the 1832 version, Smith went into the grove in his "sixteenth year."[51]

> **Notable and Quotable:** "The First Vision of 1820 is of first importance in the history of Joseph Smith. Upon its reality rest the truth and value of his subsequent work" (LDS apostle John A. Widtsoe.
>
> "The First Vision of the Prophet Joseph Smith constitutes the groundwork of the Church which was later organized. If this First Vision was but a figment of Joseph Smith's imagination, then the Mormon Church is what its detractors declare it to be— a wicked and deliberate imposture" (LDS apostle Hugh B. Brown).
>
> "We declare without equivocation that God the Father and His Son, the Lord Jesus Christ, appeared in person to the boy Joseph Smith....Our whole strength rests on the validity of that vision. It either occurred or it did not occur. If it did not, then this work is a fraud" (LDS president Gordon B. Hinckley).*

Moreover, there is no allusion to "two personages" in Smith's 1832 version. Joseph, instead, sees only "the Lord" (Jesus). God the Father is mentioned nowhere. And the phrase "This is my beloved Son, hear him" also is missing. In its place is a simple admonition from Christ: "[M]y son thy sins are forgiven thee. [G]o thy way walk in my statutes and keep my commandments."[52]

Even the main message of today's version—that all the churches in Joseph's day were false—is absent. Instead, Jesus rails against a world that has "turned aside from the Gospel" and "lieth in sin."[53] Smith briefly

---

* Respectively, Widtsoe, *Joseph Smith—Seeker After Truth*, page 19; Brown, *An Abundant Life*, pp. 310-311; Hinckley, "The Marvelous Foundation," Oct. 6, 2002, available at www.lds.org.

mentions Christianity's fallen state only in passing. But instead of claiming that this news came from Christ, Smith says he learned about Christendom's errors through personal Bible study at the age of 12—*two years before his vision supposedly occurred.*[54]

Other early accounts of the First Vision, contrary to Faust's claim, are equally inconsistent with today's *official* version of the story (Table 1.1).[55] LDS apostle Orson Pratt, for instance, during one lecture (about 1839), reportedly said that two personages had indeed appeared to Joseph, but that they "declared themselves to be angels."[56]

As late as 1888, LDS Church historian Andrew Jenson still held this understanding of the First Vision. In *The Historical Record* he wrote, "The angel again forbade Joseph to join any of these churches." Jenson then quoted Smith's *History of the Church* account (1842), but added the qualifying word "angel" as follows: "Many other things did he (the angel) say unto me which I cannot write at this time."[57]

Did You Know? Smith came precariously close to losing his church in 1838 through the defection of several high-ranking leaders. They included First Presidency counselor Frederick G. Williams, Book of Mormon witness Martin Harris, and LDS apostles John F. Boynton, Luke Johnson, Lyman Johnson, and William McClellin, as well as some 30 other elders (for example, Oliver Cowdery, David Whitmer, Hiram Page, and Jacob Whitmer). It was after this traumatic year that Smith dictated a new history—one that was decidedly more impressive than anything he had thus far told.

For decades most Mormons seemed rather confused about the First Vision. They often blended it with today's *official* version of yet another sacred encounter—Smith's 1823 vision of an unidentified angel, later to be named Moroni (see chapter 2). This angelic visit was probably the *real* first vision, since for many years it was the *only* vision about which Smith, his family, or his followers ever spoke.

FIRST VISION VERSION	Date? Location	Smith's Age	A Revival?
June 1830[58] by Joseph Smith UNPUBLISHED UNTIL 1833	No date specified No location specified	No age specified	No revival mentioned
Jan. 6, 1831[59] by Lucy M. Smith (hand-written) UNPUBLISHED UNTIL 1906	No date specified[60] No location specified	No age specified	No revival mentioned
1832[61] by Joseph Smith (handwritten) UNPUBLISHED	1821/22 implied "in the wilderness"	"in the 16th year of my age"[62]	No revival mentioned
Feb. 1835[63] by Oliver Cowdery (Book of Mormon Scribe) PUBLISHED in *Messenger & Advocate*	1823 specified Smith's bedroom	"in the 17th [year of age]"[64]	Revival added, but incorrect date implied[65]
Nov. 9, 1835[66] by Joseph Smith (transcribed) UNPUBLISHED	No date specified "silent grove"	"about 14 years old" Smith explicitly calls this event his "first" encounter	No revival mentioned
Nov. 14, 1835[67] by Joseph Smith (transcribed) UNPUBLISHED	No date specified No location specified	"about 14 yrs. old"	No revival mentioned
1839[68] by Joseph Smith (transcribed) PUBLISHED IN 1842 OFFICIAL	1820 implied No location specified	"in my fifteenth year" (that is, 14 yrs. old)	Revival (added)
Sept. 1840[69] by Orson Pratt (apostle) FIRST PUBLISHED VERSION	No date specified "a secret place, in a grove"	"about fourteen or fifteen years old"	No revival
June 1841[70] by Orson Hyde (apostle) PUBLISHED 1842 GERMAN EDITION	No date specified "a small grove of trees"	"his fifteenth year" (that is, 14 yrs. old)	No revival

Table 1.1—Several of the earliest versions of Smith's First Vision

Personages Appearing	Corrupt Churches Information	Primary Message(s)
No mention of Father or Son	No mention of corrupt churches	No messages specified Joseph *first* repented of his sins
No mention of Father or Son	No mention of corrupt churches	No messages specified Joseph *first* repented of his sins
"the Lord" (that is, Jesus Christ)	Smith decided at age 12 that all the churches were corrupt and believed incorrect doctrines	"thy sins are forgiven thee"
"a messenger sent by commandment of the Lord"	The messenger gave Smith a "special message" about his call to obtain and translate the Book of Mormon	"his sins were forgiven, and his prayers were heard"
Two *unidentified* personages, and also saw "many angels" Second personage testifies that Jesus "is the son of God," but does *not* say, "This is my beloved Son, hear him"	No mention is made of any message received about all of the churches being corrupt or teaching false doctrines; but Smith does note that when he was "17 years old" he saw *another* "vision of angels in the night"	"thy sins are forgiven thee" Jesus is the "son of God"
"visitation of Angels"	No mention is made of any message received about all churches being corrupt or teaching false doctrines	No messages specified
Two personages—one of them says, "This is my beloved Son, hear him" (added)	Smith is told by the personages that all sects are corrupt; he contradicts his 1832 version by stating, "at this time it had never entered my heart that all were wrong"	Sins forgiven message (deleted) Churches in error (added)
Two *unidentified* "personages, who exactly resembled each other in their features"	Smith is told by the personages that all the churches are believing "incorrect doctrines" and that God acknowledges "none of them"	"his sins were forgiven" Churches in error (added)
Two *unidentified* "glorious heavenly personages... resembling each other exactly in features"	Smith decided for himself that all churches were corrupt, believed incorrect doctrines, and did not teach "unadulterated truth"	Sins forgiven message (deleted) Churches in error (added)

Table 1.1 (continued)

An Interesting Fact: Not a single piece of published literature (Mormon, non-Mormon, or anti-Mormon) from the 1830s mentions Smith having a vision of the Father and Son.[71] The most striking fact is that many important LDS works were published during this decade, yet none of them refer to the Father and Son appearing to Smith. Such works include *The Evening and the Morning Star* periodical (1832–1834); the *Book of Commandments* (1833); the *Latter-day Saints Messenger and Advocate* publication (1834–1836); the "Lectures on Faith" series of teachings (1834–1835); Doctrine and Covenants (1835); and Parley Pratt's *Voice of Warning* missionary pamphlet (1837).

Joseph's own mother, in an 1831 letter to her older brother (Solomon Mack Jr.), explained that her son's first vision was indeed that of a "holy Angel."[72] Lucy makes no mention of either God the Father or Jesus Christ appearing to Joseph.[73] Within a year, however, Joseph *privately* began reworking his tale into a vision of Christ (the 1832 account). This vision later turned into a visit by Jesus and the Father.[74]

Something to Consider: Doctrine and Covenants 84:21-22, which is an 1832 revelation from God to Joseph Smith, tells us that without Mormonism's so-called "Melchizedek Priesthood" (see chapter 10) "no man can see the face of God, even the Father, and live." But according to today's version of the First Vision, Joseph Smith saw the face of God in 1820—many years *before* he supposedly received the Melchizedek Priesthood. Oddly, no one seems to know with any certainty just when or how Smith received this "priesthood," since LDS references to the event are not only vague, but also contradictory. None of Smith's earliest converts had even heard about this priesthood or seen it conferred on any LDS leaders until 1831.*

But to make room for this Father–Son vision *and* the angel vision, Smith had to backdate his Father–Son vision to 1820. That change was finalized in 1839, perhaps in response to the dissent then plaguing the LDS church (see sidebar, page 31).[75] This easily explains the discrepancy

* See "Restoration of the Melchizedek Priesthood," online at www.lds-mormon.com/mph.shtml.

between today's *official* First Vision and the versions of it told by early Mormons, who taught that the First Vision involved an angel (or angels).[76] Historical data also suggests that there was no 1820 revival in Palmyra that converted "great multitudes." Church records only show revivals in 1816 to 1817 and 1824 to 1825.[77] The latter event actually prompted Smith and several members of his family to join Christendom. This would have been an odd thing to do if Jesus had already told young Joseph that all of the churches were wrong.[78]

Finally, there is evidence (from 1829 and 1830) that Smith's first experience may have been a *dream* about a spirit that visited him three times in one night. This story is strikingly similar to what is today presented by Mormons as Smith's *second* vision. In one of the earliest public references to Smith (August 1829), a New York newspaper reported, "In the fall of 1827, a person by the name of Joseph Smith, of Manchester, Ontario county, reported that he had been visited in a dream by the spirit of the Almighty."[79]

Another local paper ran a similar story, this time attributing the "spirit of the Almighty" aspect of Smith's tale to Martin Harris (Smith's early benefactor).[80] Then, in May 1830, this same publication explained that Smith himself had said he " 'was commanded of the Lord in a dream' " to find some golden plates.[81] Such language would have been consistent with the way people in Smith's day, including Mormons, often spoke of their dreams as visions and vice-versa.[82]

> **Did You Know?** In 1893, Edward Stevenson noted in his *Reminiscences of Joseph, the Prophet, and the Coming Forth of the Book of Mormon* that in 1834 he heard Smith testify "with great power concerning the visit of the Father and the Son, and the conversation he had with them" (page 4). The significance of his recollection, however, is questionable since it is a very late reference that may have been tainted by the *official* First Vision version, which by 1893 had been circulating for many years.

Even more intriguing are the recollections of several persons who claimed that Smith's first tale had nothing to do with God *or* an angel. These persons maintained that Smith's original story involved a dream or vision of a bloody ghost dressed as a Spaniard.[83] (Such a phantom, coincidentally, would have been consistent with the beliefs of that era's money-diggers, who often sought treasure buried by Spaniards.[84])

These multiple reports certainly trouble evangelicals, but of even greater concern is the fact that Smith was an occultist. He, along with many early Mormons, regularly engaged in divination, astrology, fortune-telling, magick, and other occult practices.[85]

Mormon Magick

John L. Brooke of Tufts University has noted that early Mormons were not just superstitious, but "attuned to the supernatural powers of witchcraft."[86] Historian D. Michael Quinn has made a similar observation, citing numerous documents as proof of his position.[87] One piece of evidence was written by Joseph's own mother, who unflinchingly refers to how her whole family engaged in ritual magick. She revealed their occult practices while making a defense for her family against charges of laziness:

> [L]et not my reader suppose that…we stopt our labor and went at trying to win the faculty of Abrac[,] drawing Magic circles or sooth saying to the neglect of all kinds of business[—]we never during our lives suffered one important interest to swallow up every other obligation but whilst we worked with our hands we endeavored to remember the service of & the welfare of our souls.[88]

Soothsaying is foretelling the future by means of occult tools (for example, tarot cards). It was quite popular among early LDS women, many of whom practiced it in various ways (for example, palmistry and tea-leaf reading).[89]

Drawing magic circles relates to a ritual used to gain power over spirits invoked by an occultist. *The Ancients Book of Magic* explains that when contacting these spirits, a magician must draw a circle within a circle, which forms a barrier impassable by demons.[90] This is exactly what Joseph Smith Sr. and Joseph Smith Jr. did while money-digging.[91]

Finally, Lucy mentions the "faculty of Abrac," which refers to the deity regarded by the second-century Basilidians* as the "chief of the 365 genies

---

* Followers of the teachings of Basilides, a gnostic who was active in Alexandria from about A.D. 120 to 140.

ruling the days of the year."[92] It is from the name *Abrac* (or *Abraxas*) that we get the word *abracadabra*.

An Interesting Fact: Peasants in the Middle Ages believed that the word *abracadabra* guarded them from injury, danger, demons, and disease, especially the plague. *Abracadabra* was written in a triangle, dropping one letter in each line until only one letter remained. The parchment on which this formula had been inscribed was then worn around the neck by someone who had fallen ill. Then, it was thrown backward over one's shoulder into a stream running eastward. The bearer hoped his or her malady or other troubling circumstance would likewise depart. The "faculty of abrac" refers to the seventh line down from the top:

```
a b r a c a d a b r a
a b r a c a d a b r
a b r a c a d a b
a b r a c a d a
a b r a c a d
a b r a c a
a b r a c
a b r a
a b r
a b
a
```

The depths to which Joseph and his family were immersed in occultism is best illustrated by the objects they used in conjunction with their beliefs: 1) a magick dagger,[93] 2) three magick parchments,[94] and 3) a Jupiter talisman (which Joseph had with him for protection, ironically, on the day he was murdered in 1844).[95]

Each of these artifacts contains magick markings. Consider the parchments (owned by Joseph's brother Hyrum). Although they contain symbols copied from various occult sources, most of the drawings were lifted from astrologer Ebenezer Sibly's 1784 *New and Complete Illustration of the Occult Sciences.*[96]

The symbols were used not only in connection with magick, but also with the occult beliefs associated with Jewish kabbalism. And it is now believed by researchers of Mormonism that this mystical religious system, which influenced medieval magick, inspired several of Smith's ideas about God, humanity, creation, and salvation.[97]

The Smiths also believed in astrology, as did most early Mormons. Consequently, Hyrum's dagger and Joseph's talisman are inscribed with astrological markings.[98] The talisman bears the sign of Jupiter, a cross for the spirit of Jupiter, and the Jupiter orbital path. Why? Because Smith was born under Jupiter's astrological influence.[99]

> **Notable and Quotable:** "The God of Joseph Smith is a daring revival of the God of some of the Kabbalists and Gnostics, prophetic sages who, like Smith himself, asserted that they had returned to the true religion" (Renowned literary critic Harold Bloom, *The American Religion*, 1992, page 99).

Interestingly, Joseph chose to organize his church on April 6, 1830, a day known in folk magick as the beneficial "DAY-FATAL-ITY," which in 1830 coincided with an alignment of Jupiter and the Sun. He even entered into various marriages and introduced new doctrines on days that had astrological significance to him.[100]

Joseph the Glass-Looker

As for his money-digging, Joseph Smith was not alone in this pursuit.[101] Many of his associates, before and after converting to Mormonism, used seer stones to hunt for buried treasure.[102] These stones were thought to be enchanted tools by which anyone could locate lost items, missing people, or hidden wealth.[103]

But such exploits often brought consequences. In 1826, for example, Smith was arrested in Bainbridge, New York, for being a "disorderly person and an impostor."[104] He had broken the law by hiring himself out as a money-digger to a Josiah Stowell.[105] Consequently, he was brought to court as a glass-looker—"one who, by peering through a glass stone, could see things not discernible by the natural eye."[106]

During the court "examination," Smith admitted to having "a certain stone" that he used to find buried treasure. Several witnesses were then produced, which led to a "guilty" judgment.[107] However, because of his age, he was allowed to make "leg bail."[108] In other words, he was released on the condition that he get out of town.[109]

For years Mormons decried this story, including in their objections a court transcript published by *Fraser's Magazine* (1873). It was all anti-LDS propaganda concocted to smear Smith's good name, they said.[110] Then, in 1971, evidence for the validity of the 1873 transcript was unearthed by religion researchers, who found the bill for the 1826 court case presided over by a Justice Albert Neely.[111] Its authenticity was beyond dispute.[112]

Interestingly, before Neely's bill surfaced, LDS apologist Hugh Nibley noted that if the previously published transcripts of the court case (for example, in *Fraser's Magazine*) were ever proved authentic, it would be "the most damning evidence in existence against Joseph Smith."[113] Popular LDS author Francis Kirkham echoed the same sentiment.[114] Both Kirkham and Nibley knew, of course, that Scripture condemns divination and many other occult practices.*

So when it comes to the occultism in LDS history, it is not just a matter of evangelicals refusing to excuse a few minor errors of judgment by Smith and others. It also is an issue of mainstream Christians agreeing with the pre-1971 observations made by Mormons like Kirkham and Nibley. Their comments remain applicable since no statements of repentance by Smith have ever been found.[115]

According to history professor Alan Taylor, it was by Smith's agency that "treasure-seeking evolved into the Mormon faith."[116] Jan Shipps, history professor emeritus at Indiana–Purdue University, agrees that there is "little room for doubting" that Smith's seer stone use "was an important indication of his early and *continued* interest in extra-rational phenomena and that it played an important role in his spiritual development."[117]

---

* See Exodus 7:11; 22:18; Leviticus 19:26; Deuteronomy 18:10-12; Joshua 13:22; 2 Kings 17:17; 2 Chronicles 33:6; 1 Samuel 15:23; Isaiah 44:25; 47:13-15; Jeremiah 27:9; 29:8; Ezekiel 13:9,23; 22:28; Zechariah 10:2; Acts 16:16-18.[118]

LDS RESPONSES

Mormons handle concerns about Smith in varying ways. For example, when it comes to the different versions of the First Vision, some Latter-day Saints feel perfectly satisfied in saying that each version is merely emphasizing a different aspect of the event.[119] Granted, this might explain some *minor* deviations, but it cannot reconcile versions so at odds with each other that an evolution of the story is obvious.

LDS author Richard Bushman disagrees. He has no problem with the First Vision, explaining, for example, that the 1832 version fails to mention God the Father because in 1832 Joseph did not see that as a very significant element of the story.[120] Bushman also suggests that in 1838, Joseph suddenly realized "how significant it was that the Father had appeared."[121] Then, according to Bushman, once Smith grasped the importance of having seen God the Father, he began talking about it.

But this kind of after-the-fact defense seems not only desperate, but far-fetched. Is it reasonable to assume, without any corroborating statements from Smith, that he simply overlooked such a monumental event as God the Father appearing? Is it reasonable to assume that the contradicting versions of the vision are just descriptions of different aspects of the event? Evangelicals think not.

> **Notable and Quotable:** "[W]e cannot be certain about the First Vision. We cannot know that it occurred or, if it occurred, when or what Joseph experienced....Neither Joseph Smith nor any other Latter Day Saint analyst has satisfactorily accounted for the discrepancies among the accounts on the point of the number and identity of the personage(s) appearing to him in the First Vision" (Richard P. Howard, historian for the Reorganized Church of Jesus Christ of Latter Day Saints Church*).[122]

It also should be noted that a few Mormons have responded to critics by falsely citing documentation in hopes of proving the story. Consider LDS president Gordon B. Hinckley's popular book *Truth Restored*, which boldly depicts the 1820 revival as a historically verified event:

---

* The Reorganized Church of Jesus Christ of Latter Day Saints is now known as the Community of Christ. See also abbreviation guide on page 325.

One week a Rochester paper noted: "More than 200 souls have become hopeful subjects of divine grace in Palmyra, Macedon, Manchester, Lyons, and Ontario since the late revival commenced." The week following it was able to report "that in Palmyra and Macedon...more than four hundred souls have already confessed that the Lord is good."[123]

Although the reference to "a Rochester paper" seems to add some validity to Smith's tale, the citation is highly misleading since the periodical quoted (the *Rochester Religious Advocate*) did not even exist in 1820! It began publication in late 1824. As for the text Hinckley quotes, it is from an early 1825 article wherein a revival of 1824 to 1825—not 1820—is being discussed (see this chapter's notes 68, 74, 76–78, and 130 for a brief discussion of this revival and its relation to the LDS story about Smith).[124]

Using Paul's Vision

The propagation of such erroneous information is but one reason why evangelicals view the First Vision with so much consternation. Mormons, however, cannot understand the problem. They see virtually no difference between the First Vision accounts and the experience of Paul the apostle on the road to Damascus. Here is the argument presented by LDS apologist Michael Hickenbotham:

> Historical evidence indicates that Joseph Smith was reluctant to speak or write of the first vision because of the ridicule he received about it when he first shared it with others and because of its sacred nature.... [T]hose who are critical of Joseph's delay in recording the first vision should consider the fact that Paul's "first known mention of the Damascus appearance [of Christ] is in 1 Corinthians 9:1, written about two dozen years after it happened."...It is interesting to compare later, more complete accounts of Paul's vision as found in Acts 9:3-8; 22:6-11; and 26:13-18. Not only do they differ in details but they conflict in some of these details. Similar problems may be found in the Gospel narratives of the crucifixion and resurrection.[125]

But Hickenbotham's claim about "historical evidence" is inaccurate. There is no evidence at all from that period (about 1820 to 1824) verifying persecution against Smith. In fact, there is none before 1827 to 1828 (in other words, when he began to claim he had experienced visions of an angel).[126] This absence of historical data suggests that "no one at that time and for a long time thereafter was aware that he was supposed to have had the vision."[127]

Hickenbotham's remark about the time gap between Paul's vision and 1 Corinthians 9:1 no way relates to Smith's First Vision. The problem is not that Joseph was *not* talking about his vision, but that he *was* talking about it. And it did not match today's *official* version about the Father and Son appearing in 1820.

Finally, Hickenbotham's appeal to the discrepancies in Paul's accounts cannot be compared to Smith's First Vision. The alleged contradictions in Acts were long ago resolved by scholars analyzing the Greek texts. The discrepancies in Paul's account involve modern ignorance of the Greek wording used (see sidebar, page 43). Unlike Paul's accounts, Smith's tales were told in English.[128]

And it should not be forgotten that Joseph's mother, a sister, and two brothers joined the Presbyterians during the 1824–1825 revival and remained members until 1828.[129] Joseph himself, during this same period, may have gotten involved with several denominations—in opposition to the supposed 1820 vision, wherein he learned that all of the churches were corrupt and that he should join none of them.[130]

Explaining the Origin of the First Vision

Mormons, however, are quick to accept rationalizations for Smith's contrasting stories. Their alternative is not pleasant, according to Gordon B. Hinckley: "If the First Vision did not occur, then we are involved in a great sham. It is just that simple."[131]

Of course, no one can say with certainty how Smith created his tales. But non-LDS explanations are more plausible than those offered by Mormons. Fawn Brodie (author of the famous biography of Joseph Smith *No Man Knows My History*) speculated that the First Vision was perhaps "the elaboration of some half-remembered dream stimulated by the early revival excitement and reinforced by the rich folklore of visions circulating in his neighborhood."[132]

Brodie's theory would satisfactorily explain things. The 1800s produced many religious tales bearing great similarity to the *official* First Vision—the version Smith ultimately adopted. Interestingly, many of these accounts were circulating in and around Palmyra, both in print and by word of mouth—*and they predated Smith's story by years.*[133] That Smith blended elements of these stories into his own tale is plausible.

Something to Consider: Acts 9:7 states that the men with Paul "heard" Christ's voice, while Acts 22:9 says they "heard not" his voice. A contradiction? Hardly. The Greek word *akouo* that is translated as "heard" and "heard not" actually means "to hear." But in English we lose the Greek nuances. The meaning of *akouo* depends on how it is used (whether it is followed by the accusative or the genitive case). In Acts 9:7, *akouo* is used with the noun "voice" in the partitive genitive case, which indicates that those with Paul "heard" the *sound* of the voice. In Acts 22:9, *akouo* is used with the noun "voice" in the accusative case, which relates to the hearing of something *with an understanding of the message being relayed.**

Therefore, the verses are saying different things—that is, Paul's companions *heard* the sound of the voice (9:7), but they *heard not* the voice's message (22:9). As an analogy, one might think of hearing someone shouting from another room. One may *akouo* (partitive genitive case) the sound, but not *akouo* (accusative case) the message.

As for other minor variations in Paul's accounts, they are not at all like those in Smith's tale, because they create no fundamental change in Paul's account. At most, they are expansions of the story to include what happened to others (for example, in Acts 22:9 we are told that those with Paul also fell down). But Paul never substantially altered what he said happened to him. Joseph, however, did indeed make such a change—much to the confusion of early Mormons.

---

* W.E. Vine, *Vine's Expository Dictionary of New Testament Words* (McLean, VA: MacDonald Publishing Co., n.d.), p. 544.

Such a theory boldly challenges LDS apostle James Faust's contention that critics of the First Vision "find it difficult to explain away."[134] His assertion is further weakened by yet another theory of Brodie's, which posits that Smith's story might have been "created some time after 1830 when the need arose for a magnificent tradition" to cancel out the stories of his fortune-telling and money-digging."[135]

Smith's Occultism

With regard to Joseph Smith's occultism and money-digging, in 1987 Gordon B. Hinckley simply opted to criticize those who had begun investigating such matters, accusing them of trying to "ferret out every element of folk magic and the occult in the environment in which Joseph Smith lived to explain what he did and why."[136] He went on to seriously downplay Smith's questionable activities:

> [T]here were superstitions and the superstitious. I suppose there was some of this in the days when the Savior walked the earth. There is even some in this age of so-called enlightenment.... [S]ome hotels and business buildings skip the numbering of floor thirteen. Does this mean there is something wrong with the building? Of course not. Or with the builders? No. Similarly, the fact that there were superstitions among the people in the days of Joseph Smith is no evidence whatever that the Church came of such superstition.[137]

This response, however, does not take into consideration the intensity of Smith's occult beliefs and practices. He spent his life immersed in occultism, its rituals, its principles of magick, and its so-called powers of protection. Spiritually speaking, there was far more being embraced by Smith than some harmless superstition comparable to the tradition of skipping a building's thirteenth floor.

Similar arguments, though, have come from LDS defenders such as Sam Katich, whose work has been distributed by the Foundation for Apologetic Information & Research (FAIR).*

---

* FAIR describes itself as a group "dedicated to providing well-documented answers to criticisms of LDS doctrine, belief and practice."[138]

In one article focusing on Smith's Jupiter talisman, Katich challenges the very idea that Smith even owned it.[139] (This argument has been refuted by a variety of persons, including respected scholar D. Michael Quinn.[140]) Most interesting about Katich's article, however, is his response to the disconcerting what-if scenario—that is, what if Smith did indeed possess the Jupiter talisman?

> [T]he presence of such artifacts are meaningless from the perspective of our current culture and understanding and they do not serve to prove or disprove Joseph as a prophet.....[S]uch an item would have been a protection against enemies, witchcraft, and sorcery. It could also have been used as an amulet of luck, love, protection, healing, astrology, or ritual magic as it was used by thousands of other Americans *who customarily wore the then in-vogue amulets or talismans.* One must wonder, if Joseph were to have had a lucky rabbit's foot in his pocket, would it be argued that he had a bizarre fascination with rabbits and worshiped the Velveteen Rabbit god?[141]

Like Hinckley, Katich dismisses Smith's occultism as trivial—as if it existed independently of an all-encompassing occult worldview. The truth is that Smith, in his forays into occultism, was hardly on par with someone who lightheartedly carries a rabbit's foot. He and his family, friends, and followers were full-blown occultists who, as part of their religious faith and practice, engaged in activities condemned by God.

Other Mormons have sought to distance Smith from occultism by suggesting that 1) his work as a money-digger is comparable to the labor undertaken by "gold miners, or silver miners, or coal miners";[142] and 2) his association with magick and occultism was limited to those years prior to his call from God and guidance of the LDS Church.

First, however, money-diggers were not miners. They were nonprofessionals seeking buried treasure via divination and magick. As researcher Dan Vogel has noted, it was Smith's "unparalleled reputation as a treasure seer that drew Josiah Stowell to hire Smith, not as a digger, but as a treasure seer to locate treasure."[143] Second, Joseph, his family, and many of his followers *continued* practicing magick, divination, astrology, and soothsaying long after the LDS Church was founded in 1830.[144]

Did You Know? Brigham Young used a divining rod to find "where the Temple should be built" in Salt Lake City (*Anthon H. Lund Journal,* under July 5, 1901). A 1981 *Sunstone* magazine article revealed that the divining rod came from Oliver Cowdery via Phineas Young (brother-in-law of Oliver Cowdery and brother of Brigham Young), and that Brigham "had it with him when he arrived in this (Salt Lake) valley and that it was with that stick that he pointed out where the Temple should be built."*

D. Michael Quinn notes,

> The most prominent use of a rod in Utah occurred in 1847 when Brigham Young evidently used Oliver Cowdery's rod, which he had received from his brother Phineas Young, and "pointed out" where the Saints' new temple should be built (Lund, 1901). But in the twentieth century, church leaders have largely ignored divining rods, and there is no evidence that they were used in divination after…1868. Still, some rural Mormons have continued to use rods in searching for underground water, minerals, and gas (Quinn, *Early Mormonism and the Magic Worldview,* page 206).

Surprisingly, some Mormons have used false statements to defend Smith. One example of this approach comes, again, from Sam Katich, who wrote, "Joseph certainly was never one to advocate or encourage Church members to engage in magical arts."[145] He adds, "The magical heritages of some early nineteenth-century members quickly faded into what most certainly did not persist in later LDS culture."[146]

In reality, though, Smith did indeed encourage occultism among his followers, many of whom used divining rods to find buried treasure.[147] In fact, Brigham Young and Heber C. Kimball were given their rods by Smith "as a symbol of gratitude for their loyalty."[148] And in April 1829, Smith actually received a revelation praising Oliver Cowdery's divining talents as a God-given "gift" (see chapter 3, pages 88–89)[149]

Smith also encouraged use of seer stones *after* the church had been organized. On December 27, 1841, he went so far as to display one of his own stones to the Quorum of the Twelve Apostles. Brigham Young later

---

* "The Psychological Needs Of Mormon Women," *Sunstone,* volume 6, number 2, page 67.

reminisced that Smith said that "every man who lived on the earth was entitled to a seer stone, and should have one."[150]

The Magick Continues

As for Katich's assertion that the magical practices of "some" members "quickly faded" from "LDS culture," this also is false. He attempts to prove his point by noting that early LDS Church discipline was meted out to individuals for using seer stones, fortune-telling, and magic. For example, he cites the case of a William Mountford, who was disfellowshipped for practicing "black art."[151]

But a number of points contradict Katich's argument and render his example irrelevant. First, LDS leaders routinely went public with condemnations of activities that they themselves privately practiced (for example, polygamy—see chapter 9). So their public actions in this case mean little.

Second, notice the reason for Mountford's condemnation. It was for "black art"—magic used for purposes not ordained by God. Early Mormons viewed occult practices that were properly handled as white magick. Hence, it was not Mountford's activities that were intrinsically wrong to LDS leaders, but rather his misplaced motives and wrong uses of magickal arts.

Third, Mountford was not simply involved with divination. He, along with several Mormons from Staffordshire, England, were actually building their own personal altars and praying to a deity they addressed as SAMEAZER. This conflicted with LDS teachings about God.

Fourth, LDS leaders believed that some practices (for example, polygamy, seer stone use, receiving revelations) were *only* for leaders who had the spiritual maturity and right to engage in such things.[152] Moreover, LDS tools of divination were supposed to be consecrated to God. In fact, when Joseph Smith was given some Staffordshire seer stones, he did not condemn them, but said that they were an "Urim and Thummim as good as ever was upon the earth." However, they had been "consecrated to devils."[153]

The truth is that *many* early Mormons, particularly those who founded the church, practiced occultism.[154] And many Mormons practiced occultism well into the 1900s, contrary to Katich's claim.[155] Smith himself continued his occult activities until his death. He used his seer stone not only to "translate," but also to receive revelations and give blessings (for example, in 1830, 1835, and 1842).[156]

As late as May 1844, Smith gave a seer stone to LDS apostle Lyman Wight "as part of a secret ordination for Wight to perform a special mission."[157] Even Brigham Young knew the value of seer stones to Smith, explaining in 1855 that Joseph had five stones, three of which he used throughout his entire religious life.[158]

These facts flatly contradict LDS apologists, who maintain that "no type of stone [was] involved in receiving revelation or translation" after 1829 and that Smith's seer stone was "not operational in Joseph's religious activities."[159] Rather, according to D. Michael Quinn, "Smith did not regard his seer stones simply as relics of his youth. Rather, as church president Smith continued to discover new seer stones."[160]

It is history itself, therefore, that refutes LDS claims that God took young Joseph Smith, "a man innocently caught up in the superstition of his day, and turned him in the right direction."[161] Smith began his career as an occultist, and he never stopped being one.

But seeking to distance Smith from the occult is understandable. Today's LDS Church denounces all divination, astrology, magick, wizardry, necromancy, séances, and spiritualism.[162] The *Encyclopedia of Mormonism* notes the following:

> Latter-day Saints reject magic as a serious manipulation of nature and are advised to avoid any practice that claims supernatural power apart from the priesthood and spiritual gifts of the Church (see Devils; Satanism). They are also counseled against using any fortune-telling devices. Both so-called white and black magic can be Satanic.[163]

Equally relevant is a 1992 letter signed by the LDS Church's First Presidency and sent to all general and local priesthood leaders:

> We caution all members of the Church not to affiliate in any way with the occult or those mysterious powers it espouses. Such activities are among the works of darkness spoken of in the scriptures. They are designed to destroy one's faith in Christ, and will jeopardize the salvation of those who knowingly promote this wickedness. These

things should not be pursued as games, be topics in Church meetings, or be delved into in private, personal conversations.[164]

In other words, the beliefs and practices of early Mormons (including
Smith and his entire family) were, at best, contrary to modern LDS teachings. At worst, their activities were satanic. Christians can only view such
a spiritually dark and doctrinally inconsistent past as irreparably dam-
aging to all LDS claims of being a biblically sound church whose founding
prophet–leader was led by God.

FINAL OBSERVATIONS

A concluding word must be said about Smith's various moral and
ethical failures (see notes 28–30 for this chapter). Faithful Latter-day
Saints either 1) justify them, or 2) view them, on the whole, as no more
disconcerting than Abraham's lying (Genesis 12:10-16), David's adultery
(2 Samuel 11), or Peter's betrayal (Matthew 26:69-75).

But what Mormons seem to be missing is that the moral lapses of these
biblical characters were *exceptions* in their lives. In Smith's case, however,
there appears to have been an ongoing pattern of ungodly behavior and
attitudes. This pattern seems to have been linked to what historian D.
Michael Quinn has labeled "theocratic ethics."[165]

This philosophy, which was adopted by Smith and other early LDS
leaders, placed early Mormon concepts of right and wrong on a level *above*
both civil laws and biblical mandates. In other words, since Smith was
directly receiving divine guidance, it followed that right and wrong were
whatever Smith said was right and wrong. This subjective standard of
morality became particularly useful when Smith began to secretly practice polygamy (see chapter 9 and appendix A).

Evangelicals see such actions as a further indication that Joseph Smith
could not have been a prophet. Scripture tells us that those who habitually practice sin in an unrepentant manner and make sin their normal
pattern of life are not of God (1 John 3:6-10).

And yet it cannot be denied that this same Joseph Smith somehow
produced a quite remarkable book, the Book of Mormon—which in many
ways not only points to Jesus Christ, but also exhorts the world to live
righteously before God. This fascinating volume of LDS scripture will be
the focus of our next chapter.

2

AND IT CAME TO PASS

*Just as the arch crumbles if the keystone is removed, so does all the
Church stand or fall with the truthfulness of the Book of Mormon.... [I]f it
can be discredited, the Prophet Joseph Smith goes with it.* [1]
—Ezra Taft Benson (1899–1994), Mormon president

Everyone loves a good story. And the Book of Mormon, truth be told,
offers a fairly good tale. It has all the makings of a bestseller: action, adventure, intrigue, spirituality, and a cast of characters that puts many modern
thrillers to shame. And it sounds so biblical. But this is also its downfall.
It is so much like the Bible that it is *too much* like the Bible. In fact, it is
chock-full of lengthy passages lifted straight from the Old and New
Testaments. Although these segments lend a biblical feel to the book, they
also indicate that plagiarism was a major component in the Book of
Mormon's creation. [2] In addition, a number of Bible stories seem to have
simply been reworked to fit the volume. [3]

Evangelicals find these aspects of Smith's Book of Mormon very disconcerting. Other concerns about this LDS standard work relate to its
origin, claims, gradual and continual evolution, and overall message.
Before examining these concerns, however, someone must at least know
what the volume is about. Consequently, we will begin our look at the
Book of Mormon by taking a brief glance at its story line. As with everything else in Mormonism, one must travel back to the days of Joseph Smith
to find the truth.

✠ ✠ ✠

As I noted in chapter 1, Joseph Smith's First Vision originally involved
just an angel. This story, however, was turned into a visit from Jesus. That

experience then became a tale about the Father and Son appearing in
1820.[4] So what happened to the original angel story? It became Smith's
second vision—that of the angel Moroni.

This event, according to today's *official* LDS history, unfolded on
September 21, 1823, as Smith prayed at night near his bedside. A light
filled the room until it "was lighter than at noonday."[5] Then an angel
appeared. He announced that God had a mission for Smith—one
involving golden plates said to contain the fullness of the Gospel "as delivered by the Savior" to America's ancient inhabitants.[6]

The plates had been buried centuries earlier in a stone box under the
Hill Cumorah, about a mile from Smith's home.[7] They contained *not* the
corrupt dogmas of Christendom, but Christ's pure teachings.[8] So the next
day, Smith went to where the treasure lay hidden. However, he was not
allowed to take the ancient cache just yet.

Instead, Moroni ordered him to return to the location every year on
September 22. He reportedly obeyed this directive; and each time he found
Moroni, who gave him "instruction and intelligence."[9] Finally, on
September 22, 1827, the angel let Joseph retrieve the plates, along with
two stones set in silver bows. He was told that these stones, the "Urim
and Thummim," "were what constituted 'Seers' in ancient or former times;
and that God had prepared them for the purpose of translating the book."[10]

Smith now had all that was necessary to produce another testament
of Jesus Christ: the Book of Mormon; the "keystone" of Mormonism.

MORMON QUOTES

"[The Book of Mormon] is approved by the highest authority in the
universe, the Lord himself" (Marion G. Romney, LDS apostle, 1949).[11]

"There is no greater issue ever to confront mankind in modern times
than this: Is the Book of Mormon the mind and will and voice of God
to all men?" (Bruce McConkie, LDS apostle, 1982).[12]

"[T]he Book of Mormon is the keystone of our religion. It is the keystone in our witness of Christ. It is the keystone of our doctrine. It is
the keystone of testimony" (Ezra Taft Benson, LDS president, 1986).[13]

"Either the Book of Mormon is what the Prophet Joseph said it is, or this Church and its founder are false, a deception from the first instance onward" (Jeffrey R. Holland, LDS apostle, 1997).[14]

A CLOSER LOOK

The Book of Mormon is supposed to be a translation of the "reformed Egyptian" characters engraved on Moroni's plates.[15] The book itself purports to be God's dealings with the inhabitants of America from "2,200 years before the birth of Jesus Christ to 421 years after the death of Jesus Christ."[16] These inhabitants allegedly arrived via three migrations.

The first migration—that of the "Jaredites"—took place soon after the events of the Tower of Babel (see Genesis 11). These voyagers to the New World produced a great civilization that lasted about 2000 years until it was "destroyed by internal conflicts" and war.[17]

The second migration—that of the "Nephites"—occurred during the reign of Judah's King Zedekiah (about 600 B.C.), when two friends named Lehi and Ishmael led their families from Jerusalem. This group, like the Jaredites, traveled by ship to the Americas, where they began a thriving society.

The final group—the "Mulekites"—subsequently arrived from the east under the leadership of Mulek. According to the Book of Mormon, Mulek was a son of King Zedekiah. But unlike the Jaredites and Nephites, the Mulekites did not establish their own culture. They simply joined the flourishing Nephite society founded by Lehi and Ishmael.

The Nephites, named after their mightiest prophet, Nephi, were "faithful members of the Church" and "believed the revelations and sought to keep the commandments of God."[18] Depending on their lineage, some Nephites also were known as Jacobites, Josephites, or Zoramites.

But the Lamanites, named after Laman (their most powerful leader), were rebellious. Their minds "were darkened by unbelief" and they "were apostates from the Church."[19] Some Lamanites also were known as Lemuelites or Ishmaelites, after persons to whom they were related by blood or marriage (see "The DNA Dilemma," page 69).

The Lamanites were so evil that God prohibited marriage between them and the Nephites, reinforcing his wishes by pronouncing a curse on the Lamanites: "a skin of blackness." This he did so they "might not be enticing" to the "white" Nephites.[20] The Lamanites thus became "loathsome" to look upon.[21]

Mercifully, God promised that repentant Lamanites who joined the Nephites would have the curse removed, and their skin would become "white like unto the Nephites" and their young men and their daughters would become "exceedingly fair."[22]

For centuries the Lamanites and Nephites lived in strife, until around A.D. 34, when Christ appeared to them and offered his gift of salvation.[23] He told them about his crucifixion and resurrection and taught them the same things he had taught in Galilee.[24] Everyone responded by following Christ, which brought peace and unity.

Soon afterward, however, war again erupted between the groups, who traveled northward. Millions were killed, until all the remaining warriors met for a final battle in New York, near Cumorah (see "Archaeology and Geography," page 65). The Lamanites won the showdown, leaving only a handful of Nephites alive and scattered abroad.

These Lamanites subsequently became so vile that they actually began warring among themselves and lost all knowledge of their spiritual heritage. By the time Columbus found them, these so-called American Indians had even forgotten they were Israelites.[25]

According to Smith, this Native American saga would have been lost forever if it had not been for faithful prophet–historians like Mormon, who etched the tale on golden plates. He then gave these plates to his son, Moroni, who in turn "added a few words of his own," and buried them "in the hill Cumorah."[26] There they remained until Joseph found them, thus fulfilling Book of Mormon prophecies.[27]

EVANGELICAL THOUGHTS

It is very difficult for evangelicals to accept the divine origin and historicity of the Book of Mormon. Even the story surrounding its coming forth through Moroni's visit is problematic. This "Second Vision," like Smith's First Vision, seems to have been manufactured over time. For instance, there is a discrepancy over the very identity of Smith's angel.

The 1839 *History* of the church, reportedly dictated by Smith himself, states that the angel was "Nephi"—not "Moroni."[28]

Mormon point: Early references to "Nephi" as the angel mean nothing. They simply reflect an early clerical error in the 1839 *History*—an error that was repeated a few times.

Counterpoint: Early uses of "Nephi" are actually quite significant. Smith had plenty of time to correct these "errors," but never did so. Instead, his 1839 *History* was reprinted in the LDS publication *Times and Seasons* (1842). Then, throughout the rest of his life, he made no correction or retraction of the name "Nephi," which had appeared in the periodical.

More remarkable, however, is how Mormons try to explain "Nephi" as a scribal "error" from 1839 by pointing to Doctrine and Covenants, section 50 (1835). This revelation was received in 1830 and does mention "Moroni." The LDS argument is that Moroni was obviously known as the angel's name all the way back in 1830.

But what many Mormons seem not to know is that when the revelation was *originally* given in 1830 and printed in the *Book of Commandments* as section 28 (1833), it contained no reference to Moroni. That name was later inserted. This can be seen by examining copies of the original revelation in the *Book of Commandments*, in the non-LDS newspaper *The Telegraph* (Painesville, Ohio, April 19, 1831), and in the LDS periodical *The Evening and the Morning Star* (March 1833, page 78). Another source to consult is H. Michael Marquardt, *The Joseph Smith Revelations Text and Commentary*, pages 72–75.

And in Smith's 1832 account (see chapter 1), it is an *unidentified* "angel of the Lord" who imparts the news about plates "engraven by Maroni."[29] Obviously, if the angel spoke *about* Moroni, then he could not have *been* Moroni.[30] Historian LaMar Petersen—18-year member of the Advisory Board of Editors for the *Utah Historical Quarterly*—has commented, "Notice that the angel did not say 'engravings which was engraven by me' or 'I, Moroni, engraved these plates.'"[31]

A contradiction? Perhaps not. The issue may instead relate to the occult beliefs that at the time were part of Smith's theological system. According to D. Michael Quinn, the name "Nephi" has close ties to various generic terms used by nineteenth-century occultists for spirit messengers " 'called out by *Magicians* and *Necromancers*.' "[32]

> **Notable and Quotable:** "Joseph had a stone which was dug from the well of Mason Chase....It was by means of this stone that he first discovered these plates....He found them by looking in the stone."*

Another element of the Second Vision rarely discussed is the means by which Joseph found his plates. Today's *official* version says he was directed to them by Moroni. But for years it was understood that Smith found the plates by means of his seer stone.[33] This was commonly known during the 1800s.[34] This scenario coincides with what may have been Smith's initial intent—to convince other money-diggers that there existed a golden book about hidden treasure.[35] Only later did Smith add a religious twist to his story.[36]

Smith's money-digging companions, of course, did not just idly sit by while their former associate enjoyed possession of a golden book.[37] So they tried to steal it. Fortunately for Smith, their attempts failed. His next hurdle was translating the plates, which relates to yet another problem Christians have with the Book of Mormon.[38]

A Stone, a Hat, and a Scribe

Early Latter-day Saints, unlike many of today's Mormons, knew that Smith had "translated" his Book of Mormon without even looking at the golden plates.[39] Instead of truly *translating* the symbols on them in an academic fashion, he gazed into his seer stone and read the text aloud as it appeared to him. A scribe then wrote down his words. As Isaac Hale (Smith's father-in-law) said, Smith translated "the same as when he looked for the money-diggers, with the stone in his hat, and his hat over his face, while the Book of Plates were at the same time hid in the woods."[40]

---

* Martin Harris, 1859 interview, *Tiffany's Monthly* (www.utlm.org/onlineresources/ sermons_talks_interviews/harrisinterviewtiffanysmonthly.htm).

Many witnesses described this process: Joseph Knight Sr. (a convert), Michael Morse (Smith's brother-in-law), and David Whitmer (Book of Mormon witness).[41] Even Smith's wife and brother confirmed the seer stone's use.[42] LDS apologist B.H. Roberts also affirmed Smith's use of a seer stone to translate the Book of Mormon.[43]

BYU scholar Noel B. Reynolds as well has conceded that Smith translated the Book of Mormon with a stone, adding that Smith read text off of it like we "might read lines off a computer screen."[44] But to Reynolds, this is a point in *favor* of the Book of Mormon:

> For any mortal to dictate a 500-page book in this way, off the top of his head, would inevitably lead to wandering, repetition, contradiction, non sequiturs, and pointlessness.[45]

Ironically, the "mortal" source Reynolds refers to is exactly what is evidenced in the Book of Mormon. The 1830 first edition for instance, contained atrocious grammar. In other places, Smith failed to correctly use the archaic English of the King James Bible.[46] These slip-ups, of course, were ultimately resolved by edits (for example, in the 1837 edition).

The corrections, however, present yet another dilemma—since every sentence and word in the 1830 edition had supposedly come directly from God.[47] Edward Stevenson related how Martin Harris explained the translation process during an 1870 meeting:

> By aid of the seer stone, sentences would appear and were read by the Prophet and written by Martin, and when finished he would say, "Written," and if correctly written, that sentence would disappear and another appear in its place, but if not written correctly it remained until corrected, so that the translation was just as it was engraven on the plates, precisely in the language then used.[48]

In other words, no changes (barring correction of printer errors) should have been made to the Book of Mormon, especially in light of what happened when Smith prayed about the volume. A voice spoke from heaven, telling him that the translation of the text was correct. "'These plates have been revealed by the power of God, and they have been translated by the power of God,'" said the voice. "'The translation of them which you have seen is correct, and I command you to bear record of what you now see and hear.'"[49]

> **Did You Know?** The Book of Mormon states, "[T]here were no envyings, nor strifes....There were no robbers, nor no murderers, neither were there Lamanites, nor no manner of Ites; but they were in one, the children of Christ" (Book of Mormon, 1830 edition, page 515; 4 Nephi 1:16-17, modern edition). Joseph Smith's use of "Ites" in this passage reveals his notion that the suffix "ites" could be used as a descriptive proper noun for a group of people. LDS leaders corrected this error in subsequent editions by rewriting the term as a hyphenated word: "-ites." This is only one example of the poor grammar that LDS leaders had to conceal in later editions of this allegedly divine text.

Whether or not the original 1830 edition should have been changed is almost a moot point, however, since other errors involving zoology, botany, history, anthropology, geography, and archaeology remain in modern editions. These errors alone are enough to give evangelicals pause when it comes to LDS claims about the book.

Concerning history, for instance, the Book of Mormon Israelites leave Jerusalem *before* the Babylonian captivity and build synagogues in the New World "after the manner of the Jews."[50] But the Jews did not build synagogues until *after* the Babylonian captivity began.[51] And then there are the references to cows, oxen, horses, and goats in the New World 600 years before Christ.[52] But these animals were not present for man's use in the area until Europeans imported them hundreds of years later.[53]

Of Ancient Origin?

Despite its many problems, Mormons firmly believe that the Book of Mormon is an account revelatory of American Indian origins. In reality, however, the volume is simply a rehashing of nineteenth-century speculations linking Native Americans to the Israelites. These ideas were very popular during the 1800s, especially around Smith's locale.[54]

Something to Consider: In the original 1830 Book of Mormon, Joseph Smith consistently inserted an unnecessary "a" before participles, incorrectly used "no" instead of "any" (creating a double negative), erroneously formed past participles, and used incorrect forms of the past tense. These grammatical flaws are some of the most obvious indications that the Book of Mormon is a product of Smith's mind—not God's. Consider the following examples (page numbers refer to the 1830 edition):

- "As I was a journeying to see a very near kindred....I was a going thither" (page 249)
- "...they did not fight against God no more" (page 290)
- "...no man can look in them...lest he should look for that he had not ought" (page 173)
- "...this they done throughout all the land" (page 220)
- "...and they had began to possess the land of Amulon" (page 204)
- "...and also of Adam and Eve, which was our first parents" (page 15)
- "...they was angry with me" (page 248)
- "...thus ended the record of Alma, which was wrote upon the plates" (page 347)
- "...when they had arriven in the borders of the land" (page 270)
- "...the Lamanites did gather themselves together for to sing" (page 196)
- "they did cast up mighty heaps of earth for to get ore" (page 560)
- "we depend upon them for to teach us the word" (page 451)

By 1823, in fact, Palmyra residents were being inundated with notions about American Indians and Israelites. One 1825 article in the *Wayne Sentinel* of Palmyra printed a speech wherein Native Americans were labeled "'descendants of the lost tribes of Israel.'"[55] A subsequent article added, "Those who are most conversant with the public and private economy of the Indians, are strongly of opinion that they are the lineal descendants of the Israelites."[56]

Smith undoubtedly came into contact with many works advancing such theories.[57] In fact, research has shown that he drew great inspiration from a number of relevant books, going so far as to actually incorporate text from some of them into his Book of Mormon.[58] Perhaps most striking are the parallels existing between Joseph's work and Ethan Smith's *View of the Hebrews* (1823).

There are dozens of textual similarities in these two volumes (see note 59 for a partial listing).[59] Both books even share the same basic story line and premise about a large group of Israelites who arrived in the New World and separated into warring factions, the more violent of which prevailed, but then ended up in a "savage state."[60]

Joseph's saga about finding a buried book written by the ancestors of Native Americans also may have been lifted from *View of the Hebrews,* which declared, "If the Indians are of the tribes of Israel, some decisive evidence of the fact will ere long be exhibited."[61] Ethan Smith then noted a discovery in Massachusetts of parchments containing Hebrew characters. These had been found buried in a place called Indian Hill.[62] Both the Book of Mormon and *View of the Hebrews* also share the following characteristics:

- they begin with frequent references to Jerusalem's destruction
- they tell of inspired prophets among the ancient Americans
- they quote heavily from the biblical book Isaiah
- they describe the ancient Americans as a highly civilized people
- they declare that it is the mission of the American nation in the last days to gather Native Americans into Christianity, thereby hastening the day of the glorious millennium.[63]

Interestingly, when *View of the Hebrews* was first published in 1823, and again in 1825, one resident of the same small town in which the book was released (Poultney, Vermont) was a teenager named Oliver Cowdery—Joseph Smith's third cousin and future scribe.[64] The Cowdery family also happened to be associated with the Poultney Congregational Church, the very church led by none other than Pastor Ethan Smith, author of *View of the Hebrews.*[65]

An Interesting Fact: The idea that Native Americans were descended from Israelites appeared in numerous books that predated Joseph Smith's Book of Mormon:

- *Jews in America* (Thomas Thorowgood, 1650), which "promoted the idea that the Indians were descendants of the lost tribes of Israel"*
- *The History of the American Indians* (James Adair, 1775)
- *Essay Upon the Propagation of the Gospel, in which there are facts to prove that many of the Indians in America are descended from the Ten Tribes* (Charles Crawford, 1799)
- *A Star in the West; or, a Humble Attempt to Discover the Long Lost Tribes of Israel, Preparatory to Their Return to Their Beloved City, Jerusalem* (Elias Boudinot, 1816)

Smith's "Witnesses"

Another issue surrounding the reliability of the Book of Mormon relates to whether or not Smith ever had any gold plates. He always took great pains to ensure that no one saw them, explaining that the angel would take them away if he allowed this to happen.[66] Moreover, anyone who physically looked upon the plates allegedly would perish.[67]

But what about those men who said they *did* see and handle the plates? Their statements, which preface the Book of Mormon, appear in two groups: 1) The Three Witnesses (Oliver Cowdery, David Whitmer, and Martin Harris); and 2) The Eight Witnesses (Christian Whitmer, Jacob Whitmer, Peter Whitmer Jr., John Whitmer, Hiram Page, Joseph Smith Sr., Hyrum Smith, and Samuel Smith).

These joint declarations imply that the signers *physically* saw the plates with their eyes and handled them with their hands. According to BYU professor Daniel C. Peterson, this virtually proves that Smith had the plates.

---

* John L. Brooke, *The Refiner's Fire* (New York: Cambridge University Press, 1994), page 35.

Their existence, says Peterson, "is among the most securely established facts in Latter-day Saint history."[68]

But a look at additional data reveals something still unknown to many Mormons: The witnesses did not *literally* see or handle the plates. They beheld them in visions. Grant Palmer, former director of the LDS Institutes of Religion in California and Utah, explains the cause of today's incorrect notions about the witnesses:

> [W]e tend to read into their testimonies a rationalist perspective rather than a nineteenth-century magical mindset....More specifically, they believed in what has been called second sight. Traditionally, this included the ability to see spirits and their dwelling places within the local hills and elsewhere....Ezra Booth, an early Mormon convert, reported of Joseph: "He does not pretend to see them [spirits and angels] with his natural, but with his spiritual eyes; and he says he can see them as well with his eyes shut, as with them open."...The eleven witnesses to the Book of Mormon claimed second-sight as well.[69]

As for the various additional remarks made by these witnesses, they are usually taken to mean that the men saw or handled the plates just as anyone might see or handle any object in the material world. But as Palmer notes, their oft-quoted words "tell only part of the story."[70] The question is not, Did they ever say they saw or handled the plates? Rather, the question is, What did they *mean* when they said they saw or handled them?

It is fairly obvious that Cowdery, Whitmer, and Harris saw or handled the plates during *visions* they had while in the woods.[71] And contrary to the general impression given by their joint Book of Mormon statement, the men were not all together when they saw the plates.[72] Their experiences came separately, in response to a revelation wherein God promised that Cowdery, Whitmer, and Harris would see the plates (D&C 17:2).

The subsequent vision transpired as the men prayed. At first, nothing happened. Again, they prayed. But still, no plates. Harris left, thinking he was the problem. Suddenly, while he was gone, the angel appeared and showed the plates to Smith, Cowdery, and Whitmer.[73]

Smith then hunted down Harris, who had walked "a considerable distance" from the trio and was "fervently engaged in prayer."[74] After the two men prayed together, "the same vision was opened," causing Harris to cry out, " 'Tis enough; 'tis enough; mine eyes have beheld."[75]

> **Did You Know?** Once the Book of Mormon translation was complete, the plates were supposedly returned to Moroni. According to Brigham Young,
>
> When Joseph got the plates, the angel instructed him to carry them back to the hill Cumorah, which he did. Oliver [Cowdery] says that when Joseph and Oliver went there, the hill opened, and they walked into a cave, in which there was a large and spacious room....They laid the plates on a table; it was a large table that stood in the room. Under this table there was a pile of plates as much as two feet high, and there were altogether in this room more plates than probably many wagon loads; they were piled up in the corners and along the walls.*

It must be remembered that we are not dealing here with whether or not these men ever denied their experiences or recanted their belief that the visions were real *to them*. The more important questions are, Did they witness the plates on the physical plane as opposed to in an inner, second-sight vision? Were their experiences objectively real and tangible or subjectively metaphysical and spiritual?

According to all three men, their heavenly encounter was a vision.[76] For instance, during an 1880 interview with journalist John Murphy, Whitmer explained that his viewing of the angel and plates was similar to how a Quaker might have impressions " 'when the spirit moves,' or as a good Methodist might experience 'a feeling.' "[77]

Martin Harris made similar allusions to the spiritual nature of the event, explaining to Palmyra resident John H. Gilbert (typesetter for the Book of Mormon) that he had seen the plates only " 'with a spiritual [sic] eye."[78] Likewise, according to Reuben P. Harmon, a highly respected citizen of

---

* Brigham Young, June 17, 1877, in *Journal of Discourses*, volume 19, page 38.

Kirtland, Ohio, Martin "never claimed to have seen them [the plates] with his natural eyes, only spiritual vision."[79]

Notable and Quotable:

[W]hen I came to hear Martin Harris state in public that he never saw the plates with his natural eyes only in vision or imagination, neither Oliver [Cowdery] nor David [Whitmer] & also that the eight witnesses never saw them & hesitated to sign that instrument [that is, statement] for that reason, but were persuaded to do it, the last pedestal gave way, in my view our foundations was sapped & the entire superstructure fell a heap of ruins.*

As for Cowdery, he apparently saw the plates in a vision even before meeting Smith, whose 1832 history reads, "[The] Lord appeared unto a young man by the name of Oliver Cowdery and shewed unto him the plates in a vision."[80]

Yet there are several statements by Cowdery, Whitmer, and Harris that suggest they *did* physically see and handle the plates.[81] What are we to make of these comments? Apparently, such remarks were in reference to those occasions on which Smith allowed the men to handle and "heft" the plates—but only as long as the plates were either 1) covered with a cloth or 2) in a closed wooden box.[82]

As for the Eight Witnesses, controversy has surrounded their testimony since 1838, when, during a public meeting, Martin Harris not only confirmed his own "spiritual" vision of the plates, but declared that *none* of the eight witnesses had literally seen or handled the objects.[83] This caused many Mormons—including several apostles—to leave Smith's church.[84] In an August 11, 1838, letter, apostle Warren Parrish recounted that

> Martin Harris, one of the subscribing witnesses; has come out at last, and says he never saw the plates, from which the book purports to have been translated, except in vision; and he further says that any man who says he has seen them in any other way is a liar, Joseph not excepted.[85]

---

* LDS apostle Stephen Burnett, letter to Lyman E. Johnson, April 15, 1838, in Dan Vogel, *Early Mormon Documents,* volume 2, page 291.

Grant Palmer has made one of the most fascinating of all observations about the Book of Mormon witnesses by noting that other religious leaders have produced witnesses to divine objects as well. Of particular relevance is James Strang, a former devotee of Smith's, who maintained that he was supposed to have been Smith's successor.

Strang, like Smith, said he had found ancient plates and translated them. He, too, claimed that he had received the Urim and Thummim from an angel. He used them to produce a holy volume titled *The Book of the Law of the Lord*. It, too, contains a joint statement signed by "witnesses" to the genuine nature of the metal plates from which his book allegedly came forth. The Book of Mormon, therefore, can hardly be considered unique.[86]

LDS RESPONSES

Mormons have earnestly sought to validate Smith's claim that the Book of Mormon is historically accurate. But such efforts have forced them to 1) revise previous interpretations of several passages in the book; and 2) depart from long-held LDS beliefs about the book's geography, archaeology, and anthropology.

Only this approach has enabled LDS apologists to bring the book's mistakes into line with facts about the Book of Mormon era. However, according to LDS history researchers, these new approaches do not at all resolve the numerous problems tied to the book's factual errors.

Archaeology and Geography

Especially disturbing is how today's LDS defenders, in order to get around the Book of Mormon's inaccuracies, have chosen to pay little heed to the words Smith actually used in the text. They have redefined many of his terms, in effect restating what he *must* have meant. Consider the following observations by authors Dan Vogel and Brent Metcalfe about this tactic:

> [S]teel is actually iron; horses are deer; wheat is amaranth; goats are brockets [small deer]; cows are deer, brockets, camelidae [that is, llamas], or bison; and tents are makeshift huts. In short, things are

not what they appear. Never mind that Mesoamerica had no met-
allurgy to speak of until after the Book of Mormon times, that the
Nephites used the horse to pull chariots in battle and over long distances, or that tents are described as being "pitched," portable, and
usable. Only with increasing difficulty do apologists accept the Book
of Mormon at face value.[87]

Of great interest to Mormons has been the archaeology of their book.
Countless LDS works have been published in hopes of offering some evidence for it. But to date, there exists no *definitive* archaeological confirmation
of anything in the Book of Mormon. Some LDS scholars, such as Dee F.
Green, have conceded as much: "The first myth we need to eliminate is that
Book of Mormon archaeology exists."[88] Consider, too, the words of renowned
non-LDS anthropologist Michael Coe:

> [N]othing, absolutely nothing, has ever shown up in any New World
> excavation that would suggest to a dispassionate observer that the
> Book of Mormon, as claimed by Joseph Smith, is a historical doc-
> ument relating to the history of early migrants to our hemisphere.[89]

Although Green and Coe made their comments in 1969 and 1973,
little has changed. Book of Mormon archaeology is still "non-existent."[90]
Bradley Lepper, Assistant Professor in the Department of Sociology and
Anthropology at Denison University (Granville, Ohio), made a similar
criticism in 1997, saying, "There is no archaeological evidence for Old
World culture in the Americas."[91]

Such remarks cannot be easily dismissed, even by Mormons, as evidenced in a 2002 admission by Terryl L. Givens (BYU graduate, author
of *By the Hand of Mormon,* and professor of religion and literature at the
University of Richmond):

> [N]ot one single archaeological artifact has been found that con-
> clusively establishes a direct connection between the record [that is,
> the Book of Mormon] and any actual culture or civilization of the
> Western hemisphere.[92]

Equally troublesome has been finding geographical consistency between the real world and the Book of Mormon. Mormons at one time held that the book's saga encompassed the entire Western hemisphere.[93] Now, however, LDS defenders are claiming that the events took place in a "limited region of Mesoamerica (the area surrounding the Isthmus of Tehuantepec in Southern Mexico)."[94]

Such a view helps offset the vast distances that the Book of Mormon peoples would have had to travel to get from their homelands to the Hill Cumorah in New York, where the golden plates were buried. But this new approach is defensible only through "specialized" arguments that "cannot bear rigorous scrutiny."[95] It also does violence "to the Book of Mormon text, early Mormon history, Joseph Smith's divine edicts, and Mesoamerican archaeology."[96]

As an example of the claims of today's LDS apologists, BYU professor John L. Sorenson maintains that the Nephite saga "played out in a limited area probably less than 500 miles in diameter" and that the "LDS assumption that the New York hill where Moroni buried the gold plates was the same as the Book of Mormon's Hill Cumorah, where Mormon had his great records repository, doesn't work very well."[97]

In other words, even the long-held belief about the final Nephite–Lamanite battle in New York has been jettisoned by modern LDS apologists.[98] They have gone so far as to suggest that *not a single* early Mormon, including Joseph Smith, ever bothered reading the Book of Mormon "closely enough to grasp the fact that the plates Mormon gave to Moroni were never buried in the hill of the final Nephite battle."[99]

Oddly, LDS apologists also are now claiming, "We face a lack of detail in our historical sources as to what the earliest Latter-day Saints thought about Book of Mormon geography."[100] In truth, however, a wealth of data shows precisely what early Mormons believed about this geography. Smith and his associates understood the Book of Mormon to be hemispheric.[101] The LDS founder–prophet even drew maps detailing the Nephite journey from Central America to Missouri and Illinois and then to New York's Hill Cumorah.[102]

As recently as 1990, a letter from the LDS Church's Office of the First Presidency was still advocating the standard LDS teaching that "Cumorah" in the Book of Mormon is the New York Hill Cumorah:

The Church has long maintained, as attested to by references in the writings of General Authorities, that the Hill Cumorah in western New York state is the same as referenced in the Book of Mormon.[103]

Does this mean that today's LDS leaders have still not read the Book of Mormon closely enough to understand it? This question remains unanswered by BYU apologists. Meanwhile, however, they continue to steadily undercut long-held LDS beliefs.[104] This is their only option because defending the geography of the Book of Mormon demands that modern Mormons refute what Joseph taught. Put another way, according to Sorenson and others, Smith was wrong. That is a remarkable criticism of the LDS prophet that would never have been tolerated by church authorities in the early 1800s.[105]

Finally, an additional observation must be made about the 1990 letter above. It was modified in 1993 by another letter from the LDS First Presidency. The latter communication, which was sent to Brent Hall of FARMS, said something quite different:

> While some Latter-day Saints have looked for possible locations and explanations because the New York Hill Cumorah does not readily fit the Book of Mormon description of Cumorah, there are no conclusive connections between the Book of Mormon text and any specific site that has been suggested.[106]

This letter can be taken two ways. It is either 1) supporting old Book of Mormon geography theories and letting traditionally minded Mormons know they can hold on to the views of past LDS leaders since there are "no conclusive connections" to any newly suggested locations for the book's events; or 2) supporting the new Mesoamerican theories about limited Book of Mormon geographical sites by implying that all statements made by past leaders were just opinions, since there are "no conclusive connections" to any locations for the events.

The second choice, of course, would make the 1993 letter an attempt by LDS leaders to support FARMS opinions about a limited Book of Mormon geography. As the letter says, "the New York Hill Cumorah does not readily fit the Book of Mormon description of Cumorah." But it also uses a caution about "no conclusive connections" between any new site and the actual text.

Perhaps a future letter will clarify what the First Presidency is saying. But who should Mormons listen to when it comes to opinions and theories about something as major as where Book of Mormon events took place? Which opinions are more authoritative in Mormonism—those of LDS prophets and apostles, or those of current BYU professors?[107] If an LDS prophet or apostle makes a statement about any Book of Mormon event or historical fact, then do Mormons have to wait to accept that opinion until after it has been approved by BYU professors and professional Mormon apologists?

The DNA Dilemma

One of the harshest blows to the Book of Mormon has come through DNA research. It has verified that Native Americans are not of Israelite origin. They are Asiatic.[108] This has required a mass exodus from the false assumption long held by Mormons—that Israelites are the "principal ancestors" of Native Americans.[109]

LDS apologists and BYU professors are advocating a new *unofficial* opinion that Lehi and his people (see pages 53-54) represented only a "small band" of Israelites, compared to a larger population of indigenous people in the New World.[110] Consequently, only a small number of Native Americans *might* be related to Israelites.

Some Mormons are now going so far as to say that a biological link between Israelites and Native Americans will *never* be found.[111] This admission is possible because, according to the updated, BYU-based view of Native Americans, those genetic markers that *would* have been passed down from Israelites were lost (or "diluted"). The dilution supposedly occurred via "an extensive intermingling [by intermarriage] with the other peoples in the region who were not Israelites [in other words, Asians who had migrated to the Americas]."[112] LDS professor Jeffrey Meldrum articulated this new mindset rather well during a 2003 lecture:

> The necessary experiment simply cannot be designed that would refute the historicity of the Book of Mormon as the record of a small

population (small intermingled population) on the basis of DNA studies and population genetics.[113]

But according to Mormon 1:7 in the Book of Mormon, the Nephite and Lamanite populations were hardly small: "The whole face of the land had become covered with buildings, and the people were as numerous almost, as it were the sand of the sea [about A.D. 322]." Helaman 3:8 adds,

> And it came to pass that they did multiply and spread, and did go forth from the land southward to the land northward, and did spread insomuch that they began to cover the face of the whole earth, from the sea south to the sea north, from the sea west to the sea east.[114]

Joseph Smith himself said that *all* American Indians were "literal descendants of Abraham."[115] He publicly advocated this belief as early as 1833. Smith even claimed that this understanding came from God via an angel.[116] But as previously noted, DNA studies have totally discredited Smith's assumptions.[117]

Notable and Quotable:

The Book of Mormon is a record of the forefathers of our western tribes of Indians; having been found through the ministration of an holy Angel, and translated into our own language by the gift and power of God, after having been hid up in the earth for the last fourteen hundred years, containing the word of God which was delivered unto them. By it we learn that our western tribes of Indians are descendants from that Joseph which was sold into Egypt, and that the land of America is a promised land unto them (Joseph Smith, 1833).[118]

In the face of such scientific data, Mormons have been able to salvage their faith in the Book of Mormon only by use of the aforementioned twists on Smith's views. Predictably, this damage-control spin on traditional LDS thought is quickly gaining popularity, even though Smith's initial theory still appears in the introduction of current editions of the Book of Mormon.[119] (Old beliefs are very difficult to replace overnight.)

Into the Twenty-First Century

It is nothing less than radical for Mormons to now be departing from what was originally taught by LDS leadership. Smith and his associates clearly founded their "Restored Church" on the belief that *all* Native Americans (as well as the inhabitants of Central and South America) are descendants of Israelites.[120]

This doctrine was for years intrinsic to Mormonism.[121] To quote LDS president Spencer W. Kimball, "The term Lamanite includes all Indians and Indian mixtures, such as the Polynesians, the Guatemalans, the Peruvians, as well as the Sioux, the Apache, the Mohawk, the Navajo, and others."[122] As recently as 2003, LDS president Gordon B. Hinckley was still voicing similar ideas.[123]

Notable and Quotable:

[T]he land was left to the possession of the red men, who were without intelligence, only in the affairs of their wars; and having no records, only preserving their history by tradition from father to son, lost the account of their true origin, and wandered from river to river, from hill to hill, from mountain to mountain, and from sea to sea, till the land was again peopled, in a measure, by a rude, wild, revengeful, warlike and barbarous race.—Such are our Indians.*

Modern LDS apologists, however, are trying to not only change this belief, but downplay its significance in their community. During the 2003 lecture mentioned on page 69, for example, LDS professor Jeffrey Meldrum said that early Mormons suffered from "misconceptions about the scope and context" of the Book of Mormon by believing that "all Native Americans are solely Lehi's direct descendants."[124] He then added,

---

* Oliver Cowdery, letter to W.W. Phelps, *Messenger & Advocate*, July 1835, volume 1, number 10, page 158.

This assumption seems to have been held by *some* early members
of the Church. And may still be held by *some* today—that all Native
Americans are exclusively descended from lineal remnants of Laman;
the Lamanites.[125]

In truth, *all* early Mormons held this view.[126] And virtually *all* modern
Mormons advanced the same notion until science showed it to be erroneous.[127] Even now, relatively few Mormons have adopted the new and
revised opinion. This may be due to one very controversial aspect of the
updated LDS paradigm—that non-Israelite natives were already living
in the New World when Lehi arrived. It is with these people that the
Nephites are said to have intermarried, thus enabling their Israelite DNA
to be diluted.[128]

However, the Book of Mormon makes no mention of these non-
Israelites. And that silence contradicts BYU professor Noel B. Reynolds'
claim that the book "describes various ebbs and flows of ethnic interaction without ever losing track of even the most minor groups."[129] The
silence also reveals what has always been the LDS view—namely that
Israelites were the *first* ones to populate the Americas.[130]

The clear implication of modern DNA research is that the Book of
Mormon is neither an authentic nor a historical account of either the
ancient Israelites or Native Americans. This assessment, which is commonly used by secular critics of the church, is very troubling to Mormons.
But according to BYU professor Daniel Peterson, such an observation
against the Book of Mormon is even more irritating when it comes from
"evangelical Protestants."[131]

Like Peterson, many LDS apologists feel that Christians' use of the
DNA argument is akin to spiritual "suicide bombing."[132] How so? Because
the DNA argument, Mormons maintain, can also be turned around and
applied just as effectively to the Bible. But this LDS claim is flawed because
it rests on the erroneous assumption that most Christians believe the world
was created around 4000 B.C. (at the beginning of the Adamic era) and
that the Great Flood occurred around 2000 B.C. (during the Noahic
period)—which would mean that all of us should have some genetic material traceable to Noah.[133]

Such dates, if they were explicitly noted in the Bible, would seem to contradict much of what Scripture recounts as history since DNA studies at their current state of development cannot trace any of us back to either date. (And this is not to mention we have evidence that apparently points to human existence before 4000 B.C.) Consequently, the 4000 B.C.–2000 B.C. response has become almost the standard LDS reply to Christians wanting to discuss the DNA issue.[134] As Peterson says, "[I]f you're going to use DNA evidence as a weapon against the Latter-day Saints because it proves that Indian migrations came tens of thousands of years before the present era, intellectual honesty demands that you let the other shoe drop. . . . DNA is a double-edged sword."[135]

The truth of the matter, however, is that not many Christians embrace these exact dates as being accurate, let alone rest their faith in the Bible on them. The majority of traditional Christians understand that the world is older than 6000 years, although no one really knows how much older. Consequently, the LDS argument about DNA, Christians, and the Bible is irrelevant. It is a straw-man argument—and it in no way eradicates the DNA evidence against the Book of Mormon.

Jettisoning More Junk

Another belief now being discarded in response to the new BYU-based theories on the Book of Mormon and the Lamanites involves the destiny of Native Americans. These cursed Lamanites, according to early LDS teachings, were supposed to become "white like unto the Nephites" once they converted *en masse* to Mormonism.

Although this doctrine has in recent years been downplayed, its existence in Mormonism cannot be denied.[136] In fact, the Book of Mormon, originally stated that the Lamanites would indeed turn white-skinned ("white and delightsome") upon returning to God.[137] But then in 1981, the term "white" was changed to "pure."

LDS leaders claimed that the alteration had nothing to do with the absurd notion that "Indians" would physically turn white. However, similar Book of Mormon passages indicate otherwise.[138] And numerous pre-1981 statements from LDS officials indeed taught that the curse of dark skin upon Native Americans would one day be removed.

In 1960, LDS president Spencer W. Kimball reported that Indians were *already* "becoming a white and delightsome people." He added that Indian children "in the home placement program in Utah are often lighter than their brothers and sisters in the hogans on the reservation." Kimball also said he knew one Indian girl who, because she was LDS, was "several shades lighter than her parents."[139]

In *Why I Believe,* Mormon writer George Edward Clark noted that he himself had been privileged to see the miraculous change in the skin pigmentation of LDS American Indians. In reference to the Catawba tribe of South Carolina, Clark wrote,

> That tribe, or most of its people, are members of the Church of Jesus Christ of Latter-day Saints (Mormon). Those Indians, at least as many as I have observed, were white and delightsome; as white and fair as any group of citizens of our country. I know of no prophecy, ancient or modern, that has had a more literal fulfillment.[140]

Despite such straightforward remarks—which clearly contradict scientific knowledge and discovery—today's LDS apologists continue to support the historicity of the Book of Mormon. But as we have seen, out of necessity they have been altering key LDS beliefs in opposition to what Mormonism's founders taught.

Who are we to believe? If we adhere to Joseph Smith's teachings, then the Book of Mormon is out of step with history, geography, anthropology, archaeology, and other sciences. If we embrace the views of today's LDS apologists and professors, then we can only wonder how many more of Smith's views are flawed. Other questions relating to LDS authority are equally disturbing to evangelicals:

- Who defines Mormon beliefs—Joseph Smith, living prophets, or modern BYU professors and LDS apologists? If it is BYU professors, then why is there a need for LDS prophets?

- What other teachings espoused by Smith might future LDS apologists, BYU professors, or both dismiss in an effort to make Mormonism compatible with scientific findings?

- Where is there any consistency of faith in Mormonism if basic beliefs such as the identity of Native Americans can be jettisoned so easily?

- Who speaks for Mormonism? Why should Mormons believe the *unofficial* opinion of modern LDS apologists over the teachings of Joseph Smith? Even if Smith was merely expressing his "opinion," as Mormonism's founding prophet–leader he would certainly be in a better position to know the meaning of the Book of Mormon—especially since he additionally stated that it was the angel who told him the Indians were "the literal descendants of Abraham."

For evangelicals, these questions build an impenetrable barrier to accepting the Book of Mormon. Mormons, on the other hand, remain unmoved by such issues. Faithful Mormons do not even seem bothered by the words of respected biological anthropologists such as Michael Crawford of the University of Kansas, who has said, "I don't think there is one iota of evidence that suggests a lost tribe from Israel made it all the way to the New World. It is a great story, slain by ugly fact."[141]

A Tale of Two Scholars

After years of research, LDS apologist and scholar B.H. Roberts reached a shocking conclusion about the Book of Mormon—a conclusion that diametrically opposed his previous position. This shocking reversal came to light in *Studies of the Book of Mormon,* edited by Brigham D. Madsen and Sterling M. McMurrin, which brought to light a manuscript wherein Roberts expressed doubt about the authenticity of the Book of Mormon. In reference to certain characters in the book, he wrote,

> The evidence, I sorrowfully submit, points to Joseph Smith as their creator. It is difficult to believe that they are the product of history, that they come upon the scene separated by long periods of time, and among a race which was the ancestral race of the red man of America.[142]

Then, shortly before his death in 1933, he told Wesley P. Lloyd, former dean of the BYU graduate school, that he had come to realize that the Book of Mormon was a nonhistorical document. Lloyd wrote in his diary that Roberts said the plates "were not objective but subjective with Joseph Smith, that his exceptional imagination qualified him psychologically for the experience which he had in presenting to the world the Book of Mormon."[143]

Popular LDS scholar Thomas Stuart Ferguson reached a similar conclusion. He had dedicated his life to finding objective proof for the Book of Mormon, going so far as to found the New World Archaeology Foundation at BYU. It was established specifically for the purpose of unearthing archaeological evidence supporting the book.

Did You Know? LDS apologists have tried to refute the idea that B.H. Roberts changed his position on the Book of Mormon. For example, FARMS representatives have alleged that the editors of *Studies of the* Book of Mormon—Brigham D. Madsen and Sterling M. McMurrin—misrepresented Roberts' final views. Madsen and McMurrin responded by offering to hold a public panel discussion of the issues. Their offer, however, was refused by members of FARMS, who simply continued to maintain that Roberts was indeed misrepresented and that, by making the statements he had made, he was only playing the "devil's advocate" role. However, no documentation was ever provided by FARMS to prove such an assertion.

Other LDS writers have sought to disprove the Roberts-lost-his-faith opinion by citing several instances of his affirming the Book of Mormon after he began his in-depth study of it.* But these attempts fail to adequately address some of Roberts' later statements because they focus on declarations he made *before* he had reached his final conclusion.

But by 1972, Ferguson's expectations had been all but utterly destroyed.[144] This led to his preparation in 1975 of a 29-page report that

---

* See Truman G. Madsen, "B.H. Roberts and the Book of Mormon," *BYU Studies* (Summer 1979), volume 19, pages 427-445.

responded to papers written by LDS apologists John Sorenson and Garth Norman, both of whom were claiming that archaeological evidence for the Book of Mormon existed. Ferguson wrote,

> With all of these great efforts, it cannot be established factually that anyone, from Joseph Smith to the present day, has put his finger on a single point of terrain that was a Book-of-Mormon geographical place. And the hemisphere has been pretty well checked out by competent people....I must agree with Dee Green, who has told us that to date there is no Book-of-Mormon geography. I, for one, would be happy if Dee were wrong.[145]

In a 1976 letter, however, Ferguson explained that he had decided to keep quiet about his findings because to do otherwise might destroy the faith of others. He suggested that like-minded Mormons do the same, because he saw Mormonism as a well-conceived "myth-fraternity" to be enjoyed.[146] "[Smith] can be refuted," he wrote, "[b]ut why bother...? It would be like wiping out placebos in medicine, and that would make no sense when they do lots of good."[147]

FINAL OBSERVATIONS

Today, the ongoing struggle by Latter-day Saints to verify the Book of Mormon continues. But as one LDS critic has noted, they have so far had "little success."[148] The best they have yet been able to do is to revise and edit the volume and its teachings to bring LDS more in line with so-called "facts" that appear in the text.[149]

As for other LDS attempts to find parallels between the Book of Mormon and ancient Mesoamerica, some of these have been decidedly peculiar. For example, BYU Professor John L. Sorenson, like many Latter-day Saints, seems rather captivated by the "similarities between certain characteristics of the god Quetzalcoatl, as known from native traditions in Mexico and Guatemala, and Jesus Christ, whose visit to Lehi's descendants is described in 3 Nephi."[150] Likewise, LDS defender Dr. Joseph Allen—founder of Book of Mormon Tours—has asserted that "the deity Quetzalcoatl apparently had its origin in the visit of Jesus Christ to the American continent."[151]

There are indeed several minor similarities between Jesus and Quetzal-coatl. The latter, for instance, was said to be a bearded, fair-skinned god who left his people, promising to one day return. He also was born of a virgin. But what LDS apologists tend to not mention are a few additional aspects of Quetzalcoatl, none of which seem very consistent with Jesus Christ:

- He also was known as the Serpent Dragon, or Feathered Serpent god: "The first myth he appears in, he is called 'Precious Serpent.'"[152] "His temples were circular with conical roofs and often had serpent maws acting as a doorway."[153] Hence, Quetzalcoatl was connected to snake worship.

- Human sacrifices were made to Quetzalcoatl in the Toltec, Aztec, Inca, and Mayan cultures.[154] According to the Quetzalcoatl–Tohil myth, Quetzalcoatl–Tohil gave instruction for worship of the gods (that is, human sacrifices) so that humanity could be created.[149] In his compassion, however, he demanded only one human sacrifice a year.[156]

- Although he was a son of the virgin goddess Coatlicue, Quetzal-coatl had a twin brother—Xolotl. As for Coatlicue, she was eventually decapitated by her other children. She, like Quetzalcoatl, was a serpent deity. Hence, she often was depicted wearing a skirt of snakes. The intricate system of Mesoamerican mythology also described her as a female monster of sorts that devoured others. In one version of creation, she is killed by the gods Quetzalcoatl and Tezcatlipoca, who changed themselves into serpents and ripped her in two. Her lower half rose to form the heavens and her upper part descended to form the earth. Coatlicue also had a gory food craving—human hearts and blood.

Evangelicals cannot help but see LDS arguments about limited Book of Mormon geography, Quetzalcoatl, and diluted DNA as little more than misguided and desperate efforts to salvage their cherished faith. To traditional Christians, Mormons are only clinging to what their thirteenth president, Ezra Taft Benson, said: "We do not have to prove the Book of Mormon is true. The book is its own proof. All we need to do is read it and declare it! The Book of Mormon is not on trial."[157]

Indeed, this idea was reiterated in a 2003 FARMS article by Jeffrey Meldrum and Trent D. Stephens: "[T]he veracity of the claims of the Book of Mormon lies beyond the ken of modern DNA research," said the two scholars. "[T]he book, as a witness of the prophetic calling of Joseph Smith and as another testament of the divinity of Jesus Christ, remain[s] within the realm of faith and individual testimony."[158]

THUS SAITH JOSEPH

[Joseph shall] be called a seer, a translator, a prophet....
[The Church shall] give heed unto all his words,
and commandments, which he shall give unto you,
as he receiveth them, walking in all holiness before me:
For his word ye shall receive, as if from mine own mouth,
in all patience and faith. [1]

—revelation to Joseph Smith, April 6, 1830, *Book of Commandments*

God speaks to me," said the LDS missionary.

"God speaks to me too," I responded.

Elder Banks was stunned. Speechless.

"What's the problem?" I asked.

He hesitated, but finally explained. "I thought you didn't believe in revelation. In The Church of Jesus Christ of Latter-day Saints we believe in revelation. Our church is founded upon the revelations of Joseph Smith. God spoke to him. And God has spoken to me. And I bear you my testimony that Joseph was a prophet, that the Book of Mormon is true, and that The Church of Jesus Christ of Latter-day Saints is God's true church."

I paused. "Did God tell you that?"

"Yes, he did."

"But Elder Banks," I continued, "we have a few problems. First, I already said God speaks to me too. Second, God has told me that Joseph was *not* a prophet, that the Book of Mormon is *not* true, and that The Church of Jesus Christ of Latter-day Saints is *not* God's true church. Now what? Third, insofar as God speaking to Joseph, if that is true, then my question is, Which versions of the things he said to Joseph are you going to believe?"

"What do you mean, 'versions'?" he asked.

This final question launched my new friend and me into a very long discussion about truth, Scripture, LDS history, and a host of other things relating to what is one of the most important features of Mormonism—revelation. Its significance to Mormons cannot be overstated. It is seen as God's stamp of approval on his true followers.[2]

Evangelicals also accept that God can speak to us in many ways: for example, through Scripture, dreams and visions, and impressions he imparts to our spirit. More problematic, though, is another kind of revelation that is accepted by Latter-day Saints but rejected by evangelicals. This particular type of revelation allegedly is communicated to us through a "living prophet" (the LDS president), whose task is to lead the church and impart messages bearing scriptural authority.[3] Here we have one of the deepest divides between evangelicals and Mormons, as the following pages will show.

⌗ ⌗ ⌗

Joseph Smith is said to be the first prophet ordained by God in our modern era. His revelations and extrabiblical writings, therefore, are the source of most LDS beliefs. Smith's first work, as already noted, was the Book of Mormon. His two additional volumes of scripture were the Doctrine and Covenants (D&C) and the Pearl of Great Price (PGP).

> **Mormon Point:** Anyone can easily find out what the LDS Church teaches by reading "The Articles of Faith," which are found not only in the Pearl of Great Price, but also on the official Church Web site at lds.org.
>
> **Counterpoint:** "The Articles of Faith" is a list of 13 LDS beliefs that, from an evangelical perspective, do not at all explain what Mormons actually believe. The terminology used may sound thoroughly evangelical, yet the meanings ascribed to the terms are radically different than the ones that would normally be applied to them by evangelicals (see chapters 4–8). This has often confused the general public by making it appear as if Mormonism is just another denomination of traditional Christianity.

The Doctrine and Covenants is primarily a collection of revelations.[4] The Pearl of Great Price is a compilation of several works, including the *official* narrative detailing Smith's First Vision, Smith's tale about Moroni, and the story involving the gold plates (titled "Joseph Smith—History"). The Pearl of Great Price also contains

- selections from the Book of Moses
- the Book of Abraham
- a retranslation of Matthew 23:39 and Matthew 24 ("Joseph Smith—Matthew")
- "The Articles of Faith," which lists 13 basic LDS doctrines

Did You Know? The Doctrine and Covenants also includes a revelation to Brigham Young (section 136), a vision received by LDS president Joseph Fielding Smith (section 138), the 1890 LDS Manifesto banning polygamy (Official Declaration 1), and the 1978 LDS policy change that allowed blacks to hold the Mormon priesthood (Official Declaration 2). Other documents contained are minutes of the meeting wherein the LDS High Council was organized (section 102), a statement on LDS beliefs concerning earthly governments (section 134), and an eyewitness account of Joseph Smith's murder (section 135).

Both the Pearl of Great Price and Doctrine and Covenants, like the Book of Mormon, are rejected by evangelicals for many reasons. Mormons, however, see them as examples of God's ongoing communication to us.

—— MORMON QUOTES ——

"The Bible, Book of Mormon, Doctrine and Covenants, and Pearl of Great Price do not contain the wisdom of men alone, but of God" (George Albert Smith, LDS apostle, 1917).[5]

"Through revelation we have received the Book of Mormon, the Doctrine and Covenants, and the Pearl of Great Price, which contain the words of God to us" (M. Russell Ballard, LDS apostle, 1998).[6]

"[God] provided a guide—a spiritual road map—to help us achieve success in our journey. We call that guide the standard works...the

Holy Bible, the Book of Mormon, the Doctrine and Covenants, and the
Pearl of Great Price—[they] constitute the *standard* by which we should
live" (Russell M. Nelson, LDS apostle, 2003).[7]

A Closer Look

On April 6, 1830, the Mormon church was formally organized in New
York by 24-year-old Joseph Smith Jr. Within a year he and his initial followers had gained hundreds of converts from Pennsylvania, New York,
and Ohio. All of them embraced the divine authenticity of the Book of
Mormon and implicitly believed the revelations Smith had started
declaring in the first person, as if God himself were speaking.[8]

These revelations, after being carefully transcribed by his followers,
were initially published in *The Evening and the Morning Star,* an LDS periodical first printed in Missouri (June 1832 to July 1833). They were subsequently arranged, edited by Smith for accuracy, then printed as *A Book
of Commandments* (1833).[9]

But because very few copies of the *Book of Commandments* were produced, it remained unavailable to most Mormons. So in 1835 LDS leaders
republished the revelations. But by that time the declarations were showing
their age. Many contained outdated information. Some included erroneous statements. Others presented abandoned doctrines. A few of the
revelations simply revealed too much information about LDS beliefs,
which in turn had caused critics to respond negatively.

Smith's solution was simple. He rewrote the revelations so they would
conform to his needs and those of the church.[10] The texts were extensively
edited "without regard for earlier documents."[11] Key phrases were altered.
Crucial words were deleted. And never-before-seen text was added in such
a way as to make it seem as if the new verbiage had always been part of
the divine messages received by Smith some years earlier.

These *revised* revelations were first published individually in Ohio in
the *Evening and Morning Star* (a reprint of the earlier newspaper). Soon
afterward they were collected and published in a new book of doctrine
titled the Doctrine and Covenants (1835).[12] The degree of text alteration
was highlighted in 1955 by Melvin J. Petersen, who calculated the changes
made as follows: 703 words had been changed, 1656 words had been
added, and 453 words had been deleted.[13]

So drastic were these revisions that some of the revelations ended up containing material inconsistent with the historical time frame in which they were initially given (about 1830 to 1832). Oddly, in 1835 no one paid much attention to the changes that had been made to God's words. No explanations were requested. No questions were asked. And no objections were raised, at least not at first. This event illustrates how Mormons view divine truth—it is "not absolute or fixed; it is changeable, flexible."[14] Evangelicals find such manipulations intolerable. Either God said what he said, or he did not say it.

As for the Pearl of Great Price, two of the works it contains are especially interesting: the Book of Moses and the Book of Abraham. Both of these works advocate teachings that are radically opposed to traditional Christianity. And yet they are crucial to Mormonism.

The Book of Moses is a rewrite of the first several chapters of Genesis, which, according to Smith, needed rewriting because the biblical text had been so corrupted. This project began after God himself directed Smith to correct Genesis. His revision (by revelation) not only deleted so-called mistakes in the Bible's first book, but also inserted a great deal of material that had supposedly been excised by evil men.[15]

Something to Consider: When Smith received his revelations, they were recorded by scribes in a manner that suggests his words were understood as coming directly from God. Popular LDS writer John Stewart noted, "Several of his associates, sitting in his presence when some of the revelations were received, reported that Joseph would dictate them to a clerk at as fast and steady a pace as the clerk was able to write, maintaining an even flow of delivery, and never altering the words spoken."[16]

The Book of Abraham is supposedly the "translation" of some ancient Egyptian records that Smith obtained in 1835. These ancient artifacts came into his hands after the arrival in Kirtland, Ohio, of a traveling exhibitor named Michael H. Chandler, who owned four mummies and several ancient papyrus scrolls. Smith's followers bought the entire exhibit for $2400. The scrolls, said Smith, contained knowledge directly traceable to Abraham (the Hebrew patriarch) and Joseph (the son of Jacob).

So important were these documents and their alleged teachings that Smith put illustrations of the papyri images ("Facsimiles 1, 2, 3") into his new Book of Abraham. The drawings, Smith's interpretation of them, and the translation of the text on his scrolls were first published in 1842.[17] Then, after being republished and redistributed in 1851 and 1878, the Book of Abraham was canonized in 1880 and placed in the Pearl of Great Price.

It is now known, however, that Smith's papyri were common Egyptian funerary texts. And rather than being composed during Abraham's era, the writings date back to only around 100 B.C. Nevertheless, Mormons have continued to accept the Book of Abraham as proof of Smith's powers to translate.

According to BYU professor of ancient scripture Andrew Skinner, the Book of Abraham "is a unique and priceless gem in our treasury of revealed scripture...a most remarkable book."[18] Skinner says it is "so dynamic that it can reveal the historical and cultural origins of ancient Egyptian civilization...and yet, in the turn of a phrase, teach us profound truths about eternity."[19]

EVANGELICAL THOUGHTS

Was Joseph Smith a prophet or not? Were the revelations and scriptures he produced of God or not? To answer these questions, the remainder of this chapter will focus not only on the Doctrine and Covenants and Pearl of Great Price themselves, but also on how these texts were received.

Doctrine and Covenants

Smith's revelations began in 1828, before his Book of Mormon "translation" was complete. At that time, of course, he was still using his seer stone, which he later called his "Urim and Thummim." Not surprisingly, he began receiving revelations through this device. His first 15 revelations were obtained in this way (D&C 3–12, 14–18).[20] In 1842, he admitted as much in a published explanation of how he and Oliver Cowdery settled a disagreement about whether the apostle John had ever died. They agreed to settle it by "the Urim and Thummim"—the seer stone.[21]

Smith continued to use his stone for revelations after the publication of the Book of Mormon, but only on occasion.[22] One reason for this change may have been a false revelation he received in 1830. David Whitmer related the details of this event in 1887:

> Joseph looked into the hat in which he placed the stone, and received a revelation that some of the brethren should go to Toronto, Canada, and that they would sell the copyright of the Book of Mormon. Hiram Page and Oliver Cowdery went to Toronto on this mission, but they failed entirely to sell the copyright, returning without any money. Joseph was at my father's house when they returned. I was there also, and am an eye witness to these facts. Jacob Whitmer and John Whitmer were also present when Hiram Page and Oliver Cowdery returned from Canada. Well, we were all in great trouble; and we asked Joseph how it was that he had received a revelation from the Lord and the brethren had utterly failed in their undertaking....[H]e enquired of the Lord about it, and behold the following revelation came through the stone: "Some revelations are of God: some revelations are of man; and some revelations are of the devil."[23]

But the above prophecy, which for understandable reasons never found its way into print, was not the only problematic revelation. As mentioned, even the divine messages that got published in the 1833 *Book of Commandments* had to be dramatically altered for the 1835 Doctrine and Covenants. These changes "introduced concepts, people, names, and structures which did not [even] exist in the original revelations and historical documents."[24]

D. Michael Quinn has observed, "In some instances these unannounced changes altered or reversed the original meaning of the various statements."[25] According to David Whitmer, Smith had to make the changes because he and other LDS leaders "had gone away ahead of the written word" as it was originally given.[26]

> **Something to Consider:** In 1842, Joseph Smith said that a bad angel would be revealed if he were to contradict a former revelation. In this same *Times and Seasons* editorial, Smith also explained that another way to tell the difference between a good angel and a bad angel was by the color of his hair (*History of the Church*, volume 4, page 581).

One of the changed revelations was *Book of Commandments* 44:32. It initially read, "[F]or I will consecrate the riches of the Gentiles, unto my people which are of the house of the Israel." But this verse created strife with non-Mormons in Missouri, who feared that the Latter-day Saints were going to take their property and goods by force if necessary.

So in 1835 Smith changed the passage to read, "[F]or I will consecrate of the riches of those who embrace my gospel among the Gentiles, unto the poor of my people who are of the house of Israel" (D&C 13:11—1835 edition; D&C 42:39—modern edition). Obviously, the whole thrust of the message was changed to be less controversial.

> **Did You Know?** "[Joseph] received several revelations to which I was a witness by means of the Seerstone," said LDS apostle Orson Pratt in 1878. "But he could receive also without any instrument."* The LDS Church's *official* history reports,
>
> > [Pratt] explained the circumstances under which several revelations were received by Joseph, the Prophet, and the manner in which he received them, he being present on several occasions of the kind. Declared [that] at such times Joseph used the Seerstone when inquiring of the Lord, and receiving revelation, but that he was so thoroughly endowed with the inspiration of the Almighty and the spirit of revelation that he often received them without any instrument.†

Consider, too, the changes to *Book of Commandments* 4 and 7 (Tables 3.1 and 3.2). The first passage was changed to allow for Smith's expanded responsibilities and new "gifts" he apparently wanted to begin exercising. The second passage, however, was reworded to *conceal* a "gift"—that of Oliver Cowdery's occult divination by a rod, which God had originally blessed.

Oddly, despite the hundreds of changes that were made to Smith's revelations, 12 LDS apostles apparently approved an 1835 joint statement certifying the "Truth of the Book of Doctrine and Covenants" (D&C, 1835 edition, page 256).[27] They bore testimony that "these commandments were given by inspiration of God."

---

* Orson Pratt, *Millennial Star,* December 16, 1878 (volume 40, number 49).

† *History of the Church,* introduction, volume 5, page xxxi.

Book of Commandments 4:2 (1833)	D&C 32:1 (1835) / 5:4 (modern)
"I the Lord am God, and I have given these things unto my servant Joseph.... [A]nd he has a gift to translate the book, and I have commanded him that he shall pretend to no other gift, for I will grant him no other gift."	"I the Lord am God, and have given these things unto you, my servant Joseph.... And you have a gift to translate the plates; and this is the first gift that I bestowed upon you, and I have commanded that you should pretend to no other gift until my purpose is fulfilled in this; for I will grant unto you no other gift until it is finished."

Table 3.1
Many words were added to this revelation in order to expand Joseph's role as a religious leader. A literal interpretation of the initial revelation suggests that Joseph originally "had one and only one task, that of translating the plates, when he had completed that task, he would have 'no other gift.' In this interpretation, Joseph would have changed the phrase to justify his later actions: he was not called to be a prophet or to organize a church, but assumed those roles on his own."[28]

Book of Commandments 7:3 (1833)	D&C 34:3 (1835) / 8:6-9 (modern)
"[Y]ou have another gift, which is the gift of working with the rod: behold it has told you things: behold there is no other power save God, that can cause this rod of nature, to work in your hands, for it is the work of God; and therefore whatsoever you shall ask me to tell you by that means, that will I grant unto you."	"[Y]ou have another gift, which is the gift of Aaron: behold it has told you many things: behold there is no other power save the power of God that can cause this gift of Aaron to be with you; therefore, doubt not, for it is the gift of God, and you shall hold it in your hands, and do marvelous works; and no power shall be able to take it away out of your hands; for it is the work of God.... [W]hatsoever you shall ask me to tell you by that means, that will I grant unto you."

Table 3.2
D. Michael Quinn writes, "Church authorities published this 'rod of nature' revelation in 1832 and again in 1833, but after E.D. Howe's 1834 *Mormonism Unvailed* ridiculed the Smiths' previous use of divining rods, the 1835 edition of the Doctrine and Covenants changed these references."[29]

H. Michael Marquardt notes, "It seems that Cowdery obtained revelations as he worked with a divining rod, but, with the change, the allusion to Aaron's rod which budded (Num. 17:8), is obscurantist."[30]

However, LDS apostle William E. McLellin (whose name *still* appears on the statement) later labeled this testimony a "base forgery."[31] In reality, it was the 1831 testimony to the *Book of Commandments*—simply given "a few minor changes in wording" and inserted.[32] When the Doctrine and Covenants text was approved at a Kirtland, Ohio, conference in August 1835, most of the senior LDS leaders (for example, the Mormon apostles) were not even there! They had left Ohio on a mission and were out of state until October.[33]

McLellin left the church because, as the *Salt Lake Tribune* reported, his faith had been "shaken by the changes made in the revelations."[34] The former apostle consistently told the same story about the Doctrine and Covenants throughout the remainder of his life.[35] David Whitmer leveled equally harsh charges against the book.[36]

Today's Mormons, however, have no problem with the tinkering that has been done with their prophet's original words. Nor do they seem concerned over some of the less-than-accurate comments made by various LDS leaders about these changes. Evangelicals, on the other hand, even without considering the content of Smith's revelations, find their alterations to be reason enough for rejecting them.

The alterations can easily be seen using photocopies of the 1833 *Book of Commandments*. The following graphics show exactly how and where the 1835 changes were made. Boxed text indicates added words. Underlines show rewrites. A strikethrough has been made over deleted words.

> **Did You Know?** Faithful Latter-day Saints have stated that "the fact that Joseph Smith expanded some of the revelations he received is evidence for, not against, his prophetic calling."* This reflects the LDS belief that a prophet, because he is a prophet, can simply add to or take away from divine revelation (see pages 103–104).
>
> Mormons allege this is what the biblical writers did. LDS apologist Stephen Gibson reasons, "Since we don't have the original manuscripts used for the books of the Bible, nor do we have records of their writing processes, critics cannot claim that Biblical prophets never revised nor added to their revelations."† But this type of reasoning is known as an "argument from silence." It is actually meaningless because arguments from silence can be used to prove nearly anything.

---

*†Stephen W. Gibson, *One-Minute Answers to Anti-Mormon Questions* (Bountiful, UT: Horizon Publishers, 1995), page 82.

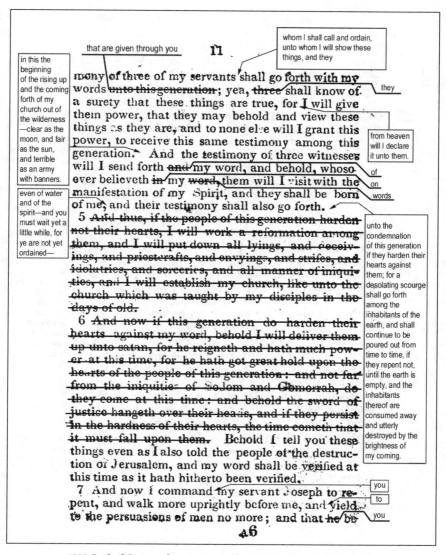

in this the beginning of the rising up and the coming forth of my church out of the wilderness —clear as the moon, and fair as the sun, and terrible as an army with banners.

even of water and of the spirit—and you must wait yet a little while, for ye are not yet ordained—

that are given through you

11

whom I shall call and ordain, unto whom I will show these things, and they

mony of three of my servants shall go forth with my words unto this generation; yea, three shall know of a surety that these things are true, for I will give them power, that they may behold and view these things as they are, and to none else will I grant this power, to receive this same testimony among this generation. And the testimony of three witnesses will I send forth and my word, and behold, whosoever believeth in my word, them will I visit with the manifestation of my Spirit, and they shall be born of me, and their testimony shall also go forth.

they

from heaven will I declare it unto them.

of
on
words

5 And thus, if the people of this generation harden not their hearts, I will work a reformation among them, and I will put down all lyings, and deceivings, and priestcrafts, and envyings, and strifes, and idolatries, and sorceries, and all manner of iniquities, and I will establish my church, like unto the church which was taught by my disciples in the days of old.

6 And now if this generation do harden their hearts against my word, behold I will deliver them up unto satan, for he reigneth and hath much power at this time, for he hath got great hold upon the hearts of the people of this generation: and not far from the iniquities of Sodom and Gomorrah, do they come at this time: and behold the sword of justice hangeth over their heads, and if they persist in the hardness of their hearts, the time cometh that it must fall upon them. Behold I tell you these things even as I also told the people of the destruction of Jerusalem, and my word shall be verified at this time as it hath hitherto been verified.

unto the condemnation of this generation if they harden their hearts against them; for a desolating scourge shall go forth among the inhabitants of the earth, and shall continue to be poured out from time to time, if they repent not, until the earth is empty, and the inhabitants thereof are consumed away and utterly destroyed by the brightness of my coming.

7 And now I command my servant Joseph to repent, and walk more uprightly before me, and yield to the persuasions of men no more; and that he be

you
to
you

46

1833 *Book of Commandments*, page 11 (D&C 5:11-22, modern edition).

23

plan, that he may destroy this work; for he ~~has~~ put
it into their hearts to do this, that by lying they may
say they have caught you in the words which you
have pretended to translate.
3 Verily I say unto you, that I will not suffer that
satan shall accomplish his evil design in this thing,
for behold he has put it into their hearts to tempt the
Lord ~~their~~ God; ~~for~~ behold they say in their hearts,
We will see if God has given him power to translate, if so, ~~he will~~ also give him power again; and
if God giveth him power again, or if he ~~translate~~
again, or in other words, if he bringeth forth the
same words, behold we have the same with us, and
we have altered them: Therefore, they will not
agree, and we will say that he has lied in his words,
and that he has no gift, and that he has no power:
therefore, we will destroy him, and also the work,
and we will do this that we may not be ashamed in
the end, and that we may get glory of the world.
4 Verily, verily I say unto you, that satan has
great hold upon their hearts; he stirreth them up ~~to~~
~~do~~ iniquity against that which is good, that he may
lead their souls to destruction, and thus he has laid
a cunning plan to destroy the work of God; yea, he
stirreth up their hearts to anger against this work;
yea, he saith unto them, Deceive and lie in wait to
catch, that ye may destroy: behold this is no harm,
and thus he flattereth them and telleth them that it
is no sin to lie, that they may catch a man in a lie,
that they may destroy him, and thus he flattereth
them, and leadeth them along until he draggeth their
souls down to hell; and thus he causeth them to
catch themselves in their own snare; and thus he
goeth up and down, to and fro in the earth, seeking
to destroy the souls of men.

hath
in asking to translate it over again, and then,
to get thee to
thy
and think
translates
and their hearts are corrupt, and full of wickedness and abominations; and they love darkness rather than light, because their deeds are evil; therefore they will not ask of me. Satan stirreth them up,
thinking
But I will require this at their hands, and it shall turn to their shame and condemnation in the day of judgment.

1833 *Book of Commandments*, page 23 (D&C 10:12-27, modern edition).

18

CHAPTER VI.

1 *A Revelation given to Joseph and Oliver, in Harmony, Pennsylvania, April, 1829, when they desired to know whether John, the beloved disciple, tarried on earth. Translated from parchment, written and hid up by himself.*

AND the Lord said unto me, John my beloved, what desirest thou? and I said Lord, give unto me power that I may bring souls unto thee.— And the Lord said unto me: Verily, verily I say unto thee, because thou desiredst this, thou shalt tarry till I come in my glory:

2 And for this cause, the Lord said unto Peter:— If I will that he tarry till I come, what is that to thee? for he desiredst of me that he might bring souls unto me: but thou desiredst that thou might speedily come unto me in my kingdom: I say unto thee, Peter, this was a good desire, but my beloved has undertaken a greater work.

3 Verily I say unto you, ye shall both have according to your desires, for ye both joy in that which ye have desired.

(marginal notes:)

For if you shall ask what you will, it shall be granted unto you

over death

until

desired

desired

unto him

live and

and shalt prophesy before nations, kindreds, tongues and people.

mightest

that he might do more, or

yet among men than what he has before done. Yea, he has undertaken a greater work; therefore I will make him as flaming fire and a ministering angel; he shall minister for those who shall be heirs of salvation who dwell on the earth. And I will make thee to minister or him and for thy brother James; and unto you three I will give this power and the keys of this ministry until I come.

1833 *Book of Commandments,* page 18 (D&C 6:1-8, modern edition).

The Book of Abraham

Until recently there existed no way to ascertain whether Smith's Book of Abraham translation was accurate. His papyri fragments had been destroyed, it was thought, in the Chicago fire of 1871. Then, in 1967, 11 pieces of his original scrolls were rediscovered in the New York Metropolitan Museum of Art. One of the fragments even contained the drawing Smith used for Facsimile 1. Egyptologists, religion scholars, and historians hailed the discovery as momentous.

But the jubilation for Mormons was short-lived. The scrolls did not vindicate Smith. They were Egyptian—but were merely funerary texts belonging to the Book of Breathings (which Smith turned into the Book of Abraham) and the Book of the Dead (which Smith said had been written by Joseph). And the Book of Breathings drawings that Smith had copied had nothing to do with his explanation of them (see Figure 3.1).

Moreover, it was learned that the original source of Smith's Facsimile 1 was missing its top portion. Someone's solution was to arbitrarily fill in how they thought the missing piece had looked. But when the amended scroll is compared to other copies of the Book of Breathings, it is obvious that the guesses were terribly wrong (see Figures 3.2, 3.3, and 3.4).

> **Did You Know?** The first challenge to Smith's Book of Abraham came in 1860 and 1861 in the comments of French Egyptologist Theodule Deveria. He examined Smith's facsimiles and "dismissed Joseph's explanations as rambling nonsense."[37] According to Deveria, the "Facsimile from the Book of Abraham" was really "a funeral illustration for a corpse named Horus."*
>
> Other early scholarly responses (around the early 1900s) to the Book of Abraham came from W.M. Flinders Petrie (London University), James H. Breasted (University of Chicago), Author C. Mace (Assistant Curator, Metropolitan Museum of Art, Department of Egyptian Art), and S.A.B. Mercer (Western Theological Seminary). All of them denounced Smith's work as an absurdity and a fraud.†

---

* H. Michael Marquardt, "The Book of Abraham Revisited," online at www.xmission .com/~research/about/abraham.htm.

† F.S. Spalding, *Joseph Smith, Jr. As a Translator,* pages 23–29. Quoted in Richard Abanes, *One Nation Under Gods* (New York: Four Walls Eight Windows, 2003), pages 450–451.

Figure 3.1

Facsimile 3 from the Book of Abraham like Facsimile 1 and 2, has numbered explanations of the images represented. But the drawing was completely misinterpreted by Joseph Smith (see comparison chart below). The original of this papyrus used by Smith has not been found. However, it is one of the most common funeral scenes represented in Egyptian burial texts.

Smith's Identifications of Images (Abraham in the king's court)	Accurate Egyptian Scene (Court of Osiris in underworld)
1. Abraham sitting on throne.	1. Osiris, wearing a double-plumed crown, holding royal flail and crook across chest.
2. King Pharaoh.	2. Isis, wearing customary solar disc and cow horn.
3. Signifies Abraham in Egypt.	3. Standard libation platform common in all Egyptian sketches featuring major deities.
4. Prince of Pharaoh, King of Egypt.	4. Maat, goddess of justice.
5. Shulem, one of the king's principal waiters.	5. Deceased individual wearing traditional perfumed cone and lotus flower on head, being led by Maat to Osiris.
6. Olimlah, a slave belonging to the prince.	6. Anubis, guide of the dead.

Figure 3.2

Facsimile 1 from the Book of Abraham. Smith's original papyrus (Figure 3.3) found at New York's Metropolitan Museum of Art, reveals that this section was missing its top segment. So he drew in the missing parts (barely visible on the backing paper), which were then reproduced in the official version of the Book of Abraham (Figure 3.2). But when compared to how the papyri *should* appear, based on modern Egyptology and other copies of the Book of Breathings (see Figures 3.3 and 3.4), it is clear that Smith seriously erred in completing it. He gave the standing figure a human head instead of a jackal head (3). He gave the flying bird a bird's head instead of a human head (1). He missed drawing in the falcon altogether. And he incorrectly drew the hand position of the figure lying down (2). Smith also mislabeled every part of the Egyptian scene, apparently having no clue what the images actually meant (see comparison chart after Figure 3.4).

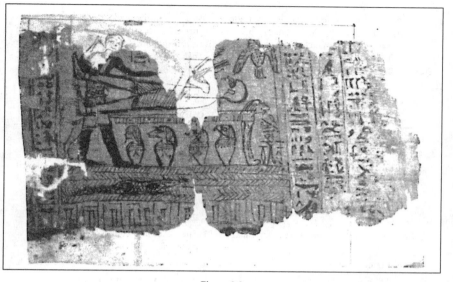

Figure 3.3

Figure 3.4

Figure 3.4 (see previous page) is a common reconstruction of the Book of Breathings papyrus segment used by Smith. Unlike Smith's papyrus (Figure 3.3—see previous page), the Book of Breathings reconstruction includes the portions that were missing from Smith's scroll (from Charles M. Larson, *By His Own Hand Upon Papyrus: A New Look At the Joseph Smith Papyri*, 1985, 1992 edition). The following chart shows Smith's faulty interpretation of the Egyptian papyrus.

Smith's Identifications of Images (Abraham on an Altar)	Accurate Egyptian Scene (Osiris' embalming and resurrection)
1. Angel of the Lord.	1. The soul *(ba)* of Osiris hovering over the body, waiting to enter it.
2. Abraham fastened on altar.	2. The god Osiris, one hand pointing upward (palm down as a sign of grief), and one hand holding his phallus, in preparation for the impregnation of his wife, Isis (in the form of a falcon).
3. Evil priest Elkenah attempting to sacrifice Abraham.	3. The jackal-headed god, Anubis, who is embalming Osiris.
4. The altar of sacrifice.	4. Traditional lion-headed embalming couch.
5. The idolatrous god Elkenah.	5. A grandson of Osiris and Isis.
6. The idolatrous god Libnah.	6. A grandson of Osiris and Isis.
7. The idolatrous god Mahmackrah.	7. A grandson of Osiris and Isis.
8. The idolatrous god Korash.	8. A grandson of Osiris and Isis.
9. The idolatrous god Pharaoh.	9. The crocodile god, Sobek.
10. Abraham in Egypt.	10. A libation platform bearing wines, oils, and a stylized papyrus plant.
11. Pillars of heaven, as understood by Egyptians.	11. Stones bordering the front of a pool of water.
12. Represents the height of the heavens.	12. A pool in which Sobek is swimming.

Many books have been written cataloguing and explaining the inaccurate information, mistranslated text, and erroneously interpreted drawings in Smith's Book of Abraham. But such information has had little effect on faithful Mormons, who have come up with remarkably inventive arguments in the face of overwhelming evidence. In *Mormonism: Shadow or Reality?* Jerald and Sandra Tanner have observed that such stick-to-itiveness "is almost beyond belief."[38]

LDS RESPONSES

Obviously, Latter-day Saints cannot simply declare some of their most sacred works of scripture to be fraudulent. Such an admission would destroy Joseph Smith's standing as a prophet and eradicate a number of doctrines crucial to Mormonism.[39] Consequently, a significant number of works by LDS apologists focus on one main purpose—explaining away any and all criticisms that might damage the validity of Smith's writings.

Answers for Abraham

Since 1967, Latter-day Saints have made a concerted effort to explain just how the Book of Abraham could possibly be a validly "translated" book of divine truth. Many of these arguments are far too complex to even address in a chapter of this length, let alone be thoroughly discussed. Two of the most popular ones, however, can be mentioned:

- *The recent papyrus argument:* The scrolls were not actually handwritten by Abraham. Only the textual *content* of the scrolls came from Abraham. Hence, it can legitimately be said that the scrolls (although they may have been created as recently as 100 to 50 B.C.) came *from* Abraham.[40]

- *The translation argument:* Whatever scrolls Smith used, he did not translate them in the same way "university scholars" translate texts. He relied on divine revelation to understand them.[41]

The first LDS argument downplays the fact that Smith's Facsimile 1 (see page 96) source document does not date back to Abraham's day. But this response cannot erase early Mormon belief that the papyri did indeed date back to Abraham. Early Mormons were unsure *only* about exactly how the papyri had been preserved in Egypt.

The second argument is an attempt to explain away the obvious and severe discrepancy between the Book of Abraham text and the writing on Smith's papyri. It is the most effective of all LDS responses because it is essentially irrefutable—it is based on a definition of *translation* that does not mean *to translate* in any academic or usual sense.

The word *translate,* as used by Mormons about the Book of Abraham, has nothing to do with a process in which word-for-word equivalents are determined in order to transfer a specific message from one language into another. Smith "never did a document-to-document translation based on knowledge of two languages."[42]

This is evident from another example, that of Doctrine and Covenants 7, which includes "translated" text that Joseph supposedly gleaned from an ancient parchment written by John the apostle and hidden away somewhere. He produced this "translation" using his seer stone—without the document even being in his possession!

It must be recognized, then, that the LDS definition of *translation* was, and continues to be, different from the commonly accepted definition used by others. In relation to the Book of Abraham, it refers, rather, to revelatory information received independent of exact meanings attached to the hieroglyphs or words of another language.[43]

But even this unique type of "translation" may not apply to the Book of Abraham. Documents produced by Smith and his scribes show the hieroglyphs from the papyri that were matched to Book of Abraham text (Table 3.3).[44] These documents suggest that Smith's narrative was indeed built from paragraphs he composed and attributed to the hieroglyphs—each of which represents only one or two words or ideas in Egyptian.[45]

So how did Smith receive his revelatory information? He may have used one of his seer stones to do the "translating."[46] This seems to have been the belief of LDS apostle Parley P. Pratt. In 1842, Pratt explained that the Book of Abraham was being translated "by means of the Urim and Thummim."[47] (Smith also used his seer stone to obtain other revelations.[48])

Pratt was once again using the common LDS euphemism for Smith's seer stone. As LDS president Joseph Fielding Smith said, such post-1829 references could not have been to "the biblical Urim and Thummim or the instrument by that name found with the gold plates of the Book of Mormon, but had to refer to the seer stone."[49]

Correct Egyptian Translations	Joseph Smith's "Translation" (Book of Abraham 1:11-15)
"the, this" ⼤	11. Now, this priest had offered upon this altar three virgins at one time, who were the daughters of Onitah, one of the royal descent directly from the loins of Ham. These virgins were offered up be-cause of their virtue; they would not bow down to worship gods of wood or of stone, therefore they were killed upon this altar.
"pool" ⼤	and it was done after the manner of the Egyptians. 12. And it came to pass that the priests laid violence upon me, that they might slay me also, as they did those virgins upon this altar; and that you may have a knowledge of this altar, I will refer you to the representation at the commencement of this record.
"water" ⼆	13. It was made after the form of a bedstead, such as was had among the Chaldeans, and it stood before the gods of Elkenah, Libnah, Mahmackrah, Korash, and also a god like unto that of Pharaoh, king of Egypt. 14. That you may have an understanding of these gods, I have given you the fashion of them in the figures at the beginning, which manner of the figures is called by the Chaldeans Rahleenos, which signifies hieroglyphics.
"great" ⼤	15. And as they lifted up their hands upon me, that they might offer me up and take away my life, behold, I lifted up my voice unto my God, and the Lord hearkened and heard, and he filled me with the vision of the Almighty, and the angel of his presence stood by me, and immediately unloosed my bands.

Table 3.3

Debating the Doctrine and Covenants

In a 1966 letter, LDS apologist Hugh Nibley, blithely noted, "Revelations have been revised whenever necessary. That is the nice thing about revelation—it is strictly open-ended."[50] Not every Mormon, however, has been so forthright. Also in 1966, for example, LDS apostle Hugh B. Brown wrote, "None of the early revelations of the Church have been revised, and the Doctrine and Covenants stands as printed including sections 5 and 7."[51] Other prominent sources have said likewise, not only

downplaying the extent of changes to Smith's revelations, but on occasion claiming the very opposite of what Nibley admitted (see note 52
to this chapter).[52]

The apparent LDS desire to conceal Smith's changes to his revelations
moved some Mormon officials in the 1960s to actually suppress a copy
of the *Book of Commandments* in their church archives. At one point LDS
leaders even contacted BYU, telling the school to not allow microfilmed
pages of the rare book to be distributed to the public.[53]

Today's LDS apologists are taking a different approach. Rather than
seeking to deny the changes, they are trying to explain why those changes
are no cause for concern or doubt about Smith's prophetic role. The
responses are quite straightforward:

1. The *Book of Commandments* revelations were *inaccurate* copies
   of the text transcribed by those who had heard Smith speak forth
   God's word. Consequently, the revelations had to be corrected for
   publication in the 1835 Doctrine and Covenants.

2. "Smith did not receive all these revelations as word-for-word dic-
   tations from the Lord (although he may have received some this
   way). Rather, he received inspiration and wrote the revelations
   using his own words, often couched in Victorian English."[54] That
   is, Smith was not speaking God's words but was only speaking
   forth the general ideas God was placing in his mind. His dictated
   words were his *interpretations* of God's thoughts. Hence, changes
   to the revelations are examples of Smith fine-tuning what God
   had said to him (clarifying God's messages, that is).

3. Because Smith was a prophet, he had absolute authority to revise,
   update, change, or expand any revelation.

The first response is certainly legitimate and can account for a large
number of changes to the revelations involving grammar, punctuation,
spelling, minor word revisions, and other cosmetic alterations. However,
it cannot account for large portions of inserted or deleted text. It is
extremely doubtful that so much text could be overlooked or wrongly
copied from the originals.

The second argument relates more directly to the many *substantive*
changes made to Smith's revelations. But there is a problem with this, given

the manner in which Smith received and recorded his divine messages. The revelations were carefully transcribed, and each word was treated as a verbatim communication from God, either through the seer stone or simply by direct revelation to Smith's spirit and mind.

Evangelicals cannot understand how anyone can tamper with divine messages that were spoken by a prophet in the first person as if God himself were speaking—for example, "Behold I Jesus Christ, your Lord and your God, and your Redeemer, by the power of my Spirit, have spoken it" (D&C 18). Such language suggests that God dictated his message instead of just giving Smith a generalized idea that he had to put into his own words.

Something to Consider: LDS leader M. Russell Ballard, in seeking to explain just how carefully Smith's revelations were copied, quoted LDS apostle Parley Pratt, who said,

> Each sentence was uttered slowly and very distinctly, and with a pause between each sufficiently long for it to be recorded by an ordinary writer in long hand. This was the manner in which all his written revelations were dictated and written. There was never any hesitation, reviewing or reading back to keep the thread of the subject; neither did any of these communications undergo revisions, interlinings, or corrections. As he dictated them, so they stood, so far as I have witnessed; and I was present to witness the dictation of several communications of several pages.[55]

Lastly, Melvin J. Petersen—BYU professor of Church History and Doctrine—expressed in very clear terms the third response: "A prophet cannot be justly criticized when he rewrites the commandments he received from God, for he is only doing that which is part of his role as prophet."[56]

Orson Pratt alluded to this idea, arguing that the wisdom of man may certainly not alter revelations, but "[i]f they need altering, God alone has the right to alter them, or to add to them."[57] Pratt then referred to the case of the prophet Jeremiah, whose revelation was burned by the king of Judah. Afterwards "Jeremiah was commanded to write all the words again, and there were added besides unto them many like words."[58]

The problem evangelicals have with this last LDS solution to the Doctrine and Covenants changes is threefold. First, Smith is not at all seen by traditional Christians as a legitimate prophet of God. Second, such a view of revelation leaves open a very dangerous loophole by which an unscrupulous "prophet" could manipulate followers with one stroke of his revelation-changing pen.

And third, Smith's alterations to his original revelations cannot at all be compared to Jeremiah's action. Smith *internally* changed his revelations, and in so doing altered their meaning in many places. Mormons suggest that this is what Jeremiah did.[59] However, a careful reading of Jeremiah 36:32a reveals that the prophet rewrote "all the words of the book" that had been burned—that is, the same words, the same book. Then "there were added besides unto them many like words" (verse 32b).

Now there are two ways to interpret this passage: 1) words were added *throughout* the book; or 2) words were added *to* the completed book as an addendum—in the same way one might add a postscript to a new edition of a previously published work. No one knows which option is correct.

But even if, for the sake of discussion, we opt for the former choice, this still does not mean that Jeremiah's additions substantially changed the meaning of what he had originally written (as Smith's changes did). Moreover, the Jeremiah reference speaks only of *adding* to a revelation. It says nothing about deleting large portions of it, let alone reversing its main message.

FINAL OBSERVATIONS

Ultimately, criticisms of the Doctrine and Covenants and Pearl of Great Price—specifically, the Book of Abraham—amount to little in the minds of most Mormons. The very existence of these revelatory texts is what matters most to Mormons. Robert J. Woodford made this clear in a 1985 article for the LDS Church magazine, *Ensign:*

> The most important thing that must be kept in mind is that we accept the revelations as they are now written. Knowing about earlier texts

and changes which have occurred may aid the researcher in his studies of Church history, but the earlier versions have no claim upon our faith—it is the current edition upon which we rely.[60]

However, despite this apparent dismissal of worries about changes to revelations, there continue to be more attempts to conceal aspects of the early revelations. In the above article, for example, Woodford provides a side-by-side comparison of *Book of Commandments* 7:3 and Doctrine and Covenants 8:6-8 (see pages 88–89), then makes the following comment:

> The meaning of this revelation as recorded in the Book of Commandments and in the Doctrine and Covenants is not clear. History does not record that Oliver Cowdery or anyone else living at the time it was given had a problem understanding it, but today some of the revelation is unclear to us.[61]

The truth is, for decades the meaning of this revelation has been widely known to be a reference to Oliver Cowdery's occult practice of divining by a rod, as we saw earlier. This is just one more example of what seems to be a willingness on the part of LDS Church leaders to be less than completely up-front about some very important issues.

Of course, the most important issues of all are those that touch upon the actual religious doctrines espoused by Mormons. These beliefs, which come primarily from the holy writings thus far discussed, will be the focus of the next five chapters.

ONE GOD VERSUS MANY GODS

Some who write anti-Mormon pamphlets insist that the Latter-day Saint concept of Deity is contrary to what is recognized as traditional Christian doctrine. In this they are quite correct. [1]
—William O. Nelson, Director of the LDS Church's
Melchizedek Priesthood Department

For Christians, sharing our faith in God is usually a very joyful experience. But when it comes to communicating with Latter-day Saints, discussing theology can be a frustrating venture. For example, anyone who has spent a lot of time talking to Mormons has probably endured a conversation very similar to the one I had with an LDS bishop not too many years ago.

It all started out rather simply, with me saying, "Look, I can appreciate a lot of things about Mormon ethics and morality, but we disagree on some highly important matters when it comes to God."

"Like what?" the bishop replied.

Hoping to avoid any serious controversy, I simply stated what I thought would be the obvious: "Well, for example, I believe there exists only one God. Mormons, however, believe there exists more than one God, and—"

"Wait a minute," he interrupted. "That is not true. We believe in only one God."

"Don't you believe in the Father, Son, and Holy Ghost?"

He confidently answered, "We certainly do, and they are one God."

At this point, I was forced to seek a bit of clarification. "Don't you believe the Father is a god?" I asked.

"Yes, of course."

"And the Son is a god?"

"Yes."

"And the Holy Ghost is a god."

"Yes."

"That's three gods."

"No, they're one God."

I couldn't believe my ears. "But you just said each one is a god."

"Yes."

"Then, that's three."

"No, that's one."

At this point I felt like I had entered, via some *Twilight Zone*–like rift in the universe, an alternate-reality version of the famous Abbott and Costello skit "Who's On First?" However, instead of talking about baseball players, I was discussing God.

We continued our debate for I don't know how long, actually arguing over the meaning of what would otherwise be extraordinarily simple words: "one," "three," and even the term "God." This interaction illustrates just how crucial it is for Christians to have some working knowledge of the way Latter-day Saints view these concepts. Consequently, this chapter will deal with whether, for Mormons, there exists one God, or many gods.

⚜ ⚜ ⚜

Mormonism preaches a personal God who knows our needs, hears our prayers, and guides our steps. Mormons also see God as "merciful and gracious, slow to anger, abundant in goodness."[2] The LDS manual *Gospel Principles* adds, "God is perfect....He is a God of love, mercy, charity, truth, power, faith, knowledge, and judgment."[3]

Obviously, Mormons share with evangelicals a number of key observations about God. But Mormons and mainstream Christians quickly part company with regard to one of the most basic of all questions concerning deity—namely, How many gods are there?

Traditional Christians say there is only one God. Mormons, on the other hand, assert that there are many gods. This is the most fundamental difference between the two faiths. Christians adhere to *monotheism,* which is defined as "belief in one God," whereas Mormons embrace *polytheism,* which is "belief in a plurality of gods."[4]

Mormons also reject the traditional Christian concept of the Holy Trinity.[5] This doctrine affirms that the one and only *true* God exists eternally as three distinct Persons (or centers of self-consciousness)—namely, the Father, Son, and Holy Ghost. These three Persons, although they each possess individuality, simultaneously share the same divine substance, or essence. Hence, the three Persons *are* the one God.

Did You Know? According to philosophy professor Francis Beckwith, the Book of Mormon "seems to teach a strongly Judaic monotheism with modalistic (God is only one person manifesting in three modes) overtones (*see* Alma 11:26-31, 38; Moroni 8:18; Mosiah 3:5-8; 7:27; 15:1-5), while the equally authoritative Pearl of Great Price...clearly teaches that more than one God exists (*see* Abraham 4-5). This is why a number of Mormon scholars have argued that their theology evolved from a traditional monotheism to a uniquely American polytheism"*—for example, James B. Allen, Thomas G. Alexander, and Boyd Kirkland.[6] Other LDS scholars, however, deny that Joseph Smith's theology evolved.†

Mormons, however, claim that the Father, Son, and Holy Ghost are three gods. "God the Father" goes by the name *Elohim* in the Old Testament. He is the "God above all gods." Jesus ("God the Son") is usually identified as *Jehovah* of the Old Testament. "God the Holy Ghost," to whom no name is given, is referred to as simply the Holy Ghost.[7] According to Paul E. Dahl, director of the LDS Tucson Institute of Religion, "[T]hese three gods form the Godhead."[8]

This further shows that Mormons are polytheists. Moreover, the term *polytheism* itself comes from the Greek words *polus* ("many") and *theos*

---

* Francis Beckwith, "Philosophical Problems with the Mormon Concept of God," DM 410, www.equip.org/free/DM410.htm.

† See Barry R. Bickmore, "Does the Book of Mormon Teach Mainstream Trinitarianism or Modalism?" [FAIR], www.fairlds.org/pubs/BoMTrin.pdf.

("God"). These Greek words provide the most basic and widely accepted definition of polytheism, which is "belief in many gods."[9]

MORMON QUOTES

"I have always declared God to be a distinct personage, Jesus Christ a separate and distinct personage from God the Father, and that the Holy Ghost was a distinct personage and a Spirit: and these three constitute three distinct personages and three Gods" (Joseph Smith, LDS founder and president, 1844).[10]

"How many Gods there are, I do not know. But there never was a time when there were not Gods" (Brigham Young, LDS president, 1859).[11]

"We have already shown that the Father, the Son, and the Holy Ghost are three separate and distinct persons, and, so far as personality is concerned, are three Gods" (B.H. Roberts, LDS apostle, 1903).[12]

"There are three Gods—the Father, Son, and Holy Ghost."[13] "[T]here is an infinite number of holy personages, drawn from worlds without number, who have passed on to exaltation and are thus gods" (Bruce McConkie, LDS apostle, 1958).[14]

"[Jesus] acted in concert with other Gods to create our world: 'Then the Lord said: Let us go down. And they went down at the beginning, and they, that is the Gods, organized and formed the heavens and the earth'" (*Ensign,* LDS Church publication, 1989).[15]

"[U]nder *God the Father:*...3. He is named Elohim....4. He is 'God above all Gods.'...'Elohim...is also used as the exalted name-title of God the Eternal Father, a usage that connotes his supremacy and omnipotence, he being God above all Gods'" (LDS *Aaronic Priesthood Manual,* 1995).[16]

A CLOSER LOOK

Latter-day Saints greatly resent being labeled polytheists. In fact, LDS leaders have often stressed that they are not polytheists and that Mormonism is not polytheistic.[17] (This may be in part because of polytheism's association with non-Christian religious systems such as Hinduism, Wicca, neopaganism, and ancient mystery religions.)

Some Christians, not realizing that Mormons tend to redefine terms, view such denials as disingenuous. Another difficulty stems from the evolving character of LDS theology and teachings. Consequently, it is often difficult for non-LDS onlookers to discern what Mormons are saying. Mormons, on the other hand, fail to see the problem.

Redefining Polytheism

Mormons often defend their denial that Mormonism is polytheistic by pointing out that polytheism means either 1) belief in, *and worship of,* more than one god;[18] or 2) belief in, and worship of, *false* gods or pagan deities.[19] Granted, the worship of more than one god is intrinsic to *some* definitions of polytheism.[20] But what Mormons often fail to address is how their denials square with the fact that they *do* indeed worship more than one god.

BYU professor Robert Millet confirms this: "God [the Father] and Christ are the objects of our worship."[21] LDS apostle Bruce McConkie actually included the Holy Ghost among the gods worshiped by Mormons. "Three separate personages—Father, Son and Holy Ghost—comprise the Godhead," McConkie wrote. "As each of these persons is a God, it is evident, from this standpoint alone that a *plurality of Gods* exist. To us, speaking in the proper finite sense, these three are the only Gods we worship."[22]

As for the second definition of polytheism (belief in, and worship of, *false* gods), this would indeed separate Mormonism from polytheism—*if* that definition were widely substantiated by non-LDS scholars. But no add-on clauses are usually offered that restrict polytheism to the worship of *false* gods or *pagan* deities.

> **Notable and Quotable:** "[T]here are now, and will continue to be, many gods who will rule and reign throughout eternity on an ever increasing number of worlds which they will create. This is not in opposition to the Biblical concept of 'one God,' for an earth serves as the dwelling place for the children of only one God" (Duane S. Crowther, LDS author, *Life Everlasting*, page 361).

A New Dictionary of Religions defines polytheism as "[b]elief in, or worship of, many GODS." This same work defines monotheism thus: "Belief that there is one, but only one, divine being."[23] F. Max Müller (1823–1900), one of the most respected religious scholars of his day, offered a stricter definition of monotheism: "[B]elief in one god, excluding the very possibility of other gods."[24]

Based on these definitions, Mormons are polytheists. Their recognition of other gods, coupled with their admitted worship of more gods than one, makes any alternate classification unjustified. As for their excessively narrow redefinitions of the term "polytheism," evangelicals see them as not only illegitimate, but a basis of confusion for the general public.

Redefining Monotheism

Other Mormons, rather than redefining polytheism, redefine monotheism to mean the worship of one *primary or supreme* god above "all other gods." In LDS theology, the Father is this supreme God—at least for this planet, in this universe.[25] He is the only god with whom Mormons interact, the only *supreme* god they worship.[26]

This redefinition of monotheism allows Mormons to comfortably say there is only "one God" while still believing that other gods exist.[27] A 2003 article from the Foundation for Ancient Research and Mormon Studies essentially agreed:

> [T]here is only one God because the Father is the supreme monarch of our universe. There is no other God to whom we could switch our allegiance, and there never will be such a thing. He is "the eternal God of all other gods" (D&C 121:32).[28]

This article then quotes LDS apostle Boyd K. Packer: "The Father is the one true God....He is Elohim, the Father. He is God; of Him there is only one."[29] Interestingly, Packer here is not only redefining "one God" to mean one "supreme monarch," but also seems to be redefining "one true God" to mean something more akin to "the one God that we call *our* God."

But monotheism does not mean the worship of one god above other gods. It means, as F. Max Müller wrote, "belief in one god, excluding the very possibility of other gods."[30] Likewise, *The Oxford Dictionary of World Religions* states, "Monotheism. Belief that there is one God (and only one), in contrast to Henotheism or Polytheism."[31] And the *Dictionary of Religion and Philosophy* reads, "Belief in the existence of one God who alone is to be worshipped."[32] Mormonism clearly does not measure up to commonly accepted definitions of monotheism.

Mormonism does, however, match the definition of *tritheism*, a subcategory of polytheism. The distinctions between these views—monotheism, polytheism, and tritheism)—are noted in *The Blackwell Companion to Philosophy*:

> [C]ontexts may arise when it will be quite important to note explicitly the differences between monotheism (there is one God), polytheism (there are many gods), and tritheism (there are three Gods or gods—this usage comes into play in philosophical work on the Trinity in Christianity).[33]

Mormons, given their own remarks, are tritheists. Interestingly, a certain level of acceptance of this label has been voiced by BYU professors Daniel C. Peterson and Stephen D. Ricks.[34] They recognized LDS tritheism in *Offenders for a Word* (1998), saying that it is "probably not an inappropriate term for Mormon teaching."[35] But Peterson and Ricks then defend tritheism, arguing that it "was taught by a number of prominent theologians in late antiquity, and can be considered 'a definite phase in the history of Christian thought.'"[36]

The two scholars further claim that tritheism is never termed "non-Christian," adding, "In the sixth century A.D., its leading exponent is John Philoponus.…[H]e is always described by Christian scholars as a Christian."[37] In their footnote to this assertion, they write, "The reader will find no contrary opinions."[38]

Tritheism, however, has indeed been condemned by "Christian scholars" and church leaders as non-Christian and heretical. As for Philoponus (c. 490-575), he was no mere tritheist. He embraced *monophysitism:* that is, that Christ had *only* a divine nature—one separate from the Father and Holy Ghost, who have their own natures.[39]

The appeal to Philoponus highlights yet another problem in LDS material that seeks to defend Mormonism as biblical and historical. Mormons often point to early church quotes that have been lifted out of their historical, political, and social contexts (see chapter 8). Such quotes, on their surface, seem to support LDS claims that Mormonism is much closer to the original church founded by Christ. But upon closer examination, the quotes are actually saying something quite different than what Mormons are trying to prove.

The development of the early church is rife with political complexities, multifaceted disputes about theology, and interlocking socioeconomic events that would make anyone's head spin. All such things affected early church writings. No one, therefore, can legitimately isolate comments from the early church, transport them into our era, then reinterpret them according to our contemporary mindset in a way totally divorced from their historical setting. The results, although they may serve a particular agenda, are far from reliable.

Redefining "One God"

A third way that some Mormons try to explain why their faith should be considered monotheistic involves redefining "one God" to mean a single *group* of gods—specifically the LDS triumvirate of Father, Son, and Holy Ghost (also known as the Godhead).[40] These three gods are "one in purpose, one in mind, one in glory, one in attributes and powers."[41]

The Godhead, therefore, is *one*. And worshiping one *Godhead,* so the argument goes, is tantamount to worshiping only one God. Mormons, according to this explanation, are not polytheistic.[42] In 1998, LDS apostle M. Russell Ballard used the argument as follows:

> A fourth area of misunderstanding among some of our friends in Christianity is that they refer to us as "polytheists," meaning that we believe in a plurality of Gods. Much misunderstanding would be avoided if they understood that we worship only one Godhead, consisting of God the Father, God the Son, and God the Holy Ghost.[43]

Although such thinking is logically convoluted and linguistically untenable, it is airtight—at least from an LDS perspective. Given its parameters, the only way a Mormon could be accused of polytheism would be if he or she worshiped a god or godhead *outside* of their Godhead. But this is something a faithful Mormon would never do.[44]

To evangelicals, this "three-gods-are-really-one-God-because-they-are-one-Godhead" approach is merely an arbitrary dismissal of accepted definitions for *one* and *god*. In the real world, *one* means a single unit, while *god* means a divine being. Together they mean *one God*. They do not, nor can they, refer to *three* gods—no matter how united in purpose, will, and power they may be. Three gods are three gods. One God is one God.

Even if we accept the LDS redefinition of "one God" to mean three gods in a single "Godhead," the redefinition would not erase LDS teachings about the existence of other gods. Mormons would still be practitioners of yet another subcategory of polytheism known as *monolatry*— "the worship of only one god [or in LDS-speak, one Godhead], while the existence of other gods is admitted or not questioned."[45]

Oddly, it was none other than BYU's widely quoted professor emeritus of philosophy and religion, Truman Madsen, who in 1996 told the *San Francisco Chronicle*, "People tell us, 'You don't believe in one God: you believe in three Gods.' And the answer is 'Yes, we do.' If that's polytheism, then we are (polytheists)."[46]

EVANGELICAL THOUGHTS

Much of the conflict between evangelicals and Mormons results from arguments over the nature of the Trinity. Mormons find the concept patently offensive and see it as a hopelessly confused notion that is based on little more than pagan philosophy. Sadly, the doctrine is very often misunderstood by Mormons (and Christians), which is one reason why so much animosity gets built up around it. It is crucially important, therefore, that Christians and Mormons be informed in their understanding of Trinitarianism so that both groups can better interact when discussing its strengths and weaknesses.

The Trinity is "one of the most important doctrines of the Christian faith,"[47] and as such, lies at "the heart of the Christian conception of God."[48] It asserts that there is only one true God, who, within his eternal nature, exists as three distinct Persons (or centers of self-consciousness)—namely, the Father, Son, and Holy Ghost.

These co-equal and co-eternal Persons, while somehow retaining their distinctness, share the same divine substance or essence. Hence they are neither three gods, nor three parts of God. They *are* the one God. In other words, God exists as three Persons in one substance. In dealing with the concept, though, we must realize a couple of things.

First, "Persons" should not be understood in any contemporary way that denotes utter separateness or individual centers of consciousness (as in three people). That is tritheism. In Trinitarianism, "Persons" expresses three centers of *self*-consciousness within the one God. "The unity is in his essence (what God is), and the plurality is in God's persons (how he relates within himself)."[49] This is unlike any other kind of life-form we know. But this is to be expected since God is a unique being (Psalm 71:19; 89:6).[50]

Second, "the infinite truth of the Godhead lies far beyond the boundaries of logic, which deals only with finite truths and categories."[51] The doctrine may be beyond logic, which means we will never fully grasp *how* it is, but this does not mean we cannot grasp *what* it is—or *that* it is. Trinitarianism, in other words, does not go against logic or run contrary to it. Southern Evangelical Seminary president Norman Geisler explains:

> The philosophical law of non-contradiction informs us that something cannot be both true and false at the same time and in the same sense. This is the fundamental law of all rational thought. And the doctrine of the Trinity does not violate it. This can be shown by stating first of all what the Trinity is not. The Trinity is not the belief that God is three persons and only one person at the same time and in the same sense. That would be a contradiction. Rather, it is the belief that there are three persons [that is, centers of self-consciousness] in one *nature*....Further, the Trinity is not the belief that there are three natures in one nature or three essences in one essence. That would be a contradiction. Rather, Christians affirm that there are three persons in one essence.[52]

Mormons, however, see the complexity of Trinitarianism as good enough reason for rejecting it. But their prejudice against the doctrine is inconsistent since every day we find ourselves accepting various concepts while at the same time failing to fully comprehend exactly *how* those concepts could be true. These are compatible states of mind as long as the "law of noncontradiction" remains unbroken.

For instance, I may understand that the Earth is orbiting the sun at thousands of miles per hour, but I certainly do not fully comprehend *how* that can be. I also may understand that my chair is comprised of millions of molecules moving so fast that they are forming what looks like a solid object, but I certainly do not fully comprehend at every level and from every angle *how* that could be. (This is an extremely important point to stress to Mormons so that they can see how Trinitarians can accept the Trinity.)

Further, some concepts actually do seem to go *against* logic, and yet they are still accepted! Scientists, for instance, are discovering a whole realm of never-before-known aspects of creation using theoretical physics, non-communicative geometry, and quantum mechanics. Experiments in these highly intricate, and often baffling, fields of study have shown that not everything is as it appears to be. Certain apparent truths seem quite contradictory and rather bizarre. Consider these mind-boggling theories, discoveries, and observations about our universe:

- In the microworld, when numbers are multiplied, their answer depends *on the order* in which they are multiplied.[53]

- Time is relative. "The question *What time is it?* has no single answer."[54]

- "Gravity is not a force, but the effect of the curvature of space-time, so that not only motion but also gravity causes clocks to slow down."[55]

Such truths push our finite minds to the very limits of what we can comprehend. As theoretical physicist Lee Smolin of Pennsylvania State University has noted, "[D]oing cosmology requires a radical revision of our way of doing science—a revision that goes even to the foundation of logic."[56] Should we not expect God, who created the universe, to be infinitely more complex than the universe itself? After all, it is commonly understood that any created thing must have been created by a more complex thing. (A human, for instance, can design a computer, but a computer cannot design a human.)

Trinitarianism 101

It is critical to know that the Trinity is a terribly difficult concept for Mormons to accept. And yet, oddly, Mormons admit that many of their own beliefs are beyond full comprehension, complete explanation, and total understanding (see sidebar below). Ironically, the LDS willingness to embrace ideas that cannot fully be comprehended even extends to God! Mormon apostle Dallin Oaks has publicly stated that Latter-day Saints do not "claim sufficient spiritual maturity to comprehend God."[57]

Did You Know? Even though Mormons severely criticize evangelicals for not being able to completely comprehend how the Trinity is possible, Mormons themselves embrace numerous beliefs that their own leaders have said are incomprehensible, including the following:[58]

- God's glory and God's majesty (Gordon B. Hinckley, LDS president)
- The effects of the atonement (Gordon B. Hinckley, LDS president)
- The nature of the atonement (James E. Faust, First Presidency)
- Our state of existence before birth (Victor L. Ludlow, BYU professor)
- The succession of gods (B.H. Roberts, LDS apostle)
- Christ taking our sins (Jeffrey Holland, LDS apostle)
- The begetting of spirit children (Joseph Fielding Smith, LDS president)
- Why unchastity is so sinful (Bruce Hafen, First Quorum of the Seventy)
- God's works (Richard C. Edgley, LDS bishop)
- Christ's resurrection and its effects (Bruce McConkie, LDS apostle)

Evangelicals feel it would be only fair for Mormons to allow Trinitarians the same leeway when it comes to the Trinity. God, in fact, told us that certain aspects of his nature would be unsearchable (Psalm 145:3; Isaiah 40:28; Romans 11:33). The question to ask then is not, *How* does the Trinity exist; but, *Does* the Trinity exist? According to Scripture, as understood by evangelicals, the answer to the latter question is *yes*.

For those readers whose thoughts cannot be so easily pulled away from the *how* question, a few analogies may be helpful. One is the mathematical formula 1 x 1 x 1 = 1. (In Mormonism, however, the formula would be 1 + 1 + 1 = 3.) Sunlight is a second analogy. It consists— at least to us nonphysicists—of three distinct aspects: visible light, ultraviolet rays, and warmth.[59] All are distinct, but all are sunlight—just as the Father, Son, and Holy Ghost are all distinct, but are all the one God.

I believe the best analogy, however, is our concept of time. Like the Trinity, time consists of three distinct things: past, present, and future. These aspects of time correspond well to the Father, Son, and Holy Ghost. In both cases (Trinity–Time), the three particulars being discussed (past, present, future–Father, Son, Holy Ghost) are distinct, yet share the same nature and substance of what they represent.

The past, present, and future may be called "time" individually or collectively, just as the Father, Son, and Holy Ghost may be called "God" individually or collectively. And if any element of "time" were removed, then "time" would no longer exist. God, similarly, would not be "God" without a Father, Son, and Holy Ghost. All three Persons *are* "God," just as all three time aspects *are* "time."[60]

No analogy, of course, can perfectly illustrate the Trinity. But seeking helpful analogies in order to better understand Trinitarian thought is worthwhile to everyone. As Augustine reportedly said in reference to the Trinity, "In no other subject is error more dangerous, or inquiry more laborious, or discovery of truth more profitable."[61] (For a brief study of the biblical passages about the Trinity, see appendix C.)

LDS RESPONSES

To evangelicals, only the Trinity doctrine can effectively (and logically) reconcile the hundreds of biblical passages—Old Testament and New

Testament—that present two seemingly contradictory teachings: 1) There is only one God; and 2) the Father, the Son, and the Holy Ghost should be addressed and worshiped as God.

Yet Latter-day Saints see the Trinity doctrine as unquestionably false. Furthermore, they find their understanding of multiple gods to be a far more biblical view, given the scriptures that mention "gods," "lords," or both. Consider *The Missionary's Little Book of Answers*, which is sold in LDS bookstores:

> The reality of many gods in the eternal realms is made clear in the Bible when it speaks of "God of gods" and "Lord of lords" as Paul and other prophets taught (Deut. 10:17; Ex. 15:11; 1 Cor. 8:5-6; Rev. 19:16).[62]

Such verses do seem to suggest, at least on the surface, that there are many gods. But the key to understanding all such passages is a third verse—1 Corinthians 8:5—which speaks of things "that are *called* gods" (emphasis added). Anything can be "called" a god: sex, drugs, money, fame, beauty. But that does not make it a true god. Such things are, in reality, false gods: idols of our worship.

Such an idol can be something made with our hands (Leviticus 19:4; Deuteronomy 27:15), a person who thinks he or she is godlike (Ezekiel 28:9), or any spiritual entity to whom a person is obedient (2 Corinthians 4:4). But all of these so-called gods are not *true* gods, or gods "by nature" (Galatians 4:8). There is only one true God (2 Chronicles 15:3; Jeremiah 10:10; John 17:3).

This is why Psalm 86:8 declares, "Among the gods there is none like unto thee, O LORD." In other words, there is no other true God; no other being that is truly a god by nature. The true God is above all other *so-called* gods (Deuteronomy 4:35,39; 32:39; 2 Kings 19:19; Psalm 86:10; Isaiah 43:10; Mark 12:29). The Bible leaves no room for the existence of more than one true God (one divine being who by his nature is deity).

Polytheistic Jews?

Thanks to BYU-based apologists, many Latter-day Saints are now using a fairly new argument to defend their belief in multiple gods. They are claiming that the early Israelites were polytheistic.[63] Therefore, according to this argument, Mormons are only returning to what was once accepted as true in ancient Israel.

This claim rests on the *theory* that Israel initially held to polytheism, which gave way to monolatry, which in turn evolved into monotheism. Such a scenario matches what is taught by most non-Christians and liberal scholars—the same scholars quoted by LDS apologists when discussing Israel's so-called polytheism.

Did You Know? In an article for the Apologetics Resource Center, Christian apologist Steve Cowan comments,

> Those who doubt Israel's early monotheism sometimes point to biblical texts that seem to recognize the existence of gods other than Yahweh (Genesis 35:2; Exodus 18:11; Joshua 24:14-15; Judges 11:23-24), as well as to the fact that the Israelites did worship other gods (Exodus 32:1-4; Judges 2:11; 3:7; 1 Kings 16:30-33). As for the former, these texts do not necessarily imply that pagan gods were thought to be real by the authors of these texts, but only that those who actually worshiped them thought so. Concerning the latter, there is no reason to believe that Israel's idolatry points to an original Israelite polytheism rather than to what the biblical author claims, namely, that Israel fell away from her devotion to Yahweh. Israel's increasingly pervasive apostasy during the later monarchy also explains the more clear and more dogmatic assertions of monotheism found in the prophets. Rather than introducing an innovation, the prophets (by their own admission) were calling God's idolatrous people to return to their original faith in the one true God.*

Significantly, these also are the same scholars who assert that the Bible is a product of dubious edits, clandestine revisions, and mythology. But such accusations are inconsequential to Mormons, who likewise assert that the biblical text is terribly marred. (As LDS apostle Orson Pratt noted,

---

* Steve Cowan, "Monotheism," unpublished manuscript forwarded to Richard Abanes, no date.

"Who knows that even one verse of the whole Bible has escaped pollution, so as to convey the same sense now that it did in the original?"[64])

As to whether or not the ancient Israelites were polytheistic, it cannot be denied that *some* Israelites continued to worship various deities (engage in polytheism) long after Moses' era.[65] And it also is true that other Israelites, although they may not have *worshiped* other gods, apparently recognized them as true gods (monolatry).[66] The rest of the Israelites, most notably the prophets, advocated monotheism.

Mormon Point: Many verses in the Bible show that the Israelites believed that more than one god existed. For example, Judges 11:24 shows that Jephthah believed in other gods, because he speaks to the Ammonites about their god, Chemosh.

Counterpoint: The verses commonly cited by Mormons as proof that most Israelites practiced either polytheism or monolatry are often read out of context. Judges 11:24, for instance, nowhere says that Jephthah considered Chemosh a *true* god. In his *Introduction to the Old Testament,* Dr. Roland Kenneth Harrison observes, "Jephthah is not speaking as a theologian but as a foreign diplomat, negotiating with them in terms which they could understand as he appealed to their sense of fair play" (pages 389–390).

In *A History of Israel,* John Bright explains,

> Certainly Israel's faith was no polytheism. Nor will henotheism or monolatry do, for though the existence of other gods was not expressly denied, neither was their status as gods tolerantly granted.... To Israel only one God was God: Yahweh, whose grace had called her into being, and under whose sovereign overlordship she had engaged to live. The other gods, allowed neither part in creation, nor function in the cosmos, nor power over events, nor cult, were robbed of all that made them gods and rendered nonentities, in short, were "undeified" (pages 159–160).

Ancient Israel was a spiritual hodgepodge of polytheism, monolatry, and monotheism. There never was an *official* state religion. At the same time, however, according to Dr. Jeffrey Tigay (professor of Hebrew and Semitic languages, University of Pennsylvania), "[S]o far as we can tell from the Bible and from archaeological evidence, most Israelites were de facto monotheists ever since the time of Moses."[67]

All we really see in Scripture is the Israelites emerging from pagan, polytheistic Egypt and going into the pagan, polytheistic promised land. And in the midst of this story is Moses declaring that Yahweh alone is God. Then, we see Israel not heeding the words of Moses and other prophets. Instead, many Israelites continued to either worship other gods or, at the very least, acknowledge other gods as true deities.

All the while, however, Yahweh's prophets continued to declare that the Israelites needed to forsake their pagan views and practices. There was no gradual evolution from polytheism to monotheism. They existed side-by-side, both fighting for dominance, until monotheism finally vanquished its rival.

The crucial question, then, is not whether polytheism or monolatry existed in Israel. The question is, Was polytheism or monolatry *sanctioned* or *accepted* by Yahweh, his representative Moses, or faithful followers of Yahweh? According to the Bible, the answer to this question is *no*. Moreover, the archaeological data suggests that there were not even that many Israelites, relatively speaking, who succumbed to polytheism.[68]

It also is noteworthy that the whole notion of an ancient society like Israel evolving from polytheism to monotheism goes against what is now known about ancient cultures. A variety of respected scholars hold the opinion that primitive cultures tend to devolve from monotheism into polytheism.[69] And once a culture is polytheistic, it tends to multiply gods, not eradicate them (for example, Hinduism in India).

Councils and Creeds

Unlike LDS tritheism, which exalts God's plurality at the expense of his unity, Christian Trinitarianism preserves God's unity without sacrificing his plurality. Trinitarianism is the only path that is centered on the fine line between an overemphasis of one attribute or the other. And it does not rely on subjective redefinitions of terms.

Mormons, on the other hand, view the Trinity with an aversion that is traceable to their founder, Joseph Smith. He rarely hesitated to belittle it as belief in a "strange god," "a wonderfully big god," or "a giant or a monster."[70] In a less polemic condemnation, BYU professor of ancient scripture Stephen Robinson has explained that Mormons reject the Trinity because 1) "it is not biblical"; 2) "words central to the orthodox understanding of the Trinity [for example, the very word *Trinity*]...are not found in scripture"; and 3) it reflects a capitulation to Hellenistic (pagan–Greek) philosophy.[71]

Whose Understanding?

First, the Trinity doctrine is indeed "biblical." Its various component teachings are found in Scripture (see appendix C). The Bible tells us 1) there exists only one true God; 2) there are three distinct Persons called the Father, Son, and Holy Ghost; and 3) all three Persons mentioned are either called God or described in ways only applicable to the *one* God.

Robinson's "it is not biblical" objection, therefore, is actually somewhat misleading. It is more accurate to say that Mormons disagree with the Trinitarian *interpretation* (understanding) of the aforementioned biblical components. This is because Mormons have chosen to follow Joseph Smith's interpretation (understanding) of the components. Evangelicals, however, have chosen to follow the interpretation (understanding) of the components that was reached by early church leaders who attended the church councils of their era.

The councils, interestingly, were never called upon to define the Trinity. Rather, Christ's claims had understandably raised a number of questions. And so the councils met in order to find a way to explain *how* Jesus could have been who he was. The attenders asked, How could Jesus have been the human and divine savior of the world when there is only one God?

Their answers took the form of creeds, which were accepted as the formalized and finalized expressions of the Christian faith. The creeds took shape only after learned Christians "speculated, reasoned, argued, fought, and agonized over the doctrine of Christ."[72]

Notable and Quotable: Christian philosophy professor Francis Beckwith has observed that there are a number of concepts for which no explicit scriptural language is found. For example, he writes that

> the language of "rights" does not appear in the Scriptures, for such language has its origin in the political philosophy of such Enlightenment thinkers as John Locke, Thomas Hobbes, and John Stuart Mill. Nevertheless, one could say that the Bible teaches rights. For instance the command not to steal implies a "right to property," and the command not to murder implies a "right to life." Thus, it would not be necessarily wrong for a Christian to say that the Bible teaches a "right to property," even though such a right is not literally spelled out in Scripture....
>
> Many Mormons are quite active in the Right to Life movement. Although "rights" language does not literally appear in the Bible, Mormon scholars surely would not deny that the Bible teaches that the unborn have a right to life on the grounds that the language of rights does not appear in Scripture and is merely the product of Enlightenment philosophy.[73]

Mormons, however, have no such councils upon which to base their biblical interpretations. They have no "multitude of counsellers" as a safety net, so to speak (Proverbs 11:14); no discussions by early church theologians from which they draw their conclusions (although they have recently begun appealing to early church fathers); no bodies of philosophical thinkers in their formative years who wrestled with pressing issues.

Instead, the LDS Church has only Joseph Smith, a man whose reputation and activities were questionable at best. From his First Vision came LDS beliefs about God. From his revelations came LDS concepts of Christ, salvation, and eternity. From his so-called "translations" came LDS views of history, the cosmos, and creation. Evangelicals find this dependency on one man, especially a man such as Joseph Smith, to be much too weak a foundation for faith.

The Simple Represents the Complex

Second, regarding the absence of the word *trinity* in Scripture, this objection is irrelevant since *trinity* is merely a simple term used to represent a complex reality. Using *trinity* is akin to using the term *water*, which represents two molecules of hydrogen and one molecule of oxygen (H_2O). For convenience, we simply ask for *water*. Likewise, we use *trinity* when speaking of God's nature.

Consider, too, the word *Bible*. It is not in Scripture either, but we use it for the 66 books of the Old and New Testaments that represent God's thoughts to man and his revealed plan of salvation.

Scripture also does not contain such LDS terms and doctrines as *Heavenly Mother, premortal, eternal progression, First Estate, Second Estate,* and *intelligences* (see chapter 6). These beliefs are "not biblical," yet Mormons accept them. They even point to various *non*explicit verses to substantiate the doctrines.

But when Trinitarians use the word *Trinity*, which to mainstream Christians easily expresses how numerous biblical verses fit together, Mormons decry it as an evolution away from pure biblical teachings.[74] Evangelicals, on the other hand, see Trinitarianism as simply a logical *development* of biblical truths.

Transforming Pagan Thought

Third, a word also must be said about Robinson's use of the popular accusation that the Trinity is a result of early Christians accommodating Hellenistic thinking (Platonism, Stoicism, paganism, and Eastern mystery religions).[75] Robert Millet similarly claims that the Trinity is "a doctrine that evolved from efforts to reconcile Christian theology with Greek philosophy."[76]

Although many early converts to Christianity did indeed come from a Hellenistic background, there exists no concrete evidence that today's evangelical doctrines are either 1) *exclusively* pagan, or 2) the product of a *corrupting* imposition of Greek philosophy on the developing church.

Did Greek philosophy and pagan thought have *any* influence at all on how early Christians ultimately understood and explained God? Of course. But this is not necessarily a negative thing. During the first several centuries of the church's development, some Christian thinkers simply took various truths from Hellenistic thought and used them to express how biblical components are cohesive and make sense.

Misrepresentations

Finally, it must be noted that LDS leaders, on numerous occasions, have misrepresented the Trinity doctrine. For example, LDS philosopher David Paulsen recently made use of popular Mormon theologian James Talmage's words:

> The one-ness of the Godhead, to which the scriptures so abundantly testify, implies no mystical union of substance, nor any unnatural and therefore impossible blending of personality. Father, Son, and Holy Ghost are as distinct in their persons and individualities as are any three personages in mortality.[77]

However, Paulsen does not acknowledge that Talmage is inaccurately defining Trinitarianism. The Trinity doctrine does *not* teach that there is any "blending of personalities." Moreover, Talmage is failing to recognize that Mormons are *interpreting* Scripture just as much as Trinitarians are. Most telling is how Talmage, like many Mormons, is so quick to say what is "unnatural" and "impossible." (But as we have already seen, dogmatic declarations about what may or may not be possible are growing more questionable in light of the many new discoveries scientists, biologists, and physicists are making.)

Mormons have been equally imprecise in other lectures and writings, alleging that the Trinity presents an "unknown and unknowable"[78] God, who is "indefinable"[79] and beyond being "comprehended."[80] In *Not My Will, But Thine*, LDS apostle Neal Maxwell compared Christianity's traditional God to "a distant cosmic presence," a "'cosmic force,'" and "a vague 'life force' somewhere in space."[81]

Latter-day Saints have gone so far as to say that, by the time Smith came along, the Trinitarians of Christendom no longer worshiped a "personal" or "compassionate" God,[82] but had turned to a deity resembling a pagan idol—unable to "see," "hear," or "speak."[83]

All of these charges are false. Trinitarianism does not deny one's capacity to *know*, *define*, or *comprehend* God. Trinitarians (just like Mormons) simply believe that we, as finite creatures, can only know, define, or comprehend God *to a certain point*. Moreover, the Trinity doctrine, contrary to LDS claims, does indeed affirm that God is not only a *personal* and *compassionate* God, but is One who can indeed *see*, *hear*, and *speak*.

FINAL OBSERVATIONS

The intertwining of Christianity, Scripture, the creeds, and Hellenistic thought is perhaps the most troubling thing about the Trinity from an LDS perspective. Therefore, it is extremely important that evangelicals seek to clarify for Mormons that the blending of these things in no way compromises the correctness of orthodox perceptions of God.

Mormons must be helped to understand that faith in God and submission to the Bible is wholly compatible with Hellenistic influence. Such a blending only parallels what was advocated by Brigham Young. He said that it mattered not where "truth" was found, even if found among "infidels."[84] He added that LDS elders were "to gather up all the truths in the world pertaining to life and salvation, to the Gospel we preach, to mechanism of every kind, to the sciences, and to philosophy, wherever it may be found."[85]

This is merely a repetition of what early church leaders knew—that all truth is God's truth. They saw that the pagans and philosophers of the Hellenistic world had made many astute observations about God and indeed possessed some truth. For Greek converts, Christianity provided a far deeper understanding and fuller expression of the truths upon which they and other Hellenistic thinkers had stumbled. The LDS First Presidency has admitted as much:

> The great religious leaders of the world such as Mohammed, Confucius, and the Reformers, as well as philosophers including Socrates, Plato, and others received a portion of God's light. Moral truths were given to them by God to enlighten whole nations and to bring a higher level of understanding to individuals.[86]

The truth of this comment is evident as early as Paul's sermon to the Athenians (Acts 17:22-34). He mentions their altar to "THE UNKNOWN GOD," adding, "Whom therefore ye ignorantly worship, him declare I unto you." He goes on to say,

> [He] hath made of one blood all nations of men...[t]hat they should seek the Lord, if haply they might feel after him, and find him, though he be not far from every one of us: For in him we live and move, and have our being; as certain also of your own poets have said. For we are also his offspring (verses 23,26-28).

An Interesting Fact: The Greek poem that Epimenides wrote to the Supreme God reads, *They fashioned a tomb for Thee, O holy and high One, The Cretens, always liars, evil beasts, idle bellies! But thou art not dead; for ever Thou art risen and alive, For in Thee we live and move and have our being.*

Paul's words "we live and move, and have our being" are from a poem by Epimenides of Crete (around 600 B.C.) to the Supreme God. The assertion, "For we are also his offspring," is from *Phenomena* by the Greek poet Aratus of Cilicia (third century B.C.) and reflects the teachings of Cleanthes, a Stoic philosopher (also third century B.C.). Paul again cites Epimenides in Titus 1:12. And in 1 Corinthians 15:33 he even quotes a proverb from *Thaïs*, a comedy by the Greek playwright Menander (342–292 B.C.).

Did You Know? Justin Martyr "believed that the Word or Reason is what gave men knowledge of God. Even before the coming of Christ, men had seeds of that Reason within them; therefore, fragments of the truth could be reached by even pagans. The philosopher Socrates, Justin claimed, was a Christian (*I Apology* 46). He even went so far as to say that the Greek philosophers copied ideas from the books of Moses."*

---

* Mark Mattison, "Jesus and the Trinity," www.auburn.edu/~allenkc/openhse/trinity1.html#Introduction.

So does modern Christianity have *any* doctrines in common with Greek philosophy, first-century paganism, and Eastern mystery religions? Certainly. But such was already the case during the apostolic era, as Paul demonstrated. The early church fathers likewise understood that pagans had grasped certain ideas about God (see sidebar on previous page).

> Such ideas not only formed a point of contact to which the Christian preacher might appeal, as St. Paul does in the speech attributed to him in Athens…they would also shape the expression of *biblical truth* as it was elaborated by Christian thinkers schooled in the classics of Greece and Rome.[87]

And logically speaking, similarity of belief systems does not necessarily mean that those belief systems are of the same origin. Most religions have many similarities. For example, Christianity and numerous primitive religions scattered throughout the world share belief in the existence of an afterlife and a Creator–Father. Does this mean that the concepts of life after death and God as our heavenly Father are pagan? Surely not.

This brings out yet another extraordinarily ironic fact. Mormonism, too, shares many beliefs with pagan Hellenistic thought: for example, the eternality of matter, the pre-existence of spirits, and human deification. The LDS acceptance of many gods also mirrors the pagan beliefs of several ancient cultures: among others, the Assyrians, Babylonians, and Sumerians. Even BYU professor Robert Millet has admitted that Mormons should not be surprised by finding LDS concepts within pagan traditions.[88]

Indeed, one of the most important of all LDS beliefs—the pre-existence of the soul (see chapter 6)—is actually pure Greek philosophy, traceable to Plato and his theory of "Forms" (see page 153). Should we now assert that there has been a Hellenization, or a paganization, of Mormonism? Using LDS logic, we would have to say so.

But how many Mormons would see this charge as fair or logical? Consequently, similar charges against classic Christianity should be withdrawn by Mormons—unless, of course, they are willing to condemn their own faith for promoting beliefs, views, and attitudes that were not only embraced but also propagated throughout the Hellenistic world by Greek philosophers and pagans.

HEAVENLY FATHER IS A MAN

*If men do not comprehend the character of God,
they do not comprehend themselves.*[1]

—Joseph Smith Jr. (April 7, 1844)

I had been speaking to the Latter-day Saint woman on the phone, long-distance, for more than an hour. Our discussion was continuing to revolve around one very crucial question about Heavenly Father: Is he a man? Of course, I knew that she, as a Mormon, rejected the idea that God, in his essence, is spirit (an incorporeal being). And this was confirmed by her repeated claim that God is indeed an immortal man with a body of flesh and bones.[2] This belief, she told me, was proved by Smith's First Vision.

This is one thing that evangelicals must remember when talking to Mormons. Their view of God is firmly rooted in the First Vision. Smith's alleged experience is seen as an indisputable historical event that serves as a sort of final arbiter in disputes over God's nature, as Stephen Robinson notes:

> [T]he doctrine of the nature of God is established more clearly by the First Vision of the Prophet Joseph Smith than by anything else.... For Latter-day Saints, no theological or philosophical propositions about God can override the primary experience of the Prophet.[3]

Even more significant is the way Mormons identify so closely with Heavenly Father because he is a man. I realized this after speaking to my LDS friend, Cindy, for another 45 minutes. It didn't matter that I had shown her verse after verse in the Bible clearly stating that God is not a man.

"Can you really not see what I'm trying to say?" I finally asked her.

She paused, then admitted, "Okay, I see what you're saying. But it doesn't matter."

I couldn't yet understand her point. "So you're still going to remain a Mormon, even though I have shown you—and you have admitted—that the Bible does not teach that God is a man?"

"Yes," she replied.

"But why? Why would you remain faithful to the Mormon God if that is not the God clearly talked about in the Bible?"

Cindy paused, then finally answered. "Because I like the Mormon God. I like the idea of God being a man just like us."

⚹ ⚹ ⚹

Mormons often begin their quest for knowledge about God by accepting Joseph Smith's First Vision, as the above story demonstrates. Only then do they turn to Scripture, or to reason and logic, to confirm the beliefs that have emerged from that vision: beliefs they "know" are true; beliefs that include the revealed "truth" that God is a man and that he has a body of flesh and bones.

In other words, anything that might contradict the LDS view of God is dismissed by Mormons in favor of the "truth" obtained through Joseph's vision. The miraculous visitation is *proof* that the Father is a man—a physical being rather than an incorporeal one.[4] LDS apostle Stephen L. Richards explained,

> When Joseph came out of the grove, he had no need to argue for a theory—he knew the facts. God is in form like a man....The testimony is direct and positive and irrefutable.[5]

So once a Mormon accepts the historicity of Smith's vision, faith in that vision takes precedence over all other data. As the old cliché says, "Seeing is believing." This does not mean that Mormons reject or ignore philosophical musings, logical thought, intellectual reasoning, or biblical arguments. But these things take a backseat, so to speak, to Joseph's heavenly encounter.

Mormons also believe that God has not always been God. "Heavenly Father" *progressed* to godhood, beginning at some point in the distant past when he lived on an earthlike planet.[6] God actually worshiped and served a god above him, who likewise had a god...and so on and so on, in a successive line of gods.

Heavenly Father, before reaching godhood, also had to die and be resurrected. Then, he continued to learn truth and pursue righteousness by means of obedience to truth. Finally, after untold aeons of diligence, Elohim (Heavenly Father's name) reached the exalted state of a God.

─── MORMON QUOTES ───

"God himself was once as we are now, and is an exalted man....I say, if you were to see him today, you would see him like a man in form—like yourselves in all the person, image, and very form as a man;...We have imagined and supposed that God was God from all eternity. I will refute that idea....He was once a man like us; yea, that God himself, the Father of us all, dwelt on an earth, the same as Jesus Christ Himself did" (Joseph Smith Jr., 1843 or 1844).[7]

"God undoubtedly took advantage of every opportunity to learn the laws of truth and as He became acquainted with each new verity He righteously obeyed it....As he gained more knowledge through persistent effort and continuous industry, as well as through absolute obedience, His understanding of the universal laws continued to become more complete. Thus he grew in experience and continued to grow until He attained the status of Godhood" (Milton R. Hunter, LDS apostle, 1958).[8]

"God is a perfected, saved soul enjoying eternal life" (Marion G. Romney, LDS apostle, 1977).[9]

"God the Father is an exalted man, a corporeal being, a personage with flesh and bones....Smith taught in 1844 that God our Father was once a mortal, that he lived on an earth, died, was resurrected and glorified, and grew and developed over time to become the Almighty that he now is." (Robert L. Millet, BYU professor, 1998).[10]

"Not much has been revealed about this concept beyond the fact that God was once a man and that over a long period of time he gained the knowledge, power, and divine attributes necessary to know all things and have all power" (Robert L. Millet and Noel B. Reynolds, BYU professors, 1998).[11]

"God is a man, a Man of Holiness...who possesses a body of flesh and bones....These concepts are clearly part of the doctrinal restoration" (Robert L. Millet, BYU professor, 1998).[12]

A CLOSER LOOK

As noted, the LDS belief that God is a man stems primarily from the First Vision—not the Bible. Mormons, however, do use the Bible as *secondary* confirmation of their beliefs. They usually appeal to those verses that refer to God in anthropomorphic terms (terms that ascribe physical characteristics to God).[13]

Latter-day Saints interpret such verses in an extremely literal way. Evangelicals, however, interpret them metaphorically, believing that they are meant to either 1) make God more understandable to human beings; or 2) illustrate certain aspects of God's personality. After all, there are only so many words at our disposal. And since we are human, one of the best ways to picture God is though anthropomorphisms.

The evangelical perspective is plausible, given the Bible passages in which God, Christ, or both are described in *non*human terms. To read these verses literally would make God a ball of flame (Deuteronomy 4:24), a bird (Psalm 17:8; 36:7; 57:1; 61:4; 91:4), and a slab of stone (2 Samuel 22:47; Psalm 89:26); would make Jesus a flashlight (John 1:7), a baguette (John 6:51), a door (John 10:9), and a vine (John 15:1); and would make the Holy Ghost a dove (Matthew 3:16).

Mormons see things differently when it comes to anthropomorphic passages (for example, Genesis 1:26-27; 1 Corinthians 11:7; Hebrews 1:3; Exodus 33:11; John 14:9; and Acts 7:55-56).[14] In all fairness, these verses that speak of images and faces do seem to suggest that God *might* be a man with a body. But the teaching is nowhere openly stated (as Robinson admits). So what does "image" mean (Genesis 1:26-27)? What does "face to face" mean (Exodus 33:11)? Why should such terms be taken nonliterally?

Something to Consider: There is so much back-and-forth speculation in Mormonism that contraditions among LDS leaders, Mormon apologists, or both are relatively easy to find. One example relates to whether or not the LDS concept of God having a physical body is explicitly taught in the Bible. BYU professor Stephen Robinson says no:

> We believe this not because it is the clear teaching of the Bible but because it was the personal experience of the prophet Joseph Smith in his first vision and because the information is further clarified for us in modern [LDS] revelation....It is understandable that some Latter-day Saints would want to find this view of God the Father explicitly taught in the Bible, but I think Prof. Blomberg is correct in pointing out that it is not there.[15]

BYU professor Robert Millet, however, says yes:

> [Mormons] believe that God the Father is an exalted man, a Man of Holiness who possesses a physical (corporeal) body. This, of course, is soundly rejected by other Christian denominations....Latter-day Saints believe this not just because it is taught in the Bible but also because modern prophets have so declared it.[16]

These questions are central to LDS–evangelical disagreements over God's nature. BYU geology professor Barry Bickmore agrees that terms for God such as "wings" and "feathers" are metaphorical.[17] But he changes his view when it comes to anthropomorphisms:

> [W]hat is the metaphorical interpretation of God's "back parts" that Moses saw [Exodus 33:23]? When Stephen reported his vision, the text gives no clue as to any metaphorical interpretation; he simply reported what he saw [Acts 7:55-56].[18]

Admittedly, the above verses are difficult to interpret and require careful study. Most vital is realizing that the cardinal rule of biblical interpretation is to *always* interpret the debatable passages in light of the clear (or explicit) ones. Consequently, the first step toward either verifying or invalidating the LDS concept of God is to look at any *explicit* scriptures relating to the proposition that God is an exalted man with a tangible body—a man who progressed to godhood.

EVANGELICAL THOUGHTS

Using the most explicit words available, various biblical verses seem to say that God, far from being an exalted man, is an incorporeal entity who has always been, and always will be, just as he now is

- "God is not a man, that he should lie; neither the son of man, that he should repent" (Numbers 23:19).
- "[T]he strength of Israel will not lie nor repent: for he is not a man, that he should repent" (1 Samuel 15:29).
- "I will not return to destroy Ephraim: for I am God, and not man; the Holy One in the midst of thee" (Hosea 11:9).

Despite the clarity of language used in these verses, Mormons do not see them as definitively saying that "God is not a man." The passages cannot mean, indeed they *must* not mean, what they appear to mean. The words, taken at face value, utterly contravene Joseph's vision. Each passage, therefore, is reinterpreted by Mormons to mean that God is not a man *like us*. In other words, he is not mortal (a man who is sinful, subject to death, or imperfect).

This leaves room for Mormons to accept that God is not a *mortal* man while at the same time maintaining that God is indeed an exalted, or *immortal,* man.[19] In reference to Numbers 23:19, for instance, Stephen Robinson says, "I do not believe God is a (mortal) man—or the son of one, or that God ever changes his mind."[20]

Another Mormon, who might best be described as a lay apologist of sorts for the LDS faith, expressed his understanding of the various "God is not a man" verses as follows:

This verse [Numbers 23:19], as well as similar verses in the Bible, are contrasting the imperfections of man as we are now to the glorious perfect God we worship. For example, 1 Samuel 15:29 says "And also the Strength of Israel will not lie nor repent: for he is not a man that he should repent." This passage, like the one from Numbers 23:19, illustrates the differences between man and God *now*.[21]

However, these passages, contrary to the LDS view, do not say that "God is not *a mere mortal* man" or that "God is not a *nonexalted, earthly* man." They say "God is not a man"—period. Such verses may indeed be affirming that God neither lies nor repents. But why is that? It is because he is "not a man." *That* is the pivotal reason why God does not behave like us. These verses are not only contrasting what we do as opposed to what God does, but also what we *are* (man) as opposed to what God *is* (*not* man).

Does God Have a Body?

But if God is not a man, then what is God? And whatever God is, does he have a tangible form? These questions can be answered most succinctly using only two Bible passages, John 4:24 and Luke 24:39. The first verse reads, "God is a Spirit: and they that worship him must worship him in spirit and truth." But what is a spirit, or rather, what is *not* a spirit? In the second verse, Jesus tells us that "a spirit hath not flesh and bones, as ye see me have." These verses seem to be saying that God is spirit, not flesh and bone. In a 1986 message, LDS president Gordon B. Hinckley, however, explained away the obvious in this way:

> I opened my Bible to the verse he had quoted [John 4:24] and read to him the entire verse: "God is a Spirit: and they that worship him must worship him in spirit and in truth." I said, "Of course God is a spirit, and so are you, in the combination of spirit and body that makes of you a living being, and so am I." Each of us is a dual being of spiritual entity and physical entity....Jesus' declaration that God is a spirit no more denies that he has a body than does the statement that I am a spirit while also having a body.[22]

Hinckley changes the text's meaning by reinterpreting what it says to what it *must* say in order to remain consistent with LDS teachings—namely, that God *has* a spirit. This is a mere repetition of D&C 93:33-34, where Joseph Smith said that man "is spirit." But the Greek text *(pneuma ho theos)*, which does not have the indefinite article "a," leaves no room for such a view. It literally says God *is* spirit—or rather, spirit is God's quality of being; it is his very essence or substance. As for Hinckley's parallel about God being "a spirit" and a person being "a spirit," this is a particularly egregious error for three reasons.

First, his comparison asserts that someone who *possesses* a spirit may have their entire self (spirit *and* body) properly referred to as "a spirit." But this is not an accepted use of the terms. One cannot rightfully point to someone else and say, "You are a spirit." To do so is like pointing to a peach and saying, "That is a pit." It would only be proper to say "You *have* a spirit" or "That peach *has* a pit."

Second, Hinckley has arbitrarily redefined "spirit" to mean a spirit *in* a body. To draw another analogy, his argument is like a chemist claiming that "water" really means "water in a bucket."

Third, there is no reason to read this fairly straightforward text in such a convoluted way. Shandon Guthrie, adjunct professor of philosophy at the University of Nevada, Las Vegas, explains:

> The interpretation of 4:24 is simple, God is proposed to have the nature of *spirit*....It is just as feasible to translate 4:24 as, "God=spirit." Now, when one "worships in spirit," one [that is, we as humans] is not being described. The word "spirit" here is in the dative case, thereby denoting a medium through which the worship is carried out. This is different from the subject of those who are told to worship Him! In this context [that is, in reference to us], "spirit" is the means of how we are to worship God, not a description of our ontological status [what our natures are like].[23]

Stephen Robinson, however, insists differently:

> Just as God is not limited to being light and nothing else by 1 John 1:5, or to being love and nothing else by 1 John 4:8, so he is not limited to being spirit and nothing else by John 4:24—unless one *assumes* with the Greeks that spirit and matter are mutually exclusive, opposing categories. That God *is* spirit does not limit him to being

a spirit any more than his being worshipped *in* spirit (John 4:24) requires worshippers to first jettison their physical bodies.[24]

But Robinson is setting up a straw-man argument because no one is saying that the attribute of "spirit" limits God to being "nothing else." God, in fact, is many more things than just spirit. But the designation "spirit" seems to be excluding him from the *physical* category—just as "light" and "love" exclude him from the categories of darkness and unlovingness.

Robinson also has somehow missed a key point being made here by John with regard to the attributes mentioned. Each passage is stating a truth in such a way as to reveal, at the same time, an opposing truth: 1) God is light—and conversely, he is not darkness; 2) God is love—and conversely, he is not unloving; 3) God is spirit—and conversely, he is not physical or corporeal. The "light" and "love" verses only bolster the evangelical claim that God is, in his essence or substance, spirit rather than flesh and bone.

It is not surprising that Mormons adamantly seek to defend the idea of God's corporeality. They believe that the traditional Christian view of God, as expressed through the "creeds of Christendom," is nothing less than "what Lucifer wants so-called Christian people to believe about Deity, in order to be damned."[25]

Notable and Quotable:

I thought of the many ways in which God's true nature is distorted in the teachings of so many Christian churches. Joseph Smith taught that not only does God have a body, but that he "dwells in everlasting burnings."...But many—perhaps the majority—of churches teach that it is the *devil* who has a body (often pictured with horns, tail, and cloven hoof) and dwells in everlasting burnings....Satan must surely enjoy the visual irony that much of Christianity has reversed his position with that of God! For the truth of the matter is that it is the devil who is but a spirit (John Tvedtnes, BYU ancient language professor).*

---

* John Tvedtnes, "Children of the Most High," *Tambuli*, July 1984, www.lds.org.

However, God's nonphysicality easily squares with those scriptures describing God as nonlocalized (Acts 17:24); omnipresent (1 Kings 8:27; Psalm 139:7-10; Isaiah 66:1-2; Jeremiah 23:23-24; Amos 9:1-4; Acts 7:48, 17:28); invisible (1 Timothy 1:17; 6:15-16), and beyond sight (John 1:18; 1 John 4:12). God himself said, "Thou canst not see my face: for there shall no man see me, and live" (Exodus 33:20).

LDS President Joseph Fielding Smith refuted these verses with what has remained perhaps the most direct argument: "There are too many passages which declare very definitely that God did appear, 'face to face,' with his ancient servants. Therefore, passages which declare that no man has seen him, must be in error."[26]

Mormons find the entire concept of an invisible God very distasteful. It not only cuts across their ideas of what is understandable, but goes against what they see as possible. "How can a God who is invisible exist?" they ask. But again, it is science that gives us examples of concrete realities paralleling the evangelical concept of God. Many things are real that also are invisible, the most common being space itself.[27]

Has God Always Been God?

According to traditional Christianity, God has always been God. There never was a time when he was not God. This is known as the doctrine of God's eternality, or infinity. Wayne Grudem, research professor of Bible and theology at Phoenix Seminary, explains it thus:

> God has no beginning, end, or succession of moments in his own being, and he sees all time equally vivid, yet God sees events in time and acts on time....The doctrine is also related to God's unchangeableness.[28]

God's eternality and his unchangeableness should be understood with respect to his nature, or *essential being,* not to the varying ways he deals with people. As theologian Louis Berkhof noted, "There is change round about Him, change in the relations of men to Him, but there is no change in His Being, His attributes, His purpose, His motives of action, or His promises."[29]

In other words, God may make certain pronouncements (for example, stating his intent to destroy the city of Nineveh) and then act in an opposite way (for example, removing his wrath from Nineveh after its people repented of their sins). But this does not mean he changed. "In reality, the change is not in God, but in man and in man's relations to God."[30] Similarly, Christ's incarnation did not change God, because his eternal nature and purpose were not altered.

The evangelical perspective is that God, in his essence, has eternally been God. Several scriptures speak of God as existing "from everlasting to everlasting" (Deuteronomy 33:27; Psalm 90:2; 93:2; Isaiah 48:12).

Mormons, however, understand "eternity" and "from everlasting to everlasting" to mean from an age before creation to a future age. BYU professor Robert Millet explains that, because God has "held his exalted status for a longer period than any of us can conceive, he is able to speak in terms of eternity and can state that he is from everlasting to everlasting."[31] To Mormons, then, these terms say nothing about whether God has always been God, or how he existed "before the clock started ticking."[32]

Such a concept of "eternity" in relation to God is legitimate, says BYU professor Stephen Robinson, because there is some ambiguity as to the meaning of "forever" and "eternal."[33] On the other hand, Denver Seminary professor Craig Blomberg sees no evidence for interpreting the verses "to mean anything other than that God has always existed as the one supreme, uncaused being who alone is worthy of worship."[34]

LDS RESPONSES

Genesis 1:26-27 ("God created man in his own image") is perhaps the most popular text used by Mormons to prove that God is a man with a body. And it must be admitted that the passage can be unclear, as Yeshiva University Rabbi Joseph Telushkin notes: "This description has confused more than a few people and been interpreted in widely disparate ways."[35]

What Does "Image" Mean?

To Rabbi Telushkin, "image" merely refers to our human ability to make moral choices via reason.[36] He also makes the following remark:

A Mormon religious teacher once told me that it means that God
has a body, and that the human form is created in the image of God's
body. Jewish teachings hold, however, that God is incorporeal,
without a body (see Deuteronomy 4:12,15).[37]

Traditional Christianity agrees with Telushkin. In their *Commentary
on the Old Testament,* Keil and Delitzsch offer a refined version of the
rabbi's thoughts in the observation that the very ability to reason is only
possible by virtue of man's spiritual personality (said another way, the
spirit given to him by God). Hence, "the man endowed with free self-
conscious personality possesses, in his spiritual as well as corporeal nature,
a creaturely copy of the holiness and the blessedness of the divine life."[38]

Other attributes also are sometimes seen as part of the divine image:
for example, love, forgiveness, goodness. As for the LDS view, though,
Stephen Robinson asserts an altogether different opinion:

> As Adam is created in the likeness and image of God, so after the
> Fall Adam begets Seth in *his* own likeness and image (Gen. 5:3).
> The language of orthodox Christians in making the "image" in
> which Adam was created a nonphysical image, a spiritual image,
> necessitates taking the word *image* figuratively. This is fine with
> me—the passage can be coherently interpreted that way—but it is
> another instance of the LDS's taking Scripture *literally* where the
> "orthodox" make it merely figurative and then charge *us* with being
> unbiblical![39]

First, however, Genesis 5:3 in no way contradicts the evangelical view
of Genesis 1:26-27. In fact, it supports it. When read with a traditional
understanding of "image," Genesis 5:3 makes it clear that Seth was begotten
in Adam's image (a spiritually sinful image). Although Seth's image retains
some of the divine image of God, it has been marred, perverted, twisted,
misdirected, and corrupted. Seth was indeed in Adam's image rather than
in God's.

Second, Robinson's charge about not taking the passage at face value
is groundless. The word *image* has no rigid definition that is being spir-
itualized away by evangelicals. Mormons are presupposing that the word
must mean a physical duplicate. Then they insert their meaning into the

text to make it consistent with LDS theology. But no such definition of the term exists in Hebrew. In fact, two different words are used: *tselem* ("image"); and *demut* ("likeness").

Understanding Hebrew Thought

Tselem means "statue," and by inference, an "image" or "copy."[40] Does this necessitate accepting Adam as a duplicate of God? No. The word can mean image in the sense of a thing's "essential nature," or as a representation of something while lacking its "essential characteristics."[41] For example, *tselem* (Genesis 1:27) is used in Psalm 39:6 to describe men walking as "a phantom" ("vain shew" in the KJV). In Psalm 73:20, *tselem* is the remaining "image" of what was in a dream.

The word *demut* literally means "likeness; shape; figure; form; pattern."[42] Its uses are even broader than those of *tselem*. In fact, "[a]ll but 5 of the 25 appearances of this word are in poetical or prophetical books."[43] In 2 Kings 16:10 it "means 'pattern,' in the sense of the specifications from which an actual item is made."[44] It also is used for the actual "shape" of an item. Describing "the original after which a thing is patterned" is a third use.*[45]

What does all of this mean? The significance may lie in the fact that *tselem* and *demut* are used interchangeably (see Genesis 1:26,27; 5:1-3; 9:6). In *Nelson's Expository Dictionary of the Old Testament*, Merrill F. Unger and William White Jr. explain:

> This plus the fact that in other contexts the words are used exactly the same leads to the conclusion that the use of both [words] in passages such as Gen. 1:26 is for literary effect.[47]

Thus, no opinion about the *exact* meaning of *image* or *likeness* is absolute. The terms, in their most literal senses, "are simply explanatory of each other. The simple declaration of Scripture is that man at his creation was like God."[48] That's it. No more information is provided. As theology professor Wayne Grudem says, the words "simply informed the original readers that man was *like* God, and would in many ways *represent* God."[49]

---

* *Demut* can even be used, as it is in Psalm 58:4, "to extend the form but not the meaning of the preposition *ke:* 'Their poison is like the poison of a serpent.'"[46]

Noteworthy is the fact that in the ancient Near East, a representative was often called the "image" of the one represented. Some inscriptions, for instance, identify kings and pharaohs as the "image" (or representative) of their culture's deity. Old Testament professor Phyllis Bird of Garrett Evangelical Theological Seminary also has noted that *tselem elohim* ("image of God") is "the exact counterpart of the Akkadian expression… [that] appears as an epithet of the Mesopotamian kings":[50]

> The king in ancient Babylonia and Assyria was understood to be a special representative of the god or gods, possessing a divine mandate to rule, and hence divine authority.…The epithet "image of the god" served to emphasize his divinely sanctioned authority and godlike dignity.[51]

In the Bible, however, Bird notes that "all men carry the image and likeness; the image is 'not an identity of substance of being, but of character or function (and power).'"[52] (This is, she adds, a "portrait of human dignity and responsibility in creation that counters the picture presented by the creation myths of surrounding cultures."[53])

Whatever the view taken of "image," one must bear in mind that all theories (Evangelical, Jewish, and LDS) built upon the word *image* are to some degree speculation. Some Mormons, however, assert that they alone understand *image* correctly—that is, allegedly according to the intended literal way, as Robinson claimed (see page 142).

This assertion is not only groundless, but ironic, since Mormons are the ones who claim that "God is not a man" does not *really* mean that "God is not a man." It is Mormonism, too, that teaches "there is one God" does not *really* mean "there is one God." Mormons seem to be doing what they accuse evangelicals of doing. One difference, however, is that Mormons are willing to adopt metaphorical and figurative interpretations even when the grammar and language of Scripture does not allow for such interpretations.

Seeing Jesus, Beholding God

If we look at 1 Corinthians 11:7 ("the image and glory of God") and Hebrews 1:3 ("the express image" of God), we have a situation comparable to the Genesis verses. Two Greek words are used for image: *eikōn* (1 Corinthians 11:7) and *charaktēr* (Hebrews 1:3).

The word *eikōn*, does not exclusively mean a carbon-copy duplicate, although it can mean as much. The word more importantly suggests "the two ideas of representation and manifestation" (see, for comparison, Colossians 1:15).[54] For example, 2 Corinthians says that Christians, as they mature, are gradually changed into the "image" *(eikōn)* of Christ.

Well-known Greek scholar William Barclay remarked that an image "can be two things which merge into each other. It can be a representation; but a representation, if it is perfect enough, can become a manifestation."[55] Thus, in Paul's words, Jesus is a perfect manifestation *(eikōn)* of God.

As for *charaktēr*, this word does indeed connote, most forcefully, an exact duplication.[56] The pressing question is, How was Christ an exact duplication of God? Hebrews 1:2,3 tells us that God spoke "unto us by his Son, whom he hath appointed heir of all things....Who being the brightness of his glory, and the express image *[charaktēr]* of his person *[hupostasis]*."

Now, in order for Mormons to be correct in their interpretation, the word *hupostasis* would have to mean physical form. But that word actually means substance, essence, or the real nature of something. Hence, this verse is an affirmation of Christ's deity. It is saying that whatever may be the substance, or essence, of God, that also is Christ.[57] Hebrews 1:3 is thus picturing Christ as "exactly equal to God."[58]

And Hebrews 1:3 leads us to John 14:9, where Jesus tells his disciples that "he that hath seen me hath seen the Father." Contrary to the LDS belief that Christ's words were referring to his physical shape, the declaration highlights the fact that Jesus was both the *eikōn* (representation) of God and the *charaktēr* (duplication) of God's divine essence or substance. Nothing in John 14:9 refers to bodily form.

Face to Face

Perhaps the most often quoted and difficult-to-explain verse used by Mormons to "prove" God is a man is Exodus 33:11. It mentions Moses speaking to God face to face "as a man speaketh unto his friend." There are two alternatives here concerning "face to face": 1) It could mean that, as friends, they spoke *physically* face to face, which would include actually seeing each other; or 2) it could mean they communicated openly, honestly, and lovingly with each other, as friends would do during a face-to-face meeting.

Mormons opt for the former interpretation. But doing so goes against other passages that explicitly state that no one has ever seen God (John 1:18), who is, in fact, unseeable (Exodus 33:20; 1 Timothy 6:16). So we are left with only the latter choice as an acceptable explanation of the passage. Moreover, this understanding of the verse seems more appropriate in light of Numbers 12:8, where God says he spoke to Moses "mouth to mouth." Obviously, God and Moses were not standing with their mouths touching.

This verse, like Exodus 33:11, is employing a figure of speech. "[T]o 'see the face of' a person was a regular Hebrew idiom for being received in audience by someone of consequence (for example, Genesis 43:3,5; 2 Samuel 14:24)."[59] (See note 59 for further explanation.)

Complicating the issue further is Exodus 33:23, which talks about God's "back parts." Contrary to the LDS understanding of the verse, however, ("back parts" = God's back), the Hebrew text indicates that "back parts" is an expression meaning God's "afterglow," or some kind of residual aspect of God's glory that was left behind for Moses to see.

In His Presence

To understand these verses, one must recall Moses' request: "I beseech thee, shew me thy *glory*" (verse 18, emphasis added). God responded by saying, "I will make all my *goodness* pass before thee" (verse 19, emphasis added). Then suddenly, in verse 20, the references to "glory" and "goodness" are equated with "face" when God says, "Thou canst not see my face: for there shall no man see me, and live."

What is occurring here? The answer lies in the Hebrew word *panim*, which is translated as "face." Its most basic meaning, of course, is literally one's face. But more important are the many passages wherein *panim* ("face") means "presence." (See note 60 for a discussion of examples.) [60] In this light, we can see exactly what is happening between Moses and God in Exodus 33:18-23. Moses, in asking to see God's glory, was boldly requesting to see all that God is: his total presence.

We know this from the Hebrew word for "glory," *kabod*, which literally refers to "the great physical weight or 'quantity' of a thing....*Kabod* can also have an abstract emphasis of 'glory,' imposing presence or position."[61] This same term is used in Exodus 40:34-35, where God's glory *[kabod]* "filled the tabernacle."[62]

The unveiled presence of God, therefore, is what Moses wanted to see. But the Lord replied, "Thou canst not see my face [that is, presence]: for there shall no man see me, and live." God, however, promised that his glory would pass by and that Moses would behold his *achor* ("back parts"). This Hebrew word, far from meaning someone's back, has an extremely broad spectrum of application that simply relates in some way to the back of, or the leftover aspects of, something.

To sum up, the text is merely saying that "Moses did not see the glory [unveiled presence] of God directly, but once it had gone past, God did allow him to view the results, the afterglow, that his presence produced."[63] The word "face" is thus a synonym for God's unveiled "glory" (verse 18) and "goodness" (verse 19), while the word "back" (NIV) or "back parts" is a synonym for God's residual glory; glory similar to the *shekinah* glow that illuminated Moses' face after he interacted with God (Exodus 34:29; 2 Corinthians 3:7).

At His "Right Hand"?

At this point a brief word must be said about Acts 7:55-56, where Stephen sees Jesus at the "right hand" of God. Once again, Mormons like to interpret this in a rigid manner—at the expense of what is quite probably another idiom. The "right hand" commonly referred to one's might or power in Hebrew culture (see Exodus 15:6; Psalm 89:13).[64] In a more contemporary, albeit cruder fashion, one would not be far off the mark in saying that Jesus is the Father's "right-hand" man (his representative of power and might).

Stephen seems to be making reference to the messianic identity of Jesus by making a statement that closely parallels Psalm 110:1, which is a messianic psalm. Being at the "right hand" of a king represented the highest place of honor, authority, and power.[65] One's physical location (that is *literally* by someone's right hand) was not the point.

The verse has nothing to do with God being a man or having a body. Stephen saw Jesus standing to receive him into heaven—standing in the position of one having the Father's power and might.

A Man of War; A Son of a Man

Finally, I must mention two of the oddest ways I have heard some Mormons try to biblically validate their belief that God is a man. The first involves Exodus 15:3, which refers to God as "a man of war." The second involves the numerous New Testament passages wherein Christ is called "Son of Man." The former passage, say Mormons, literally calls God a man. And the latter passage calls Jesus the "Son" of a man—and so God the Father, obviously, must be a man.

But once more, such simplistic reasoning seems to stem from a severe lack of familiarity with biblical studies. I mention these verses not only because they are truly used by Latter-day Saints, but also because their use shows how Mormons tend to read into Scripture all kinds of ideas and preconceived notions that are completely unsupported by biblical scholarship.

Regarding Exodus 15, is it really saying that God is literally a "man" (Hebrew, *ish*) who is warlike? Or is it trying to say he is a warrior (metaphorically, a "man of war")? The key to arriving at the correct answer has to do with the verse's context, which is a hymn being sung by Moses and the children of Israel "unto the LORD." In other words, these are lyrics to a song![66]

From the standpoint of good biblical interpretation, song lyrics are not an ideal source of doctrine. If interpreted literally, lyrics often say something, that is not only absurd, but may actually contradict what the writer is trying to express. If taken metaphorically and figuratively, however, the lyrics make sense and can be very encouraging.[67]

Thus, Exodus 15:1-19 is poetic in nature, using imagery and phrasing to creatively communicate various truths. One cannot legitimately rip the word "man" from a song to prove that God is man. The lyrical and poetical nature of this passage is why so many translations render the phrase in question "The Lord is a warrior."[68] That is what these lyrics are communicating. God is the one who will fight for his people.

Note that this song also says that God's right hand "dashed in pieces the enemy" (verse 6). Did God *literally* punch and smash the Egyptians? Verse 8 reads, "[W]ith the blast of thy nostrils the waters were gathered together." Did God *literally* huff and puff at the Red Sea? As for Israel's enemies, verse 16 explains that "[b]y the greatness of thine arm they shall be as still as a stone." Is it *literally* true that God's biceps and triceps appeared so enormous that the Egyptian army froze in their tracks and became as motionless as rocks?

Now concerning the title "Son of Man," there are several ways to interpret this phrase. But none of them imply that God the Father is a man. One might notice, for instance, that contrary to what Mormons may assert, the phrase does not say "son of *a* man." There are no indefinite articles in the Greek. Each instance simply reads, "Son of Man."

This appears to be yet another Hebrew idiom, one meant to designate the Christ as one who is of humankind (Psalm 144:3). The expression simply means a human—or put a different way, one who possesses a human nature. "Son of Man" might just as easily be read "human." Moreover, "Son of Man" is a messianic title based on Daniel 7:13-14. Of particular interest is how "son of man" in this verse distinguishes the messiah (in appearance) from the form of the *beasts*. The messiah's humanity is being shown.

Throughout the gospels, Jesus applies the title to himself in three ways: 1) as the Son of Man serving on earth; 2) as the Son of Man suffering and dying; and 3) as the Son of Man in future end-time glory. Interestingly, only Jesus uses the term to describe himself. Christian theologian George Eldon Ladd writes that

> by use of the term "Son of Man," interpreted in the light of its historical and religious background, Jesus laid claim both to messianic dignity and to a messianic role....[I]t carried overtones of supernatural character and origin. He did not call himself messiah because his mission was utterly different from that connoted to the popular mind by this messianic term. He called himself Son of Man because this title made an exalted claim and yet at the same time permitted Jesus to fill the term with new meaning. This he did by coupling the role of the "Son of Man" with that of the Suffering Servant.[69]

Therefore, this descriptive phrase is not saying that Jesus is the *literal* son of a *literal* man. The word "man" suggests humanness—as in the modern term "mankind," or in the cliche "love your fellow man." As Christian scholar Robert M. Bowman observes, "And if 'man' in 'Son of Man' meant God, wouldn't it at the very least include the definite article 'the' (i.e., 'Son of *the* Man')?"[70]

Appealing to the Church Fathers

In addition to the many biblical interpretation problems facing LDS notions about God, there is a more difficult quandary unique to Mormon understandings of anthropomorphic language. Consider Isaiah 66:1, which says that heaven is God's throne and earth is his footstool. Exodus 33:22 reveals that God used his hand to entirely cover Moses. And Isaiah 40:12 says that God measured the waters of earth "in the hollow of his hand" and measured out the heavens with the "span" of his hand (in other words, the distance between the tip of the little finger to the end of the extended thumb). A consistent LDS reading of these passages would make God gigantic.

Interestingly, rigid literalism is what actually led some Jews to believe in an immense God. One reference to this huge God appears in the *Shiur Komah* (second century A.D.). The mystical work, now associated with kabbalistic Judaism (an occult religious system), claims that God's height is "236 ten thousand thousands parasangs [1 parasang = 3.6 feet]" with a span of "30 ten thousands [parasangs]" between his eyes![71]

The above-noted Jewish belief in a gigantic God is even reported in the writings of early church fathers, who speak of God's "body."[72] This raises a final issue that needs to be briefly explored. As we saw in our discussion of the Trinity, Mormons quote early church fathers in support of modern LDS beliefs—but unknown to many rank-and-file Mormons is how LDS apologists often take such quotes out of context (see page 113).

In "Does God Have A Body In Human Form?" for example, Barry Bickmore writes, "[T]he great Christian writer, Tertullian (ca. 200 A.D.) wrote, 'For who will deny that God is a body, although "God is a Spirit"? For Spirit has a bodily substance of its own kind, in its own form.'"[73]

Although Bickmore accurately quotes Tertullian's words, he provides only a partial understanding of the church father's view.

Notice that in his statement about God's "body" (or "bodily substance") Tertullian gives two qualifying phrases: "its own kind" and "its own form." These qualifiers are important in the context of other remarks by Tertullian. Why? Because Tertullian equated substance with existence. He felt that all *real* things must have substance *of some kind*. Consequently, God also must have substance (of some kind)—but not necessarily flesh and bone.

Yet Bickmore's title implies that Tertullian is speaking of God having a "human body." As it turns out, though, Tertullian's view bears little resemblance to LDS beliefs. Other statements not quoted by Bickmore reveal that when Tertullian used words like *body* and *corporeality* in reference to God, he only meant that God, *in a limited sense*, has some kind of substance or form.

Notable and Quotable:

Tertullian declared,

> Reason herself expressly forbids the belief in more gods than one, because the self-same rule lays down one God and not two, which declares that God must be a Being to which, as the great Supreme, nothing is equal; and that Being to which nothing is equal must, moreover, be unique. What new god is there, except a false one? Not even Saturn will be proved to be a god by all his ancient fame, because it was a novel pretence which some time or other produced even him, when it first gave him godship. On the contrary, living and perfect Deity has its origin neither in novelty nor in antiquity, but in its own true nature. Eternity has no time. It is itself all time. It acts; it cannot then suffer. It cannot be born, therefore it lacks age. God, if old, forfeits the eternity that is to come; if new, the eternity which is past. The newness bears witness to a beginning; the oldness threatens an end. God, moreover, is as independent of beginning and end as He is of time, which is only the arbiter and measurer of a beginning and an end.[74]

"We read, indeed, of God's right hand, and eyes, and feet," Tertullian said. "[T]hese must not, however, be compared with those of human beings, because they are associated in one and the same name."[75] He also contradicted the LDS view of what "created in God's image" means.[76] And he explicitly said that God is "not human."[77]

Further, Tertullian believed in the Trinity as well (albeit in a slightly different manner than is commonly accepted today). And he condemned polytheism, along with the belief that God has not always been God (see sidebar, page 151). Bickmore's appeal to Tertullian is another example of how a growing number of Mormons are too eagerly taking the words of early church writers out of context.

FINAL OBSERVATIONS

It must be conceded that Mormon apologists have been very faithful in seeking to defend their beliefs. However, all these efforts have not succeeded in negating the validity of what journalist Kenneth Woodward observed in a 1980 *Newsweek* article: "[U]nderneath their *Reader's Digest* image, the Mormons espouse a radical, anthropomorphic conception of God that sets them far apart from other religions."[78] This radical concept, as we will see in the next chapter, includes "the belief that God is literally a procreating father and that he is married to a Mrs. God, or divine mother."[79]

SIBLINGS FROM ETERNITY PAST

From a Latter-day Saint perspective, we did not suddenly spring into existence at the time of our mortal birth. We have always lived. [1]

—Robert Millet (1998), BYU professor of Ancient Scripture

In his famous ode "Intimations of Immortality," the poet William Wordsworth (1770–1850) wrote that our birth "is but a sleep and a forgetting." The verse refers to the Greek philosophical theory of Forms voiced by Plato (427–347 B.C.). He asserted that our world of sense "never really is" because it is always *becoming*. Consequently, things of constancy, such as Ideas, must have their origins in another realm—a realm that is eternal, a realm of pure essences. This domain, according to Plato, was also the place of our origins. He theorized that we existed there as spirits before coming to Earth.

This notion, coincidentally, is essentially what Mormonism teaches. The irony, of course, is that Mormons tend to despise any hints of Greek philosophy in orthodox Christianity, but seem to have no problems accepting its influence in their own faith. Moreover, their views on our pre-existence in the spirit world are deeply woven into their teachings about human origins.

All of us, according to Mormon thought, are *literal* spirit-children of God.[2] Moreover, God is married to an exalted woman known as Heavenly Mother.[3] She is *literally* the mother of our spirits.[4] These notions are central to the LDS worldview, which, like all worldviews, explains where we came from, why we are here, and where we are going.[5]

The LDS perspective on these issues is based primarily on a single presupposition voiced by Joseph Smith—namely, that only two things are eternal: 1) spirit matter (or "element"); and 2) "intelligence." These ideas are basic to the LDS claim that nothing has ever been "created" by God. He has merely *organized* everything out of pre-existing spirit matter.[6] Only "the elements are eternal," said Smith. Hence, the word "created" in Genesis *should* read "formed or organized."[7]

Thus, Mormons believe that even humans are not created by God but, like everything else, are simply "organized." Unlike objects, however, we are supposedly formed out of disorganized "intelligence(s)." Even God sprang from "intelligence." Consequently, he is "an organized being just as we are."[8] All of us, therefore, are "of the same species as God."[9] Again, it was Smith who advanced this idea.[10] It is perhaps the most fascinating of all LDS notions, and it is deeply intertwined with almost every Mormon doctrine.[11]

⎹ ⌨ ⎹

What exactly is "intelligence"? Mormons usually define it as "the eternal essence of our being....[I]t is the nucleus of our identity and individual personality....Intelligence is an eternal gift of the universe, the essence of our reality."[12] BYU professor of Near East studies Victor Ludlow explains it thus: "Identity or intelligence is the unique characteristic of human personality—it is the core element that makes each person original, individual, and distinct."[13]

Building on these doctrines, Mormons assert that before being born on earth, we made the transition from *disorganized* intelligences to *organized* intelligences ("spirit children") thanks to Heavenly Father and Heavenly Mother—who, through some kind of sexual union, "clothed" each of us with a spirit-body.[14]

Mormons believe that we existed in this "First Estate" for countless years, during which time we were reared into "grown spirit men and women."[15] We dwelt somewhere in the cosmos near the as-yet-undiscovered planet Kolob, where one day equals 1000 earth years.[16] We lived there much like any family would on this planet, until it finally came time for us to become mortal (our "Second Estate").

The first of Heavenly Father's spirit-children to make the journey to Earth were Adam and Eve. They arrived in order to do what all of us are supposed to do—travel along the path of "eternal progression" toward all that God wants us to be. Their first task was to "be fruitful and multiply," which was supposed to provide a way for the rest of God's offspring to assume physical bodies.

According to LDS teachings, however, Adam and Eve could not have children when they arrived on Earth because they were not yet mortal. (In other words, they were not flesh and blood—not subject to death.) They were only spirit beings with bodies formed from the earth. This presented a problem, since mortality, in LDS thought, is essential for progressing toward Mormon "salvation."

Adam and Eve ultimately saw that their only choice was to disobey God and eat the forbidden fruit. Thus, they "died." And in so doing, they became flesh-and-blood mortals subject to death. But they also became capable of reproducing. The Fall, therefore, was a spectacular blessing— "Adam fell that men might be."[17]

Further, say Mormons, this act of disobedience was not even a sin.[18] Coke Newell, media spokesperson for the LDS Church, explained: "The 'transgression' of Adam and Eve was in fact a brilliant move, a bit of prescient genius (on the part of Eve primarily)."[19]

--------- **MORMON QUOTES** ---------

"Intelligence is eternal and exists upon a self-existent principle. It is a spirit from age to age, and there is no creation about it" (Joseph Smith, 1844).[20]

"[M]an, as a spirit, was begotten and born of heavenly parents, and reared to maturity in the eternal mansions of the Father, prior to coming upon the earth in a temporal body....[Thus, we know that] All men existed in the spirit before any man existed in the flesh, and that all who have inhabited the earth since Adam have taken bodies and become souls in like manner....God Himself is an exalted man, perfected, enthroned, and supreme. By His almighty power He organized the earth, and all that it contains, from spirit and element, which exist co-eternally with Himself" (LDS First Presidency, 1909).[21]

"There is no way to make sense out of life without a knowledge of the doctrine of premortal life. The idea that mortal birth is the beginning

is preposterous. There is no way to explain life if you believe that" (Boyd
K. Packer, LDS apostle, 1983).[22]

"Latter-day Saints believe that all the people of earth who lived or will
live are actual spiritual offspring of God the Eternal Father. In this perspective, parenthood requires both father and mother, whether for
the creation of spirits in the premortal life or of physical tabernacles
on earth. A Heavenly Mother shares parenthood with the Heavenly
Father" (*Encyclopedia of Mormonism*, 1992).[23]

"[M]en and women are literally the spirit sons and daughters of God,
we lived in a premortal existence before our birth…we grew and progressed in that 'first estate,' all in preparation for this 'second estate'"
(Robert Millet, BYU professor, 1998).[24]

A CLOSER LOOK

Three important beliefs are represented in the preceding quotes: those
of 1) Heavenly Mother, 2) our premortal life, and 3) the Fall. All of them
have ramifications and deserve attention. But before showing why evangelicals view such doctrines with concern, we need to further explore LDS
justifications for them.

Our Heavenly Mother

One of the oddest aspects of the LDS teaching about Heavenly Mother
teaching is that no mention of her is made in *any* of the Mormon Standard
Works.[25] LDS president Joseph Fielding Smith reasoned, "If we had a
Father, which we did, for all of these records speak of him, then does not
good common sense tell us that we must have had a mother there also?"[26]
In other words, Latter-day Saint leaders feel there simply *must* be a lit-
eral Heavenly Mother because they already know there exists a literal
Heavenly Father.[27]

This belief, therefore, once more rests on Joseph's Smith's visions and
teachings, rather than Scripture.[28] It seems to have come about as a necessary addition to LDS theology so Smith's views about God would make
sense. Hence, the *Encyclopedia of Mormonism* tells us that Mormons "*infer*

from authoritative sources of scripture and modern prophecy that there is a Heavenly Mother as well as a Heavenly Father."[29] Bruce McConkie expressed this same sentiment, albeit in more detail, in his popular book *Mormon Doctrine*.[30]

LDS President Gordon B. Hinckley also has said that the Heavenly Mother concept is based mostly on "logic and reason," which, he says, "suggest that if we have a Father in Heaven, we have a Mother in Heaven."[31] Evangelicals feel that such reasoning is fragile at best, since it begs the underlying, pivotal question: Are we, in fact, God's *literal* offspring who were born as spirit-children before coming to Earth?

Born Before Birth

Mormons insist that God merely formed or organized, everything, including all of us, out of pre-existing spirit material. Most crucial to this concept is the idea of "intelligence." To Mormons this belief is nothing less than the "glory of God," and it is equated with "light and truth" (D&C 93:36-37).[32] Mormons do not know in "what particular form or capacity our original intelligence existed."[33] Nevertheless, they assert that our "existence as unorganized intelligence comprised the major portion of our first estate."[34]

Then, from some collective source of unorganized intelligence in the universe, each of us advanced to being an *individual* intelligence in a spirit-body.[35] "This creation of our spirit body was our first, or spiritual 'birthday,' the highlight of our first estate in the premortal world."[36] According to Brigham Young, our spirit body was created via a sexual union of Heavenly Father and Mother. "[God] created man, as we create our children," said Young, "[f]or there is no other process of creation in heaven, on the earth, in the earth, or under the earth, or in all the eternities, that is, that were, or that ever will be."[37]

More recently, Angel Abrea—a member of the First Quorum of the Seventy—declared, "God is the actual father of the spiritual bodies possessed at that time. This is not a case of creation but of procreation."[38] In other words, we became spirit-babies, so to speak, then matured and prepared ourselves for our trip to Earth.

Every newborn babe is another spirit-child entering mortality. This is why LDS leadership, until 1998, officially encouraged Mormons to have large families and condemned birth control as "contrary to the teachings of the Church."[39]

Did You Know? Previous to 1998, LDS leaders harshly condemned birth control:

- LDS president David O. McKay (1873–1970) said, "All such efforts too often tend to put the marriage relationship on a level with the panderer and the courtesan. They befoul the pure fountains of life with the slime of indulgence and sensuality" (as quoted in *Encyclopedia of Mormonism,* volume 2, page 961).
- In 1987, LDS president Ezra Taft Benson declared, "Do not curtail the number of children for personal or selfish reasons. Material possessions, social convenience and so-called professional advantages are nothing compared to a righteous posterity" (quoted in *Encyclopedia,* volume 2, page 961).
- In 1955, LDS president Joseph Fielding Smith, went so far as to teach that "Birth Control Leads to Damnation" (Joseph Fielding Smith, *Doctrines of Salvation,* volume 2, page 88).
- In 1917, Smith had previously stated that birth control was "one of the greatest crimes of the world today, this evil practice" (Smith, *Relief Society Magazine,* volume 4, page 314).

Further, Mormons also believe that every *thing,* as well as every person, pre-existed in a spirit form.[40] In fact, some Latter-day Saints maintain that a near-duplicate of every physical object first came to be in the realms of eternity. (Bruce McConkie elaborated on this concept in his 1982 book *The Millennial Messiah.*)[41]

Joseph Smith claimed that this bit of knowledge came from God himself, who allegedly said, "I, the Lord God, created all things, of which I have spoken, spiritually, before they were naturally upon the face of the earth.... [A]ll things were before created, but spiritually were they created and made according to my word."[42]

Falling Up?

As we noted earlier, unlike traditional Christians, Latter-day Saints embrace the Fall as a blessed event. They see it as a forward step on the road to eternal life (see chapter 7)—which involves 1) becoming mortal, 2) dying, and 3) being resurrected. God supposedly gave Adam and Eve the go-ahead to start this whole process by saying to them, "Be fruitful and multiply." (Put another way, "Go ahead and give bodies to all of those spirits waiting in the heavenly realms for an opportunity to come to Earth.")

But as we saw, this presented a dilemma to Adam and Eve, who when they first came to Earth, were "not yet mortal, they could not grow old and die."[43] And they could not have children.[44] There needed to be "a significant change before they could fulfill the commandment to have children and thus provide earthly bodies for premortal spirit sons and daughters of God."[45] How did this change occur through the Fall? LDS apostle Dallin Oaks explains that

> this transition, or "fall," could not happen without a transgression—an exercise of moral agency amounting to a willful breaking of a law....This would be a planned offense, a formality to serve an eternal purpose....It was Eve who first transgressed the limits of Eden in order to initiate the conditions of mortality. Her act, whatever its nature, was formally a transgression but eternally a glorious necessity to open the doorway toward eternal life. Adam showed his wisdom by doing the same. And thus Eve and "Adam fell that men might be" (2 Ne. 2:25).[46]

So "by partaking of the forbidden fruit, Adam and Eve opened the way for us to enter into mortality."[47] This is why the Fall was allegedly a "Great Blessing."[48] In the words of LDS apostle James Talmage, it is from our first parents that we have received "the means of winning title to glory, exaltation and eternal lives."[49]

EVANGELICAL THOUGHTS

A few key observations about the previously mentioned doctrines will sufficiently show why traditional Christians reject them. Consider, for example, the LDS belief in Heavenly Mother. It has already been shown that there are no explicit references to a Heavenly Mother in any LDS Standard Works. Nevertheless, some Mormons claim that the Bible does include at least a few suggestions or "hints" of her existence.[50] *The Missionary's Little Book of Answers* cites Genesis 1:27: "It is possible that since God created male and female in His image that this verse means God patterned the first earthly couple after His own heavenly marriage."[51]

In truth, however, this passage neither hints at nor suggests any such possibility. Nowhere in it is anything said about Adam and Eve being created as a reflection of God and his wife. The verse simply reads, "God created man in his own image, in the image of God created he him; male and female created he them."

To assert that this verse is implying the existence of God's "own heavenly marriage" is to drift into the realm of pure conjecture. A better case actually could be made that the verse implies God is a hermaphrodite since it states that he created male and female in *his own* image. This option, of course, is absurd. It is only presented to show the tenuous nature of the LDS claim that Genesis 1:27 might be hinting at God's role as a heavenly husband.

There also is no biblical support for LDS teachings on pre-existence. For Mormons, however, a more important issue may be the kind of comfort that can be derived from such a doctrine. Not only does it reveal how we came to be, but it goes so far as to explain, in part, the suffering we endure in life. According to LDS apostle Neal Maxwell, "[S]ome of our present circumstance may reflect previous agreements" that we "freely made" with God during our pre-earth life.[52] We allegedly "accepted the very conditions of challenge" we now find ourselves in.[53]

This belief can be a great source of strength since it places the cause of some of our suffering on our own shoulders. Our pain is something we ourselves, while in our pre-existence, accepted. In other words, what we are enduring is partially our own doing. This doctrine, therefore, provides a way to escape feelings of victimization that may stem from either the actions of others or the actions of God.

Biblically speaking, though, as with Heavenly Mother, the idea of pre-existence comes primarily from LDS prophets. BYU scholar Stephen Robinson admits as much, saying that it is "[o]n the basis of modern revelation" that Mormons believe all spirits "were organized in a premortal existence and that they lived for a time in the presence of God *before* they came to earth."[54]

Regarding the Fall, it must be acknowledged by traditional Christians that God clearly chose to create beings that he knew would rebel. He also knew, however, that after the Fall a significant number of lost souls would turn to him for forgiveness (Romans 8:29-30; 9:14-26; Ephesians 1:5,11; 1 Peter 2:9-10) and choose the precious gift of eternal life offered in the death and resurrection of Christ (Romans 3:21-26; Ephesians 2:13-22; Colossians 1:13-14). In this way, God would be able to display "the exceeding riches of his grace in his kindness toward us" (Ephesians 2:7).

We also must accept that God allows evil and suffering to exist so his power and glory can be manifested (for example, John 9:1-5). And so, in a *general* sense, we can agree with Mormons that the Fall and our redemption has "always been part of the plan."[55] But this does not mean that the actions of Adam and Eve were not sinful.

The scriptures make it very plain that the first couple disobeyed a direct command *not* to eat of the tree of knowledge of good and evil. Their disobedience was a tragically poor choice that brought physical–spiritual death (Romans 5:12; 6:23; 8:10). Eve was deceived, and Adam deliberately sinned (Genesis 3:13; 1 Timothy 2:14).

God responded to Adam and Eve's choices by 1) cursing the serpent that had deceived Eve, 2) multiplying Eve's pain in childbirth, 3) cursing the earth on which humanity would walk, 4) adding sorrow to the activity of work, and 5) driving the first human couple from his presence. Despite the obvious fact that these acts were obvious punishments, LDS leaders such as Dallin Oaks maintain a highly inappropriate opinion of the dreadful scene:

> Some Christians condemn Eve for her act, concluding that she and her daughters are somehow flawed by it. Not the Latter-day Saints! Informed by revelation, we celebrate Eve's act and honor her wisdom and courage in the great episode called the Fall.[56]

Equally disconcerting is the LDS claim that Adam and Eve could not bear children before the Fall. That notion is utterly foreign to the Bible. Moreover, the claim puts God in an unflattering light since he was the one who commanded the first human couple to "be fruitful and multiply" *before* the Fall. Mormons basically present God as commanding Adam and Eve to do something they could not do—which forced them to sin.

LDS RESPONSES

For many years, Latter-day Saints have sought to validate their belief in Heavenly Mother through the Bible. One such attempt was voiced as far back as 1884 by LDS leader George Q. Cannon. Like other Mormons, he taught that God "is a married Being" and that all men "were born in the spirit world of the union of the sexes, having a literal father and a literal mother before coming to this world."[57] But Cannon also declared that veiled references to God's wife could be found in Jeremiah, where the prophet (according to Cannon) makes reference to how "the angels were offering incense to the queen of heaven" (Jeremiah 7:17-19; 44:17-19,25-27).[58]

A Pagan "Queen of Heaven"

These verses, however, say nothing about angels, but instead refer to those Hebrews who were devoted to a *pagan* "Queen of Heaven" deity, not any kind of Judeo–Christian Heavenly Mother. And Jeremiah is not condoning their behavior—he is condemning it as idolatry. Moreover, their offerings brought wrathful judgments from God, not heartfelt blessings.

This "queen of heaven" could have been any one of several deities, including the ancient goddesses Anat, Asherah, Astarte, or Ishtar/Inanna. Each of them was associated with the others, and all were described as Queen of Heaven, Sovereign of Heaven, Lady of Heaven, and so on. For example, an Egyptian stele found in a temple built by Ramses III[59] describes Anat as "the queen of heaven, the mistress of all the gods."[60]

Jeremiah seems to have deliberately used a title that was applicable to many different goddesses.[61] Thus it is impossible to know for certain which goddess he was referencing.[62] In fact, these goddesses were essentially the same deity, differing slightly only in traits and mythologies as found in different cultures.[63]

Despite their varying traits, they shared one thing in common—a radical dissimilarity from Mormonism's Heavenly Mother. Astarte, for example, functioned as a fertility goddess who, along with Anat and Asherah, was closely linked to Baal, the chief Canaanite deity, whose worship included child sacrifice (Jeremiah 19:5 and 32:35).[64]

Astarte, whom most scholars believe was a sex goddess, also served as a war goddess. She is mentioned in 1 Kings 11:5-6 as the deity of the Sidonians, to whom Solomon's heart was turned. In 2 Kings 23:13 she is called an "abomination." The plural of her name, Ashtoreth, was used as a collective term "for the female divinities of the Canaanites (Judges 2:13; 1 Samuel 12:10)."[65]

Nonbiblical references to Astarte indicate she was often identified with the planet Venus, which explains her ultimate transformation into the Roman goddess Venus and the Greek goddess Aphrodite, both goddesses of sexual pleasure. This may be why her Hebrew name, Ashtoreth, means "shameful thing." *The New Book of Goddesses and Heroines* comments, "What seems to have been shameful to the patriarchal Hebrews was the untrammeled sexuality of the goddess."[66]

Like Astarte, the other goddesses also do not resemble any kind of Heavenly Mother:

- **Asherah** was commonly depicted in the form of "upright posts or living trees"—objects in which her followers "perceived her essence."[67] This is why the King James Version renders *asherah* as *grove(s)*. Worship of her was accompanied by what has been described as "joyfully orgiastic rites."[68] She is mentioned in the condemnation of Baal altars (Judges 6:25-30), Moses' command for the destruction of her images (Deuteronomy 7:5; 16:21), and God's praise for King Hezekiah's obedience to Moses' directive (2 Kings 18:4).

- **Anat** was a Canaanite warrior goddess "of violence and sexuality,"[69] whose "bloodthirsty nature is shockingly explicit in one well-known text (KTU 1.3 ii:3-30) in which she is described as joyously wading thigh-deep in the blood of slain warriors."[70] During this battle scene

"Anat fastens severed heads and hands to her waist."[71] Although not specifically mentioned in the Bible—except in the form of a place name (*Beth-Anat,* Joshua 19:38; Judges 1:33), and a personal name (*Shamgar ben Anat,* Judges 3:31)—her popularity clearly permeated Hebrew culture.[72]

- **Ishtar/Inanna,** the patroness of prostitutes, was perhaps "the most revered and popular goddess of ancient Mesopotamia."[73] As a goddess of love and excessive sexuality, she possessed "strong powers of sexual attraction."[74] She was usually depicted in statue form, nude and with her hands holding her huge breasts. Although Ishtar/Inanna had many traits, she was most often seen as "the wanton [goddess], constantly plotting to find a new lover—divine, human, bestial, it did not matter."[75] But she also tended toward "anger and rage," which fell in line with her role as yet another goddess of war. Most relevant at this point may be an ancient hymn to her in which she praised herself as the "queen of the heavens."[76] Her very name (in-an-na) literally means "lady of Heaven."[77]

Therefore, contrary to Cannon's assertions, Jeremiah was not picturing any Heavenly Mother as the Mormons understand such a figure. Nevertheless, some of today's LDS apologists continue to insist that the Jeremiah verses allude to her.

The Search for Heavenly Mother

In *Restoring the Ancient Church,* LDS apologist Barry Bickmore attempts to prove the acceptance of a Heavenly Mother in ancient Israel by citing two articles (see Table 6.1)—one by British language scholar Theodore Robinson (from 1933) and one by Swedish history of religion scholar George Widengren (from 1958).[78]

According to Bickmore, these quotes provide scholarly confirmation that 1) the Israelites worshipped a goddess "who was believed to be the consort of 'Yahweh'"; and 2) the Queen of Heaven "received officially sanctioned worship in Jerusalem" that was connected to year-rites in which "a sacred marriage was performed for the god and goddess, who then gave birth to a Savior-King."[79]

Robinson, as quoted by Bickmore	**Widengren, as quoted by Bickmore**
"From our Old Testament alone we should never have guessed that Israel associated a goddess with Yahweh, even popularly, but the conclusion is irresistible, and we are justified in assuming that she played her part in the mythology and ritual of Israel."[80]	"In much later times there was a goddess called the Queen of Heaven(s), to whom official sacrifices were offered by kings and princes, both in Jerusalem and in other cities of Judah, Jer. xliv. 17...That the sacred marriage should bring as its fruit the birth of the Savior-king is in accordance with the general myth and ritual pattern..."[81]

Table 6.1

Unfortunately, Bickmore's misrepresentation of what is being discussed in the articles only shows how *some* Latter-day Saints, although well-meaning and sincere, are not being very careful in investigating the biblical and historical material related to their faith. In this case, Bickmore's readers are left with the false impression that Robinson and Widengren are lending support to LDS beliefs. But nothing could be more untrue.

Bickmore's approach is not only an example of poor scholarship, but borders on deceptive manipulation of information. He fails to mention, for example, that both Robinson and Widengren held views of Scripture that were quite liberal—too liberal, in fact, not only for evangelicals, but probably for most Mormons, especially LDS leaders.[82]

An Interesting Fact: Devotion in various ways to a Queen of Heaven continued well into the Christian era, as Cornelius Houtman noted in the *Dictionary of Deities and Demons in the Bible:* "Epiphanius (4th century) criticized certain women in Thracia, Scythia, and Arabia, on account of their habit of adoring the Virgin Mary as a goddess and offering to her a certain kind of cake....Isaac of Antioch (5th century) equates the Queen of Heaven of the book of Jeremiah with the Syr goddess Kaukabta, 'the Star' (= Venus). He also identifies the Arab goddess Al-Uzza with the Queen of Heaven."[83]

Widengren, for instance, was part of the "Myth and Ritual School" of religious study, which taught that "a distinctive set of rituals and myths were common to all Near Eastern peoples, including the Hebrews."[84] These pagan myths and rituals (for example, the New Year Festival) allegedly explained Hebrew faith and practice.[85] In other words, Widengren felt that much of the Old Testament was little more than pagan mythology in Hebrew garb, especially the poetical books and Genesis.[86] He went so far as to say that many descriptions of God were *borrowed* descriptions of Baal.[87]

This decidedly non-Mormon view was earlier advocated by none other than Theodore Robinson, who in his 1921 book *A Short Comparative History of Religions* declared, "In short, Yahweh became Baal."[88] Robinson also accepted the liberal *documentary hypothesis* view of the Old Testament, which denies Moses' authorship of the Bible's first five books, postulating rather that at least four non-Mosaic sources appear in Genesis through Deuteronomy. Some as-yet-unknown revisionist then compiled and edited the text into its current form.

It is noteworthy that this hypothesis is often employed by liberals, atheists, and agnostics to undermine the credibility of Scripture.[89] Also crucial is the fact that this approach to the Old Testament—as articulated by its most influential proponents Karl Graf (1865) and Julius Wellhausen (1878)—has been rejected by a host of key LDS leaders and scholars of the past: B.H. Roberts, Sidney B. Sperry, Hugh Nibley, Bruce McConkie, J. Reuben Clark, Mark E. Petersen, and Joseph Fielding Smith, for example.

Even Bickmore's own BYU colleagues reject this theory,[90] as do current LDS authorities. High-ranking apostle James E. Faust has made this clear: "Moses was one of the greatest prophets who ever lived and was the author of five books in the Old Testament."[91] It is difficult to understand why Bickmore would resort to quoting sources that are based in part on a viewpoint widely rejected by his own church's leaders and scholars—*and by the Book of Mormon* (1 Nephi 5:11).[92]

Robinson and Widengren Dissected

Concerning the actual content of Theodore Robinson's article, Bickmore neglected to reveal that the whole point of the book in which it appeared *(Myth and Ritual)* was to discover if any pagan practices and beliefs had crept *into* Hebrew worship and faith. Robinson thought so, explaining that "a certain amount of *assimilation* with Canaanite religious practices was taking place as Israel gradually passed from a semi-nomadic and pastoral way of life to an urban and agricultural civilization."[93]

Samuel Hooke, editor of *Myth and Ritual,* noted that "the prophets regarded these *borrowings* as a deliberate attempt on the part of Israel to make itself like its surrounding pagan neighbors."[94] This explains Robinson's reference to a goddess in association with Yahweh. The pairing reflected an aspect of paganism that had influenced ancient Israel.

B.S.J. Isserlin—former Head of the Department of Semitic Studies and Reader in Semitic Studies at the University of Leeds—verified this in his 1998 text *The Israelites:*

> Israelites worshipped, in particular, the Baals, Ashtoroth (Astarte) and Asherah. These were local manifestations of Canaanite deities....In the Canaanite pantheon, Asherah was the wife of the wise and kindly, if at times lascivious, chief god El. She was the great mother goddess.... Baal and Astarte were worshipped, following Canaanite precedent.[95]

The ebb and flow of paganism within Israel, according to Hooke, created "levels of religion in Israel, widely spread throughout the country, in which Yahweh was spoken of as Baal and was associated in popular thought with those sexual elements in the fertility cults of Canaan whose existence is well attested."[96] Such a perversion of Moses' teachings resulted in the now famous succession of prophets who tirelessly called for Israel to return to worship of the one true God (see Ezekiel 20).[97]

This unquestionably conflicts with Bickmore's implication that Israelite devotion to the Queen of Heaven somehow reflected a kind of lost truth that was once inherent to Moses-derived worship. The Queen of Heaven, according to both Hooke and Robinson, found a place among ancient Israelites as a direct result of *pagan* influence:

> What are we to say when we find…women weeping for Tammuz, women declaring that since they ceased baking cakes for the Queen of heaven nothing has gone well with them, the *masseboth,* the asherehs, the divinations, the seeking unto the *elohim,* and numerous

other practices? It is surely impossible to deny that all these are foreign elements, some Canaanite, some presumably Assyro-Babylonian,
and some possibly Egyptian, and that all of these enter into the picture of "the religion of Israel as it appears in the Old Testament."[98]

Further, Robinson's comment about "a goddess with Yahweh" (as
quoted by Bickmore) is part of his discussion of the presence in Israel of
a *pagan* cult ritual "involving a dying God, a divine marriage, and a ceremonial procession."[99] He was claiming that this "divine marriage" between
a *pagan* god and goddess could be found in the Old Testament book of
the Song of Solomon. And who did Robinson name as the goddess? Anat![100]

In other words, Robinson's "sacred marriage" between a goddess and
Yahweh was clearly something he believed had come *into* Israel from
pagan nations. Research as recent as 2001 has confirmed that there was
indeed a pagan cult in Israel linking Yahweh to a goddess. Joseph
Blenkinsopp, biblical studies professor at the University of Notre Dame,
has posited that the goddess was Asherah.[101] This same opinion has
appeared in many other studies as well.[102] Ishtar/Inanna also has been
linked to Yahweh.[103]

As for the second quote by Bickmore in Table 6.1—that from George
Widengren—that writer did indeed comment on "official sacrifices" being
"offered by kings and princes" in Jerusalem to the Queen of Heaven. But
Bickmore's claim that Widengren meant the Queen "received officially
sanctioned worship in Jerusalem" is misleading.[104] In reality, Widengren's
use of the word "official" has more to do with how the widespread practice, which was a pagan ritual, had reached the highest levels of Hebrew
society. This may have happened because so many of Yahweh's attributes
were mirrored in the attributes that Canaanites ascribed to Baal and El
(the supreme Canaanite deity whose position was usurped by Baal).

Immediately after Widengren's remark about "official sacrifices" to the
Queen of Heaven, Bickmore used his first set of ellipses (see Table 6.1)
to delete the following qualification:

> Now, this Queen of Heaven(s) *cannot possibly* be any other goddess
> than Astart, who accordingly as late as c. 600 enjoyed official wor-
> ship in the Kingdom of Judah.[105]

The significance of Widengren's qualifier is obvious—the Queen of Heaven was an *imported pagan* goddess, rather than a Heavenly Mother intrinsic to Jewish faith and Mosaic beliefs. But this is not the message Bickmore's readers receive.

Equally misleading is the citation of Widengren's comment "the sacred marriage should bring as its fruit the birth of the Savior-king." Bickmore implies that this somehow reflects a once-cherished Hebrew notion about Heavenly Father and Mother bringing forth Christ. But again, a set of ellipses is used by Bickmore to alter Widengren's intended meaning, which again has to do with a *pagan* marriage ritual that had infected Israel's devotion to Yahweh.

Like Robinson, Widengren pointed to the Song of Solomon, theorizing that it is a collection of pagan poems. He reiterated Robinson's findings that a significant number of pagan-influenced Hebrews taught that Yahweh had a consort—"the goddess Anat."[106] But just as he had done with the Robinson quote, Bickmore left out Widengren's explicit naming of Anat as the goddess being discussed.

Clearly, neither Robinson nor Widengren were stating what Bickmore was trying to prove.[107] This only shows the BYU scholar's lack of care with his sources, and it demonstrates all the more strongly that Heavenly Mother is a doctrine for which there is no support—especially from Jeremiah.

Rather, the Old Testament prophet simply presented in a most striking way the fact that a pagan mother–goddess was "the most common and pluriform deity of the religions of the ancient Near East."[108] And in this twenty-first century, although Mormons may not worship Heavenly Mother (the Queen of Heaven), they nevertheless espouse the same ancient pagan belief that plagued Israel—that God has a consort.

Our Premortal Years

The *Encyclopedia of Mormonism* tells us that Mormonism "accepts literally the vital scriptural teaching as worded by Paul: 'The spirit itself beareth witness with our spirit, that we are the children of God.'"[109] The significance of this verse in relation to premortal life was highlighted in 1992 by Victor Ludlow:

God the Father took what is called primal or unorganized intelligence, combined it with other spirit elements, and organized them into intelligent spirit personages—each unique, independent, and endowed with the power to think and act for itself as his spirit child. The process by which this spirit came into being is called a spirit birth, for "the Spirit itself beareth witness with our spirit, that we are the children of God [Rom. 8:16]."[110]

However, contrary to Ludlow's assertions, Romans 8:16 is actually highlighting a Christian's postconversion realization that through Christ he or she has *become* a child of God by *adoption* (verse 15). Paul's main point relates to how we, by adoption, become "heirs of God, and joint-heirs with Christ" (verse 17)—just as someone adopted by the head of a household becomes their heir. It was Paul's way of picturing our position before God as Christians, as opposed to our preconversion standing before the Lord as children of sin and death.[111]

Interestingly, Paul adds a qualifier. Verse 14 says "as many as are led by the Spirit of God, *they* are the sons of God" (emphasis added). Thus, conversely, those who are *not* led by God's Spirit are *not* God's sons—which contradicts the view that all of us are God's literal offspring.[112] Paul says the same thing in Galatians 3:26: "For ye are all the children of God by faith in Christ Jesus." The apostle is not making a statement about our pre-existence as literal children of God. Rather, the subject of these passages is salvation and ongoing growth in Christ.

More "Proof" for Pre-Existence?

Other verses used by Mormons to prove human beings' pre-existence as spirit-children of the Father are Matthew 6:9, Acts 17:28-29, Ephesians 4:6, Hebrews 12:9, Numbers 16:22, and Numbers 27:16.[113] Malachi 2:10 is cited as well. But these passages, in reality, provide no support for the LDS position.

In Matthew 6:9, for instance, Jesus is speaking about the Father in reference to teaching his disciples how to pray. (The same thought behind Romans 8:16 may be applied here.) Other biblical references to God as "Father" also do not mean that God is our *literal* father in the way that Mormons propose. Actually, there are three basic ways Scripture uses the word *father:* 1) in regard to a literal father; 2) in regard to a father by adoption (for example, Romans 8:14-17 above); and 3) in reference to God as "Creator."

It is in this latter sense that "father" and related terms are being used in Acts 17:28-29, Ephesians 4:6, Hebrews 12:9, Numbers 16:22, and Numbers 27:16. This is evident from Malachi 2:10: "Have we not all one father? hath not one God *created* us?" (emphasis added). As with the English word *father*, it is quite appropriate to use both the Hebrew equivalent *(ab)* and the Greek, *(pater)* in figurative or metaphorical ways (see note).[114]

Two more verses cited in connection to pre-existence are Job 38:4-7 and Ecclesiastes 12:7. In the first passage, God asks Job, "Where wast thou when I laid the foundations of the earth? declare, if thou hast understanding....or who laid the corner stone thereof; When the morning stars sang together, and the sons of God shouted for joy?" In the second verse, Solomon tells us that at death "the spirit shall return unto God who gave it."

Mormons are quick to attribute the concept of premortal life to these passages. But neither one gives clear confirmation of the doctrine. The Ecclesiastes verse, for instance, may simply be saying that there is an afterlife wherein we return to our Creator.

This interpretation seems more plausible than the LDS view, especially in light of Zechariah 12:1, which says that God "formeth the spirit of man within him." Zechariah makes no mention of our spirits being fashioned out of "intelligence" or being clothed with a spirit body during a premortal life.

And in Job the question being posed by God appears within a strong rebuke he is delivering. It is clearly rhetorical, and the answer is so obvious—namely, Job was nonexistent when God created—that a verbal answer is neither expected nor required.

As for the "sons of God" in Job, Mormons again opt for a rigid interpretation in order to substantiate their beliefs.[115] To them the phrase means the *literal* sons of God. As one popular lay apologist in the LDS community has explained, "Our spirits existed before we were born into mortality. As sons and daughters of God, we witnessed the creation of the world and shouted for joy."[116]

But evangelicals understand such terms to mean angels rather than pre-existing spirit babies. In fact, the phrase "sons of God" (Hebrew, *bene ha elohim*) was routinely used throughout the Ancient Near East to describe all manner of heavenly entities, divine beings, minor divinities, or various types of subdeities.[117]

Evangelicals also feel that Mormons are inconsistent in where and when they interpret verses literally. For instance, regarding the "sons of God" issue, a shift occurs in the LDS mode of Bible interpretation with passages like John 8:42-44. Here, Jesus says to the unbelieving Jews, "If God were your Father, ye would love me....ye are of your father, the devil, and the lusts of your father ye will do."

To be consistent, Mormons would have to interpret this verse to mean that Heavenly Father is not the spiritual sire of those who do not love Jesus. Mormons also would have to believe that those who do not love Jesus were born as the spirit-children of Satan in the premortal life. And that would mean that Satan, too—like God—has a wife, albeit a demonic one. But such doctrines do not fit the LDS paradigm. So Mormons interpret John 8:42-44 figuratively.

God's Omniscience, Not Our Pre-Existence

Perhaps the most common verse used by Mormons to support pre-existence is Jeremiah 1:5: "Before I formed thee in the belly I knew thee; and before thou camest forth out of the womb I sanctified thee, and I ordained thee a prophet..."

This verse does indeed say that God knew us before we were born. Mormons, therefore, reason that for us to have been known, we must have existed. Although this is an understandable conclusion, it is not necessarily accurate. A careful reading of the verse indicates it is saying only that God *knew* us before our births, not that we existed before our births.

The verse, therefore, is likely speaking of God's omniscience (see Psalm 139:11-12; 147:5; 1 John 3:19-20)—specifically, his foreknowledge. In other words, because God is omniscient, even before our birth he knew all about us—including our identity. He knew us as if we already existed. As Romans 4:17 puts it, God "calleth those things which be not as though they were."

In summary, Scripture nowhere even suggests that before being born on Earth we are procreated in heaven as literal sons and daughters of a god and goddess. Instead, we are described in the Bible as God's children by adoption (Romans 8:15). Paul reinforces this by noting the progression: "[T]hat was not first which was spiritual, but that which is natural; and afterward that which is spiritual" (1 Corinthians 15:46).

Finally, it should be noted that the LDS doctrine of pre-existence, like several other Mormon beliefs, is not fully understood by Latter-day Saints. For example, although Heavenly Mother and Heavenly Father have resurrected bodies of flesh and bone, they have *spirit*-babies. Why is it, and how is it, that this occurs? Mormons cannot answer such a question, but are content to simply believe the doctrine based on what they consider "sufficient reasons."[118] This admission is intriguing since—as we discussed in chapter 4—Mormons reject the Trinity partly because certain aspects of it are a mystery.

Feeling the Fall

In 1990, Gerald N. Lund—bishop for the fifty-second Mormon ward in Bountiful, Utah—said, "One of the most misunderstood and misinterpreted doctrines in all of Christianity is the doctrine of the Fall of Adam."[119] Unfortunately, this statement is true for many Christians also, who view the Fall as if it were an accident that forced God to resort to a Plan B of sorts.

God, though, being omniscient, knew what would happen. And his long-range plan, for some as yet undisclosed reason, included the Fall. This aspect of God's plan for humanity, however, need not trouble evangelicals, who maintain that God is not only in control of his creation, but also is good and loving. He has a purpose for those of us who love him and who are called by him (Romans 8:28).

But such an admission does not open a doorway for the Mormon explanation of the Fall. Evangelicals see LDS beliefs on this issue to be little more than unwillingness to accept that Adam and Eve committed a grave sin. This is best seen in the novel distinction Mormons have made, in regard to the Fall, between what is a *sin* and what is a *transgression*. Joseph Fielding Smith said, "This was a transgression of the law, but not a sin in the strict sense, for it was something that Adam and Eve had to do!"[120] LDS apostle Dallin Oaks explains it this way:

> Some acts, like murder, are crimes because they are inherently wrong. Other acts, like operating without a license, are crimes only because they are legally prohibited. Under these distinctions, the act that produced the Fall was not a sin—inherently wrong—but a transgression—wrong because it was formally prohibited....Modern revelation shows that our first parents understood the necessity of the Fall. Adam declared, "Blessed be the name of God, for because of my transgression my eyes are opened, and in this life I shall have joy, and again in the flesh I shall see God" (Moses 5:10).[121]

Oaks is making a delineation here that comes not from the Bible, but rather from LDS "modern revelation." Paul explicitly declares that it was through Adam that "sin entered the world" (Romans 5:12-15,19). How so? The New Testament Greek word for transgression, *parabasis,* is used for any act that breaks a law.[122] And it is applied both to Adam (Romans 5:14) and to Eve (1 Timothy 2:14).

In sum, what this means is that in order to transgress (or break a law), one must sin. This is why John said, "[W]hosoever committeth sin transgresseth also the law: for sin is the transgression of the law" (1 John 3:4). Hence, the Bible says "by one man's disobedience many were made sinners," worthy of spiritual death and separation from God (Romans 3:23; 5:19; 6:23).

FINAL OBSERVATIONS

Although Mormonism advances numerous ideas compatible with traditional Christianity, it also disagrees with a variety of extremely important doctrines, among them what has been one of the subjects of this last chapter: the Fall.

According to LDS thought, the actions of Adam and Eve actually made us far more than just fallen humans—they made us mortals able to obtain the coveted blessing of *godhood.* Closely associated with this belief are those doctrines surrounding that personage who allegedly makes our deification possible: Jesus Christ, our elder brother, the firstborn son of Elohim.

Here is where some of the most serious disagreements arise between Mormons and evangelicals. Of course, just as Latter-day Saints share with traditional Christians certain general ideas about God, so too do they embrace some traditional observations about Jesus, salvation, and the afterlife. But upon closer examination, the LDS faith offers to the world a very different kind of Jesus Christ. This difference between the Mormon Jesus and the traditional Christ, as well as related doctrines, will be the subject of chapter 7.

AFTER ALL WE CAN DO

[I]t is by grace that we are saved, after all we can do.

—Book of Mormon, 2 Nephi 25:23

More than 60,000 Mormon missionaries are actively spreading the LDS message throughout the world. They are young, energetic, clean-cut, and hardworking. What are they working for? The simple answer is, eternal life—the opportunity to return to Heavenly Father and dwell for all eternity in celestial realms of glory. But for many Mormons, the idea of having to work their way back to God is a crushing burden that produces doubt, fear, guilt, and no end of anxiety.

I had never realized how difficult it was to live the Mormon life until I had spent a whole summer getting to know Steven, an LDS missionary. I lived in New York, and he was there only temporarily on his mission, far away from his home in Utah. We talked a lot about his faith, which was very different from mine.

"I know I'm going to heaven when I die," I told him once. "How about you?"

Steven seemed like he was not sure. "I hope," he finally answered, "I hope that if I work hard enough, learn all I can learn, and do all I can do, then maybe Heavenly Father will grant me a place in the Celestial Kingdom—if I'm worthy."

"You—worthy of heaven?" I joked. "Man, I can already tell you that's never going to happen."

He laughed. "Yeah, you're probably right."

"Seriously," I continued, "how can you live like that? I mean, no one is worthy of eternal life. All you gotta do is look around to know that. The Bible says we're saved by grace, Steve. It's all God."

"Yeah…well, the Book of Mormon says we're saved after all we can do."

"But how can you ever know if you've really done all you can do?"

Steve thought for a moment, then realized his dilemma. "I guess I can't. Maybe that's why I'm so stressed all the time."

"That's why we need Jesus. He did it it all for us. Paid the price for our sins. Canceled out the debt against us. Opened up a way, free and clear, to eternal life."

"That sounds nice. But that's not my faith."

"It could be," I hinted.

"Hey," he responded. "I thought I was the missionary here."

I had several more conversations like this one with Steve, but eventually he had to leave for other lands. We kept in touch for a while through letters. But in those days there was no such thing as e-mail, and ultimately we lost touch. To this day, however, I still hope and pray that Steve found peace…and some kind of certainty that there is indeed a way to be secure about his eternal destiny.

This chapter will focus not only on the issue Steve and I discussed so long ago, but also on the figure central to the faith of Mormons and evangelicals—Jesus Christ.

⌗ ⌗⌗⌗ ⌗

Mormons believe that Christ was fully divine and look exclusively to him as the one in whom forgiveness for sins may be obtained.[1] Mormons also believe that good works done in Jesus' name are only possible by God's grace, which equips, strengthens, and empowers them for such acts. Mormons even acknowledge that it is only by Christ's life, death, and resurrection that heaven may be accessed.

As for the afterlife, Mormons steadfastly maintain that there are rewards to be received and rewards to be lost. The LDS Church additionally teaches that only by being a Christian can one dwell in God's presence for all eternity. And in such a state there will be endless peace, joy unspeakable, and unimaginable glory to behold.

Notable and Quotable: "President Hinckley spoke of those outside the Church who say Latter-day Saints 'do not believe in the traditional Christ.' 'No I don't. The traditional Christ of whom they speak is not the Christ of whom I speak'" (LDS *Church News,* week ending June 20, 1998, page 7).

Despite these doctrinal similarities, the LDS concept of Christ contradicts evangelicalism. Regarding Jesus' eternality, for example, Mormons see him as having been created ("organized") just as we were created—as a spirit-child from intelligence. The main difference between us and Jesus is that he was begotten not only in the spirit by Heavenly Father, but also *in the flesh* by him.

Concerning salvation, Mormons believe that eternal life is attained not "by grace alone through faith alone," but by a kind of grace–works syncretism. In Mormonism, "eternal life" is a reward to be gained, not a gift to be received. But even this does not adequately express LDS thinking, which advances two kinds of salvation: 1) *universal,* a free gift received by all (resurrection); and 2) *individual,* also known as exaltation or "eternal life"—a reward to be attained by effort (godhood).[2]

Moreover, there are three heavenly kingdoms: Celestial, Terrestrial, and Telestial (see pages 200–201). And the Celestial Kingdom itself has three levels, each of which offers differing rewards. Only in the highest level may one obtain the greatest reward—deification (see chapter 8). This reward was first "attained" by Jesus, who "marked the path and led the way for others likewise to become exalted divine beings by following him."[3]

——— MORMON QUOTES ———

"[Jesus] is the Son of the living God, the Firstborn of the Father, the Only Begotten in the flesh" (Gordon B. Hinckley, LDS President, 2002).[4]

"The Resurrection is unconditional and applies to all who have ever lived and ever will live. It is a free gift" (James E. Faust, Second Counselor in the First Presidency, 2001).[5]

"[T]here has been much debate regarding the relationship of grace and works....[B]oth are core doctrines....[T]he Lord's grace and our works of faith in Christ, personal repentance, and receiving saving ordinances are required for eternal life [that is, godhood]" (M. Russell Ballard, LDS apostle, 1998).[6]

"After all we can do to pay to the uttermost farthing and make right our wrongs, the Savior's grace is activated in our lives through the Atonement, which purifies us and can perfect us....All of us have sinned and need to repent to fully pay *our* part of the debt. When we sincerely repent, the Savior's magnificent Atonement pays the *rest* of that debt" (James E. Faust, LDS apostle, 2001).[7]

A CLOSER LOOK

According to Mormons, the "greatest salient truth of life is that the Son of God came into the world and atoned for the sins of mankind."[8] Even more mainstream-sounding is their belief that the atonement offered "God's greatest gift, eternal life."[9] Although such remarks seem compatible with evangelicalism, they are actually quite far from anything traditional. Consequently, the general public is now more confused than ever.

Mormon Point: "We do believe things about Jesus that other Christians do not believe, but that is because we know, through revelation, things about Jesus that others do not know. It is a twisting of language to call this a 'different Jesus,' as though we have created some other individual by that name."*

Counterpoint: It is a great misunderstanding for Mormons to think that evangelicals are saying Latter-day Saints believe in a "Jesus" that is another Jesus than Jesus of Nazareth. No one is claiming that a "different Jesus" means a separate individual. The phrase "another Jesus" refers to the nonbiblical way Mormons describe the historical person of Jesus. Hence, evangelicals see the Mormon Jesus as "another" Jesus, who has a nature contrary to that revealed in the Bible.

Latter-day Saints have redefined several key doctrinal terms in nonevangelical ways: *atonement, gift, eternal life,* and *salvation.* These

---

* M. Russell Ballard, "Building Bridges of Understanding," February 17, 1998, available at www.lds.org.

redefinitions effectively conceal, perhaps quite unintentionally, the very *non*traditional LDS views of Christ's eternal nature, pre-existence, relationship to us, atoning work, and ultimate mission. In other words, although Mormons recognize the historical person of Jesus, their Jesus is a qualitatively "different Jesus" (2 Corinthians 11:3-4).

BYU professors Daniel Peterson and Stephen Ricks admit that there are "undeniable differences between the attributes ascribed to Jesus by the Mormons and those ascribed to him by other Christians."[10] Even LDS president Gordon B. Hinckley has agreed, "There is some substance" to what critics say when they point out that Mormons "do not believe in the traditional Christ of Christianity."[11]

Various LDS leaders obviously understand that Mormonism conflicts with mainstream Christianity in substantial ways. Mormons teach, for instance, that Christ, just like us, pre-existed as a disorganized "intelligence" until being organized by Heavenly Father and Heavenly Mother into an individual spirit.[12] But unlike God's other offspring, Jesus achieved a higher degree of advancement in the premortal world than the rest of us, his spirit brothers and sisters.[13]

Mormonism's Jesus demonstrated his supremacy in godliness at a so-called Grand Council in heaven to which Elohim allegedly called his spirit-children.[14] It was here, before creation, that we are said to have learned of Heavenly Father's plan for how we, if we followed his plan, could become "like him" (that is, gods).[15]

But we were also told that in order for the plan to succeed, we would have to go to earth as mortals, gain knowledge and experience, choose between good and evil, endure suffering and trials, and follow God. Sadly, the weakness of mortality would cause us to be sinners with no memory of our pre-earth life. A "veil of forgetfulness" would be over us so we could choose God's way *by faith,* rather than *by knowledge.*[16]

This condition of amnesia would necessitate that a savior be sent to rescue us from eternal death—a savior who could lead us on the path of righteousness.[17] Who would it be? In answer to this question, two spirit brothers stepped forward and volunteered to redeem humanity: Jesus, Elohim's firstborn son, and his brother, Lucifer.[18]

One crucial difference separated them. Jesus, like Heavenly Father, wanted to ensure that all men and women on earth would be given the opportunity to choose *freely* whether or not to accept salvation.[19] Lucifer, however, wanted to *force* all men and women on earth to accept Heavenly Father's plan.

God chose Jesus (who, according to Mormons, appears in the Old Testament "as Jehovah, or Yahweh"[20]). But the choice did not sit well with Lucifer, who responded by rebelling. This caused a "war in heaven" between Jesus and his supporters against Lucifer and his supporters.[21] In the end, Lucifer was "cast down from heaven."[22] Moreover, he and his rebellious army were denied mortal bodies, which meant that they would never progress toward godhood.

And so the plan of Heavenly Father proceeded:

1. The world was created (not just by Jesus, but by all of God's spirit offspring).[23]

2. Adam and Eve fell "that man might be."

3. Jesus, as Yahweh, appeared to Old Testament believers to help them follow God.

4. Christ was born of Mary, after being "begotten" by her and Heavenly Father.[24]

5. Christ suffered, died, and rose again in fulfillment of his premortal guarantee to redeem humanity from sin and death.

EVANGELICAL THOUGHTS

Mormons consider Jesus the "central figure" of their faith.[25] But to evangelicals that means very little if it is not the right Jesus. There are, after all, many different ideas about Jesus, which are being promoted by various religions. But according to BYU president Merrill J. Bateman, Mormons "are blessed through modern revelation to know more about Christ and His purposes than any other people on earth."[26] Christ's relationship to us is described "in terms of his divine roles in the three phases of existence: premortal, mortal and postmortal."[27] Each phase is crucial to the LDS faith.

But LDS views about Jesus are difficult for evangelicals to share because these views are not gleaned primarily from the Bible. They are received through Joseph Smith's teachings and the extrabiblical revelations he produced (Doctrine and Covenants, Book of Mormon, Pearl of Great Price). As Victor Ludlow explained in his *Principles and Practices of the Restored Gospel,* it is through "the revelation of the Prophet Joseph Smith" that Mormons declare "Jesus is literally the Son of God—his spirit child, his only begotten in the flesh, and his fully obedient offspring."[28]

The same can be said for LDS doctrines relating to *individual* salvation (grace plus works), the states of heaven (three kingdoms), and the nature of "eternal life" (deification, also known as godhood).

Did You Know? Evangelical beliefs rejected by Mormons include the following:

- God the Son—Second Person of the Trinity—is eternal, uncreated/unorganized, and co-equal with the Father (John 1:1). Then, at the start of Earth's last days, or latter-days (Hebrews 1:2), this *uncreated* Word "became flesh and dwelt among us" as Jesus (John 1:14).

- Christ was born of the virgin Mary, who, when the Holy Ghost came upon her, miraculously conceived the promised messiah (Isaiah 7:14).

- Christ's atoning sacrifice *entirely on the cross* (Ephesians 5:2) and his subsequent resurrection (John 20) provided the way whereby all of us were reconciled to God (Romans 5:10; 2 Corinthians 5:19). And for those who accept him as their Savior and Lord, their faith is accounted to them as righteousness (2 Corinthians 5:21). All one's sins, along with the penalty for them, are washed away by his sacrifice (Isaiah 53:10; Jeremiah 31:34; Matthew 26:28; Mark 14:24). Through him we receive eternal life (dwelling eternally in God's presence) as an utterly *free* gift, "not by works, lest any man should boast" (Ephesians 2:8-10).

Concerning biblical support for these views, Mormons tend to look for vague passages into which LDS beliefs can be pressed. Scriptures that contradict LDS thought are usually treated in one of the following ways:

1. dismissed as errors

2. accepted only as far as modern LDS revelations allow

3. interpreted contrary to the language, grammar, or context of the passage

4. read in light of Smith's interpretations

5. rewritten using arbitrary textual insertions that reflect LDS belief (for example, Smith's corrected "translation" of Matthew 24 in the Pearl of Great Price)

It is this LDS method of finding biblical support that often leads Mormons and evangelicals to a sudden impasse during discussions. It is perhaps best, therefore, to simply hope for an accurate understanding of the differences that exist between the two faiths.

Jesus, Mary, and Elohim

Both Mormons and evangelicals believe that God the Son existed prior to his birth. Evangelicals, however, see no scriptures in which it is even suggested that Jesus was an eternal "intelligence" organized into a spirit-child by an exalted god-man (and his wife). Such a view, in fact, contradicts a number of Bible verses that depict Jesus as the uncreated, eternal Son (John 8:58; Revelation 1:17-18; Isaiah 44:6).

Also unbiblical is the traditional LDS view concerning the means by which Jesus was conceived "in the flesh." Until recently, the common belief clearly implied throughout the history of Mormonism—based on Luke 1:35 and the Book of Mormon (1 Nephi 11:14,16-18,20,24,26-28,32-33)—was that Jesus' conception occurred via sexual intercourse between Heavenly Father (Elohim) and Mary.

Allusions to this idea can be seen in the remarks of LDS leaders, who have described God the Father as the *literal* father of Jesus Christ.[29] Some of the plainest expressions of the doctrine appear in the sermons of Brigham Young. He asserted that the Father literally had to come "down from heaven" in order to beget Jesus.[30] Christ "partook of flesh and blood— was begotten of his Father, as we were of our fathers," said Young.[31]

Young also stated, "[Jesus] was begotten of the Father, and he was born of the virgin Mary as my mother bore me and as my father begot me and as you begot your children."[32] He went so far as to say that, although the New Testament's Joseph did not have another wife, Mary "had another husband."[33] And that husband, said Young, was Heavenly Father, who impregnated Mary "instead of letting any other man do it."[34]

As if there were any question remaining about how early LDS leaders understood the term "begotten," Mormon apostle Heber C. Kimball drew an analogy that perfectly illustrated Jesus' conception: "I was naturally begotten; so was my father, and also my Saviour Jesus Christ....[H]e is the first begotten of his father in the flesh, and there was nothing unnatural about it."[35]

Some twentieth-century comparisons between how Jesus was conceived and how we are conceived remain the commonly accepted explanations given by LDS leaders of the sexual union that must have taken place between Heavenly Father and Mary. As LDS president Joseph Fielding Smith said, "Christ was begotten of God. He was not born without the aid of Man, and that Man was God!"[36] Similar comments came from Heber J. Grant (1921 and 1938),[37] Bruce R. McConkie (1958, 1978 and 1979),[38] and the LDS *Family Home Evenings* (1972).[39]

Many researchers, however, have found such statements puzzling in light of other LDS comments that refer to Mary as a "virgin" *after* she was visited by Heavenly Father.[40] But the apparent contradiction is easily resolved. Early LDS leaders redefined "virgin" to mean a woman who has never known a *mortal* man. Heavenly Father, of course, is *immortal*.[41] Hence, Mary was still a "virgin" after her union with the Father. This subtle distinction appears as far back as 1878, in remarks by LDS apostle Erastus Snow:

> Christ was born of the Virgin Mary.... [T]he record teaches us that
> he was begotten by the power of God, and not of man, and that she
> had no intercourse with *mortal* man in the flesh until after she gave
> birth to the Savior, who is called the Son of God.[42]

Then, in the mid-twentieth century, Bruce McConkie explained that Christ "was Begotten by an immortal Father in the same way that mortal men are begotten by mortal fathers."[43] More recently, a reference to Jesus being sired by an *immortal* father appeared in *The Encyclopedia of Mormonism* (1992).[44]

This pseudo-official work also explains that it is "LDS doctrine that Jesus Christ is the child of MARY and GOD THE FATHER, 'not in violation of natural law but in accordance with a higher manifestation thereof.' "[45] In other words, the natural law of procreation through sexual union was not suspended but was apparently elevated to a higher level of glory, honor, and sacredness.

As for the Holy Ghost, LDS leaders have understood his role as being that of Mary's protector, so to speak. The Holy Ghost enabled Mary to endure the rather intense and immediate presence of God the Father. LDS authority Melvin J. Ballard detailed the event in a sermon in which he also assured listeners that Heavenly Father's procreative act with Mary was in no way debased, but was instead sacred.[46]

Although references to sex between Heavenly Father and Mary are now even more subtle, implications of it can still be seen in recent comments about the *condescension* of God. For instance, the current LDS Church–published *Book of Mormon Gospel Doctrine Teacher's Manual* reads, "The condescension of God (meaning the Father) consists in the fact that… he became the personal and literal Father of a mortal Offspring born of mortal woman."[47] Interestingly, the manual is referencing Bruce Mc-Conkie's *Mormon Doctrine* (1958 and 1966).[48] McConkie, of course, advanced a sexual-union view of the virgin birth.

McConkie's "virgin" birth views also were quoted in 2001 by Bishop Richard C. Edgley (First Counselor in the Presiding Bishopric) in an article published by the LDS Church magazine *Ensign*.[49] Also in 2001, *Ensign* republished an article by former LDS president Ezra Taft Benson, who said that Christ was God's son "in the most literal sense." He added, "The body in which He performed His mission in the flesh was *sired* by that same Holy Being we worship as God, our Eternal Father."[50]

The Atonement

Christ's atonement is another area where evangelicals and Mormons disagree. Evangelicals claim it took place entirely on the cross (1 Peter 2:24; Colossians 1:20). Mormons, however, believe it was "worked out in

Gethsemane and on the cross."[51] As Neal Maxwell said, Jesus "suffered for each of us in Gethsemane and on Calvary!"[52] This LDS claim has been voiced many times.[53]

Theologian Dr. Cky J. Carrigan of the North American Mission Board, Southern Baptist Convention, has noted that the Mormon view of the atonement is usually presented "in a way that emphasizes the suffering and bleeding of the Son in Gethsemane."[54] Why is this important? Because, as Carrigan adds, although the LDS Church does not *reject* the atonement on the cross, it does seem to *minimize* it. More importantly, Mormonism "rejects the teaching that the Son's very point of death itself was an act of atonement."[55]

Perhaps more significant than the specifics of how and where the atonement occurred is the nature and extent of the atonement—that is, what did Christ's death accomplish? Mormonism teaches that it 1) blessed everyone with *unconditional salvation* (immortality), or resurrection from the grave, regardless of their beliefs;[56] and 2) made *individual salvation* (exaltation, or godhood) possible for those who, through self-effort, prove themselves worthy of that reward (also called "eternal life"), which is available only through Jesus.[57]

Evangelicals, though, recognize only one kind of salvation—eternity in God's immediate presence. All who accept Jesus' sacrifice for them will receive this benefit of Christ's death and resurrection (Romans 10:9). Forgiveness of personal sins (Acts 10:43) and entrance to heaven (Romans 3:24) is the twofold free gift that God offers (Romans 6:23) to those who will simply receive his salvation by grace through faith (Ephesians 2:8-10). Any conditions, from an evangelical perspective, are unbiblical.

To LDS leaders, however, individual salvation (which includes removal of personal sins) "is conditional."[58] The LDS Church manual *Gospel Principles* provides the following information:

> We accept Christ's atonement by [1] repenting of our sins, [2] being baptized, [3] receiving the gift of the Holy Ghost, and [4] obeying all of the commandments. In this way we are cleansed from sin and we become worthy to return and live forever with our Heavenly Father....Christ's atonement makes it possible to be saved from sin *if* we do our part.[59]

Put another way, Christ's mercy and love, as demonstrated by his death and resurrection, makes LDS eternal life (godhood) merely *possible*. According to BYU professors Robert Millet and Noel B. Reynolds, "Mormons believe there are certain things individuals must do for divine grace to be fully activated in their lives."[60]

This syncretism between Christ's work and LDS personal effort for eternal life appears in countless statements from Mormon leaders.[61] In addition, LDS leadership has added conscientious spreading of the Mormon gospel as a factor in securing "eternal life." As LDS apostle Neal Maxwell notes, "The forgiveness we seek and need is correlated with our steadfastness in the work of the Lord."[62]

Mormon commandments are numerous, even including adherence to their Word of Wisdom, which entails abstinence from coffee and tea.[63] And finally, according to LDS apostle Boyd K. Packer, "to restore our innocence after serious transgressions, there must be confession to our bishop, who is the appointed judge."[64]

LDS RESPONSES

Regarding the virgin birth, evangelicals must realize that Mormons have greatly softened their former position. Even subtle references to a sexual union between Heavenly Father and Mary have virtually disappeared from LDS literature. Although some Mormons may still embrace the belief, most Mormons view it as offensive.

In other words, when it comes to Jesus, Mary, and Elohim, today's Latter-day Saints are far more comfortable with simply accepting that God the Father is *somehow* Christ's literal father. But Mormons no longer really pursue ways of explaining how such a miracle occurred. They are content to say, "How the conception of Mary was accomplished we do not know."[65]

The Mormon Jesus

LDS author Gilbert Scharffs has revealed that in conversations with LDS authorities, he found the common position to be that "Latter-day Saints have no doctrine concerning the method of procreation on the deity level."[66]

An Interesting Fact: As of 2004, the Mormon Church had not yet issued any *official* repudiation of those former LDS leader statements wherein it was clearly suggested that God and Mary had sexual relations in order to procreate Jesus.

This toned-down view of the virgin birth has been echoed by BYU professor Stephen Robinson, who asserts, "Mary was in some unspecified manner made pregnant by God the Father, through the power of the Holy Ghost (Lk 1:32-35)."[67] Robinson, like BYU professors Daniel C. Peterson and Stephen D. Ricks, has tried to downplay the remarks previously cited by LDS leaders, implying that the controversial comments were isolated to the "nineteenth century" (Table 7.1).

Stephen Robinson	Peterson and Ricks
"While it is true that certain LDS leaders (mostly in the nineteenth century) have offered their opinions on the conception of Jesus, those opinions were never included among the official doctrines of the church and have, during my lifetime at least, not appeared in official church publications—lest they be taken as the view of the church."[68]	"[T]hese scattered nineteenth-century speculations were never canonized by the Mormon Church.... While certain early Mormon leaders may occasionally have interpreted the concept of 'virgin birth,' they never for a moment suggested that Jesus was begotten by a mortal man, nor that his father was any other personage than God....And for a denial, it cannot be repeated too often, that the Latter-day Saints have never accepted [this] as official doctrine."[69]

Table 7.1

Being overlooked, of course, is the fact that when these "nineteenth-century" leaders made their statements, the comments were indeed official—at least in some loose sense of the word. After all, the statements were made by LDS prophets, apostles, scholars, and theologians. Some of the pronouncements would have even been considered "scripture" (according to the LDS Church instructional manual *Gospel Principles*, pages 51–53). As such, they could only have been understood as important expressions of the LDS faith *at that time*.

Also disturbing is the implication that all of the offensive remarks were made in the "nineteenth century"—when in reality, many of the comments were made by *twentieth*-century presidents (Joseph F. Smith, Joseph Fielding Smith, Ezra Taft Benson) and apostles (James Talmage, George Romney, M. Russell Ballard, Bruce McConkie).

Son of God; Son of the Father

The LDS notion that Jesus is a literal son of God in the way we are children of our parents determines how Mormons interpret "Son of God" (or "Son of the Father") in the Bible (for example, Matthew 14:33; Luke 4:41; 2 John 1:3). To Latter-day Saints the phrase means a *literal* son, in support of which they note that Jesus is never called "son of the Holy Ghost."[70] This understanding deserves some attention.

Although Jesus rarely applied "Son of God" to himself (see Matthew 27:43; Luke 22:70; John 10:36), others used it quite often (Matthew 26:63-64; 27:42-43; Romans 1:3; Galatians 2:20; Ephesians 4:13; Hebrews 6:6; 1 John 4:15; 5:5,13). Must it be taken literally? No, especially given that the term is used for the nation of Israel (Exodus 4:22-23; Hosea 11:1) and Israel's king (2 Samuel 7:14).

Moreover, just the words "son of" had various nonliteral connotations in Hebrew culture—for example, they were often used in reference to moral kinship. "Thus, Paul can assert that all who believe God as Abraham did are the true sons of Abraham, whether they are physical descendants or not."[71] In this same vein, peacemakers are called "sons of God" (Matthew 5:9).

As for the Bible's use of the definite article "the," it seems to carry messianic implications.[72] In other words, Jesus is uniquely qualified to be called *the* "son" by virtue of his perfect obedience, knowledge of the Father, service, position above other men, angels, and prophets.[73] More importantly, Christ's identity as *the* Son of God communicated nothing less than his equality with God, a claim considered blasphemous by the Jews (John 5:18; 8:58; 10:33).

Begotten, Not Made

Christ's unique status is also demonstrated by another term Mormons use to prove that Jesus is God's literal son: "only begotten" (John 1:14,18).

But the Greek word for *only begotten (monogenēs)* does not mean begotten in the sense we beget children. It means "having no peer, unique," or perhaps more precisely, "one of a kind."[74] This term is applied to Jesus five times: John 1:14,18; 3:16,18; and 1 John 4:9.[75]

John seems to be portraying Jesus, especially in John 1:14,18, as unique. Princeton scholar B.B. Warfield noted that *only begotten* "conveys the idea, not of derivation and subordination, but of uniqueness and consubstantiality: Jesus is all that God is, and He alone is this."[76]

Only in the three remaining passages (John 3:16,18 and 1 John 4:9) is Jesus actually called the only begotten "son." But these words still need not be interpreted in the LDS way. According to Greek scholars, the verses communicate Christ's unique identity, not some literal, biological sonship.[77]

According to Christian New Testament professor Craig Blomberg, *monogenēs (only begotten)* comes from the root words *monos (only)* and *ginomai (to be)*. Blomberg comments "[H]ence, 'only existing.'...There is nothing here to suggest God created (or 'begat') Jesus."[78] For instance, Hebrews 11:17 says Isaac was Abraham's "only begotten" *(monogenēs)* son. Yet Abraham had other children. Obviously, *begotten* and *only begotten* can be applied nonliterally.

LDS scholar Stephen Robinson, however, responds that Blomberg's *monogenēs* argument "is moot since there are other Bible passages that refer to Jesus as 'begotten,' and from [the Greek root] *gennaō* rather than *ginomai*."[79] He cites 1 John 5:18 as proof, adding that many Christian scholars (for example, F.F. Bruce and I.H. Marshall) "have held that 'the One begotten by God' (1 Jn. 5:18) is Jesus."[80] Robinson notes that even the Nicene Creed says Jesus is "begotten," concluding that "it isn't just the Mormons standing alone here!"[81]

Unfortunately, Robinson seems to not know that *gennaō* can mean more than just offspring. Its variants are used in Scripture 1) metaphorically, for instigation or impartation of something (for example, strife, 2 Timothy 2:23); 2) figuratively, for the relationship of a teacher and student (1 Corinthians 4:15; Philemon 1:10), or of evil men who are brute beasts (2 Peter 2:12); and 3) spiritually, to highlight the rebirth of those who receive new life in Christ (John 3:3-7; 1 John 2:9; 1 John 5:1).[82]

Some evangelical scholars do interpret 1 John 5:18 ("whosoever is *begotten of God* sinneth not"—ASV) as a reference to Jesus. But in context, these scholars are speaking about John's discussion of spiritual issues, including relationships to the Father. John is not hinting at a literal procreation of Christ. Neither Bruce nor Marshall has ever cited 1 John 5:18 to show that Jesus was *literally* "begotten" by God. Nor does the Nicene Creed use the word "begotten" as Mormons use it. The two forms of this creed (A.D. 325, 381) use "begotten" to indicate that Jesus "is different, utterly different, from any of the created beings. He is not out of any other substance, but out of the Father."[83]

Mormon Point: "If Jesus were truly a *human* being, then he had forty-six chromosomes, a double strand of twenty-three. If he was truly human, he got one strand of twenty-three chromosomes from his mother. Where did the other strand come from, if not from his Father?" (Stephen Robinson, in *How Wide the Divide,* page 139).

Counterpoint: Jesus' chromosones are not even an issue with evangelicals in regard to whether Jesus was literally begotten by God the Father as we beget our children. The other chromosomes obviously came from God the Father by the power of the Holy Ghost. This was a miraculous act, but that does not mean the Father is an exalted man or a father in the same sense that we are fathers (which is the implication of Robinson's comment). God could easily have just created the chromosomes. Moreover, Robinson's remark directly conflicts with that of BYU president Richard Draper, who said that Jesus, in fact, was *not* human![84]

The "Begats"

In seeking to prove the procreation of Jesus, Robinson also has pointed to the "begats" in Matthew, where Mary is "referred to as she 'out of whom was begotten *(egennethe)* Jesus.'" He reasons that since this reference "appears as the last string of forty consecutive occurrences of that verb, all unmistakably having the sense of paternal 'begetting,'" then Christ, too, was "begotten," like Isaac was begotten of Abraham.[85]

But such reasoning is a double-edged sword. If Robinson wants to make a consistent parallel of words used in these verses, then he also will have to admit the very thing that he so strongly wants to deny—that Heavenly Father and Mary had sexual intercourse, which was the same natural means by which "Abraham begat Isaac."

Moreover, Robinson has either not noticed, or deliberately ignored, a significant detail in the Greek. *Egennethe* ("begotten") is the word used of Jesus. But this is not the same word used for all of the other "begats" (*egennēsen*) in Matthew 1:2-16. The switch suggests a change in concept. In other words, Jesus was *born* of Mary, rather than begotten of a man. Hence, "was born" of Mary is a more accurate rendering than "was begotten."[86]

Robinson then notes that "God was the immediate cause of the conception of Jesus" and caused Mary "to become pregnant."[87] Evangelicals agree, but would stop short of saying that "father" is meant in a literal way (see chapter 6). Interestingly, according to LDS teachings, even Jesus can be figuratively and metaphorically called our "father," although he is not our *literal* father (for example, see Isaiah 9:6).[88]

God's Firstborn?

Yet another term Mormons often use to try to biblically prove that Jesus is literally God's first spirit-child is "firstborn" (Colossians 1:15).[89] But contrary to how Latter-day Saints read "firstborn," the Greek term from which it is translated—*prōtotokos*—does not have to mean one who is literally born first.

The term "firstborn" can also mean, and often does mean, the pre-eminent one. David, for instance, is called God's "firstborn" although he was not a son who was born first (Psalm 89:27). Similarly, Ephraim was younger than Manasseh, but is called "firstborn" (Jeremiah 31:9).

Combining these LDS interpretations with Colossians 1:15 would mean that David, Ephraim (Joseph's son, Genesis 41:52), and Jesus were all the "firstborn" spirit-children of Heavenly Father. The evangelical interpretation makes far more sense. As Greek scholar F.F. Bruce noted, "Firstborn came to denote (among the ancients) not priority in time but preeminence in rank."[90]

Most disconcerting are the incessant LDS charges that, when it comes to Jesus' sonship, evangelicals do not accept the Bible—in contrast with how Mormons supposedly *do* accept it. Stephen Robinson chided "'orthodox' Christians," saying that they, "in the interest of truth in advertising, ought to clarify that they believe the Bible only as amended and interpreted by later voices [namely, the Christian creeds]."[91]

But again, Robinson has used a double-edged sword. To use his reasoning, Mormons, "in the interest of truth in advertising, ought to clarify that they believe the Bible only as amended and interpreted by" their *living* prophets (as opposed to dead prophets, whose teachings are no longer binding) and Joseph Smith's extrabiblical revelations (the interpretations of which are subject to alteration, revision, and re-interpretation).

Grace and Works

Moving into the realm of salvation, it is obvious that "good works" play a crucial role in Mormonism. But evangelicals interpret this LDS stress laid on acts of righteousness and right behavior as an affront to not only Scripture, but also God's love, grace, and mercy. Traditional Christians are especially troubled by the LDS idea that their personal sins cannot be forgiven (cleansed) by Christ until they have proven themselves worthy by "individual effort."[92] Mormons refer to many biblical passages to justify this teaching, particularly James 2:14-17, which says that faith without works is dead.

> **Notable and Quotable:** "The Individual Effect of the Atonement makes it possible for any and every soul to obtain absolution from the effect of personal sins, through the mediation of Christ; but such saving intercession is to be invoked by individual effort as manifested through faith, repentance, and continued works of righteousness....[T]he blessing of redemption from individual sins, while open for all to attain, is nevertheless conditioned on individual effort" (James Talmage, *A Study of the Articles of Faith,* page 89).

But in declaring that a *professed* faith without works is a dead faith, James is not saying that acquiring salvation is linked to good works. He is merely asserting that someone who has real faith will produce good works as a natural consequence of the supernatural working of the Holy Ghost in his or her life. Anyone who has truly been saved will naturally manifest the kind of good works that are consistent with salvation. In other words, if no good works are seen, then the faith being professed is dead. It is a false faith.

Two analogies may be helpful. Consider an apple tree. It does not bear apples to become an apple tree. It bears apples because it already is an apple tree. Likewise, a dog barks because it already is a dog. It does not bark to become a dog. Similarly, Christians do good works *because of* salvation, not *for* salvation (Romans 4:5).

As James says, real faith will produce a changed life that others will be able to see. This is not to say that every Christian changes in the exact same ways or at the exact same speed. God deals with each person individually. For one Christian, good works may entail no longer getting drunk or being promiscuous. For another Christian, good works may mean being more patient or kinder.

A related LDS argument that favors a grace–works formula for "eternal life" involves James 2:22-24. This passage says that Abraham was justified by works. But to understand the verses, one must read them in context and in light of Romans 4:2,4-5. James, first of all, is speaking of justification before men: "I will show *you* my faith by my works" (emphasis added). Paul, on the other hand, in the Romans passage, is discussing justification "before God." In context, then, our justification *before God* (Romans 4:2) is by grace alone through faith alone, while our justification *before men* (James 2:22-24) must be demonstrated by our good works.

As for those who attempt to be justified before God by good works, those works will be counted against them as debt (Romans 4:4). "But to him that worketh not, but believeth on him that justifieth the ungodly, his faith is counted for righteousness" (verse 5).

The Bible consistently depicts the *gift* of eternal life as an act whereby God declares righteous those who, in fact, are unrighteous (Romans 4:5-8; 5:8-10). Justification imparts something (a righteous standing before

God), while forgiveness removes something (sin and its penalty). And it is all done by grace alone. Nothing we do can add anything to what has already been done for us by God.

Christians, though declared righteous by God, remain within a body of sin. This is why no Christian can live perfectly. However, by God's grace, we can be more conformed to Christ's image (this process is called *sanctification*). But our growth in holiness is not a prerequisite for attaining salvation. It is just an outworking or application of salvation (consider the words of Philippians 2:12-13). Concerning "righteousness" as it pertains to eternal life, God imputes to us by faith the righteousness of Christ—the righteousness by which we have access to God, apart from good works or the law (Romans 3:21-26).

This is not to say that our faith *causes* our justification. To say otherwise would make faith itself a work that earns salvation. Faith is more like a channel through which justification comes to a sinner. Faith is not an action, it is an attitude of openness to receive.[93] A good illustration occurs every Christmas, when we shower our loved ones with gifts. Those gifts belong to the recipients even before they are received. They are purchased, wrapped, and waiting to bring joy. The recipients need only receive their gifts to benefit from them.

In a similar way, sinners need only receive the gift of eternal life offered to them by God, in effect saying, "Yes, I believe you have that gift for me. I accept it." God, in turn, gives us the *individual salvation* he purchased for us by his own blood (Ephesians 1:7-8). That is the good news of the gospel—eternal life imparted as a free gift.

To sum up, Do good works contribute *anything* to securing the gift of eternal life with God? Scripture says no—as evidenced by 2 Timothy 1:9, which says that God "saved us, and called us with an holy calling, not according to our works, but according to his own purpose and grace, which was granted us in Christ Jesus before the world began."

Repentance Brings...

The great enduring truth of Christianity we have just discussed was presented by Paul, who forsook everything for the knowledge of Christ. "I count all things but loss," he said, "that I may win Christ, and be found in him, *not having mine own righteousness,* which is of the law, but that which is through the faith of Christ, the righteousness which is of God by faith" (Philippians 3:8-9, emphasis added).

Interestingly, when the law-bound Jews pressed Jesus for a list of do's and don'ts by asking, "What shall we do, that we might work the works of God?" Jesus replied, "This is the work of God, that ye believe on him whom he hath sent" (John 6:28-29). To do all that God has for us to do, there is only one step to take—belief, which brings us into a right relationship with God. This truth is echoed in 1 John 5:12-13, which tells us that those who have the Son "have eternal life."[94]

...Assurance?

Herein is the tragedy of the LDS concept of justification by grace through faith *plus* works: A Mormon can never be sure of whether he or she will ever receive eternal life. As Robert Millet has observed, the best that Mormons can hope for in mortality is to be treated by Christ *as if* they were "fully qualified to inherit eternal life."[95]

In this present world, Mormons are only justified in a limited, theoretical sense—and for only as long as they remain worthy. According to Millet, the Book of Mormon teaches that there is a "need for retaining a remission of sins from day to day" (Mosiah 4:25). We must "labor to maintain our justified, sin-free condition," Millet says.[96]

To keep their guiltless stand before God, Mormons must, at the very least, do two basic things according to the Book of Mormon: 1) acknowledge God's greatness and goodness while recognizing their "absolute ineptitude without divine assistance," and 2) participate in "care of the needy"[97] (Mosiah 4:11-12; Moroni 7:42-44).

It must be stressed, however, that Mormons *do not* hold to a works-righteousness route to salvation that is divorced from Christ. Jesus is essential for obtaining eternal life.[98] Like Roman Catholics, Latter-day Saints believe that it is through God's grace that they "receive strength and assistance to do good works that they otherwise would not be able to maintain if left to their own means."[99]

But even obtaining God's "grace" is predicated upon Mormons proving to God that they are entitled to it. That proof might best be summarized in one word—*repentance.* To borrow Millet's explanation, the Book of Mormon (Moroni 10:32) teaches, "For us to enjoy the strength, enabling power, and purifying influence [of God]...we must do all in our power to receive it."[100]

...Justification?

Unlike evangelicals, who see justification as a "declarative act of God" coinciding with one's faith in Christ and based on his atoning work,[101] Mormons see justification and sanctification as a single ongoing *process.*[102] One difficulty arising out of this view is the consequences of not toeing the line, so to speak:

> I, the Lord, will not lay any sin to your charge; go your ways and sin no more; but unto that soul who sinneth shall the former sins return, saith the Lord your God (D&C 82:7).

In 1984, LDS president Spencer W. Kimball explained,

> The forsaking of sin must be a permanent one. True repentance does not permit making the same mistake again....There can be no holding back. If the sinner neglects his tithing, misses his meetings, breaks the Sabbath, or fails in his prayers and other responsibilities, he is not completely repentant.[103]

Did You Know? Mormons share with Roman Catholics the notion that works purify us to make us fit for heaven (or acceptable to God and ready for eternal life). LDS apostle M. Russell Ballard explains that both grace and works "are core doctrines. Just as a pair of scissors requires two blades to function, the Lord's grace and our works of faith in Christ, personal repentance, and receiving saving ordinances are required for eternal life in God's presence."* Also reminiscent of Roman Catholicism are LDS communion and baptism, both of which are seen as channels of grace.†

---

* M. Russell Ballard, "Building Bridges," available at www.lds.org.

† See D. Todd Christofferson, "Justification and Sanctification," *Ensign,* June 2001, page 18, available at www.lds.org; compare Robert Millet, *Grace Works,* page 76).

This same issue was addressed in a 1991 *Ensign* magazine article by S. Michael Wilcox, instructor for the Institute of Religion adjacent to the University of Utah. According to Wilcox, full justification will only come at some point in the distant future, after we have perfected ourselves through the empowering of the Holy Ghost.[104]

Some LDS leaders, such as Mormon apostle LeGrand Richards, have actually called the Christian doctrine of salvation by grace alone through faith alone a satanic deception![105] As if there were any doubt about how Mormons see the traditional Christian view of justification, consider Wilcox's 1991 assessment that

> much of the Christian world has been confused by this doctrine. Many believe that justification comes by faith in Christ's grace alone, that an acceptance of him as their Savior is all that is necessary. But is it consistent with reason and the testimony of the scriptures and the Spirit to think that Christ would extend the full measure of his atonement, having suffered all that he has suffered, to those who merely give lip service to him?[106]

...Forgiveness?

As is clear from the above, unlike evangelicalism (in which repentance is marked by simply turning to Christ and relying on his unmerited grace), Mormonism teaches that believers must strive to prove their repentance by not repeating a sin.[107] D&C 58:43 reads, "By this we know if a man repenteth of his sins—for behold, he will confess them and forsake them." This is why no Mormon can ever *truly* know if he or she has been totally forgiven. As LDS president Kimball pointed out,

> It could be weeks, it could be years, it could be centuries before that happy day when you have the positive assurance that the Lord has forgiven you. That depends on your humility, your sincerity, your works, your attitudes.[108]

Forgiveness in Mormonism entails, first, working hard at the commandments and second, doing one's best, which is a decidedly intangible concept. It is impossible for many Mormons to rest in what God has done for them.[109] Forgiveness for them is an ever-fleeting ideal. Not even God's love is a sure thing for Mormons. LDS leaders actually teach that God's love is *not* unconditional. To Latter-day Saints, God's love for us is "predicated upon our obedience to eternal law."[110]

Russell M. Nelson of the Quorum of the Twelve Apostles made this very clear in a 2003 *Ensign* magazine article, in which he explained "the conditional nature of divine love for us."[111] This teaching appears even in Doctrine and Covenants 95:12, where God declares through Joseph Smith, "If you keep not my commandments, the love of the Father shall not continue with you."

Such views have no doubt troubled many Mormons. Consider the 2003 admission made by BYU professor of Church History and Doctrine, Roger Keller. After quoting 2 Nephi 25:23, Keller humorously noted that there are "a lot of Latter-day Saints who are trying to figure what the 756.5 things you have to do are, before grace kicks in—and they're all on Prozac."[112]

But this should not be. Scripture tells us that we have been raised to life with Christ, who has *already* forgiven us "all our sins," and has nailed our debt to his cross (Colossians 2:13-15). "[B]y one offering he hath perfected for ever them that are sanctified" (Hebrews 10:14).

Mormons are quite aware of these passages, as evidenced by the remarks of Gerald N. Lund (LDS Church Educational System) about Romans 3:20,28; Romans 10:9; and Galatians 3:16.[113] According to Lund, however, justification actually means the *opportunity* to secure justification and eternal life.[114] Scripture, though, contradicts this notion. Justification does not need to be secured by one's good works in fulfillment of "preconditions" that activate Christ's atonement. Our justification is a completed act (Romans 8:29-30).

...Godhood?

At this point, a word must be said about the LDS concept of three heavens (or three kingdoms of glory), the highest one being what Mormons hope to attain through the process of justification, sanctification, and repentance. The first kingdom, which provides a limited amount of glory and reward, is reserved for non-Mormons whose lives are marked primarily by immorality and wickedness.[115]

The second kingdom is for non-Mormons, and for Mormons whose lives were marked by kindness, goodness, and trying to live the best life possible, but who were "not valiant in the testimony of Jesus."[116]

The third and highest kingdom is reserved for faithful Mormons who lived exemplary lives. This kingdom itself has three levels, and only those who reach the highest level in this kingdom become gods.[117] They receive what is known as exaltation. This is the core element of the LDS gospel.[118] As Mormon apostle Bruce McConkie declared in 1958, "That exaltation which the saints of all ages have so devoutly sought is *godhood* itself."[119]

The three-heaven doctrine has no basis whatsoever in the Bible, but can be solely attributed to yet another vision by Joseph Smith.[120] BYU professors Robert Millet and Stephen Robinson agree that Mormons "do not derive their belief in the three degrees of glory [telestial, terrestrial, and celestial] primarily from the Bible."[121]

Although most Mormons will readily agree with Robinson and Millet, many would also say that 1 Corinthians 15:40-42 and 2 Corinthians 12:2 at least allude to Joseph's three heavens. In truth, however, neither text relates to LDS ideas about the afterlife.

When in 1 Corinthians 15 Paul speaks of celestial bodies and terrestrial bodies, he is merely comparing the characteristics of various material objects. The context is the nature of our resurrection bodies. Paul first points out that animal flesh differs from human flesh (verse 39). Next, Paul compares celestial (heavenly) bodies to terrestrial (earthly) bodies, then contrasts the glory of various celestial bodies (sun, moon, stars).[122] He ends his analogy by showing how our resurrected body will differ from our current one (verse 42).

Although 2 Corinthians 12:2 does speak of a "third heaven" seen by Paul in a vision, nothing in the passage adds credence to the LDS concept of three heavens. It is true that in the minds of some first-century Jews there existed a plurality of heavens. And Paul *might* have been referring to the highest of these eternal abodes. But they would not have been analogous to LDS concepts of the afterlife.

Furthermore, there is reason to suspect that Paul was merely using "a Jewish expression for the immediate presence of God, and for Paul a phrase to convey the idea of the most sublime blessedness."[123] Yet another possibility is that Paul was referring to the abode of God (the third heaven) in contrast to the place of stars and planets (the second heaven) and the Earth's own atmosphere (the first heaven).[124]

Whatever Paul meant, it certainly had nothing to do with the Mormon hope of reaching the highest level of their third heaven—godhood. To attain this goal is why Mormons, contrary to the message preached by Paul, so consistently stress works of righteousness and the pursuit of "perfection" for eternal life. After all, one *must* be perfect in order to be a god.

Spencer W. Kimball noted, "All transgressions must be cleansed, all weaknesses must be overcome, before a person can attain perfection and godhood."[125] He also declared that "progress toward eternal life is a matter of achieving perfection. Living all the commandments guarantees total forgiveness of sins and assures one of exaltation."[126]

FINAL OBSERVATIONS

As of the twenty-first century, some Mormons are finally beginning to actually preach against the traditional call to LDS perfection. For example, Roger Keller's 2003 explanation of forgiveness and entrance into heaven does not sound that far removed from classic Christianity:

> Perfection is not a reality in this life unless it is through Jesus Christ.... We come to him first in faith, which shows us that we need to repent. And then he asks us to do something very simple, which is to be baptized. And if we do those three things, we're in the Kingdom of God. And he gives us a gift to prove that we stand in okay with him. And that's the gift of the Holy Ghost. If the Holy Ghost is in our lives, that is God's personal affirmation to us that we are okay with him; that we would go to the Celestial Kingdom tonight were we to die.[121]

This statement—strictly in regard to the mode of receiving "eternal life"—would be acceptable to many evangelicals. Hopefully, views like the one being espoused by Keller will spread throughout the LDS community. If so, then at least in the area of salvation, the LDS Church will begin to drift quite close to traditional Christianity. Still problematic, however, is the LDS idea that we, as followers of Christ, can hope to attain godhood. This will be the subject of our next chapter.

YE ARE GODS

If you could hie to Kolob in the twinkling of an eye,
And then continue onward with that same speed to fly,
Do you think that you could ever, through all eternity,
Find out the generation where Gods began to be?[1]
—"If You Could Hie to Kolob," Mormon Hymn #257

Throughout my last year of high school, *Battlestar Galactica* was my favorite TV show. This program told the tale of Adama (commander of the spaceship *Galactica*) and his followers. They were the only survivors of the 12 "Colonies of Man," which had been annihilated by a race of evil, robotlike beings called Cylons. The series followed the intrepid adventurers as they set out across the universe in hopes of finding the mythical planet Earth, which they hoped would be a new and safe home.

Little did I realize that the whole series was based on Mormonism. But today the parallels are obvious to me: episode titles such as "War of the Gods," plot elements including the "Council of the Twelve," and character names like Adama, Cain, and the Prince of Darkness. But back in 1978 and 1979, I had no idea what these things indicated.

The series idea actually originated in the late 1960s, when Mormon Glen Larson made a pitch to TV studios for a new sci-fi show he wanted to call *Adam's Ark*. That title was eventually changed, but the basic plot was kept. The show's opening prologue explained,

> There are those who believe that life here began out there, far across the universe, with tribes of humans who may have been the forefathers of the Egyptians, or the Toltecs, or the Mayans. They may have been the architects of the great pyramids, or the lost civilizations of Lemuria or Atlantis. Some believe that there may yet be brothers of man who even now fight to survive far, far away, amongst the stars.

The similarities between *Battlestar Galactica* and LDS thought almost leap out of the screen…for anyone who knows LDS ideas about the universe. For example, in the series the 12 colonies were founded by 12 tribes of humans who left their home planet of "Kobol." This, of course, is reminiscent of the Mormon "Kolob" (see page 154), which, according to the Pearl of Great Price, is the planet nearest to "the throne of God" (Abraham 3:9). It is the place where the gods came forth. Interestingly, the name of the *Battlestar Galactica* episode about "Kobol" was titled "Lost Planet of the Gods."

Equally intriguing is the episode "War of the Gods," in which the character Starbuck meets advanced beings (godlike angel entities) in a ship of lights. These entities show a keen interest in Adama and his followers, but it is a mystery as to why.

"Why are you bothering with us?" asks Starbuck. "We are from a simple handful of human survivors."

The entity answers, "Because, as you are now, we once were. As we are now, you may become." This little couplet, as we shall see, is actually one of the most popular of all LDS encapsulations of what Mormonism is about—becoming a god.[2]

※ ※ ※

Mormonism advances what might best be termed practical universalism. Nearly everyone will end up in some kind of heaven (or kingdom)—telestial, terrestrial, or celestial—each having its own glory (D&C 76:70-98).[3] The highest kingdom, of course, is the one in which godhood may be secured.

The Mormon path to godhood received its most popular expression in the famous couplet by LDS president Lorenzo Snow (which, as we noted above, was quoted nearly verbatim in *Battlestar Galactica*): "As Man is, God once was; as God is, man may become."[4] In 1921, LDS apostle Melvin J. Ballard declared his agreement with this phrase, explaining, "It is a Mormon truism that is current among us and we all accept it, that as man is God once was and as God is man may become."[5]

—————— MORMON QUOTES ——————

"Here, then, is eternal life—to know the only wise and true God; and you have got to learn how to be gods yourselves, and to be kings and priests to God, the same as all gods have done before you" (Joseph Smith Jr., 1844).[6]

"The lowest degree is the telestial domain of those who 'received not the gospel, neither the testimony of Jesus, neither the prophets.'... Its occupants receive the Holy Spirit and the administering of angels, for even those who have been wicked will ultimately be 'heirs of [this] salvation' (D&C 76:88). The next higher degree of glory, the terrestrial,...is the abode of those who were the 'honorable men of the earth' (D&C 76:75)....[T]hose who qualify for terrestrial glory 'receive of the presence of the Son' (D&C 76:77). Concepts familiar to all Christians might liken this higher kingdom to heaven because it has the presence of the Son....[W]e join with Paul in affirming the existence of a third or higher heaven...the celestial kingdom" (Dallin Oaks, LDS apostle, 1995).[7]

"Deification is accomplished finally through the grace and goodness of Jesus" (Robert L. Millet, BYU professor, 1998).[8]

A CLOSER LOOK

Many Bible verses refute the notion of deification (for example, Isaiah 43:10; 44:8; 1 Timothy 2:5; James 2:19). But Mormons usually interpret these fairly straightforward passages in a way that allows for their views. For example, 1 Timothy 2:5, rather than meaning there is only one God, is understood by Mormons to be saying, "[T]here is one [Supreme] God [for this planet], and one mediator between God and men."

As a result, Mormons readily embrace the idea of multiple gods in the universe and their own potential godhood. Consider the 1994 article "Don't Drop the Ball," in which LDS president Gordon B. Hinckley revealed that "the whole design of the gospel is to lead us onward and upward to greater achievement, even, eventually, to godhood."[9]

Why do Mormons take such a view? "We are the sons and daughters of celestial Beings," said Brigham Young, "and the germ of the Deity dwells within us."[10] This reflects the most common LDS argument raised in defense of our potential godhood. It is based on the presupposition that we are *literal* children of a god. Hence, we are capable "by experience through ages and aeons, of evolving into a God."[11]

LDS reasoning stems from the like-begets-like principle, which says a living entity reproduces "after his kind" (Genesis 1:24). The *Encyclopedia of Mormonism* couples this principle with the assumption that God would want us, his children, to enjoy all that he enjoys, including his divine nature, glory, creative capabilities, and omnipotence.[12]

It should be noted, however, that Mormons do *not* feel they will ever be "co-equal, or on the same level, with God and no longer worship him."[13] We will forever be "subject to and worship the God of Heaven, which is represented as the Father, the Son, and the Holy Ghost" and will only "be like them and enjoy a quality of life similar to theirs."[14]

According to LDS apologist W. John Walsh, deification is "a doctrine which the Bible clearly teaches."[15] Indeed, Mormons use many biblical verses to bolster LDS claims for deification. None of them, however, explicitly teach LDS deification.

EVANGELICAL THOUGHTS

When it comes to the issue of deification, what is most disturbing to evangelicals is the way LDS apologists misapply so many scriptures by

- lifting them out of context
- divorcing them from Hebrew culture
- reading them according to a modern mindset

For example, Robert Millet contends that godhood is alluded to in various scriptural promises about how Christ will transform us (Romans 8:29; 1 Corinthians 15:49; 2 Corinthians 3:18; 1 John 3:2).[16] And during a 2002 conference at BYU, Mark D. Ellison (coordinator for the LDS Church's Church Educational System, Tampa, Florida) asserted that "Paul repeatedly used the language of adoption to teach that in Christ we can become 'heirs of God' (Romans 8:14-18; Acts 17:28-29; Galatians 4:7)."[17]

Going After Godhood

Regarding Millet's set of verses, they all deal with various issues relating to our sanctification, spiritual growth, and resurrected state. None of them even hints at deification. But Millet, like many other LDS apologists, is content with imposing the idea of deification on any verse that in any way speaks of believers becoming like Christ. But nothing could be further from the actual case. Romans 8:29, for instance, says only that we will be "conformed to the image" of Christ at the resurrection. No mention is made of godhood or deification. The passage is simply saying that all we are, including our bodies, will be glorified and made fit for eternity (compare this to Philippians 3:21).

Similarly, 1 Corinthians 15:49 says *nothing* about becoming a god, but merely asserts that "as we have borne the image of the earthy, we shall also bear the image of the heavenly." Verses 47-48 set the context with a comparison of earthly bodies to heavenly bodies. Paul even goes on in verse 50 to pinpoint his subject exactly: "Now this I say, brethren, that flesh and blood cannot inherit the kingdom of God; neither doth corruption inherit incorruption."

The same topic is found in 1 John 3:2. John tells us that when Christ appears "we shall be like him, for we shall see him as he is." In other words, the unveiling of Christ to us will be the event that marks our change from earthly vessels to glorified, heavenly vessels.

Millet's use of 2 Corinthians 3:18 is most puzzling. The context begins with the blindness of the Jews and the liberty enjoyed upon removal of that blindness (verses 12-17). Verse 18 refers to how believers, although saved, are still unable to fully see Christ's glory ("beholding as in a glass [for example, a dull mirror]"). Yet as we go on beholding him, even imperfectly, we will be changed into his "image" (or *eikōn* in Greek, which means resemblance). So it relates to sanctification, not godhood.

Desiring Deification

Mark Ellison's selection of passages is equally irrelevant to the LDS doctrine of deification. In Romans 8:14-18, Paul does indeed reveal that

Christians, as children of God, are "heirs of God, and joint-heirs with Christ" (verse 17). But what do these phrases mean? In order to answer this question, we must first look at the context of the phrases.

The subject of this passage is our spiritual sonship through the "Spirit of adoption," by which we may cry, "Abba, Father." Verse 14 then reveals that the "sons of God" are those who are "led by the spirit of God" (see Galatians 5:18).

Now, as for the terms "heirs" and "joint-heirs," these correspond to the Greek words *klēronomos* and *sunklēronomos* respectively. Mormons interpret them to mean that we will inherit all that is Christ's, including his godhood. But this assumption is simply a mistake.

The term *klēronomos* "denotes one who obtains a lot or portion," while *sunklēronomos* is used of a "co-inheritor."[18] Their import bears on the Christian's changed relationship to God (from estrangement to sonship), which includes inheritance. And that which is to be inherited is not godhood. It is a portion of Christ's "glory" (verse 18)—*doxa*, in Greek. This word relates not to deification, but "primarily signifies an opinion, estimate, and hence, the honour resulting from a good opinion."[19] Greek scholar Spiros Zodhiates comments,

> The true glory *[doxa]* of man, on the other hand, is the ideal condition in which God created man. This condition was lost in the fall and is recovered through Christ.... The believer waits for this complete restoration.[20]

Galatians 4:7 draws a similar comparison between the believer's transformation from a "servant" to a "son." Hence, a Christian is "an heir of God." But this is speaking only of man's glory (that is, all that he is and can be). Mormons, of course, assume this means godhood—but of course, the words "godhood," "deification," or "exaltation" appear nowhere.

In Acts 17:28-29, Paul simply refers to pagan poets who spoke of us as God's offspring (see page 126). Again, no hint is made about Christians becoming gods. Such a concept must be read into the text by Mormons as they interpret the verse in light of their doctrine of premortal existence as God's literal children destined for godhood.

Two other verses often cited include,

- *Matthew 5:48*—Christ's command to "be ye therefore perfect, even as your Father which is in heaven is perfect" is interpreted to mean "It is possible in the eternities to know all things and have the capacity to endure all things and live according to all truth." Perfection allegedly equals godhood.[21]

- *2 Peter 1:3,4*—Peter "spoke of our being 'partakers of the divine nature.'" This supposedly means we will become gods.[22]

But once more, LDS apologists have not adequately studied these verses. In Matthew 5:48, the Greek word for "perfect"—*teleios*—means completeness, or wholeness. It signifies that the thing being spoken of has reached a point where nothing that belongs to its essence is lost or left out. In other words, just as God is all that he can be, Christ wants us to reach our full potential and be everything that we were created to be.

God wants us to be *teleios*—perfect, complete, not lacking, fully all that we were meant to be. This does not mean perfect in the sense of *absolute* perfection, or godhood. This is an assumption that Mormons must add into the text—an assumption based on their preconceived belief in human deification.

And being a *partaker* of God's divine nature (2 Peter 1:3-4) does not mean being a *taker* of God's nature. Mormons habitually tend to quote only the portion of this passage that says we "might be partakers of the divine nature." In context, this is dealing with how we, as Christians, may share in numerous communicable attributes of God: for example, goodness, kindness, holiness, purity, and righteousness.

Verse 3 explains that God gives us all things pertaining to "life and godliness, through the knowledge of him" who called us. By this knowledge of God we are able to partake of His nature. Partake how? By becoming gods? Hardly. We become partakers of God's nature "having escaped the corruption that is in the world through lust" (verse 4).

To traditional Christians, these are all standard interpretations of some fairly basic and uncomplicated scriptures. LDS apologists, however, go in quite another direction, opting for unconventional interpretations of the Bible to prove that we can become gods. Robert Millet, for instance, has actually stated that "it is neither robbery nor heresy for the children of God to aspire to be like God."[23] But the Bible passage to which Millet is clearly alluding (Philippians 2:6) is about Jesus Christ, not us!

But Jesus Called Us Gods

The most oft-repeated and grossly misinterpreted deification scriptures used by Mormons are John 10:34-36 and Psalm 82:6. In reference to the latter passage, Gordon B. Hinckley has noted, "Something of the very nature of God is within you. The Psalmist sang, 'I have said, Ye are gods; and all of you are children of the most High.'"[24] Boyd K. Packer has asserted that the passages offer the "strongest" support for human deification:

> [Christ] quoted that very clear verse from the Eighty-second Psalm: "Is it not written in your law, *I said, Ye are gods*? [See Ps. 82:6.] If he called them *gods*, unto whom the word of God came, *and the scripture cannot be broken*; Say ye of him, whom the Father hath sanctified, and sent into the world, Thou blasphemest; because I said, I am the *Son* of God?" (John 10:34-36; italics added [by Packer].).[25]

But both Packer and Hinckley have completely missed what is taking place between Jesus and the Jewish leaders in these verses. Shandon Guthrie, adjunct professor in philosophy at the University of Nevada, Las Vegas, makes the following observations:

> Does this text [John 10:34-36] advocate deification? I think some reasons can be given to demonstrate that it does not. (i) Jesus was catching them at one of their hypocritical declarations. The scenario that unfolds is this: Jesus claims absolute deity (v. 30). The Jews attempt to assassinate him once again on the grounds of blasphemy (v. 31). Jesus points out their hypocrisy by noting that these same Jews were called "gods" by virtue of their having God's power move through them (cf. Psalms 82:6); yet they do not consider that blasphemy. (ii) Certainly men are not "gods" currently. (iii) Jesus would not have declared that his own adversaries were deities by nature. It must not be that Jesus was being sincere in the statement. Jesus was merely demonstrating their hypocrisy when it came to the law and their own biases. But, more importantly, why would the Jews scoff at Jesus for claiming a

special relationship with God the Father when the Jews were comfortable being called "gods" themselves?

The second argument given in favor of human deification is found in Psalm 82:1-6, where there is said to be a judgment "among the gods." We see that the "mighty men" were called "gods" according to verse 6. But there are a couple of problems with the Mormon interpretation. First, the context is clear that God is mocking the rulers, not praising them. Second, the reason God called the mighty judges "gods" was due to their perception by the nation. When the Lord of lords moved through men, the skeptical world saw this power and falsely attributed it to those men exercising it.[26]

In addition to Guthrie's observations, the text being quoted by Jesus (Psalm 82:6) says of the Jews, "Ye *are* gods" (present tense), which conflicts with LDS beliefs that godhood will only be obtained after aeons of time in the afterlife. Christ obviously is not teaching Mormonism's doctrine of deification. He is saying something entirely different, as Guthrie explains above.

LDS RESPONSES

Becoming a god is one of the most sacred and beloved beliefs embraced by Mormons. Consequently, LDS apologists exert a great deal of effort trying to support the doctrine. As already shown, they most often appeal to a number of Bible verses.

But in addition to using Scripture, Mormons commonly seek to validate deification through various statements made by early church fathers. According to the *Encyclopedia of Mormonism*, "From the second to eighth centuries, the standard Christian term for SALVATION was *theopoiesis* or *theosis*, literally, 'being made God,' or deification."[27]

BYU professor Stephen Robinson has been especially ardent in asserting that the LDS position on deification was shared by early church leaders in their idea of *theosis*. He has claimed, for example, that belief in deification was "part of mainstream Christian orthodoxy for centuries."[28]

Robinson and other Mormons, it must be conceded, are partly right. But they also are partly wrong. The doctrine of "deification" was indeed an important concept in early Christianity. The words "deification," "deify," "divinization," as well as similar terms, appear often in the writings of our early church fathers, including Irenaeus (about 180), Clement (about

195), Hippolytus (about 225), Theophilus (about 180), Origen (about 248), Cyprian (about 250), Eusebius (about 315), and most notably Athanasius (about 325).

As BYU professors Daniel C. Peterson and Stephen D. Ricks have rightly noted, the concept of deification "remained very much alive in the Eastern Orthodox faith, which includes such Christian sects today as the Greek Orthodox and Russian Orthodox churches."[29] Eventually, however, such terminology fell out of use in Western churches. So the question is not, Did the early church fathers teach deification? The question is rather, What did the early church fathers mean by the words they used when they taught it? LDS apologists are either unwilling, or unable, to answer this question accurately. Instead, they repeatedly resort to offering *theosis*-related quotes from early church fathers that, when taken out of their historical and theological context, seem to support Mormon beliefs.

The Term *Theosis*

Before analyzing the words of the church fathers, a few things about the term *theosis* must be noted:

- it was used inconsistently in early church writings
- it was a product of Eastern thought—which was, and still is, different than Western thinking
- it grew out of Greek philosophical ideas about humanity (which is most ironic, considering LDS disdain for the influence that Hellenistic and pagan thinking had on Christianity—see chapter 4)

Regarding the term *theosis* itself, professor Nathan Ng of the University of Edinburgh has observed that to this day "we still do not possess a single clear theological definition of deification" from the early church fathers.[30] A similar assessment, according to Ng, was made by Jules Gross in the book *The Divinization of the Christian According to the Greek Fathers*. Gross found that no church father had ever given "a precise definition" for "divinization" or its equivalents.[31]

Not a single treatise solely dealing with *theosis* was ever written by an early church father.[32] Moreover, the most significant man to teach "deification," Athanasius, did so quite inexactly.[33] He sometimes used the term in a very narrow sense to describe our partaking of God's nature. On other occasions he spoke of divinization in broader terms, referring to "everything a Christian may obtain on the way to God."[34]

More to the LDS point, Athanasius taught that Christ was "made man that we might be made God."[35] Irenaeus said, "[W]e have not been made gods from the beginning, but at first merely men, then at length gods."[36] Justin Martyr noted that "those only are deified who have lived near to God in holiness and virtue."[37] And Tertullian observed,

> For we shall be even gods, if we shall deserve to be among those of whom He declared, "I have said, Ye are gods," and, "God standeth in the congregation of the gods." But this comes of His own grace, not from any property in us, because it is He alone who can make gods.[38]

What do these statements mean? Properly interpreting them is not as simple as reading today's newspaper. An extremely complex issue is being articulated. In fact, *theosis* was viewed as a kind of "mystical event" almost beyond words or logical expression.[39] These individuals also were writing from a wholly different mindset—Greek, philosophical, and Eastern. Only a close examination of the issue reveals what early Christians were actually communicating.

Theosis and Theology

To a certain extent, notions of deification may be traced to various Bible verses (for example, Genesis 1:26-27; Deuteronomy 33:1; 2 Kings 1:9-13; 2 Kings 4:1-44; 1 Samuel 9:7-10; 2 Peter 1:4). But there is no doubt that the fully developed idea of *theosis* flourished as a result of pagan philosophical speculation on the state of humanity:

> The principal influence here came from the Greek definition of deity as possessing immortality, so that the promise of receiving immortality in Christ was expressed by the idea of deification.[40]

In other words, the roots of the concept of deification are embedded in Greek beliefs that equated incorruptibility (or in other words, immortality) with godhood: "W.R. Inge, for example, suggests that the attribute of divinity which was chiefly in the minds of the Greek fathers when they talked about deification was that of *imperishableness*."[41] Likewise, B. Drewery has asserted that the "true pedigree of deification" is Greek philosophy.[42]

This idea is closely associated with how the Greeks viewed Christ's incarnation. They felt that "God" could only have become a man if the mortal, fleshly body had somehow been deified, or in other words, raised to a level of immortality.[43] Christ, in other words, was an archetype of us. His life illustrated what would happen to our flesh when we, through union with him, became fit for immortal life. We, to coin an alternate term, would be "Christified": made like Christ; made immortal.[44]

Linked to the immortality aspect of *theosis* was the hope that Christians would mirror God's virtues and his divine goodness via union with his Spirit. In this way—through a spiritual union with God, that is— the early church fathers indeed felt that believers could be deified. Evangelicals have no problem agreeing with this definition of deification— that we are "a god, in the sense that we reflect His glory and holiness."[45]

For example, during a 1994 presentation for Concordia Theological Seminary, Lutheran D. Richard Stuckwisch made the following remarks:

> Deification is the process of becoming "as much as possible like and in union with God"—a "participation through grace in that which surrounds the nature of God." It was realized perfectly and fully in the Incarnation of the Son of God, in Whom "generic" human nature was deified. This nature of man had been established in the Creation for communion with God, but it was "darkened by its existential condition subsequent to Adam's sin." Deification is the restoration of the intended communion between God and man, beginning with the human life and death of Christ.
>
> Thus, Deification describes the Eastern understanding of *salvation in Christ*. It lies behind the Christology of Athanasius, the Cappadocian Fathers, Cyril of Alexandria, John of Damascus, *etc.* "God became man, that man might become divine." At the Council of Nicaea, the confession of the Son as *homoousios* ["of one substance"]

with the Father ensured that fellowship with Christ must be understood as communion with God, i.e., as Deification. Likewise, at the Council of Constantinople, the confession of the Holy Spirit as divine was also required, since "deification of man as sanctification is rooted in the work of the Holy Spirit." If the Spirit was not true God, then "man would be neither sanctified nor deified."[46]

Far from the LDS belief that we can be divine in nature—or become "a god" just like Heavenly Father became "a God" (which can be termed *ontological* deification)—the early church fathers were merely seeking to find a familiar way to express "the richness and sublime content" of salvation.[47] They were groping for some way to describe the glory and wonder of immortality and union with God, as well as the blessedness of sanctification by (and union with) Christ.[48] Christian scholar Robert M. Bowman Jr. comments,

> It may surprise some to learn that a monotheistic doctrine of deification was taught by many of the church fathers, and is believed by many Christians today, including the entire Eastern Orthodox church. In keeping with monotheism, the Eastern Orthodox do not teach that men will literally become "gods" (which would be polytheism). Rather, as did many of the church fathers, they teach that men are "deified" in the sense that the Holy Spirit dwells within Christian believers and transforms them into the image of God in Christ.... Thus, it should not be argued that anyone who speaks of deification necessarily holds to a heretical view of man. Such a sweeping judgment would condemn many of the early church's greatest theologians (for example, Athanasius, Augustine), as well as one of the three main branches of historic orthodox Christianity in existence today.[49]

Unfortunately, many Latter-day Saints are under the false impression that relatively few evangelicals know about *theosis* in the early church. But this is not the case. (See note 50 for several Protestant quotes).[50]

Clearly, "deification" as taught by the early church fathers poses no problem to evangelicals. Equally acceptable are similar teachings being espoused by members of Eastern churches today. Even Roman Catholics would not object to beliefs relating to deification. In fact, Roman Catholic

doctrine is very accepting of *theosis*, as evidenced by references in the
Roman Catholic Catechism to believers being "divinized." [51]

> **Did You Know?** The 1994 Roman Catholic catechism reads, "The
> Word became flesh to make us *'partakers of the divine nature':* 'For
> this is why the Word became man, and the Son of God became
> the Son of man: so that man, by entering into communion with
> the Word and thus receiving divine sonship, might become a son
> of God.' 'For the Son of God became man so that we might
> become God.' 'The only-begotten Son of God, wanting to make
> us sharers in his divinity, assumed our nature, so that he, made
> man, might make men gods'" (*Catechism of the Catholic
> Church*, 1994, page 116).

Defenders of the Gods

Christendom's unity on *theosis*, past and present, has nothing to do
with the polytheistic brand of deification preached by Mormons.
Unfortunately, some persons have misunderstood *theosis*—and in an
apparent effort at fostering ecumenical dialogue, have taken up defending
Mormonism as a sort of crusade for truth.

One notable example is David Waltz, who professes to be a Roman
Catholic but actively defends Mormonism via Internet postings and
articles.[52] Waltz eagerly stresses that he is "not a member of the Church
of Jesus Christ of Latter-day Saints."[53] This, of course, infuses his comments with an air of objectivity. His non-LDS standing lulls the uninformed into assuming that he, as a non-Mormon, would be unbiased and
reliable—especially in his defenses of Mormonism.

Waltz is best known at Zion's Lighthouse Message Board (ZLMB).
It is there that he has posted most of his support for LDS beliefs, particularly those related to deification.[54] In support of the LDS concept of
deification—which, as we have seen, entails obtaining true divinity within
our own nature—Waltz forcefully answered one critic as follows:

> I am truly amazed that you say, "the ECF [early church fathers] DID
> NOT…believe that God and Man were or ever could be ontolog-
> ically the same."…When the CF's [church fathers] of the second,

third and most of the fourth centuries said that "God became man that man might be God" they meant it!!!...[E]ven after Athanasius many CF's still believed that man through grace could become ontologically one with God....I have well over 100 quotations from the CF's concerning the doctrine of deification.[55]

And yet Waltz is at odds here with even LDS apologists (including professors Daniel Peterson and Stephen Ricks), who are "under no illusions that such figures as Athanasius and the Byzantine fathers—given their very different metaphysical and theological presuppositions—understood theosis in precisely the same way as do the Latter-day Saints."[56] Peterson has publicly noted that

there are differences, even highly significant differences, between patristic views of theosis and the Latter-day Saint notion of eternal progression....I have repeatedly said, in print, that the view of theosis in the Fathers is distinct from that held by Latter-day Saints.[57]

BYU professor Robert Millet has echoed Peterson's admission:

Latter-day Saints would probably not agree with most of what was taught about deification by the early Christian church leaders because they believe that many of the plain and precious truths concerning God and man had been lost by then.[58]

Even Barry Bickmore has acknowledged that *after* the so-called total apostasy of the Christian church around the second or third century (see pages 254, 257–258), many, even most, of the doctrines being advanced were "out of harmony with revealed truth." He adds, "Therefore, we don't expect our doctrines to exactly match all the doctrines of any of the fathers."[59]

Such a response, although understated, corresponds to what has previously been shown in this chapter—that the statements made by early church fathers about deification and divinization do not reflect Mormon beliefs about exaltation. So why do Latter-day Saints still quote these Greek fathers?

One of the ways Mormons and their supporters attempt to downplay the differences between modern LDS beliefs on deification and those of the earliest church fathers is by claiming that Athanasius (around 297 to 373) was the first one to "deny that redeemed and glorified mankind would be ontologically one with God."[60]

This claim is crucial because it leaves room for interpreting in a more LDS-friendly way the *theosis*-related remarks dated *before* Athanasius. Others at ZLMB have noted as much: "Waltz showed that Athanasius marked a *turning point* in the doctrinal evolution, with *earlier* Fathers holding to the idea that 'ontological sameness' could be achieved with God."[61]

In reality, however, the pre-Athanasian church fathers did not define their *theosis*-related terms in this way. In fact, they did not define their terms *at all*. Hence, Athanasius did not represent any kind of a "turning point" in Christian deification thought—rather, he offered in his writings a documentation of a gradual evolution of deification thought and a refinement of it.

The earliest of the early church fathers (for example, Irenaeus) simply used a wide variety of terms and phrases to describe the Christian hope—of becoming immortal, incorruptible, like God, like Christ, and so forth.[62] Such terminology was somehow—we do not know exactly how—linked to *theosis*. We do know, however, that eventually the concept was necessarily clarified, perhaps out of the confusion that *theosis* terminology caused. And it was not seen as ontological deification.[63]

The very best a Mormon can argue from the writings of the earliest church fathers is that they used *theosis* terminology but never defined its meaning. A Latter-day Saint can then at least have the freedom to 1) infuse—despite the absence of any real evidence—LDS beliefs into those undefined terms; or 2) suggest that the earliest church fathers *probably* believed as Mormons believe, but that their teachings were lost because of Christianity's total apostasy. Both of these views have been voiced by Mormons.[64]

But this is not how Protestants, Roman Catholics, or members of Eastern churches seem to have ever understood *theosis*. Their writings about *theosis* do not match the definition that Mormons have sought to give the word. Conveniently, however, Mormons dismiss any incompatible views evidenced in early church writings as nothing more than results of the great apostasy—which allegedly caused a change in what *must* have been the *real* beliefs of *theosis* espoused by the earliest church fathers.

Mormon Point: Evangelicals are a bit hypocritical in criticizing Mormon beliefs about reaching godhood—because even the great Christian writer C.S. Lewis believed that humans can become gods! In fact, he talked about becoming gods and human deification on several occasions, saying that it was not only possible, but was part of God's plan for us.

Counterpoint: As previously demonstrated in this chapter, churches in all sectors of Christendom—Protestant, Eastern, and Roman Catholic—accept *theosis* (or deification) *as taught by the early church fathers*. This acceptance mirrors what Lewis was referring to in his writings. He was not talking about the kind of deification embraced by Mormons. Rather, "Lewis simply offers rhetorical riffs on classical Christian teaching and in no way suggests an ontological equivalence between Creator and creature."[65]

Such reasoning highlights one particularly troubling practice among *some* Latter-day Saints—selective acceptance of historical data. Deification is a good case in point. Mormons are more than ready to accept any and all statements from early church fathers that *seem* to support LDS views—because these writings allegedly represent the church's original teachings, which are now once more being taught through Mormonism. At the same time, however, other statements made by the very same church leaders will be dismissed by Mormons if their words conflict with LDS ideas—because *these* writings suddenly are evidence of the great apostasy (and proof that traditional Christianity is corrupt).

In sum, anything that supports Mormonism from early centuries is proof of the Christian doctrines *restored* by Joseph Smith. Anything that contradicts Mormonism is proof of the false teachings that are linked to the church's apostasy—which, again, was taught by Smith. This is an airtight method of historical analysis that perfectly fits the LDS agenda to prove the validity of Joseph Smith and his restored church.

Such a practice has been observed by numerous scholars, researchers of Mormonism, and religious leaders, including the well-known Roman Catholic priest, Richard John Neuhaus. In his very enlightening 2000 article titled "Is Mormonism Christian?" Neuhaus concluded that it is certainly a Christian derivation—but "by way of sharpest contrast, in radical discontinuity with historical Christianity."[66]

FINAL OBSERVATIONS

Clearly, evangelicals and Mormons hold divergent views of the afterlife and our condition and nature in it. Linked to this issue is yet another LDS doctrine that is utterly foreign to evangelicals—that "Christ has the power to bind men and women together for eternity."[67] In other words, Mormons believe their families go on for eternity and marriage is part of achieving godhood.[68]

Not only do families formed in this life continue, but additional spirit-children will be birthed in heaven by those who reach exaltation.[69] Latter-day Saints believe they will "dwell again with God the Father, and live and act like him in endless worlds of happiness, power, love, glory...above all, they will have the power of procreating endless lives."[70]

Historian B.H. Roberts wrote that God's followers will continue to have children "the same as our God, who is the Father of our spirits." He further explained that through faithfulness, Mormons may become parents "the same as our heavenly Father is Father to us."[71] Using more explicit terms, in 1880 LDS apostle George Q. Cannon declared that

> if we obtain celestial glory in the fullest sense of the word, then we have wives and children in eternity, we have the power of endless lives granted unto us, the power of propagation that will endure through all eternity, all being fathers and mothers in eternity; fathers of fathers, and mothers of mothers, kings and queens, priests and priestesses, and shall I say more? Yes, all becoming gods.[72]

It was this doctrine, in part, that led to polygamy during the early years of Mormonism, which caused no small amount of anguish to many LDS women. The practice also led to some odd doctrinal, social, and political problems in the 1800s and early 1900s. But with great finesse, Mormon leaders successfully steered their church through this public-relations nightmare.

Polygamy, however, remains a fascinating study and a topic that continues to shed light on LDS thinking. More efforts are now being made throughout America to make polygamy legal. Consequently, I have chosen to make it the subject of chapter 9.

MORE THAN ONE WIFE

[I]n attaining the highest degree of glory in the celestial kingdom, the man cannot enter without the woman, neither can the woman enter without the man. The two are inseparable as husband and wife in eligibility for that highest degree of glory.[1]

—Gordon B. Hinckley, LDS President

Polygamy. The word has been in the news almost constantly since 2002, when 14-year-old Elizabeth Smart was abducted from her Utah home by a deranged religious zealot named David Mitchell. Fortunately, she was found alive and well—at least in body—but only after being forced to endure nine months as Mitchell's wife. Mitchell, an excommunicated Mormon, believed that God had told him young Elizabeth was meant to be his bride. In fact, he believed God had said he would eventually have seven wives.

The crime immediately placed The Church of Jesus Christ of Latter-day Saints into the media spotlight, which in turn moved LDS authorities to respond in a public statement denying any connection to Mitchell or his views. But the forceful denials only caused more talk and speculation about polygamy and its continuing presence in America, especially in relation to Mormonism.

Coincidentally, in the very midst of the Elizabeth Smart tragedy, the LDS Church was also having to deal with the publicity and controversy being generated by *More Than One: Plural Marriage*, an uncomfortable polygamy-promoting book that had been published by a faithful Mormon, Shane LeGrande Whelan.[2] The volume, which eventually led to Whelan's excommunication, blatantly supported the doctrine of earthly polygamy and drew far too much public attention to the practice of it by early Mormons.

Then, in 2004, headlines were captured by the polygamy-practicing Fundamentalist Church of Jesus Christ of Latter Day Saints in Colorado City, Arizona, when teenagers began escaping from that group's enclave.[3] The seriousness of the situation escalated as reports of church rivalries, weapon stockpiles, and possible attempts at revenge surfaced. ABC even televised a *Primetime Thursday* special segment on the group (on March 4, 2004).

Finally, also in 2004, three Utahans filed a lawsuit in federal court "seeking to overturn a century-old ban on polygamy, claiming the pro-hibition against taking plural spouses violates their constitutional rights."[4] This lawsuit has brought polygamy "back in the public consciousness for the first time in years because of wrangling over the legal definition of marriage and several high-profile criminal cases."[5] In other words, it is a very real possibility (given cases such as Lawrence v. Texas, which over-turned anti-sodomy laws) that polygamy will become legal at some point in the near future.[6]

So, unlike in years past, when debates about polygamy and Mor-monism were more academic than anything else, today we must be more careful in discussing the issue. Is polygamy godly? Is it commanded in the Bible? Has God ever ordained it as a holy practice? These questions will now be covered—based on the understanding that polygamy is some-thing that, at one time, was both widespread and legal in America.

❄ ❄ ❄

Mormons, generally speaking, believe that marriage is essential for deification.[7] Finding a mate, therefore, is critically important to Latter-day Saints, especially Mormon women, whose "eternal life" is *uniquely* dependent upon a faithful LDS husband. In a 1988 article in *Dialogue: A Journal of Mormon Thought*, Melodie Moench Charles noted that

> a husband helps his wife attain salvation in a way that a wife does not do for her husband.... *The Melchizedek Priesthood Personal Study Guide* from 1984 included the following: "Elder Bruce R. McConkie wrote: '[Husbands] must...love their wives, sacrifice for their well-being and salvation, and guide them in holiness until they are

cleansed, sanctified, and perfected, until they are prepared for exaltation in that glorious heaven where the family unit continues. Husbands thus become in effect the saviors of their wives' (*Doctrinal New Testament Commentary* 2:519)."[8]

Something to Consider:

In order to attain the highest rank and reward in this Mormon heaven a person must be married in the temple. The unmarried and people married in any way other than a sealing ceremony are doomed to the fate outlined in Doctrine and Covenants 132:16-17: "To minister for those who are worthy of a far more, and an exceeding, and an eternal weight of glory."...Mormon leaders teach an exception to the harsh penalty presented in this scripture: people who had no fair chance to be married correctly get a chance to marry after mortal life.

In mortality Mormonism offers single adults an awkward and isolated social status that evokes either suspicion or pity in other Mormons. It condemns them to a life of sexual frustration and encourages feelings of unrighteousness, guilt, and inadequacy. For single men it offers significantly fewer chances to serve in high management positions in the Church....

Why does Mormon theology do this to single people? Because of the idea that the highest glory in heaven includes becoming a god and reigning over the kingdoms which we create by procreating....Creating includes not only making a world, but peopling it through procreating, through sexual union with one's spouse.[10]

Once an LDS couple agrees to marry, they are wed *for time* (life on earth) and *for eternity* (the afterlife). Their "sealing" (marriage) is how they will continue their union in heaven and beget children throughout all eternity.[9] This sacred ceremony must take place in an LDS temple, and it is available only to *Temple Mormons*—Mormons who have proven themselves worthy of the temple. (Only with a *Temple Recommend,* which must be shown at the temple door, can a Mormon use a temple. This, of course, means that in order to even attend a temple wedding, one must be a Temple Mormon. It is one of Mormonism's holiest ceremonies.)

A Brief History of LDS Polygamy

For decades the Mormon marriage concept was inextricably linked to polygamy. It all began in the 1830s after Joseph Smith claimed that God *commanded* him to take more wives.[11] He reportedly did not *want* to start polygamy, but God made him an offer he could not refuse.[12] The Lord, according to Smith, sent an angel carrying a drawn sword with which he would be slain if he did not obey God's directive.[13]

Polygamy, also called the "Law of Abraham" by Smith, allegedly was a terrible burden for him to bear. He also felt that its sacredness would be impossible for some people to discern. So he initially shared it with only trusted allies (those who "could bear it").[14]

But LDS critics soon found out what was going on, which stirred up trouble. No doctrine, in fact, created more conflict for the Latter-day Saints than polygamy (originally referred to as either *plural marriage*, or *celestial marriage*).

One of Joseph's first polygamous unions occurred in 1832 or 1833 with Fanny Alger, the 16-year-old daughter in a neighboring Mormon family.[15] He actually married Alger in a secret ceremony and then had her move into his home in 1835 as a maidservant and adopted daughter.[16] Smith, however, had not yet *officially* introduced the doctrine of polygamy, nor had any high-ranking leaders publicly sanctioned the practice.

Nevertheless, several Saints sought multiple partners, which in turn left the Mormons open to outside persecution and internal strife. LDS officials decided to stop the unsanctioned marriages by reprimanding anyone found indulging in Smith's privilege. Then, perhaps in an attempt to conceal Smith's affair, LDS leaders drafted section 101 for the 1835 Doctrine and Covenants, which boldly condemned polygamy.[17]

Smith took his next wife in 1838. In 1841 he acquired 3 more wives. He married 11 women the next year. Finally, in 1843, he took at least 17 wives. Meanwhile, Joseph's original wife, Emma, tried opposing her husband's amorous activity.[18] To silence her, Smith simply issued a revelation in which God commanded her to stop complaining and accept Joseph's actions—or else be damned.[19] This 1843 revelation was read to Emma privately and given to several of Smith's trusted followers—but was still kept secret from the vast majority of Saints living in Nauvoo, Illinois (about 1845 to 1846).

Public repudiations of polygamy continued even after Joseph Smith's death in 1846. Mormons also concealed the fact that some 30 other men were enjoying the Law of Abraham, which resulted in about 84 plural marriages in the early 1840s. This privilege was gradually extended to others in the LDS community under Brigham Young, who took the Latter-day Saints to Utah in 1847.

It was only then that Mormons began to talk openly about polygamy, as evidenced by Young's public acknowledgment of his "wives" in 1851.[20] Once in Utah, away from the government's prying eyes, polygamy became *the* standard of righteousness.[21]

> **Interesting Fact:** Although Joseph Smith received his revelation commanding polygamy in 1843, it would not be publicly released until 1852—and not printed in the Doctrine and Covenants until 1876. But by that time the Mormons, then in Utah, had openly engaged in the practice for many years. Back in 1845, however, only about 25 families among the 20,000 people living in Nauvoo knew about polygamy. The others thought that the charges being leveled against LDS Church elders were slanderous attempts to bring down Mormon leaders in the community.

Plural marriage continued in Utah until statehood became an issue in the late 1800s. It was a chaotic time, with U.S. politicians seeking prosecution of polygamous Mormons, new antibigamy legislation being passed, some LDS leaders fleeing federal authorities, and other LDS leaders actually being imprisoned.[22]

Eventually, the U.S. government gave Mormons only two choices: 1) continue practicing polygamy and face closure of the Church; or 2) stop polygamy and enjoy the benefits of Utah statehood.[23] Obviously, there was only one course of action. So on September 25, 1890, LDS president Wilford Woodruff released an official Manifesto admonishing every Mormon to no longer enter into plural marriage.

This Manifesto, however, did not condemn polygamy *in principle*, but prohibited it only *in practice* on Earth. Hence, today's Mormons still view polygamy as a godly activity. In fact, a form of it is *still* practiced in Mormonism:

> Those husbands who have lost a beloved spouse and are left alone in this world can still be married for time and eternity to another wife....It is clear that all marriages continued in heaven will involve participation in plural marriage. Whether instituted in this life or the next, it will be a part of our eternal existence.[24]

If all goes well, then, each LDS male will find a wife, reach godhood, and take his place among the gods. It is a "gradually unfolding course of advancement and experience," said LDS apostle Bruce McConkie, "a course that began in a past eternity [that is, pre-existence] and will continue in ages future."[25] And as we shall see, polygamy was at one time an indispensable part of that advancement.

——— MORMON QUOTES ———

"[A]s touching the principle and doctrine of their having many wives and concubines....I reveal unto you a new and everlasting covenant; and if ye abide not that covenant, then are ye damned" (D&C 132:1,4).

"[M]y wives will be mine in eternity" (Joseph Fielding Smith, LDS President, 1955).[26]

"[P]lural marriage is the patriarchal order of marriage lived by God and others who reign in the Celestial Kingdom" (John J. Stewart, LDS author, 1961).[27]

"My lovely Joan was sent to me: So Joan joins Fern[,] That three might be, more fitted for eternity" (Harold B. Lee, LDS president, 1974).[28]

"[P]lural marriage is not a product of man's sinful nature. It is a higher law of marriage which was practiced by prophets and other worthy men when directed by the Lord" (Michael W. Hickenbotham, LDS apologist, 1995).[29]

"[M]arriage must be monogamous and does not accept into its membership those practicing plural marriage" (Gordon B. Hinckley, LDS President, 1998).[30]

A Closer Look

Polygamy has always been a chief source of contention between Mormons and traditional Christians. Plural marriage is abhorrent to Western sensibilities as something that not only degrades women, but indulges and multiplies men's worst proclivities. Mormons, however, have long viewed it as a glorious principle of *true* Christianity.

> **Notable and Quotable:** In his diary, William Clayton related how Smith initiated him into the circle of leaders allowed to practice polygamy:
>
> > [T]he Prophet invited me to walk with him. During our walk, he said he had learned that there was a sister back in England, to whom I was very much attached. I replied there was, but nothing further than an attachment such as a brother and sister in the Church might rightfully entertain for each other. He then said, "Why don't you send for her?" I replied, "In the first place, I have no authority to send for her, and if I had, I have not the means to pay expenses." To this he answered, "I give you authority to send for her, and I will furnish you with means," which he did....
> >
> > He informed me that the doctrine and principle was right in the sight of our Heavenly Father, and that it was a doctrine which pertained to celestial order and glory. After giving me lengthy instructions and information concerning the doctrine of celestial or plural marriage, he concluded his remarks by the words, "It is your privilege to have all the wives you want."[33]

William Clayton, for example, who served as Joseph Smith's clerk, recalled, "From him I learned that the doctrine of plural and celestial marriage is the most holy and important doctrine ever revealed to man on the earth."[31] Other LDS leaders, after admitting to their participation in the practice, also assured everyone that it all had nothing to do with gratifying "carnal lusts and feelings of man."[32]

Robbing the Cradle

Polygamy, according to early Mormon males, was a necessary trial that would produce not only spiritual maturity, but also populate God's kingdom on earth. And as a side benefit, mortal bodies would be provided for Heavenly Father's spirit children who were still waiting in heaven for their chance at mortality.

But history professor Jan Shipps, one of the world's foremost authorities on Mormonism, has stated that after Smith allowed polygamy for a select number of LDS men, these Mormon leaders "came to resemble children suddenly told that eating candy was good for them."[34] This seems to be a quite accurate assessment of the practice.

According to Peter Wood, associate professor of anthropology at Boston University, polygamy leads to a host of abuses. One "essential truth" of polygamy, says Wood, is that it "is inseparable from older men imposing themselves on young women."[35] In other words, it "is a system by which powerful older men assemble a household of young desirable women."[36] Wood asks,

> But why?...The answer lies in something anthropologists don't like to talk about: human nature. The human sexes accommodate fairly easily to a dominant male hierarchy; human males are biologically primed to seek sexual variety; and the systems of reciprocity on which all human societies are based lend themselves very easily to dominant males consolidating their status by taking young wives.[37]

The validity of Wood's observation is apparent in LDS history. Fanny Stenhouse, who fled life as a plural LDS wife in Utah, described what she witnessed in *Tell It All* (1875). This book, which featured a preface by the prestigious Harriet Beecher Stowe, noted that "old men tottering on the brink of the grave have been united to little girls scarcely in their teens."[38] Stenhouse added,

I know also another man who married a widow with several children; and when one of the girls had grown into her teens he insisted on marrying her also...and to this very day the daughter bears children to her step-father, living as wife in the same house with her mother.[39]

Such unions were common during Mormonism's polygamous period. Bishop Aaron Johnson of Springville, Utah, for instance, claimed six of his own nieces as wives—the eldest being only 15 years old when he wed her. The younger nieces ranged downward in age to 2 years old. Johnson asked that they be given to him as they matured, which is exactly what happened. He was finally sealed to the littlest girl when she reached about 13.[40]

Did You Know? Brigham Young said sexual desire had very little to do with taking wives:

The time is coming when the Lord is going to raise up a holy nation....[H]e has introduced a plurality of wives for that express purpose, and not to gratify lustful passion in the least....I never entered into the order of plurality of wives to gratify passion. And were I now asked whether I desired and wanted another wife, my reply would be, It should be one by whom the Spirit will bring forth noble children.*

Patterned After the Prophet

Johnson, like numerous other Mormons, was only following in the prophet's footsteps. Of Smith's wives, eleven were teenagers (14 to 20 years old). Nine were 21 to 30 years old. Only eight were in Smith's own age group (31 to 40). Five women fell in the 41 to 60 age range. Brigham Young, too, acquired many young wives, several of whom were just teenagers (Table 9.1).

---

* Brigham Young, April 7, 1861, in *Journal of Discourses*, volume 9, page 36.

Young Wives of Brigham Young

Plural Wife	Wife's Age at Marriage	Young's Age at Marriage
Lucy Ann Decker	20	41
Harriet Campbell	18	42
Clarissa Decker	15	42
Emily Dow Partridge	20	43
Emmeline Free	19	43
Ellen Rockwood	16	44
Margaret Maria Alley	20	45
Lucy Bigelow	16	45
Mary Jane Bigelow	19	45
Harriet Amelia Folsom	24	61
Mary Van Cott	22	63
Ann Eliza Webb	23 or 24	66 or 67

Table 9.1[41]

Unfortunately, after the Mormons had been several years in Utah, the supply of young girls there had dwindled. To remedy the situation, missionaries were told to bring back eligible females to replenish the reservoir from which aging LDS leaders could draw mates. But this caused a slight problem. The missionaries were young and handsome bachelors. The concern was that they would take the best women. Hence, safeguards were put in place.

Missionaries, for instance, received warnings about not being greedy concerning women. Heber C. Kimball advised departing men to "not make a choice of any of those sheep; do not make selections before they are brought home."[42] At times, Kimball spoke even more plainly:

> The brother missionaries have been in the habit of picking out the prettiest women for themselves before they get here, and bringing on the ugly ones for us; hereafter you have to bring them all here before taking any of them, and let us all have a fair shake.[43]

Such attitudes continued unabated for decades. And to assist older men, LDS leaders often urged young girls to choose experienced husbands, who had the power to resurrect them after death, rather than young men "whose position in the church was not fixed."[44]

The More, the Better

Plural marriage, in other words, became a measure of status in the church. All bishops, stake presidents, and other ecclesiastical authorities were expected to abide by the Law of Abraham. This expectation fostered an atmosphere in which men almost *had* to take more wives, or else suffer the consequences of perpetual low status.[45]

But unlike polygamy in other cultures, LDS plural marriage developed very rapidly, had few societal regulations, and presented no detailed methods for acquiring wives. There also existed no courtship patterns or limits on how many wives could be taken. In the mad rush to acquire wives and solidify polygamous bonds, LDS family units became a tangled mass of incestuous interfamilial unions:

> Uncles and nieces were married; one man would marry several sisters; and it was a very common thing for a mother and daughter to have the same husband. In one family, at least three generations were represented among the wives—grandmother, mother, and daughter; and a case actually occurred in Salt Lake City where a man married his half sister, and that, too, with the full knowledge and approval of Brigham Young.[46]

Until the major LDS doctrinal shift that occurred in 1890 because of the change in polygamy practice, faithful Mormons believed plural marriage was necessary for deification in the Celestial Kingdom.[47] And the more wives acquired in this life, the better it would be in the next life.

Wives for Exaltation

Brigham Young declared, "The only men who become Gods, even the Sons of God, are those who enter into polygamy."[48] Anyone who wanted the Celestial Kingdom had to be a polygamist, at least in their faith.[49] This understanding prompted Utahans to send an 1870 memorial to Congress calling polygamy a divine principle "underlying our every hope of eternal salvation and happiness in heaven."[50]

Ten years later, in 1880, LDS president Wilford Woodruff received a revelation that depicted polygamy as absolutely essential to godhood. This blatantly contradicts the view held by modern Mormons, who mistakenly think that only *eternal* marriage was seen by early Saints as essential for exaltation, but that *plural* marriage was not so viewed.[51] This modern misconception has enabled Mormons to very easily rationalize the 1890 banning of polygamy.

Yet the historical evidence tells a different story. Woodruff's 1880 divine communication, for instance, went so far as to damn anyone who would even *hinder* Mormons from obeying plural marriage.[52] The entire LDS First Presidency admitted as much in appealing to the government for amnesty in 1891:

> We formerly taught to our people that polygamy or Celestial marriage as commanded by God through Joseph Smith was right; that it was a necessity to man's highest exaltation in the life to come. That doctrine was publicly promulgated by our president, the late Brigham Young, forty years ago, and was steadily taught and impressed upon the Latter day Saints up to September, 1890.[53]

As mentioned earlier, those who only believed in polygamy but did not actually practice it were destined to be servants in the Celestial Kingdom rather than gods.[54] An LDS male had to *participate* in plural marriage to achieve deification because monogamy was thought to be a "lower law" than the "higher law" of polygamy.[55] And "a man obeying a lower law is not qualified to preside over those who keep a higher law."[56]

LDS leaders went so far as to threaten other men, saying that if they refused another wife, then in the afterlife the wife they did possess would go to another man—a polygamist—for all eternity.[57] As Young said in 1873 of a "man who did not have but one wife in the Resurrection[,] that woman will not be his but taken from him & given to another."[58] (This aspect of polygamy, however, was also changed after 1890.)

Denials, Denunciations, and Deception

Given the controversial nature of plural marriage, it is hardly surprising that Joseph Smith Jr. resorted to blatant deception in order to hide his glorious principle. He not only refused to endorse polygamy publicly, but actually went so far as to condemn it. He consistently and vehemently denounced the practice as sinful, maintaining that monogamy was God's perfect design for marital relationships.

Privately, however, the spiritual walk of Smith and other high-ranking LDS men was not matching their public talk. For example, on March 4, 1843, Smith married 19-year-old Emily Partridge, after which time he waited only four days before taking her 22-year-old sister, Eliza, as a wife. But then, only a week later, Smith's *Times and Seasons* published an LDS letter denying polygamy.[59]

Joseph's pretense at monogamy continued until his death. As late as 1837—some four to five years after Smith's first polygamous union—Daniel S. Miles was stating through the *Saints' Messenger and Advocate* that polygamy was indeed against the Doctrine and Covenants:

> [W]e will have no fellowship whatever with any Elder belonging to the quorums of the Seventies who is guilty of polygamy or any offence of the kind, and who does not in all things conform to the laws of the church contained in the Bible and in the Book of Doctrine and Covenants.[60]

Ebenezer Robinson recalled that the doctrine of multiple wives was talked about privately in Nauvoo as early as 1841 and that he was invited to join the select participants in 1843. Robinson recalled how Smith's brother Hyrum

> instructed me in Nov or Dec 1843 to make a selection of some young woman and he would seal her to me, and I should take her home, and if she should have an offspring [I was to] give out word that she had a husband, an Elder, who had gone on a foreign mission.[61]

Because secrecy had to be maintained, church leaders actually designated a place in Iowa (about a dozen or so miles from Nauvoo), where impregnated plural wives were sent to be shielded from inquisitive Gentiles.[62] Another subterfuge Joseph used to protect himself was to have his women feign marriage to other men.[63]

Not every woman, however, yielded to polygamy. Orson Pratt's first wife, Sarah, after leaving her husband and the church, declared it the "direst curse": one that completely demoralized "good men," and made "bad men correspondingly worse."[64] She herself had been propositioned by Joseph, which in part led to her rejection of Mormonism. An 1886 interview with her enlightened many readers:

> [Joseph] used to state to his intended victims, as he did to me: "God does not care if we have a good time, if only other people do not know it." He only introduced a marriage ceremony when he found out he could not get certain women without it....If any woman, like me, opposed his wishes, he used to say: "Be silent, or I shall ruin your character. My character must be sustained in the interest of the Church."[65]

Despite such conduct, Mormonism's founder boldly denied all reports linking him to polygamy, adultery, or both, especially if they came from dissidents, whom he denounced as liars. Consider, for example, Joseph's May 26, 1844, public response to his accusers:

> [William Law] swears that I have committed adultery. I wish the grand jury would tell me who they are...I am quite tired of the fools asking me. A man asked me whether the commandment was given that a man may have seven wives....I am innocent of all these charges....What a thing it is for a man to be accused of committing adultery, and having seven wives, when I can only find one. I am the same man, and as innocent as I was fourteen years ago; and I can prove them all perjurers.[66]

When Smith made these statements, he indeed did not have 7 wives. He had at least 33 wives. And using a more liberal estimate from *Dialogue: A Journal of Mormon Thought,* he had perhaps as many as 40 wives![67]

Another rarely discussed aspect of Smith's polygamy is that 11 of his wives were already wed to other men "and cohabitating with them when

Smith married them."[68] Nine of his first dozen wives were the spouses of some of his closest friends, many of whom were important LDS leaders.[69] Although the wives continued to live with their husbands, they would receive conjugal visits from Smith whenever the need arose.[70]

Other Mormons followed suit. Consider Lucinda Pendleton. She is widely known for having married first Smith, then Brigham Young after Smith's murder. But what is commonly overlooked is that she married Smith and Young while still married to a George Harris. And Zina Huntington married Brigham Young while still married to Henry Jacobs. Jacobs, in fact, stood as a witness![71]

Wife-swapping was eventually looked upon as wholly acceptable if an influential church authority was involved. Jedediah M. Grant, for example, admitted, "If President Young wants my wives I will give them to him without a grumble, and he can take them whenever he likes."[72] Grant also explained,

> What would a man of God say, who felt aright, when Joseph [Smith] asked him for his money? He would say, "Yes, and I wish I had more to help to build up the kingdom of God." Or if he came and said, "I want your wife?" "O yes," he would say, "here she is; there are plenty more."[73]

The *Confessions of John D. Lee* confirmed wife-swapping in Utah, saying, "Some have mutually agreed to exchange wives."[74] One of Brigham's own brothers, Lorenzo Young, engaged in just such a trade with a Mr. Decker, whose wife was wanted by Lorenzo. The two men simply swapped mates.[75]

EVANGELICAL THOUGHTS

Did God command polygamy? That is the key question, especially since Smith seemed to get his ideas about plural marriage from Old Testament patriarchs, kings, and leaders (for example, Abraham, Jacob, David, Solomon). Their polygamous conduct apparently led Smith to believe that having many wives was ordered by God.

But nowhere in Scripture does God actually sanction, let alone command, polygamy. At best, the Lord tolerated humanity's stubborn refusal to adhere to what appears to have been his ideal—monogamy. This form of marriage was set forth in Genesis, where the Lord created one woman for Adam. God then underscored his desire for a one-to-one pairing of men and women: "Therefore shall a man leave his father and mother, and shall cleave unto his wife [singular]: and they shall be one flesh [singular]" (Genesis 2:24).

Old Testament Polygamy

Noteworthy is Genesis 4:19, the first place polygamy appears in the Bible. Here we find Lamech, the first polygamist. Far from being an admirable character, he is a violent Cainite—a descendant of the infamous Cain (Genesis 4:1-8). He is a man in whom we see "[t]he powerful development of the worldly mind and of ungodliness."[76] In his "sword song," for instance, Lamech boasts of murder, then brags that he will avenge himself upon anyone harming him (Genesis 4:23-24).

After Lamech's era (previous to 2100 B.C.), polygamy slowly spread, but it seemed to be largely confined to the ruling and upper classes of the ancient Near East. Although a social institution by Moses' time, there are "no examples given of large polygamous marriages in the families of commoners."[77] Most Israelites were monogamous.

In fact, monogamy remained not only the norm, but was viewed by the Israelites as the most acceptable form of marriage, as implied by various Hebrew laws (Exodus 20:17; 21:5; Leviticus 18:8,16,20; 20:10; Numbers 5:12; Deuteronomy 5:21). Herein lies another departure that the Mormons made from the Old Testament in relation to polygamy. The Hebrews never considered it a *standard* practice.

It also is significant that virtually every Old Testament story involving polygamy includes some tragedy, punishment, or suffering directly related to plural marriage:

- Incessant fighting, bitterness, anger, and jealousy plagued Abraham's two wives—Sarah and Hagar—both of whom suffered great emotional anguish, especially Hagar (Genesis 21:8-16).

- Jacob's wives, Rachel and Leah, though sisters, were relationally torn by bitterness (Genesis 30:15).

- Friction between Elkanah's wives, Hannah and Peninnah, caused heartbreak and anger in Hannah (1 Samuel 1:1-10).

- David resorted to murder so he could have another wife (2 Samuel 11).

- Solomon's polygamy turned him into an idolater (1 Kings 11:1-8).

These stories, far from being intended as a promotion of polygamy, seem to represent a discouragement of the practice. The Bible provides not a single instance of polygamy being extolled as virtuous. (For more information, see appendix A). Rather, the Hebrew kings were warned against multiplying wives because it would turn their hearts away from God (Deuteronomy 17:17). Even in Proverbs, verses about marriage do not enjoin polygamy, but suggest monogamy.[78]

And although Mormons call polygamy the Law of Abraham, the story of Abraham portrays his acceptance of plural marriage as a mark of disobedience to, and a lack of faith in, God. He accepted another wife from his first wife, Sarah, in order to father a child solely because he did not trust God's promise to give him a son by Sarah.

Moreover, Abraham embraced polygamy by listening to Sarah's counsel—not God's counsel. Afterward, Sarah recognized her mistake, saying, "My wrong be upon thee" (Genesis 16:5). So, far from being Abraham's *Law*, polygamy reflected Abraham's *sin*—his willingness to accept the pagan custom of ancient Mesopotamia instead of obeying the marriage pattern established at creation.[79]

New Testament Polygamy?

Early Mormon leaders further erred in believing that the New Testament teaches polygamy—more specifically, that Jesus and his apostles were polygamists.[80] Jedediah M. Grant, Brigham Young's Second Counselor, asserted, "A belief in the doctrine of a plurality of wives caused the persecution of Jesus and his followers."[81] LDS apostle Orson Hyde taught that Jesus "was married at Cana of Galilee, that Mary, Martha, and others were his wives."[82] And LDS apostle Orson Pratt declared that "the great messiah who was the founder of the Christian religion, was a polygamist."[83]

But nothing in the New Testament remotely suggests that Jesus and his disciples were polygamists. According to the Gospel accounts of Christ's life, Jesus was persecuted and crucified for committing what the Jews considered to be blasphemy, not for practicing polygamy (Matthew 26:63-66). Further, several New Testament verses clearly teach that monogamy is the Judeo-Christian pattern of marriage:

- "A bishop then must be blameless, the husband of one wife" (1 Timothy 3:2).
- "[O]rdain elders in every city, as I had appointed thee: If any be blameless, the husband of one wife...For a bishop must be blameless" (Titus 1:5-6,7).
- "Let every man have his own wife" (1 Corinthians 7:2).

The Bible also depicts the church as *the* bride of Christ: *one* bride cared for by Jesus (John 3:29; 2 Corinthians 11:2; Ephesians 5:24-31; Revelation 19:7; 21:2-9). The marital relationship between one man and one woman is a picture of this. But this illustration is rendered meaningless by polygamy. It invalidates the Christ/Church–husband/wife analogy (see Ephesians 5:33).[84]

> **Did You Know?** Even the Book of Mormon seems to condemn polygamy (Jacob 1:15; 2:24-27; 3:5). Latter-day Saints, however, deny that this is the case. They claim that, although God did indeed forbid polygamy for the people he was addressing in the Book of Mormon, he was not making a blanket condemnation of it. They assert that the appropriateness of polygamy is somewhat of a fluid issue—meaning that when God says it is acceptable, then it is acceptable and must be obeyed (for example, from 1841 to 1890). But when God says it is not acceptable, then it must not be practiced, otherwise one is in disobedience to God (for example, from 1890 onward). Although this answer makes their God appear somewhat fickle, it is how Mormons view the discrepancy in the earthly practice, which at one time was necessary for righteous living, but then suddenly was not necessary—indeed, it was forbidden.

Other New Testament passages, again in direct contrast to Mormonism, say that in certain instances it is better for a person to remain unmarried (1 Corinthians 7:8-9,11,27). And in one passage Jesus specifically declares that in the afterlife individuals "neither marry, nor are given in marriage" (Matthew 22:30; Mark 12:25; Luke 20:35).[85]

An Interesting Fact: Whether or not Jesus was and is married continues to be a confusing issue for Mormons. Why? Because according to LDS teachings a person *must* enter into eternal marriage to be exalted to godhood. Yet Jesus, although he seems to have had no wives on Earth, is a god. In fact, Jesus was a god even before coming to Earth. Does this mean he married someone in the eternities *before* being born?

A related problem involves the very idea that Jesus was a god before his birth in Bethlehem. Mormonism clams that a person can *only* become a god by first entering mortality, then being resurrected, then progressing on to godhood. But Jesus, in LDS thought, was already a god before being begotten in the flesh. How is this possible? (The same question might be asked of the Holy Ghost, who also is a god. But he has *still* not even taken a body—or entered mortality. So how can he be a god?) These are questions for which Mormons have no answers.

Even if just for the sake of discussion it is conceded that Scripture tolerates, even advocates, polygamy, Smith and early Mormons blatantly disobeyed Old Testament prohibitions against a man marrying either his wife's sister (Leviticus 18:18) or his wife's mother (Leviticus 20:14). Smith and other LDS leaders, including Brigham Young, did both (see this chapter's note 46 for a discussion of such pairings).

Despite all of these passages from the Bible, modern Mormons still assert that their spiritual forefathers were following God's command to take multiple wives. LDS author John J. Stewart, for instance, explained in 1961 that "for a person to say that he believes the Bible but does not believe the doctrine of plural marriage is something akin to saying that he accepts the Constitution but not the Bill of Rights."[86]

LDS Responses

As previously noted, Mormons still embrace the *principle* of polygamy even though *practicing* it is forbidden. This has put LDS leadership in an extraordinarily difficult position. On the one hand, they must uphold polygamy as a righteous principle. On the other hand, they must discourage church members from practicing it while avoiding any suggestion that Smith was wrong for instituting it. Simultaneously, they must not defend the doctrine too vigorously or else some Saints might again start indulging in it.

Mormon authorities usually end up resolving this dilemma by either 1) avoiding the issue altogether or 2) revising LDS history so as to downplay the significance of polygamy in Mormonism's past. The LDS Church–published *Deseret News 2001-2002 Church Almanac* provides a prime example of the first option in its "Historical Listing of General Authorities" section, where all past presidents are listed.[87]

Each is given a brief biography. But only the monogamists have a wife listed: George Albert Smith (died 1951) and onward. Polygamist presidents Brigham Young, John Taylor, Wilford Woodruff, Lorenzo Snow, Joseph F. Smith, and Heber J. Grant have no wives or marriages mentioned *at all*. Joseph Smith's entry, however, does include the following: "Married Emma Hale Jan. 18, 1827." But none of his other wives are noted.

An example of the second option—the revisionist—appeared as recently as 1997–1998 in the form of *Teachings of Presidents of the Church: Brigham Young*. This volume, which is based on select teachings of Young, makes no mention of polygamy. The publication lists only Young's first wife, Miriam Works. After noting Works's death, it then says Young married Mary Ann Angell in 1834 (page vii), making it appear as if the widower, Brigham Young, remarried only once. The volume subsequently says that "six children were born into their family" (page 4).

Nowhere, however, does it mention the more than 50 additional women Young married or the approximately four dozen children he fathered by them. Such omissions were so glaring that the *Salt Lake City Tribune* ran a story on the book.[88]

And references to polygamy that appeared in Young's sermons were deleted in the excerpt contained in the manual.[89] Ron Priddis, vice president of Signature Books, who published the work, noted that "about 10 percent of the quotes are overtly lifted out of context, with about another 10 percent that are more subtly altered."[90] Craig Manscill, chairman of the writing committee for the manual, admitted the following:

> Was it in the material that we reviewed? Oh, it was there. And did we ellipse in certain places? Of course we did. But we were following what our leaders had asked us to do. [91]

Despite these alterations to LDS history, LDS elder Merrill C. Oaks had the temerity to tell attendees of the 1998 semiannual LDS General Conference that the Brigham Young book provided "wonderful continuity and agreement" with "current prophets."[92] Oaks, of course, neglected to mention that the agreement on marriage issues was only as a result of significant editing of Brigham Young's remarks.

Controversial Concealment

Similar tactics were used in *The Truth About the Church of Jesus Christ of Latter-day Saints,* a pamphlet published by the LDS Church's Public Affairs Department. This publication, which is often given to non-Mormons, reads,

> During the early years in Utah, some members of the Church practiced polygamy, patterned after similar Old Testament practices, which they considered to be a religious principle revealed by God to the Church founder, Joseph Smith. In 1890 Church President Wilford Woodruff announced the end of the Church's practice of polygamy. No one practicing polygamy today can be a member of the Church.[93]

First, polygamy was not practiced just "[d]uring the early years in Utah." It was an integral part of Mormonism from *before* the LDS migration to Utah (1847) until several years *after* the Manifesto (1890). And plural marriage was not confined to Utah. It was practiced by Mormons in Ohio, Missouri, Illinois, Canada, and Mexico.

Second, "some members" is hardly an accurate accounting of how many Mormons participated in polygamy. All high-ranking leaders were involved. According to the *Encyclopedia of Mormonism*, "studies suggest a maximum of from 20% to 25% of LDS adults were members of polygamous households."[94]

Third, LDS polygamy was not "patterned" after Old Testament practices. In the ancient Near East, polygamy was not illegal. And as we saw earlier, nowhere in the Old Testament is polygamy linked with any mandates to practice it. Moreover, also as already noted, the Old Testament prohibited marriage to either two sisters or a mother and daughter.

Fourth, although it is true that Woodruff "announced the end" of polygamy as a practice, this is only a half-truth. Mormon leaders did not cease practicing plural marriage until many years after the 1890 Manifesto. Historical evidence suggests that it may have been adopted merely as a temporary, stop-gap solution that LDS leaders intended to repeal after statehood had been secured.[95]

The Manifesto's wording, for instance, and the way leaders publicly released it differed from every other "revelation" that had ever been given to the Saints.[96] The Manifesto even included false statements reminiscent of Smith's denials of polygamy. Consider the following excerpt, which can be found in the current Doctrine and Covenants 132:

> [They] allege that plural marriages are still being solemnized and that forty or more such marriages have been contracted in Utah since last June or during the past year, also that in public discourses the leaders of the Church have taught, encouraged and urged the continuance of the practice of polygamy. I, therefore, as President of the Church of Jesus Christ of Latter-day Saints, do hereby, in the most solemn manner, declare that these charges are false. We are not teaching polygamy or plural marriage, nor permitting any person to enter into its practice, and I deny that either forty or any other number of plural marriages have during that period been solemnized in our Temples or in any other place in the Territory.

In reality, the LDS church had for years been doing exactly what this statement is denying. Like Taylor, Young, and Smith before him, Woodruff apparently saw no problem in saying one thing publicly while privately behaving otherwise. He himself continued practicing plural marriage after 1890, as did many other Saints. Supporting such an assertion are numerous historical records of more than 200 plural marriages contracted *after* the Manifesto was issued.[97]

The Smoot Hearings

Much of the above information about LDS deception came out during the Senate subcommittee hearings on, and debate over, Reed Smoot (1904–1907). This LDS leader had been elected senator in 1903, but various politicians were concerned about LDS polygamy and Smoot's loyalty to America. Consequently, hearings were held to determine what was going on in Utah and Smoot's involvement with it.

The first witness called was LDS president Joseph F. Smith. He confirmed that some church leaders had been violating federal laws by living with their plural wives and marrying additional women in direct disobedience to the Manifesto. Smith even defended his own illegal cohabitation with five wives:

> I have cohabited with my wives—not openly, that is, not in a manner that I thought would be offensive to my neighbors—but I have acknowledged them; I have visited them.[98]

What Smith did not reveal was how he had encouraged others to do likewise.[99] While serving under Wilford Woodruff, he performed the plural marriage of Abraham H. Cannon to Lillian Hamlin in 1896—a marriage that occurred because Woodruff had told Cannon in 1894 that he could take a plural wife with God's blessings.[100] Under president Lorenzo Snow, Smith continued to approve of plural marriages.[101]

Then, during his own administration, Smith approved two polygamous unions solemnized in Mexico by Mormon authority Alexander F. MacDonald. In fact, when presented with MacDonald's marriage records by Orson Pratt Brown (LDS bishop in the Mexican colonies), Smith said the work had been "duly authorized" by him. He told Brown to make sure the records stayed in Mexico "so that a search in Salt Lake City could not unearth the records if federal marshals were to get permission to look for just such materials."[102] Further, as late as 1903 he sent a letter to Anthony

W. Ivins authorizing a plural marriage.[103] He ended up giving tacit approval to at least 63 plural marriages from 1902 to 1904.[104]

But the public received a different story.[105] Smith's testimony included evasive answers, half-truths, and responses wherein he claimed not to recall his own statements, meetings with LDS leaders, the words of other Mormon authorities, and documents being circulated throughout the church.[106] Smith even denied knowledge of the beliefs and practices of LDS missionaries and elders![107]

The LDS president additionally used narrowly-defined words to obscure facts. For example, he claimed not to "know" certain plural wives of an LDS apostle, only to quickly admit he had *seen* them.[108] He then said the Manifesto was not a "law" of the church, only to subsequently state that it was a *rule* of the church.[109] When pressed, however, Smith admitted that he had broken not only U.S. laws (contrary to biblical revelations about obedience to the government), but also God's laws (as given in the 1890 Manifesto).[110]

"To Protect the Church"

Oddly, today's Mormons seem to have no problem with the illegal actions and lies of Smith or any other LDS polygamists. Modern Latter-day Saints usually equate such actions with the sporadic law-breaking by God's people that is seen in the Old Testament—for example, when the God-fearing midwives in Exodus 1:15-20 refused to murder the sons of Hebrew women, then lied to Pharaoh about it.

But this justification is flawed since the two situations are not analogous. In the case of the Hebrew midwives, the government was seeking to compel God's people to do something sinful (murder). They could only disobey. Murder has always been, and always will be, wrong. No divine revelation had been given to the midwives that murder was now mandated (or, in the LDS context, monogamy is now mandated). Finally, the Hebrew midwives were in a life-or-death situation. They were *compelled* to disobey the laws and lie based on a moral imperative—saving life. (It was akin to what people in World War II Germany did when they told the Nazis that no Jews were hidden in their basements.)

Decades ago, before modern LDS apologists, Mormons had no need to justify Smith's actions. They simply believed that he "had to say what he did in Washington to protect the Church."[111] Other LDS authorities, in seeking to protect the church before the Senate subcommittee, acted with equal disreputability. Mormon testimony was both absurd and humorous.[112] Apostle John Henry Smith, for example, could not remember much of anything after 1890, including how many of his children had been born since that year.[113]

And then there was LDS polygamist George Reynolds, who claimed to not know when his own daughter had been born, her age, or when she had become a plural wife. He also could not recall when he found out about her marriage, and said that after he did find out about it, he never asked her anything regarding it. He could not even remember *why* he had chosen not to question her.[114] Reynolds further said that since 1890 he had spoken neither for, nor against, polygamy—to anyone! And that he had *never in his life* preached either for, or against, polygamy.[115]

The Manifesto—A Camouflage?

It was obvious to the Committee on Privileges and Elections that the LDS hierarchy had for many years been practicing, encouraging, and solemnizing polygamy. The Manifesto, according to Walter M. Wolfe (a teacher for Brigham Young College and Brigham Young Academy), had been a ruse. During his testimony Wolfe stated that apostle John Henry Smith had told him, "'Brother Wolfe, don't you know that the manifesto is only a trick to beat the devil at his own game?'"[116] Wolfe also revealed that the Manifesto was being used by high-ranking LDS leaders as an excuse to bar undeserving males from entering into plural marriage, while at the same time giving an opportunity "for worthy men to take more wives."[117]

Not surprisingly, the Senate committee voted seven to five *against* accepting Smoot as a senator. But by the time this report was debated before the full Senate in 1907, Smoot already had been in Congress for several years. He had formed political alliances, no doubt made quid pro quo agreements with various congressmen, and most importantly, during a private meeting he had convinced U.S. president Teddy Roosevelt of his innocence. So when the full Senate voted, Smoot came out on top and retained his seat.

But what was not known at that time was that Smoot had lied under oath. He claimed he had never heard a discussion of plural marriage in meetings of the apostles and had never himself "promulgated or advised the promulgation of the practice of polygamy."[118] In truth, however, Smoot had been present at 16 pre-1904 meetings in which polygamy was discussed by apostles. The meetings included a January 1902 gathering during which Smoot said that plural marriage "if universally practiced would save the world much sorrow and distress."[119]

Then, in October 1903, Smoot was present when LDS leader Marriner W. Merrill told three apostles to marry plural wives. Moreover, in 1904 Smoot advised the First Presidency to have post-Manifesto plural wives hide in order to avoid arrest.[120] Yet it was during this very same year that Smoot told the Senate he had never heard a discussion about plural marriage in the Temple.

Many Mormons, as it turned out, continued to *illegally* practice polygamy in direct violation of the 1890 Manifesto—even during and after the Smoot hearings. Approximately 262 additional plural marriages occured between October 1890 and December 1910.[121] And as we noted, LDS president Joseph F. Smith himself tacitly approved many of these.

In the end, however, the Smoot hearings basically forced LDS leaders to finally begin adherence to the Manifesto. It was the beginning of drastic steps, such as widespread excommunications, to curtail polygamy among fellow Mormons. Today's Latter-day Saints are left with the unenviable task of having to put a positive spin not only on polygamy, but on the actions of their leaders.

Gordon B. Hinckley, for instance, did his best to downplay polygamy on *Larry King Live*. He stated that only 2 to 5 percent of Mormons in early Utah practiced it. [122] Then he added, "It was a very limited practice; carefully safeguarded. In 1890, that practice was discontinued."[123] Hinckley also condemned polygamy as illegal in *Ensign* magazine (1998), saying that today's polygamists "are not members of this Church....They are in violation of the civil law. They know they are in violation of the law. They are subject to its penalties."[124]

However, Hinckley, has never publicly addressed several relevant questions. Was it proper for LDS prophets and apostles to disobey the laws of the land throughout the 1800s and into the early twentieth century?

If yes, then why was it acceptable *for them* to disobey anti-polygamy laws, but not acceptable *for others* to disobey those same laws today? If no, then were they in sin and did this disqualify them from being leaders? Finally, if the Manifesto was a revelation to be obeyed, then why was it disobeyed by LDS president Joseph F. Smith and so many of his apostles?

FINAL OBSERVATIONS

Despite all LDS efforts, polygamy cannot be justified from the Bible (again, see more on this issue in appendix A). Rather than appealing to solid biblical exegesis or historical fact, Mormon pro-polygamy arguments are based primarily on half-truths, misapplication of biblical texts, straw-man arguments, historical revisionism, and silence. The long history of LDS deception and ungodly behavior surrounding polygamy also suggests that it has had nothing to do with God.

I hope this chapter has assisted honest truth-seekers to understand more clearly the issue of polygamy, its place in the Bible, the Christian view of it, and how some Mormons have sought to defend it. Still unanswered, however, is the way in which all of these issues relate to one of the most fundamental questions now being asked: Are Mormons Christians? This delicate topic will be approached in our final chapter.

THE "CHRISTIAN" QUESTION

[T]he accusation that we are not Christians is probably the most commonly heard criticism of the LDS Church and its doctrines today. Why would anyone say such a thing? Isn't the name of our church The Church of Jesus Christ of Latter-day Saints? Do we not worship Christ? Is not the Book of Mormon another testament of Jesus Christ? How could anyone seriously doubt that Latter-day Saints are Christians? [1]

—Stephen E. Robinson, BYU professor, 1998

I landed in Salt Lake City and was met at the baggage claim by a new Mormon online friend of mine, who had volunteered to pick me up and drive me to my hotel. We had e-mailed each other countless times and discussed all kinds of issues from the veracity of the Book of Mormon to the trustworthiness of Joseph Smith. He was, and still is, a faithful Temple Mormon. Most exciting to me, however, was the day we had planned. I was going to go over to his house and enjoy a backyard barbeque with his whole family.

Their modest home was a joyous place to be—comfortable, cozy, and full of obvious love. And they had laid out a terrific spread of food for me—hot dogs, hamburgers, fresh-cut vegetables, chips, and copious amounts of soda. We ate and drank until none of us could move. Then, we listened to my self-produced CD of inspirational Christian music. Afterward, they gathered all of the brothers together (quite a few of them of varying ages) and sang for me as a chorus the beloved LDS hymn "If You Could Hie to Kolob." I can still remember the look of love and pride on the face of their wonderfully kind mother.

It was a day I will never forget. It contradicted everything I had ever heard about Mormons. They were, from everything I could see, just about as "Christian" as anyone can get. And yet, theologically speaking, we continued to part company, with very different views about God, Jesus, salvation, and eternity. I confess that after all of this time, I still have not been able to sort it all out. And so I have decided to write this final chapter as an expression of my thoughts on, and an examination of, the most troubling of all questions, at least to me: Are Mormons Christian?

☷ ☷ ☷

What is a Christian? The answer to this question often depends on who you ask. Some say a Christian is anyone who goes to church. Others think a Christian is anyone who subscribes to one or more teachings traceable to Jesus. The responses are seemingly endless. And most of them are usually intertwined with intense emotions.

Consequently, it is with great hesitation that I even approach such a volatile issue. Yet this subject deserves attention because whether or not Mormons are Christian is linked to gaining a better understanding how all of us fit into God's plan and how we relate to his way of salvation. My hope is that I will, at the very least, help Mormons and evangelicals understand the varying opinions concerning this topic.

——— MORMON QUOTES ———

"Mormonism is Christianity; Christianity is Mormonism; they are one and the same, and they are not to be distinguished from each other in the minutest detail" (Bruce McConkie, LDS apostle, 1958).[2]

"We are Christians. We want the whole world to know that we are. Sometimes we are accused of not being Christians, but such is not the case" (Hartman Rector Jr., First Council of the Seventy, 1972).[3]

"My message is for those who teach and write and produce films which claim that The Church of Jesus Christ of Latter-day Saints is not a Christian church and that we, the members, are not Christians....I find it difficult to respond without saying that such individuals are uninformed and unfair and not consistent with the spirit of Christian brotherhood" (Boyd K. Packer, LDS apostle, 1998).[4]

A Closer Look

Evangelicals find it difficult to understand how Mormons can call themselves "Christian" when their beliefs differ so radically from those of mainstream believers. How can all of us be "Christian" if Mormons neither recognize, nor worship, the same kind of God? Someone *must* be wrong. To say otherwise, at least to evangelicals, is a striking inconsistency. It would be more consistent for Mormons to say that either 1) they *alone* are Christians, or 2) they represent a new religion that *sprang* from Christianity.

Jan Shipps, history professor and renowned expert on Mormonism, agrees that Latter-day Saints might, at best, be able to *trace their roots* to Christianity. Thereafter, however, they should consider themselves members of "a new religion."[5] On the other hand, Shipps appears to contradict herself in her unwillingness to excise them from Christianity because, in her opinion, to do so would be both "mean-spirited" and "wrong."[6] Therefore, despite the fact that Mormons "have an entirely different understanding of deity," she still sees LDS Church members as merely "different kinds of Christians."[7]

Most mainstream Christian denominations, however, are united in their outright rejection of Mormonism.

Something to Consider: In 2001, the Roman Catholic Church, which recognizes the baptisms of most denominations, "decided that Mormons who convert to Catholicism must be rebaptized." The Church determined that the LDS view on the nature of God "was too different from its own," according to *L'Osservatore Romano,* the Vatican's daily newspaper. Most Protestants agree. The Southern Baptists, for instance, "evangelize" Mormons, which implies that Latter-day Saints are in need of salvation. The Lutheran Church, Missouri Synod, has asserted that Mormonism is not Christian. And the Presbyterian Church (USA) published a 1990 study showing where Mormons diverge theologically from Protestants. They subsequently issued guidelines in 1995 "stating that the Mormons were not 'within the historic apostolic tradition of the Christian Church.'"[8]

Their reason for this is inextricably linked to the fact that Mormons worship a differently defined "Christ" than the one preached throughout Christendom. This has been admitted by LDS leaders.[9] The truth of this admission is quite apparent. For example, Mormons are instructed to *not* pray to Jesus, which is completely unlike mainstream Christianity, wherein prayers to Christ are desirable and proper.

Christian prayers to Christ are considered appropriate because of the "personal relationship" Christians have with Christ. LDS apostle Bruce McConkie, however, adamantly discouraged prayers to Christ during a 1982 BYU speech that is still available from the BYU "Speeches and Devotionals" Internet site.[10] This is a drastic departure from Christianity, which has always included the freedom to address Christ directly in prayer.

After Jesus' resurrection, for example, Stephen prayed to him (Acts 7:59), as did Paul (2 Corinthians 12:8-9), and John (Revelation 22:20). Jesus himself said that after his departure, his disciples would be free to ask anything of him. A literal translation of the oldest Greek copies of John 14:14 reads, "If anything ye ask me in the name of me, I will do."[11]

Mormons, as previously noted, also view the Godhead differently. In 1995, LDS apostle Dallin Oaks noted that Christians see God as an entirely different kind of being than the kind of being acknowledged as God throughout Christendom.[12] "[We] testify that God the Father is not just a spirit but is a glorified person with a tangible body, as is his resurrected Son, Jesus Christ," said Oaks.[13]

Christian Versus Mormon Versus Apostate

Rejecting Mormonism as not Christian may sound harsh, but it all began when early LDS leaders themselves distanced Mormonism from mainstream Christianity. The so-called Great Apostasy highlights the reason why most evangelicals feel that they cannot view Mormonism as Christian. In other words, the real division between Mormonism and Christianity was erected by Mormons. They were the ones to initially separate their church from, in their view, *apostate* Christendom.

Since Mormonism's earliest years, Latter-day Saints have been leveling attacks against the faith of those in Christendom—beginning with Joseph Smith, who said all denominations were wrong and all Christian creeds were an "abomination" (see chapter 1). As an 1987 LDS *Ensign* article explained about Smith's era, "God the Father and his Son were greatly displeased with the doctrines being taught in the churches."[14]

For decades LDS leaders not only railed against mainstream Christianity as an institution, but denounced Christian doctrines, pastors, priests, churches, and believers (see note 15 for quotes from various leaders).[15] Mormons often downplay the gravity of these remarks by dismissing them as mere shadows of past animosity. And to be fair, overtly harsh condemnations have not only ceased, but have been replaced with a more acceptable call for toleration among rank-and-file Mormons.[16]

As far back as 1987, LDS authorities themselves were starting to qualify their criticisms of Christendom: "In rejecting false creeds and unauthorized ordinances, we do not pass judgment on people."[17] Still, however, well into the 1980s LDS leaders were attacking Christians as believers in a false god whom they worship "in vain," followers of the "precepts of men," and persons disconnected from the "*real* God."[18]

One very disturbing remark was made in 1984 by BYU professor Kent P. Jackson, who said that "Satan sits in the place of God in Christianity," although not "all that is in it is satanic."[19] Given the seriousness of such judgments, it is difficult to hear Mormons claim that they do not, nor have they ever, attacked anyone's church or religion.[20]

Notable and Quotable: "President Hinckley has asked us to be tolerant of those of other faiths: 'We must not be clannish. We must never adopt a holier-than-thou attitude. We must not be self-righteous. We must be magnanimous, and open, and friendly. We can keep our faith. We can practice our religion. We can cherish our method of worship without being offensive to others.' These attitudes, coupled with a sincere Christlike love, patience, and trust, are the answers to sharing the gospel."[21]

And despite decades of harsh comments, Latter-day Saints continue to argue that they, unlike mainstream Christians, do not tear down the faith of others.[22] In a 2003 Internet post, for instance, one faithful Mormon voiced this common response, while at the same time implying that Mormons behave better than traditional Christians:

> I can't remember one instance when my priesthood Quorum put together a project to stand out in front of the first Baptist church to hand out tracts on the evils of the Baptist cult. We have not had any classes outlining the evils of mainstream [C]hristianity yet....I see no comparison between Mormonism's uplifting message and the hateful propaganda of the anti-Mormon activists.[23]

But such an argument is at best contradictory to the evidence, and at worst, disingenuous. Why? Because Mormons do not have to hold "classes" to outline "the evils of the Baptist cult." They are repeatedly taught at LDS General Conferences and through LDS publications that Christendom is swimming in a veritable ocean of false beliefs.

"The Only True and Living Church"?

There is no room for Mormons to misunderstand the LDS view of Christianity. The Book of Mormon (1 Nephi 13:4-9, 24-29; 14:10-13) teaches that there are only two churches: 1) the false church of the devil, and 2) the true church of the Lamb.[24] The latter church is Mormonism. The former church is represented by nearly all else, including *all* of Christendom's denominations (see D&C sections 19-21).[25] LDS apostle B.H. Roberts described this kingdom of evil as "the whole empire of Satan."[26]

In other words, Mormons are in God's true church, while all mainstream Christians fall into the world system known as the devil's church (or Satan's kingdom). LDS leaders have for decades preached the reality of this scenario—making sure to note, however, that God still might be "pleased" with many persons "born under an environment that has led them into those churches which are not of God."[27]

Today, anyone can verify this ongoing Mormon belief by simply going to his or her nearest LDS bookstore and purchasing a current edition of any number of books—for example, *Mormon Doctrine*, which declares that "virtually all the millions of apostate Christendom have abased themselves before the mythical throne of a mythical Christ."[28]

Or a Mormon could just visit the LDS Church's lds.org Web site and download dozens of articles with titles such as "Strange Creeds of Christendom," "Apostasy and Restoration," "The Great Apostasy as Seen by Eusebius," or "Early Signs of the Apostasy."[29]

These articles, some of which date back to the 1970s, are united in saying that "Christ's church was gradually lost and that the churches today do not teach the doctrine taught by the Master."[30] Consider BYU professor Stephen Robinson's 1988 remarks about traditional Christianity, which are still available online for Mormons:

> The historical abominable church of the devil is that apostate church that replaced true Christianity in the first and second centuries, teaching the philosophies of men mingled with scriptures. It dethroned God in the church and replaced him with man by denying the principle of revelation and turning instead to human intellect. As the product of human agency, its creeds were an abomination to the Lord, for they were idolatry: men worshipping the creations, not of their own hands, but of their own minds.[31]

And for the benefit of Mormons studying Scripture, the "Topical Guide" in LDS copies of the Bible lists 39 alleged biblical references to "Apostasy of the Early Christian Church."[32] This is in accord with the ongoing condemnation of Christianity built into the very core of Mormonism as a central tenet—the doctrine of the restoration.

Although overtly hostile remarks from LDS pulpits are now rare, the ungodly portrait of Christendom that LDS leaders have consistently painted since 1830 has not changed. Mormons still view Christendom as nothing less than a fallen, apostate, factious network of persons who have no authority to act in God's name. Bruce McConkie explained it in 1975:

> 1820 [the alleged year of the First Vision], like the 1,400 years which preceded it, was one in which darkness covered the earth and gross darkness the minds of the people....That gospel preached by Paul, and for which Peter died, was no longer proclaimed from the pulpits of Christendom....In short, apostasy reigned supreme; it was universal, complete, all pervading. The religion of the lowly Nazarene

was nowhere to be found. All sects, parties, and denominations had gone astray. Satan rejoiced and his angels laughed. Such were the social and religious conditions of the day.[33]

An Interesting Fact: LDS children are taught about the Great Apostasy of Christianity just as evangelical children are commonly taught about such things as the Tower of Babel, Noah's flood, or Christ's resurrection. This is evident from the LDS Primary Instruction text for children, which reads, "Remind the children that after the Apostasy, the gospel of Jesus Christ was no longer on the earth. The priesthood was not on the earth either, so no one could properly be baptized, be confirmed, or partake of the sacrament. The gospel and the priesthood had to be restored in the latter days."[34]

Mormons still declare that their church is "the only true and living church upon the face of the whole earth," with which God is "well pleased" (D&C 1:30). This statement, however, betrays what evangelicals feel is another LDS misunderstanding—that Christ's "church" is a single, visible, monolithic organization.

Not an Organization

The Bible does not portray the church as Mormons portray it. According to Scripture, all Christians (that is, those who have put their faith in Jesus and trusted him for salvation) *are* the one church. In Matthew 16:18, where Christ says he will build his church, the Greek word for "church" is *ekklēsia*, which means "called out ones."[35] (The term was used by the Greeks for "a body of citizens gathered to discuss affairs of State."[36])

The true "church," therefore, is neither a single denomination nor an isolated group of people. It crosses denominational lines and is made up of Methodists, Catholics, Presbyterians, nondenominationalists, Pentecostals, Lutherans, and others. It is because *all* believers constitute the true church that all Christians can remain unified, yet participate in different denominations.

Put another way, Christ was not saying that his "church" would be an organization. The use of the term *ekklēsia* suggests that he was building up a group of chosen persons whom God had "called out" of the world. Hence, no denomination or organization is the church of Christ. *We* (all true believers) are the church of Christ.[37] (Significantly, *ekklēsia* is even used in Acts 19:32,41 for a riotous mob—definitely no organization.)

Even more compelling is how *ekklēsia* is used in the Septuagint (the Greek translation of the Old Testament) and other relevant New Testament passages. It designates either all of Israel when called together, or a specific group of God's people who represent the entire nation (Deuteronomy 4:10, 23:2; Acts 7:38; Hebrews 2:12). Again, the clear message is that God's church is not an organization.

Priesthood Authority

According to LDS belief, a church is only a true church if God

1. "establishes it"
2. "authorizes it"
3. "recognizes its works as valid and binding"[38]

The irrefutable sign that these qualifications are present is possession by that church of what Mormons call priesthood authority. This authority, which Mormons claim is the authority to act on behalf of God toward man, is supposedly available only within Mormonism.

The LDS Church received its authority, as the story goes, during Joseph Smith's day. It came in the form of the Aaronic Priesthood (the lesser one) and the Melchizedek Priesthood (the higher one). The former was given to Smith by John the Baptist, who allegedly appeared to him. The latter was imparted by Peter, James, and John, who also paid Smith a visit. Smith subsequently introduced these priesthoods to all LDS males within his church.

The importance of the LDS priesthoods cannot be overstated. Only by priesthood authority, which Mormons claim to alone possess, can people legitimately "act in God's name for the salvation of the human family.... [T]hey can be authorized to preach the gospel, administer the ordinances of salvation, and govern God's kingdom on earth."[39] Such authority was lost after Christ's apostles died, and it remained lost until Joseph Smith.[40]

Here is where we find some of the most significant LDS accusations against mainstream Christianity. Consider the LDS answer to the question "Why Do We Need the Priesthood on the Earth?"

> We must have priesthood authority to act in the name of God when performing the sacred ordinances of the gospel, such as baptism, confirmation, administration of the sacrament, and temple marriage. If a man does not have the priesthood, even though he may be sincere, the Lord will not recognize ordinances he performs (see Matthew 7:21-23). These important ordinances must be performed on the earth by men holding the priesthood....Another reason the priesthood is needed on the earth is so we can understand the will of the Lord and carry out his purposes.[41]

At first glance, the meaning of these words may go unnoticed. But they bring to light the *current* LDS teaching that the ministers and priests of Christendom do not have proper authority to

1. effectively baptize converts

2. administer the sacrament of communion

3. confirm people in a truly saving faith.[42]

This threefold teaching explains why Mormons believe that

1. all non-LDS Christian baptisms are invalid

2. no traditional Christian has yet experienced the new spiritual birth or received the gift of the Holy Ghost

3. non-Mormons cannot achieve true forgiveness of sins

These accusations, in fact, are precisely what high-ranking LDS officials have been articulating in recent years (see quotes in note 43).[43] So, although modern Mormons now express themselves using more politically correct verbiage, the Church's underlying perspective on traditional Christianity remains unchanged.

In the eyes of evangelicals, mainstream Christians were first attacked by Mormons, who still say we are the ones lacking valid baptisms, the gift of the Holy Ghost, and true forgiveness of sins. From the orthodox Christian perspective, then, our ongoing unwillingness to admit Mormons into the household of faith is first a defensive response to the ever-present LDS accusation embodied in the Great Apostasy. Traditional Christians, in other words, are making a *counter*charge against Mormonism by saying that it is not Christian.

EVANGELICAL THOUGHTS

Despite the LDS stand on orthodox Christianity, Mormons often fail to connect all of the dots, so to speak, especially in public discourse. To go ahead and "connect the dots" otherwise would lead them down the same verbally antagonistic path their forefathers walked. To avoid this, LDS apologists and Mormon leaders have therefore been almost forced to agree that all professing Christians are "Christian," but that they practice a different "form" of Christianity.[44]

This seems terribly inconsistent and illogical to evangelicals. Mormons and traditional Christians are obviously in two very different camps. One or the other may be Christian, but not both—not if we define "Christian" as one who holds to the *essential* doctrines of Christianity as expressed in the creedal understandings of the Bible (for example, that there is one true God, as opposed to one true Godhead—see chapter 4).

As for the creeds, these were fashioned during a time when *everyone* was competing for the title "Christian": Gnostics, Monophysites, Sabellians, Docetists—the list goes on and on. All of them could not have been "Christian," since they were all teaching different things about God and Jesus Christ. So God led the leaders of the church to step in. "What is the true faith here?" they asked. Their codified answers in the creeds left Mormons, and many others, out of God's flock. As an evangelical, I see no reason (rationally or biblically) to think that God allowed a false system to inherit his precious church—the church set up by Christ himself.

The creeds, of course, are rejected by Mormons, which is why they can so easily call themselves Christian. In their eyes, *they* are the truest

Christians. *Their* church, as the restored church, is the true church, complete with Christ's pure doctrines. To Mormons, we evangelicals and other mainstream Christians are the ones in error.

This leads us back to our two fundamental questions: 1) What is a Christian? 2) Whatever a Christian is, do Mormons fit into that category? There are actually two ways to answer these questions: from a narrow viewpoint, and from a broad viewpoint.

The Narrow Viewpoint

As noted in chapter 4, the councils held throughout the early centuries of the church were called specifically to formalize and finalize the Christian faith. The creeds these councils drafted were the first official statements outlining the world's newest religion. Prior to the earliest creeds—the Apostles' (A.D. 215–340), the Niceno–Constantinopolitan (A.D. 325 and 381), and the Chalcedonian (A.D. 451)—there existed no widely accepted or official codification of the faith. The New Testament, at best, contains only the beginnings of creedal formulations and ideas (for example, 1 Corinthians 8:6; 15:3-4).

The creeds define "Christianity" for the world. They present "Christianity" as it exists in this space–time continuum—like it or not. Joseph Smith, however, came along and basically declared, "No. The creeds do *not* accurately define 'Christianity.' God himself has appeared to me, and I will define it for you as he reveals it to me, his latter-day prophet."[45] This is why early Mormons stated so blatantly that Christianity was wrong, corrupt, satanic, and dead.

Mormons and traditional Christians cannot even agree on one of the most crucial of all Christian beliefs—the identity of Christ.[46] As far back as 1977, high-ranking LDS leader Bernard P. Brockbank acknowledged, "It is true that many of the Christian churches worship a different Jesus Christ than is worshipped by the Mormons."[47]

The narrow viewpoint of what a "Christian" is, is based on the same principle used by others to determine what is a "Muslim," a "Buddhist," a "Hindu," or a "Jew." All world religions, in fact, are defined by specific beliefs as outlined in various statements of faith. And adherence to those beliefs makes a person a Buddhist, a Muslim, a Hindu, a Jew, or something else.

To be a Buddhist, one must believe certain things. Likewise, to be a Hindu or a Muslim, one must believe certain things. If one does not believe the necessary doctrines, then one is not a member of that world religion.

So it is with Christianity. Shortly after its beginning, everyone began asking, "What is Christianity?" The faith was then formally defined—and from that time on, holding a certain set of beliefs has been necessary for one to be accepted under the wide umbrella of Christianity. (Of course, there are variations in thought under that umbrella—hence, denominations.)

But for the most part, generally speaking, all Christians hold to what are known as the "essentials" of the faith—doctrines that relate directly to one's identification of, and relationship to, God. These essentials, from a logical standpoint, most certainly include the nature and identity of the God we worship, and the nature and identity of the Christ by whom we are saved.

In comparison to Christianity, Mormonism advocates opposing essentials: for example, many gods (rather than one God); Jesus as a being organized from "intelligence" (rather than an uncreated, eternal Son); an atonement that provides only the opportunity for us to achieve the *reward* of "eternal life" (rather than providing "eternal life" as an utterly free gift).

So from the narrow viewpoint, no—Mormons are not Christian. Taking such a position, of course, rests on accepting the creeds as legitimate expressions of Christianity. But to reject the creeds as standard definitions of Christianity would be as wrong and illogical as rejecting the official definitions of any other world religion. Moreover, a legitimate question is, Does it make sense that God would allow Jesus to die for our sins, establish his church, and send out his faithful followers after the glorious resurrection...only to then allow the world to be plunged into spiritual darkness through the creeds?

By way of analogy, it would be as if someone were to announce that he was an enlightened teacher called to restore true Buddhism as taught by Siddhartha Gautama (Buddha)—then his teachings drastically contradicted what had for centuries been taught as Buddhism (in its main forms). Would Buddhists embrace this teacher and his followers as true Buddhists? That is doubtful.

Or imagine someone proclaiming that he is going to restore *true* Islam, which, he declares, was lost after the death of Muhammad and his followers. But then he proceeds to advocate doctrines opposed to the beliefs that Muslims have always attributed to Muhammad. And to make matters worse, the new Muslim prophet also condemns the Qur'an as a book full of errors—a book that has lost many "plain and precious" truths. Would Muslims around the globe acknowledge this new prophet and his followers as fellow Muslims? Probably not.

Interestingly, the Muslim world actually does have this sort of theological thorn in its side—the Nation of Islam (NOI), now under the direction of Louis Farrakhan. The media, mainstream Muslims, and world religious leaders all reject the NOI as being part of Islam. Why? Because it diverges significantly from Islamic beliefs.

According to Ibrahim Hooper of the Council on American–Islamic Relations, the NOI is definitely "outside mainstream Muslim beliefs because of Farrakhan's racist views."[48] According to the *Los Angeles Times,* the NOI has "always been regarded by serious Muslim organizations as a fringe group of heretics."[49]

Yet Mormons expect to be treated differently by mainstream Christians than the Nation of Islam is treated by traditional Muslims. LDS apostle Boyd K. Packer has said,

- "It is one thing to say that we are not their kind of Christian. It is another entirely to characterize us as not being Christian at all."

- "There is more to it than simply writing a definition of what a Christian is and then rejecting anyone who does not conform to it."[50]

But imagine the response from Muslims if Louis Farrakhan were ever to declare, "It is one thing to say that we are not their kind of Muslim. It is quite another to characterize us as not being Muslims at all"—or "There is more to it than simply writing a definition of what a Muslim is and then rejecting anyone who does not conform to it." To Muslims such arguments would be no more legitimate than those offered by Packer are to many evangelicals.

The Broad Viewpoint

Having made all of the above clear, it would be negligent of me not to mention that a legitimate argument can indeed be made for calling Latter-day Saints "Christian." How? Clearly, they do not follow a religious leader of any other world religion (for example, Buddha). Nor do they look to a decidedly non-Christian god of another world religion (for example, Shiva of Hinduism). Mormons do in fact seek salvation within the historical person known to the world as Jesus of Nazareth, as they see him.

This seems to be one sense in which Mormons see themselves as Christian. For instance, in 1996 LDS apostle Joseph B. Wirthlin cited the *American Heritage Dictionary* as saying that a Christian is "'one who professes *belief* in Jesus as the Christ'…and 'one who *lives* according to the teachings of Jesus.'"[51] According to such a broad definition, Mormons would have to be considered Christian. Their doctrines certainly did not spring from any other world religion.

This does not mean that Mormons are "Christian" in an objective theological sense. It merely means there exists no other category in which they can be placed. Allowing for the broad viewpoint, however, opens up a large can of worms. What about the Branch Davidians, who called themselves "Christian" but stored illegal weapons, abused children, and murdered law enforcement officers?[52] What about The Family, a "Christian" group that currently engages in premarital "sharing" with multiple partners and allows adultery with consent?[53] How about so-called "Christian" witches?[54] There are also a significant number of liberal "Christians" (for example, John Shelby Spong, members of the Jesus Seminars, and others) who deny the virgin birth, the deity of Jesus, and Christ's physical resurrection. And let us not forget "Christian" nudists.[55]

Should all of these groups be called "Christian"? Apparently so, according to BYU professors Daniel C. Peterson and Stephen D. Ricks, who have stated that if "anyone claims to see in Jesus of Nazareth a personage of unique and preeminent authority, that individual should be considered Christian."[56] In all fairness, such a position is often taken by secular scholars, who broadly sort out religions into general categories.

Along this line, particularly interesting is a comment Peterson made to this author in late 2003:

> I don't mind being called a heretical Christian, or a Christian whose theology is unbiblical and mistaken. We can debate that. But I do very much object when some say that I'm not a Christian at all.[57]

Likewise, LDS apologist Barry Bickmore has said, "[C]all us 'heretical Christians,' or 'apostate Christians,' or whatever. Our point is that 'Christianity' is the general category in which we fit."[58] Bickmore (and Peterson) offer an option that is attractive to evangelicals since it would be proper, broadly speaking, to refer to Mormons as "heretical" Christians. Christian scholar Robert Bowman has defined "heresy" as follows:

> Doctrine which is erroneous in such a way that Christians must divide themselves as a church from all who teach or accept it; those adhering to heresy [heretics] are assumed to be lost, although Christians are unable to make definitive judgments on this matter.[59]

Among traditional Christians, this is a standard and widely accepted understanding of heresy. Of course, if it were to be accepted in reference to Mormons, from the evangelical point of view little would change since Scripture instructs believers to 1) separate themselves from false teachers and teachings (Romans 16:17; 2 John 9-11), and 2) firmly oppose heresy (Jude 3). In other words, calling Mormons "heretical Christians" (rather than insisting they are not Christians at all) would still leave evangelicals free to raise concerns about the doctrine and history of Mormonism.

So if Daniel Peterson and Barry Bickmore, for example, have no problem being called "heretical Christians," then I have no problem obliging them. Eventually, we might have some fruitful interaction and at least better understand each other (2 Timothy 2:24-26).

Robert Bowman's definition of heresy also leaves open a theological door that is important to keep ajar—namely, "those adhering to heresy [heretics] are assumed to be lost, although Christians are *unable to make definitive judgments* on this matter."[60] In other words, *some* Mormons may be saved despite their false doctrines (see note 61 for some thoughts on this topic).[61]

LDS RESPONSES

All LDS responses to the "Are Mormons Christian?" question ultimately rest in the Mormon view of priesthood authority and the apostasy. According to LDS thought, Mormonism is the one true church (and hence, Christian) because

- Christ's church went into total apostasy,[62] which caused the "loss of plain and precious doctrinal truths"[63]
- God's "proper priesthood was lost due to the death of the apostles"[64]

A Total Apostasy?

There is little evidence to suggest that a worldwide Christian apostasy necessitated a total restoration of God's church. Mormons, however, see evidence of it everywhere, both in and out of Scripture. The Great Apostasy supposedly "marked the first time in history that the entire world labored in spiritual darkness."[65]

One of the most comprehensive LDS attempts to document the Great Apostasy is Barry Bickmore's *Restoring the Ancient Church* (1999). The historicity of the apostasy, according to Bickmore, is crucial to Mormonism because, "had there been no 'apostasy,' or 'falling away,' from Christ's original Church, there would have been no need for God to restore the Church through Joseph Smith."[66]

False Teachers, False Doctrine

Bickmore, like most Mormons, list several Bible verses that allegedly show how the New Testament writers foresaw an apostasy. These include the warnings about false doctrine and false teachers and apostles in Galatians 1:6-8; 2 Corinthians 11:4,13; 3 John 9-10; and Jude 3-4,17-18.[67] Other passages often cited by Mormons also mirror those quoted and discussed by Bickmore:

- "Peter also warned the saints that 'there shall be false teachers among you, who privily shall bring in damnable heresies, even denying the Lord that bought them....(2 Peter 2:1-2)."[68]

- "Paul spoke of this apostasy ('falling away') when he told the elders at Ephesus that 'after my departing shall grievous wolves enter in among you, not sparing the flock....to draw away disciples after them' (Acts 20:29-30)."[69]

- "Paul had serious concerns about the Church's stability when he wrote to Timothy...(2 Timothy 4:3-5). Notice how Paul entreated Timothy to do *his* duty as an evangelist, but indicated that the Church in general would forsake the faith....Paul intimated that 'all they which are in Asia be turned away from me' (2 Timothy 1:15)—Asia Minor was exactly where most of the Christian converts lived."[70]

- "Paul told the Thessalonians not to worry about Christ coming back...'Let no man deceive you by any means; for that day shall not come, except there come a falling away [Greek *apostasia*] first, and that man of sin be revealed, the son of perdition.' (2 Thessalonians 2:3). This apostasy was already underway....(2 Thessalonians 2:7 NEB). Who was the 'Restrainer' Paul spoke of? When we remember [Acts 20:29-30]...it becomes clear that this was a reference to the Apostles themselves."[71]

None of these verses, however, actually mention a *total* apostasy of Christ's church. They are merely cautions designed to alert believers to the reality of heresies and heretics, both present and future.[72] In Galatians, Paul indicates only that a number of Galatians were being removed "unto another gospel." In Corinthians, Paul simply states that he is concerned about those in the church, fearing that they might have their minds "corrupted from the simplicity that is in Christ" and "might well bear with" someone preaching a false Jesus, gospel, and Spirit. Neither verse prophesies a total apostasy of the church.

John and Jude also issued limited warnings. John, for instance, rather than foretelling a churchwide apostasy, names one false teacher—Diotrephes. Jude refers only to "certain men" who had crept into the church (verse 4) and "mockers" of the faith (verse 18). Nothing in these verses suggests a total apostasy.

In the warning Peter writes, he mentions "false teachers" (2 Peter 2:1-2). But where is there any reference to a totally apostate church? Where does he predict that these false teachers will lead the whole church astray to the point of utter apostasy? Nowhere.

Bickmore's reference to Acts 20:29-30 is equally flawed. Paul mentions an unspecified number of "grievous wolves" who would enter the church in order to "draw away disciples after them." That is the extent of Paul's dire news. It would have been a perfect moment for him to reveal a coming total apostasy. Yet no such revelation is imparted.

Paul Forsaken

As for 2 Timothy 4:3-5, it does indeed include an admonition for Timothy to continue *his* work. However, contrary to Bickmore's assertion, Paul nowhere indicates "that the Church in general would forsake the faith."[73] He does not say "the church." To extend his words here to include the entire Christian church is reading LDS doctrine into the text.

Concerning 2 Timothy 1:15, Paul does state that "all they which are in Asia be turned away from me." But is this Paul's way of saying that all, or nearly all, of the "Christian converts" in Asia Minor had forsaken the faith and were already in apostasy? Not at all. The context of the passage is loyalty and opposition. Notice, Paul did not say that all in Asia had turned away from "the truth," "the gospel," or "Christ's teachings." He said "turned away from me"—in other words, turned from Paul after his arrest and imprisonment.

A reading of the next four verses (15-18) reveals what Paul is discussing. He first mentions two persons, Phygellus and Hermogenes. These men apparently helped solidify the decision by Asian churches to turn their backs on Paul, who had been taken as a prisoner to Rome. Paul then contrasts their conduct with that of Onesiphorus, who "oft refreshed" Paul and "was not ashamed" of his "chains." Of him, the apostle explains, "[W]hen he was in Rome, he sought me out very diligently, and found me." This passage, therefore, has *nothing* to do with the churches falling away into apostasy.[74]

The Antichrist and the "Restrainer"

Only in 2 Thessalonians 2:3 does Paul actually use the word *apostasy* ("falling away"). But even then, it is not characterized as a *total* apostasy, or even one so extensive that God's church would have to be restored.

Moreover, Latter-day Saints tend to overlook the fact that the apostasy to whatever extent predicted in Thessalonians would be accompanied by the unveiling of "that man of sin"—the "son of perdition," usually called Antichrist. Who then is the Antichrist supposed to be?

Most peculiar, however, is Bickmore's interpretation of 2 Thessalonians 2:7. In this verse, he identifies the "Restrainer" (singular)—"he who now letteth," in the Bible text—as the apostles (plural). Although this interpretation validates LDS preconceptions, it cannot be supported from the text. The Greek word used in this verse is *katechōn* ("the restraining one").[75] It can indeed mean "a number of persons representing the same characteristics."[76] But does *katechōn* really provide an undeniably "clear" reference "to the Apostles"? No, it does not.

"Restrainer" could be a reference to "the principle of human government manifest in the Roman state."[77] This interpretation easily fits with Paul's view of law and social authority. The government, to Paul, was "a means of maintaining law and order so that the church may do its work (cf. Romans 13:1-7; Titus 3:1; 1 Peter 2:13,14,17)."[78]

Two final apostasy-related passages cited by Mormons, including Bickmore, are 1 John 2:18 and 2 Thessalonians 2:1-4. They involve the Antichrist. Use of these verses is especially odd from an evangelical perspective. Consider Bickmore's argument surrounding 1 John 2:18:

> (1 John 2:18) Did Jude and John believe it was "the last time" because Christ was about to come back or because the Church was filled with antichrists, and would not long survive?…[I]t was not the "last time" because the Lord was about to return…but because the Antichrist had come and the Church was about to be taken from the earth.[79]

According to Bickmore, then, the advent of the Antichrist marked the "last days," which was a sign of the Great Apostasy.[80] In reality, however, Jude and John described their era as the "last days" because the "last days" began with Jesus' first advent (Hebrews 1:2). We are *still* in the "last days" and will be until Jesus returns. In 1973, LDS president Ezra Taft Benson agreed: "[T]he Bible tells us that in the last days in which we live, the wickedness of the people will become comparable to the wickedness of the people in Noah's day."[81]

So like Jude and John, LDS authorities have said we are in the "last days." They also have given public warnings to Mormons about falling away, into apostasy.[82] Does this not mean that a total LDS apostasy is near?[83] Following Bickmore's logic, Mormons would have to say yes. But such an admission will never be made. Hence, Bickmore's "last days" argument is an inconsistent application of a particular line of reasoning, designed to benefit LDS claims.

One More Passage

Bickmore takes a similar approach to 2 Thessalonians 2:4, which he claims is "[t]he most specific reference to the totality of the apostasy."[84] This verse, of course, speaks of the "son of perdition" who would sit as God "in the temple of God, shewing himself that he is God." Bickmore argues, "It is difficult to imagine how this prophecy was to be fulfilled if the Church was to remain."[85] In truth, however, the prophecy's fulfillment has nothing to do with a total apostasy in centuries immediately after Christ.

First, Paul said that the "son of perdition" would set himself up as God "in the temple of God"—the Jerusalem temple. Early Christians, however, did not meet in the temple, nor do today's mainstream Christians meet in temples. (Ironically, Mormons *do* meet in temples.) So, even if the Antichrist had set himself up in the temple, this would not have affected the church's purity.

Second, although Paul said the unveiling of the "son of perdition" (also known as the "beast" in Revelation) would indeed correspond to a "falling away," or an "apostasy," he gives no information whatsoever as to the extent of the apostasy. Why are Mormons so quick to assume that this falling away would be total? Because doing so paves the way for Smith's restoration of the LDS Church in the early 1800s.

Third, going back to the issue of the Antichrist exalting himself "in the temple of God"—when did this happen? According to Bickmore, it should have coincided with the Great Apostasy. So it must have occurred *before* the Jerusalem temple's destruction (A.D. 70). However, if the Antichrist has not yet exalted himself in the temple, then the apostasy has not yet happened—which in turn means that there was no need for Smith's restoration.

Of course, any Latter-day Saint could argue that the "temple of God" is metaphorically the Christian church itself.[86] But then they would have to show that an Antichrist of some kind had proclaimed himself "God" in Christendom. Attempting to make such an identification, however, would prove to be a futile task.

Equally relevant to this Great Apostasy issue are the many other Bible passages that discuss a falling away from the faith. Passages such as 1 Timothy 4:1-3 and 2 Peter 2:1-3 clearly say that "some shall depart from the faith" and that "many shall follow" false teachers. But these verses do not demand the occurrence of an apostasy "extensive enough that the earthly Church organization was in a shambles, and was taken over by hostile forces."[87]

Dead Baptisms

All of the LDS arguments above do not mean that today's Mormons believe the "falling away" resulted in *no* Christians existing anywhere on earth between the Great Apostasy and Joseph Smith.[88] They admit that even before Smith's restoration, there were indeed pockets of true Christians scattered across the globe. But this admission conflicts with the LDS teaching that all other churches since the Great Apostasy have lacked proper priesthood authority to baptize. And baptism is essential for "eternal life."

According to Mormonism, the only legitimate baptism that exists in the world—the one that opens the way for "eternal life"—is LDS baptism. But that authority was not restored to any church until Joseph Smith. This doctrine is why Mormons baptize the dead by proxy. They believe that such baptisms provide those in the afterlife the choice to join, or reject, the LDS faith. The baptisms must be performed here on earth by proxy because it is only LDS priests who can offer valid, properly authorized baptism.

Although the rite is intended primarily as a way of offering salvation to non-LDS ancestors, sometimes "more zealous Mormons have sought baptism for prominent historical and religious figures."[89] They have baptized the Declaration of Independence signers, Abraham Lincoln, Paul Revere, Shakespeare, Napoléon, Christopher Columbus, Frederick the Great (King of Prussia), John Wesley (the Christian evangelist), Genghis Khan, Joan of Arc, Josef Stalin, and Buddha.

The Church's computerized International Genealogical Index lists some 400 million names! This practice of baptizing dead individuals by proxy, which must take place inside LDS temples, is the prime reason for Mormonism's current push to build more temples worldwide. Such a practice, however, is unbiblical.

To attempt to biblically justify baptism of the dead by proxy, Mormons cite a single passage: "Else what shall they do which are baptized for the dead, if the dead rise not at all? why are they then baptized for the dead?" (1 Corinthians 15:29). But this verse, far from commanding baptism for the dead, is merely stating that some group of persons were baptizing for the dead—which would be absurd if they also did not believe in a resurrection. The emphasis is on the resurrection, not baptism for the dead.[90]

Interestingly, when BYU professor Robert L. Millet attempted to justify baptism for the dead using the Corinthians verse, he actually changed the second sentence of biblical text, replacing the word "they" with "we." The substitution, of course, makes it seem as if Paul was saying that he and all the Corinthians were baptizing the dead.[91]

Although Mormons' motivation may be honorable, LDS baptisms for the dead have caused considerable controversy throughout the general public. Many Americans were shocked, for example, when it was learned in 1993 that Mormons had baptized by proxy Adolf Hitler and sealed him for eternity to his mistress, Eva Braun.[92] Other Nazis baptized included Hermann Goering and Heinrich Himmler.[93]

As odd as this practice may seem to outsiders, it has become nothing less than an *idée fixe* with Mormons, which accounts for their unwavering focus on genealogies and genealogical research.[94] Names are being taken unrelentingly from obituaries, tombstones, state death records, and historical documents. As of 2004, nearly 400 million deceased persons in the Church's International Genealogical Index had been baptized by proxy.[95]

Any and all persons are fair game, so to speak, despite the faith they professed during their lives. It must be noted here that the *official* policy of the LDS church is that Mormons may submit only the names of persons in their ancestral line for proxy baptism. Nevertheless, in their zeal to give lost souls an opportunity for salvation, many Mormons ignore the policy and end up submitting names simply pulled from death records. In fact, it is very possible that many readers of this book have had their ancestors proxy baptized into Mormonism. (See note 96 for more information).[96]

Mormon Authority

As previously noted, Mormonism's priesthood authority is crucial to many LDS claims, including their identification of the Latter-day Saint Church as "Christian." The pivotal issue, then, is whether or not Scripture mandates that God's church possess either an Aaronic or Melchizedek priesthood—or both.

Evangelicals see no need for either because Scripture indicates that 1) the need for the Aaronic priesthood ceased when Christ established his new covenant of grace; and 2) the Melchizedek priesthood was *never* a literal order of priests. The Aaronic priesthood was replaced by a new one that is now held by *all believers*—God's royal priesthood (1 Peter 2:9). As for the Melchizedek priesthood, it is a symbolic one, referred to by David in Psalm 110 and now expressed perfectly in Christ.

The Aaronic Priesthood

The priesthood of Aaron "was for the priests of the temple, as defined in the books of Moses known as the Pentateuch."[97] Their main responsibility was to present offerings and sacrifices to God.[98] These sacrifices foreshadowed and symbolized "the ultimate sacrifice—that of God's Son."[99] As Scripture says, they were "the example and shadow of heavenly things" (Hebrews 8:5).

The eighth, ninth, and tenth chapters of Hebrews plainly teach that the Aaronic priesthood, as part of the Mosaic covenant, was "replaced by a superior covenant, under which God will be able to work a full transformation of believers and so perfectly forgive that he 'will remember their sins no more' (8:12)."[100] The entire reason God set up his priesthood disappeared with Christ's final sacrifice. *Literal* sacrifices pointing *forward* to Christ's death were replaced by *figurative* sacrifices that look *backward* to his death.

Now, we ourselves are living sacrifices (Romans 12:1), able to offer up sacrifices of praise for what Christ did (Hebrews 13:15). We offer such sacrifices to God as members of his royal priesthood. This is why Scripture pictures the Old Testament priesthood has having been "changed," which in turn necessitated a "change also of the law" (Hebrews 7:12). Consequently, the Aaronic priesthood is perpetuated *nowhere* in the New Testament.

Mormons recognize this absence, but they dismiss its significance.[101] They do so by appealing to Joseph Smith, who claimed that in this dispensation (era of God's dealings with humankind) there is a "welding together of dispensations, and keys, and powers, and glories" (D&C 128:18).[102] But Smith's assertion does not alleviate one very serious problem with the LDS priesthood—its holders do not meet the Old Testament criteria for priests (Table 10.1). In other words, even if God *has* infused the current dispensation with aspects of all other "dispensations, and keys, and powers, and glories," the LDS priesthood is still corrupt.

The most serious and obvious corruption of the LDS priesthood relates to its basic purpose, which according to LDS president Gordon B. Hinckley is to act "in behalf of God our Eternal Father and Jesus Christ."[103] LDS apostle Angel Abrea explains that

> the priesthood is power and authority delegated by God to man on earth to act in His behalf in the name of Jesus Christ...to possess the priesthood is to have the privilege of calling down the powers of heaven to assist in fulfilling sacred responsibilities and opportunities.[104]

But according to Hebrews 5:1, "Every high priest taken from among men is ordained *for men* in things pertaining to God, that he may offer both gifts and sacrifices for sins" (emphasis added). In other words, the LDS Aaronic priesthood is in actuality a reversal of the Old Testament Aaronic priesthood.

Interestingly, because the priests of Aaron's line had to be descended from the tribe of Levi, even Jesus himself could not hold the Aaronic priesthood. He "sprang out of Juda; of which tribe Moses spake nothing concerning priesthood" (Hebrews 7:14). So although Mormons may call their priesthood "Aaronic," even a cursory look at the Old Testament reveals that there is nothing Aaronic about it.

Old Testament Aaronic Priesthood	Mormonism Aaronic Priesthood
• Held by men from the Hebrew tribe of Levi, in the genealogical line of Aaron. (Oddly, even D&C 107:16 states that one must be a "literal descendant of Aaron" in order to hold keys of the priesthood.)	• Any worthy LDS male.
• Received into priesthood only after a ceremonial washing and anointing.	• Received into priesthood by the laying on of hands by another LDS priest.
• No physical defilements or defects allowed (for example, tattoos, disfigurement, or lameness).	• Physical defilements and defects allowed.
• Only allowed to function during the prime of manhood—no children or aged men.	• Allowed to function during their teen years and into extreme old age.
• No bodily defilement allowed (for example, contact with a dead body, shaving of beard—which was worn by all priests).	• Bodily defilement allowed.
• High priests could marry only a virgin.	• No need to marry a virgin.
• Wore white linen robes.	• No white linen garments or robes.

Table 10.1

The Melchizedek Priesthood

As for the Melchizedek Priesthood, it is allegedly a higher priesthood that is over the Aaronic Priesthood (see D&C 107:13-14).[105] But this idea is found nowhere in the Bible. Hebrews 6:20 simply says that Jesus is a "high priest" after the order of Melchizedek. And since he lives forever, he holds his priesthood eternally (Hebrews 7:24).

But what exactly is the biblical priesthood of Melchizedek? Most important, it was *unique*—never activated as a priesthood of succession or transference. It belonged only to Melchizedek and Christ.[106] Its first holder, the priest–king Melchizedek, appears in Genesis 14:18-20, where he meets Abram (Hebrews 7:1-2). Nothing is said of him except that he is "[w]ithout father, without mother, without descent, having neither beginning of days, nor end of life" (Hebrews 7:3).

These are Hebrew figures of speech for Melchizedek's importance and status. No ancestry, birth record, time of death, or successor is noted—rather, "he is made, by the very silence of scripture, to resemble the *Son of God*...who *has neither beginning of days nor end of life*."[107] (Now, Jesus—God's Son, who also has no *beginning of days nor end of life*—is "a High Priest after this order, unique and *for ever*."[108]) Melchizedek's priesthood is symbolic of kingship and ultimate priesthood, as is indicated by David (Psalm 110). The priesthood is then applied to Christ, who holds his kingship eternally.

But Mormons take these verses in a different way. They think that the "order" of Melchizedek means a "priesthood class" or "priesthood organization." Barry Bickmore asks, "[W]hat kind of priesthood did Melchizedek hold? Was his priesthood 'after the order of Melchizedek?'" He answers his question, "If so, then obviously people other than Christ can belong to this order."[109] Bickmore then supports his line of reasoning as follows:

> [T]here are statements in the early Christian literature in the third century AD that speak of "the Apostles also and their successors, priests according to the great High Priest." Of course, the "great High Priest" was Christ, and He was High Priest after the order of Melchizedek.[110]

But this argument reveals a misunderstanding of the term "order" as applied to Melchizedek. Although the Greek word for "order" *(taxis)* usually does mean "class" of priests, it can also mean, in a more figurative way, "rank, or quality," of a priest. And in Scripture, it does not seem to be applicable to Melchizedek in the usual, *literal* sense.[111] Why? Primarily because nothing in Scripture indicates that he had any successors.

There is no record of any line of priests succeeding Melchizedek. Rather, Scripture is presenting him as a type—a precursor—of Christ, who was and is a priest after the "order" (manner, quality, rank) of Melchizedek. Like Melchizedek, whose death was not recorded, Jesus retains his priesthood "after [according to] the power of an endless life" (Hebrews 7:16).

We, as Christ's followers, have nothing to do with the Melchizedek priesthood since it is after the "order" (quality, rank) of Melchizedek himself—a priest and king "without father, without mother, without descent, having neither beginning of days, nor end of life" (Hebrews 7:3). Melchizedek represents qualifications that only Jesus could and can meet.

Christ alone now holds this symbolic priesthood that is after the order of Melchizedek. Jesus, who made the final sacrifice (Hebrews 10:1-14), was, and forever will be, the last High Priest. Believers can possess only the royal priesthood, which was the same priesthood possessed by all of God's followers in Israel (Exodus 19:6).

The Royal Priesthood

Understandably, some Latter-day Saints are hostile to this idea since it seriously undermines Mormons claims. Consider the remarks of Kevin Graham, a frequent LDS participant on the Internet's Mormon-run Zion's Lighthouse Message Board:

> The Bible teaches nothing about "Priesthood of believers." This is a Protestant invention that relies on a poor interpretation of scripture. 1 Peter 2:9-10....Where does this say anything about "believers"? This verse is simply quoting the Old Testament: Exodus 19:5-6.[112]

> I asked you once, and now I'll ask you twice. Where does it say anything about "believers"?...[W]here does it assume priesthood authority by each and every one of them? Such a doctrine is completely alien to early Christianity....Protestants simply want to let their poor exegesis recreate history, as usual.[113]

Graham's twice-asked question is answered in verse 7 of 1 Peter 2. It gives context to the royal priesthood and makes a fitting conclusion to our discussion: "Unto you therefore *which believe[,]* he is precious" (emphasis added). Verse 9 then reads, "But ye are a chosen generation, a royal priesthood, an holy nation, a peculiar people; that ye should shew forth the praises of him who hath called you."

FINAL OBSERVATIONS

When it comes to whether or not Mormons are Christian, a simple yes or no answer will never do. As we have seen, there are two ways to arrive at an answer. And our considerations do not even address the myriad issues surrounding the complexities of a hurting heart, the confusions that are possible in a human mind, or the motivations of a seeking soul.

What we do know is that no one who wants to follow God will be kept from a saving knowledge of his love, grace and mercy (John 10:27-28). Our Lord is not willing that any should perish (2 Peter 3:9). As far back as the Old Testament, the God of Israel promised that those who *truly* seek him would find him (Deuteronomy 4:29).

I think everyone will be more than a little surprised once the graves have been opened, the resurrection is over, the judgment is complete, and the new heavens and new earth have come to be. Some souls whom we assumed would be in heaven will not be there. And many more whom we thought would *never* make it will be at our side.

At the same time, however, it cannot be forgotten that we must be saved on God's terms, not ours. John 4:24 tells us that those who worship God must do so in spirit and "in truth." And John 8:32 promises that it will be "the truth" that sets us free. Jesus himself declared: "I am the way, the truth, and the life: no man cometh unto the Father, but by me (John 14:6).

Someone cannot receive salvation through a God or a Christ who does not really exist; in other words, through a God and a Christ whose nature and identity are seriously misunderstood (for example, the LDS notion that Heavenly Father is merely an exalted man). But exactly how God will sort this all out on judgment day is something no one will ever know until that blessed event transpires.

Until then, perhaps the most important issue is that of our own hearts—namely, the manner in which we share our faith with those who may not be on their way to a glorious eternity with God. Are we speaking words of life as Christ would speak them? Are we being upright—not manipulative—in our presentation? Are we willing to say, "I'm sorry, I was wrong"?

Are we trying to minister to Mormons with integrity? Are we attempting to truly evangelize (spread the good news) to them...or just anger them, hurt them, or bully them theologically? Are we really trying to listen to what a Mormon might be saying—to the point of even learning something from that person? Are we genuinely concerned about each Mormon with whom we disagree? Do we see every Mormon as an individual person...or have they all just become a part of the impersonal enemy we so easily label "The Mormons"?

Defending Our Faith

Concerning apologetics (the defense of one's faith), BYU professor Daniel Peterson has astutely observed, "If you believe it's true and you believe it's really important...then it's worth defending."[114] Peterson, whom I consider a personal friend, has also given the following advice, which, I believe, demonstrates a keen understanding of the current state of LDS–evangelical interaction and how we need to take it to another level:

> [Some] take this as just, "it's a competition, you can score points." You know, you can "win on this"—gratify your ego by defeating somebody on that point or something. That's not what it's really about. Resist that temptation. These issues are vastly important. Intrinsically. Not just because you're on one team or another. [115]

Mormons and mainstream Christians will certainly remain divided for some time—perhaps always—over many important issues. But this does not mean we need to aggravate the situation by mocking each other, demeaning each other's beliefs, or being unnecessarily antagonistic while interacting with each other.

It also must be admitted that both Mormons *and* evangelicals have been far too ready to attribute the worst of motives to each other. This, too, must end, as several LDS leaders have recently stated:

- "We must never adopt a holier-than-thou attitude. We must not be self-righteous. We must be magnanimous, and open, and friendly. We can keep our faith. We can practice our religion. We can cherish our method or worship without being offensive to others. I take this occasion to plead for a spirit of tolerance and neighborliness, of friendship and love toward those of other faiths."[116]

- "Love one another. Be kind to one another despite our deepest differences. Treat one another with respect and civility."[117]

- "If the adversary can influence us to pick on each other, to find fault, bash, and undermine, to judge or humiliate or taunt, half his battle is won. Why? Because though this sort of conduct may not equate with succumbing to grievous sin, it nevertheless neutralizes us spiritually. The Spirit of the Lord cannot dwell where there is bickering, judging, contention, or any kind of bashing.... Let us open our arms to each other, accept each other for who we are, assume everyone is doing the best he or she can, and look for ways to help leave quiet messages of love and encouragement instead of being destructive with bashing."[118]

Is there any reason why both Mormons and evangelicals cannot live up to such wise counsel? Mistakes on both sides will undoubtedly continue. But if everyone tries to imitate Christ, perhaps we will at least be able to make some headway as theists living together in a decidedly atheistic world. Eternity will arrive soon enough. My hope and prayer is that on our way there, despite our differences, we will add to the world's peace, rather than its incivility, angry conflict, and intolerance.

Grace and Peace

I pray that any Mormons who have made it to this point will always understand the motivation of *most* Christians who oppose the LDS Church. It has nothing to do with "hating" Mormons, wanting to hurt them, or desiring to cause contention. Most non-LDS Christians truly care about the spiritual well-being and eternal destiny of Mormons. Confirmation of this truth has come from none other than Roger Keller, professor of Religious Understanding and Professor of Church History and Doctrine at BYU:

> There are all kinds of persons who are against the [LDS] church for one reason or another....They've learned that "If we don't evangelize the Latter-day Saints, they're in danger of going to the Nether Regions." And I think many of them see their opposition to the church as an act of love for you and me. And I don't have any problem with those persons—none at all. Because I go to Christians of other traditions for that very reason. It's an act of love to build on what they already know of Jesus, and of the Holy Ghost, and of our Heavenly Father. Because I think I have something to offer them and to give them. I think many, many, many persons who are opposed to the church are motivated by that factor....
>
> Any time we encounter a person who is opposed to the church, the question we have to ask is: "What's motivating that individual?"...I really think that at root most people are not bad people and they do what they do out of positive motivations. And so, if I can say to an individual, "How come you're so negative about the church?" And they're willing to meet me at that level of conversation, or remember, dialogue—some positive things can happen. We may still agree to disagree agreeably. But in the end, maybe we can come to an understanding.[119]

Keller has not only articulated the feelings of many evangelicals, but has also explained in a nutshell why I have offered *Becoming Gods*. My prayer is that it has been received by all readers in the spirit in which it has been written. My hope is that in the future, Mormons and traditional Christians will be able to continue talking about these crucial issues in a way that will be pleasing to Jesus. As he said,

> *"Love one another; as I have loved you, ...also love one another."*
>
> —John 13:34

APPENDIXES

MORE ON POLYGAMY

As noted in chapter 9, polygamy and Mormonism are once again sharing the media spotlight thanks to a variety of recent social and political events. Interestingly, this has led to a renewed attempt by many Latter-day Saints to defend polygamy. One of the most aggressive pro-polygamous works to appear has been "Mormonism 201: 3 Pitches, 3 Strikes, and McKeever and Johnson Are Out" (2003).

This article, produced by FAIR-affiliated writer Michael W. Fordham, contains most of the common LDS arguments for polygamy. Its goal is to refute chapter 16 of *Mormonism 101* by evangelical authors Bill McKeever and Eric Johnson. Fordham's article is full of far too many inaccuracies to be addressed here, but a few of them that relate directly to plural marriage are worth noting, especially in light of what has happened recently.

⚜ ⚜ ⚜

Fordham, like many Mormons, erroneously thinks, "Polygamy is controversial only because it is misunderstood." He further claims that it should not be so controversial because it is "practiced in many cultures throughout the world today." But both of these assertions are highly flawed.

First, polygamy is very well understood by both theologians and history scholars. LDS polygamy in particular has been discussed at length in many scholarly and popular volumes.[1] The "controversial" nature of polygamy, for traditional Christians, centers *exclusively* on whether or not it is a form of marriage that the *Christian* God condones, advocates, or commands. *That* is the issue—not whether polygamy is understood.

Second, whether polygamy is practiced in other cultures is totally irrel-evant. Other cultures also practice female circumcision, polyandry (more than one husband for a single wife), use of hallucinogenic drugs, euthanasia, abortion, social nudity, and religious nudity (for example, nat-uralists and Wiccans). Does this mean that God approves of such things, or that such things should be practiced by Christians? Of course not.

Back to Abraham and Moses

Fordham also echoes the sentiments of many Mormons when he chas-tises traditional Christians for condemning LDS polygamy, saying that they are "happy to accept Abraham and Moses as true prophets of God, yet they condemn Joseph Smith, and the rest of the early Latter-day Saints, for having plural wives." He adds, "This double standard of judgment is inconsistent with true scriptural teaching or acceptance."

In reality, most Christians do have a problem with Old Testament polygamy. The plural marriages of Abraham, David, and Solomon have never (at least to my knowledge) been depicted by mainstream Chris-tian pastors, Bible teachers, and theologians as nonproblematic. On the contrary, Old Testament polygamy is usually viewed by Christians as an ungodly lifestyle compromise that God *tolerated* due to the hardness of men's hearts, similar to the way he tolerated divorce (Mark 10:4-5).

Moreover, with regard to Abraham, he was not a prophet in the way Joseph Smith claimed to be. The Jewish patriarch had no devotees who looked to him for doctrinal instruction and leadership in the same way Smith's followers did. Abraham also did not live under explicit New Testament proscriptions against polygamy.

Abraham actually demonstrated a lack of faith in God's promises by impregnating Hagar. As with many other biblical examples, Abraham's polygamy pictured how a man can stray from righteousness (see chapter 9). His act reflected the pagan practices of the surrounding culture. *The International Standard Bible Encyclopedia* explains:

> In Mesopotamia, marriage contracts frequently specified that a wife who proved infertile should give her handmaid to her husband in order to produce children for the household. This situation under-lies the procedure whereby Sarah's handmaid Hagar was given by

her to Abraham as a wife (Gen. 16:3) for purposes of procreation. In accepting this polygamous relationship Abraham was acceding to local custom rather than obeying the divine decree or trusting God's promise to him concerning descendants.[2]

Concerning Moses, there is no biblical evidence whatsoever that he was a polygamist. The LDS assumption that Moses practiced polygamy stems from a single Bible verse that mentions an Ethiopian woman, or Cushite, as the wife of Moses (Numbers 12). But what Mormons fail to recognize is that by the time Scripture mentions this Cushite, Moses' first wife (Zipporah) was probably dead.

One must say "probably" because we know very little about Zipporah from Scripture. We do not know when she died or when the marriage of Moses and the Cushite took place. And we certainly do not know if Moses married the Ethiopian while Zipporah was still alive. No such information is actually given the Bible. To say otherwise is an assumption made by polygamy supporters.

Fordham continues, "The Bible does not condemn polygamy, and in fact clearly indicates that many God fearing men practiced it." This is an interesting argument because it juxtaposes two entirely unrelated issues. The first issue (whether or not the Bible condemns polygamy) is the subject of our discussion.

But the second issue ("that God fearing men practiced it") is not under discussion. In fact, it has no bearing whatsoever on the first issue. Just because polygamy was practiced by *some* Old Testament men (who also were sinners), it does not follow that God endorsed their behavior. Godly men in the Bible also lied (Abraham), resorted to murder (David), got drunk (Noah), and committed incest (Lot). Does this mean such practices were appropriate or God-ordained? Hardly.

For Fordham's argument to have any merit, it *should* have read, "The Bible does not *condemn* polygamy, but in fact, clearly reveals that God *commands* God-fearing men to practice it." But Fordham could not make such a statement, because nowhere does God condone, let alone command, polygamy. So he was forced to muddy the waters. He also adds,

> The problem modern day Christians have with polygamy arises in the idea that, for them, polygamy is equated with adultery. But is

> plural marriage really adultery? The Bible condemns sexual relations outside of marriage, which adultery certainly is. Polygamy is not adultery since any physical relationship would be with your married partner. Only outside of the marriage relationship is sexual relations condemned in scripture.

This is a straw-man argument since adultery does not enter into the polygamy question. In fact, the definition of adultery given by Fordham basically mirrors the definition given in *The International Standard Bible Encyclopedia:* "Adultery. In Scripture, sexual intercourse by a married man with another than his wife, or by a married woman with another than her husband."[3] Again, the real issue is whether or not God has ever condoned or commanded plural marriages.

Facing the Facts

The problem "modern day Christians have with polygamy" has more to do with New Testament passages that clearly and explicitly instruct believers, especially church leaders, to live in monogamous relationships. Additionally, a number of Old Testament passages indicate that the ideal marriage union is monogamy, not polygamy (see chapter 9).

Fordham then gives five what he calls "well-documented answers" using various LDS sources, which put LDS polygamy in a much more flattering light than does the Bible. But these answers, many of which are commonly repeated by Mormons, are inaccurate. Consider the following comparison of Fordham's "answers" with historical fact:

Mormon Answer: "Anywhere from 2%-4% of the Church membership practiced plural marriage from 1843 to 1890."[4]

Historical Fact:

> Recent studies suggest that the number of Mormons living in polygamous families between 1850 and 1890, while varying from community to community and year to year, averaged between 20 and 30 percent. In some cases the proportion was higher. The practice was especially extensive with Mormon leaders, both locally and those presiding over the entire church. These calculations would indicate that, during the entire time the principle was practiced, the number

of men, women, and children living in polygamous households amounted to tens of thousands.[5]

While estimates vary, most scholars agree that between 10 and 20 percent of Mormon marriages before 1890 were polygamous.[6]

The extent to which polygamy was practiced in Utah will probably never be known. Plural marriages were not publicly recorded, and there is little chance that any private records which might have been kept will ever be revealed....From information obtainable from all available sources, it appears that there may have been a time when 15 or possibly 20 percent of the Mormon families of Utah were polygamous.[7]

Mormon Answer: "Permission from the first wife was sought, and approval from the appropriate [priesthood] leader was required to practice plural marriage."[8]

Historical Fact: "Though the first wife's consent was supposedly required by scripture, it was not always sought or willingly given."[9]

Mormons insisted that women were not forced into plural marriages but rather controlled the process: they could refuse to enter into plural marriages, while first wives could decide whether their husbands could marry others. Of course, Mormon women were subject to heavy pressure from husbands, neighbors, and LDS officials who exhorted them to "live their religion" by contracting plural marriages or risk denying their faith. Most women in polygamous marriages apparently accepted the difficult principle, either because they believed God commanded it or because they had little other choice.[10]

[Jessie Embry] states that some first wives freely gave their consent or even encouraged their husbands to take another wife, some gave their consent *only because they feared the repercussions in the next life for saying no in this one,* and "a few" were not consulted....Orson Pratt explained in 1853 that the first wife did not have absolute veto power over her husband's entering plural marriage....[I]f her basis for refusing was insufficient, the husband would be justified in marrying again without her consent "if permitted by revelation through the prophet."[11]

Some, like Emma Smith, opposed their husbands' taking additional wives. In such instances the man had two options. Either he could respect his wife's wishes and remain monogamous, or he could, as Joseph Smith did, ignore her objections and take plural wives without her consent.[12]

Cross-examination at Read Smoot Hearings: testimony of Joseph F. Smith. *Mr. Smith.* The condition is that if she does not consent the Lord will destroy her, but I do not know how He will do it. *Senator Bailey.* Is it not true that…if she refuses her consent her husband is exempt from the law which requires her consent? *Mr. Smith.* Yes; he is exempt from the law which requires her consent. *Senator Bailey.* She is commanded to consent, but if she does not, then he is exempt from the requirement? *Mr. Smith.* Then he is at liberty to proceed without her consent, under the law. *Senator Beveridge.* In other words, her consent amounts to nothing? *Mr. Smith.* It amounts to nothing but her consent.[13]

Mormon Answer: "The man had to be able to financially support all his wives and any children involved."[14]

Historical Fact: Although it is true that the men who became polygamists tended to be wealthier than those who did not enter into it, financial care of wives was by no means a constant: "Since the number of wives permitted was never defined some men married beyond their means."[15]

Here we see another characteristic of polygamy: the men often were willing to add plural wives to their families, but after the marriage took place found they were unable to support the multiple families adequately, and the wives often had to rely on siblings and teenage sons.[16]

Poverty faced [B.H.] Roberts and his families always. Though he was offered non-church options for making a living he chose to write for church publications, and he accepted additional church callings. He was a Seventy. Proudly he saw his work as a missionary and mission president as a 'divine' calling.[17]

The Apostle Orson Pratt is one of the most persistent polygamists in Utah, and he has nothing to give his wives for their maintenance. They struggle on as best they may, striving in every way to earn a scanty sustenance for themselves and their children. Some of them live in the most wretched squalor and degrading poverty. He, in the mean while, goes on foreign and home missions.[18]

[Orson Pratt] was living in Salt Lake City. He had left his young wife and her children in Tooele—a place about forty miles distant. There they lived in a wretched little log-cabin, the young mother supporting her little ones as best she could. When her last child was born she was suffering all the miseries of poverty, dependent entirely upon the charity of her neighbors. At the time when most she needed the gentle sympathy of her husband's love that husband never came to see her.[19]

Mormon Answer: "The man had to be a member in good standing with the church."[20]

Historical Fact: Although this statement by Fordham is accurate, the reason for its accuracy is not noted. What Fordham fails to explain is that polygamous LDS men were usually "in good standing" because they were, for the most part, the more influential and powerful LDS leaders:

[C]hurch rank was more important than wealth in predicting a plural marriage....[A] man was significantly more likely to remarry or enter plural marriage in the five years subsequent to his increase in church rank than in the five years preceding it....Apparently, a man's entering plural marriage was not a prerequisite for advancement in church rank but was a responsibility accompanying the increase in rank, although some never took on the additional responsibility of plural wives.[21]

Bishops were also expected to set an example to the communities in the matter of plural marriage. New men were chosen to replace recalcitrant bishops who refused to take additional wives.[22]

Mormon Answer: "Generally plural marriage involved only two wives and seldom more than three."[23] (Interestingly, in his endnote for this citation, Fordham gives no page number for the *Encyclopedia of Mormonism*, from which he quotes [page 1094]. He may have chosen to not include the page number because, coincidentally, the opposing page—page 1095—states, "The exact percentage of Latter-day Saints who participated in the practice is not known, but studies suggest a maximum of from 20% to 25% of LDS adults were members of polygamous households." This comment, of course, directly contradicts Fordham's contention.)

Historical Fact: It is true that LDS polygamy in general involved only two wives. But Fordham's use of the decidedly subjective terms "generally" and "seldom" communicates the message that there were *not* a lot of men who took more than two wives. In actuallity, although the majority of LDS polygamous males took only one extra wife, there still were many men who took more women:

> Of 1,784 polygamists, 66.3 percent married only one extra wife [approx. 1182 men], Another 21.2 percent were three-wife men [approx. 378 men], and 6.7 percent went as far as to take four wives [approx. 119 men]. This left a small group of less than 6 percent who married five or more women [approx. 105 men].[24]

Tolerated Versus Commanded

In response to the evangelical claims that God merely tolerated polygamy, Fordham repeats an oft-made LDS request for "Biblical references" to prove the assertion. "Where does the Bible say polygamy was only 'tolerated' by God?" asks Fordham. He continues, "Since when does God allow mankind to make up his own laws of morality? What scripture says God allows man to do as he pleases and God will tolerate it? This is really an absurd statement."

Contrary to what Fordham seems to think, God indeed "allows man to do as he pleases and God will tolerate it." He has allowed mankind to make up his own laws for thousands of years—for example, the Code of Hammurabi (about 1700 B.C.) and the Assyrian law code (about 2000 B.C.). Although no scripture explicitly "says" God tolerates man's sinfulness, it is an obvious fact.

This can also be seen in numerous Bible accounts wherein God's followers lied, engaged in incest, committed murder, betrayed the Savior, and succumbed to all manner of human weaknesses and frailties. Abraham, for instance, lied by telling a king that Sarah was his sister. Did God tolerate this behavior? Yes. But because Abraham lied and God tolerated it, does that mean God condones or advocates lying? No.

Moreover, God tolerated divorce to the point where Moses actually provided a writ of divorce for the Israelites because of the hardness of their hearts. But that was never God's ideal for marriage (see Matthew

19). God even tolerated slavery to the point of providing rules for taking care of slaves.[25] The same holds true for polygamy.

As for Fordham's most curious comment about wanting a scripture wherein it explicitly "says" God *tolerated* polygamy, this borders on disingenuous. Why? Because there also exists no scripture wherein God explicitly condoned, advocated, or commanded polygamy—which is the LDS claim. No verse reads, "Thus says God, you shall multiply wives unto yourself for it is a godly thing in my sight."

And yet Mormons are willing to infer quite a bit from some fairly unclear and nonexplicit passages that, at best, picture God *permitting* polygamy, in contrast to his clear commands to not practice it. So the real question is, Which inference is more likely: 1) that God *commanded* polygamy; or 2) that God *tolerated* polygamy?

The biblical evidence for God *tolerating* polygamy is much more substantial from an evangelical perspective. Many Mormons, however, do not accept the biblical indications that God's ideal for marriage is monogamy. Like many others, Fordham asserts,

> Plural marriage was part of the Law of Moses (Exodus 21:10, Deuteronomy 21:15, 25:5). God gave David his wives (2 Samuel 12:8). God said that polygamists will inherit the kingdom of heaven (Matthew 8:11, Luke 13:28). Does this sound like God "merely tolerated" plural marriage? On the contrary, what McKeever and Johnson should have said, if they wanted to be honest, truthful, and accurate, is, "Christians today merely tolerate the fact that God sanctioned polygamy in ancient days, and refuse to accept that He would do so today."

With regard to Exodus 21:10, Fordham seems to have missed its context. This passage is referring to *slavery*. It has nothing to do with condoning or advocating polygamy, but rather, is simply talking about slaves and their proper treatment. Verse by verse, Exodus 21:7-10 reads,

- *Verse 7*—"And if a man sell his daughter to be a maidservant [a slave], she shall not go out as the menservants do."
- *Verse 8*—"If she [the daughter] please not her master, who hath betrothed her to himself, then shall he let her be redeemed [bought back]"….

- *Verse 9*—"And if he [the master] have betrothed her unto his son, he shall deal with her after the manner of daughters."

- *Verse 10*—"If he [the son] take him another wife; her food, her raiment, and her duty of marriage, shall he not diminish."

To paraphrase, God is simply saying, "Look, *if* you're going to have a slave as a wife, and *if* you then take another wife, don't you *dare* cast that slave wife out onto the street. You'd better take care of her too." Rather than advocating taking another wife, God is just trying to protect a slave, slavery being yet another thing that was tolerated by him.

This same principle of protecting innocent parties is at work in Deuteronomy 21:15, which demanded that a man needed to treat his offspring with equality, irrespective of which wife had birthed them. God is commanding that provisions be made for children. And as previously mentioned, Moses also made provisions for divorce. But that certainly was not what God intended for the marriage relationship.

Nowhere do we see God advocating polygamy. In fact, if one is going to use the Exodus 21 passage to justify polygamy, it also should be used to justify slavery and divorce—especially slavery, since the two issues *in context* are related and inseparable. But saying that God condoned slavery because he made provisions for it in the law is absurd. To summarize, then, polygamy (like slavery and divorce) was *tolerated,* even to the point of making provisions in the law that would protect women and children.

Levirate Marriages

Deuteronomy 25:5-10 is a particularly popular verse used by Mormon defenders. For example, David Waltz (who might best be termed a Catholic–Mormon—see page 216) has picked up on this passage, which discusses the levirate marriage law. This law governed the action of a man toward his brother's widow. He was supposed to take her as his wife and, if she was childless, raise up children by her. In a 2004 Internet post, Waltz referred to *The International Standard Bible Encyclopedia,* pointing out that volume 3, page 901, clearly refers to levirate marriage "in the law." Waltz commented, "Now if polygamy 'was provided for in the Law' then it was commanded by YHWH."[26]

Several points must be made here about how Waltz and like-minded defenders of Mormonism sometimes take liberties with the sources they quote. First, Waltz never mentioned in his post that the author of this article, evangelical R.K. Harrison, additionally stated that polygamy in the Old Testament existed "despite the marital ideal laid down in Gen. 2:24." Harrison further explained that "the Genesis dictum established monogamy as a working principle for mankind." So this is the context of his later comment about levirate marriage.

Waltz also used ellipses to excise a very crucial part of Harrison's comment about the presence of levirate marriage "in the law." According to Harrison, the purpose of the provision was to protect widows. A woman without an heir or a husband would never survive. In other words, a levirate marriage was contrary to God's original plan and desire for men and women, but was consistent with a higher moral imperative—preservation and protection of life. To use an analogy mentioned previously, the act would be roughly akin to lying (a moral wrong) in order to protect Jews from Nazis in World War II Germany (a moral imperative to protect life), as Harrison explains:

> Levirate marriage appears to contravene the legislation prohibiting marriage with one's brother's wife...but in other respects was actually a humane way of dealing with what was frequently the desperate plight of widows by keeping them within the family and tribe, without which they would almost certainly have starved or been callously exploited.[27]

Clearly, this is not a normal type of command by God (such as, for example, observing the Sabbath or not committing murder). It was to be followed only under extenuating circumstances, rigid controls, and specific conditions. As Harrison noted in summary about this and other reasons for polygamy, "These factors notwithstanding, the ideal Hebrew marriage continued to be monogamous."[28]

From Bad to Worse

Another Old Testament passage similarly misunderstood by Mormons is 2 Samuel 12:7-9, which Fordham also uses to justify polygamy:

> And Nathan said to David, Thou art the man. Thus saith the LORD
> God of Israel, I anointed thee king over Israel, and I delivered thee
> out of the hand of Saul; And I gave thee thy master's house, and *thy*
> *master's wives into thy bosom*, and gave thee the house of Israel and
> of Judah; and if that had been too little, I would moreover have given
> unto thee such and such things (emphasis added).

For King David to have been given the "wives" of Saul would have been
extremely difficult since we know, first, that Saul had only one wife and
one concubine (1 Samuel 14:50); and second, that Abner appropriated
Saul's concubine for himself (2 Samuel 3:7).

Further, in the East it was the custom for a king's successor to take
everything possessed by the former king. His country, his throne, his
harem, his treasures—his everything! Enumerating such things indicated
a complete turnover of power and authority. What we have here, then,
is God saying to David, "What is your problem? I gave you everything
there was to give. I gave you all of Saul's kingdom. Nothing was held back,
yet you still behave like this." No documentation indicates that David actually took any wives from Saul.

Lastly, even if for the sake of discussion we say that God did give David
some as-yet-unknown wives of Saul, they would constitute an aspect of
Saul's kingdom that would naturally go to David. This statement, then,
would still be less a promotion of polygamy than an act of God used to
communicate to the people, through a well-known Eastern tradition, the
transfer of kingly authority.

It is at this point that one of Fordham's most bizarre comments appears:
"God said that polygamists will inherit the kingdom of heaven (Matthew
8:11, Luke 13:28)."

In reality, these straightforward verses about Abraham, Isaac, and Jacob
simply say that they will be in the kingdom of heaven. The passages are
not, as Fordham seems to think, some kind of tacit endorsement of polygamy. Nor are they doctrinally significant verses that are somehow saying
polygamists (as a group) "will inherit the kingdom of heaven." The passages are merely declaring that the patriarchs will be in heaven. As for
their lifestyles and personal actions while alive, contextually, the verses
are not addressing any such issues.

Clearly, the patriarchs will be saved *despite* their polygamy, just as they will be saved despite their other sins. Abraham will be in heaven *despite* his lying (Genesis 20); Isaac, *despite* his lying (Genesis 26:6-11); and Jacob, *despite* his deceptive nature (Genesis 27). Using Fordham's reasoning, we also would have to say, "God said that liars will inherit the kingdom of heaven" (so we can lie), and "God said that deceivers will inherit the kingdom of heaven" (so we can deceive).

More Old Testament Problems

Fordham goes on to list a number of Bible verses, none of which includes any explicit *sanction* of polygamy by God.[29] One interesting reference "proving" that God sanctioned polygamy is Isaiah 4:1—"In that day seven women shall take hold of one man." This verse has for many years been touted by Mormons seeking to legitimize polygamy using the Bible. Unfortunately for them, this passage predicts the rise of polygamy as a result of divine *condemnation,* not divine blessing. And the location of the prophecy's fulfillment is Israel, not America.

Moreover, the context of Isaiah 4:1 is judgment on Israel. God denounces the women of Jerusalem in chapter 3, verse 16: "Because the daughters of Zion are haughty, and walk with stretched forth necks and wanton eyes...the LORD will discover their secret parts." The Lord's condemnation continues through the remainder of chapter 3, which concludes, "Thy men shall fall by the sword, and thy mighty in the war. And her gates shall lament and mourn; and she being desolate shall sit upon the ground." Isaiah 4:1 then explains the ultimate result of the judgment and condemnation:

> And in that day seven women shall take hold of one man, saying,
> We will eat our own bread, and wear our own apparel: only let us
> be called by thy name, to take away our reproach.

Biblical scholars Keil and Delitzsch make the following remarks in their well-known commentary on the Old Testament:

> When war shall thus unsparingly have swept away the men of Zion,
> a most unnatural effect will ensue, namely, that women will go in
> search of husbands, and not men in search of wives....

> The division of the chapters is a wrong one here, as this verse is
> the closing verse of the prophecy against the women, and the daugh-
> ters of Zion, every one of whom now thought herself the greatest
> as the wife of such and such a man, and for whom many men were
> now the suitors, would end in this unnatural self-humiliation, that
> seven of them would offer themselves to the same man, the first man
> who presented himself, and even renounce the ordinary legal claim
> upon their husband for clothing and food (Ex. 21:10)....if he would
> only take away their reproach (namely, the reproach of being unmar-
> ried, ch. 54:4, as in Gen. 30:23, of being childless) by letting them
> be called his wives....
>
> In ch. 4:1 the threat denounced against the women of Jerusalem
> is brought to a close. It is a side-piece to the threat denounced against
> the national rulers. And these two scenes of judgment were only parts
> of the general judgment about to fall upon Jerusalem and Judah, as
> a state or national community.[30]

Also very telling is how Fordham quotes "in that day seven women
shall take hold of one man," but leaves off the rest of the prophecy: "We
will eat our own bread, and wear our own apparel: only let us be called
by thy name." But contrary to this verse, the wives of early LDS leaders
never agreed *not* to take any financial support from their husbands.

And was there any war that made men so scarce that multiple LDS
women began seeking out a single man to marry? No. Furthermore, it
was LDS men seeking more wives, not the other way around. Finally, why
does Fordham not mention that this is actually a passage describing the
results of judgment on Israel? LDS arguments for polygamy are clearly
weak. Much remains to be explained regarding the issue.

One Final Puzzle

Also needing explanation is how Mormons could possibly practice
monogamy today at God's command when their prophets and apostles
depicted monogamy as a social evil that actually causes sinful behavior.[31]
It is quite probable that Mormons would simply dismiss this as either
1) mere opinion, or 2) the obsolete words of dead prophets.

For example, in a recent polygamy-related statement referenced by
the LDS Church, BYU professor Robert Millet diametrically opposed these

past opinions, declaring, "Church leaders then and now are quick to observe, however, that monogamy is the rule and polygamy is the exception."[32] In reality, in 1865 Brigham Young—a church leader from Millet's "then" era—said the very opposite of what Millet asserts. Young declared, "Those who are acquainted with the history of the world are not ignorant that polygamy has always been the general rule and monogamy the exception."[33]

MORMON QUESTIONS

One of the best decisions I made after publishing my first book on Mormonism in 1992 *(One Nation Under Gods)* was to become part of the Mormon-run online community called Zion's Lighthouse Message Board (ZLMB).[1] I visited ZLMB after receiving an e-mail saying that the Mormons there were "appalled" by my book—and me.

Unfortunately, as is so often the case when discussing religion, things quickly got out of hand upon my arrival. My presence (and posts), in fact, sparked some rather nasty exchanges. Eventually, however, after months of generating more heat than light, all sides seemed to call for a truce and began civil dialogue.

Although sometimes emotionally and spiritually difficult, my continuing interaction at ZLMB has motivated me to wrestle with some very thought-provoking issues. I now enjoy many conversations at ZLMB, and I count as friends several of its LDS participants.[2]

Then, in late 2003 I asked my ZLMB friends what questions they might like to ask an evangelical if given the opportunity. The following pages represent their responses, and for the first time, my answers to them.[3] Some of the questions are rather surprising.

✠ ✠ ✠

Do you believe in personal revelation through the gift of the Holy Ghost?

Yes. A belief in personal revelation is held by many evangelicals. God can personally communicate to his people via the Bible, dreams, visions, a word of wisdom through a fellow believer, or a spoken word to one's spirit. Few evangelicals would have a problem with the Book of Mormon's statement "[B]y the power of the Holy Ghost ye may know the truth of all things" (Moroni 10:5). This idea simply reflects John 8:32 and 14:26.

This does not mean that all "revelations" we think we receive from God are truly divine. We are sinful, fallible human beings, and as such, are open to deception. So we must test all things and accept only those revelations that are, as Scripture says, "good" (1 Thessalonians 5:21). Even if an angel or a great teacher were to appear before us and give so-called revelatory truths, we would still have to "try the spirits" to see if the message being imparted was of God.

Of course, the primary way of testing such things is by comparing them to the Bible. It is God's secure standard by which we can measure revelations that may come from other sources. God will not contradict himself, and so any true revelations to us will be in harmony to what God has already said in Scripture.

Do evangelicals believe that the family unit can exist for eternity? Are we together forever as a family, or do we part at death forever?

Evangelicals do believe that Christian families will exist together for all eternity, but not in an earthly way. As noted on pages 241 and 307–308, there is no marriage in heaven. The afterlife will be infinitely more than earthly life. Families, as they exist now, are a temporary picture of the kind of love and togetherness all of us will enjoy as part of God's heavenly family.

Since God has dealt with holy prophets since Adam, shouldn't he have prophets in these latter days?

Just because God did things in a certain way during one era does not mean that he must do things in exactly that same way in every era. Moreover, evangelicals believe that the purpose for the law and the prophets—to point the people forward to the Messiah—passed away with the coming of John the Baptist (Luke 16:16).

The prophets (and the apostles), according to the New Testament, were laid as a foundation for the church, which was built upon Jesus Christ, "himself being the chief corner stone" (Ephesians 2:20-21). Since that foundation was completed in the first century, it is believed by evangelicals that the era of apostles and prophets is no more.

Do you believe in the gifts of tongues, prophecy, revelation, visions, healing, interpretation of tongues?

Some evangelicals believe in these things, others do not. Such issues are commonly referred to as nonessentials of the Christian faith. In other words, they are not part of the key doctrines that form the heart of Christianity. It is on the key doctrines that Christians must agree, largely because they determine our understanding of who God and Christ are, as well as the means of our salvation and its authenticity in our lives. But there is room for evangelicals to differ on a variety of nonessential issues, none of which really impact our spiritual standing with God from the standpoint of salvation.

Do evangelicals believe that Jesus Christ was resurrected and that he now has a body of flesh and bones that is glorified and perfected?

Yes. This is a very important essential belief of the Christian faith, according to the creeds. After his resurrection, Jesus was touched (Matthew 28:9; John 20:17,27; 1 John 1:1). He ate food (Luke 24:30,42-43; John 21:12-13; Acts 10:41). He said he had flesh and bones (Luke 24:39). In John 2:19,21-22, he spoke of the temple of his body (Greek, *soma*—for physical body) being restored in three days. And Colossians 2:9 (written after the resurrection) uses the *present tense* to say that in Jesus the fullness of deity dwells bodily.

Do evangelicals believe in the second coming of our Savior and of the signs of the times?

Eschatology is another nonessential of the Christian faith. All evangelicals believe in the second coming, even though they all may not agree on the details of when, how, or in what order the end-time events may occur. There are four major evangelical views, each of which embraces the reality of the second coming and the signs of the times: historic premillennialism; dispensational premillennialism; amillennialism; and postmillennialism. Countless books have been written discussing these issues (see note 4).[4]

Do evangelicals tithe?

Many evangelicals do tithe. However, there is no total agreement among evangelicals on whether or not a ten-percent "tithe" is a New Testament command. Consequently, although most evangelicals give financially, they do not necessarily "tithe." Others who do tithe may do so on either their gross or net earnings.

Do evangelicals believe in the atonement of Christ?

Yes (see Romans 5:11).

Are evangelicals missionary-minded?

Yes (see Matthew 28:19-20).

Do evangelicals believe in taking care of our bodies as temples?

Yes (see 1 Corinthians 6:19-20).

Do evangelicals believe that there was gender before birth and after we die?

Before birth, yes. Before conception, no. After we die, probably so, since we will be physically resurrected in a body that is in some way connected to the bodies we now possess (see 1 Corinthians 15:35-44).

Do evangelicals get baptized by immersion by those having authority?

Yes. But it must be remembered that the evangelical concept of both "authority" and "baptism" is very different from the LDS concept of "authority" and "baptism." To evangelicals, the authority to baptize is included in the priesthood of all believers. And baptism is not for forgiveness, but rather is an outward sign that one has already been forgiven.

Do evangelicals believe that we have a spirit?

Yes. Of course. But not a spirit that was pre-existent (see chapter 6).

Do evangelicals remember our Savior through the ordinance of the sacrament?

Yes. Absolutely. In fact, unlike the LDS Church, which uses water, all evangelical churches use bread and wine or grape juice. Most evangelical churches partake either weekly or monthly.

Do evangelicals have modern apostles? Have they been ordained like the apostles of old? Can they trace their priesthood authority to Christ through the laying on of hands as was done in the Bible?

No. Most evangelicals do not accept the legitimacy of modern apostles (see question on pages 302–303). However, when one moves out of evangelical circles and into the Charismatic–Pentecostal community, one can find churches that believe in, and sustain, modern "apostles."

Which version of the Holy Bible is the "most" correct to evangelicals?

Most Bible versions (that is, translations) say essentially the same thing with minor variations. These variations are mainly a result of the different manuscript "families" on which a particular translation is based. Other variations are due to style, translation methods, and interpretive choices. For its timeless beauty, some evangelicals prefer the King James Version (based on one set of manuscripts). Many prefer the New American

Standard Bible (based on an older set of manuscripts) for its greater word-for-word accuracy. Some might prefer any number of other translations. It is an issue of personal preference.

There are different versions of the Bible, some of which include material not included by other versions. Are evangelicals obliged to accept all of these disputed portions? None of them? Some of them?

A comparison of the manuscripts used to produce the various Bible translations shows that there are no significant differences—certainly none that would lead to conflicting interpretations of Christian doctrines. Consequently, evangelicals—after making their own investigation of the material—are free to accept the variants with which they feel most comfortable.

Do all evangelicals believe in ex nihilo *creation?*

Creation *ex nihilo* (or creation of all that is out of nothing) is a standard belief throughout evangelicalism. But it is not an essential of the faith. One could technically be a Christian and hold to some view of creation wherein God used spirit matter.

Do evangelicals believe that the great apostasy spoken of by the apostle Paul has occurred?

Some evangelicals believe it has already taken place. Others maintain it is yet to come. All evangelicals, however, do agree that the apostasy of which Paul spoke would never result in a complete disappearance from the earth of the true church (that is, Christianity).

Can evangelicals answer these questions: 1) Where did I come from? 2) Why am I here? 3) After this life, what is there?

Yes. 1) Scripture teaches that the spirit is formed within the body (Zechariah 12:1). 2) To know, love, serve, and glorify God. 3) There are only two states of existence after death—eternity in God's immediate presence (heaven), and eternal separation from God (hell).

What if a sincere and prayerful evangelical arrives at different viewpoints from his religious leaders, such as perhaps understanding a critical scripture differently? Is the seeker who arrives at a divergent, unorthodox viewpoint expected to be obedient to his leaders ("follow the brethren," in Mormon-speak), or is an individual who is looking for a deep understanding (and who arrives at individual conclusions) accepted? Where do evangelicals draw the line between following their orthodoxy (whatever that may be) and individual truth-seeking?

There is great freedom given to evangelicals when it comes to personal understanding of Scripture. Even the phrase "obedient to his leaders" is understood differently within the evangelical mind and church life. "Obedience," in the truest sense of the word, is rendered to God alone—not a pastor, leader, or minister. These persons are merely guides to help God's people grow in the grace and knowledge of God. If any kind of line is ever drawn, it only pertains to the essentials of the faith as outlined in the church creeds. If, when you use the word "unorthodox," you mean a "viewpoint" contrary to these essentials of the faith, then such an individual would indeed be encouraged to rethink his or her views—but not necessarily encouraged to leave a church. True disciplinary action usually becomes an issue only when an individual's personal sin starts to adversely affect the church, or perhaps when a "leader" is approached for assistance.

Do you believe in eternal maleness and femaleness?

Certainly. Evangelicals believe that we retain our gender identity just as Christ has retained his gender identity (Acts 17:31). And yet we also understand Matthew 22:23-33 to mean that, in eternity, we will neither marry nor be given in marriage, and will live as the angels. As for Matthew 18:18, which deals with binding and loosing and is often used by Mormons to prove eternal marriage, this passage has nothing to do with couples being bound in heaven because they were bound together on earth. In context, the passage deals with church discipline. First Corinthians 11:11

also does not relate to marriage, but instead, refers to man's authority in relation to woman.

Do most evangelicals believe in the Calvinistic doctrine as formulated in "TULIP" [Total depravity, Unconditional election, Limited atonement, Irresistible grace, Perseverance of the saints]? Is this a major doctrine that can cause schisms among evangelicals?

No one knows exactly how many evangelicals believe all five points of Calvinism, although it would certainly be true that most evangelicals embrace one or more of them. Calvinism is not considered a "major doctrine" worthy of causing schisms. Calvinists and non-Calvinists enjoy full fellowship. Only extremists from either camp would use TULIP as an excuse to break fellowship.

Do evangelicals believe that they can sin after they have been "saved"? Can they get "saved" again and again and again?

Of course evangelicals can sin after they are saved. Every Christian will commit sins until he or she is released from this body of death. But ethical–moral failures do not rip one's salvation away as if it were transitory (Romans 8:38-39). Most evangelicals believe in eternal security (the "P" in TULIP) based on (among others) the scripture stating that "whom he did predestinate, them he also called: and whom he called, them he also justified; and whom he justified, them he also glorified" (Romans 8:28-30). These are all past tense. In other words, those who *are* saved will without a doubt *be* saved. Some evangelicals, however, may subscribe to an *Arminian* view of salvation, which does indeed teach that one can lose one's salvation. But this particular view, as your question implies, seems flawed on many levels (for example, 1 John 5:13).

How do evangelicals reconcile God's eternal condemnation with his eternal love?

Love is only one aspect of God's character. He is also holy and just. These qualities demand that unrighteousness be punished. Human courts, although imperfect, hand down punishments. Should we expect any less of God, who is perfectly just? Evangelicals take comfort in knowing that God is neither unfair nor cruel. In other words, no one will be condemned who does not deserve to be condemned. God's justice is evident in the fact there will be *degrees* of punishment in the afterlife (Matthew 11:21-24; Luke 12:45-48), just as there will be degrees of reward (2 Corinthians 5:10). Though it is not an attractive teaching, Scripture does indicate that those who die without Christ will continue to exist in a state of conscious eternal separation from God (2 Thessalonians 1:6-10; Hebrews 10:27).

Do evangelicals believe in being honest, true, chaste, benevolent, and virtuous, and in doing good to all men?

Yes. Those who do not seek after these things are in sin. Of course, evangelicals are not perfect and will invariably fail in living out their righteousness before God. But failing is a far cry from not trying at all and just surrendering to our sinfulness.

Do evangelicals believe that homosexuality is a sin?

Yes. However, in recent years a number of extremely liberal denominations and churches have been attempting to legitimize homosexuality. These liberals, many of whom also deny a number of essential Christian beliefs (such as the deity of Christ), are being opposed by mainstream—traditional—believers.

Why do bad things happen to good people? What is the evangelical take on this? Since God knows everything, why did he create a world and put his children through all types of pain and grief? Why didn't he just create his children to live in heaven or in hell and skip this earth?

Because we live in a fallen world—a world in which Adam and Eve, in the Garden of Eden, chose to pursue and enjoy life on their own terms instead of God's terms—we are surrounded by many things that are in opposition to God, including Satan. And Satan can have a very real impact on our world and our lives. Sin's presence in this world means that sometimes bad things do happen to good people (see the book of Job). But our comfort comes from knowing several things: 1) God loves us; 2) he sees the big picture; 3) one day the suffering for those who love him will end; and 4) suffering can bring blessings and growth.

Can evangelicals explain why God had temples built in ancient times; and if he is the same yesterday, today, and forever, why he wouldn't have us build temples today?

Temples were built for the purposes and activities outlined in the Old Testament. They are no longer needed because of Christ's final sacrifice on the cross. As for God being the same yesterday, today, and forever (Hebrews 13:8), this verse actually says, "Jesus Christ the same yesterday, and to day, and for ever." The context of the verse is the conduct of church leaders that the writer of Hebrews was telling his readers to emulate (verse 7). Then, in verse 8, Christ is presented as the ultimate example: one who does not change—in purpose, goal, motivation, or righteousness. This has nothing to do with temples.

Do evangelicals believe that a person can be forgiven for murder after being "born again"?

Yes. Christ's death on the cross paid the price for all sins past, present, and future. However, when it comes to something as heinous as murder, I would think that a true Christian would have to be under extreme mental and emotional trauma to commit such a crime.

Are Catholics and Eastern Orthodox (Russian Orthodox, Romanian Orthodox, and so on) saved?

Persons in these denominations who hold to a true faith in Jesus Christ are saved. This does not mean that all individuals in these churches are saved. Nor are all persons in Protestant churches saved. The key issue is whether or not someone knows the true Jesus as their Lord and Savior.

How can Christians avoid fighting about scriptural interpretations?

The best way to avoid religious arguments is to strive to be like Christ in all we say, think, and do, and to be a good student of God's Word, which is "profitable for doctrine, for reproof, for correction, for instruction in righteousness" (2 Timothy 3:16).

Do evangelicals believe that there are other worlds that are popu-lated? If so, do evangelicals believe that these people are sinners?

There is no evangelical position on this issue, nor does the Bible comment on it. A wide variety of opinions exist among evangelicals. Personally, I think the chances are quite high that other forms of life do exist elsewhere in the universe. Whether or not these life-forms might be "sinners" is something that is impossible to know. Even if they were "sinners," this would not necessitate God dealing with them in the same way he chose to deal with us (the human life-form).

With the proliferation of books on the subject (not to mention advances in resuscitation technology), the "near-death experience" is becoming well known. Mormonism seems to be fairly comfort-able with the reported experiences of NDEs. Do evangelicals believe that near-death experiences (as reported in numerous publications) are true accounts, mistaken accounts, inevitably fabrications, or the works of darkness? Why?

There is no consensus among evangelicals regarding NDEs. Some believe they are hallucinations. Others accept them as true glimpses of the afterlife. Some consider them to be "real," but subjective in nature. In other words, they occur within the mind as a result of biochemical changes, which produce vivid internal scenes created from a person's religious beliefs, memories, sounds in the environment, and psychological trauma.

Do all evangelicals believe in a literal hell where people stay forever if they fail to become saved while alive?

Most evangelicals probably hold to a literal hell, but not all of them. Some Christian denominations (for example, the Seventh-Day Adventists) and various individual evangelicals embrace what is known as "eternal annihilation" of those who do not accept Christ as Savior. There are actually several views of hell advanced by various individuals and churches within Christianity: literal, metaphorical, purgatorial, and conditional.[5]

Do evangelicals really try to understand other religions, or do they just judge and compartmentalize them into the "you're all going to hell" category?

As with any large group of people, evangelicals include all types of people. Many evangelicals, at least in my experience, are indeed concerned with understanding people of other religions and fostering tolerance as well as mutual respect. Unfortunately, there are some evangelicals—no one knows how many—who do "judge and compartmentalize" people. But hopefully, as these people grow in Christ, they will better represent Jesus to those who do not know God.

Do evangelicals claim the privilege of worshiping Almighty God according to the dictates of their own conscience, and allow all men the same privilege of worshiping how, where, or what they may?

Yes. But this does not mean that persons do not have the right to raise concerns about other faiths, or make valid and responsible criticisms of other faiths.

Many evangelicals seem to ignore or even denounce liturgical rites. How do you reconcile this ambivalence (hostility?) with the abundance of liturgical practices which are condoned and even commanded in the Bible?

Actually, many evangelicals in various denominations (for example, Lutheran and Presbyterian) have great respect and admiration for liturgical practices. It is true, however, that *some* evangelicals connected with independent, nondenominational churches tend to view liturgical practices as either too confining or as sterile. But again, these are nonessential issues evangelicals can view differently, depending on individual tastes and personalities.

Why don't you focus on sharing your religious views rather than on criticizing ours?

Evangelicals do share their views. But sometimes sharing one's own views necessitates raising concerns about, and making comparisons to, another person's beliefs, especially if the beliefs being discussed differ on important points. This is not inherently wrong. However, the way one communicates certainly can be either sinful or Christlike.

What about the hundreds of millions (perhaps billions) of people throughout history who—by circumstance and through no fault of their own—never had the opportunity to hear and accept the Gospel? For example, a person who lived in an area where Christ was never taught, grew up without hearing anything about Christ or the gospel, but he lives a good life—according to evangelical beliefs, does this person go to hell since he didn't accept Christ, or can he go to heaven in spite of the fact that he didn't accept Christ?

First, this question assumes that some persons who did not hear about Christ would have accepted him if only they had heard about him. But this a false assumption. Many people hear about Christ and still reject him. Second, all of God's followers in the Old Testament era were saved by faith by looking *forward* to Christ's atonement, just as we are saved by faith by looking *back* to it. Third, Scripture tells us that Jesus is the Creator (John 1:3; Colossians 1:16), which means that anyone who truly worships the Creator is saved. Hence, it is possible for someone in the remotest part of the world who has never heard the actual gospel story—*but who would accept it if they were to hear it*—to look up into the heavens, call upon the Creator, and obtain salvation by the most basic of beliefs (Romans 1:18-21). Fourth, evangelicals believe that God is absolutely sovereign. Consequently, it is a common evangelical belief that anyone in the world open to the gospel will eventually hear the gospel, whatever their location. Those who seek God will find him.

Who besides evangelicals is saved?

Anyone who accepts Christ as their Lord and Savior is saved. This is not to say, however, that everyone who simply *claims* to worship and follow someone *named* Jesus is saved. Even demons, for example, believe there is one God (James 2:19). Are they saved? Of course not. According to evangelicals, "saved" describes anyone who has by faith accepted the sacrifice of Christ for their sins. Many others besides evangelicals are saved.

THE BIBLICAL TRINITY

A good starting point for studying the Trinity is Deuteronomy 6:4: "Hear, O Israel! The LORD our God is one LORD." This verse, known as the *shema*, was the cornerstone of Israel's view of God. Other Old Testament verses articulating Jewish monotheism are 1 Kings 18:18-39, 2 Samuel 7:22, and Isaiah 45:2-22.

By preaching one God, the prophets reminded Israel "of the vast gulf that separated the Lord from pagan idols and the many so-called gods they represented (Hosea 4:12; Isaiah 2:8,20; 17:8; 31:7; Jeremiah 10:5, 10)."[1] At the same time, many Old Testament passages suggest a plurality in God's nature. Genesis 1:26 reads, "And God [singular] said, Let us [plural] make man in our [plural] image, after our [plural] likeness."

Even more thought-provoking is verse 27: "So God [singular] created man in his own [singular] image, in the image of God [singular] he created him; male and female created he [singular] them."[2] Christian scholar Gleason Archer observed that the verse is implying that "the plural equals the singular. This can only be understood in terms of the Trinitarian nature of God."[3]

Moreover, the Old Testament contains some verses wherein one Person called God (or Lord) is interacting in some way with another Person called God (or Lord). Consider Psalm 45:6,7: "Thy throne, O God, is for ever and ever...therefore God, thy God, hath anointed thee with the oil of gladness above thy fellows."

Like the Old Testament, the New Testament affirms the existence of just one God (see Galatians 3:20; 1 Timothy 1:17; 2:5; James 2:19; Jude 25). At the same time, it identifies three persons: the Father (1 John 1:1), Son (1 John 1:1-3), and Holy Ghost (John 14:16,26; 15:26; 16:13-14). And each of them are called *God* (*Father*—John 6:27; Romans 1:7; 1 Thessalonians 1:1; *Son*—John 20:28; Hebrews 1:8-9; and *Holy Ghost*—Acts 5:3-4).

Did You Know? The biblical foundation of the Trinity can be seen in the many passages that not only designate the Father, Son, and Holy Ghost as God, but also ascribe to them the same attributes and divine acts. All three dwell in believers (John 14:17,20,23). All three possess and impart eternal life (*Father*—John 5:26; *Son*—John 1:4; 5:21,26; 10:28; 11:25; *Holy Ghost*—2 Corinthians 3:6; Galatians 6:8). And all three were active in the resurrection of Christ (*Father*—Galatians 1:1; *Son*—John 2:19-20; 10:17; *Holy Ghost*—Romans 8:11), even though we are told that it was "God" who raised Jesus from the dead (1 Corinthians 6:14).

The New Testament also presents Father, Son, and Holy Ghost as having an incomparably intimate union. All are named in the Great Commission (Matthew 28:19), Paul's benediction to the Corinthians (2 Corinthians 13:14), and Peter's salutation to Christians (1 Peter 1:2). Jesus' baptism also provides a vivid picture of the Trinity (Matthew 3:16-17). And in the New Testament, many Old Testament titles and prerogatives reserved to God are applied to Jesus and the Holy Ghost.[4]

APPENDIX D

"Why I Am a Mormon"

I first met Daniel C. Peterson, BYU professor of Islamic Studies, via e-mails in 2003. We discussed a number of issues through online correspondence, eventually deciding to follow up our electronic communications with a series of phone calls. He sounded not at all how I thought he would sound. I found, much to my surprise, that we saw eye-to-eye on a number of issues. Not every issue, of course, but this did not stop us from appreciating each other as individuals sincerely seeking to do the right thing in life.

We met not long afterward, during a trip I made to Utah later that year. It was an extremely cordial meeting that led to our having a nearly three-hour dinner together. BYU professor emeritus of political science Lou Midgley dined with us. The evening was one of the most enlightening and enjoyable nights I have ever had in connection to my work. I continued my contact with Peterson, often e-mailing him about his faith—even asking some rather pointed questions. I gradually came to consider him a friend, and I believe he feels the same way about me.

Then, while writing this book, I realized that one way to help my readers better understand Mormons would be to actually have a faithful Mormon share his faith—his testimony—his heart. I immediately thought of Dan. He is not only a reputable scholar, but also an articulate and well-respected Latter-day Saint—whose heart, I believe, is set on furthering communication between Mormons and evangelicals. Therefore, I offer to you his gracious reply to my request for a brief word that explains why he is a Mormon.

瑞 瑞 瑞

Dear Richard,

I am a Christian. I also am a Mormon. I not only believe in God, but I also happen to believe in the truthfulness of The Church of Jesus Christ of Latter-day Saints.

I believe in God partly because I don't believe that the universe can be explained by random chance. It cannot be accounted for naturalistically. I also believe in God because, intuitively, high in the mountains or under star-studded desert nights, I simply know that God lives. In Christian terms, the Spirit testifies to my spirit.

I call myself a Christian because the New Testament speaks powerfully to me, because I consider the atonement of Jesus Christ the pivotal point of history, and because I believe in Jesus' resurrection, which confirms him as the Son of God, my Savior and Lord. These convictions are fundamental and indispensable to my faith. But, necessary though they are, they don't explain why I've chosen my particular church.

I'm a Mormon out of confidence that the events of the Restoration—the appearances of the Father and the Son and of Moroni to Joseph Smith, the translation of the Book of Mormon, angelic bestowals of priesthood authority—literally occurred, as recounted by eyewitnesses. In other words, I not only believe that God established The Church of Jesus Christ of Latter-day Saints, but I also have reasons for the hope that lies within me.

The grand sweep of Mormonism captured my heart because it offers an intellectually satisfying, even exhilarating, vision of the universe and of the significance of human life. (I cannot imagine a more exciting destiny for humankind.) Among the many teachings that I love, I mention two. First, openness to truth everywhere, recognizing that God has worked and does work among all peoples. Second, the principle of salvation for the dead, which, offering Christ's redemption even to those who never heard his name, vindicates God's merciful justice, demonstrates the irreducible worth of every soul, and inspires a serene confidence that, ultimately, all will be well.

Mormonism opens the scriptures to me, making the ancient saints my contemporaries. It roots me in a history and a people. I share my life with a community of believers that, even in its imperfections, forcefully reminds me of the New Testament church. This fellowship is deeply fulfilling. It offers limitless opportunities for service and calls upon me, often against my nature, to learn to care and sacrifice. I have both witnessed and experienced the comfort that the gospel and its ordinances give in seasons of bereavement, the quiet understanding they provide in times of pain.

Finally, my encounters with the Spirit of God nourish and sustain my faith. My prayers have been answered. I've sensed profound holiness in the temple. I've enjoyed glimpses, fleeting but immensely powerful, of the eternities. Several times, I've been granted specific knowledge of the future. Having received revelation, I can believe in continuing revelation through living prophets and apostles. Although in this life we all see through a glass darkly, I can see further and more clearly because of the restored gospel of Jesus Christ. And what I see, through Mormonism, is inexpressibly good.

Daniel C. Peterson
Professor of Islamic Studies and Arabic, BYU

Research Resources

I. Online Secular (LDS doctrine, Mormon history, Christian responses)

- *American Religions,* http://religion.rutgers.edu/vri/america.html
- *Anti-Mormon Preservation Society,* http://antimormon.8m.com/
- *Beliefnet,* http://www.beliefnet.com/
- *Dr. Shades' Mormonism Page,* http://www.fiber.net/users/drshades/mormon.htm
- *Ex-Mormons,* http://www.exmormon.org/
- *LDS-Mormonism,* http://www.lds-mormon.com/
- *Making of America Books,* http://www.hti.umich.edu/m/moagrp/ (click on either "Go to MoA Books" or "Go to MoA Journals"). At these two sites, either browse the collection titles, or run keyword searches on Mormon-related words or phrases (for example, Mormon, Brigham, "Joseph Smith," and so on).
- *Mormon Central,* http://www.xmission.com/~research/central/index.htm
- *Mormon Classics,* http://SidneyRigdon.com/Classics1.htm
- *Mormons in Transition,* http://www.irr.org/mit/
- *Real Mormon History,* http://www.realmormonhistory.com/
- *Saints Without Halos,* http://www.saintswithouthalos.com/
- *2think Online Discussion Forum,* http://2thinkforums.org/

II. Online Christian (apologetics, counter-LDS, world religions, cults)

- *Alpha & Omega Ministries,* http://aomin.org/Mormonism.html
- *Answers In Action,* http://answers.org/
- *Apologetics Index,* http://www.apologeticsindex.org/
- *Apologetics Resource Center,* http://www.apologeticsresctr.org/
- *Christian Research Institute,* http://www.equip.org/
- *FactNet,* http://www.factnet.org/
- *Institute of Religious Research,* http://www.irr.org/
- *Mormonism Research Ministries,* http://www.mrm.org/

- *Religious Information Center,* http://www.abanes.com/RIC.html
- *Tekton Apologetics Ministries,* http://tektonics.org/index.html
- *Utah Lighthouse Ministry,* http://www.utlm.org/
- *Watchman Fellowship,* http://watchman.org/watchman.htm
- *Wellington Christian Apologetics Society,* http://www.christian-apologetics.org/ index.html

III. ONLINE LDS / FUNDAMENTALISTS / RLDS

- *BYU Speeches,* http://speeches.byu.edu/index.php?/
- *Church of Jesus Christ of Latter-day Saints,* http://www.lds.org/
- *Community of Christ,* http://CofChrist.org/
- *Deseret News,* http://deseretnews.com/dn
- *FAIR (Foundation for Apologetics Information Resources),* http://www.fairlds.org
- *FARMS (Foundation for Ancient Research and Mormon Studies),* http://farms.byu.edu/splash4.html
- *Kingdom of Zion,* http://www.kingdomofzion.org
- *LDS Church News,* http://www.desnews.com/cn/
- *Meridian Magazine,* http://www.meridianmagazine.com/
- *Restoration Website,* http://restoration.org/
- *SHIELDS (Scholarly & Historical Information Exchange for Latter-Day Saints),* http://www.shields-research.org/
- *Zion's Lighthouse Message Board,* http://pub26.ezboard.com/bpacumenispages

IV. MULTIMEDIA, CD-ROM

- *GospeLink 2001* (SLC: Deseret Book Co., 2001), available at Deseret Bookstores
- *The Mormon Puzzle* (Southern Baptist Convention, video), available online at http://www.utlm.org/booklist/titles/xv001_mormonpuzzle.htm
- *The Mormon Historical Reference Library,* available online at http://antimormon.8m .com/storeA.html
- *New Mormon Studies CD-ROM: A Comprehensive Resource Library* (Smith Research Associates), available online from numerous outlets.
- *The Personal Gospel Library* (LDS Palm Pocket Software, 2003), a Mormon CD of materials that can be downloaded to a PDA, available online from numerous outlets and from 1-800-585-3188.
- *Selected Collections from the Archives of The Church of Jesus Christ of Latter-day Saints* (Brigham Young University Press), available exclusively from BYU, online at http://byustudies.byu.edu

NOTES
INDEXES

NOTES

Abbreviations

AOF The "Articles of Faith." Thirteen statements of belief outlining basic LDS beliefs in non-offensive terms. None of the statements deal with doctrines that might be viewed as controversial. The AOF appears in the Pearl of Great Price and online at http://scriptures.lds.org/a_of_f/1.

BMO Book of Moses. Received by divine revelation to Joseph Smith, it is a "correction" and revision of the first several chapters of Genesis. It appears in the Pearl of Great Price, and online at http://scriptures.lds.org/moses/ contents.

BOA Book of Abraham. Said to have been written by Abraham on papyri scrolls that Joseph Smith acquired in 1835. Smith claimed to have translated this volume into English from the Egyptian writing on the scrolls. It has since been learned that the scrolls were nothing but common funerary texts from the Egyptian Book of Breathings (see chapter 3). The BOA appears in the Pearl of Great Price and online at http://scriptures .lds.org/abr/contents.

BOC *Book of Commandments.* First published in 1833, it contained Joseph Smith's earliest revelations. It was republished in 1835 as the Doctrine and Covenants. Online at http://www.irr.org/mit/BOC/1833boc-1835d&c-index.html.

BOM Book of Mormon. Published in 1830, it is the translation of gold plates Joseph Smith said he found in the Hill Cumorah (Palmyra, New York). The plates supposedly contained the history of America's ancient inhabitants and the fullness of God's everlasting gospel. The BOM has gone through major revisions and edits. It is online at http://scriptures.lds .org/bm/contents.

BYU Brigham Young University.

CHC *A Comprehensive History of the Church.* Produced by LDS historian B.H. Roberts.

CR *Conference Report,* the annual publication containing speeches delivered at LDS conferences.

D&C Doctrine and Covenants. Published in 1835, it contains the words of God to Joseph Smith. It has been repeatedly revised and edited to reflect unforeseen changes in LDS doctrine, practices, and history. The Doctrine and Covenants also includes 1) the 1890 Manifesto by LDS president Wilford Woodruff that banned polygamy; and 2) the 1978 "revelation" allowing blacks to hold the LDS priesthood. It is online at http://scriptures.lds.org/dc/contents.

E&MS *The Evening and the Morning Star.* The first LDS periodical, initially published in Missouri (June 1832–July 1833). After being destroyed by a mob, its publication site was relocated to Ohio (1833–1834).

EJ *Elders' Journal of the Church of Latter Day Saints.* An early LDS periodical first published in Ohio (1837), then in Missouri (July 1838–August 1838).

EMD *Early Mormon Documents.* Five volumes, edited by Dan Vogel.

FAIR The Foundation for Apologetic Information & Research. An Internet-based Mormon apologetic organization that provides material defending the LDS faith and seeks to refute evangelical criticisms of Mormonism.

FARMS The Foundation for Ancient Research and Mormon Studies. A BYU-affiliated organization of highly trained LDS scholars who provide scholarly defenses of the LDS faith and refutations of literature critical of the Mormon Church.

HC *History of the Church.* The history of Mormonism presented by the LDS Church. It was written by Joseph Smith, various scribes, and later historians, who "updated" the text in an effort to conceal events that reflected badly on Smith, other LDS leaders, and the church.

HR *The Historical Record.* An LDS periodical published to give the historical, biographical, chronological, and statistical matters of the church (9 volumes, 1882–1890). Edited by LDS church historian Andrew Jenson.

JOD *Journal of Discourses.* Published by the LDS Church, this is a compilation of the lectures and sermons given by LDS leaders from 1843 to 1886 (26 volumes).

LDSC The Church of Jesus Christ of Latter-day Saints.

LDSCA The Church of Jesus Christ of Latter-day Saints Church Archives. Located in Salt Lake City, Utah.

MD *Mormon Doctrine.* An extremely popular volume written by LDS apostle Bruce McConkie (1915–1985).

MH *Manuscript History* of the LDS Church.

MS *Millennial Star.* An early LDS periodical that was published in England.

MS&AD *The Latter-day Saints' Messenger & Advocate.* An early LDS periodical that was published in Kirtland, Ohio (October 1834 to August 1837).

n, nn, fn, fnn Abbreviations for "endnote," "endnotes," "footnote," and "footnotes."

NT New Testament.

OT Old Testament.

PGP Pearl of Great Price. A compilation of documents: BMO, BOA, a section from the *HC*, Smith's retranslation of Matthew 23:39 to Matthew 24, and the AOF.

PJS *The Papers of Joseph Smith.* Two volumes of important historical documents compiled and edited by Dean Jessee.

Proceedings The *Proceedings Before the Committee On Privileges and Elections of the United States Senate in the Matter of the Protests Against the Right of Hon. Reed Smoot.* The testimony given to a committee called to determine if LDS apostle Reed Smoot could retain his senatorial seat (1904).

RLDSCA The Reorganized Church of Jesus Christ of Latter Day Saints Church Archives (Independence, Missouri). Now known as the Community of Christ. However, when citing documents from previously published resources, I have chosen to retain the RLDS designation.

SLC Salt Lake City, Utah.

T&S *Times and Seasons.* An early LDS periodical issued from Commerce/Nauvoo, Illinois (November 1839 to February 1846).

ULM The Utah Lighthouse Ministry (Salt Lake City). A veritable storehouse of information on Mormonism, collected by Jerald and Sandra Tanner. Jerald is a descendant of John Tanner, who was an associate of Joseph Smith in the 1800s. Sandra is the great-great-grandchild of Brigham Young.

ZLMB Zion's Lighthouse Message Board. An LDS-run Internet message board community.

"Can't We All Just Get Along?"

1. J. Reuben Clark. Quoted in D. Michael Quinn, *J. Reuben Clark: The Church Years* (Provo, UT: BYU Press, 1983), p. 24.

2. See Richard Abanes, *One Nation Under Gods* (New York: Four Walls Eight Windows, 2002; rev. paperback, 2003), pp. 311-353. Mormons claim that the cessation of polygamy occurred in response to a "revelation" given to LDS leadership. Historical evidence, however, suggests that the policy change came as a direct response to U.S. government threats to disband the LDS Church and seize its property if polygamy was not stopped. Debate remains over the exact nature of the 1890 Manifesto—Was it a revelation? For a discussion of this issue, see chapter 9, pp. 243ff.; see also D. Michael Quinn, "LDS Church Authority and New Plural Marriages, 1890-1904," *Dialogue: A Journal of Mormon Thought* (Spring 1985), vol. 18, no. 1, pp. 10-11, www.lds-mormon.com/quinn_polygamy.shtml.

3. See Keith B. McMullin, "An Invitation with Promise," Apr. 1, 2001, in *CR*, p. 78, available at www.lds.org; Dallin Oaks, "Focus and Priorities," Apr. 1, 2001, in *CR*, p. 109, available at www.lds.org; David E. Sorenson, "You Can't Pet A Rattlesnake," Mar. 31, 2001, in *CR*, p. 95, available at www.lds.org.

4. Richard Mouw, foreword in Francis J. Beckwith, Carl Mosser, and Paul Owen, *The New Mormon Challenge* (Grand Rapids, MI: Zondervan, 2002), p. 12.

5. Mouw, in Beckwith, et al., p. 12.

6. A "theist" is anyone who believes in a God.

7. Notable among these BYU professors are: Stephen E. Robinson, Robert L. Millet, Noel B. Reynolds, Stephen D. Ricks, Barry R. Bickmore, Daniel C. Peterson, Brent L. Top, John W. Welch, John Tvedtnes, William J. Hamblin, and Larry E. Dahl.

8. FARMS, "About FARMS," www.farms.byu.edu/aboutfarms.php. Many LDS lay apologists have followed the lead of FARMS by seeking to provide their own answers to evangelical concerns about Mormonism. The two most notable nonprofessional organizations, each of which enjoys an influential Internet presence, are the Foundation for Apologetic Information & Research (FAIR) at www.fairlds.org/home.html; and the Scholarly & Historical Information Exchange for Latter-day Saints (SHIELDS) at www.shields-research.org/.

9. I agree with BYU professors Robert L. Millet and Noel B. Reynolds, who see "a pressing need in today's world for people of various religious denominations to better understand one another. Nothing good comes from misrepresenting another's beliefs" (Robert L. Millet and Noel B. Reynolds, *Latter-Day Christianity: 10 Basic Issues* [Provo, UT: FARMS, 1998], p. v, http://farms.byu.edu/10basic/10basicissues.php?chapter=preface.

10. Excellent resources can be obtained from the following: Answers In Action (Gretchen Passantino, PO Box 2067, Costa Mesa, CA 92628, 949-646-9042, www.answers.org/); Christian Research Institute (Hank Hanegraaff, PO Box 7000, Rancho Santa Margarita, CA 92688-7000, 949-858-6100, www.equip.org/); Mormonism Research Ministries (Bill McKeever, PO Box 1746, Draper, UT 84020-1746, 801-572-2153, www.mrm.org/); and Utah Lighthouse Ministries (Sandra Tanner, PO Box 1884, Salt Lake City, UT 84110, 801-485-8894, www.utlm.org/).

11. Carl Mosser and Paul Owen, "Mormon Scholarship, Apologetics, and Evangelical Neglect: Losing the Battle and Not Knowing It?" *Trinity Journal* (Fall 1998), pp. 179-205, www.cephasministry.com/mormon_apologetics_losing_battle.html.

12. Carl Mosser and Paul Owen. Quoted in Justin Hart, "Winning the Battle and Not Knowing It," *Meridian Magazine*, www.ldsmag.com/voices/020529winning.html.

13. Beckwith, et al., p. 25.

14. John Taylor, Apr. 13, 1862, in *JOD*, vol. 9, p. 342.

15. BYU history professor Thomas G. Alexander has explained, "Perhaps the main barrier to understanding the development of Mormon theology is an underlying assumption by most Church members that there is a cumulative unity of doctrine. Mormons seem to believe that particular doctrines develop consistently, that ideas build on each other in hierarchical fashion. As a result, older revelations are reinterpreted by referring to current doctrinal positions. Thus, most members would suppose that a scripture or statement at any point in time has resulted from such orderly change. While this type of exegesis or interpretation may produce systematic theology and while it may satisfy those trying to understand and internalize current doctrine, it is bad history since it leaves an unwarranted impression of continuity and consistency" (Thomas G. Alexander, "The Reconstruction of Mormon Doctrine: From Joseph Smith to Progressive Theology," *Sunstone* [July-Aug.1980], vol. 5, issue 4, p. 24, excerpt at www.lds-mormon.com/changod.shtml).

16. Jason Gallentine, "Internet Mormonism vs. Chapel Mormonism," www.fiber.net/ users/drshades/imvscm.htm.

17. Beckwith, et al., p. 22. These categories of belief are further broken down by Beckwith, Mosser, and Owen into "doctrinally binding Mormon theology, traditional Mormon theology, common Mormon beliefs, and that which is permissible as Mormon theology."

18. The Church of Jesus Christ of Latter-day Saints, *AOF*, www.scriptures.lds.org/a_of_f/1.

19. Joseph Smith, Oct. 15, 1843, in *HC* (SLC: LDS Church, 1950; 1980 ed.), vol. 6, p. 57. The place of importance and authority of the Bible amid the other Standard Works was articulated by LDS apostle Bruce McConkie, who stated that "aceptance of the Bible is coupled with a reservation that it is true only insofar as translated correctly (Eighth Article of Faith.) The other three, having been revealed in modern times in English, are accepted without qualification" (*MD*, p. 764). McConkie also said that today's Bibles "do not accurately record or perfectly preserve the words, thoughts, and intents of the original inspired authors" (*MD*, p. 383).

   BYU professor Robert L. Millet has likewise stated: "Occasionally we hear certain Latter-day Saint teachings described as *unbiblical* or of a particular doctrine being *contradictory* to the Bible. Let us be clear on this matter. The Bible is one of the books within our standard works, and thus our doctrines and practices are in harmony with the Bible. There are times, of course, when latter-day revelation provides clarification or enhancement of the intended meaning in the Bible. But addition to the canon is not the same as rejection of the canon. Supplementation is not the same as contradiction" (Robert L. Millet, "What We Believe," Feb. 3, 1998, BYU devotional, http://speeches.byu.edu/ htmlfiles/MilletW98.html).

20. Millet, http://speeches.byu.edu/htmlfiles/MilletW98.html. Millet also noted that Smith did not "believe in either the inerrancy or the infallibility of the Bible."

21. "[W]e love the Bible and cherish its messages. But the Bible is not the source of our doctrine or authority, nor is much to be gained through efforts to 'prove' the truthfulness of the restored gospel from the Bible. Ours is an independent revelation. We know what we know about the premortal existence, priesthood, celestial marriage, baptism for the dead, the postmortal spirit world, degrees of glory, etc., because of what God has made known through latter-day prophets, not because we are able to identify a few biblical allusions to these matters. Some of our greatest difficulties in handling questions about our faith come when we try to establish specific doctrines of the Restoration from the Bible alone" (Millet, http://speeches.byu.edu/htmlfiles/MilletW98.html).

22. *Gospel Principles* (SLC: LDSC, 1978; rev., 1979; Missionary Reference Library Edition, 1990), pp. 51-52. But even this statement can be challenged. First, *Gospel Principles* is not itself a Standard Work. Hence, a Mormon might object to its assertions, even though it has been written by the LDS Church. Second, a Mormon may fix on the word "inspired," which is a vague term. What does it mean for a comment to be inspired? Who decides if a comment is inspired? Does a comment have to be announced as inspired *before* it is made? These questions still have not been *officially* answered.

   BYU professor Stephen E. Robinson, meanwhile, has defined official doctrine thus: In addition to the Standard Works, the only other binding words on Latter-day Saints are the official *interpretations* and *applications* of these doctrinal sources, which "are those that come to the church over the signatures of the First Presidency or the Quorum of the Twelve Apostles (collectively). All the rest is commentary" (Stephen E. Robinson, "Christ and the Trinity," in Craig L. Blomberg and Stephen E. Robinson, *How Wide the Divide?* [Downers Grove, IL: InterVarsity Press, 1997], p. 140); cf. this chapter's n30. But Robinson's explanation itself is open to dismissal since it, too, is not a Standard Work, nor does it appear "over the signatures" of LDS authorities. Such difficulties highlight the problem within Mormonism over who speaks for the LDS faith, when their words are *really* official, and which statements should be quoted when discussing Mormon beliefs.

23. Ezra Taft Benson, "Jesus Christ—Gifts and Expectations," *New Era*, May 1975, p. 16, available at www.lds.org. Portions of this comment have been quoted as recently as 2003 (LDS Sunday School Curriculum, "We Thank Thee, O God, for a Prophet," *Doctrine and Covenants* and *Church History Gospel Doctrine—Teacher's Manual* [SLC: LDSC, 2003], Chapter 37, available at www.lds.org).

24. James E. Faulconer, review of Francis J. Beckwith and Stephen E. Parrish, *The Mormon Concept of God: A Philosophical Analysis* (Lewiston, NY: Edwin Mellen, 1991), in *BYU Studies* (1992), vol. 32, no. 4, p. 187. Quoted in Stephen Parrish [with Carl Mosser], "A Tale of Two Theisms," in Beckwith, et al., p. 195.

25. Blake Ostler. Quoted in Kevinchill, "Open message to Richard Abanes," Nov. 12, 2003, Internet post at ZLMB.

26. BYU scholar Marvin S. Hill explained such a mindset among Smith's followers during the mid-nineteenth century (c. 1839–1844): "Relatively few Mormons seemed to care whether what had been prophesied was perfectly consistent with what happened afterward. It did not matter how often the prophet altered or expanded theology; the Saints valued the process of revelation more than the product. Although Joseph Smith revised his revelations from time to time, including the Book of Mormon, few elders ever objected" (Marvin S. Hill, "Religion in Nauvoo: Some Reflections," in Roger D. Launius and John E. Hallwas, eds., *Kingdom on the Mississippi Revisited: Nauvoo In Mormon History* [Urbana, IL: University of Illinois Press, 1996], p. 123).

27. Ezra Taft Benson, "Fourteen Fundamentals In Following The Prophet," Feb. 26, 1980, reprinted in *Classic Speeches* (Provo, UT: BYU, 1994), vol. 1, p. 20.

28. Ostler, in Kevinchill, Internet post at ZLMB.

29. David Paulsen, "Are Mormons Trinitarians?: An Interview with Dr. David Paulsen," *Modern Reformation* (Nov./Dec. 2003), www.christianity.com/partner/Article_ Display_Page/0,,PTID307086|CHID581342|CIID1671522,00.html.

30. For a definition of *official* LDS doctrine, see Stephen E. Robinson, *Are Mormons Christian?* (SLC: Bookcraft, 1991), pp. 13-18, excerpted online as "The Exclusion of Misrepresentation," www.lightplanet.com/mormons/response/general/christians/ser2.htm (compare this chapter's n22).

31. "DNA and the Book of Mormon Various Media Outlets," Nov. 11, 2003, available at www.lds.org. This document was provided in response to recent news reports about DNA studies that debunked the long-held Mormon claim that ancient Israelites are the principal ancestors of the American Indians (see chapter 2).

32. Although many LDS beliefs have remained constant, many doctrinal teachings and extremely important beliefs have come and gone with the living prophets. These may

now be considered only opinions and speculation by modern Mormons, but they certainly were not taken as mere opinions and speculation when originally spoken by LDS leaders (for example, Joseph Smith, Brigham Young, Orson Pratt, Parley Pratt). In other words, in Mormonism, doctrine and belief can be changed to mere opinion by additional and contradictory pronouncements of future leaders.

33. Robert Millet, for example, has stated that remarks by nineteenth-century LDS leaders about "blood atonement"—the idea that Christ's death did not pay for every kind of sin, and so a person's own blood must be spilled (they must be killed) in order for these particular sins to be forgiven—was merely "a kind of 'revival rhetoric' in which the leaders of the Church were striving to 'raise the bar' in terms of obedience and faithfulness" (Robert Millet, "What Is Our Doctrine?" Sept. 12, 2003, http://home.uchicago.edu/ ~spackman/millet.doc). However, historical documents and events reveal that such comments were far more than rhetoric, and the teachings probably led to some horrific violence in Utah under Brigham Young (see Abanes, pp. 231-254; and Will Bagley, *Blood of the Prophets* [Norman, OK: University of Oklahoma Press, 2002]).

34. A view may be held, or might have *been* held, by virtually everyone in Church, promoted by most LDS leaders, repeated in numerous LDS publications, and seen as foundational to LDS life—and for all intents and purposes be indeed a "doctrine"—but when criticized for that view, a Mormon may say it is not and never has been a "doctrine," but simply a "belief" (e.g., Brigham Young's view, now seen as heretical by modern Mormons, that Adam was actually Heavenly Father) or a "practice" (e.g., polygamy).

35. For example, I have often spoken of the LDS belief in eternal "Celestial Sex" (i.e., the process by which Mormons believe they will procreate spirit children in eternity with their spouses, see chapter 6). But this has brought LDS criticisms because the actual phrase "Celestial Sex" is not used by LDS leaders—even though sexual union is how many Mormons believe they will procreate in the Celestial Kingdom.

36. Millet, "What is Our Doctrine?" see this chapter's n33 for Internet availability.

37. Gordon B. Hinckley, Feb. 21, 1995, National Conference of Christians and Jews Banquet. Quoted in Gordon B. Hinckley, *Teachings of Gordon B. Hinckley* (SLC: Deseret Book Co., 1997), p. 665.

38. McConkie, *MD*, p. 352.

39. M. Russell Ballard, Oct. 6, 2001, in *CR*, p. 45, available at www.lds.org.

40. Neal A. Maxwell, "But for a Small Moment" (SLC: Bookcraft, 1986), p. 82, reprinted in Neal A. Maxwell, *The Collected Works of Neal A. Maxwell* (SLC: Eagle Gate, 2001), vol. 4.

41. George A. Smith, Aug. 13, 1871, in *JOD*, vol. 14, p. 216.

Chapter 1: God's Latter-day Prophet

1. B.H. Roberts, *Defense of the Faith and the Saints* (SLC: Deseret News, 1907), vol. 1, p. 59. Quoted in LaMar Petersen, *The Creation of the Book of Mormon* (SLC: Freethinker Press, 2000), p. xx.

2. Jeffrey R. Holland, *Christ and the New Covenant* (SLC: Deseret Book Co., 1997), pp. 345-346. Quoted in Joseph B. Wirthlin, "The Book of Mormon: The Heart of Missionary Proselyting," *Ensign*, Sept. 2002, p. 13, available at www.lds.org.

3. LDS president Joseph Fielding Smith said Mormonism "must stand or fall on the story of Joseph Smith. He was either a prophet of God, divinely called, properly appointed and commissioned, or he was one of the biggest frauds this world has ever seen" (Joseph Fielding Smith, *Doctrines of Salvation* [SLC: Bookcraft, 1954], vol. 1, p. 188).

4. The business boom occurring in this region was a result of the Erie Canal construction.

5. For a more complete picture of the Smiths and the hardships they endured, see Richard L. Bushman, *Joseph Smith and the Beginnings of Mormonism* (Urbana, IL: University of Illinois Press, 1984), p. 29.

6. Money-digging was a popular American pastime in the early 1800s. "Money-diggers" often spent most of their time trying to "dig up treasure that supposedly had been buried throughout the land by pirates, Spaniards, or ancient inhabitants of the country" (David Persuitte, *Joseph Smith and the Origins of the Book of Mormon* [Jefferson, NC: McFarland & Co., 2000], p. 35).

7. Smith was well-known as a money-digger throughout western New York and northern Pennsylvania.

8. Fifty-one citizens of Palmyra signed a joint statement against the whole Smith family (Citizens of Palmyra, statement of Dec. 4, 1833, in E.D. Howe, *Mormonism Unvailed* [Painesville, OH: author, 1834], pp. 261-262, www.solomonspalding.com/docs/1834howf.htm#pg261). Howe's book catalogued statements of nearly 100 persons acquainted with the Smiths. Each individual gave their negative impressions of the family to Howe's investigator, Philastus Hurlbut.

   Mormons have consistently sought to discredit the volume (see Richard L. Anderson, "Joseph Smith's New York Reputation Reappraised," *BYU Studies* [Spring 1970], vol. 10, pp. 283-314; and Milton V. Backman, *Joseph Smith's First Vision* [SLC: Bookcraft, 1971; sec. ed., 1980], p. 116). But an examination of Howe's documents by non-LDS historians has upheld the probability of their accuracy:

   Nineteenth-century religion specialist Rodger I. Anderson has listed numerous reasons to trust Howe's accounts (see *Joseph Smith's New York Reputation Reexamined* [SLC: Signature Books, 1990], p. 6).

   German historian Eduard Meyer (1855–1930), a nonreligious man who was neither hostile nor partial to Mormonism, also believed that Hurlbut's reports presented the opinions of Smith's neighbors "in their true, essential form" (Eduard Meyer, *Urspung und Geschichte der Mormonen* [Halle: Max Niemeyer, 1912], tr. Heinz F. Rahde and Eugene Seaich, *The Origin and History of the Mormons* [SLC: University of Utah, n.d.], p. 3).

   Jan Shipps, professor emeritus of history and religious studies at Indiana University–Purdue University at Indianapolis, has likewise affirmed that the statements, although unfavorable, are not "necessarily wrong, because newspaper articles and first-hand accounts written by Obadiah Dogberry [a.k.a. journalist Abner Cole], the Reverend Diedrich Willers, and James Gordon Bennett, which contain precisely the same information, were published in 1831—a full two years before the preparation of *Mormonism*

Unvailed" (Jan Shipps, "The Prophet Puzzle: Suggestions Leading toward a More Comprehensive Interpretation of Joseph Smith," in Bryan Waterman, ed., *The Prophet Puzzle: Interpretive Essays on Joseph Smith* [SLC: Signature Books, 1999], p. 36).

9. Nathaniel Lewis, statement of Mar. 20, 1834, in "Mormonism," *The Susquehanna* (Pennsylvania) *Register,* May 1, 1834, www.lavazone2.com/dbroadhu/PA/penn1820.htm #050134. Lewis was a lay minister for the Methodist Episcopal church. Neighbor Parley Chase (b. 1806) said, "Joseph Smith Jr. to my knowledge, bore the reputation among his neighbors of being a liar" (Parley Chase, statement of Dec. 2, 1833, in Howe, p. 248, www.solomonspalding.com/docs/1834howf.htm#pg248).

10. A recent article wherein Smith is portrayed in such glowing terms is "The Character of Joseph Smith" by Richard L. Bushman (*BYU Studies* [2003], vol. 42, no. 2, pp. 23-34).

11. *PGP—JSH* 1:5,10; cf. *HC* (SLC: Deseret Book Co., 1976/1980), vol. 1, p. 4.

12. For a detailed look at the First Vision, see Richard Abanes, *One Nation Under Gods* (New York: Four Walls Eight Windows, 2002; rev. paperback, 2003), pp. 11-22.

13. *PGP—JSH* 1:17.

14. *PGP—JSH* 1:19.

15. Alan Taylor, "Rediscovering the Context of Joseph Smith's Treasure Seeking," in Waterman, p. 147; and Dan Vogel, "'The Prophet Puzzle' Revisited," in Waterman, p. 51; cf. Abanes, pp. 28-33.

16. Gordon B. Hinckley, July 12, 1996, lecture at New York Rochester Missionary Meeting, reprinted in Gordon B. Hinckley, *Teachings of Gordon B. Hinckley* (SLC: Deseret Book Co., 1997), p. 226. Hinckley stated, "Every claim that we make concerning divine authority, every truth that we offer concerning the validity of this work, all finds its roots in the First Vision of the boy prophet."

17. Gordon B. Hinckley, "What Are People Asking About Us?" *Ensign,* Nov. 1998, pp. 70-71, available at www.lds.org.

18. Gordon B. Hinckley, "The Marvelous Foundation of Our Faith," Oct. 6, 2002, in *CR,* available at www.lds.org.

19. LDS apostle Neal Maxwell has made such comparisons (see Neal A. Maxwell, *Meek and Lowly* [SLC: Deseret Book Co., 1987], pp. 77-81; and Neal A. Maxwell, *But for a Small Moment* [SLC: Bookcraft, 1986], pp. 106-107. Both are reprinted in Neal A. Maxwell, *The Collected Works of Neal A. Maxwell* [SLC: Eagle Gate, 2001], vol. 4). BYU professor Richard L. Anderson has compared Smith to Paul (see Richard L. Anderson, "Parallel Prophets: Paul and Joseph Smith," *Ensign,* Apr. 1985, p. 12, available at www.lds.org).

20. I do not mean to say that Mormons hold Joseph Smith on an equal par with Jesus Christ. Smith holds a place just *below* Christ. He is associated with LDS salvation in that he restored all of the truths lost by Christianity (for example, God, Christ's mission, our pre-existence, salvation). In a 1961 letter, for example, LDS leader Levi Edgar Young commented on the importance of Smith's story being made available to the general public: "The grandeur of Joseph Smith's life must become known to the people of the world, and I am praying daily that people by the thousands may turn to him" (Levi Edgar Young, Apr. 14, 1961, quoted in Jerald and Sandra Tanner, *The Case Against*

Mormonism [Salt Lake City: ULM, 1967], vol. 1, p. 75); cf. quotations in this chapter's nn21, 40-42.

21. Joseph Fielding Smith, *Doctrines of Salvation* (SLC: Deseret News Press, 1955), vol. 2, p. 302. This is a subheading penned by Smith's editor, LDS apostle Bruce R. McConkie. But under the section, Smith did say, "We must have faith in the mission of Joseph Smith. Because the world had lapsed into spiritual darkness, changed the ordinances and broken the everlasting covenant, the Church of Jesus Christ had to be brought again from the heavens. Where there is no faith in these truths, there is no faith in Jesus Christ who sent the Prophet Joseph Smith. This knowledge is vital to our eternal salvation" (p. 303).

22. Brigham Young, Aug. 3, 1862, in *JOD*, vol. 9, p. 332.

23. Bruce R. McConkie, *The Millennial Messiah* (SLC: Deseret Book Co., 1982), p. 334.

24. Dallin H. Oaks, "Joseph, the Man and the Prophet," *Ensign*, May 1996, p. 71, available at www.lds.org.

25. James E. Faust, "The Importance of Bearing Testimony," *Liahona*, Mar. 1997, p. 3, available at www.lds.org.

26. This same sentiment was expressed almost verbatim in 1977 by Mark E. Petersen in "It Was a Miracle!" *Ensign*, Nov. 1977, p. 11, available at www.lds.org.

27. Joseph Smith has been described as "one of the most controversial and enigmatic figures ever to appear in American history" (Persuitte, p. 1). Some exalt Smith as a prophet whose basic character and behavior easily outshined that of other men. Others paint him as nothing but a clever charlatan who followed a reprehensible code of ethics in pursuit of power, wealth, and fame. Dean Jessee, former historian for the LDS Church, has rightly observed, "Such widespread disagreement makes the Prophet an intriguing subject for historians' scrutiny" (Dean Jessee, "Joseph Smith's Reputation," *Ensign*, Sept. 1979, p. 56, available at www.lds.org).

28. One of Smith's negative traits was his tendency to use violence against those whom he felt had offended or contradicted him. Historian D. Michael Quinn has noted that Smith was a "church president who physically assaulted both Mormons and non-Mormons for insulting him" (D. Michael Quinn, *The Mormon Hierarchy: Origins of Power* [SLC: Signature Books, 1994], pp. 261-262). For a look at this aspect of Smith's character, see Abanes, pp. 178-180.

    Joseph's willingness to use force against critics eventually led to his murder. His final act of aggression was to order the *Nauvoo* (Illinois) *Expositor* newspaper destroyed for printing an issue that had severely criticized him and publicly exposed many of his secret activities—for example, polygamy (A copy of this issue is at www.solomon spalding.com/docs/exposit1.htm. Easier to read text excerpts are at www.utlm.org/onlineresources/nauvooexpositor.htm). Community outrage led to Smith's arrest and incarceration at Carthage, Illinois. Vigilantes, after breaking into the jail, murdered Smith and his brother Hyrum on June 27, 1844.

29. A number of Smith's comments suggest that he was rather arrogant and may have even suffered from delusions of grandeur. Some have speculated that he possessed what contemporary psychiatrist Robert Anderson has labeled a "narcissistic personality" (Robert D. Anderson, *Inside the Mind of Joseph Smith* [SLC: Signature Books, 1999], pp. xxxix, 222-242).

According to Anderson, who created a psychological profile of Smith, the LDS prophet may have suffered from the mental pathology associated with narcissism, as outlined in 1980 by the American Psychiatric Association (see "Diagnostic Criteria for 301.81 Narcissistic Disorder," *Diagnostic and Statistical Manual of Mental Disorders*, 4th ed. [Washington, DC: American Psychiatric Association, 1994], p. 661).

Smith exhibited his condition in the form of grandiose statements about himself (see Abanes, pp. 174-178). Jan Shipps, however, who is one of the world's foremost authorities on Mormonism, has suggested that Smith's habitual posturing may have been a response to his insecurities dating back to when he was a youth who did not quite fit into society (see Shipps, in Waterman, ed., p. 35).

30. In response to dissension that arose among the Mormons in the mid-1800s, Smith likened apostates to salt that had lost its savor, adding that such individuals were "good for nothing but to be cast out and trodden under foot of men" (D&C 103:10). On one occasion he verbally attacked detractors: "Such characters as McLellin, John Whitmer, David Whitmer, Oliver Cowdery, and Martin Harris, are too mean to mention; and we had liked to have forgotten them" (*HC*, vol. 3, p. 232). Smith also referred to David Whitmer in connection to William McLellin: "I would remember William E. McLellin,…[he] has no other dumb ass to ride but David Whitmer…he brays out cursings instead of blessings. Poor ass! Whoever lives to see it, will see him and his rider perish" (*HC*, vol. 3, p. 228).

Smith also sanctioned a band of LDS ruffians called Danites, whose job it was to silence opposers—violently, if necessary, even to the point of murder (see Abanes, pp. 151-154, 188).

31. An 1843 *New York Sun* article titled "Joe Smith, the Mormon Prophet," reportedly said, "Joe Smith, the founder of the Mormons, is a man of great talent, a deep thinker, an eloquent speaker, an able writer, and a man of great mental power, no one can doubt who has watched his career" (Quoted in *HC*, vol. 6, p. 3).

32. In reference to Smith, Josiah Quincy (mayor of Boston) remarked, "*A fine-looking man* is what the passer-by would instinctively have murmured upon meeting the remarkable individual" (Josiah Quincy, *Figures of the Past* [Boston: Roberts Brothers, 1883], p. 381, www.olivercowdery.com/smithhome/1880s-1890s/1883Quin.htm).

33. In 1886, a one-time follower of Smith's revealed this telling bit of information: "[Joseph] acquired knowledge very rapidly, and learned with special facility all the tricks of the scoundrels who worked in his company….He learned by heart a number of Latin, Greek and French common-place phrases, to use them in his speeches and sermons…. Joseph kept a learned Jew in his house for a long time for the purpose of studying Hebrew with him….I taught him the first rules of English Grammar in Kirtland in 1834. He learned rapidly" (C.G. Webb. Quoted in W. Wyl, *Mormon Portraits* [SLC: Tribune Printing & Publishing Co., 1886], p. 25). A reprint of this volume is at www.utlm.org/booklist/titles/up016_mormonportraits.htm.

34. Vogel, in Waterman, p. 50.

35. Vogel, in Waterman, p. 50. Vogel goes on to cite *Mormon Answer to Skepticism* (St. Louis: Clayton Publishing House, 1980) by Robert N. Hullinger, who observed that even if one thinks the worst of Smith's motives, "one still must account for the Book of Mormon" (Hullinger, p. xvi). Vogel notes: "Indeed the book's religious appeal—its defense of God,

Jesus Christ, and spiritual gifts, and its call to repentance—argues strongly against presuming that Smith's motives were malicious or completely self-serving (Vogel, in Waterman, p. 50). Vogel presents evidence that Smith believed it was appropriate to use deception to further God's purposes—for example, to get people saved or to build up God's kingdom (Vogel, in Waterman, pp. 55-56).

36. *T&S*, Mar. 15, 1843, vol. 4, no. 9, p. 143.

37. In reference to Smith, early LDS leader Heber C. Kimball said, "It is not for us to reproach the Lord's anointed, nor speak evil of him; all have covenanted not to do it" (Heber C. Kimball, cited in Helen Mar Whitney, "Scenes and Incidents from H.C. Kimball's Journal," *Woman's Exponent*, Aug. 1, 1883, vol. 12, p. 34).

38. Wilford Woodruff, in Scott G. Kenney, *Wilford Woodruff's Journal* (Midvale, UT: Signature Books, 1983), under Apr. 9, 1837, vol. 1, p. 138.

39. Heber C. Kimball, July 26, 1857, in *JOD*, vol. 5, p. 88.

40. Brigham Young, Sept. 9, 1860, in *JOD*, vol. 8, p. 176; cf. Brigham Young, "October Conference Minutes (Oct. 6, 1844)," *T&S*, Oct. 15, 1844, vol. 5, no. 19, p. 683. Young also said, "[No one] in this dispensation will ever enter into the celestial kingdom of God without the consent of Joseph....[E]very man and woman must have the certificate of Joseph Smith, junior, as a passport to their entrance into the mansion where God and Christ are....He reigns there as supreme a being in his sphere, capacity, and calling, as God does in heaven" (Brigham Young, Oct. 9, 1859, in *JOD*, vol. 7, p. 289).

41. In 1966, for example, popular LDS author John J. Stewart repeated the common LDS belief that Smith was "perhaps the most Christ-like man to live upon the earth" (John J. Stewart, *Joseph Smith: The Mormon Prophet* [SLC: Mercury Publishing, 1966], p. 1); cf. this chapter's n42.

42. A 1922 LDS religious lesson plan, for example, compared Smith's life to Christ's life ("Weber Stake Ward Teachers' Lesson," 1922, reprinted in "News of Mormonism," *Light On Mormonism*, Sept. 1922, vol. 1, no. 2, p. 5, The Utah Gospel Mission of Cleveland, Ohio. For a photo of this document, see Abanes, p. 177).

43. See second footnote on p. 25.

44. See this chapter's nn28-30 and the end of this chapter ("Final Observations").

45. David O. McKay, *Gospel Ideals* (SLC: Deseret News Press, 1953), p. 85.

46. Gordon B. Hinckley, Oct., 1, 1961, in *CR*, p. 116.

47. Preston Nibley, *Joseph Smith the Prophet* (SLC: Deseret News, 1944), p. 30.

48. James B. Allen, "The Significance of Joseph Smith's 'First Vision' in Mormon Thought," in D. Michael Quinn, ed., *The New Mormon History* (SLC: Signature Books, 1992), pp. 38-39. The earliest *unpublished* reference to "two personages" appearing to Smith can be found in a Nov. 9, 1835, version of the event transcribed in Joseph Smith's Journal (see this chapter's Table 1.1). But even in this version, neither personage is identified. And the second personage does not point to the other, saying, "This is my beloved Son, hear him." Instead, the second personage merely testifies "that Jesus Christ is the son of God" (see this chapter's n66).

49. James E. Faust, "The Magnificent Vision Near Palmyra," *Ensign*, May 1984, p. 67, available at www.lds.org.

50. Joseph Smith, *1832 History*, original manuscript, contained in Joseph Smith Letterbook 1, pp. 1-6, Joseph Smith Papers, LDSCA, reprinted in Dean Jessee, ed., *PJS* (SLC: Deseret Book Co., 1989), vol. 1, pp. 5-7; and in Dan Vogel, *EMD* (SLC: Signature Books, 1996), vol. 1, pp. 27-29.

51. Smith, *1832 History*, in Jessee, *PJS*, vol. 1, p. 6; and in Vogel, *EMD*, vol. 1, p. 28. Smith probably meant when he was 16 years old (see this chapter's nn62, 64, 74, 76).

52. Smith, *1832 History*, in Jessee, *PJS*, vol. 1, p. 6; and Vogel, *EMD*, vol. 1, p. 28.

53. Smith, *1832 History*, in Jessee, *PJS*, vol. 1, pp. 6-7; and Vogel, *EMD*, vol. 1, p. 28.

54. Smith, *1832 History*, in Jessee, *PJS*, vol. 1, p. 5; and Vogel, *EMD*, vol. 1, p. 27.

55. The text of the earliest versions of Smith's First Visions can be found www.lds-mormon.com/fv.shtml.

56. Orson Pratt, sermon (c. 1837 to 1839), as recorded by William I. Appleby, "Biography and Journal of William I. Appleby, Elder in the Church of Latter Day Saints," 1848, pp. 30-33, LDSCA, SLC, reprinted in Vogel, *EMD*, vol. 1, pp. 146-147. Similarly, in 1836 early Mormon leader Parley Pratt converted John Taylor (who would eventually be an LDS president) apparently without making *any* reference to Smith being visited by the Father and Son. He instead told Taylor about Smith's angelic visitations (Parley P. Pratt, *Autobiography of Parley P. Pratt* [SLC: Deseret Book, 1961], pp. 136-151).

57. Andrew Jenson, "Joseph Smith, The Prophet," *HR*, Jan. 1888, vol. 3, nos. 1-3, p. 355. When this document was reprinted two years later by the church, LDS leaders attempted to cover up the discrepancy by changing "The angel" to "The Holy Being" and "(the angel)" to "(the Christ)." The rest of the text and formatting remained as printed in the original version. No notation was made regarding the edits.

58. Joseph Smith, June 1830, *BOC* XXVI:6, pp. 58-59 (modern D&C 20:5).

59. Vogel, *EMD*, vol. 1, p. 216.

60. A later account written by Lucy (c. 1845) indicates that her understanding was that this episode took place in Joseph's bedroom (see Lucy's account in this chapter's n76).

61. Joseph Smith, *1832 History*, in Jessee, *PJS*, vol. 1, pp. 5-7; and Vogel, *EMD*, vol. 1, pp. 27-29.

62. Although Smith implies 1821 by stating that he was *in* his 16th year (i.e., 15 years old), I believe that what he was trying to say was that he was 16 years old, which would have put him *in* his 17th year (i.e., 1822). The same kind of error was made in Smith's *1839 History* (in the handwriting of James Mulholland), where Smith states, "My father Joseph Smith Senior…left the State of Vermont and moved to Palmyra, Ontario, (now Wayne) County, in the State of New York when I was in my tenth year [i.e., 1815]." But Smith Sr. actually moved to Palmyra in 1816 (*after* Joseph had turned 10 years old). It is obvious that what Joseph intended to say was that his father moved to Palmyra when he was 10 years old (which would have been *in* his 11th year).

63. Oliver Cowdery, letter to W.W. Phelps, "Letter IV," Feb. 1835, *MS&AD*, pp. 77-90, reprinted in Dan Vogel, *EMD*, vol. 2, pp. 427-430.

64. The date of Sept. 21, 1823 that Cowdery gives in this account would have put Smith *in* his 18th year (after turning 17 years old in Dec. 1822). Smith may have told Cowdery that he was *in* his 17th year when the vision took place (see this chapter's nn62, 74, 76), and Cowdery misinterpreted that to mean that Smith was 17 years old, which would match Cowdery's date of Sept. 21, 1823. Cowdery may not have understood that when one is *in* a certain year of their age, they are actually a year younger. In other words, Smith told Cowdery the vision took place *in* his 17th year (i.e., when 16 years old, on Sept. 21, 1822), but Cowdery thought he was saying 17 years old (i.e., Sept. 21, 1823).

65. For information on the revival in Palmyra, see this chapter's n77.

66. Joseph Smith, *Joseph Smith Diary* (Ohio Journal, 1835-1836), relevant segment transcribed by Warren Parrish, Nov. 9, 1835, Joseph Smith Papers, LDSCA, reprinted in Jessee, *PJS,* vol. 2, pp. 68-69; and Vogel, *EMD,* vol. 1, pp. 43-45. The First Vision given here took place during a meeting between Smith and Robert Matthews.

67. Smith, *Joseph Smith Diary,* Nov. 14, 1835, relevant segment transcribed by Warren Parrish, Joseph Smith Papers, LDSCA, reprinted in Jessee, *PJS,* vol. 2, p. 79. The First Vision account given here took place during a meeting between Smith and Erastus Holmes. It is an abbreviated summary of the First Vision that was detailed on Nov. 9.

68. Jessee, *PJS,* vol. 1, pp. 267-273; and Vogel, *EMD,* vol. 1, pp. 57-61. This version is significant in that Smith told his scribe that the religious revival ("unusual excitement on the subject of religion") leading to his First Vision took place "[s]ometime in the second year after our removal to Manchester." That would place the time of the revival in approximately 1824, not 1820, since the Smiths finished their Manchester cabin in 1822. Two years later would be 1824, which coincides with historical documents about a revival in that year; one that caused Smith's family to join the Presbyterian church (Vogel, *EMD,* vol. 1, pp. 58-59 [fns19-20]; cf. this chapter's nn76-77).

69. Orson Pratt, *Interesting Account of Several Remarkable Visions, and of the Late Discovery of Ancient American Record* (Edinburgh: Ballantyne and Hughes, 1840), pp. 3-5; reprinted in Vogel, *EMD,* vol. 1, pp. 149-160 (for specific sections quoted, see Vogel, *EMD,* vol. 1, pp. 150-151).

70. Orson Hyde, *Ein Ruf aus der Wüste, eine Stimme aus der Schoose der Erde (A Cry from the Wilderness, A Voice from the Dust of the Earth,* Frankfurt: 1842), reprinted in Jessee, *PJS,* vol. 1, pp. 402-425 (for specific sections quoted, see Jessee, pp. 405-409). Although published in 1842, this work actually was completed by Hyde in 1841, as evidenced by a letter he wrote to Smith informing him of the pamphlet's completion (see Orson Hyde, letter to Joseph Smith, June 15, 1841, published in *T&S,* Oct. 1, 1841, vol. 2, no. 23, pp. 551-555; cf. *HC,* vol. 4, pp. 372-374).

71. It should be noted that in one 1831 newspaper article about the activities of LDS missionaries (i.e., Oliver Cowdery and three others) there is a vague reference to Smith seeing God. The journalist wrote, "Smith (they affirmed) had seen God frequently and personally" ("God Bible No. 4: Book of Mormon," *Palmyra Reflector,* Feb. 14, 1831, www.lavazone2.com/dbroadhu/NY/wayn1830.htm#021431). This remark indicates that as early as 1831 Smith *might* have been starting to privately tell select persons that he had at some point seen God. But at this early date there cannot be found any *formal* "First Vision" account that parallels today's *official* First Vision. Moreover, there can be found no corroboration for what these missionaries allegedly were saying.

72. Lucy Mack Smith, letter to Solomon Mack Jr., Jan. 6, 1831, reprinted in Vogel, *EMD*, vol. 1, p. 216.

73. Several other examples can be found in Dan Vogel's *EMD*, volumes 1, 2, and 3. Dozens of similar stories were printed in old newspaper articles on Mormonism, money-digging, and Smith's early visions (c. 1829 to 1836). These are available at www.lava zone2.com/dbroadhu/artindex.htm. As late as 1845, Lucy was still declaring that Smith's First Vision was of an angel, who had said to her son, "I perceive that you are enquiring in your mind which is the true church[,] there is not a true church on Earth" (Lucy Mack Smith, *Biographical Sketches of Joseph Smith the Prophet, and His Progenitors for many Generations*, unedited "Preliminary Manuscript" [1845], reprinted in Vogel, *EMD*, vol. 1, pp. 289-291).

74. The Feb. 1835 issue of the *MS&AD*, for example, placed the year of the so-called revival and its accompanying First Vision in 1823 (Oliver Cowdery, "Letter IV," *MS&AD*, Feb. 1835, vol. 1, no. 5, pp. 77-80, www.centerplace.org/history/ma/v1n05.htm, reprinted in Dan Vogel, *EMD*, vol. 2, p. 427). The text of Cowdery's letter reads, "I mentioned the time of a religious excitement, in Palmyra and vicinity to have been in the 15th year of our brother J. Smith Jr's, age—that was an error in the type—it should have been in the 17th.—You will please remember this correction, as it will be necessary for the full understanding of what will follow in time. This would bring the date down to the year 1823" (p. 78; Vogel, *EMD*, vol. 2, p. 427). See this chapter's n64 for a discussion about Smith's age as noted by Cowdery.

75. According to Palmer, Smith "announced that this initial calling had not come from an angel in 1823, as he had said for over a decade, but from God the Father and Jesus Christ in 1820....This earlier date established his mission independent of the troubling questions and former witnesses associated with the Book of Mormon" (Grant Palmer, *An Insider's View of Mormon Origins* [SLC: Signature Books, 2002], p. 251).

76. Such accounts include those provided by William Smith (Joseph's brother), George A. Smith (Joseph's cousin), Lucy Smith (Joseph's mother), Brigham Young (Brigham Young, Feb. 18, 1855, in *JOD*, vol. 2, p. 171), John Taylor (John Taylor, Mar. 2, 1879, in *JOD*, p. 167), and Heber C. Kimball (Heber C. Kimball, Nov. 8, 1857, in *JOD*, vol. 6, p. 29).

    William Smith placed the First Vision, as well as the alleged revival that led to it, in about 1822 to 1823—not 1820. He also put Joseph at "about seventeen" years old (i.e., in 1823), not fourteen, and makes no mention of either God the Father or Jesus appearing. Instead, William says that it was "an angel" who met Joseph *in the woods* (William Smith, *William Smith on Mormonism* [Lamoni, IA: Herald Steam Book and Job Office, 1883], pp. 6,7-10, www.olivercowdery.com/smithhome/1883Wilm.htm; cf. reprint in Vogel, *EMD*, vol. 1, p. 495).

    William Smith also recounted his brother's First Vision during a June 1884 sermon. It matched what he had stated in 1883 (William Smith, "The Old Soldier's Testimony" [reported by C.E. Butterworth], *Saints Herald*, Oct. 4, 1884, vol. 31, no. 40, pp. 643-644; cf. reprint in Vogel, *EMD*, vol. 1, pp. 503-505). In this account, William additionally revealed that Joseph was indeed 18 years old (i.e., 1824, which would match the year of the revival that did indeed take place in Palmyra–Manchester) and that he went to pray at *the suggestion of a Christian minister!*

    William's final recollection in print, which appeared in 1893, confirmed his prior statements that the First Vision took place in 1824, that it involved an angel, and that it occurred during a revival started by Rev. Lane (William Smith, "Statement of William Smith, Concerning Joseph, the Prophet," *Deseret Evening News*, Jan. 20, 1894, no. 27, p. 11, reprinted in Vogel, *EMD*, vol. 1, pp. 510-513).

George A. *Smith* also combined into one episode the revival, Joseph at 14 to 15 years old, an angelic visitation *in the woods*, and the *angel* being the one who met Joseph in the woods to convey the message that Christendom was in error (George A. Smith, Nov. 15, 1863, in *JOD*, vol. 12, pp. 333-334; cf. George A. Smith, June 20, 1869, in *JOD*, vol. 13, pp. 77-78).

Lucy Smith, although she did not date the First Vision, did recount that it was "an angel of the Lord" that appeared to Joseph—not the Father or Jesus. She also said that this encounter took place not in the woods, but in Joseph's bedroom (Lucy Smith, *Biographical Sketches*, reprinted in Vogel, *EMD*, vol. 1, pp. 289-291. Lucy's text has recently been republished in Lavina Fielding Anderson, ed., *Lucy's Book: A Critical Edition of Lucy Mack Smith's Family Memoir* [SLC: Signature Books, 2001]).

77. Although rare, a few historical sources at least make reference to various religious meetings in or near Palmyra around 1820. The June 28, 1820, *Palmyra Register*, for example, mentions a Methodist "camp-meeting that was held in this vicinity." But whether such a meeting and others like it amounted to a true "revival" is doubtful. (The LDS Church's official Internet site clearly refers to the event that led to Smith's First Vision as being "a religious revival" in the "rural community of Palmyra" [see "History: Joseph Smith," available at www.lds.org].)

In 1824, however, there was indeed a true revival. This religious event, therefore, may have been the "excitement" Smith *later* incorporated into his story as he finished crafting it some time after 1832—the date of the earliest written version of his First Vision (see H. Michael Marquardt and Wesley P. Walters, *Inventing Mormonism: Tradition and Historical Record* [San Francisco: Smith Research Associates, 1994], pp. xxvi-xxviii, 15-41, 36n13; cf. Wesley Walters, "New Light on Mormon Origins From the Palmyra Revival," *Dialogue: A Journal of Mormon Thought* [Spring 1969], vol. 4, no. 1, p. 67).

Various pieces of historical evidence seem to indicate that the actual event preceding Smith's original First Vision tale was the revival of 1824—not 1820. According to Oliver Cowdery's 1834 or 1835 *MS&AD* version of Smith's First Vision, the Palmyra–Manchester revival began when a Rev. Lane, presiding Elder of the Methodist church, "visited Palmyra, and vicinity" (Oliver Cowdery, "Letter III," Dec. 1834, *MS&AD*, vol. 1, no. 3, p. 42, www.centerplace.org/history/ma/v1n03.htm, reprinted in Vogel, *EMD*, vol. 2, p. 424). But Methodist church records show that Rev. Lane did not receive an appointment to "serve as Presiding Elder of the Ontario District in which Palmyra is located" until July 1824.

Moreover, Lane's own account of the Palmyra–Manchester revival, which appeared in *The Methodist Magazine* (Apr. 1825, vol. 8, p. 159ff), states that it began in 1824, rather than 1820. In 1819 to 1820, Reverend Lane was still serving the Susquehanna District in Central Pennsylvania, more 150 miles from Palmyra!

LDS apologists claim that a revival involving Rev. Lane did occur from 1819 to 1820, but that it took place in Vienna, some 13 miles from Joseph's home (see Bushman, *Joseph Smith*, p. 53). Although historical records show that Lane was indeed at Vienna in July 1819 to attend the annual meeting of the Methodist Genesee Conference, there is no indication that he preached there or that any camp meetings were held in connection with the conference. Nor is there any evidence that there was a revival at that time due to the event. Walters and Marquardt have shown that the idea of a revival at Vienna during these years can only result from a misreading and conjoining of two unrelated sources (see Marquardt and Walters, pp. 28-31).

And regarding the "great multitudes" of converts that supposedly came into the Methodist, Presbyterian, and Baptist churches during the "1820" revival, no such numbers exist in church records for that year. Walters found membership records from each of these churches that actually list the number of converts for 1820. Palmyra's Presbyterian church lists no baptisms and no revival. The Palmyra Baptist church, which also did not report a revival, baptized only six people. Baptist churches in nearby Farmington, Lyons, and Canandaigua actually lost members. The Methodist churches in the entire circuit recorded a net loss of six people for 1820 (cf. Persuitte, p. 300, endnotes).

Jan Shipps, a widely respected scholar who is decidedly nonhostile toward Mormonism, finds LDS arguments on this issue inadequate. She has stated, "[T]he Reverend Walters's construction of the events surrounding the 1824 revival, his argument that this was the 'war of words and the tumult of opinions' the prophet spoke of, is more convincing than the counter-argument that Smith was referring to an awakening that took place, not in the immediate Palmyra–Manchester area, but nearby, around 1820" (Shipps, in Waterman, p. 32).

It should be noted, however, that some evidence does exist for 1820 revivals that took place about 25 to 30 miles away from Palmyra. Some LDS scholars have asserted that these events easily qualify as the "religious excitement" to which Smith alluded (for example, a June 7, 1820, front page headline for the *Palmyra Register* read, "Great Revivals in Religion." The accompanying story discussed a wave of revivals across the U.S.). This is certainly a possibility, but in no way proves that the First Vision occurred in 1820.

As BYU professor Marvin S. Hill has noted, "I am inclined to agree that the religious turmoil that Joseph described which led to some family members joining the Presbyterians and to much sectarian bitterness does not fit well into the 1820 context....For one thing, it does not seem likely that there could have been heavy sectarian strife in 1820 and then a joint revival where all was harmony in 1824. In addition, as Walters notes, Lucy Mack Smith said the revival where she became interested in a particular sect came after Alvin's death, thus almost certainly in early 1824" (Marvin Hill, "The First Vision Controversy: A Critique and Reconciliation," *Dialogue: A Journal of Mormon Thought* [Summer 1982], vol. 15, no. 2, p. 39).

For a point–counterpoint article on this issue, see Wesley P. Walters and Richard L. Bushman, "The Question of the Palmyra Revival," *Dialogue: A Journal of Mormon Thought* (Spring 1969), vol. 4, pp. 59-100.

Additional Sources:

An 1820 Revival?—NO: Wesley P. Walters, "New Light on Mormon Origins From Palmyra (N.Y.) Revival," *Bulletin of the Evangelical Theological Society* 10 [Fall 1967], p. 238; Dan Vogel, *EMD,* vol. 1, pp. 58 n19, 61 n25, 288 n87, 306 n103, 494-495; Marvin S. Hill, *Quest for Refuge: The Mormon Flight from American Pluralism* [SLC: Signature Books, 1989], p. 193n54.

An 1820 Revival?—YES: Milton V. Backman, *Joseph Smith's First Vision* (SLC: Bookcraft, 1971; 2nd ed., 1980), pp. 67-71, 79-89, 157-166; Richard L. Bushman, "Just the Facts Please," *FARMS Review of Books* (1994), vol. 6, no. 2, pp. 126-129; Larry C.

Porter, "Reinventing Mormonism: To Make or Redo?" *FARMS Review of Books* (1995), vol. 7, no 2, pp. 129-131.

78. See this chapter's n130. Smith may have joined the Baptists in 1824 and sought membership with the Methodists in 1828.

79. "From the Palmyra Freeman: Golden Bible," *Niagra Courier*, Aug. 27, 1829, vol. 2, no. 18, www.lavazone2.com/dbroadhu/NY/miscNYS1.htm#082729. This article was a reprint of a news piece that had appeared a few days earlier in the *Palmyra Freeman*. It goes on to say, "After having been thrice thus visited, as he states, he proceeded to the spot [of the gold plates]." The exact date of the original *Palmyra Freeman* article is unknown, but was most certainly within a day or two of the *Niagra Courier* reprint. The article was subsequently reproduced as "The Gold Bible," *Rochester Advertiser and Telegraph*, Aug. 31, 1829, www.lavazone2.com/dbroadhu/NY/miscNYSf.htm#083129.

80. "A Golden Bible," *The* [Rochester, New York] *Gem of Literature and Science*, Sept. 5, 1829, vol. 1, no. 9, www.lavazone2.com/dbroadhu/NY/miscNYSf.htm#090529. Harris was Smith's financial benefactor in the early 1800s and became one of the Three Witnesses to the BOM (see chapter 2).

81. "Imposition & Blasphemy: Money-Diggers, &c," *The* [Rochester] *Gem of Literature and Science*, May 15, 1830, www.lavazone2.com/dbroadhu/NY/miscNYSf.htm#051530. Equally relevant is a subsequent *Painesville* (Ohio) *Telegraph* article wherein LDS "proselytes" are credited with explaining that the BOM came forth as a result of Smith being "visited in a dream by the spirit of the Almighty, and informed that in a certain hill in that town, was deposited this Golden Bible" ("Golden Bible," *Painesville Telegraph*, Sept. 22, 1829, www.lavazone2.com/dbroadhu/OH/painetel.htm#092229).

As late as 1830 it was still being reported in letters to newspapers that LDS missionaries were "preaching" about their new gospel, saying that it "was discovered by an Angel of light, appearing *in a dream* to a man by the name of Smith" (Letter from Amherst, OH, Nov. 26, 1830, in "Beware of Imposters," *Painesville Telegraph*, Dec. 14, 1830, p. 2, www.lavazone2.com/dbroadhu/OH/painetel.htm#121430; cf. "The Golden Bible," *Ohio Star* [Ravenna, OH], Dec. 9, 1830.) This latter article states that several prominent Mormons "preached" that it was in the fall of 1827 when "a man named *Joseph Smith* of Manchester, Ontario county, N.Y. reported that he had three times been visited in a dream, by the spirit of the Almighty."

82. Leading scholars involved in Mormon studies recognize the dream–vision connection, as Jan Shipps has said: "[T]he elder Smith like the father of Nephi in the Book of Mormon regarded dream and vision as synonymous" (Shipps, in Waterman, p. 32). Lucy Smith, too, in recalling her husband's *visions*, said that he experienced them while *asleep* at night—i.e., they were dreams (see "Joseph Senior's Visions," www.saintswithouthalos. com/n/visions_js_sr.phtml).

Likewise, Abinade Pratt, in his preface to Parley P. Pratt's *The Angel of the Prairies* (1880), used the words "dream" and "vision" interchangeably (A. Pratt, Preface to Parley Pratt, *The Angel of the Prairies: A Dream of the Future* [SLC: Deseret News Printing and Publishing Establishment, 1880], www.rexresearch.com/articles/pratt.htm and www.zianet.com/collier/prairies.htm).

Even the BOM equates visions with dreams, saying, "Behold, I have dreamed a dream; or, in other words, I have seen a vision" (1 Nephi 8:2). Smith himself employed such language in relating a dream that took place the night before his murder (*HC*, vol. 6,

p. 610). It must be noted, however, that Cowdery said Smith did *not* see the angel in a dream (Oliver Cowdery, "Letter VII," *MS&AD*, vol. 1, no. 10, July 1835, p. 156, www.cen terplace.org/history/ma/v1n10.htm, reprinted in Vogel, *EMD*, vol. 2, p. 446).

83. These persons include Hiel Lewis (Smith's cousin-in-law) and New York neighbor Fayette Lapham.

 Lewis, who was a cousin of Smith's wife Emma, said he heard Smith tell a Rev. N. Lewis that a dream led to his discovery of the golden plates (Hiel Lewis, letter to James T. Cobb, *Amboy Journal,* Apr. 30, 1879, p. 1, reprinted in Wyl, pp. 79-80. A reprint of Wyl's volume is available for purchase online at www.utlm.org/booklist/titles/up016_ mormonportraits).

 Lapham heard the same scenario from Joseph Sr.—Joseph's father—however, he additionally revealed that the very same bloody ghost that appeared to Joseph at the location of the plates had also been the messenger to appear in young Joseph's dream (see Fayette Lapham, "Interview with the Father of Joseph Smith, the Mormon Prophet, Forty Years Ago. His Account of the Finding of the Sacred Plates," *Historical Magazine,* May 1870, 2nd Series, vol. 7, pp. 305-307, reprinted in Vogel, *EMD*, vol. 1, p. 459).

84. For more information on these tales told by Smith before his initial angel vision, see Abanes, pp. 46-53, 59-60.

85. Lance Owens, who specializes in the study of gnosticism and Western religious history, has noted that researchers have now found a "wealth of unquestionably genuine historical evidence—much of it long available but either misunderstood, suppressed, or ignored—substantiating that Smith and his early followers had multiple involvements with magic, irregular Freemasonry, and traditions generally termed occult" (Lance S. Owens, "Joseph Smith: America's Hermetic Prophet," *Gnosis,* Spring 1995, no. 35, p. 60).

86. John L. Brooke, *The Refiner's Fire: The Making of Mormon Cosmology, 1644-1844* (New York: Cambridge University Press, 1994; paperback edition, 1996), pp. 71-72.

87. D. Michael Quinn, *Early Mormonism and the Magic World View* (SLC: Signature Books, 1998), p. xxii. Quinn writes, "[T]he first generation of Mormons included people with a magic world view that predated Mormonism." He also lists those first-generation Mormons involved in occultism as being "the witnesses to the *Book of Mormon*, nearly half of the original Quorum of the Twelve Apostles, and some of the earliest converts from New York and New England."

88. Lucy Smith, reprinted in Vogel, *EMD*, vol. 1, p. 285. This paragraph, which appears in the 1845 preliminary manuscript version of *Biographical Sketches,* did not make it into the 1853 published edition. "One possible reason is that Lucy alludes to folk magic, which was a sensitive subject for those not wishing to give credence to claims made in affidavits collected in 1833 by Philastus Hurlbut" as Dan Vogel writes (Vogel, *EMD*, vol. 1, p. 285; see this chapter's n8). It should be noted that Lucy nowhere in this quote denies that occult practices were part of her family's spiritual routine. She is merely saying these practices did not distract any of them from taking care of more temporal responsibilities—e.g., daily work.

89. These practices continued sporadically among LDS women well into the 1960s.

90. Lewis de Claremont, *The Ancients Book of Magic,* p. 10. Cited in Jerald Tanner and Sandra Tanner, *Mormonism, Magic and Masonry* (SLC: ULM, 1988), p. 3.

91. Two eyewitnesses to such activities include William Stafford (William Stafford, statement of Dec. 9, 1833, in Howe, pp. 238-239, www.solomonspalding.com/docs/1834 howf.htm#pg238); and Joseph Capron (Capron, in Howe, pp. 259-260, www.solomon spalding.com/docs/1834howf.htm#pg259).

92. Julien Tondriau, *L'OCCULTISME* (Verviers, France: Gerard & Co., 1964), tr. edition by Bay Bocks Pty. Ltd., *The Occult: Secrets of the Hidden World* (New York: Pyramid Communications, 1972), p. 127. The "Faculty of Abrac" was well-known in the early 1800s among folk magicians and Freemasons (see Abanes, pp. 34-36).

93. This dagger is inscribed with the magick symbols for the "Intelligence" and "Seal" of Mars. It also has a Jupiter sign etched on it. These planets were important to Smith because they held astrological significance over his birth year.

94. The "Holiness to the Lord" parchment, which may have been used in ceremonial magick to procure visits from good angels, reveals its probable date of creation to be Sept. 1823—the very same month Joseph allegedly received his first visit from the angel Moroni (see chapter 2). Its many symbols include four pentagrams, which are the symbols necessary for invoking spirits.

    The "Saint Peter Bind Them" parchment, which was designed for personal protection, includes the phrase "Saint Peter bind them, In the name of [sic] Jesus Christ, may every hair of their head be as heavy as a millstone that desires to set fore or destroy this body."

    The "Jehovah, Jehovah, Jehovah" parchment, which was probably used as a means of warding off evil spirits, includes a central disk bordered by four Maltese crosses (located at points north, south, east, and west). The symbol closely resembles an "Earth seal" pictured in *Occult Sciences* (Sibly, p. 1102, www.esotericarchives.com/solomon/sibly4.htm). Sibly explains that these are the seals "without which no Spirits will appear."

95. Smith was murdered on June 27, 1844 (see this chapter's n28).

96. This text is available online at www.esotericarchives.com/solomon/sibly4.htm. For images of the parchments, see Abanes, pp. 91-92.

97. Lance S. Owens, "Joseph Smith: America's Hermetic Prophet," in Waterman, pp. 155-171.

    During a lecture at the 1993 Sunstone Symposium, Owens noted, "By 1844, it appears Smith was not only cognizant of Kabbalah, but ready to enlist elements of Kabbalistic theosophy into his most important doctrinal pronouncement, the 'King Follett Discourse,' Joseph Smith's concepts of God's plurality, his vision of God as *anthropos* [man], and his possession by the issue of sacred marriage all might have been cross-fertilized by intercourse...with Kabbalistic theosophy" (Quoted in "Was Mormonism's Founder a Kabbalist?" *Gnosis*, Spring 1994, no. 31, p. 7).

    Some LDS scholars have attempted to downplay the significance of the kabbalah's influence on Smith by distancing the kabbalah from the occult, referring to it instead as simply an esoteric—i.e., secret, confidential, or difficult to discern—system of belief (see William J. Hamblin, "'Everything is Everything:' Was Joseph Smith Influenced by Kabbalah?" *FARMS Review of Books*, vol. 8, issue 2, www.farms.byu.edu/display .php?id=229&table=review.htm. This is a review of the article "Joseph Smith and Kabbalah: The Occult Connection," by Lance Owens, *Dialogue: A Journal of Mormon Thought*, 1994, vol. 27, no. 3, pp. 117-194, www.gnosis.org/jskabb1.htm).

But redefining kabbalah as simply an esoteric religion is misleading. As D. Michael Quinn has pointed out, making this distinction is "creating a false dichotomy between the occult and the esoteric, as Edward A. Tiryakian indicated in his 1972 essay on esoteric culture. The occult is a group of 'practices, techniques or procedures,' and the esoteric is 'those religiophilosophic belief systems which underlie occult techniques and practices.' That has become an internationally accepted view among reputable scholars" (see Quinn, *Early Mormonism*, xxxvii-xxxviii; cf. Edward A. Tiryakian, "Toward the Sociology of Esoteric Culture," *American Journal of Sociology*, Nov. 1972, pp. 498-499).

98. For images of Joseph's talisman, see Abanes, p. 91.

99. There is little doubt among non-LDS scholars that this Jupiter talisman was indeed owned by Smith. As history professor Alan Taylor has noted, "[Smith] earnestly wanted to become godlike. So he wore a silver Jupiter talisman inscribed, 'Make me, O God, all powerful' " (Taylor, in Waterman, pp. 147-148).

100. For a detailed look at this issue, see Quinn, *Early Mormonism*, pp. 76-79, 278-280.

101. One early document referring to Smith's money-digging reputation is an 1830 letter from Rev. John Sherer to the American Home Missionary Society. Sherer described Smith as a person who looked "through a glass, to see money underground." Sherer also labeled Smith a "juggler," a term used for someone who defrauded people—i.e., a con man (John Sherer, letter to American Home Missionary Society, Nov. 18, 1830. Quoted in Persuitte, p. 36).

Before assuming his prophetic role, Smith formed a money-digging company. This was explained by Martin Harris: "There was a company there in that neighborhood, who were digging for money supposed to have been hidden by the ancients. Of this company were old Mr. Stowel—I think his name was Josiah—also old Mr. Beman, also Samuel Lawrence, George Proper, Joseph Smith, Jr., and his father, and his brother [Hyrum] Smith. They dug for money in Palmyra, Manchester, also in Pennsylvania, and other places" ("Mormonism—No. II" [an interview], *Tiffany's Monthly*, Aug. 1859, vol. 5, p. 164, www.utlm.org/onlineresources/sermons_talks_interviews/harrisinter viewtiffanysmonthly.htm).

102. For example, David Whitmer, Hiram Page, Philo Dibble, and W.W. Phelps (see Ogden Kraut, *Seers and Seer Stones*, p. 55, www.helpingmormons.org/SeerStones.htm).

Joseph's mother, Lucy Mack Smith, apparently used seer stones as well (see Samantha Payne, affidavit, June 29, 1881, Ontario County Clerk's Office, Canandaigua, New York, published in *Ontario County Times*, July 27, 1881, p. 3, photocopy in fd 31, box 149, Marquardt papers, Marriott Library).

The brother of Mormon bishop Newel K. Whitney recalled how "Mormon elders and women often searched the bed of the river for stones with holes caused by the sand washing out, to peep into" (Samuel F. Whitney, statement of Mar. 6, 1885, reprinted in A.B. Deming, ed., *Naked Truths About Mormonism* (Jan. 1888), vol. 1, no. 1, p. 3, www.lava zone2.com/dbroadhu/CA/natruths.htm).

Joseph Smith, his father, and many other prominent Mormons (for example, Martin Harris, Orrin Porter Rockwell, Joseph and Newel Knight, and Josiah Stowell) also used divining rods to find buried treasure (Marvin S. Hill, "Brodie Revisited: A Reappraisal," *Dialogue: A Journal of Mormon Thought* [Winter 1972], vol. 7, p. 78).

103. Oliver Cowdery, Smith's closest ally during Mormonism's formative period, became extremely proficient at using a divining rod (see this chapter's n150). In Apr. 1829, in fact, Joseph went so far as to receive a revelation praising this "gift" of Oliver's as something of divine origin (see chapter 3, p. 85).

   Like Cowdery, other prominent members of early Mormonism used divining rods: for example, Martin Harris, Orrin Porter Rockwell, Joseph and Newel Knight, and Josiah Stowell. Brigham Young and Heber C. Kimball were given their divining rods by Joseph Jr. himself "as a symbol of gratitude for their loyalty" (Stanley B. Kimball, *Heber C. Kimball: Mormon Patriarch and Pioneer* [Urbana: University of Illinois Press, 1981], pp. 248-249).

104. Dan Vogel, "Rethinking the 1826 Judicial Decision," *Mormon Scripture Studies: An E-Journal of Critical Thought*, www.mormonscripturestudies.com/ch/dv/1826.asp. Vogel explains that the term *impostor* "points to a specific section of the New York statute that describes various kinds of offenses under the definition of 'disorderly persons.' The section of the statute applicable...states: 'All jugglers [*deceivers*—Noah Webster's *Compendious Dictionary of the English Language*, Hartford, CT: Hudson & Goodwin, 1806, defines a juggler as "one who juggles, a cheat, a deceiver," and juggling as "the act of playing tricks, deceit," p. 168] and all persons *pretending* to have skill in physiognomy, palmistry, or like crafty science, or *pretending* to tell fortunes, or to discover where lost goods may be found...shall be deemed and adjudged disorderly persons.'"

105. Money-diggers would often hire themselves out to persons who believed that they, too, might find wealth in the ground. Such activity, however, was illegal because money-diggers habitually defrauded clients out of hard-earned cash by not delivering on their promises to find large caches of buried treasure. Smith had been hired by a Josiah Stowell, as Joseph's mother remembered: "A short time before the house was completed [1825], a man, by the name of Josiah Stoal, came from Chenango county, New York, with the view of getting Joseph to assist him in digging for a silver mine. He came for Joseph on account of having heard that he possessed certain keys, by which he could discern things invisible to the natural eye" (Lucy Smith, *Biographical Sketches*, pp. 91-92, in Vogel, *EMD*, vol. 1, pp. 309-310).

106. Leonard J. Arrington and David Bitton, *The Mormon Experience* (Champaign, IL: University of Illinois Press, 1992), pp. 10-11.

107. There has been debate over the term "guilty" as used in court documents relating to this case. It is clear that the verdict was not part of a formal trial decision. The term, as used in connection to nineteenth-century preliminary hearings, basically meant that the examination judge had found enough evidence to hold a prisoner over for a formal trial (see Vogel, "Rethinking the 1826 Judicial Decision," www.mormonscripture studies.com/ch/dv/1826.asp).

108. In an 1831 letter to the *Evangelical Magazine and Gospel Advocate*, Bainbridge resident A.W. Benton recounted what he witnessed at Smith's trial: "[C]onsidering his youth, (he then being a minor,) and thinking he might reform his conduct, he was designedly allowed to escape. This was four or five years ago. From this time he absented himself from this place, returning only privately, and holding clandestine intercourse with his credulous dupes, for two or three years" (A.W. Benton, letter to editor, *Evangelical Magazine and Gospel Advocate* [Utica, NY], Apr. 9, 1831, New Series 2, p. 120).

109. Joel K. Noble, a justice of the peace during that era, corroborated Benton's account, stating, "Jo. was condemned. [The] Whisper came to Jo. 'off, off'—[He] took Leg Bail....Jo was not seen in our town for 2 years or more (except in Dark Corners)" (Joel K. Noble, letter to Jonathan B. Turner, Mar. 8, 1842. Wesley P. Walters discussed this document and provided a copy of it in "From Occult to Cult with Joseph Smith, Jr.," *Journal of Pastoral Practice* [Summer 1977], vol. 1, pp. 121-137).

110. LDS author Francis Kirkham, for example, adamantly declared that "no such record was ever made, and therefore, is not in existence" (Francis Kirkham, *A New Witness for Christ in the America* [SLC: Utah Printing Co., 1942; 1960 ed., p. 386.)

   The LDS church–owned *Deseret News* called the court transcript a "fabrication of unknown authorship and never in the court records at all" (*Deseret News,* Church Section, May 11, 1946, as cited in Kirkham, enlarged edition, pp. 430-431. Quoted in Jerald Tanner and Sandra Tanner, "State of New York vs. Joseph Smith," *Salt Lake City Messenger* (#68), July 1988, p. 1, www.utlm.org/newsletters/no68.htm).

   LDS apostle John Widtsoe stated, "This alleged court record...seems to be a literary attempt of an enemy to ridicule Joseph Smith....There is no existing proof that such a trial was ever held" (*Joseph Smith—Seeker After Truth* [SLC: Deseret News, 1951], p. 78).

111. See Wesley P. Walters, "Joseph Smith's Bainbridge, N.Y., Court Trials," *Westminster Theological Journal* (Winter 1974), vol. 36, p. 125.

112. This bill references "Joseph Smith the Glass Looker." Neely's charges, $2.68, exactly matches the figure given in the 1873 *Fraser's Magazine* reprint of the hearing's transcript. The date also was the same—March 20, 1826. In response, Mormons began casting aspersions on the legitimacy of the Neely bill. Finally, in 1992, LDS church historian Leonard J. Arrington conceded that the bill was indeed drawn up by Judge Neely and that it referred to Smith "as a 'glass looker'" (Arrington and Bitton, p. 10). For a photo of this document, see Abanes, p. 45.

113. Hugh Nibley, *The Myth Makers* (SLC: Bookcraft, 1967), vol. 1, p. 42.

114. Kirkham, p. 387: "If any evidence had been in existence that Joseph Smith had used a seer stone for fraud and deception, and especially had he made this confession in a court of law as early as 1826, or four years before the *Book of Mormon* was printed, and this confession was in a court record, it would have been impossible for him to have [legitimately] organized the restored Church."

115. See this chapter's nn145, 151.

116. Taylor, in Waterman, p. 150.

117. Shipps, in Waterman, p. 37 (emphasis added). The influence of occultism on Smith's doctrines can still be seen in modern editions of the D&C. Consider D&C 129:8, received by Smith in 1843. It relates to God's instructions involving how to distinguish an angelic messenger from a demonic one. The passage says that one should shake hands with the messenger. Feeling air means the messenger is demonic.

   Interestingly, a similar test was used by occultists of the mid-1800s, as evidenced by a quote from the 1896 edition of *The Ritual of Transcendental Magic*: "[S]pirits, or at least the spectres pretended to be such, may indeed touch us occasionally, but we cannot touch them, and this is one of the most affrighting characteristics of these apparitions, which are at times so real in appearance that we cannot unmoved feel the hand pass through that which seems a body and yet make contact with nothing" (Eliphas Levi, *The Ritual of Transcendental Magic,* tr. A.E. Waite [London: William Rider and Co., 1896], p. 74, in modern 2002 PDF online file, www.hermetics.org/pdf/DogmaEtRituel_ Part_II.pdf).

118.   Other OT passages forbidding magick, astrology, and soothsaying include Gen. 41:8, 41:24; Ex. 7:22; 8:7,18,19; 9:11; Dan. 1:20; 2:2,10,27; 4:7,9; 5:11. This also may be why those who helped compile the LDS Church's official *History of the Church* "were anxious not to emphasize the prophet's early connection with the divining art" (Shipps, in Waterman, p. 37). Shipps also noted, "It seems reasonable to conclude that the motive for playing down this part of the prophet's background was the knowledge that it could be used as the basis for charges that might endanger his reputation" (Shipps, in Waterman, p. 37).

119.   Milton V. Backman, "First Vision," in Daniel H. Ludlow, ed., *Encyclopedia of Mormonism* (New York: Macmillan Publishing Co., 1992), vol. 2, p. 516. Backman states, "On several occasions between 1832 and 1842, the young Prophet wrote or dictated accounts of the vision, each in a different setting, the last two for publication. Each record omits or adds some details."

       A similar rationalization appeared in a 2003 article published by FAIR: "[E]ach account emphasizes different details" (Michael R. Ash, *The First Vision* [Redding, CA: FAIR, 2003], p. 1, www.fairlds.org/apol/brochures/firstvision.pdf).

       James B. Allen has made the same point: "The variations in these and other accounts suggest that in relating his story to various individuals at various times, Joseph Smith emphasized different aspects of it and that his listeners were each impressed with different details. This, of course, is to be expected, for the same thing happens in retelling any story" (Allen, in Quinn, *The New Mormon History,* pp. 48-49).

120.   Bushman, *Joseph Smith,* p. 54.

121.   Bushman, *Joseph Smith,* p. 57.

122.   Richard P. Howard, "An Analysis of Six Contemporary Accounts Touching Joseph Smith's First Vision," in Maurice L. Draper, ed., *Restoration Studies 1: Sesquicentennial Edition* (Independence, MO: Herald Publishing House, 1980), p. 112.

123.   Gordon B. Hinckley, *Truth Restored* (SLC: LDSC, 1947; revised, 1979, as printed in the 1990 Missionary Reference Library edition), pp. 1-2. The 1969 edition of Hinckley's book gives no endnote for this reference. The 1990 Missionary Library edition, however, does give a reference. But it is not the original source document. Hinckley instead cites Preston Nibley, *Joseph Smith, the Prophet* (SLC: Deseret News Press, 1946), pp. 21-22. As of 2003, Hinckley's book was still being distributed by the LDS Church as part of its Missionary Reference Library.

124.   The article published by the *Religious Advocate* was reprinted by Palmyra's newspaper the *Wayne Sentinel,* Mar. 2, 1825, www.lavazone2.com/dbroadhu/NY/miscNYSg.htm.

125.   Michael Hickenbotham, *Answering Challenging Mormon Questions* (Bountiful, UT: Horizon Publishers, 1995; third printing, 1999), p. 45. The quotation Hickenbotham cites is from Richard Anderson, "Parallel Prophets," pp. 4-5.

126. Vogel, *EMD*, vol. 1, p. 29. No eyewitnesses have been found who stated that they remembered Smith talking about angelic visions any time before 1827 to 1828.

127. Persuitte, p. 21. As late as 1840, few people had heard about Smith meeting God and Jesus Christ in the woods. For example, in a letter to the editor appearing in the *Ohio Observer* (Hudson, Ohio, Aug. 11, 1836) and reprinted in the *Cincinnati Journal and Western Luminary* (Aug. 25, 1836), Kirtland, Ohio, resident Truman Coe detailed his knowledge of Smith's visionary experiences. Coe makes no mention whatsoever of any 1820 vision of the Father and the Son (see Vogel, *EMD*, vol. 1, pp. 46-47).

128. Variations within the Bible's crucifixion and resurrection stories are likewise complementary rather than contradictory. Nevertheless, similar arguments against these biblical passages also have been raised by LDS scholars such as Milton V. Backman ("Joseph Smith's Recitals of the First Vision," *Ensign*, Jan. 1985, p. 8, available at www.lds.org) and LDS apologist Michael Ash (see *The First Vision*, cited in this chapter, n119).

    Ash, for example, points to the number of angels at Christ's tomb as mentioned by Matthew, Mark, Luke, and John. Of course, this analogy is flawed because the biblical accounts are four different versions as told by four *different* people—not four different versions told by the *same* person (Joseph Smith). Hence, in the Bible accounts we have several eyewitnesses, not just one (as in Smith's case).

    Ash also has claimed that the sign above Christ's head is described in contradictory ways (see Matt. 27:37; Mark 15:26; Luke 23:38; and John 19:19). But this is yet another language issue. The words above Christ's head were in three languages: Latin, Aramaic, and Greek. Consequently, the three different readings in Matthew, Luke, and John. Mark's wording seems to be "an abridged form of the Latin wording" (Gleason Archer, *Encyclopedia of Bible Difficulties* [Grand Rapids: Zondervan, 1982], p. 346. Archer's book also deals with the alleged contradictions within the accounts of Christ's resurrection (pp. 347-356). Of course, there is no language issue with Smith's accounts.

    As for Backman, he additionally cites the so-called contradictions in Paul's visionary meeting with Christ on the road to Damascus (see sidebar, p. 43, for a response).

129. Wesley Walters, "New Light On Mormon Origins From the Palmyra N.Y. Revival," originally published in the *Evangelical Theological Society* (Fall 1967), vol. 10, no. 4, pp. 227-244; cf. the revised version of this article published in *Dialogue: A Journal of Mormon Thought* (Spring 1969), vol. 4, no. 1, pp. 60-81.

130. According to Joseph Sr., it also was in 1824 that Joseph Jr. "was baptized, becoming thus a member of the Baptist Church" (Joseph Smith Sr. Quoted by Lapham, "Interview," pp. 305-306, reprinted in Vogel, *EMD*, vol. 1, p. 458). The 1824 date is derived from the explanation of Joseph Sr., who stated to Lapham that his son turned to the Baptists about two years after digging a well for Willard Chase (the well-digging occurred in 1822).

    Joseph's involvement with the Baptist church is supported by an article about the history of the Manchester Baptist Church, which in part reads, "Joe occasionally attended the stone church; especially the revivals, sitting with the crowds—the 'sinners'—up in the gallery" (Mitchell Bronk, "The Baptist Church at Manchester," *The Chronicle: A Baptist Historical Quarterly* [January 1948], vol. 11, pp. 23-24). This article's contents included reminiscences of conversations with old Manchester townspeople (reprinted in Vogel, *EMD*, vol. 3, p. 259).

    Three years earlier (c. 1820 to 1821) Joseph apparently caught a "spark of Methodism" in a camp meeting and became an exhorter. This information comes from Orasmus

Turner, who knew Smith in Palmyra and had accompanied Smith to Methodist camp meetings. According to an article by Turner that was published in the *Lockport* (New York) *Daily Courier*, May 5, 1854, Turner left the Palmyra area in 1822, which would put his experiences with Smith as an "exhorter" before that date. The "Deeds of Ontario Co. Bk G, 345" show that the Methodists did not acquire their property in the woods until July of 1821, which would mean that the camp meetings were held sometime between 1821 and 1822 (see Wesley P. Walters, "A Reply to Dr. Bushman," *Dialogue: A Journal of Mormon Thought* [Spring 1969], vol. 4, p. 99).

Then, as late as June 1828, Smith sought membership in the Methodist Episcopal class in Harmony, Pennsylvania, perhaps in response to his first child being stillborn (Sophia Lewis, *Susquehanna* [Pennsylvania] *Register,* May 1, 1834, reprinted in Howe, 269, www.solomonspalding.com/docs/1834howf.htm#pg269). According to Hiel and Joseph Lewis—cousins of Emma Hale (who became Smith's wife)—Smith requested that his name be put on a roster for membership class. But it was removed three days later when church members asked Smith to either renounce his previous money-digging and occult activities or strike his name from the book. He chose to do the latter (see Persuitte, p. 76).

131. Hinckley, July 12, 1996, lecture at New York Rochester Missionary Meeting, in Hinckley, *Teachings,* p. 227.

132. Fawn M. Brodie, *No Man Knows My History* (New York: Vintage Books, 1995; original edition by Alfred A. Knopf, 1945), p. 25.

133. Norris Stearns' 1815 account of his own vision reads, "I saw two spirits, which I knew at the first sight. But if I had the tongue of an Angel I could not describe their glory, for they brought the joys of heaven with them. One was God, my Maker, almost in bodily shape like a man. His face was, as it were a flame of Fire, and his body, as it had been a Pillar and a Cloud....Below him stood Jesus Christ my Redeemer, in perfect shape like a man—His face was not ablaze, but had the countenance of fire, being bright and shining" (Norris Stearns, *The Religious Experience of Norris Stearns* [Greenfield, MA: 1815], quoted in Richard Bushman, "The Visionary World of Joseph Smith," *BYU Studies* [1997–1998], vol. 37, no. 1, p. 191). For a list of several more stories and accompanying excerpts, see Abanes, pp. 19-22.

134. Faust, available at www.lds.org.

135. Brodie, p. 25. Testimony describing Smith as a fortune-teller appears in several statements from various individuals. For example, C.M. Stafford recalled, "Jo claimed to have revelations and tell fortunes. He told mine by looking in the palm of my hand and said among other things that I would not live to be very old" (C.M. Stafford, statement of Mar. 23, 1885, reprinted in A.B. Deming, ed., *Naked Truths About Mormonism,* Apr. 1888, vol. 1, no. 2, 1, www.lavazone2.com/dbroadhu/CA/natruths.htm; cf. Henry Harris, statement to Justice of the Peace Jonathan Lapham, n.d., reprinted in Howe, p. 251, www.solomonspalding.com/docs/1834howf.htm#pg251).

136. Gordon B. Hinckley, "Lord, Increase Our Faith," *Ensign,* Nov. 1987, p. 51, available at www.lds.org.

137. Hinckley, "Lord, Increase Our Faith," available at www.lds.org.

138. FAIR further describes itself as a group "[s]eeking to assist the lay member and scholar alike to respond to intentional and well-meaning attacks on individual faith, FAIR helps publish articles and books that defend the LDS church, operates a Web site that receives thousands of visitors each day, and sponsors research projects and conferences that provide the LDS scholarly community an outlet for getting information into the hands of the average member" (Barry R. Bickmore, *Does God Have A Body In Human Form?* [Redding, CA: FAIR, 2003], p. 5, www.fairlds.org/pubs/GodHaveBody.pdf).

139. Sam Katich, "The Jupiter Talisman Myth," www.angelfire.com/sk2/ldsdefense/talis.html.

140. Quinn, *Early Mormonism*, pp. 84-92.

141. Katich, www.angelfire.com/sk2/ldsdefense/talis.html.

142. Hickenbotham, p. 40.

143. Vogel, in Waterman, p. 51.

144. The use of seer stones among Mormons continued well into the late 1800s, due in part to Smith's failure to condemn them. As for Joseph's own use of seer stones, he utilized at least two during his money-digging years (c. 1820 to 1827). He eventually obtained two additional seer stones, and perhaps more, before his death in 1844. There is no solid information, however, as to how he may have used these other stones.

145. Sam Katich, "Joseph Smith," www.fairlds.org/apol/morm201/m20117b.html.

146. Katich, "Joseph Smith," www.fairlds.org/apol/morm201/m20117b.html.

147. Marvin S. Hill, "Brodie Revisited: A Reappraisal," *Dialogue: A Journal of Mormon Thought* (Winter 1972), vol. 7, p. 78.

148. Stanley B. Kimball, *Heber C. Kimball: Mormon Patriarch and Pioneer* (Urbana: University of Illinois Press, 1981), pp. 248-249; cf. Sarah M. Kimball, statement of June 21, 1892, in Solomon F. Kimball, "Sacred History," LDSCA. Quoted in Quinn, *Early Mormonism*, p. 256; cf. Brooke, p. 143.

149. *BOC* VII:3, p. 19.

150. "I met with the Twelve at Brother Joseph's. He conversed with us in a familiar manner on a variety of subjects, and explained to us the Urim and Thummim which he found with the plates, called in the Book of Mormon the Interpreters. He said that every man who lived on the earth was entitled to a seer stone, and should have one, but they are kept from them in consequence of their wickedness, and most of those who do find one make an evil use of it; he showed us his *seer stone*" (Brigham Young, Dec. 27, 1841, in Elden J. Watson, ed., *Manuscript History of Brigham Young;* cf. "History of Brigham Young," *MS*, Feb. 20, 1864, vol. 26, p. 118).

151. Katich, "Joseph Smith," www.fairlds.org/apol/morm201/m20117b.html. Mountford was disfellowshipped for "practicing fortune telling, magic, black art, etc." Katich writes, "In 1841, Elder Woodruff explained the Church's position on the Mountford case. Woodruff said, 'we ha[ve] no such custom or practice in the Church, and that we should not fellowship any individual who practiced magic, fortune telling, black art, etc., for it was not of God.'"

152. A relevant example would be Hiram Page, a founding member of Mormonism, who had his own seer stone and started using it in 1830 to receive revelations that contradicted

Smith's revelations. Smith quickly responded with a revelation in which God condemned Page: "[T]hose things which he hath written from that stone are not of me...Satan deceiveth him" (D&C 28:11).

153.   *Wandle Mace Journal*, p. 66, microfilm in LDSCA.

154.   "At the new religion's founding, non-Mormons claimed that its converts had occult beliefs and practiced folk magic....A Survey of prominent early Mormons also confirms these non-Mormon assessments. Joseph Smith...used divining rods, a talisman, and implements of ritual magic....His father....His older brother, Hyrum....His younger brothers Samuel and William....The Three Witnesses....Magic belief and practice also influenced the first Quorum of the Twelve Apostles in 1835....[T]wo-thirds of Mormonism's first apostles had some affinity for folk magic" (Quinn, *Early Mormonism*, pp. 239-240).

155.   History professor Alan Taylor has noted that "magic persisted within early Mormonism, as Michael Quinn has so thoroughly documented....Early Mormons persisted in practicing magic because they nurtured a magical world view where the material and the spiritual were interwoven in the same universe" (Taylor, in Waterman, p. 149). Consider the following examples of LDS occultism that support Taylor's assertion:

   1841—LDS apostle Orson Hyde uses his divining rod to dedicate the Holy Land ("Interesting News from Alexandria and Jerusalem," *MS*, Jan. 1842, p. 135, reprinted in *T&S*, Apr. 1, 1842, p. 741).

   1860—LDS apostle John Taylor explains recent comments by Brigham Young, saying: "[Brigham] was speaking of men being born Natural Prophets & seers. Many have the gift of seeing through seer stones without the Priesthood at all" (John Taylor. Cited by Woodruff, in Kenney, *Wilford Woodruff's Journal*, under Feb. 11, 1861, vol. 5, p. 550).

   1888—Wilford Woodruff "[c]onsecrated upon the [Manti Temple] Altar the seer Stone that Joseph Smith found by Revelation some 30 feet under the Earth [and] Carried By him through life" (Woodruff, in Kenney, *Wilford Woodruff's Journal*, under May 18, 1888, vol. 8, p. 500).

   1890s—Well-known southern Utah resident John Steele continues to practice sorcery and witchcraft as a means of warding off evil. Nevertheless, "in the 1880s and 1890s John Steele remained an honored citizen of Parowan, where stake authorities knew of his occult ceremonies and residents throughout southern Utah petitioned him for horoscopes" (Quinn, *Early Mormonism*, pp. 293, 565 n430; cf. p. 565 n426).

   1920s—LDS women were still practicing various forms of divination, especially tarot card reading and palm-reading (see Quinn, *Early Mormonism*, pp. 294-296).

   1969—Popular astrologer Jeanne Dixon reveals, "Of the Bibles that are sent to me with requests to write a short message on the flyleaf, more come from Mormons than any others" (Jeanne Dixon, *My Life and Prophecies* [New York: Morrow and Co., 1969], p. 208).

   1998—LDS apostle David B. Haight "reinvoked the astrological principle that people should 'do nothing without the assistance of the moon'" (Quinn, *Early Mormonism*, p. 291). Haight's remark "do nothing without the assistance of the moon" was made during his lecture at the 168th Annual General Conference. But when the transcribed text of the speech was made available online through the LDS Church's official Internet site, the phrase had been deleted.

156. Smith used his seer stone to translate the Book of Mormon (1829 and 1830) and possibly the Book of Abraham (1842). For information on the BOM, see chapter 2. Regarding the BOA, LDS Church historian and eventual president, Joseph Fielding Smith, said that Joseph used his seer stone to translate it (Joseph Fielding Smith, *Doctrines of Salvation* [SLC: Bookcraft, 1956, vol. 3, p. 225].

Others who indicated that Smith translated the BOA using his seer stone include Wilford Woodruff and Parley Pratt. Orson Pratt claimed to have been present "on several occasions" when Smith received revelations and that "sometimes Joseph used a seer stone when enquiring of the Lord, and receiving revelation" ("Report of Elders Orson Pratt and Joseph F. Smith," *Deseret Evening News*, Nov. 23, 1878, reprinted in *MS*, Dec. 16, 1878, vol. 40, p. 787). In Oct. 1835, Smith used his stone to give a patriarchal blessing to Newel K. Whitney and his wife (see Quinn, *Early Mormonism*, pp. 244, 538 n51). For information on how today's LDS apologists and BYU professors are seeking to downplay Smith's use of the seer stone in the production of the BOA, see Quinn, *Early Mormonism*, pp. 244, 539 n60.

157. Quinn, *Early Mormonism*, p. 245. Citing Lyman Wight, letter to Cooper and Chidester, July 1855, Wight Letterbook, p. 23, RLDSCA.

158. Smith possessed three stones until moving to Nauvoo in 1839, where he found two additional stones.

159. Anderson, "The Mature Joseph Smith," pp. 538-539.

160. Quinn, *Early Mormonism*, p. 200.

161. Gilbert Scharffs, *The Truth About "The Godmakers"* (SLC: Publishers Press, 1986), p. 138. Some Mormons, it should be noted, have admitted that Smith continued his occult practices after the alleged 1820 vision. BYU professor Marvin S. Hill, for example, has stated, "[T]here was certainly more continuity between the money-digging religious culture and the early Mormon movement than some historians have recognized. Joseph Smith began receiving revelations as a prophet in 1823, and thus began assuming the role central to his religious movement long before he abandoned his money digging in 1827" (Marvin S. Hill, *Quest for Refuge: The Mormon Flight from American Pluralism* [SLC: Signature Books, 1989], p. 20).

162. Robert J. Matthews, "What the Scriptures Say about Astrology, Divination, Spirit Mediums, Magic, Wizardry, and Necromancy," *Ensign*, Mar. 1974, p. 26, available at www.lds.org; cf. *Aaronic Priesthood Manual 2* (SLC: LDSC, 1995, online edition), "Satan and His Temptations," chapter 11, p. 37, available at www.lds.org.

163. Janet Thomas, "Magic," in Ludlow, ed., vol. 2, pp. 849-850.

164. "News of the Church," *Ensign*, June 1992, p. 74, available at www.lds.org.

165. Quinn, *The Mormon Hierarchy*, p. 88.

Chapter 2: And It Came to Pass

1. Ezra Taft Benson, "The Book of Mormon—Keystone of Our Religion," *Ensign*, Nov. 1986, p. 4, available at www.lds.org.

2. Smith plagiarized text not only from the 1611 King James Version of the Bible, but he also lifted passages from the Apocrypha (a set of religio-historical books not

canonized as Scripture). For a side-by-side comparison of plagiarized BOM passages, see Richard Abanes, *One Nation Under Gods* (New York: Four Walls Eight Windows, 2002; rev. paperback ed., 2003), pp. 71-72.

3. Fawn Brodie, in her landmark biography of Smith, noted, "The daughter of Jared [in the *Book of Mormon*], like Salome, danced before a king and a decapitation followed [cf. Matthew 14:1-12]. Aminadi, like Daniel, deciphered handwriting on a wall [cf. Daniel 5:13-30], and Alma was converted after the exact fashion of St. Paul [cf. Acts 9:1-19]. The daughters of the Lamanites were abducted like the dancing daughters of Shiloh [cf. Judges 21:19-23]; and Amon, the American counterpart of David, for want of a Goliath, slew six sheep-rustlers with his sling [cf. 1 Samuel 17:1-54]" (Fawn Brodie, *No Man Knows My History* [New York: Vintage Books, 1995; original edition by Alfred A. Knopf, 1945], pp. 62-63).

4. Such a scenario has been outlined by many researchers of LDS history, including Dan Vogel, D. Michael Quinn, Brent Metcalfe, and surprisingly, Grant Palmer, long-time institute director for the Church Educational System (CES) of the LDS Church (see Grant Palmer, *An Insider's View of Mormon Origins* [SLC: Signature Books, 2002], pp. 239-240, 251, 253-254; cf. pp. 255-256).

5. *HC* (SLC: Deseret Book Co., 1976/1980), vol. 1, p. 11.

6. *HC*, vol. 1, p. 12.

7. The plates were later described as being about six inches wide by eight inches long, and bound together with three huge rings.

8. See John A. Tvedtnes and Matthew Roper, "One Small Step," *FARMS Review of Books* (2003), vol. 15, no. 1, http://farms.byu.edu/display.php?table=review&id=472.

9. *HC*, vol. 1, p. 16.

10. *HC*, vol. 1, p. 12.

11. Marion G. Romney, in *CR*, Apr. 3, 1949, p. 37.

12. Bruce McConkie, *The Millennial Messiah* (SLC: Deseret Book Co., 1982) pp. 159, 170, 179. Quoted in Ezra Taft Benson, "Flooding the Earth with the Book of Mormon," *Ensign*, Nov. 1988, p. 4, available at www.lds.org.

13. Benson, available at www.lds.org.

14. Jeffrey R. Holland, *Christ and the New Covenant* (SLC: Deseret Book Co., 1997), p. 345. Quoted in Joseph B. Wirthlin, "The Book of Mormon: The Heart of Missionary Proselyting," *Ensign*, Sept. 2002, p. 13, available at www.lds.org.

15. See BOM, Mormon 9:32-33.

16. *Gospel Principles* (SLC: LDSC, 1978; rev., 1979; Missionary Reference Library Edition, 1990), p. 351; cf. John Widtsoe and Franklin S. Harris Jr., *Seven Claims of the Book of Mormon* (Independence, MO: Zion's Printing and Publishing Co., 1937), pp. 13-14.

17. *What is the Book of Mormon?* (SLC: LDSC, 1982), p. 1.

18. Bruce McConkie, *MD* (SLC: Bookcraft, 1958; rev. ed., 1966; 23rd printing, 1977), p. 528.

19. McConkie, *MD*, p. 528.

20. BOM, 1830 ed., p. 73 (2 Nephi 5:21, modern edition).

21. BOM, 1830 ed., p. 73 (2 Nephi 5:22, modern edition); cf. 1 Nephi 12:23, modern edition. They also became "an idle people, full of mischief and subtlety." Moreover, God declared, "[C]ursed shall be the seed of him that mixeth with their seed: for they shall be cursed even with the same cursing" (BOM, 1830 ed., p. 73; 2 Nephi 5:23, modern edition).

22. BOM, 1830 ed., p. 456 (3 Nephi 2:14-16, modern edition).

23. BOM, 1830 ed., pp. 473-474 (3 Nephi 9:14-21, modern edition).

24. BOM, 1830 ed., pp. 476-477 (3 Nephi 11:1-17, modern edition).

25. See Oliver Cowdery, letter to W.W. Phelps, *MS&AD*, July 1835, vol. 1, no. 10, p. 158, reprinted in Dan Vogel, ed., *EMD* (SLC: Signature Books, 1998), vol. 2, p. 450.

26. BOM, modern ed., introduction.

27. BOM, 1830 ed., pp. 512-513 (3 Nephi 29, modern edition).

28. *Which angel appeared to Joseph Smith?*

Nephi	Unidentified	Moroni
1839 (Joseph Smith)	1832 (Joseph Smith)	Apr. 1835 (Oliver Cowdery, *MS&AD*)
Apr. 1842 (Joseph Smith, *T&S*)	1833 *(BOC)*	1835 (Joseph Smith, D&C)
Aug. 1842 *(MS)*	Feb. 1835 (Oliver Cowdery, *MS&AD*)	1838 *(EJ)*
1851 (PGP)		1878 (PGP)
1853 (Lucy Mack Smith)		
1888 (J.C. Whitmer)		

The documentation for the above citations is as follows:

Unidentified:

- *1832*—Joseph Smith, *1832 History*, original manuscript, contained in Joseph Smith Letterbook 1, pp. 1-6, Joseph Smith Papers, LDSCA, reprinted in Dean Jessee, ed., *PJS* (SLC: Deseret Book Co., 1989), vol. 1, p. 8; and Dan Vogel, *EMD* (SLC: Signature Books, 1996), vol. 1, p. 29.

- *1833*—Joseph Smith, revelation received on June 1830, *BOC* 24:6-7. (This version is consistent with Smith's 1832 account, wherein he says he first received forgiveness for his sins, but then fell into sins for which he had repent. Only after doing so was he visited by the "holy angel" during the night.)

- *Feb. 1835*—(Oliver Cowdery, "Letter IV," *MS&AD*, Feb. 1835, vol. 1, no. 5, p. 79, www.centerplace.org/history/ma/v1n05.htm, reprinted in Vogel, *EMD*, vol. 2, p. 429). In this account, Cowdery states that the angel, rather than declaring himself to be Moroni, simply declared himself "to be a messenger sent by commandment of the Lord."

Moroni:

- *Apr. 1835*—Oliver Cowdery, "Letter VI," *MS&AD*, Apr. 1835, vol. 1, no. 7, p. 112, www.centerplace.org/history/ma/v1n07.htm, reprinted in Vogel, *EMD*, vol. 2, p. 443.

- *1835*—Joseph Smith, *D&C* 50:2 (1835 edition), as reprinted in Wilford C. Wood, *Joseph Smith Begins His Work* (SLC: Wilford Wood, 1962), vol. 2.

- *1838*—Joseph Smith, "Answers to Questions," *EJ*, vol.1, no. 3, p. 42, reprinted in Vogel, *EMD*, vol. 1, p. 52.

- *1878*—*PGP*, "Joseph Smith History," 1:33.

Nephi:

- *1839*—Joseph Smith, *1839 History*, reprinted in Vogel, *EMD*, vol. 1, p. 63. Near the turn of the century (c. 1900), the name "Moroni" was written, possibly by LDS scholar–historian B.H. Roberts, over the original *1839 History* text. An explanatory note stated, "Evidently a clerical error; see Book Doc. & Cov., Sec 50, par 2 [1835 Kirtland edition]" (see Jessee, *PJS*, vol. 1, p. 277 n1). Likewise, LDS apostle Orson Pratt explained in an 1876 letter to John Christensen that the name "Nephi" resulted from a careless scribe, who probably pulled the wrong name from his memory. Pratt added, "[T]he items probably were not sufficiently scanned by Bro. Joseph, before they got into print" (Orson Pratt, letter to John Christenson, Mar. 11, 1876, Orson Pratt Letterbook, LDSCA, quoted in Jessee, *PJS*, vol. 1, p. 277 n1; Apr. 1842—*T&S*, "History of Joseph Smith," Apr. 15, 1842, vol. 3, p. 753, www.centerplace.org/history/ts/v3n12. htm. It should be noted that Smith never called for a retraction of "Nephi" being used in this account).

- *Aug. 1842*—*MS*, vol. 3, no. 12, pp. 53, 71.

- *1851*—*PGP*, "Joseph Smith History," p. 41.

- *1853*—Lucy Mack Smith, *Biographical Sketches of Joseph Smith the Prophet, and His Progenitors for many Generations* (Liverpool: S.W. Richards, 1853), p. 79.

- *1888*—John C. Whitmer, "The Eight Witnesses," published in Andrew Jenson, *HR*, Oct. 1888, vol. 7, p. 621. Whitmer stated, "I have heard my grandmother, Mary M. Whitmer [mother of five BOM witnesses] say on several occasions that she was shown the plates of the Book of Mormon by an holy angel, whom she always called Brother Nephi."

29. Smith, *1832 History*, in Vogel, *EMD*, vol. 1, p. 29.

30. Abanes, p. 25.

31. LaMar Peterson, *The Creation of the Book of Mormon* (SLC: Freethinker Press, 2000), p. 18. Petersen also noted, "Oddly enough there is no reference to the angel by name in any account prior to 1835" (Peterson, p. 17). Even the 1833 *BOC* speaks only of a "holy angel" appearing to Smith (*BOC* XXVI:7, p. 48; cf. D&C 20:6).

32. D. Michael Quinn, *Early Mormonism and the Magic World View* (SLC: Signature Books, 1998), pp. 198-199. Quinn is quoting here from John Beaumont, *Historical, Physiological, and Theological Treatise of Spirits* (London: Printed for D. Browne, 1705), p. 90. Whether or not Quinn's observation explains the Nephi–Moroni inconsistency is debatable. But Smith certainly had no problem using the names interchangeably (Quinn, p. 199).

33. Smith's vision of Moroni may actually have taken place through the medium of his seer stone—i.e., *in* the stone, as one would see a vision in a crystal ball (see Richard S. Van Wagoner and Steven C. Walker, "Joseph Smith: 'The Gift of Seeing,'" in Bryan Waterman, ed., *The Prophet Puzzle* [SLC: Signature Books, 1999], p. 97).

34. Even Brigham Young knew that Smith used his seer stone in such a way. LDS pioneer Hosea Stout recorded in his diary that Young actually "exhibited the Seer's stone with which the Prophet Joseph discovered the plates of the Book of Mormon" (Hosea Stout, *On the Mormon Frontier: The Diary of Hosea Stout,* Juanita Brooks, ed. [SLC: University of Utah Press, 1964], vol. 2, p. 593).

35. Smith originally attached no religious significance to the volume, but instead touted the book as a volume that would, according to neighbor Parley Chase, *"tell him how to get money that was buried in the ground"* (Parley Chase, letter to James T. Cobb, Apr. 3, 1879, in Wilhelm Ritter von Wymetal, *Joseph Smith, the Prophet, His Family, and His Friends* [SLC: Tribune Printing and Publishing Co., 1886], p. 276, reprinted in Dan Vogel, ed., *EMD* [SLC: Signature Books, 2000], vol. 3, p. 135).

36. Smith's cousin-in-law Hiel Lewis, recalled: "The heavenly visions and messages of angels, etc., contained in Mormon books were after-thoughts, revised to order" (Hiel Lewis, *The Amboy Journal,* Apr. 30, 1879, quoted in Wesley P. Walters, "The Mormon Prophet Attempts to Join the Methodists," www.utlm.org/onlineresources/josephsmithmethodist.htm).

37. According to Martin Harris, Smith's money-digging companions believed "they had as much right to the plates as Joseph." In their eyes, he had been a "traitor and had appropriated to himself that which belonged to them" (Martin Harris, interview in *Tiffany's Monthly,* 1859, p. 167, www.utlm.org/onlineresources/sermons_talks_inter views/ harrisinterviewtiffanysmonthly.htm).

   David Whitmer, one of the three "witnesses" to the BOM, may have first heard about the golden plates from some of Smith's money-digging companions. During an 1881 interview with the *Kansas City Journal,* Whitmer related that he had "had conversations with several young men who said that Joseph Smith had certainly golden plates, and that before he attained them he had promised to share with them, but had not done so, and they were very much incensed with him" (David Whitmer, interview, *Kansas City Journal,* June 5, 1881, reprinted in Fred C. Collier, ed., *Unpublished Revelations* [SLC: Collier's Publishing, Co., 1993], vol. 2, p. 114).

38. Van Wagoner and Walker, in Waterman, pp. 87-112.

39. The plates alternately were 1) covered up and lying nearby, 2) in another room, or 3) hidden elsewhere (for example, outside in a tree stump). For documentation, see David Whitmer, in Collier, vol. 2, p. 116; Emma Smith, interview with Joseph Smith III, Feb. 1879, reprinted in Vogel, *EMD,* vol. 1, p. 539; Martin Harris, interview with Anthony Metcalf, in A. Metcalf, *Ten Years Before the Mast* (Malad City, ID: n.p., 1888), pp. 70-71, reprinted in Vogel, *EMD,* vol. 2, pp. 346-347; and Noel B. Reynolds, "The Authorship of the Book of Mormon," May 27, 1997, lecture in BYU's de Jong Concert Hall, www.speeches.byu.edu/htmlfiles/ReynoldsSp97.html.

40. Isaac Hale, statement of Mar. 20, 1834, in "Mormonism," *Susquehanna Register, and Northern Pennsylvanian,* May 1, 1834, p. 1, http://speeches.byu.edu/htmlfiles/Reynolds Sp97.html.

41. Joseph Knight Sr. used the term "Urim and Thummim" as a euphemism for Smith's seer stone (see Joseph Knight, quoted in Richard S. Van Wagoner and Steven C. Walker, "Joseph Smith: The Gift of Seeing," *Dialogue: A Journal of Mormon Thought* [Summer 1982], vol. 15, pp. 52-53); cf. similar usage of "Urim and Thummim" in Michael Morse, interview with William W. Blair, letter to editor, June 15, 1879, *Saints Herald*, vol. 26, no. 12, pp. 190-191, quoted by Van Wagoner and Walker, in Waterman, p. 52; and David Whitmer, *An Address to All Believers in Christ* (Richmond, MO: author, 1887), p. 12, www.utlm.org/onlinebooks/address1.htm. Also see this chapter's n42.

42. Emma Smith recalled, "In writing for J.S. [Smith] I frequently wrote day after day, often sitting at the table close to him, he sitting with his face buried in his hat, with the stone in it and dictating [the Book of Mormon] hour after hour with nothing between us" (Emma Smith Bidamon, as quoted in the unpublished notes of her interview with Joseph Smith III, Feb. 1879, Miscellany, RLDSA, Independence, MO, reprinted in Vogel, *EMD*, vol. 1, p. 539).

    Smith's brother William, like Joseph Knight, used the term "Urim and Thummim" as a euphemism for Smith's seer stone (cf. this chapter's n41 on Joseph Knight Sr.). William recalled, "The manner in which this was done was by looking into the Urim and Thummim, which was placed in a hat to exclude the light, (the plates lying near by covered up), and reading off the translation, which appeared in the stone by the power of God" (William Smith, *William Smith On Mormonism* [Lamoni, IA: Herald Steam Book and Job Office, 1883], p. 11. Quoted in Francis Kirkham, *A New Witness for Christ in America* [SLC: Utah Printing, Co., 1951], vol. 2, p. 417).

43. B.H. Roberts, *CHC* (SLC: Deseret News Press, 1930), vol. 1, pp. 128-129. The highly regarded LDS scholar Richard Bushman has said, "Mormons first applied the word seer to Joseph and combined the words 'seer' and 'stone.' Martin Harris, David Whitmer, Oliver Cowdery, Brigham Young and Orson Pratt described Joseph using a seerstone to translate and receive revelations….The word seer elevated the stones, symbolizing the redirection of the Smith family's interest in magic toward a more serious religious end….Although treasure-seeking was left behind, the magical culture of the stones played an important part in the development of Joseph's identity as seer and translator….In fact, as work on the Book of Mormon went on, a seerstone took the place of the Urim and Thummim, blending the culture of magic with divine culture of translation" (Richard L. Bushman, "Joseph Smith As Translator," *The Prophet Puzzle* [SLC: Signature Books, 1999], pp. 78-79).

44. Reynolds, http://speeches.byu.edu/htmlfiles/ReynoldsSp97.html.

45. Reynolds, http://speeches.byu.edu/htmlfiles/ReynoldsSp97.html.

46. Wesley P. Walters, *The Use of the Old Testament in the Book of Mormon* (SLC: ULM, 1990), p. 30. Walters writes, "Since the Elizabethan style was not Joseph's natural idiom, he continually slipped out of this King James pattern and repeatedly confused the norms as well. Thus he lapsed from 'ye' (subject) to 'you' (object) as the subject of sentences (e.g., Mos. 2:19; 3:34; 4:24), jumped from plural ('ye') to singular ('thou') in the same sentence (Mos. 4:22) and moved from verbs without endings to ones with endings (e.g. 'yields…putteth,' 3:19)."

47. LDS president Joseph F. Smith gave his understanding of Smith's "translation" in an 1881 sermon (as reported by Oliver B. Huntington): "The Lord caused each word spelled

as it is in the book to appear on the stones in short sentences of words, and when Joseph had uttered the sentence or word before him the scribe had written it properly, that sentence would disappear and another appear. And if there was a word wrongly written or even a letter incorrect the writing on the stones would remain there. Then Joseph would require the scribe to spell the reading of the last spoken and thus find the mistake and when corrected the sentence would disappear as usual" (Oliver B. Huntington, *Journal of Oliver Huntington,* p. 168, typed copy at Utah State Historical Society).

48. Martin Harris. Cited in Edward Stevenson, "Letter to the Editor," Nov. 30, 1881, published on Dec. 28, 1881, *Deseret Evening News,* p. 763; cf. Reynolds, http://speeches .byu.edu/htmlfiles/ReynoldsSp97.html. Reynolds stated, "As Joseph dictated without the aid of notes, papers, or even the plates themselves, relying solely on the Urim and Thummim or the seerstone, the scribes carefully recorded every word."

49. *HC,* vol. 1, pp. 54-55.

50. BOM, 1830 edition, p. 268 (Alma 16:13, modern edition).

51. J.D. Douglas, rev. ed., and Merrill C. Tenney, gen. ed., *The New International Dictionary of the Bible* (Grand Rapids: Zondervan, 1987), p. 972.

52. 1 Nephi 18:25.

53. Thomas D.S. Key, "A Biologist Looks at the Book of Mormon," *Journal of the American Scientific Affiliation,* June 1985, XXX-VIII, p. 3. Dr. Thomas Key, Box 43, East Central Community College, Decatur MS 39227-0129. This article has since been expanded and renamed *The Book Of Mormon In The Light Of Science.* It is sold by Utah Missions, Inc. (UMI), PO Box 348, Marlow, OK 73055, 1-800-654-3992, www.umi.org/.

    In an attempt to reconcile this problem, LDS apologist John Sorenson has suggested that Smith mistranslated numerous words from the BOM golden plates. For example, *cattle* and *oxen* should have been rendered *deer* and *bison.* Moreover, *horses* should also have been translated *deer,* while *swine* allegedly refers to the wild pig. Other supposed mistranslations are also listed by Sorenson (John L. Sorenson, *An Ancient American Setting for the Book of Mormon* [SLC: Deseret Book, 1985], 191-276, p. 299; cf. comment by Vogel and Metcalfe about use of such argumentation, this chapter's n87). As appealing as this resolution may be to some Mormons, it is countered by Joseph Smith himself, who claimed that a voice spoke to him from heaven, saying that the translation of the BOM was correct as written (see this chapter's nn47-48).

54. This was due, in part, to the many burial mounds dotting the land. Curiosity about them "made an amateur antiquarian of almost everyone in the area" (Brodie, p. 34).

55. Mordecai M. Noah, *Wayne Sentinel,* Oct. 4, 1825. Quoted in Vogel, *EMD,* vol. 3, p. 279 n3.

56. *Wayne Sentinel,* Oct. 11, 1825, reprinted in Larry Jonas, *Mormon Claims Examined,* p. 45. Quoted in Jerald Tanner and Sandra Tanner, *The Changing World of Mormonism* (Chicago: Moody, 1981), p. 126, www.utlm.org/onlinebooks/changech5b.htm. Joseph Smith Sr. subscribed to this newspaper and even ran advertisements in it, which means Joseph Jr. would have had access to the publication.

57. Brodie, p. 46. Theories about Israelites in America were so common by 1833 that Josiah Priest wrote, "The opinion that the American Indians are descendants of the Lost Ten

Tribes is now a popular one and generally believed" (Josiah Priest, quoted in Brodie, p. 45). Brodie noted, "Fantastic parallels were drawn between Hebraic and Indian customs, such as feasts of first fruits, sacrifices of the first-born in the flock, cities of refuge, ceremonies of purification, and division into tribes. The Indian 'language' (which actually consisted of countless distinct languages derived from numerous linguistic stocks) was said to be chiefly Hebrew. The Indian belief in the Great Spirit (which originally had been implanted by French and Spanish missionaries) was said to be derived in a direct line from Jewish monotheism. One writer even held that syphilis, the Indian's gift to Europe, was an altered form of Biblical leprosy" (Brodie, p. 45).

58. Smith seems to have lifted text from Josiah Priest's *The Wonders of Nature,* published in 1825. Interestingly, Priest's 1835 *American Antiquities* was actually quoted in the LDS publication *T&S* ("From Priest's American Antiquities," June 1, 1842, vol. 3, no. 15, pp. 813-814). Moreover, *The Wonders of Nature* (1825) was available in Smith's neighborhood prior to the time the BOM was translated.

Jerald and Sandra Tanner have a photograph of an original copy of *The Wonders of Nature* that contained a sticker showing it belonged to the library in Manchester, New York (where Smith lived). For a side-by-side comparison chart of BOM passages plagiarized from *The Wonders of Nature,* see Abanes, p. 68.

59. For a side-by-side comparison chart of BOM passages plagiarized from *View of the Hebrews,* see Abanes, p. 69.

60. Ethan Smith, *View of the Hebrews* (Poultney, VT: 1st ed., 1823; 2nd ed., 1825), p. 172. Quoted in Persuitte, p. 107.

61. Quoted in Persuitte, p. 122.

62. Persuitte, p. 122.

63. An extremely detailed look at the many similarities between the BOM and *View of the Hebrews* can be found in Sandra Tanner, "Where Did Joseph Smith Get His Ideas for the Book of Mormon?," www.utlm.org/onlineresources/bomindianorigins.htm. For another in-depth comparison of the BOM and *View of the Hebrews,* see Persuitte.

64. According to LDS historian Andrew Jenson, Oliver Cowdery did not leave Poultney, Vermont, for New York until about 1825 (Andrew Jenson, "The Three Witnesses," *HR,* May 1887, vol. 6 nos. 3-5, p. 196).

65. Ethan Smith was installed as minister of the church on Nov. 21, 1821. Records of the Poultney Congregational Church indicate that on Aug. 2, 1818, a "Mr. Cowdery" (i.e., William) had three of his four daughters (Rebecca, Maria, Lucy, and Phoebe) baptized "on the faith of their mother," which would have been a Mrs. Keziah Pearce Austin, to whom William was wed in 1810 after his first wife died in 1809. Under the date of May 26, 1810, the church's records also reveal that a vote was taken "to give Mrs. Keziah Cowdery a letter of recommendation" (Persuitte, pp. 7, 298 n3).

66. William Smith, Joseph's brother, recounted, "'I did not see them uncovered, but I handled them and hefted them while wrapped in a tow frock and judged them to have weighed about sixty pounds....Father and my brother Samuel saw them as I did while in the frock. So did Hyrum and others of the family.' When the interviewer asked if he didn't want to remove the cloth and see the bare plates, William replied, "No, for father had just asked if he might not be permitted to do so, and Joseph, putting his hand on

them said; 'No, I am instructed not to show them to any one. If I do, I will transgress and lose them again.' Besides, we did not care to have him break the commandment and suffer as he did before"'" (*Zion's Ensign*, Jan. 13, 1894, p. 6, cited in Church of Christ broadside, www.exmormon.org/ file9.htm).

67. Harris, www.utlm.org/onlineresources/sermons_talks_interviews/harrisinterviewtiffanysmonthly.htm. He stated, "[W]e had a command to let no man look into them, except by the command of God, lest he should 'look aught and perish.'"

68. Daniel C. Peterson, "Mounting Evidence for the Book of Mormon," *Ensign*, Jan. 2000, p. 19, available at www.lds.org. He adds, "Meticulous research on these witnesses has confirmed their good character and the truthfulness of their accounts."

69. Palmer, pp. 175-176. Palmer also notes, "Joseph reported that the antediluvian prophet Enoch beheld 'things which were not visible to the natural eye' and explained that he, like Enoch, could 'see' with the spiritual 'mind' (Moses 6:36; D&C 67:10). Joseph Smith and Oliver Cowdery would later perceive Jesus, Moses, Elias, and Elijah in a worship service in Ohio while congregants discerned 'convoy after convoy of angels,' all 'with eyes of our understanding'" (see Palmer, p. 176).

70. Palmer, p. 175.

71. The separate experiences of the Three Witnesses came in response to a June 1829 revelation to Smith wherein God promised that Cowdery, Whitmer, and Harris would see the plates (D&C 17:2): "[I]t is by your faith that you shall obtain a view of them."

72. Perhaps as a guard against possible criticism, a revelation given by Smith *before* the visions set a limit on the men's testimony should they ever see the plates. They were to make only one affirmation: "I have seen [the plates], for they have been shown unto me *by the power of God*" (*D&C* 5:25, emphasis added). In other words, no specifics were to be given. The vagueness of this declaration conveniently caused a number of misunderstandings about their experience to circulate.

73. Palmer, p. 85.

74. *HC*, vol. 1, pp. 52-57.

75. Jessee, *PJS*, vol. 1, pp. 296-297.

76. Dan Vogel, "The Validity of the Witnesses' Testimonies," in Dan Vogel and Brent Metcalfe, *American Apocrypha* (SLC: Signature Books, 2002), p. 86. This in no way conflicts with their descriptions of the event using naturalistic language (for example, seeing with their "eyes"). Such wording would fit well with their nineteenth-century spiritual mindset.

77. Vogel, "The Validity," p. 87. Although David Whitmer released a statement in response to the article, saying that he was an honest and respectable man, he did not contradict Murphy's description of how he had described his viewing of the plates.
    Then, during an 1885 interview with James Henry Moyle, a faithful Mormon, Whitmer said he did indeed see the plates and angel and heard the angel, but that he "did not handle the plates." According to Moyle, Whitmer said the experience "was through the power of God....[H]e then spoke of Paul hearing and seeing Christ but his associates did not. Because it is only seen in the Spirit." Moyle noted that Whitmer "was somewhat spiritual in his explanations. He was not as materialistic in his descriptions as I wished" (Quoted in Vogel, "The Validity," p. 87). Moyle expressed his own

disappointment in the interview, saying, "I was not fully satisfied with the explanation. It was more spiritual than I had anticipated" (Vogel, "The Validity," p. 87; cf. Palmer, p. 197 and James Henry Moyle, personal journal, June 28, 1885, James Henry Moyle papers, F508:1, LDSCA. Quoted in Preston Nibley, *Witnesses of the Book of Mormon* [SLC: Stevens and Wallis, 1946], pp. 92-95).

Whitmer confirmed his "vision" of the plates not only in other interviews, but also in his own pamphlet titled *An Address to All Believers in Christ* (see Whitmer, *An Address,* p. 32).

78. Martin Harris. Quoted by John H. Gilbert, "Memorandum," Sept. 8, 1892, reprinted in Vogel, *EMD,* vol. 2, p. 548.

79. Reuben P. Harmon, statement to Arthur B. Deming, Dec. 16, 1884, in *Naked Truths About Mormonism,* Apr. 1888, vol. 1, no. 2, www.lavazone2.com/dbroadhu/CA/natruths.htm #040088-1d2, reprinted in Vogel, *EMD,* vol. 2, p. 385.

80. Jessee, *PJS,* vol. 1, p. 10.

81. Palmer, pp. 198-199.

82. Harris, www.utlm.org/onlineresources/sermons_talks_interviews/harrisinterviewtiffa nysmonthly.htm; cf. S.F. Anderick, statement of June 24, 1887, in *Naked Truths About Mormonism,* Jan. 1888, p. 2, www.lavazone2.com/dbroadhu/CA/natruths.htm#0108 8-2d2. Anderick said, "Several times I saw what he claimed were the plates, which were covered with a cloth. They appeared to be six or eight inches square. He frequently carried them with him. I heard they kept them under the brick hearth."

83. This admission came in the midst of dissension that was plaguing Smith's Church in Ohio. Out of the eight witnesses who signed the joint statement that appears at the beginning of the BOM, "only three individually reported that they saw and touched the records" (Palmer, p. 205). And only from one of them do we receive a hint of exactly *how* they saw and handled them. According to Theodore Turley, John Whitmer said he had seen and handled the plates "by a supernatural power" (*HC,* vol. 3, p. 307; cf. Theodore Turley, Memorandus, Apr. 4, 1839, LDSCA. Quoted in Palmer, pp. 205-206.)

84. Palmer, pp. 204-205. Those who left included Luke S. Johnson, Lyman E. Johnson, John F. Boynton, Stephen Burnett, and Warren Parrish.

85. Warren Parrish, letter to E. Holmes, Aug. 11, 1839. This letter was published in *The Evangelist,* Oct. 1, 1838, www.lavazone2.com/dbroadhu/OH/evan1832.htm#100138.

86. See Palmer, pp. 208-212.

87. Vogel and Metcalfe, in *American Apocrypha,* p. xiii.

88. Dee F. Green, "Book of Mormon Archeology: the Myths and the Alternatives," *Dialogue: A Journal of Mormon Thought* (Summer 1969), vol. 4, pp. 72-80.

89. Michael Coe, "Mormons and Archaeology: An Outside View," *Dialogue: A Journal of Mormon Thought* (Winter 1973), vol. 8, p. 44. Coe is Professor Emeritus of Anthropology and Curator Emeritus of Anthropology at the Peabody Museum.

90. Vogel and Metcalfe, *American Apocrypha,* p. vii.

91. Bradley Lepper. Quoted in Ben Fulton, "Burden of Proof," *Weekly Wire*, Oct. 6, 1997, www.weeklywire.com/ww/10-06-97/slc_story.html. He further said that where the BOM makes "claims around that, it's found wanting."

92. Terryl L. Givens, *By the Hand of Mormon* (New York: Oxford University Press, 2002), p. 155. Givens, however, also quoted BYU professor Daniel Peterson, who made a statement in support of the BOM's unique character (see Daniel C. Peterson, "Editor's Introduction: By What Measure Shall We Mete?" in *FARMS Review of Books* [1990], vol. 2, p. xxiii).

93. Since very early in LDS history, "an obvious interpretation was in many readers' minds. The 'land southward' they considered to be South America, the Isthmus of Panama was 'the narrow neck,' and North America was thought to be the 'land northward' " (John L. Sorenson and Matthew Roper, "Before DNA," *Journal of Book of Mormon Studies* (2003), vol. 12, no. 1, p. 10).

94. Vogel and Metcalfe, *American Apocrypha*, p. viii. Mesoamerica usually refers to that area encompassing Belize, northern Costa Rica, El Salvador, Guatemala, parts of Honduras, Nicaragua, and central to southern Mexico.

95. Vogel and Metcalfe, *American Apocrypha*, pp. viii-ix; cf. Deanne G. Matheny, "Does the Shoe Fit? A Critique of the Limited Tehuantepec Geography," in Brent Lee Metcalfe, ed., *New Approaches to the Book of Mormon: Explorations in Critical Methodology* (SLC: Signature Books, 1993), pp. 269-328.

96. Vogel and Metcalfe, *American Apocrypha*, pp. viii-ix; cf. Matheny, in Metcalfe, ed., *New Approaches*, pp. 269-328.

97. Reynolds, citing Sorenson's view, http://speeches.byu.edu/htmlfiles/ReynoldsSp97 .html. Sorenson offered his view in *An Ancient American Setting for the Book of Mormon* (SLC: Deseret Book and FARMS, 1985). The next book to appear in support of this new perspective was anthropologist F. Richard Hauck's *Deciphering the Geography of the Book of Mormon* (SLC: Deseret Book, 1988).

98. Sorenson and Roper admit, "By the beginning of the 20th century, likely not more than a handful of readers of Mormon's book questioned the interpretation that Lehi landed in Chile, that Panama was the narrow neck, and that the final battle of the Nephites took place in New York" (Sorenson and Roper, p. 10).

99. Sorenson and Roper, p. 10.

100. Sorenson and Roper, p. 10.

101. Givens, p. 99. LDS educator Kenneth W. Godfrey also has noted that "early Church leaders and saints alike believed the Book of Mormon history was broad enough and had lasted long enough to have included the peopling of both North and South America" (Kenneth W. Godfrey, "Joseph Smith, the Hill Cumorah, and Book of Mormon Geography: A Historical Study, 1823-1844," lecture at the Mormon History Association Meeting, 1989. Quoted by Matheny, in Metcalfe, ed., *New Approaches*, p. 270).

102. See Givens, p. 99. Dan Vogel has observed, "It is absolutely clear that Joseph Smith and the early Mormons associated the Book of Mormon with the Mound Builder myth and that they consistently held the belief that the Book of Mormon contained the history of a people who had landed in South America and were destroyed in the Great Lakes

region" (Dan Vogel, "The New Theory of the Book of Mormon Geography: A Preliminary Examination," private document, 1985. Quoted in Metcalfe, ed., *New Approaches*, p. 271).

103. Office of the First Presidency, letter to [LDS] Bishop Darrell L. Brooks, Oct. 16, 1990, www.utlm.org/images/cumorahletter.gif.

104. One follower of LDS apologists expressed the new BOM argument, saying in a 2003 Internet message post, "Joseph and other early LDS had very limited understanding of parts of the *Book of Mormon*....[T]hey also created misconceptions about its contents which persist today" (Cromis, Apr. 23, 2003, Internet post at ZLMB).

105. A limited geography model of the BOM story can *only* be accepted if an admission of numerous errors in the BOM is simultaneously made (see Matheny, in Brent Metcalfe, ed., pp. 277-281). In his 2003 article "Critique of a Limited Geography for Book of Mormon Events," Earl M. Wunderli has noted the following about Sorenson's work: "Sorenson notes in 'Mesoamerican Record,' 396, that 'the hundreds of statements and allusions about geography demonstrate that the volume's chief author, Mormon, held a mental map of Nephite lands that was consistent throughout, but its scale was limited to hundreds, not thousands of miles.' Nevertheless, Sorenson does recognize some apparent inconsistencies....First, he recognizes the city of Gid seems to be south of the city of Mulek in Alma 51:26 but reversed in Hel. 5:15. To resolve this, he supposes 'Mulek to have been seaward and Gid inland' even though Alma 51:26 states they were both 'on the east borders by the seashore.' Second, he recognizes that Moroni's recapturing the city of Mulek 'in the land of Nephi' is 'an evident error (mental slip) by the original scribe or Mormon,' since Mulek was in the land of Zarahemla. Third, he recognizes that at 4 Nephi 46, the Gadianton robbers were 'spread over all the face of the land,' but at Morm. 1:18, the robbers 'were among the Lamanites,' and states that it is unclear what Mormon means by 'among the Lamanites.'" (Wunderli, *Dialogue: A Journal of Mormon Thought* [Fall 2002], vol. 35, no. 3], pp. 182-183, fn51).

106. Office of the LDS First Presidency, letter to Brent Hall (FARMS), sender Carla Ogden, Apr. 23, 1993. From the files of John Sorenson.

107. One major problem, of course, is that every year the LDS Church holds its nearly sacred "Hill Cumorah Pageant" celebration in New York to commemorate the BOM tale and the church's restoration through Joseph Smith. This pageant has traditionally been viewed as the location of the last Nephite–Lamanite battle.

108. Thomas W. Murphy, "Lamanite Genesis, Genealogy, and Genetics," in Vogel and Metcalfe, eds., *American Apocrypha*, pp. 47-77; Michael Crawford, *The Origins of Native Americans* (New York: Cambridge University Press, 1998); D.C. Wallace, et al., "Dramatic Founder Effects in Amerindian Mitochondrial DNAs," *American Journal of Physical Anthropology* 68 (1985), pp. 149-155; T.G. Schurr et al., "Amerindian Mitochondrial DNAs Have Rare Asian Mutations at High Frequencies Suggesting a Limited Number of Founders," *American Journal of Human Genetics* 46 (1990), pp. 613-623; Antonio Torroni, "Mitochondrial DNA and the Origin of Native Americans," in Colin Renfrew, ed., *American Past, American Present: Genes and Languages in the Americas and Beyond* (Cambridge, UK: McDonald Institute for Archaeological Research, 2000), pp. 77-87.

109. BOM, introduction.

110. Jeffrey Meldrum, "The Children of Lehi: DNA and the *Book of Mormon*," lecture at the 2003 FAIR Conference, Aug. 8, 2003.

111. For example, during a 2003 lecture before a predominantly Mormon audience, LDS professor Jeffrey Meldrum of Idaho State University admitted in reference to Lehi's descendants, "It is very unlikely that they will be detected by genetic analysis of modern New World inhabitants" (Meldrum, see this chapter's n110). Meldrum also stated that his position is that "no genetic evidence of Middle Eastern subset has been found and probably never will be found."

112. Meldrum, "The Children of Lehi."

113. Meldrum, "The Children of Lehi."

114. In commenting on this passage, the *Book of Mormon Student Manual*, published by the LDS Church, notes, "No one knows the details of Book of Mormon geography. But the Prophet Joseph Smith revealed some information that suggests that at some time in their history the spread of the Nephites unto the 'land northward' included what we know today as North America" (1979 edition, p. 354). Similarly, D&C 54:8 explains that the borders of the Lamanites extended to the "land of Missouri."

115. Joseph Smith, *Ohio Journal—1835-1836*, Nov. 9, 1835, reprinted in Jessee, ed., *PJS*, vol. 2, p. 70; cf. reprinted in Dan Vogel, ed., *EMD*, vol. 1, p. 44.

116. Joseph Smith, Mar. 1, 1842, letter to John Wentworth, reprinted in *HC*, vol. 4, p. 537.

117. DNA studies have shown that 99.6% of Native Americans are descended from individuals who migrated to the Americas from Central and Northeast Asia. Such individuals have been categorized into what DNA researchers have designated as haplogroups A, B, C, D, and X (Meldrum, "The Children of Lehi").

118. Joseph Smith, letter to N.E. Seaton, Feb. 2, 1833, *American Revivalist and Rochester Observer*, www.lavazone2.com/dbroadhu/NY/miscNYSc.htm#020233.

119. BOM, introduction.

120. Early LDS beliefs regarding Native Americans can be clearly seen in Oliver Cowdery's Speech to the Delawares. He openly identified American Indians as descendants of Israelites (see Parley P. Pratt, *Autobiography of Parley P. Pratt* [SLC: Deseret Book Co., 1979], pp. 54-56).

121. "The Lamanites, while increasing in numbers, fell under the curse of divine displeasure; they became dark in skin and benighted in spirit, forgot the God of their fathers, lived a wild nomadic life, and degenerated into the fallen state in which the American Indians—their lineal descendants—were found by those who rediscovered the western continent in later times" (James E. Talmage, *The Articles of Faith* [SLC: LDSC, 1890; rev. ed., 1940], p. 260).

122. Spencer W. Kimball, in Edward L. Kimball, ed., *Teachings of Spencer W. Kimball* (SLC: Bookcraft,1982), p. 596.

123. Hinckley's opinion was recorded in the *LDS Church News:* "In an interview with the *Church News*, President [Gordon B.] Hinckley commented on the appreciation of the Ecuadorian members for the new temple....He noted that 'it has been a very interesting thing to see the descendants of Father Lehi in the congregations that have gathered in the [Guayaquil, Ecuador] temple. So very many of these people have the blood of Lehi

in their veins and it is just an intriguing thing to see their tremendous response and their tremendous interest.'...President [James E. Faust]...said that the 'Latin people have a special quality of softness and graciousness and kindness. They are a great people— they are sons and daughters of Father Lehi, and they have believing blood' " (Gordon B. Hinckley. Quoted in John L. Hart, "Guayaquil Ecuador Temple dedication: 'A wondrous day' for members," Aug. 7, 1999, *LDS Church News*, www.desnews.com/cgi-bin/lib story_church? dn99&9908090026). Hinckley made similar comments in 1984 during his dedicatory prayer for the Guatemala temple in Guatemala City (Gordon B. Hinckley, dedicatory prayer, Dec. 14, 1984, www.ldschurchtemples.com/cgi-bin/prayerscgi? guatemala_city&chronological).

This same view was expressed by LDS leaders Thomas Monson (dedicatory prayer for Villahermosa temple, May 21, 2000, www.ldschurchtemples.com/cgi-bin/prayers .cgi?villahermosa&chronological); James E. Faust (dedicatory prayer for the Tuxtla Gutierrez temple, Mar. 12, 2000); and Walter F. Gonzalez (quoted in "Book of Mormon Has Direct Message for Children of Lehi," *LDS Church News*, Jan 1, 2000).

124. Meldrum, "The Children of Lehi."

125. Meldrum, "The Children of Lehi," emphasis added. Interestingly, when this statement appeared in print for a FARMS article, it was changed to read as follows: "A tradition apparently has persisted in the Latter-day Saint community, from the time the Book of Mormon first appeared in print in the 19th century, that all Native Americans are Lehi's direct descendants. This assumption seems to have been held by *many* early members of the Church of Jesus Christ of Latter-day Saints and is still held by *most* today" (D. Jeffrey Meldrum and Trent D. Stephens, "Who are the Children of Lehi?" *Journal of Book of Mormon Studies*, vol. 12, no. 1, p. 40, http://farms.byu.edu/display.php ?table=jbms&id=314.

126. George Q. Cannon, in *JOD*, Apr. 6, 1884, vol. 25, p. 124. Cannon stated, "[W]e have scarcely touched the Indian races. There is an immense field spreading out before the Elders of this Church in the redemption of these poor remnants of the house of Israel....But here stretches out before us this immense continent on the south, peopled with descendants of the house of Israel" (George Q. Cannon, Apr. 4, 1897, in Brian H. Stuy, ed., *Collected Discourses* [SLC: B.H.S. Publishing, 1992], vol. 5, p. 269).

127. "And thus you shall take your journey into the regions westward, unto the land of Missouri, unto the borders of the Lamanites" (D&C 54:8). This teaching was reiterated throughout the twentieth century: **1909**—Walter C. Lyman, in *CR*, Oct. 6, 1907, p. 86; **1929**—Hyrum G. Smith, in *CR*, Apr. 7, 1929, p. 123; **1950**—E. Wesley Smith, in *CR*, Sept. 29, 1950, p. 47; **1954**—Spencer W. Kimball, in *CR*, Apr. 6, 1954, pp. 106-108; **1957**—Gordon M. Romney, in *CR*, Apr. 6, 1957, p. 80; **1970**—Neal A. Maxwell, in *CR*, Oct. 3, 1970, p. 93.

128. Cooper Johnson, "DNA and the Book of Mormon," www.fairlds.org/apol/bom/ bom01.html.

129. Reynolds, http://speeches.byu.edu/htmlfiles/ReynoldsSp97.html.

130. This teaching comes from the BOM, 2 Nephi 1:6, where Lehi prophesies, "[T]here shall none come into this land save they shall be brought by the hand of the Lord." He adds, "And behold, it is wisdom that this land should be kept as yet from the knowledge of other nations; for behold, many nations would overrun the land, that there would be

no place for an inheritance. Wherefore, I, Lehi, have obtained a promise, that inasmuch as those whom the Lord God shall bring out of the land of Jerusalem shall keep his commandments, they shall prosper upon the face of this land; and they shall be kept from all other nations, that they may possess this land unto themselves. And if it so be that they shall keep his commandments they shall be blessed upon the face of this land, and there shall be none to molest them, nor to take away the land of their inheritance" (vv. 8-9).

In 1940, LDS leader J. Reuben Clark clearly articulated this long-held Mormon belief: "The Lord took every precaution to see that nothing might interfere with this posterity of Joseph in working out their God-given destiny and the destiny of America. He provided, and so told Lehi at the very beginning of his settlement, that:...it is wisdom that this land should be kept as yet from the knowledge of other nations; for behold, many nations would overrun the land, that there would be no place for an inheritance. (2 Nephi 1:8.) The Lord so kept the land for a thousand years after Lehi landed. He so kept it in His wisdom for another thousand years after the Nephites were destroyed, perhaps to give the Lamanitish branch another chance" (J. Reuben Clark, "Prophecies, Penalties, and Blessings," *Improvement Era,* July 1940, vol. xliii., no. 7. Quoted in Bill McKeever, "DNA and the Book of Mormon Record," www.mrm.org/multimedia/text/dna-bom.html).

131. Daniel C. Peterson, FAIR Conference, untitled lecture, Aug. 8, 2003, author's private notes.

132. David Stewart, "DNA and the Book of Mormon," www.limhi.com/bookofmormondna.html.

133. Peterson, FAIR Conference; Stewart.

134. See "DNA Experts and Christians Attack the Bible as Well as the Book of Mormon," www.newrevelations.com/dna_experts_attack_the_bible.htm; cf. Stewart.

135. Peterson, FAIR Conference.

136. The origin of this doctrine can be traced to 1831, when Smith encouraged LDS men to take Indian wives. It was to be done, God said via a revelation, so Native Americans could turn white in fulfillment of BOM prophecies: "[I]t is my will, that in time, ye should take unto you wives of the Lamanites and Nephites, that their posterity may become white, delightsome and just" (Joseph Smith, "Revelation Received West of Jackson County, Missouri, July 17, 1831." Transcribed by W.W. Phelps, manuscript in LDSCA, reprinted in H. Michael Marquardt, *The Joseph Smith Revelations: Text & Commentary* [SLC: Signature Books, 1999], p. 375; cf. W.W. Phelps, letter to Brigham Young, Aug. 12, 1861, Joseph Smith Collection, LDSCA, reprinted in Fred C. Collier, comp., *Unpublished Revelations* [SLC: Collier's Publishing Co., 1979; 2nd ed., 1981], vol. 1, p. 58).

137. BOM, 2 Nephi 30:6 (pre-1981 edition).

138. BOM, 2 Nephi 5:21, which reads, "[T]hey had hardened their hearts against him, that they had become like unto a flint; wherefore, as they were white, and exceedingly fair and delightsome, that they might not be enticing unto my people the Lord God did cause a skin of blackness to come upon them."

139. Kimball, *Improvement Era*, Dec. 1960, pp. 922-923. Quoted in Bill McKeever and Eric Johnson, "Pure and Delightsome," *Mormonism Researched*, Spring 1994, p. 5.

140. George Edward Clark, *Why I Believe*, p. 129. Quoted in McKeever and Johnson, p. 5, www.mrm.org/multimedia/text/pure-white.html.

141. Michael Crawford. Quoted in Dan Egan, "BYU Gene Data May Shed Light in Origin of Book of Mormon's Lamanites," *Salt Lake Tribune*, Nov. 30, 2000, www.sltrib.com (archives).

142. B.H. Roberts, *Studies of the Book of Mormon*, Brigham D. Madsen and Sterling M. McMurrin, eds. (Urbana, IL: University of Illinois Press, 1985), p. 271. Roberts concluded, "[W]as Joseph Smith possessed of a sufficiently vivid and creative imagination as to produce such a work as the Book of Mormon from such materials as have been indicated in the preceding chapters?...That such power of imagination would have to be of a high order is conceded; that Joseph Smith possessed such a gift of mind there can be no question" (Roberts, p. 243).
    Roberts also wrote, "In the light of this evidence, there can be no doubt as to the possession of a vividly strong, creative imagination by Joseph Smith, the Prophet, an imagination, it could with reason be urged, which, given the suggestions that are found in the 'common knowledge' of accepted American antiquities of the times, supplemented by such a work as Ethan Smith's *View of the Hebrews*, would make it possible for him to create a book such as the Book of Mormon is....If from all that has gone before in Part 1, the view be taken that the Book of Mormon is merely of human origin...if it be assumed that he [Joseph Smith] is the author of it, then it could be said there is much internal evidence in the book itself to sustain such a view. In the first place there is a certain lack of perspective in the things the book relates as history that points quite clearly to an undeveloped mind as their origin. The narrative proceeds in characteristic disregard of conditions necessary to its reasonableness, as if it were a tale told by a child, with utter disregard for consistency" (Roberts, pp. 250, 251).

143. Lloyd's statement is online at www.lds-mormon.com/bhrlettr.shtml. Lloyd also noted, "These are some of the things which has made Bro. Roberts shift his base on the Book of Mormon. Instead of regarding it as the strongest evidence we have of Church Divinity, he regards it as the one which needs the most bolstering."

144. Thomas Stuart Ferguson, letter to Harold Hougey, June 5, 1972. Quoted in Stan Larson, "The Odyssey of Thomas Stuart Ferguson," *Dialogue: A Journal of Mormon Thought* (Spring 1990), vol. 23, p. 76. Ferguson said, "Ten years have passed....I sincerely anticipated that Book-of-Mormon cities would be positively identified within 10 years—and time has proved me wrong in my anticipation."

145. Thomas Stuart Ferguson, *One Fold And One Shepherd* (1962, p. 263). Quoted in Tanner and Tanner, "Ferguson's Two Faces," *Salt Lake City Messenger* (#69), Sept. 1988, p. 3, www.utlm.org/newsletters/no69.htm.

146. Thomas Stuart Ferguson, letter dated Feb. 9, 1976. For a photo of this letter, see Abanes, p. 80.

147. Ferguson, letter dated Feb. 9, 1976. Ferguson also said, "Why not say the right things and keep your membership in the great fraternity, enjoying the good things you like and discarding the ones you can't swallow (and keeping your mouth shut)?...[W]hy

try to be heroic and fight the myths—the Mormon one or any other that does more good than ill? Perhaps you and I have been spoofed by Joseph Smith. Now that we have the inside dope—why not spoof a little back and stay aboard? Please consider this letter confidential—for obvious reasons. I want to stay aboard the good ship, Mormonism."

148. Austin Cline, "By the Hand of Mormon: The American Scripture that Launched a New World Religion," www.atheism.about.com/library/books/full/aafprHandMormon .htm.

149. Reynolds, http://speeches.byu.edu/htmlfiles/ReynoldsSp97.html.

150. John L. Sorenson, "The Decline of the God Quetzalcoatl," in *Pressing Forward with the Book of Mormon* (Provo, UT: FARMS, 1999), p. 234. This argument also may be found in the writings of earlier LDS apologists such as John A. Widtsoe (see John A. Widtsoe & Franklin S. Harris Jr., *Seven Claims of The Book of Mormon* [Independence, MO: Press of Zion's Printing and Publishing Company], pp. 117-121).

151. Joseph Allen, *Exploring the Lands of the Book of Mormon* (Brigham Young University Print Services, 1989), excerpt online at www.nephiproject.com/white_ god_quetzal coatl.htm. Interestingly, Allen reproduced this statement in a 2003 article but was far more guarded in his assertion: "[I]t could be that the deity Quetzalcoatl had its origin in the visit of Jesus Christ to the American continent" (see Joseph Allen, "The White God Quetzalcoatl," *Meridian Magazine*, 2003, www.meridianmagazine.com/articles/ 030926white.html).

152. Adela Fernandez, *Pre-Hispanic Gods of Mexico* (Mexico City: Panorama Editorial, 1984), p. 68. Cited in "Quetzalcoatl the Myth," www.weber.ucsd.edu/~anthclub/quetzalcoatl/ que.htm.

153. Quetzalcoatl the Myth," www.weber.ucsd.edu/~anthclub/quetzalcoatl/que.htm.

154. The Toltec culture existed primarily in the Valley of Mexico. The Aztecs, descendants of the Toltec, lived mainly in the Central Mexico basin. The Incas populated Peru. The Mayans were spread throughout the Yucatán Peninsula. The Quiche–Mayan culture inhabited the highland valley of Guatemala. Quetzalcoatl was known to the Incas as Viracocha and to the Mayans as Kukulcan.

155. Tohil is the Quiche–Mayan name for Quetzalcoatl.

156. Burr Cartwright Brundage, *The Phoenix of the Western World* (Norman, OK: University of Oklahoma Press, 1982).

157. Ezra Taft Benson, "A New Witness for Christ," *Ensign*, Nov. 1984, p. 6, available at www.lds.org.

158. Meldrum and Stephens, p. 51, http://farms.byu.edu/display.php?table=jbms&id=314. One former member of the RLDS Church put it in these terms: "If you have faith in God and trust in Him He will let you know it is true. Those who have this faith do not need archeology or science to prove the book of Mormon true to them. It's that simple" (RockHeaded, May 2, 2003, Internet post at ZLMB).

Chapter 3: Thus Saith Joseph

1. *BOC* XXII:1-4, p. 45.

2. "Whenever the Lord had a people on the earth that he acknowledged as such, that people were led by revelation" (Wilford Woodruff, quoted in James E. Faust, "Continuing Revelation," *Ensign*, Aug. 1996, p. 2, available at www.lds.org). Ezra Taft Benson said, "The Book of Mormon is the 'keystone' of our religion, and the *D&C* is the capstone, with continuing latter-day revelation" (Ezra Taft Benson, "The Book of Mormon and the Doctrine and Covenants," *Ensign*, May 1987, p. 83, available at www.lds.org).

3. "I do not believe members of this Church can be in full harmony with the Savior without sustaining His living prophet on earth, the President of the Church. If we do not sustain the living prophet, whoever he may be, we die spiritually" (James E. Faust, available at www.lds.org).

4. See "Explanatory Introduction," D&C, www.scriptures.lds.org/dc/intro. Gordon B. Hinckley has said that the D&C "is primarily a book of revelation given through the Prophet of this dispensation" (Gordon B. Hinckley, "The Order and Will of God," *Ensign*, Jan. 1989, p. 2, available at www.lds.org).

5. George Albert Smith, Oct. 6, 1917, in *CR*, p. 43.

6. M. Russell Ballard, "Marvelous Are the Revelations of the Lord," *Ensign*, May 1998, p. 31, available at www.lds.org.

7. Russell M. Nelson, "Getting Where You Want to Go," *New Era*, May 2003, p. 4, available at www.lds.org.

8. For example, see this chapter's n1.

9. On Dec. 1, 1832, Smith recorded in his diary, "[I] wrote and corrected revelations &c" (Joseph Smith, *Ohio Journal—1832-1834*, Dec. 1, 1832, p. 3. LDSCA, in Dean Jessee, *PJS* [SLC: Deseret Book Co., 1992], vol. 2, p. 4). The press that printed the sheets of revelations was destroyed by an anti-Mormon mob. The sheets, scattered in the streets, were gathered up and assembled into a 160-page book.

10. Karl F. Best, "Changes in the Revelations, 1833-1835," *Dialogue: A Journal of Mormon Thought* (Spring 1992), vol. 25, no.1, p. 90. Best writes, "Because Joseph Smith was on the committee that 'arranged' the revelations for publication and signed the committee's letter recommending the 1835 Doctrine and Covenants to the members of the Church, we can assume that he was responsible for the 1833-35 changes, or at least knew and approved of them, even if they originated with other members of the committee."

11. H. Michael Marquardt, *The Joseph Smith Revelations: Text & Commentary* (SLC: Signature Books, 1999), p. 17.

12. In 1890, LDS president Wilford Woodruff stated that the D&C contained "some of the most sublime revelations" ever given by God "to any generation, or to any prophet or people under heaven" (Wilford Woodruff, Apr. 4, 1890, in Brian Stuy, ed., *Collected Discourses* [Burbank: B.H.S. Publishing, 1988], vol. 2, p. 29). A little more than 20 years later, LDS authority Joseph Fielding Smith declared that in the D&C there could be found "some of the most glorious principles ever revealed to the world" (Joseph Fielding Smith, Oct. 4, 1913, in *CR*, p. 9).

13. Melvin J. Petersen, "A Study of the Nature of and the Significance of the Changes in the Revelations as Found in a Comparison of the Book of Commandments and

Subsequent Editions of the Doctrine and Covenants," BYU Thesis, MS, 1955, typed copy, p. 118. See Best, pp. 90, 101-102, 109.

14. Richard N. Ostling and Joan K. Ostling, *Mormon America* (San Francisco: HarperSanFrancisco, 1999), p. 249, summarizing the views of Mark P. Leone, *Roots of Modern Mormonism* (Cambridge: Harvard University Press: 1979), pp. 204, 211.

15. David Rolph Seely, "The Joseph Smith Translation: 'Plain and Precious Things' Restored," *Ensign*, Aug. 1997, p. 9, available at www.lds.org. Smith revised Matthew 24 for similar reasons. Seely, professor of ancient scripture at BYU, noted, "To the biblical text of Matthew 24, the Prophet added 450 new words. Significantly, he also changed the order of many of the verses and repeated elements of three verses."

16. John J. Stewart, *Joseph Smith the Mormon Prophet* (SLC: Mercury, 1966), p. 57.

17. "A Translation," *T&S*, Mar. 1, 1842, pp. 703-706; "The Book of Abraham," *T&S*, Mar. 15, 1842, pp. 719-722; "A Fac-Simile From The Book of Abraham," *T&S*, May 16, 1842, p. 783.

18. Andrew Skinner, "The Book of Abraham: A Most Remarkable Book," *Ensign*, Mar. 1997, p. 16, available at www.lds.org.

19. Skinner, available at www.lds.org.

20. Marquardt, p. xiii; cf. James E. Lancaster, "The Translation of the Book of Mormon," in Dan Vogel, ed., *The Word of God: Essays on Mormon Scripture* (SLC: Signature Books, 1990). These first 15 revelations were received from July 1828 to June 1829. Then, in November 1830, Smith received yet another revelation by way of his seer stone (D&C 34). It is also believed that D&C 34 was transcribed by John Whitmer as Smith read it from his seer stone, which he had placed in his hat (see James R.B. Vancleave, letter to Joseph Smith III, Sept. 29, 1878, "Miscellaneous Letters and Papers," RLDSCA; John Logan Traughber, letter to "Dear Friend," Oct. 10, 1881, Schroeder Collection, State Historical Society of Wisconsin. Both cited in Marquardt, p. 94 fn94).

21. "History of Joseph Smith—Continued," *T&S*, July 15, 1842, p. 853).

22. In an 1874 *MS* article, Orson Pratt reported that Joseph said that "the Lord gave him the Urim and Thummim when he was inexperienced in the Spirit of inspiration." Eventually, though, he "understood the operations of that Spirit, and did not need the assistance of that instrument" (Orson Pratt, *MS*, Aug. 11, 1874).

There are some contradictory accounts on this point. David Whitmer, for example, remembered "Joseph giving the revelations of 1829 through the same stone through which the Book was translated....He then gave up the stone forever" (David Whitmer, *An Address to All Believers in the Book of Mormon* [Richmond, MO: author, 1887], p. 3, www.utlm.org/onlinebooks/addressbom.htm).

Whitmer also recorded that "after the translation of the Book of Mormon was finished, early in the spring of 1830, before April 6th, Joseph gave the stone to Oliver Cowdery and told me as well as the rest that he was through with it, and he did not use the stone any more. He said he was through the work that God had given him the gift to perform, except to preach the gospel. He told us that we would all have to depend on the Holy Ghost hereafter to be guided into truth and obtain the will of the Lord. The revelations after this came through Joseph as 'mouthpiece'; that is, he would enquire of the Lord, pray and ask concerning a matter, and speak out the revelation" (Whitmer, p. 32, www.utlm.org/onlinebooks/address3.htm).

23. Whitmer, pp. 31-32, 54, www.utlm.org/onlinebooks/address3.htm. This revelation was received around January 1830. It is believed that the written text is no longer extant (cf. *D&C* 46:7). In 1848, Hiram Page confirmed the revelation and his trip to Canada with Cowdery, Joseph Knight, and Josiah Stowell. He said Joseph wanted the copyright sold to "get a handsom[e] Sum of money which was to be...for the exclusive benefit of the Smith famaly *[sic]* and was to be at the disposal of Joseph" (Hiram Page, letter to William McLellin, Feb. 2, 1848, RLDSCA. Quoted in Marquardt, p. 372).

24. D. Michael Quinn, *The Mormon Hierarchy: Origins of Power* (SLC: Signature Books, 1994), p. 5.

25. Quinn, p. 5.

26. Whitmer, p. 59, www.utlm.org/onlinebooks/address4.htm. Whitmer also said, "Some of the revelations as they are now in the Book of Doctrine and Covenants have been changed and added to. Some of the changes being of the greatest importance as the meaning is entirely changed on some very important matters; as if the Lord had changed his mind a few years after he gave the revelations....The revelations were printed in the Book of Commandments correctly. This I know, and will prove it to you. These revelations were arranged for publication by Brothers Joseph Smith, Sydney Rigdon, Orson Hyde and others, in Hiram, Ohio, while I was there, were sent to Independence to be published, and were printed just exactly as they were arranged by Brother Joseph and the others. And when the Book of Commandments was printed, Joseph and the church received it as being printed correctly. This I know. In the winter of 1834 they saw that some of the revelations in the Book of Commandments had to be changed, because the heads of the church had gone too far, and had done things in which they had already gone ahead of some of the former revelations. So the book of 'Doctrine and Covenants' was printed in 1835, and some of the revelations changed and added to" (Whitmer, p. 56, www.utlm.org/onlinebooks/address4.htm).

27. See "Explanatory Notes," D&C, modern edition.

28. Best, p. 98.

29. D. Michael Quinn, *Early Mormonism and the Magic World View* (SLC: Signature Books, 1998), p. 206. This change also was made in today's *HC*, vol. 1, p. 37.

30. Marquardt, p. 37.

31. William McLellin, letter of Oct. 1870, published in *The True Latter Day Saints' Herald*, Aug. 1, 1872, p. 472; cf. Daniel Macgregor, *Changing the Revelations* [Independence, MO: author, n.d), p. 32. Macgregor's manuscript is available at BYU-Idaho in the Arthur Porter Special Collections, File MS 135, contact information and manuscript online at http://abish.byui.edu/SpecialCollections/Manuscripts/Collections/CollMss0.htm.

32. Robert J. Woodford, "The Story of the Doctrine and Covenants," *Ensign*, Dec. 1984, p. 32, available at www.lds.org.

33. Marquardt, pp. 14-15.

34. "The Early History of the Saints and Their Enemies," Sept. 28, 1875, in *Salt Lake Daily Tribune*, Dec. 5, 1878, www.lavazone2.com/dbroadhu/UT/tribune1.htm.

35. "In 1835 in Kirtland another committee was appointed to fix up the revelations for print again....I was often in Joseph's office, and know positively that some of the revelations were so altered, mutilated and changed that a good scholar would scarcely know them. In one revelation I counted 20 alterations! Hence, who can depend upon them? I cannot. I will not....All your trouble arises from your taking that mutilated and altered Doctrine and Covenants" (William McLellin, *Saints' Herald*, vol. 17, pp. 556-557, as quoted in Macgregor, p. 6).

36. Whitmer, p. 61, www.utlm.org/onlinebooks/address4.htm; cf. David Whitmer, letter to *Saints' Herald*, Feb. 5, 1887, vol. 34, p. 93, www.xmission.com/~country/reason/dw_let3.htm).

37. Charles M. Larson, *By His Own Hand Upon Papyrus* (Grand Rapids: Institute for Religious Research, 1985, rev. ed. 1992), p. 25.

38. Jerald Tanner and Sandra Tanner, *Mormonism: Shadow or Reality?* (SLC: ULM, 1987), p. 369.

39. The BOA "serves as a prime source for the doctrines of the premortal existence of human spirits and the plurality of Gods, stands as a halfway house in the movement toward plural marriage, and marks a stage in the development of statements about priesthood as the key to the power and knowledge of God" (Karl C. Sandberg, "Knowing Brother Joseph Again," in Bryan Waterman, ed., *The Prophet Puzzle* [SLC: Signature Books, 1999], p. 334; cf. Larson, pp. 18-21).

40. Ben McGuire, "Responding to Errors In An Anti-Mormon Film," FAIR, 2003, pp. 2-3.

41. Gordon, www.meridianmagazine.com/ideas/030528anti.html.

42. Sandberg, in Waterman, p. 322.

43. The early LDS concept of "translation" may have been related to an occult means of interpretation whereby the hidden meaning of symbols could be deciphered (Sandberg, in Waterman, p. 322; cf. Quinn, *Early Mormonism*, pp. 152-153).

44. For a photo of a page from this document, see Richard Abanes, *One Nation Under Gods: A History of the Mormon Church* (New York: Four Walls Eight Windows, 2002; paperback ed., 2003), p. 457.

45. Richard L. Bushman, "Joseph Smith As Translator," in Waterman, p. 81. Bushman discusses the implications of Smith's attempt to produce his "Grammar & Alphabet of the Egyptian Language," which was supposed to have been a kind of manual on translating Egyptian. Bushman writes, "The translations contain whole paragraphs of material for a single character, and, as the grammar went on, blend into the translation that eventually became the Book of Abraham" (Bushman, in Waterman, p. 81).

46. Smith possessed at least three seer stones for most of his life—a brown one (by which he translated the BOM); a white one (by which he translated the BOA); and a green one (which he may or may not have used).

47. Parley Pratt, *MS*, July 1842, vol. 3, p. 47; cf. Quinn, *Early Mormonism*, p. 198.

    On Feb. 19, 1842, LDS apostle Wilford Woodruff recorded in his diary that God was blessing Smith "to translate through the Urim & Thummim Ancient records & Hyeroglyphics as old as Abraham or Adam....Joseph the Seer has presented us some of the Book of Abraham" (Wilford Woodruff. Quoted in Quinn, *Early Mormonism*, p. 198).

This well-understood aspect of the BOA translation was reiterated in 1969 by a young LDS student of archaeology: "[T]his 'translation' was not a translation in the usual sense of the word (as that of the Inspired Version was not, either), and…no man, no matter how wise or imaginative, could have done it by any normal means. How then, did Joseph do it? How did Joseph Smith translate? Well, Wilford Woodruff said he translated with the Urim and Thummim. Parley P. Pratt said he translated with the Urim and Thummim. Orson Pratt said he translated with the Urim and Thummim. He translated with a divine instrument. That was the only way he could have done it" (Benjamin Urrutia, "The Joseph Smith Papyri," *Dialogue: A Journal of Mormon Thought*, vol. 4, no. 2, p. 134).

48. Smith made other use of the white stone, or "Urim and Thummim." He stated, for example, "that he had obtained the 'g[rand] key word' of the temple endowment 'by the Urim & Thummim' and began teaching this information to trusted associates as early as 1842.…In 1843 Smith said, 'Then the white stone mentioned in Revelation 2:17, will become a Urim and Thummim to each individual who receives one.…And a white stone is given to each of those who come into the celestial kingdom' (*D&C* 130:10-11). Three months later, Smith's older brother Hyrum, who had been appointed church patriarch and associate president, asked him to use the stone to dictate the previously unwritten, lengthy revelation on plural marriage and the eternal sealing of husbands and wives. William Clayton, Smith's private secretary, later stated that on 12 July 1843, 'Joseph in reply said he did not need to, for he knew the revelation perfectly from beginning to end' " (Quinn, *Early Mormonism*, p. 199).

49. Quinn, *Early Mormonism*, p. 198.

50. Hugh Nibley, letter to Morris L. Reynolds, May 12, 1966.

51. Hugh B. Brown, letter to Morris L. Reynolds, May13, 1966.

52. Consider the following remarks. They show either 1) some disingenuousness on the part of these LDS leaders or 2) an acute lack of knowledge regarding their own faith and church history:

   • "There has been no tampering with God's Word.…[T]he whole body of Church laws forms a harmonious unit, which does not anywhere contradict itself nor has it been found necessary to alter any part of it" (John Widtsoe, *Joseph Smith—Seeker After Truth* [SLC: Deseret News Press, 1951], pp. 119, 122).

   • "Inspiration is discovered in the fact that each part, as it was revealed, dovetailed perfectly with what had come before. There was no need for eliminating, changing, or adjusting any part to make it fit; but each new revelation on doctrine and priesthood fitted in its place perfectly to complete the whole structure, as it had been prepared by the Master Builder" (Joseph Fielding Smith, *Doctrines of Salvation* [SLC: Bookcraft, 1954], vol. 1, p. 170). When Smith made these comments, he was LDS Church historian.

53. Jerald Tanner and Sandra Tanner, *Major Problems of Mormonism* (SLC: ULM, 1989), p, 135. The Internet version of this volume is online at www.utlm.org/onlinebooks/changecontents.htm.

54. Robert J. Woodford, "How the Revelations in the Doctrine and Covenants Were Received and Compiled," *Ensign*, Jan. 1985, p. 27, available at www.lds.org.

55. See M. Russell Ballard, "Marvelous Are the Revelations of the Lord," *Ensign*, May 1998, p. 31, available at www.lds.org; cf. Parley P. Pratt, *Autobiography of Parley P. Pratt,* Parley P. Pratt Jr., ed. (New York: Russell Brothers, 1874; modern reprint in SLC: Deseret Book Co., 1979).

56. Petersen, p. 165.

57. Orson Pratt, "Divine Authenticity of the Book of Mormon—no. 1, 1850," pp. 4-5. Reprinted in Orson Pratt, *Orson Pratt's Works,* vol. 2 (Orem, UT: Grandin Book Co., 1990).

58. Pratt, "Divine Authenticity," pp. 4-5.

59. One example of this argument appeared in *Dialogue: A Journal of Mormon Thought:* "Note that Jeremiah was commanded by the Lord only to 'write in it [the scroll] all the former words' (Jer. 36:28). Jeremiah added more words on his own (v. 32) but makes no mention of any condemnation from the Lord. Expansion of prophetic texts by a prophet, then, is nothing new" (Best, p. 107).

60. Woodford, available at www.lds.org.

61. Woodford, available at www.lds.org.

Chapter 4: One God Versus Many Gods

1. William O. Nelson, *A Sure Foundation: Answers to Difficult Gospel Questions* (SLC: Deseret Book Co., 1988), p. 93, excerpt at www.lightplanet.com/mormons/response/qa/god_spirit.htm#won.

2. David H. Yarn Jr., "God," in Daniel H. Ludlow, ed., *Encyclopedia of Mormonism* (New York: Macmillan Publishing Co., 1992), vol. 2, p. 546. This reference work might best be described as a pseudo-official publication.

3. *Gospel Principles* (SLC: LDSC, 1978; 1979 rev., as printed in the 1990 Missionary Reference Library edition), p. 6.

4. Vergilius Ferm, ed., *The Encyclopedia of Religion* (Secaucus, NJ: Poplar Books, 1985), p. 774.

5. "The Church's first Article of Faith is 'We believe in God, the Eternal Father, and in His Son, Jesus Christ, and in the Holy Ghost.' This is a straightforward statement of belief that there are three members in the Godhead. However, Latter-day Saints do reject the doctrines of the Trinity as taught by most Christian churches today" (Daniel C. Peterson and Stephen D. Ricks, "Comparing LDS Beliefs with First-Century Christianity," *Ensign,* Mar. 1988, p. 7, available at www.lds.org).

6. See James B. Allen, "Emergence of a Fundamental: The Expanding Role of Joseph Smith's First Vision in Mormon Religious Thought," *Journal of Mormon History* 7 (1980), vol. 7, pp. 43-61; Thomas G. Alexander, "The Reconstruction of Mormon Doctrine: From Joseph Smith to Progression Theology," *Sunstone* (July/Aug. 1980), vol. 5, pp. 32-39; Boyd Kirkland, "The Development of the Mormon Doctrine of God," in Gary James Bergera, ed., *Line Upon Line: Essays in Mormon Doctrine* (SLC: Signature Books, 1989), pp. 35-52.

7. Barry R. Bickmore, *Restoring the Ancient Church* (Ben Lomond, CA: FAIR, 1999), p. 107.

8. Paul E. Dahl, "Godhead," in Ludlow, vol. 2, p. 552.

9. Lane Community College [Eugene, OR] World Religion Study Site, www.lanecc .edu/library/faith/disclaim.htm. This unscholarly reference is deliberately being used in order to show that "belief in many gods" is an extremely common definition of polytheism.

10. Joseph Smith, June 16, 1844, HC (SLC: Deseret Book Co., 1976/1980), vol. 6, p. 474.

11. Brigham Young, Oct. 8, 1859, in JOD, vol. 7, p. 333.

12. B.H. Roberts, The Mormon Doctrine of Deity (Bountiful, UT: Horizon Publishers, reprint 1976, originally published in 1903), p. 29.

13. Bruce R. McConkie, MD (SLC: Bookcraft, 1958; rev. ed. 1966; 23rd printing 1977), p. 291.

14. McConkie, p. 521.

15. Donald Q. Cannon, Larry E. Dahl, and John W. Welch, "The Restoration of Major Doctrines through Joseph Smith: The Godhead, Mankind, and the Creation," Ensign, Jan. 1989, p. 27, available at www.lds.org.

16. Aaronic Priesthood Manual 3 (SLC: LDSC, 1995, online edition), Lesson Number One, available at www.lds.org. The closing segment of the quote is from McConkie, p. 224.

17. In 1958 Bruce McConkie stated, "The saints are not polytheists" (McConkie, p. 523). More recently, Robert Millet wrote, "[Mormons], who believe in the Godhead, are no more polytheistic than are Christians who believe in the Trinity" (Robert L. Millet, The Mormon Faith [SLC: Shadow Mountain, 1998], p. 176).

18. Gilbert Scharffs, The Missionary's Little Book of Answers (American Fork, UT: Covenant Communications, Inc., 2002), p. 25. This book, which is sold through LDS bookstores, reads, "Latter-day Saints are definitely not polytheistic. Webster's Ninth Collegiate Dictionary defines polytheism as those who worship many gods. Although the LDS Church believes that there are many gods in the eternities, they do not worship many gods, which is completely different."

19. McConkie, p. 523. McConkie stated, "Primitive and pagan peoples often believe in and worship many supposed gods....[P]olytheism has reference to pagan deities to whom reverence, devotion, and worship are given. It is not to be confused with the gospel truth that there are 'gods many, and lords many.'"

    These sentiments were echoed by LDS Apostle Boyd K. Packer: "There are many other verses of scripture, at least an equal number in the Bible, that speak in plural terms of 'lords' and 'gods.'...The acceptance of this truth does not mean accepting the multiple gods of mythology nor the polytheism of the pagans, which was so roundly condemned by Isaiah and the other prophets" (Boyd K. Packer, "The Pattern of Our Parentage," Ensign, Nov. 1984, p. 66, available at www.lds.org).

20. Funk & Wagnalls Standard Dictionary (New York: Harper Paperbacks, 1983), p. 616: "[B]elief in and worship of more gods than one."

21. Millet, The Mormon Faith, p. 176; cf. Robert L. Millet, "What We Believe," Feb. 3, 1998, BYU devotional, http://speeches.byu.edu/htmlfiles/MilletW98.html. Millet stated, "[W]e do not believe we will ever, worlds without end, unseat or oust God the Eternal Father or his Only Begotten Son, Jesus Christ; those holy beings are and forever will

be the gods we worship." It should be noted, however, that there seems to be a different *kind* of worship given to each member of the godhead (see this chapter's n22). The Father is given the highest level of worship. For example, he *alone* is the god to whom Mormons pray.

22. McConkie, p. 521. McConkie later qualified the *kind* of worship given to the Father as opposed to the *kind* of worship given to the Son and Holy Ghost: "We worship the Father, and him only, and no one else. We do not worship the Son, and we do not worship the Holy Ghost. I know perfectly well what the scriptures say about worshiping Christ and Jehovah, but they are speaking in an entirely different sense—the sense of standing in awe and being reverentially grateful to him who has redeemed us. Worship in the true and saving sense is reserved for God the First, the Creator" (Bruce McConkie, "Our Relationship with the Lord," Mar. 2, 1982, BYU devotional, http://speeches.byu.edu/index.php?act=viewitem&id=602&tid=).

23. John R. Hinnells, ed., *A New Dictionary of Religions* (Cambridge, MA: Blackwell Publishers, Inc., 1984; 1995 edition), p. 323.

24. F. Max Müller, "Henotheism, Polytheism, Monotheism, Atheism," *Lectures on the Origin and Growth of Religion* (New York, 1879), p. 362. Quoted in Mircea Eliade, ed., *The Encyclopedia of Religion* (New York: Macmillan Publishing Co., 1987), vol. 5, p. 266.

25. LDS theology recognizes that other supreme gods exist for other universes and worlds. But Mormons contend that we have nothing to do with these gods.

26. This teaching may be found in several sources: "God, the Father, the supreme God, knows the equivalent of every phase of the Great Plan, which we are working out" (John Widtsoe, *A Rational Theology* [SLC: Deseret Book Co., 1915]), p. 67); "[God the Father] is the Supreme Controller of the universe" (Brigham Young, Jan. 8, 1865, in *JOD*, vol. 11, p. 41); "God is the only supreme governor and independent being in whom all fullness and perfection dwell" (Joseph Smith, *Lectures on Faith* [SLC: Deseret Book Co., 1985], lecture 2, paragraph 2).

27. Duane S. Crowther, *Life Everlasting* (SLC: Bookcraft, 1967), p. 361.

28. Barry R. Bickmore, "Of Simplicity, Oversimplification, and Monotheism," *FARMS Review of Books*, vol. 15, issue 1, http://farms.byu.edu/display.php?table=review&id=474.

29. Boyd K. Packer, *Let Not Your Heart Be Troubled* (SLC: Bookcraft, 1991), p. 293. Quoted in Bickmore, "Of Simplicity," http://farms.byu.edu/display.php?table=review&id=474.
    LDS philosopher David Paulsen agrees: "Given the plurality of divine persons, how can there be but one God?...There is only one God the Father or fount of divinity" (David Paulsen, "Are Mormons Trinitarians?: An Interview with Dr. David Paulsen," *Modern Reformation* [Nov./Dec. 2003], www.christianity.com/partner/Article_Display_Page/0,,PTID307086|CHID581342|CIID1671522,00.html).

30. Müller, in Eliade, vol. 5, p. 266.

31. John Bowker, ed., *The Oxford Dictionary of World Religions* (New York: Oxford University Press, 1997), p. 653.

32. Geddes MacGregor, *Dictionary of Religion and Philosophy* (New York: Paragon House, 1989), p. 420.

33. Charles Taliaferro, "Philosophy of Religion," in Nicholas Bunnin and E.P. Tsui-James, eds., *The Blackwell Companion to Philosophy* (Malden, MA: Blackwell Publishing, 1996; 2003 edition), p. 456.

34. Peterson is professor of Islamic Studies and Arabic and Ricks is professor of Hebrew in the Department of Asian and Near Eastern Languages.

35. Daniel C. Peterson and Stephen D. Ricks, *Offenders for a Word* (Provo, UT: FARMS, 1998), p. 67 fn204. They refer to the *Oxford English Dictionary* and the *Random House Dictionary*. Richard L. Anderson, emeritus professor of ancient scripture at BYU, also has accepted that "Latter-day Saints are not really Trinitarians but tritheists, for they bluntly hold to the individuality of each person of the Godhead" (Richard L. Anderson, *Understanding Paul* [SLC: Deseret Book Co.], 1983, p. 248).

36. Peterson and Ricks, *Offenders*, p. 67.

37. Peterson and Ricks, *Offenders*, p. 67.

38. Peterson and Ricks, *Offenders*, p. 68 fn208.

39. Monophysitism also is known as *Eutychianism*. It was denounced at the Council of Chalcedon (451) and the Second Council of Constantinople (553). Other forms of tritheism were condemned at the Council of Soissons (1092) and Reims (1148). Philoponus himself was declared heretical by John Scholasticus (Patriarch of Constantinople, 565–577) and was posthumously condemned by the Third Council of Constantinople (680–681).

40. LDS philosopher David Paulsen has noted that "there is only one perfectly united, mutually indwelling, divine community. We call that community 'God' and there is only one such" (Paulsen, www.christianity.com/partner/Article_Display_Page/0,,PTID307086|CHID581342|CIID1671522,00.html).

41. Millet, *The Mormon Faith*, p. 29.

42. Joseph Fielding Smith, in *Doctrine and Covenants* (SLC: Deseret Book Co., 1981, student manual), p. 41.
     Smith also stated, "[T]o us there is but one God. Correctly interpreted, God in this sense means Godhead, for it is composed of Father, Son, and Holy Spirit....[T]o us, the inhabitants of this world, they constitute the only God, or Godhead. There is none other besides them. To them we are amenable, and subject to their authority, and there is no other Godhead unto whom we are subject. However, as the Prophet has shown, there can be, and are, other Gods" (Joseph Fielding Smith, *Answers to Gospel Questions* [SLC: Deseret Book Co., 1958], vol. 2, p. 142).
     Most interesting is how this reasoning was used in a 1985 *Ensign* article. In this LDS magazine's "I Have A Question" section, BYU's dean emeritus of religious instruction, Roy W. Doxey, addressed what one reader thought was a peculiar passage in the *Book of Mormon* (Alma 11:21-22, 26-31)—a passage that seemed to say there is only one God. Doxey answered, "Of course Amulek knew that there are three separate personages in the Godhead and that they are one in purpose....Since the Son and the Holy Spirit are one in purpose, mission, and glory with the 'true and living God,' the three are indeed 'one Eternal God'" (Roy W. Doxey, "I Have a Question," *Ensign*, Aug. 1985, p. 11, available at www.lds.org).
     A 2003 FARMS article also took this approach, stating, "[T]he Father, Son, and Holy Spirit are so unified in mind, will, love, and covenant that they can collectively

be called 'one God' " (Bickmore, "Of Simplicity," http://farms.byu.edu/display.php?table=review&id=474).

43. M. Russell Ballard, "Building Bridges of Understanding," *Ensign*, June 1998, p. 62, available at www.lds.org.

   LDS president Joseph Fielding Smith made a very similar comment: "This reference [D&C 20:27-29], then, to the three as one God, must be interpreted to mean that they constitute one Godhead or Supreme Council, composed of three separate Personages, the Father, the Son, and the Holy Ghost" (Joseph Fielding Smith, *Melchizedek Priesthood Personal Study Guide* [SLC: LDSC, 1972/73], p. 10).

   Bruce McConkie stated the same thing: "*Monotheism* is the doctrine or belief that there is but one God. If this is properly interpreted to mean that the Father, Son, and Holy Ghost—each of whom is a separate and distinct godly personage—are one God, meaning one Godhead, then true saints are monotheists" (McConkie, *MD*, p. 463).

44. Worshiping more than one godhead is advocated nowhere in LDS literature (see Millet, *The Mormon Faith*, pp. 176-177).

45. Hinnells, p. 207.

46. Truman Madsen. Quoted in "150-Year-Old Debate: Are Mormons 'Really Christian'?" *San Francisco Chronicle*, Apr. 8, 1996, A6, available at www.newslibrary.com.

47. Wayne Grudem, *Systematic Theology* (Grand Rapids: Zondervan, 1994), p. 226.

48. Stanley Grenz, *Theology for the Community of God* (Nashville: Broadman & Holman, 1994), p. 99.

49. Norman Geisler, "Trinity," *Baker Encyclopedia of Christian Apologetics* (Grand Rapids: Baker Book House, 1999), p. 732.

50. The Lord himself made this clear by rhetorically asking, "To whom will ye liken me, and make me equal, and compare me, that we may be like?...I am God, and there is none else; I am God, and there is none like me" (Is. 46:5,9). In Exodus 9:14, God says, "I will send all my plagues on you and your servants and your people, so that you may know that there is no one like me in all the earth." And Isaiah 44:8 reads, "Is there a God beside me? yea, there is no God; I know not any."

51. Philip Schaff, ed., *The Creeds of Christendom* (Grand Rapids: Baker Book House, 1983: 1996 edition), vol. 2, pp. 66-67, vol. 1, p. 38.

52. Geisler, p. 732.

53. Brian Greene, "The Future of String Theory—A Conversation with Brian Greene," interview of Oct. 13, 2003, in *Scientific American*, Nov. 2003, www.sciam.com/print_version.cfm?articleID=000073A5-C100-1F80-B57583414B7F0103.

54. John Archibald Wheeler, *Geons, Black Holes, and Quantum Foam* (New York: W.W. Norton and Co., 1998), pp. 344-345. Wheeler is a Princeton University professor emeritus of physics.

55. Roger S. Jones, *Physics for the Rest of Us* (Chicago: Contemporary Books, 1992), p. 76. Jones is a University of Minnesota professor emeritus of physics.

56. Lee Smolin, *Three Roads to Quantum Gravity* (New York: Basic Books, 2001), p. 37.

57. Dallin H. Oaks, "Apostasy and Restoration," *Ensign*, May 1995, p. 84, available at www.lds.org.

58. *God's glory and God's majesty*—"God our Eternal Father lives....I don't understand the wonder of His majesty. I can't comprehend the glory of the Godhead, but I know that He is my Father, notwithstanding all that" (Gordon B. Hinckley, Ketchikan Alaska Fireside, June 22, 1995. Quoted in Hinckley, *Teachings*, p. 238).

    The Effects of the atonement—"I can't comprehend, in terms of eternities and the blessings of eternities, the magnitude of the Atonement, but I can sense it and appreciate it in a measure at least" (Gordon B. Hinckley, England Birmingham Missionary Meeting, August 29, 1995. Quoted in Hinckley, *Teachings*, p. 454); "I sense in a measure the meaning of His atonement. I cannot comprehend it all. It is so vast in its reach and yet so intimate in its effect that it defies comprehension" (Gordon B. Hinckley, "Jesus Christ," Dec. 4, 1994, devotional address. Quoted in Hinckley, *Teachings*, p. 28).

    The nature of the atonement—"The nature of the atonement and its effects is so infinite, so unfathomable, and so profound that it lies beyond the knowledge and comprehension of mortal man" (James E. Faust, "The Atonement: Our Greatest Hope," *Ensign*, Nov. 2001, p. 18, available at www.lds.org).

    Our state of existence before birth—"In what particular form or capacity our original intelligence existed, we cannot say....However, lacking a complete comprehension of the entity need not prohibit us from observing its influence and experiencing its effect in our own lives" (Victor L. Ludlow, *Principles and Practices of the Restored Gospel* [SLC: Deseret Book Co., 1992], p. 143).

    The succession of gods—"[T]here never was a time but what there was a Father and Son....Says one, 'this is incomprehensible.' It may be so in some respects. We can admit, though, that duration is endless, for it is impossible for man to conceive a limit to it" (Roberts, p. 277).

    Christ taking our sins—"In some way that is to our minds incomprehensible and beyond the deepest appreciation of our hearts, Jesus Christ took upon himself the burden of men's sins from Adam to the end of the world" (Jeffrey R. Holland, "Whom Say Ye That I Am?" http://farms.byu.edu/display.php?table=transcripts&id=99).

    Begetting spirit children—"Question: 'If God has a body of flesh and bones plus spirit, how is it that his children were spirits, in pre-existence?' Answer:...This question the Lord has not fully explained, but there are sufficient reasons why we should believe that he does have a tabernacle of flesh and bones" (Joseph Fielding Smith, *Melchizedek Priesthood Personal Study Guide* [SLC: LDSC, 1972/73], p. 17).

    Why unchastity is so serious a sin—"[U]nchastity is second only to murder.... Perhaps we should not expect the reasons for this commandment to be fully understandable to our finite minds" (Bruce C. Hafen, "The Gospel and Romantic Love," Sept. 28, 1982, devotional address, reprinted in *Classic Speeches* [Provo, UT: BYU, 1994], pp. 83-84).

    God's works—"The magnitude of God's work is incomprehensible....Like the vastness of God's creations, incomprehensible to the finite mind, His suffering is equally incomprehensible" (Richard C. Edgley, "The Condescension of God," *Ensign*, Dec. 2001, p. 16, available at www.lds.org.

    Christ's resurrection and its effects—"[I]n a way incomprehensible to us, he [Jesus] took up that body which had not yet seen corruption and arose in that glorious immortality.... His rising from death on the third day crowned the Atonement. Again, in some way incomprehensible to us, the effects of his resurrection pass upon all men" (Bruce

R. McConkie, "The Purifying Power of Gethsemane," *Ensign,* May 1985, p. 9, available at www.lds.org).

59. Sunlight is actually much more than these things. For example, radiation is also present. A more scientific triune description of light would be "brilliance (or amplitude), color (or frequency), and polarization (or angle of vibration)" (*Wikepedia: The Free Encyclopedia,* www.en2.wikipedia.org/wiki/Light).

60.

TIME is	**GOD** is
Past—Time	Father—God
Present—Time	Son—God
Future—Time	Holy Ghost—God

61. Augustine. Quoted in Robert Lightner, *Handbook of Evangelical Theology* (Grand Rapids: Kregel, 1995), p. 47.

62. Scharffs, p. 25.

- "For the LORD your God is God of gods, and Lord of lords..." (Deut. 10:17).

- "Who is like unto thee, O LORD, among the gods? who is like thee, glorious in holiness, fearful in praises, doing wonders?" (Ex. 15:11).

- "For though there be that are called gods, whether in heaven or in earth, (as there be gods many, and lords many,) But to us there is but one God, the Father, of whom are all things, and we in him; and one Lord Jesus Christ, by whom are all things, and we by him" (1 Cor. 8:5-6).

- "And he hath on his vesture and on his thigh a name written, KING OF KINGS, AND LORD OF LORDS " (Rev. 19:16).

63. Bickmore, *Restoring,* pp. 106-117. As an introduction to this assertion, Bickmore quotes liberal scholar Margaret Barker, who claims, "Israel's oldest religion was not monotheistic" (Margaret Barker, *The Great Angel: A Study of Israel's Second God* [Louisville: Westminster/John Knox Press, 1992], p. 162).

64. Orson Pratt, *Divine Authenticity of the Book of Mormon—No. 3,* Dec. 1, 1850, p. 47, reprinted in *Orson Pratt's Works,* vol. 2 (Orem, UT: Grandin Book Co., 1990). Joseph Smith taught, "Ignorant translators, careless transcribers, or designing and corrupt priests have committed many errors [in the Bible]" (Joseph Smith, Oct. 15, 1843, *HC,* vol. 6, p. 57).

65. See 2 Kings 21:3; 23:4-7,11-12.

66. Biblical verses often cited to show monolatry in Israel include Judges 11:14-15,24; 1 Kings 11:33; and 2 Kings 1:3.

67. Jeffrey Tigay, "Moses and Monotheism," www.myjewishlearning.com/ideas_belief/god/Overview_About_God/God_Monotheism_Tigay.htm.

68. Tigay, www.myjewishlearning.com/ideas_belief/god/Overview_About_God/God_Mono theism_Tigay.htm.

69. In "Religions of Pre-literary Societies," Edward G. Newing makes the following observations: "Most, if not all, pre-literary people have a belief in a Supreme Being which most scholars call a High God to distinguish him from the lesser divinities....It

is interesting to note that among some of the most backward peoples of the world clear and high ideas of God are to be found. W. Schmidt of Vienna built up a whole theory on it: that the original religious concept of man in his primeval state was monotheism which later became corrupted into polytheism" (Edward G. Newing, "Religions of Pre-literary Societies," pp. 11-48 in Sir Norman Anderson, ed., *The World's Religions* [Grand Rapids: Eerdmans Publishing Co., 1950; 4th rev. ed. 1975], p. 38).

Winfried Corduan notes, "[I]n almost all traditional contexts—in Africa, America, Australia, Asia, or Europe—we find belief in a God located in the sky (or on a high mountain) and almost always referred to with masculine language. This God creates the world….He provides standards of behavior….Particularly in later cultures, he stands apart from the routine worship of gods and spirits. There is a memory of a time when this God was worshiped regularly, but something intervened. Many (but not all) cultures that refer to this interruption explain that it happened because this God did not receive the obedience due him" (Winfried Corduan, *Neighboring Faiths: A Christian Introduction to World Religions* [Downers Grove, IL: InterVarsity Press, 1998], p. 33).

70. Joseph Smith, in *HC*, vol. 6, p. 476.

71. Stephen Robinson, *Are Mormons Christian?* (SLC: Bookcraft, 1991), p. 72.

Millet echoes Robinson's objections against the Trinity, listing the following reasons for rejecting the doctrine: 1) It represents a superimposition of Hellenistic philosophy on the Bible; 2) it is not the "simplest and clearest reading" of the Gospels; 3) no formal or explicit explanation of the Trinity appears in the Bible; and 4) the word "Trinity" is not found in God's Word (Millet, *The Mormon Faith*, p. 188).

72. Mark M. Mattison, "Jesus and the Trinity" (True Grace Ministries), www.auburn.edu/~allenkc/openhse/trinity1.html#Introduction.

73. Francis Beckwith, "Mormon Theism, the Traditional Christian Concept of God, and Greek Philosophy: A Critical Analysis," *Journal of the Evangelical Theological Society*, Dec. 2001, p. 690.

74. "Latter-day Saints reject the doctrines of the Trinity as taught by most Christian churches today. These creeds were canonized in the fourth and fifth centuries A.D. and do not reflect the thinking or beliefs of the New Testament Church" (Daniel C. Peterson and Stephen D. Ricks, "Comparing LDS Beliefs with First-Century Christianity," *Ensign*, Mar. 1988, p. 7, available at www.lds.org).

75. This has become *the* Mormon argument against the Trinity. One statement by LDS apostle Dallin Oaks is typical: "We maintain that the concepts identified by such non-scriptural terms as 'the incomprehensible mystery of God' and 'the mystery of the Holy Trinity' are attributable to the ideas of Greek philosophy. These philosophical concepts transformed Christianity in the first few centuries following the deaths of the Apostles….[T]here came a synthesis of Greek philosophy and Christian doctrine in which the orthodox Christians of that day lost the fulness of truth about the nature of God and the Godhead" (Dallin H. Oaks, "Apostasy and Restoration," *Ensign*, May 1995, p. 84, available at www.lds.org).

76. Millet, "What We Believe," http://speeches.byu.edu/htmlfiles/MilletW98.html.

77. James Talmage, AOF (SLC: Deseret Book Co., 1899; modern reprint, 1948), p. 37. Quoted in Paulsen, www.christianity.com/partner/Article_Display_Page/0,,PTID307086|CHI D581342|CIID1671522,00.html).

78. "[T]he man-made creeds of erring generations which describe God variously as unknown and unknowable—formless, passionless, elusive, ethereal, simultaneously everywhere and nowhere at all" (Jeffrey R. Holland, "The Grandeur of God," *Ensign*, Nov. 2003, p. 70, available at www.lds.org.
    "The true knowledge of God had been lost during the centuries following the death of Christ. When Joseph Smith went into those woods to pray, he knew no more about God than did his contemporaries. Up to that time every Christian church believed and taught of a Godhead fused into one. They believed in a God of spirit, unknown and unknowable" (Theodore M. Burton, "Thus Saith the Lord," *Ensign*, Dec. 1971, p. 78, available at www.lds.org).

79. "During the early 1800s, in the minds of self-appointed interpreters, God was vast, immaterial, unknowable, and indefinable" (S. Dilworth Young, "What Joseph Smith Teaches Us of Christ," *Ensign*, Dec. 1973, p. 41, available at www.lds.org).

80. "Orthodox Christians also emphasize that their theology is a negative approach to God, for they insist that God is a mystery who cannot be comprehended by man" (Milton V. Backman Jr., "Eastern Orthodoxy," *Ensign*, May 1971, p. 48, available at www.lds.org.

81. Respectively, on pages 2, 82, and 67. In the pages cited, Maxwell does not explicitly state that these are the characteristics of the God worshiped by traditional Christians. However, a look at the index of his six-volume compilation, *The Collected Works of Neal A. Maxwell*, reveals what he meant. The index lists each of these pages from *Not My Will, But Thy Will* under the heading "true nature vs. traditional view" (Neal A. Maxwell, "Index," in *The Collected Works of Neal A. Maxwell* [SLC: Eagle Gate, 2001], vol. 6, p. 49).

82. "In the process of what we call the Apostasy, the tangible, personal God described in the Old and New Testaments was replaced by the abstract, incomprehensible deity"; "God the Father ceased to be a Father in any but an allegorical sense. He ceased to exist as a comprehensible and compassionate being" (Oaks, "Apostasy and Restoration," available at www.lds.org).

83. "When the Prophet Joseph saw his vision, the whole Christian world believed in a God without body, parts, or passions. That means he had no eyes; he couldn't see. He had no ears; he couldn't hear. He had no mouth; he couldn't speak.... when he went to lead the children of Israel into the Promised Land, he told them that they would not remain there long, but that they would be scattered among the nations, and that they would worship gods made by the hands of man (that's man's doing) that could neither see, nor hear, nor taste, nor smell....That's exactly the kind of a god the whole Christian world was worshipping at the time Joseph Smith had his vision" (LeGrand Richards, "The Things of God and Man," *Ensign*, Nov. 1977, p. 21, available at www.lds.org).

84. Young named "professed infidels," "Universalists," and "the Church of Rome" (Brigham Young, Oct. 9, 1859, in *JOD*, vol. 7, p. 283). Joseph Smith held the same opinion: "One of the grand fundamental principles of 'Mormonism' is to receive truth, let it come from whence it may" (*HC*, vol. 5, p. 499).

85. Young, in *JOD*, vol. 7, p. 283.

86. LDS First Presidency (Spencer W. Kimball, N. Eldon Tanner, Marion G. Romney), Feb. 15, 1978. Quoted in Spencer J. Palmer, "LDSfaq About The Church of Jesus Christ of Latter-day Saints: World Religions (Non-Christian) and Mormonism," http://ldsfaq .byu.edu/emmain.asp?number=202.

87. Stuart G. Hall, *Doctrine and Practice in the Early Church* (Grand Rapids, MI: Eerdmans Publishing Co., 1991), p. 6, emphasis added.

88. Robert L. Millet, "The Eternal Gospel," *Ensign*, July 1996, p. 48, available at www.lds.org.

Chapter 5: Heavenly Father Is a Man

1. Joseph Smith, *HC* (SLC: Deseret Book Co., 1976/1980), vol. 6, p. 303.

2. "The Father has a body of flesh and bones as tangible as man's" (D&C 130:22).

3. Stephen E. Robinson, "God the Father," in Daniel H. Ludlow, ed., *Encyclopedia of Mormonism* (New York: Macmillan Publishing Co., 1992), vol. 2, p. 548.

4. "A modern prophet, Joseph Smith, Jr., provided the world with an eyewitness testimony of God's true nature" (William O. Nelson, "Is the LDS View of God Consistent with the Bible?" *Ensign*, July 1987, p. 56, available at www.lds.org).

5. Stephen L. Richards, *Where Is Wisdom?* (SLC: Deseret Book Co., 1955), p. 31.

6. Joseph F. Smith, February 17, 1884, in *JOD*, vol. 25, p. 58. Smith stated, "We are precisely in the same condition and under the same circumstances that God our Heavenly Father was when He was passing through this or a similar ordeal."

7. *HC*, vol. 6, p. 305.

8. Milton R. Hunter, *The Gospel Through the Ages* (SLC: Deseret Book Co., 1958), pp. 114-115.

9. Marion G. Romney, "How Men Are Saved," *Ensign*, Nov. 1974, p. 38, available at www.lds.org.

10. Robert L. Millet, *The Mormon Faith* (SLC: Shadow Mountain, 1998), pp. 29-30.
     Other LDS leaders are less explicit: "[T]he Father became the Father at some time before 'the beginning' as humans know it, by experiencing a mortality similar to that experienced on earth. There has been speculation among some Latter-day Saints on the implications of this doctrine, but nothing has been revealed to the Church about conditions before the 'beginning' as mortals know it" (Robinson, in Ludlow, vol. 2, p. 549).
     Some LDS apologists have further softened this belief by portraying it as pure speculation: "[M]any Latter-day Saints believe that prior to our creation God (the Father) also was incarnate on an earth in much the same way God (the Son) was incarnate on our earth. This helps us understand why the Father, in both the Old and New Testament, is consistently portrayed as a gloriously exalted embodied person, humanlike in form" (David Paulsen, "Are Mormons Trinitarians?: An Interview with Dr. David Paulsen," *Modern Reformation* [Nov./Dec. 2003], www.christianity.com/partner/Article_ Display_Page/0,,PTID307086|CHID581342|CIID1671522,00.html).

11. Robert L. Millet and Noel B. Reynolds, *Latter-day Christianity: 10 Basic Issues* (Provo, UT: FARMS, 1998), pp. 32-33, chapter 6, http://farms.byu.edu/10basic/10basicissues.php ?chapter=6).

12. Robert Millet, "What Is Our Doctrine?" Sept. 12, 2003, http://home/uchicago.edu/~spackman/millet.doc.

13. Num. 11:18 speaks of people weeping "in the ears of the LORD." Deut. 11:12, in a similar fashion, mentions "the eyes of the LORD." And in Ex. 15:8, Moses comments on the Red Sea crossing, saying to God, "With the blast of thy nostrils the waters were gathered together." God, too, was "walking in the garden in the cool of the day" (Gen. 3:8), so he must have legs. Amos 7:7 says, "The LORD stood upon a wall," so he must have feet. And Is. 6:1 pictures God "sitting upon a throne," so he must have a backside.

14. Consider the following LDS understanding of various anthropomorphic passages:

   • "Latter-day Saints perceive the Father as an exalted Man in the most literal, anthropomorphic terms. They do not view the language of Genesis [i.e., Gen. 1:26] as allegorical; human beings are created in the form and image of a God who has a physical form and image" (Robinson, in Ludlow, "God the Father," vol. 2, p. 548).

   • "Latter-day Saints take literally the many passages in the Bible that describe God as having a physical form. God created Adam 'in his own image' and 'after [his] likeness' (Genesis 1:26-27), and Paul taught that ordinary mortal men were in the 'image' of God (1 Corinthians 11:7). During his earthly life, Jesus Christ was said to be 'the express image' of God the Father (Hebrews 1:3)" (Millet & Reynolds, p. 11, chapter 2, http://farms.byu.edu/10basic/10basicissues.php?chapter=2).

   • "Another example is when God is speaking with Moses 'face to face,' which further underscores the LDS belief (Ex. 33:11)" (Gilbert Scharffs, *The Missionary's Little Book of Answers* [American Fork, UT: Covenant Communications, Inc., 2002], p. 26). "The resurrected Savior (with a physical body) said, 'He that hath seen me hath seen the Father.' This indicates that Jesus and God are alike and that God too has a perfected physical body (John 14:9)" (Scharffs, pp. 26-27).

   • "Joseph Smith saw a confirmation of what Jesus had impressed upon Philip long ago: 'Have I been so long time with you, and yet hast thou not known me, Philip? he that hath seen me hath seen the Father; and how sayest thou then, Shew us the Father?' (John 14:9). Jesus was apparently informing his disciples that he and his Father were alike in attributes, in power, and in bodily appearance" (Nelson, available at www.lds.org).

   • "[We believe] that when God the Father and Jesus Christ both visited him [Joseph Smith], and that when he viewed them, they were two separate personages... just like they were when Stephen saw them (see Acts 7:55-56)" (W.F. Walker Johanson, *What Is Mormonism All About?* [New York: St. Martin's Griffin, 2002], p. 5).

   • "[I]n Acts 7:55-56 Stephen sees a vision of both 'the glory of God' and 'the Son of man standing on the right hand of God.' This implies that God the Father has a visible human form, and this interpretation fits well with the description of Jesus as 'the brightness of his glory, and the express image of his person' (Hebrews 1:3)" (Barry R. Bickmore, "Of Simplicity, Oversimplification, and Monotheism," *FARMS Review of Books,* vol. 15, issue 1, http://farms.byu.edu/display.php?table=review&id=474).

   • "[I]f Jesus is the express image of God the Father, which we believe that He is, then God the Father has a resurrected body of flesh and bones as tangible as man's" (M.

Russell Ballard, "Building Bridges of Understanding," *Ensign,* June 1998, p. 62, available at www.lds.org).

15. Stephen E. Robinson, "God & Deification," in Craig L. Blomberg and Stephen E. Robinson, *How Wide the Divide* (Downers Grove, IL: InterVarsity Press, 1997), p. 78.

16. Millet, *The Mormon Faith*, p. 188. Oddly, when Millet co-wrote a book with BYU professor Noel Reynolds, the text agreed with Robinson: "These doctrines are not clearly stated in the Bible." They add that such knowledge concerning God's nature "has been restored through modern prophets" (Millet and Reynolds, p. 33, chapter 6, http://farms.byu.edu/10basic/10basicissues.php?chapter=6).

17. Barry R. Bickmore, "Does God Have A Body In Human Form?" FAIR, p. 5.

18. Bickmore, "Does God Have A Body," p. 2.

19. Consider this 1984 anecdote by John Tvedtnes, who now serves as senior resident scholar for FARMS. In "Children of the Most High" (*Tambuli*, July 1984, p. 18, available at www.lds.org), Tvedtnes related the following account of his interaction with an "anti-Mormon" whom he had met:

    [H]e pulled from his pocket a list of questions that he frequently asked members of the Church. "Is God a man?" he asked me confidently.

    "No," I replied, "God is not a man. It says so in the Bible." (See Num. 23:19; 1 Sam. 15:29.)

    "You're the only Mormon who believes that," he said. "Your church teaches that God is a man."

    "That's not correct," I countered. "Let me read to you from the Bible exactly what my church *does* teach." I then quoted from Psalms 82:6, which reads: "Ye are gods; and all of you are children of the most High."

    "No," I said, "God is not a man; man is a god."

20. Robinson, in Blomberg and Robinson, p. 89.

21. Kevin Hill, "Breaking Down Barriers or Building Them Up?" 1999, www.mormon fortress.com/break.html, emphasis added. On another Internet site "dedicated to the dispelling of falsehoods put forth by Mormon detractors," a third Latter-day Saint gave a similar argument: "[M]an is described as unfaithful (Hosea 5:3), stubborn (Isaiah 48:4), prideful (Isaiah 2:17), and easily deceived (Ephesians 4:14). In fact, the Bible is full of examples of man's weaknesses. No, God is definitely not a man. He does not lie and thus need repentance (Numbers 23:19) or lose his temper (Hosea 11:9). He is God, free from mortal foibles" ("Does Mormon Doctrine Contradict the Bible?" www.mormon.7p.com/contradict.html.)

22. Gordon B. Hinckley, "The Father, Son, and Holy Ghost," *Ensign,* Oct. 5, 1986; reprinted in *Liahona*, Mar. 1998, available at www.lds.org.

23. Shandon L. Guthrie, "A Discussion On Mormonism," www.sguthrie.net/MORMON IS.htm.

24. Robinson, *Are Mormons Christian?* (SLC: Bookcraft, 1991), p. 80.

25. Bruce McConkie, "Our Relationship with the Lord," Mar. 2, 1982, BYU devotional, http://speeches.byu.edu/index.php?act=viewitem&id=602&tid=.

26. Joseph Fielding Smith, *Melchizedek Priesthood Personal Study Guide* (SLC: LDSC, 1972/73), p. 16. Many Mormons, including Kent P. Jackson (a BYU professor of religion), also maintain that "the Bible gives every indication that God has a body like that of humans" (Kent P. Jackson, *From Apostasy to Restoration* [SLC: Deseret Book Co., 1996], p. 55. Quoted in James Patrick Holding, *The Mormon Defenders* [Clarcon, FL: Tekton Apologetics Ministry, 2001], p. 11).

27. Roger S. Jones, *Physics for the Rest of Us* (Chicago: Contemporary Books, 1992), p. 36. According to Jones, "[space,] whatever it may be, is invisible." He explains: "We see only images of material bodies, which we organize according to a plan or pattern that we interpret as three-dimensional space. Our perception of space is actually a construct of the mind" (Jones is associate professor of physics at the University of Minnesota).

28. Wayne Grudem, *Systematic Theology* (Grand Rapids: Zondervan, 1994), p. 168.

29. Louis Berkhof, *Systematic Theology* (Grand Rapids: Eerdmans Publishing Co., 1938; 1993 edition), p. 59.

30. Berkhof, p. 59.

31. FARMS, "What Do Latter-day Saints Mean When They Say That God Was Once A Man?" www.lightplanet.com/mormons/basic/godhead/farms_man.htm; cf. advertisement at http://farms.byu.edu/display.php?table=insights&id=55.

32. Robinson, in Blomberg and Robinson, p. 90.

33. Robinson, in Blomberg and Robinson, p. 90.

34. Blomberg, in Blomberg and Robinson, p. 97. Blomberg adds, "An expression like 'before all ages' does seem to contradict Mormon theology."

35. Joseph Telushkin, *Jewish Literacy: The Most Important Things to Know About the Jewish Religion, Its People, Its History* (New York: William Morrow and Co., Inc., 1991), p. 497.

36. Telushkin, p. 497.

37. Telushkin, p. 497.

38. C.F. Keil and F. Delitzsch, *Commentary on the Old Testament* (Peabody, MA: Hendrickson Publishers, 1996), vol. 1, p. 39.

39. Robinson, in Blomberg and Robinson, p. 80.

40. Merrill F. Unger and William White Jr., eds., *Nelson's Expository Dictionary of the Old Testament*, p. 244, as reprinted in *Vine's Complete Expository Dictionary of Old and New Testament Words* (Nashville, TN: Thomas Nelson, 1985).

41. Unger and White, p. 244.

42. Unger and White, p. 136.

43. Unger and White, p. 136.

44. Unger and White, p. 136.

45. Unger and White, p. 137.

46. Unger and White, p. 137.

47. Unger and White, p. 244.

48. Charles Hodge, *Systematic Theology* (Grand Rapids: Eerdmans Publishing Co., 1995), vol. 2, p. 96.

49. Grudem, p. 443.

50. Phyllis A. Bird, "Theological Anthropology in the Hebrew Bible," in Leo G. Perdue, *The Blackwell Companion to the Hebrew Bible* (Malden, MA: Blackwell Publishing, 2001), p. 260.

51. Bird, pp. 260-261.

52. Bird, p. 13.

53. Bird, pp. 260, 262.

54. W.E. Vine, *Vine's Expository Dictionary of New Testament Words* (McLean, VA: MacDonald Publishing Co., no date), p. 586.

55. William Barclay, *The Letters to the Philippians, Colossians, and Thessalonians* (Philadelphia: Westminster, 1975), p. 116. It should be remembered that Barclay was in no sense a conservative Christian scholar. He denied the virgin birth, deity of Christ, miracles, and the atonement. Nevertheless, given his remarkable command of the Greek language, his statement here about *image* is noteworthy.

56. Spiros Zodhiates, gen. ed., *The Complete Word Study Dictionary* (Chattanooga, TN: AMG Publishers, 1992), p. 1468.

57. See Zodhiates, p. 1468.

58. Grudem, p. 547; cf. Vine, p. 587.

59. G.B. Caird, *The Language and Imagery of the Bible* (Grand Rapids, MI: Eerdmans Publishing Co., 1980; 1997 edition), p. 74. Even the Internet's Ancient Hebrew Research Center's list of "Biblical Facts: Hebrew Idioms" reads: "Idiom—saw his face; Meaning—had access to him." Conversely, "hide your face" means "refuse to answer" (Ancient Hebrew Research Center, "Biblical Facts: Hebrews Idioms," www.ancient-hebrew.org/17_idioms.html. An alternate explanation is provided by Walter C. Kaiser Jr. in *Hard Sayings of the Old Testament* [Downers Grove, IL: InterVarsity Press, 1988], pp. 81-84). Several OT passages use "face" in this figurative way to show God favoring people (shining his face upon, Numbers 6:25), judging people (setting his face against, Leviticus 20:3-6), and rejecting people (hiding/turning his face from, Deuteronomy 31:17; Psalm 10:11).

60. Consider these examples of other meanings of *panim* in Scripture—all figurative or metaphorical:

    1. A "look on one's face," or more precisely, one's overall countenance (i.e., when someone puts a good face on a situation or is down in the face, for example, Gen. 4:5) (Unger and White, p. 75).

    2. The act of paying "something to someone's 'face' is to pay to him personally (Deut. 7:10)....The word connotes the [entire] person himself'" (Unger and White, p. 75).

    3. The "surface or visible side of a thing, as in Gen. 1:2" (Unger and White, p. 75).

    The most significant uses of *panim* are those in which the word refers to, and is translated as, "presence"—i.e., in the presence *(panim)* of God or people. Genesis 3:8

reads, "Adam and his wife hid themselves from the presence *[panim]* of the LORD God" (compare Gen. 4:16; 11:28; Ex. 35:20; 1 Kings 12:2; Job 1:12; 2:7; 23:15; Ps. 23:5; 51:11; 97:5; 139:7; Prov. 17:18; 25:6; Jer. 28:1,5,11; Jonah 1:3,10). Noteworthy, too, are the many Old Testament verses where *panim*, although it clearly means "presence," yet is still translated as "face."

Esther 1:14, for instance, speaks of "the seven princes of Persia and Media, which saw the king's face *[panim]*." Psalm 27:8 reads, "When thou saidst, Seek ye my face *[panim]*; my heart said unto thee, Thy face *[panim]*, LORD, will I seek" (see Gen. 4:14; 16:6,8; Ex. 2:15; 1 Sam. 26:20; 1 Chron. 16:11; Lam. 2:19; 3:35). Also consider the following verses where *panim* undeniably means presence:

Gen. 11:28—"before *[panim]* his father" / "in the presence of his father" (NASB)

Lev. 16:1: Deut. 14:23,26—"before *[panim]* the LORD" / "the presence of the LORD" (NASB)

Num. 14:5—"before *[panim]* all the assembly" / "in the presence of all the assembly" (NASB)

2 Kings 22:10—"before *[panim]* the king" / "in the presence of the king" (NASB)

Ps. 52:9—"before *[panim]* thy saints / "in the presence of Your godly ones" (NASB)

The word is even used for the "showbread" kept in the temple, on a table "before *[panim]* the Lord in two rows to represent the tribes of Israel" (Lawrence O. Richards, *Expository Dictionary of Bible Words* [Grand Rapids, MI: Zondervan, 1985; 1995 edition], p. 140) (see Ex. 25:30; 35:15; 39:36; Num. 4:7; 1 Sam. 21:6; 1 Kings 7:48; 2 Chron. 4:19). Use of *panim* in these verses is why some translations render it "bread of the presence" (NASB).

61. Unger and White, pp. 114-115.

62. Gleason Archer, *Encyclopedia of Bible Difficulties* (Grand Rapids: Zondervan, 1982), p. 125.

63. Kaiser, p. 84.

64. "Biblical Facts: Hebrew Idioms," www.ancient-hebrew.org/17_idioms.html. This particular idiomatic expression appears in many biblical passages such Ex. 15:6,15;15:12, Deut. 33:2, Job 40:14, Ps. 16:8, 16:11, 17:7, 18:35, 20:6, 21:8, 44:3, 45:4, 45:9, 48:10, 60:5, 63:8, 73:23, 77:10, 78:54, 80:15, 80:17, 89:13, 98:1, 108:6, 109:31, 110:1, 118:15-16, 138:7, Prov. 3:16, Ecc. 10:2, Is. 41:10, 48:13, Hab. 2:16, and Matt. 26:64.

65. Keil and Delitzsch, vol. 5, p. 695.

66. Everett Fox, *The Five Books of Moses* (New York: Schocken Books Inc., 1995), "Moses' Exultant Song at the Sea," www.jhom.com/calendar/nisan/song.html. Fox explains, "The overall effect of the poem is of fierce pride at God's victory, and exultant description of the destruction and discomfort of enemies, whether Egyptian or Canaanite. This general tone parallels many ancient war poems; what is characteristically Israelite about it is God's choosing and leading people. Therefore the last verse goes far beyond the celebration of a single military victory. The Song constitutes the founding of a theocratic people. Scholars have long noted the archaic style of the Song, which uses forms characteristic of early biblical Hebrew. Its tone is for this reason even more exalted than is usual in biblical poetry."

67. I happen to be a songwriter and so I can offer a personal example. One phrase in a song I have written reads, "Eternity is calling." However, it does not mean that eternity is a living being who is shouting my name. It means I am getting closer to death. Another set of my lyrics says: "Life's become just a violent movie." This does not mean everything and everyone I know has suddenly been transported into a film now playing at theaters across America! It means that the world has become a very violent and dangerous place.

   Regarding this verse, Mennonite minister Gary F. Daught has observed, "It is an affirmation that God is committed to the fight. And if God is committed, this is no time to be shy. This is war—the warfare of *shalom*" (Gary F. Daught, Oct. 3, 1999, "The Warfare of *Shalom:* War and peace in the Old Testament, Part 1," *Getting to Know the Bible Jesus Knew*, Part 5, sermon at Shalom Mennonite Fellowship, Tucson, AZ, www.members.cox .net/gfdaught/sermons/S9899/S062.html).

   According to Paul D. Hanson, "The freed Hebrew slaves on the far side of the Red Sea sing in celebration of their deliverance. They sing: 'Yahweh is a warrior,' literally, *ish milhamah*, 'a man of war' (Ex 15:3a). This is metaphorical language. This is not a glorification of war, nor is it a glorification of Yahweh as a god of war. It is a declaration that 'Evil [is] a reality. Its embodiment in the powerful [leads] to the suffering of the weak. [And so,] deliverance inevitably involves opposition to evil" (Paul D. Hanson, "War and Peace in the Hebrew Bible," *Interpretation,* Oct. 1984, p. 348).

68. The Holy Bible in Modern English—"The LORD is a warrior"; Knox Translation—"Javé, the warrior God, Javé"; Living Bible—"The Lord is a warrior"; Moffatt New Translation—"The Eternal knows well how to fight"; New American Bible—"The LORD is a warrior"; New Jerusalem Bible—"Yahweh is a warrior."

69. George Eldon Ladd, *A Theology of the New Testament* (Grand Rapids: Eerdmans Publishing Co., 1974; revised ed., 1993), p. 156.

70. Robert M. Bowman, Dec. 9, 2003, e-mail to Richard Abanes.

71. Rabbi Akiva and Rabbi Ishmael, *Shi'r Qoma* (Work of the Chariot, 1972 reprinting), www.workofthechariot.com/TextFiles/Translations-ShirQoma.htm. Also see David Meltzer, ed., *The Secret Garden: An Anthology in the Kabbalah* (1976), p. 3; Gershom G. Scholem, *Major Trends in Jewish Mysticism* (1941/1961), pp. 65-66.

72. Meir Bar-Ilan, "The Hand of God: A Chapter in Rabbinic Anthropomorphism," available through Marquette University, www.marquette.edu/maqom/. This article reads, "[I]n the first centuries c.e. the Jews in the Land of Israel as well as those in Babylon believed in an anthropomorphic God, as is evident in both Talmud and Hekhalot literatures. Not only that but this Jewish belief is attested also in the writings of the church fathers: Justin Martyr, Origen, Basil the Great and Arnobious of Sicca. That is to say that whatever sources are consulted—either Jewish or Christian authors about the Jews— all agree upon the anthropomorphic concept among the Jews in late antiquity....This ancient belief was elaborated as could be seen in *Shiur Qoma* and in the words attributed to R. Ishmael, R. Akiba, Rab, and R. Hisda. Apparently, not only sages, but laymen also were of the same opinion of God who has a physical form."

73. Bickmore, "Does God Have A Body," p. 2.

74. Tertullian, *The Five Books Against Marcion,* Book I, chapter 8, in Alexander Roberts and James Donaldson, eds., *The Ante-Nicene Fathers* (Grand Rapids: Eerdmans Publishing Co., 1993), vol. 3, p. 276.

75. Tertullian, Book II, chapter 16, in Roberts and Donaldson, vol. 3, p. 310.

76. Tertullian, Book II, chapter 16, in Roberts and Donaldson, vol. 3, p. 310. "[T]his, therefore, is to be deemed the likeness of God in man, that the *human soul have the same emotions and sensations as God,* although they are not of the same kind; differing as they do both in their conditions and their issues according to their nature" (emphasis added).

    Another reference to God's image reads, "[M]an was by God constituted free, master of his own will and power; *indicating the presence of God's image and likeness in him* by nothing so well as by this constitution of his nature. For it was *not by his face, and by the lineaments [i.e., features] of his body, though they were so varied in his human nature, that he expressed his likeness to the form of God;* but he showed his stamp in that essence which he derived from God Himself (that is, *the spiritual, which answered to the form of God),* and *in the freedom and power of his will*" (Tertullian, Book II, chapter 5, in Roberts and Donaldson, vol. 3, p. 301, emphasis added).

77. "Him whom you do not deny to be God, you confess to be not human; because, when you confess Him to be God, you have, in fact, already determined that He is undoubtedly diverse from every sort of human conditions" (Tertullian, Book II, chapter 16, in Roberts and Donaldson, vol. 3, p. 310).

78. Kenneth L. Woodward, "What Mormons Believe," *Newsweek,* Sept. 1, 1980, p. 68.

79. Woodward, p. 68.

Chapter 6: Siblings from Eternity Past

1. Robert Millet, *The Mormon Faith* (SLC: Shadow Mountain, 1998), p. 55.

2. Bruce R. McConkie, *MD* (SLC: Bookcraft, 1958; rev. ed., 1966; 23rd printing, 1977), p. 750. McConkie wrote, "Spirits are actually born as offspring of Heavenly Father, a glorified and exalted Man."

3. This LDS belief appears in many official and nonofficial sources, including W.F. Walker Johanson, *What Is Mormonism All About?* (New York: St. Martin's Green, 2002), p. 118; Gilbert Scharffs, *The Missionary's Little Book of Answers* (American Fork, UT: Covenant Communications, Inc., 2002), p. 181; *Achieving a Celestial Marriage, LDS Church Manual,* 1976, p. 129. LDS Apostle James E. Talmage, for example, said, "We, the human family, literally the sons and daughters of Divine Parents, the literal progeny of God our Eternal Father, and of our God Mother, are away from home for a season" (James E. Talmage, *The Philosophical Basis of "Mormonism"* [Independence, MO: Missions of LDSC, 1928], p. 9).

4. According to *some* Mormons, Heavenly Father has more than one wife. To these Mormons, although most of us were born to "Heavenly Mother," some of us *may* have been spiritually birthed by one of Elohim's other wives. LDS apostle Orson Pratt taught, "God the Father had a plurality of wives, one or more being in eternity, by whom He begat our spirits as well as the spirit of Jesus His Firstborn" (Orson Pratt, "Celestial Marriage," *The Seer,* Nov. 1853, vol. 1, no. 11, p. 172, reprinted as *The Seer* [SLC: Eborn

Books, 1990]). In 1961, Mormon writer John J. Stewart affirmed that "plural marriage is the patriarchal order of Marriage lived by God and others who reign in the Celestial Kingdom" (John J. Stewart, *Brigham Young and His Wives and The True Story of Plural Marriage* [SLC: Mercury Publishing Co., Inc., 1961], p. 41).

5. Dallin Oaks, "The Great Plan of Happiness," *Ensign*, Nov. 1993, p. 72, available at www.lds.org; cf. Millet, p. 55.

6. Victor L. Ludlow, *Principles and Practices of the Restored Gospel* (SLC: Deseret Book Co., 1992), p. 140. The 1925 First Presidency stated, "By his Almighty power God organized the earth, and all that it contains, from spirit and element, which exist co-eternally with himself" (First Presidency of The Church of Jesus Christ of Latter-day Saints [Heber J. Grant, Anthony W. Wins, Charles W. Nibley], "Mormon View of Evolution," *Improvement Era*, Sept. 1925, vol. 28, no. 11, pp. 1090-1091, http://bioag.byu.edu/botany/BOT341/Evolve.htm); cf. John A. Widtsoe, *Joseph Smith As Scientist* (SLC: The General Board, Young Men's Mutual Improvement Associations, 1908), pp. 68-69.

7. Joseph Smith. Quoted in Joseph Fielding Smith, comp., *Teachings of the Prophet Joseph Smith* (SLC: Deseret Book Co., 1938; 1973 edition), p. 181.

8. Joseph F. Smith, Feb. 17, 1884, in *JOD*, vol. 25, pp. 51-60.

9. Millet, p. 34.

10. Joseph Smith, Apr. 6, 1844, in *JOD*, vol. 6, pp. 6-7; cf. Fielding Smith, p. 353. LDS scholar B.H. Roberts made this same observation (see B.H. Roberts, *The Truth, The Way, The Life* [unpublished manuscript, printed by Smith Research Associates of San Francisco, 1994], p. 285).

11. Consider the 2001 LDS article "Before Birth," which appeared in the LDS publication *Liahona:* "Without an understanding of our premortal life we cannot correctly comprehend our relationship with our Heavenly Father, nor can we completely grasp the purpose of this earth life" (Boyd K. Packer, "The Mystery of Life," *Ensign*, Nov. 1983, p. 16, available at www.lds.org).

12. Ludlow, p. 153. Ludlow listed some LDS descriptions for *intelligence* as follows:

    • "our will, our capacity or power to make decisions; it is the part of our being with which we think; and it is our ability to reason and to form sound judgments"

    • "the light of truth expanding our understanding...our sensitivity to the reality and power of truth"

    • "an inclination to do right and to serve others"

13. Ludlow, p. 157.

14. "In our first estate, we existed as primal INTELLIGENCES until Heavenly Father provided us with spirit bodies, thus allowing us new dimensions of organization, experience, and progression" (Ludlow, p. 153). Bruce McConkie said, "Our spirit bodies had their beginning in pre-existence when we were born as the spirit children of God our Father. Through that birth process spirit element was organized into intelligent entities" (McConkie, p. 750).

    As for the sexual aspect of this event, LDS apostle John A. Widtsoe explained, "Sex Among the Gods. Sex, which is indispensable on this earth for the perpetuation of the human race, is an eternal quality which has its equivalent everywhere" (John A. Widtsoe,

A Rational Theology [SLC: Deseret News, 1915], p. 69, www.cumorah.com/etexts/rationaltheology.txt).

Today, however, Mormons are extremely reticent to talk about exactly how Heavenly Father and Mother gave spirit bodies to the intelligences they organized. Nevertheless, it is a sacred aspect of their belief system. Consider, for example, a letter written to *Dialogue: A Journal of Mormon Thought:* "Joseph Smith's spiritual experiences led him to enthrone the sex act as a point of similarity, not difference, between God and human beings. Aided by his visionary experiences, he instituted a marriage rite that celebrates the eternity and holiness of the sex act: those who endure to the end will be gods and thus enjoy the sexual privilege forever and ever" (*Dialogue: A Journal of Mormon Thought* [Fall 1989], vol.19, no. 3, p. 70).

BYU professor Eugene England has explained; "The sexual relationship perfectly represents spiritual union within polarity, that one-to-one sharing that ultimately makes possible the creativity enjoyed by the gods themselves" (Eugene England, "On Fidelity, Polygamy, and Celestial Marriage," in Brent Corcoran, ed., *Multiply and Replenish: Essays On Mormonism Series No. 7* [SLC: Signature Books, 1994], pp. 108-109).

15. Milton R. Hunter, *The Gospel Through the Ages* (SLC: Deseret Book Co., 1958), pp. 99, 127-129.

16. "Kolob means 'the first creation.' It is the name of the planet 'nearest the celestial, or the residence of God.' It is 'first in government, the last pertaining to the measurement of time....One day in Kolob is equal to a thousand years according to the measurement of this earth'" (McConkie, p. 428).

17. "Eve, his wife, heard all of these things and was glad, saying; Were it not for our transgression we never should have had seed [children], and never should have known good and evil, and the joy of our redemption" (PGP—Moses 5:11). LDS apostle Jeffrey R. Holland stated; "The privilege of mortality granted to the rest of us is the principal gift given by the fall of Adam and Eve" (Jeffrey R. Holland, *Christ and the New Covenant* [SLC: Deseret Book Co., 1997], p. 204).

18. "I never speak of the part Eve took in this fall as a sin, nor do I accuse Adam of a sin.... This was a transgression of the law, but not a sin...for it was something that Adam and Eve had to do!" (Joseph Fielding Smith, *Doctrines of Salvation* [SLC: Bookcraft, 1954], vol. 1, pp. 114-115).

19. Coke Newell, *Latter Days: A Guided Tour Through Six Billion Years of Mormonism* (New York: St. Martin's Press, 2000), p. 17.

20. Joseph Smith, in *JOD,* vol. 6, pp. 6-7.

21. LDS First Presidency (Joseph F. Smith, John R. Winder, Anthon H. Lund), "The Origin of Man," *Improvement Era,* November 1909, vol. 13, no. 1, p. 61, as quoted in *Teachings of the Latter-day Prophets* (SLC: LDS Church, 1986), p. 221, also online at http://eyring .hplx.net/Eyring/faq/evolution/FP1909.html.

22. Packer, available at www.lds.org. This statement by Packer was quoted as recently as 2001 in "Before Birth," *Liahona,* Feb. 2001, p. 36, available at www.lds.org.

23. Elaine Anderson Cannon, "Mother in Heaven," in Daniel H. Ludlow, ed., *Encyclopedia of Mormonism* (New York: Macmillan Publishing Co., 1992), vol. 2, p. 961.

24. Millet, pp. 55-56.

25. Joseph Fielding Smith, *Answers to Gospel Questions* (SLC: Deseret Book Co., 1960), vol. 3, p. 142. Smith stated, "The fact that there is no reference to a mother in heaven either in the Bible, *Book of Mormon* or *Doctrine and Covenants*, is not sufficient proof that no such thing as a mother did exist there."

26. Joseph Fielding Smith, *Answers*, vol. 3, p. 144.

27. In *A Rational Theology* LDS apostle John Widtsoe provided these thoughts: "Since we have a Father, who is our God, we must also have a mother, who possesses the attributes of Godhood. This simply carries onward the logic of things earthly, and conforms with the doctrine that whatever is on this earth is simply a representation of spiritual conditions of deeper meaning than we can here fathom" (Widtsoe, www.cumorah.com/etexts/rationaltheology.txt).

28. LDS apostle Milton R. Hunter explained, "When light burst forth from heaven in revelations to the Prophet Joseph Smith, a more complete understanding of man—especially regarding his personal relationship to Deity—was received than could be found in all of the holy scriptures combined. The stupendous truth of the existence of a Heavenly Mother, as well as a Heavenly Father, became established facts in Mormon theology" (Hunter, p. 98).

29. Cannon, in Daniel H. Ludlow, vol. 2, p. 961, emphasis added.

30. McConkie, *MD*, p. 516: "Implicit in the Christian verity that all men are the spirit children of an Eternal Father is the usually unspoken truth that they are also the offspring of an Eternal Mother. An exalted and glorified Man of Holiness could not be a Father unless a Woman of like glory, perfection, and holiness was associated with him as a Mother. The begetting of children makes a man a father and a woman a mother whether we are dealing with man in his mortal or immortal state."

31. Hinckley, "Daughters of God," *Ensign*, Nov. 1991, p. 100, as reprinted in Gordon B. Hinckley, *Teachings of Gordon B. Hinckley* (SLC: Deseret Book Co., 1997), p. 257.

32. Mormons believe that intelligence, as well as spirit matter, are the very building blocks of all that is. Their connection to us was highlighted in *Principles and Practices of the Restored Gospel:* "[T]he principle ingredients of physical and spirit elements have existed and will continue to exist in some form of organization forever. [T]he elements of the body and spirit of each human have always existed. At some point in the distant past, God brought eternal intelligence and other spirit elements together in the form of a spirit body. Later, he placed that living spirit within an embryo or fetus made of the physical elements of this earth" (Victor L. Ludlow, p. 142).

33. Victor L. Ludlow, p. 143.

34. Victor L. Ludlow, p. 145.

35. According to BYU professor of philosophy Dennis J. Packard, some LDS leaders teach that we existed as *individual* intelligent beings even before Heavenly Father clothed us with spirit bodies. Others, however, say that prior to receiving our spirit bodies, we were just "eternal intelligent matter" with no individual identity. Consequently, there is "no official position on this issue" (Dennis J. Packard, "Intelligence," in Daniel H. Ludlow, vol. 2, p. 692).

   This disagreement has resulted in a rather imprecise interpretation of how "intelligence" and "intelligences" should be used: "The term has received two interpretations by writers within the Church: [1] as literal spirit children of Heavenly Parents and [2] as individual entities existing prior to their spirit birth [i.e., being clothed with a spirit body]. Because latter-day revelation has not clarified the meaning of the term, a more precise interpretation is not possible at present" (Packard, in Daniel H. Ludlow, vol. 2, p. 692).

36. Victor L. Ludlow, pp. 146-147.

37. Brigham Young, June 18, 1865, in *JOD*, vol. 11, p. 123. More recently, LDS leader Angel Abrea stated, "Each individual born into this world has been the actual spiritual son or daughter of God the Father in the premortal world of spirits. The first major step upward made by the uncreated entities was entrance into what we call the first estate. Here the intelligences were tabernacled in bodies of spirit matter by birth through heavenly parents. In November 1909 the First Presidency declared in 'The Origin of Man': 'All men and women are in the similitude of the universal Father and Mother, and are literally the sons and daughters of Deity'" (Angel Abrea, "A Divine Nature and Destiny," June 15, 1999, devotional address, www.speeches.byu.edu/devo/98-99/AbreaSu99.html).

38. Abrea, www.speeches.byu.edu/devo/98-99/AbreaSu99.html.

39. Vern Anderson, "Family Size Is Up to Couple, LDS Handbook Says," *Salt Lake Tribune*, Dec. 5, 1998, p. A1, www.sltrib.com (archives); also posted at www.mormons.org.uk/birth.htm. This official position caused a considerable degree of anguish and suffering for an untold number of Latter-day Saints. For personal stories about the effects of this policy, see the Internet postings at www.exmormons.faithweb.com/1998/birth_con trol.html.

40. "[God] formed every plant that grows, and every animal that breathes, each after its own kind, spiritually and temporally—'that which is spiritual being in the likeness of that which is temporal, and that which is temporal in the likeness of that which is spiritual'" (First Presidency of The Church of Jesus Christ of Latter-day Saints [Heber J. Grant, Anthony W. Wins, Charles W. Nibley], "Mormon View of Evolution," *Improvement Era*, Sept. 1925, vol. 28, no. 11, pp. 1090-1091, http://bioag.byu.edu/botany/BOT341/Evolve.htm).

41. Bruce McConkie, *The Millennial Messiah* (SLC: Deseret Book Co., 1982), pp. 642-643: "Man and all forms of life existed as spirit beings and entities before the foundations of this earth were laid. There were spirit men and spirit beasts, spirit fowls and spirit fishes, spirit plants and spirit trees. Every creeping thing, every herb and shrub, every amoeba and tadpole, every elephant and dinosaur—all things—existed as spirits, spirit beings before they were placed naturally upon the earth" (Quoted in *Doctrines of the Gospel* [SLC: LDSC, 1986], p. 16; this volume was used in 1986 as the LDS Church Educational System student manual).

42. PGP—Moses 3:4-7; cf. James Talmage, *The Articles of Faith* (SLC: The Deseret News, 1890; rev. ed., 1940), p. 491.

43. Russell M. Nelson, "The Atonement," *Ensign*, Nov. 1996, p. 33, available at www.lds.org.

44. Oaks, available at www.lds.org.

45. Nelson, available at www.lds.org.

46. Oaks, available at www.lds.org; cf. Jess L. Christensen, "The Choice That Began Mortality," *Liahona*, August 2002, p. 38, available at www.lds.org.

47. *Aaronic Priesthood Manual 3* (SLC: LDSC, 1995, online edition), Lesson Number Six, available at www.lds.org.

48. *Aaronic Priesthood Manual 3*, available at www.lds.org.

49. Talmage, p. 70.

50. Cannon, in Daniel H Ludlow, vol. 2, p. 961.

51. Scharffs, p. 181.

52. Neal Maxwell, *Ensign*, May 1984, p. 22, as quoted in Corey H. Maxwell, *The Neal A. Maxwell Quote Book* (SLC: Bookcraft, 1997), p. 263, reprinted in Neal A. Maxwell, *The Collected Works of Neal A. Maxwell* (SLC: Eagle Gate, 2001), vol. 6.

53. Maxwell, pp. 263-264.

54. Stephen Robinson, *Are Mormons Christian?* (SLC: Bookcraft, 1991), p. 104.

55. Gerald N. Lund, "The Fall of Man and His Redemption," *Ensign*, Jan. 1990, p. 22, available at www.lds.org.

56. Oaks, available at www.lds.org; cf. Bruce R. McConkie, "Eve and the Fall," *Woman* (SLC: Deseret Book Co., 1979), pp. 67-68. It should be noted that evangelicals, although they condemn Eve's actions as sinful, in no way attribute any kind of inferiority to women as a result of her sinful choice.

57. George Q. Cannon, Apr. 15, 1884, *Salt Lake Herald*. Quoted in Jerreld L. Newquist, ed., *Gospel Truth: Discourses and Writings of President George Q. Cannon* (SLC: Deseret Book Co., 1957; 1974 edition), vol. 1, p. 129.

58. Cannon, in Newquist, p. 129.

59. Possible dates for the rule of Ramses III include 1180–1150 B.C., 1182–1151 B.C., and 1184–1153 B.C.

60. P.L. Day, "Anat," in Karel van der Toorn, Bob Becking, and Pieter W. van der Horst, eds., *Dictionary of Demons and Deities in the Bible* (Grand Rapids, MI: Eerdmans Publishing Co., 1999), p. 38; cf. A. Rowe, *The Four Canaanite Temples of Beth-Shan* (Philadelphia: University Museum, 1940), p. 33; H. Ringgren, tr. John Sturdy, *Religions of the Ancient Near East* (Philadelphia: Westminster Press, 1973), p. 142; and Rolan K. Harrison, "Queen of Heaven," *The International Standard Bible Encyclopedia* (Grand Rapids, MI: Eerdmans Publishing Co., 1988), vol. 4, p. 8.

61. C. Houtman, "Queen of Heaven," in van der Toorn, et al., p. 678. This corroborates an observation made by biblical scholars Keil and Delitzsch: "In the 18th verse [of chapter 7] the expression [queen of heaven] is generalized into 'other gods,' with reference to the fact that the service of the Queen of heaven was but one kind of idolatry along with others, since other strange gods were worshipped by sacrifices and libations" (C.F. Keil and F. Delitzsch, *Commentary on the Old Testament* [Peabody, MA: Hendrickson Publishers, 1996 edition], vol. 8, p. 101; cf. Deut. 31:29; 32:16).

62. Many scholars believe it was probably Anat.

63. *Asherah* (Hebrew), for instance, also was known as *Athirat* (Ugaritic) and *Asatu/Asirtu* (Mesopotamian). *Astarte* (Phoenician), meanwhile, also was referred to as *Ishtar* (Akkadian), *Athtart* (Ugaritic), and *Astoret* (Hebrew). *Ishtar* (Akkadian) also was called *Inanna* (Sumerian).

64. The predominant view among scholars is that Anat, too, was a fertility goddess as well as a consort to Baal. Recently, however, this view has been challenged by a number of other scholars. As for Baal, his devotees were a constant thorn in Israel's side. Scripture refers to his temples (1 Kings 16:32; 2 Kings 10:21, 23,25-27; 11:18), altars (Judges 6:25, 28,30-32), pillars (2 Kings 3:2; 10:27), prophets (1 Kings 18:19,22,25-26; 2 Kings 10:19), and priests (2 Kings 11:18). In response to Baal worship (for example, 1 Kings 19:18), God not only ordered Gideon to destroy his altars (Judges 6:25-26,28,30), but also prompted Elijah to execute his priests (1 Kings 18:19,38-40).

65. Manfred Lurker, *Dictionary of Gods and Goddesses, Devils and Demons* (New York: Routledge, 1987), p. 42.

66. Patricia Monaghan, *The New Book of Goddesses & Heroines* (St. Paul, MN: Llewellyn Publications, 1997), p. 57.

67. Monaghan, p. 55.

68. Monaghan, p. 56.

69. William J. Fulco, "Anat," in Mircea Eliade, ed., *The Encyclopedia of Religion* (New York: Macmillan Publishing Co., 1987), vol. 1, p. 262.

70. Day, in van der Toorn, et al., p. 37.

71. Fulco, in Eliade, vol. 1, p. 262.

72. The name *Anat,* for example, appears in the ancient writings that were unearthed throughout the Jewish settlement at Elephantine in Upper Egypt (c. 6th to 5th century B.C.).

73. Lucy Goodison and Christine Morris, eds., *Ancient Goddesses: The Myths and the Evidences* (Madison: University of Wisconsin Press, 1998), p. 72.; cf. T. Abusch in *Demons' Bible,* p. 452.

74. T. Abusch, "Ishtar," van der Toorn, et al., p. 453.

75. Monaghan, p. 164.

76. William J. Fulco, "Inanna," in Eliade, vol. 7, p. 146.

77. Goodison and Morris, p. 73.

78. Bickmore, pp. 339-340. He quotes Theodore Robinson, "Hebrew Myths," in Samuel H. Hooke, ed., *Myth and Ritual* (Oxford: Oxford University Press, 1933), p. 185; and George Widengren, "Early Hebrew Myths and Their Interpretation," in Samuel H. Hooke, ed., *Myth, Ritual, and Kingship* (Oxford: Clarendon Press, 1958), p. 183.

79. Bickmore, p. 339.

80. Barry R. Bickmore, *Restoring the Ancient Church* (Provo, UT: FARMS, 1999), p. 339.

81. Bickmore, pp. 339-340.

82. There have been at least three types of LDS responses to such modes of biblical interpretation, as exemplified by the following Mormon leaders: liberal (William H. Chamberlin), centrist (B.H. Roberts), and conservative (Joseph Fielding Smith). These three LDS perspectives were highlighted in Kevin L. Barney, "Reflections on the Documentary Hypothesis," *Dialogue: a Journal of Mormon Thought* (Spring 2000), vol. 33, no. 1, pp. 57-99, www.dialoguejournal.com/Vol33/doc_hyp_33_1.htm.

83. C. Houtman, in van der Toorn, et al., p. 679.

84. Norman Geisler, "Bible Criticism," *Baker Encyclopedia of Christian Apologetics* (Grand Rapids, MI: Baker Book House, 1999), p. 88.

85. "[T]he basic program of the New Year festival, as envisioned by Hooke, is summed in the following five points: '(a) The dramatic representation of the death and resurrection of the god. (b) The recitation or symbolic representation of the myth of creation. (c) The ritual combat, in which the triumph of the god over his enemies was depicted. (d) The sacred marriage. (e) The triumphal processions, in which the king played the part of the god followed by a train of lesser gods or visiting deities' " (S.H. Hooke, "The Myth and Ritual Pattern of the Ancient East," in S.H. Hooke, ed., *Myth and Ritual* [London: Oxford University Press, 1933], p. 8. Quoted in George Mark Elliot, "Modern Views of the Origin and Nature of the Day of Yahweh," *The Seminary Review* (Spring 1965), vol. XI, no. 3, pp. 35-78, www.dabar.org/SemReview/VOLUME11/ISSUE3/V11i3 a1.htm.

86. Widengren, in Hooke, *Myth, Ritual, and Kingship*, pp. 158-159.

87. Widengren, in Hooke, *Myth, Ritual, and Kingship*, pp. 162.

88. Theodore Robinson, *A Short Comparative History of Religions* (London: Gerald Duckworth & CO. LTD., 1926; 1951 ed.), p. 119.

89. For example, Tim Callahan, *Secret Origins of the Bible* (Altadena, CA: Millennium Press, 2002), pp. 6-14; and Richard Elliot Friedman, *Who Wrote the Bible?* (New York: Harper and Row, 1989).

90. Robert Millet, "The Ancient Covenant Restored," *Ensign*, Mar. 1998, p. 36, available at www.lds.org; and Stephen E. Robinson, "The Law after Christ," *Ensign*, Sept. 1983, p. 69, available at www.lds.org. Millet stated, "Moses—the Lord's lawgiver, the author of the Pentateuch—constructed his scriptural narrative in such a way as to lead the reader quickly through the Creation, the Fall, the Flood, and the scattering of the nations through the confounding of tongues." Robinson wrote, "Strictly speaking, the Law of Moses consists of the first five books of the Old Testament—what the Jews call the Torah. These five books of Moses (Genesis; Exodus; Leviticus; Numbers; and Deuteronomy) are also called the Pentateuch, but in the New Testament they are usually just 'the Law.'"

91. James E. Faust, "Strengthening the Inner Self," *Ensign*, Feb. 2003, p. 3, available at www.lds.org. Noteworthy is a 2003 reprint of a 1975 article by LDS president Spencer W. Kimball, who declared, "Where would we be if Moses hadn't written his history of the world, those first five vital books of the Old Testament? He had the background, the data, the record, and the inclination, and he has blessed us throughout the eternities for the service he rendered in writing the first five books of the Bible" (Spencer W. Kimball, "The Angels May Quote from It," *New Era*, October 1975, reprinted in *New Era*, Feb. 2003, p. 32, available at www.lds.org).

92. First Nephi 5:11 makes reference to the "five books of Moses." Although a few liberal Latter-day Saints have tried to assert that this passage does not say *which* five books, LDS leadership has consistently interpreted the verse to be a reference to the Pentateuch, as the following citations show:

    Boyd K. Packer: "'The five books of Moses, which gave an account of the creation of the world, and also of Adam and Eve, who were our first parents' (1 Ne. 5:11.)" (Boyd K. Packer, "The Things of My Soul," *Ensign,* May 1986, p. 59, available at www.lds.org); "Nephi had access to the Exodus account on the plates of brass, which contained the five books of Moses and an account of Israel's deliverance from Egypt. (1 Ne. 5:11, 15.)" ("Nephi and the Exodus," *Ensign,* Apr. 1987, p. 64, available at www.lds.org).

    Timothy L. Carver: "The books of Genesis through Deuteronomy are historical books, sometimes called 'the law.' They are also called the 'five books of Moses' because Moses wrote or spoke much of what is in them. These books tell us of the history of the earth as the Lord revealed it to Moses. Genesis begins with the Creation of the world and Adam and Eve. Deuteronomy finishes at the end of Moses' life" ("Enjoying The Old Testament," *Ensign,* Jan. 2002, p. 56, available at www.lds.org).

    Stephen D. Ricks: "These plates contained much of the information found in our Old Testament: 'the five books of Moses, which gave an account of the creation of the world, and also of Adam and Eve,...And also a record of the Jews from the beginning, even down to the commencement of the reign of Zedekiah, king of Judah' (1 Ne. 5:11-12.)" ("Questions and Answers," *Tambuli,* Sept. 1984, p. 13, available at www.lds.org).

93. Hooke, "Myth and Ritual: Past and Present," p. 9, emphasis added.

94. Hooke, "Myth and Ritual: Past and Present," p. 10. He further clarified the issue: "I am also of the opinion that where traces of Assyro-Babylonian influence on the religion and culture of Israel appear, and it is impossible to deny their existence, they have been received *mainly through the medium of Canaanite culture,* though some borrowings probably took place *during the period of Assyrian domination,* and later on during the Exile" (Hooke, "Myth and Ritual: Past and Present," p. 12, emphasis added).

95. B.S.J. Isserlin, *The Israelites* (London: Thames and Hudson, 1998), pp. 234-235.

96. Hooke, "Myth and Ritual: Past and Present," p. 20.

97. "[T]hey despised my judgments, and walked not in my statutes, but polluted my sabbaths: for their heart went after their idols....[W]hen I had brought them into the land, for which I lifted up mine hand to give it to them, then they saw every high hill, and all the thick trees, and they offered there their sacrifices....Thus saith the Lord GOD; Are ye polluted after the manner of your fathers? and commit ye whoredom after their abominations? For when ye offer your gifts, when ye make your sons to pass through the fire, ye pollute yourselves with all your idols, even unto this day...ye say, We will be as the heathen, as the families of the countries, to serve wood and stone" (Ezekiel 20:16,28,30-32). After citing this passage, Hooke wrote, "[T]he passage of Ezekiel just quoted shows how far deliberate assimilation of Canaanite cult practices had gone in Israel very shortly after the entry into Canaan" (Hooke, "Myth and Ritual: Past and Present," p. 15).

98. Hooke, "Myth and Ritual: Past and Present," p. 19.

99. Robinson, "Hebrew Myths," in Hooke, *Myth and Ritual,* p. 183. Quoted by Widengren, in Hooke, *Myth, Ritual, and Kingship,* p. 177. Robinson said, "the representation of the

sacred marriage involved features which were repulsive in the extreme to the mind of the nomadic element in Israel." He also felt that "some of the practices eliminated by Josiah seem to have been associated with this cult" (Robinson, "Hebrew Myths," in Hooke, *Myth and Ritual,* quoted by Widengren, in Hooke, *Myth, Ritual, and Kingship,* p. 177).

100. Anat is most likely the goddess to whom Yahweh was wed, as evidenced by an Elephantine papyrus that records an oath to Anat–Yahu, or rather, Anat of Yahu, "Anat being the name of a goddess, and Yahu a variation of Yahweh" (Goodison and Morris, p. 85). Other ancient Hebrew inscriptions at various places throughout the Semitic area also speak of "Yahweh and his Asherah." It seems, then, that some Israelites connected Yahweh with this particular goddess, rather than with Anat (Goodison and Morris, pp. 88-91).

101. Joseph Blenkinsopp, "The Household in Ancient Israel & Early Judaism," in Leo G. Perdue, *The Blackwell Companion to the Hebrew Bible* (Malden, MA: Blackwell Publishing, 2001), p. 181: "That the cult of the goddess Asherah alongside YHWH was part of the official liturgy for long periods is implicitly acknowledged in prohibitions under Deuteronomic law....The discovery of numerous figurines of the goddess and inscriptions in which Asherah is closely associated with YHWH confirm the situation which a close reading of the biblical texts insinuates."

102. B.S.J. Isserlin observed, "How the 'queen of heaven' worshiped in Judah at the time of Jeremiah may be related to Canaanite goddesses is uncertain. She may have been derived from Asherah or Astarte" (Isserlin, *The Israelites* [London: Thames and Hudson, 1998], p. 235). E.O. James, who in 1959 was the professor emeritus of the History of Religion in the University of London, suggested Anat or Astarte as the goddess whom paganized Hebrews exalted as the "consort of Yahweh" (O.E. James, *The Cult of the Mother-Goddess* [London: Thames & Hudson, 1959], pp. 78,80).

103. Goodison and Morris, p. 73.

104. Bickmore, p. 339.

105. Widengren, in Hooke, *Myth, Ritual, and Kingship,* p. 183, emphasis added.

106. Widengren, in Hooke, *Myth, Ritual, and Kingship,* p. 182.

107. It also must not be forgotten that both scholars did not even read the Old Testament as if it were a work of history, but instead saw it as a compilation of mythical stories.

108. M. Dijkstra, "Mother," in van der Toorn, et al., p. 603.

109. Cannon, in Daniel H. Ludlow, p. 961.

110. Victor L. Ludlow, p. 146.

111. J.D. Douglas and Merrill C. Tenney, eds., *The New International Dictionary of the Bible* (Grand Rapids, MI: Zondervan, 1987), pp. 17-18. The entry "adoption" reads, "An adopted son was considered like a son born in the family.... He was no longer liable for old debts.... So far as his former family was concerned he was dead. Adoption expresses both the redemption and the new relation of trust and love.... The adoption brought us from slavery to sonship and heirship."

112. Similarly, in the ASV, 1 John 3:9 and 1 John 4:7 speak of us being "begotten" of God if we follow God and abstain from sin: "Whosoever is begotten of God doeth no sin, because his seed abideth in him: and he cannot sin, because he is begotten of God";

and "Beloved, let us love one another: for love is of God; and every one that loveth is begotten of God, and knoweth God."

113.   Robert L. Millet and Noel B. Reynolds, *Latter-day Christianity: 10 Basic Issues* (Provo, UT: FARMS, 1998), p. 10, chapter 2, http://farms.byu.edu/10basics/10basicissues .php?chapter=2).

114.   *Pater* is taken from a root word "signifying a nourisher, protector, upholder" (W.E. Vine, *Vine's Expository Dictionary of New Testament Words* [McLean, VA: MacDonald Publishing Co., no date], p. 421). In the New Testament it is used figuratively not only of God as Creator, but also of one "advanced in the knowledge of Christ" (1 Jn. 2:13). It is used metaphorically of Satan (Jn. 8:28,44) and also for "the originator of a family or company of persons animated by the same spirit as himself, as of Abraham [Rom. 4:11-18]" (Vine, p. 422).
        Ab—an ancient Semitic word found in Ugaritic, Akkadian, and Phoenician languages—was used not just for father, but for grandfather, forefather, or ancestor (Merrill F. Unger and William White Jr., eds., *Nelson's Expository Dictionary of the Old Testament*, p. 244, as reprinted in *Vine's Complete Expository Dictionary of Old and New Testament Words* [Nashville, TN: Thomas Nelson, 1985], p. 78). In Scripture it is applied to an older person as a sign of respect (1 Sam. 24:11), a teacher (2 Kings 2:12), a prophet (2 Kings 6:21), a priest (Judges 17:10), a husband (Jer. 3:4), and an advisor (Gen. 45:8). Obviously there are many uses for *ab*, even in connection to God, who is described as the "father" of Israel (Deut. 32:6, i.e.—creator or source) and a "father" of the fatherless (Ps. 68:5, i.e.—a protector).

115.   Kevin Graham, Nov. 5, 2003, Internet post at ZLMB. Graham stated, "Sons of God were Gods themselves in an Old Testament setting, and that is how the NT Christians understood it." Graham is a highly contentious LDS apologist who enjoys a fairly visible presence on the Internet.

116.   Jeff Lindsay, "Do Mormons think that they will become gods?" www.jefflindsay.com/ LDSFAQ/FQ_theosis.shtml.

117.   S.B. Parker, "Sons of the Gods," in van der Toorn, p. 794. The double mention of angels as "morning stars" and "sons of God" is a Hebrew parallelism. A similar phrase has been found in an Ugaritic passage that juxtaposes "sons of El" and "assembly of stars" (KTU² 1.10 I:3-4, quoted in S.B. Parker, p. 798). (KTU² is the abbreviation for *Die keil-alpha-betisch Texte aus Ugarit*, second enlarged edition, *The Cuneiform Alphabetic Texts from Ugarit, Ras Ibn Hani and Other Places* by M. Dietrich, O. Loretz, and J. Sanmartín. This volume provides the translation of various ancient Ugaritic texts.)

118.   "Question: 'If God has a body of flesh and bones plus spirit, how is it that his children were spirits, in pre-existence?' Answer:…This question the Lord has not fully explained, but there are sufficient reasons why we should believe that he does have a tabernacle of flesh and bones" (Joseph Fielding Smith, *Melchizedek Priesthood Personal Study Guide* [SLC: LDSC, 1972/73], p. 17).

119.   Lund, available at www.lds.org.

120.   Fielding Smith, *Doctrines of Salvation*, vol. 1, p. 115.

121.   Oaks, "The Great Plan of Happiness," available at www.lds.org.

122.   Vine, p. 1172.

Chapter 7: After All We Can Do

1. Gordon B. Hinckley, "Stand True and Faithful," *Ensign*, May 1996, p. 94, available at www.lds.org. Mormons also accept the historicity of Christ's miracles, his physical resurrection, and the Gospel accounts of his birth (see Daniel C. Peterson and Stephen D. Ricks, *Offenders for a Word* [Provo, UT: FARMS, 1992], p. 57).

2. Robert L. Millet, *The Mormon Faith* (SLC: Shadow Mountain, 1998), p. 52.

3. K. Codell Carter, "Godhood," in Daniel H. Ludlow, *Encyclopedia of Mormonism* (New York: Macmillan Publishing Company, 1992), vol. 2, p. 553.

4. Gordon B. Hinckley, "We Look to Christ," *Ensign*, May 2002, p. 90, available at www.lds.org. McConkie also has said, "Christ is the Firstborn, meaning that he was the first Spirit Child born to God the Father in pre-existence" (Bruce McConkie, *MD* [SLC: Bookcraft, 1958; rev. ed., 1966; 23rd printing, 1977], p. 281).

5. James E. Faust, "The Atonement: Our Greatest Hope," Oct. 6, 2001, in *CR*, available at www.lds.org.

6. M. Russell Ballard, "Building Bridges of Understanding," Feb. 17, 1998, Logan [Utah] Institute of Religion address, available at www.lds.org. Ezra Taft Benson stated: "By his grace we receive an endowment of blessing and spiritual strength that may eventually lead us to eternal life if we endure to the end" (Ezra Taft Benson, "Redemption through Jesus Christ after All We Can Do," *Tambuli*, Dec. 1988, p. 3, available at www.lds.org).

7. Faust, available at www.lds.org.

8. Neal A. Maxwell, Apr. 1, 2001, in *CF*, p. 76, available at www.lds.org.

9. Maxwell, available at www.lds.org. LDS president Gordon B. Hinckley has spoken of this "gift" using language highly reminiscent of evangelicalism. "There is no other name given among men whereby we can be saved....He is the author of our salvation, the giver of eternal life....There is none equal to him. There never has been. There never will be" (Gordon B. Hinckley, *Teachings of Gordon B. Hinckley* [SLC: Deseret Book Co., 1997], p. 275).

10. Peterson and Ricks, p. 56.

11. Hinckley, "We Look to Christ," available at www.lds.org.

12. "Jesus was the first spirit being whom God the Father formed from the eternal intelligences that dwelt with him....Though he is not referred to as such in the scriptures, Jesus Christ has also been commonly called our 'elder brother' by modern prophets. He has been given this title because we were all with him from the beginning as intelligent entities and later and spirit personages" (Victor L. Ludlow, *Principles and Practices of the Restored Gospel* [SLC: Deseret Book Co., 1992], pp. 40, 43).

13. "[Through] obedience and devotion to the truth he [Jesus] attained that pinnacle of intelligence which ranked him as a God" (McConkie, *MD*, p. 129). "Jesus was a God in the premortal existence" (Ezra Taft Benson, *The Teachings of Ezra Taft Benson* [SLC: Bookcraft, 1988], p. 6).

14. "At the first organization in heaven we were all present, and saw the Savior chosen and appointed and the plan of salvation made, and we sanctioned it" (Joseph Smith, 1841,

in Joseph Fielding Smith, comp., *Teachings of the Prophet Joseph Smith* [SLC: Deseret Book, 1938], p. 181).

15. "In the great premortal council in heaven, God the Father presided and presented his plan for the mortality and eventual immortality of his children" (Jeffrey Holland, *Christ and the New Covenant* [SLC: Deseret Book Co., 1997], p. 198).

16. Millet, p. 59: "Before coming to earth, the sons and daughters of God were told that as mortals they would be required to walk by faith, to operate in this second estate without full knowledge of what they did and who they were in the life before. A veil of forgetfulness would be placed over their minds."

17. *Gospel Principles* (SLC: LDSC, 1978; rev., 1979; Missionary Reference Library Edition, 1990), pp. 9-12.

18. "Jehovah was the firstborn of the Father, meaning the firstborn spirit child, the heir, the one entitled to the birthright of God. In this sense, the Latter-day Saints speak of Jehovah or Jesus Christ as their 'elder brother.'...Another spirit child of God offered to save mankind by an alternative plan....Lucifer stepped forward and said, 'Behold, I here I am'" (Millet, p. 57). "Lucifer, who became Satan, was also a spirit child of Heavenly Father" (LDS Primary, "Jesus Christ Volunteered to Be Our Savior, Purpose," p. 5, available at www.lds.org). "The appointment of Jesus to be the Savior of the world was contested by one of the other sons of God. He was called Lucifer....[T]his spirit-brother of Jesus desperately tried to become the Savior" (Milton R. Hunter, *The Gospel Through the Ages* [SLC: Stevens and Wallis, 1945], p. 15).

19. "As the most righteous spirit-child of God, Jesus became the 'chief advocate' of Heavenly Father's plan of salvation" (Victor L. Ludlow, p. 43).

20. Victor L. Ludlow, p. 43.

21. *Gospel Principles*, p. 16. The phrase "war in heaven" is commonly applied by Mormons to that phase of our so-called "premortal life" when Lucifer rebelled and fought against the spirit children of Heavenly Father who chose to follow Jesus/Jehovah (see Hinckley, "We Look to Christ," available at www.lds.org).

22. *Gospel Principles*, p. 16.

23. "We know that Jehovah-Christ, assisted by 'many of the noble and great ones' (Abr. 3:22), of whom Michael is but the illustration, did in fact create the earth and all forms of plant and animal life on the face thereof" (Bruce R. McConkie, *The Promised Messiah* [SLC: Deseret Book Co., 1978], p. 69). "Christ acted in concert with other Gods to create our world: 'Then the Lord said: Let us go down. And they went down at the beginning, and they, that is the Gods, organized and formed the heavens and the earth'" (Donald Q. Cannon, Larry E. Dahl, and John W. Welch, "The Restoration of Major Doctrines through Joseph Smith: The Godhead, Mankind, and the Creation," *Ensign*, Jan. 1989, p. 27, available at www.lds.org; cf. PGP—BOA 4:3, 5, 8, 10, 26, 27).

24. "[T]he eldest and firstborn spirit child of God is Jehovah and that it was he who was later born with a physical body to MARY as Jesus Christ" (Jerry C. Giles, "Firstborn in the Spirit," in Daniel H. Ludlow, vol. 2, p. 728).

25. Robert L. Millet, "Jesus Christ: Overview," in Daniel H. Ludlow, vol. 2, p. 724.

26. Merrill J. Bateman, "Christ Is the Reason," Jan. 16, 2001, devotional address, http://speeches.byu.edu/htmlfiles/BatemanW01.html.

27. Millet, in Daniel H. Ludlow, vol. 2, p. 724.

28. Victor L. Ludlow, p. 40.

29. "Elohim is literally the Father of the spirit of Jesus Christ and also of the body in which Jesus Christ performed His mission in the flesh" (James Talmage, *The Articles of Faith* [SLC: LDSC, 1890; modern edition, 1948], p. 466). "Jesus Christ is the Son of God in the most literal sense. The body in which He performed His mission in the flesh was sired by that same Holy Being we worship as God, our Eternal Father. Jesus was not the son of Joseph, nor was He begotten by the Holy Ghost" (Benson, *The Teachings*, p. 7). "Jesus, even in mortality, was a God. And why was He a God? Because He was the literal Son of Elohim" (Richard D. Draper, "Christ's Role as Redeemer," *Liahona*, Dec. 2000, p. 11, available at www.lds.org).

30. Brigham Young, July 24, 1853, in *JOD*, vol. 1, p. 238.

31. Brigham Young, July 8, 1860, in *JOD*, vol. 8, p. 115. Young's intended message is clear from his explanation that there is only one way to create—i.e., the natural way of procreation through sex (Brigham Young, June 18, 1865, in *JOD*, vol. 11, p. 122).

32. Brigham Young, July 14, 1861, in Eldon J. Watson, ed., *Brigham Young Addresses: 1860-1864* (SLC: Elden J. Watson, 1980), vol. 4, reprinted in Eugene E. Campbell, ed., *The Essential Brigham Young* (SLC: Signature Books, 1992), p. 137.

33. Brigham Young, Aug. 19, 1866, in *JOD*, vol. 11, p. 268.

34. Brigham Young, Feb. 8, 1857, in *JOD*, vol. 4, p. 218.

35. Heber C. Kimball, Sept. 2, 1860, in *JOD*, vol. 8, p. 211.

36. Joseph Fielding Smith, *Doctrines of Salvation* (SLC: Bookcraft, 1954), vol. 1, p. 18.

37. "[Jesus] is the Son of God just as much as you and I are sons of our fathers" (Heber J. Grant, "Analysis of the Articles of Faith," a discourse in the Tabernacle on Nov. 20, 1921, in *MS* 84 [Jan. 5, 1922], p. 2. Grant said; "We believe that Jesus Christ was actually the Son of His Father, as I am the son of my father, and as you are of your father" (Heber J. Grant, "Tabernacle Address," Aug. 21, 1938, *Deseret News: Church Section* [Sept. 3, 1938], p. 1).

38. "There is nothing figurative about his [Christ's] paternity; he was begotten, conceived and born in the normal and natural course of events, for he is the Son of God, and that designation means what it says" (McConkie, *MD*, p. 742); "The Father had a Son, a natural Son, his own literal seed, the Offspring of his body" (Bruce McConkie, *The Promised Messiah* [SLC: Deseret Book, Co., 1978], pp. 355, 469); "[Jesus] is the Son of God in the same sense and way that we are the sons of mortal fathers. It is just that simple" (Bruce McConkie, *The Mortal Messiah* [SLC: Deseret Book, Co., 1979], vol. 1, p. 330); "[Jesus] is the Son of his Father in the same sense that all mortals are the sons and daughters of their fathers" (Bruce McConkie, *A New Witness for the Articles of Faith* [SLC: Deseret Book, Co., 1985], p. 68).

39. "Now, we are told in scriptures that Jesus Christ is the only begotten Son of God in the flesh. Well, now for the benefit of the older ones, how are children begotten? I answer just as Jesus Christ was begotten of his father. The difference between Jesus Christ and

other men is this: Our fathers in the flesh are mortal men, who are subject unto death: but the Father of Jesus Christ in the flesh is the God of Heaven. We must come down to the simple fact that God Almighty was the father of His Son Jesus Christ, and he was born into the world with power and intelligence like that of His Father....Now, my little friends, I will repeat again in words as simple as I can, and you talk to your parents about it, that God, the Eternal Father, is literally the father of Jesus Christ" (Joseph F. Smith, Dec. 20, 1914, "Address at Box Elder Stake Conference," in *Brigham City Box Elder News*, Jan. 28, 1915, pp. 1-2. This citation is also found in "Whom Say Ye That I Am?" *Family Home Evenings* [SLC: LDSC, 1972], pp. 125-126). *Family Home Evenings* is an official publication of the Church.

40. Ezra Taft Benson, "Joy in Christ," *Ensign*, Mar. 1986, p. 3, available at www.lds.org.

41. "...his unique status in the flesh as the offspring of a mortal mother and of an immortal, or resurrected and glorified, Father" (Joseph F. Smith, Anthon H. Lund, Charles Penrose, "Messages of the First Presidency," vol. 5, p. 34. Quoted in Rulon Burton, *We Believe: Doctrines and Principles of The Church of Jesus Christ of Latter-day Saints* [SLC: Tabernacle Books, 1994], p. 327).

42. Erastus Snow, Mar. 4, 1878, *JOD*, vol. 19, p. 271, emphasis added.

43. McConkie, *MD*, p. 547.

44. "[T]he paternity of Jesus is not obscure. He was the literal, biological son of an immortal, tangible Father and Mary, a mortal woman" (Andrew C. Skinner, "Jesus Christ: Birth of Jesus Christ," in Daniel H. Ludlow, vol. 2, p. 729). Jesus is "literally the Only Begotten Son of God the Father in the flesh....This title signifies that Jesus' physical body was the offspring of a mortal mother and of the eternal Father" (Gerald Hansen Jr., "Jesus Christ: Only Begotten in the Flesh," in Daniel H. Ludlow, vol. 2, p. 729).

45. Hansen, in Daniel H. Ludlow, vol. 2, p. 729; cf. the following: "That Child to be born of Mary was begotten of Elohim, the Eternal Father, not in violation of natural law but in accordance with a higher manifestation thereof; and the offspring from that association of supreme sanctity, celestial Sireship, and pure though mortal maternity, was of right to be called the 'Son of the Highest.' In His nature would be combined the powers of Godhood with the capacity and possibilities of mortality; and this through the ordinary operation of the fundamental law of heredity, declared of God, demonstrated by science, and admitted by philosophy, that living beings shall propagate—after their kind. The Child Jesus was to inherit the physical, mental, and spiritual traits, tendencies, and powers that characterized His parents—one immortal and glorified—God; the other human—woman" (Talmage, *Jesus the Christ* [SLC: Deseret Book Co., 1915; Missionary Reference Library Edition, 1990], p. 81).

46. "No man or woman can live in mortality and survive the presence of the Highest except by the sustaining power of the Holy Ghost. So it came upon her [Mary] to prepare her for admittance into the divine presence, and the power of the Highest, who is the Father, was present, and overshadowed her, and the holy Child that was born of her was called the Son of God....Men who deny this, or who think that it degrades our Father, have no true conception of the sacredness of the most marvelous power with which God has endowed mortal men—the power of creation. Even though that power may be abused and may become a mere harp of pleasure to the wicked, nevertheless it is the most sacred and holy and divine function with which God has endowed man. Made

holy it is by the Father of us all, and in his exercise of that great and marvelous creative power and function, he did not debase himself, degrade himself, nor debauch his daughter. Thus Christ became the literal Son of a divine Father, and no one else was worthy to be his father" (Melvin J. Ballard, *Sermons and Missionary Services of Melvin J. Ballard,* Bryant S. Hinckley, comp. [SLC: Deseret Book Co., 1949], p. 167, in *Teachings of the Latter-day Prophets* [SLC: LDSC, 1986], vol. 1, p. 301).

47. *Book of Mormon Gospel Doctrine Teacher's Manual 3,* available at www.lds.org.

48. McConkie, *MD,* p. 155.

49. "Richard C. Edgley, "The Condescension of God," Dec. 2001, *Ensign,* p. 16, available at www.lds.org.

50. Ezra Taft Benson, "Five Marks of the Divinity of Jesus Christ" (from a Dec. 9, 1979, fireside address), Dec. 2001, *Ensign,* p. 8, emphasis added, available at www.lds.org.

51. John K. Carmack, "United in Love and Testimony," Apr. 1, 2001, in *CR,* p. 100, available at www.lds.org.

52. Neal A. Maxwell, "Overcome…Even As I Also Overcame," *Ensign,* May 1987, p. 70, available at www.lds.org.

53. See James E. Faust, "The Atonement: Our Greatest Hope," Oct. 6, 2001, in *CR,* p. 20, available at www.lds.org; Robert D. Hales, "Fulfilling Our Duty to God," Oct. 6, 2001, in *CR,* p. 50, available at www.lds.org; Millet, in Daniel H. Ludlow, vol. 2, p. 725; and Bruce McConkie, "The Purifying Power of Gethsemane," *Ensign,* May 1985, p. 9, available at www.lds.org.

54. Cky Carrigan, "Did Jesus Christ Die on the Cross to Pay for Our Sins?: A Survey of Mormon Teachings on the Atonement of Christ," Annual Meeting of the Evangelical Ministries to New Religions, Biola University, Jan. 25, 2003.

55. Carrigan.

56. "The Resurrection is unconditional and applies to all who have ever lived and ever will live. It is a free gift" (Faust, "The Atonement," available at www.lds.org); "Because of his atonement all persons born on this earth will be resurrected" (*Gospel Principles,* p. 68); "[A]ll of us will at some time arise in the Resurrection, and beyond that there will be marvelous opportunities to go forward on the road of immortality and eternal life" ("Stand True and Faithful," May 1996, *Ensign,* p. 94); "Mormons believe there are two types of salvation made available through the atonement of Jesus Christ—universal and individual. All who receive a physical body—whether they are good or bad, evil or righteous—will be resurrected (see 1 Corinthians 15:22; Alma 11:41). This universal salvation….is a universal gift" (Robert L. Millet and Noel B. Reynolds, *Latter-day Christianity: 10 Basic Issues* [Provo, UT: FARMS, 1998], pp. 32-33, chapter 6, http://farms.byu.edu/10basics/10basicissues.php?chapter=6).

57. Millet and Reynolds, http://farms.byu.edu/10basics/10basicissues.php?chapter=7; cf. Robert D. Hales, "'What Think Ye of Christ?' 'Whom Say Ye That I Am?'" *Ensign,* May 1979, p. 77, available at www.lds.org. Hales stated, "We can have that same degree of glory—the celestial kingdom; if we are worthy."

58. Neal Maxwell, "The Glorious Atonement," Aug. 29, 1999, Missionary Training Center address, www.desnews.com/cn/talks/max820.htm.

59. *Gospel Principles*, pp. 68-69.

60. Millet and Reynolds, pp. 32-33, chapter 7, http://farms.byu.edu/10basics/10basic issues.php?chapter=7: "That is, they must willingly receive the Lord's gift, which is freely given. People must come unto him—accept him as Lord and Savior, have faith on his name, repent of sin, be baptized, receive the gift of the Holy Ghost, and strive to remain faithful to the end of their days."

61. *Gospel Principles*, p. 69; cf. "After all we can do to pay to the uttermost farthing and make right our wrongs, the Savior's grace is activated in our lives through the Atonement, which purifies us and can perfect us" (Faust, available at www.lds.org). In 1924 Rudger Clawson said, "[Jesus] was crucified for the sins of the world, for you and for me; and it is through that great sacrifice and our own good works that we will be saved, and not otherwise" (Rudger Clawson, Apr. 4, 1924, in *CR*, p. 30).

62. LDS president Howard W. Hunter made a similar comment in 1994: "Those of us who have partaken of the Atonement are under obligation to bear faithful testimony of our Lord and Savior. For he has said, 'I will forgive you of your sins with this command-ment—that you remain steadfast in your minds in solemnity and the spirit of prayer, in bearing testimony to all the world of those things which are communicated unto you'" (*The Atonement and Missionary Work* [New Mission Presidents' Seminar, June 21, 1994], p. 2, www.desnews.com/cn/talks/max820.htm; cf. Maxwell, "The Glorious Atonement," www.desnews.com/cn/talks/max820.htm).

63. The LDS Church's *Bishop's/Stake President's Manual* (1999 edition), under "Guidelines for Youth Interviews," states that members of the bishopric should express love, listen carefully, and discuss "the importance of *obeying the commandments*, particularly: 1. Praying regularly in private and with the family, studying the scriptures, honoring parents, and paying a full tithing. 2. Being modest in dress and action, refraining from any kind of sexual activity, and refraining from reading, listening to, or viewing porno-graphic material. 3. Obeying the Word of Wisdom and refraining from using illegal drugs and misusing other substances. 4. Refraining from using the name of the Lord in vain and from using vulgar expressions and other degrading language. 5. Attending priesthood and sacrament meetings, participating in other Church meetings and activ-ities and fulfilling assignments given by the priesthood quorum or Young Women class presidency" (emphasis added).

64. Boyd K. Packer, "The Touch of the Master's Hand," Mar. 31, 2001, in *CR*, p. 29, avail-able at www.lds.org. A rather odd textual change was made in the online edition of this lecture in variance from the hard copy version published by the church. The first sen-tence of the *online version* places the phrase "Then the conditions" into brackets as if it did not appear in the original lecture. In a hard copy of Packer's lecture, however, the text shows that he did indeed say the phrase "Then the conditions."

65. Robert Millet, interview in *The Mormon Puzzle* (Southern Baptist Convention, video, 1998).

66. Gilbert Scharffs, *The Missionary's Little Book of Answers* (American Fork, UT: Covenant Communications, Inc., 2002), p. 180.

67. Stephen E. Robinson, "Christ & the Trinity," in Craig L. Blomberg and Stephen E. Robinson, *How Wide The Divide?* (Downers Grove: InterVarsity Press, 1997), p. 135.

68. Robinson, in Blomberg and Robinson, p. 135.

69. Peterson and Ricks, pp. 129-131.

70. Robinson, in Blomberg and Robinson, p. 178.

71. F.F. Bruce, *The Spreading Flame* (Grand Rapids, MI: Eerdmans Publishing Co., 1958), p. 242.

72. The phrase was used for Christ by demons (Matt. 8:29; Mk. 3:11; 5:7; Lk. 4:41), believers (Matt. 16:16; Jn. 1:45,49; 11:27), and God's enemies (Matt. 27:40,43; Mt. 26:63; Lk. 22:67-70).

73. Peter Toon, *Our Triune God* (Wheaton, IL: Bridgepoint Books, 1996), pp. 160-164.

74. Everett F. Harrison, "Only Begotten," in Everett F. Harrison, Geoffrey W. Bromiley, and Carl F.H. Henry, eds., *Baker's Dictionary of Theology* (Grand Rapids, MI: Baker Book House, 1960; fifth printing, 1994), p. 386.

75. In John 1:14, far from saying that Christ is a begotten-in-the-flesh son of an immortal father, the Greek text simply translates as "we beheld the glory of him, glory as of an only begotten of a father." In other words, just as an only son is both precious and of the same nature as his father, so Christ is precious and like the one from whom he came— i.e., divine. Verse 18 reads, "God no man has seen never; [the] only begotten God the [one] being in the bosom of the Father, that one declared [him]."

76. B.B. Warfield, *Biblical Doctrines* (New York: Oxford University Press, 1929), p. 194; cf. W.E. Vine, *Vine's Expository Dictionary of New Testament Words* (McLean, VA: MacDonald Publishing Company, no date), p. 822.

77. Vine, pp. 822-823. As a highly respected Greek scholar, Vine observed, "In John 3:16... 'His Only Begotten Son,' must not be taken to mean that Christ *became* the Only Begotten Son by Incarnation.... The value and greatness of the gift lay in the Sonship of Him who was given. His Sonship was not the effect of His being given. In John 3:18...'Only Begotten Son of God' lays stress upon the full revelation of God's character and will, His love and grace, as conveyed in the Name of One who, being in a unique relation-ship to Him, was provided by Him as the Object of faith.... In 1 John 4:9...'Only Begotten Son'...does not mean that God sent out into the world one who at His birth in Bethlehem had *become* His Son [i.e., Christ already was the only begotten *before* his birth]" (emphasis added).

78. Blomberg, in Blomberg and Robinson, p. 123.

79. Robinson, in Blomberg and Robinson, p. 138.

80. Robinson, in Blomberg and Robinson, p. 138.

81. Robinson, in Blomberg and Robinson, p. 138.

82. Zodhiates, p. 364; cf. Vine, pp. 111-112.

83. Millard J. Erickson, *God in Three Persons* (Grand Rapids, MI: Baker Book House, 1995), p. 84. The two forms of the Nicene Creed read as follows:

   • (A.D. 325) We believe in one God....And in one Lord Jesus Christ, the Son of God, begotten of the Father [the only begotten, that is, of the essence of the Father, God of God], Light of Light, very God of very God, begotten, not made, being of one substance *(homoousios)* with the Father.

- (A.D. 381) We believe in one God....And in one Lord Jesus Christ, the only begotten Son of God, begotten of the Father before all worlds *(aeons),* Light of Light, very God of very God, begotten, not made, being of one substance with the Father.

84. Richard D. Draper, "The Mortal Ministry of the Saviour as Understood by the Book of Mormon Prophets," *Journal of Book of Mormon Studies* (Spring 1993), vol. 2, p. 1, http://farms.byu.edu/display.php?table=jbms&id=20. Draper stated, "The mortal Savior was not man, not human (Alma 34:10). Infinite and eternal, he received his physical life not from a son of Adam but from the Father of Adam, God. He took upon himself the image of man, but in truth he was the model, not the copy....Though not man, he experienced mortality....While in mortality the Savior was not man, not human....

"The question naturally arises: what kind of mortal being was he?... The Book of Mormon witnesses that this eternal yet mortal God was something special, something unique. He was different from all his mortal kin in that he was never man, and he was never human. The term *human,* as an adjective, describes that which relates to or is characteristic of man. Taken together, the terms seem to define that which is not yet God....

"Humankind was created in the image of God, not the other way around. Thus, the Savior appears to look like man, but in reality, it is man who looks like him. He set the pattern; man is but the copy. Thus, he is distinct, being the perfect model from which the image of humankind is derived....But the Savior, aside from his image or form, was still God....The Book of Mormon witnesses that we worship a God who can be touched with both our strivings and failures, for he was indeed tried, tempted, and in this way filled with mercy and compassion. Though he was neither man nor human but ever God, he knew mortality and loved mortals, perfectly understanding them because of his experience."

85. Robinson, in Blomberg and Robinson, pp. 138-139.

86. The purpose of these "begats" is not to show that all of Christ's ancestors were *literally* begotten. That would be redundant. Obviously they were begotten. The chain of people who begat *(egennēsen)* was a way to show Christ's legal right to Israel's throne—i.e., his legal descent (see R.V.G. Tasker, ed., *Tyndale New Testament Commentaries* [Grand Rapids, MI: Eerdmans Publishing Co., 1963; reprinted, 1981], vol. 1, pp. 32-33.

87. Robinson, in Blomberg and Robinson, p. 139.

88. Robert L. Millet, "Jesus Christ: Fatherhood and Sonship of," in Daniel H. Ludlow, vol. 2, p. 739. Evangelicals use the term "father" in a similarly figurative way, except in reference to the heavenly Father.

89. "He is the Son of the living God, the Firstborn of the Father, the Only Begotten in the flesh, who left the royal courts on high to be born as a mortal in the most humble of circumstances" (Hinckley, "We Look to Christ," available at www.lds.org). The LDS Church's *Ensign* said the verse describes Jesus as "the image of the invisible God, the firstborn of every creature" (First Presidency and the Quorum of the Twelve Apostles, "Gospel Classics: The Father and the Son," *Ensign,* Apr. 2002, p. 13, available at www.lds.org). Larry E. Dahl implied that Col. 1:15 is unclear, but that Mormons understand it correctly because "[m]odern revelation helps make it clear. To the Prophet Joseph,

the Savior said, 'I was in the beginning with the Father, and am the Firstborn'" (Larry E. Dahl, "The Morning Breaks, the Shadows Flee," *Ensign*, Apr. 1997, p. 12, available at www.lds.org).

90. F.F. Bruce, in Norman Geisler, ed., *Inerrancy* (Grand Rapids, MI: Zondervan, 1979), quoted in Norman Geisler, Francis J. Beckwith, Ron Rhodes, Phil Roberts, Jerald Tanner, and Sandra Tanner, *The Counterfeit Gospel of Mormonism* (Eugene, OR: Harvest House Publishers, 1998), p. 126.

91. Robinson, in Blomberg and Robinson, p. 138.

92. Talmage, *The Articles of Faith,* p. 89.

93. Robert P. Lightner, *Handbook of Evangelical Theology* (Grand Rapids, MI: Kregel, 1995), p. 201.

94. John 6:47 reads, "Verily, verily, I say unto you, He that believeth on me hath everlasting life."

95. Robert Millet, *Within Reach* (SLC: Deseret Book Co., 1995), p. 45.

96. Millet, *Within Reach,* p. 48.

97. Robert Millet, *Grace Works* (SLC: Deseret Books, 2003), pp. 60, 81.

98. Stephen E. Robinson, *Are Mormons Christians?* (SLC: Bookcraft, 1991), pp. 106-107.

99. According to the *LDS Bible Dictionary,* grace "is an enabling power that allows all men and women to lay hold on eternal life and exaltation after they have expended their own efforts" (*LDS Bible Dictionary,* p. 697. Quoted in Millet, *Grace Works,* p. 94).

100. Millet, *Grace Works,* p. 129; cf. the following: "[T]he gift of grace or mercy is received as a believer repents, enters into the specified covenants, and receives the Holy Ghost. This action of acceptance on our part opens the door for the *process of* justification (remission, or pardoning, of sins) and sanctification (cleansing from sin) to work in us—something we may refer to as being born again [emphasis added]" (D. Todd Christofferson, "Justification and Sanctification," *Ensign*, June 2001, p.18, available at www.lds.org).

101. Anthony A. Hoekema, "The Reformed Perspective," in Melvin E. Dieter, Anthony A. Hoekema, Stanley M. Horton, J. Robertson McQuilkin, and John F. Walvoord, *Five Views on Sanctification* (Grand Rapids, MI: Zondervan, 1987), p. 61.

102. "Justification, then, as defined by the Bible and the Book of Mormon, is the process by which guilt is taken away through faith in the atonement of Jesus Christ. Most students of the scriptures would agree with that definition. The confusion comes in understanding *how* the process of justification works" (S. Michael Wilcox, "I Have a Question," *Ensign*, June 1991, p. 51, available at www.lds.org).

103. Spencer W. Kimball, *Repentance Brings Forgiveness* (SLC: LDSC, 1984), p. 7.

104. "But how is this gift [i.e., justification] given and received?...As we come to Christ in faith, repenting of our sins, and covenant with him in the waters of baptism to keep his commandments, he justifies us—treats us as though we are guiltless—even though we are not yet perfect. He does this so that we might receive the gift of the Holy Ghost, which will cleanse us of sin as we repent and work out our salvation 'with fear and trembling.' (Philip. 2:12; see also Morm. 9:27.) As we progress from 'grace to grace,' receiving

'grace for grace' (see *D&C* 93:12-20), we will eventually be perfected and be able to stand before the Father fully justified as one who has become like him—guiltless, perfect, and holy" (Wilcox, available at www.lds.org).

105. LeGrand Richards, "Strange Creeds of Christendom," *Ensign*, Jan. 1973, p. 109, available at www.lds.org. Richards wrote, "I would like to mention one or two examples of Satan's deceptions. We hear constantly that all we have to do is to believe on the Lord Jesus Christ and we will be saved.... They think that they can all be saved just by acknowledging Jesus as the Christ. If they only understood the scriptures!"

106. Wilcox, available at www.lds.org.

107. "We also have to forsake the sin and never to repeat it not even in our minds, in order to remain forgiven we must never commit the sin again" (*Uniform Systems for Teaching Families*, pp. 35-36).

108. Spencer W. Kimball, *Miracle of Forgiveness* (SLC: Bookcraft, 1969), p. 325.

109. LDS president Spencer W. Kimball listed a minimum of five conditions that must be met for obtaining forgiveness: "[R]emember that to obtain forgiveness from the Lord and his Church one must: (1) realize the seriousness of the sin and pray in great humility and sorrow, (2) forsake the sin and not repeat it, (3) confess the sin to the bishop or other Church authority, (4) restore as far as possible that which was damaged, and (5) live all the commandments of the Lord. 'And when he has fasted enough, prayed enough, suffered enough, and when his heart is right, he may expect that forgiveness will come and with it that glorious peace that passeth understanding'" (Kimball, *Repentance Brings Forgiveness*, p. 12).

110. Russell M. Nelson, "Divine Love," *Ensign*, Feb. 2003, p. 20, available at www.lds.org.

111. Nelson, available at www.lds.org.

112. Roger Keller, "Q&A," Aug. 8, 2003, FAIR Conference, author's private notes.

113. These specific verses are mentioned in Gerald N. Lund, "Salvation: By Grace or by Works?" *Ensign*, Apr. 1981, p. 17, available at www.lds.org.

114. Gerald N. Lund explains: "[Christ's] sacrifice which pays the debt and frees us from the results of our own spiritual death, though it comes to us through the grace and goodness of God, *is not unconditional.* What, then, are the conditions? Very simply stated they are: first, faith in the Lord Jesus Christ, then repentance, followed by baptism. If one truly moves through those steps—mentally, spiritually, and physically—then he is prepared for the reception of the Holy Ghost. When one is given the *gift* (there's that word again) of the Holy Ghost, he has overcome spiritual death *to a degree....*

"The Holy Ghost's role, of course, is to help us *continue in the pre-conditions* of this part of the Atonement and fully overcome spiritual death by coming back into the presence of the Father and the Son [i.e., exaltation or eternal life]....We *are* saved by grace.... The atoning power of God unto salvation is a freely available gift from him—*but our works of righteousness are essential to bring the gift into power in our lives*" (Lund, available at www.lds.org, emphasis added).

115. D&C 76:82, 99-101, 103.

116. D&C 76:75-77, 79.

117. What is LDS godhood? "Those who obtain exaltation will gain all power and thus them-selves be omnipotent....Godhood is to have the character, possess the attributes, and enjoy the perfections which the Father has. It is to do what he does, have the powers resident in him, and live as he lives" (Bruce McConkie, *MD* [SLC: Bookcraft, 1958; rev. ed., 1966; 23rd printing, 1977], pp. 44, 32; cf. this chapter's n17.

118. George Q. Cannon noted, "Who is there that believes more in true evolution than the Latter-day Saints—The evolution of man until he shall become a God....That is the Gospel of Jesus Christ believed by the Latter-day Saints" (George Q. Cannon, in Jerrald L. Newquist, ed., *Gospel Truth* [SLC: Deseret Book Co., 1974], p. 9). "There is a pur-pose in the building of this earth and in the creation of man, that he might have a place in which to live, to perfect himself, that he might become perfect and...raise himself, with the help of his Father, to godhood" (Edward L. Kimball, ed., *The Teachings of Spencer W. Kimball* [SLC: Bookcraft, 1982], p. 31).

119. McConkie, p. 321.

120. This vision is recorded in D&C 76 and referenced in D&C 137 and 138. It allegedly took place on February 16, 1832.

121. Robinson, in Blomberg and Robinson, p. 153; cf. Millet, *The Mormon Faith*, p. 66.

122. Robertson, vol. 4, pp. 195-196.

123. D. Guthrie and J.A. Motyer, eds., *The Eerdmans Bible Commentary* (Grand Rapids, MI: Eerdmans Publishing Co., 1970; reprinted, 1989), p. 1086; cf. R.V.G. Tasker, ed., *Tyndale New Testament Commentaries* (Grand Rapids, MI: Eerdmans Publishing Co., 1963; reprinted, 1981), vol. 8, p. 171.

124. See *Matthew Henry's Commentary of the Whole Bible* (McLean, VA: MacDonald Publishing Co., 1985), vol. 6, p. 641. Quoted in Bill McKeever and Eric Johnson, *Mormonism 101* (Grand Rapids, MI: Baker Book House, 2000), pp. 301-302 n4.

125. Kimball, *Miracle of Forgiveness*, p. 16.

126. Kimball, *Miracle of Forgiveness*, pp. 208-209.

127. Roger Keller, "Q&A," Aug. 8, 2003, FAIR Conference, author's private notes.

Chapter 8: Ye Are Gods

1. W.W. Phelps, "If You Could Hie to Kolob," Hymn #257, in Emma Smith, ed. *A Collection of Sacred Hymns for The Church of Jesus Christ of Latter-day Saints* (Kirtland, OH: F.G. Williams & Co., 1835); cf. citation in Kent Nielson, "People On Other Worlds," *New Era*, April 1971, p. 12, available at www.lds.org.

2. For a look at the parallels between Mormonism and *Battlestar Galactica*, see Internet fan sites such as www.michaellorenzen.com/galactica.html.

3. This doctrine dates back to 1832, when Joseph Smith said he had a vision of these three kingdoms—telestial, terrestrial, and celestial—each having its own degrees of glory (D&C 76:70-98).

4. Lorenzo Snow, *MS*, vol. 54, p. 404. Quoted in Milton R. Hunter, *The Gospel Through the Ages* (SLC: Deseret Book Co., 1958), pp. 105-106.

5. Melvin J. Ballard, Apr. 6, 1921, in *CR*, p. 167.

6. *HC* (SLC: Deseret Book Co., 1976/1980), vol. 6, p. 306.

7. Dallin H. Oaks, "Apostasy and Restoration," *Ensign*, May 1995, p. 84, available at www.lds.org.

8. Robert L. Millet, *The Mormon Faith* (SLC: Shadow Mountain, 1998), p. 176.

9. Gordon B. Hinckley, "Don't Drop the Ball," *Ensign*, Nov. 1994, p. 46, available at www.lds.org. Spencer W. Kimball noted, "Our Heavenly Father has a plan for man's growth from infancy to godhood" (Spencer W. Kimball, "The Lord's Plan for Men and Women," *Ensign*, Oct. 1975, p. 2, available at www.lds.org).

10. John A. Widtsoe, ed., *Discourses of Brigham Young* (SLC: Deseret Book Co., 1954), p. 50.

11. "Man is the child of God, formed in the divine image and endowed with divine attributes, and even as the infant son of an earthly father and mother is capable in due time of becoming a man, so the undeveloped offspring of celestial parentage is capable, by experience through ages and aeons, of evolving into a God" (First Presidency of the Church of Jesus Christ of Latter-day Saints [Joseph F. Smith, John R. Winder, Anthon H. Lund], *Improvement Era*, Nov. 1909, vol. 8, no. 1).

12. K. Codell Carter, "Godhood," in Daniel H. Ludlow, *Encyclopedia of Mormonism* (New York: Macmillan Publishing Co., 1992), vol. 2, p. 553. Carter stated that "the ultimate desire of a loving Supreme Being is to help his children enjoy all that he enjoys. For Latter-day Saints, the term 'godhood' denotes the attainment of such a state—one of having all divine attributes and doing as God does and being as God is. Such a state is to be enjoyed by all exalted, embodied, intelligent beings (see Deification; Eternal Progression; Exaltation; God; Perfection)....[A]ll resurrected and perfected mortals become gods." Cf. Robert L. Millet's statement: "[God] wants his children to become and be all that he is. Godhood comes through overcoming the world through the Atonement" ("What We Believe," Feb. 3, 1998, BYU devotional, http://speeches.byu .edu/htmlfiles/MilletW98.html).

13. W. John Walsh, undated statement, in "Biblical Support for Deification," www.light planet.com/mormons/response/qa/godhood.htm#wjw.

14. Walsh, www.lightplanet.com/mormons/response/qa/godhood.htm#wjw.

15. Walsh, www.lightplanet.com/mormons/response/qa/godhood.htm#wjw.

16. Millet, BYU devotional, www.speeches.byu.edu/devo/97-98/MilletW98.html.

17. Mark D. Ellison, "CES Conference Handout 2002" (CES conference on the Doctrine and Covenants and Church History at BYU), www.ldsces.org/cesconference/2002/ CesConference2002.htm.

18. W.E. Vine, *Vine's Expository Dictionary of New Testament Words* (McLean, VA: MacDonald Publishing Co., no date), pp. 551-552.

19. Vine, p. 493.

20. Spiros Zodhiates, gen. ed., *The Complete Word Study Dictionary* (Chattanooga, TN: AMG Publishers, 1992, rev. ed., 1993), p. 478.

21. Marilyn S. Bateman, "Evolution of the Mind, the Heart, and the Soul," Sept. 7, 1999, devotional address, http://speeches.byu.edu/htmlfiles/MSBatemanF99.html.

22. Ellison, see this chapter's n22 for Internet availability.

23. Millet, BYU devotional, www.speeches.byu.edu/devo/97-98/MilletW98.html.

24. Gordon B. Hinckley, "Strengthening Each Other," *Ensign*, Feb. 1985, p. 3, available at www.lds.org.

25. Boyd K. Packer, "The Pattern of Our Parentage," *Ensign*, Nov. 1984, p. 66, available at www.lds.org.

26. Shandon L. Guthrie, "A Discussion on Mormonism," www.sguthrie.net/MORMON IS.htm.

27. Keith E. Norman, "Deification, Early Christian," in Ludlow, vol. 1, p. 369.

28. Stephen E. Robinson, *Are Mormons Christians?* (SLC: Bookcraft, 1991), pp. 62-63.

29. Daniel C. Peterson and Stephen D. Ricks, "Comparing LDS Beliefs with First-Century Christianity," *Ensign*, Mar. 1988, p. 7, available at www.lds.org.

30. Nathan K.K. Ng, "A Reconsideration of the Use of the Term 'Deification' in St. Athanasius," *Coptic Church Review* (2001), vol. 22, no. 2, p. 9, http://216.239.41.104/ search?q=cache:NcvZngbiE8kJ:home.ptd.net/~yanney/Deification_in_St_Athansius.pdf +Athansius+%22Nathan+K.K.+Ng%22&hl=en&ie=UTF-8.

31. Ng, p. 9, see this chapter's n30 for Internet availability. Ng cites the original French version of Jules Gross, *La Divinisation du Chrétien d'après les pères grecs* (Paris, 1938), p. 349. This work was translated into English by Paul A. Onica, *The Divinization of the Christian According to the Greek Fathers* (Anaheim, CA: A&C Press, 2003).

32. Ng, p. 9, see this chapter's n30 for Internet availability.

33. Ng, p. 10, see this chapter's n30 for Internet availability.

34. Ng, p. 10, see this chapter's n30 for Internet availability.

35. Athanasius, *On the Incarnation of the Word*, in Philip Schaff and Henry Wace, eds., *A Select Library of Nicene and Post-Nicene Fathers* (Grand Rapids, MI: Eerdmans Publishing Co., 1991), vol. 4, p. 65.

36. Irenaeus, *Irenaeus Against Heresies*, Book IV, chapter 38, in Alexander Roberts and James Donaldson, eds., *The Ante-Nicene Fathers* (Grand Rapids, MI: Eerdmans Publishing Co., 1993), vol. 1, p. 522.

37. Justin Martyr, *The First Apology of Justin*, in Roberts and Donaldson, vol. 1, p. 170.

38. Tertullian, *Against Hermogenes*, chapter 5, in Roberts and Donaldson, vol. 3, p. 480.

39. See Georgios I. Mantzaridis, *The Deification of Man: St. Gregory Palamas and the Orthodox Tradition*, tr. Liadain Sherrard, Contemporary Greek Theologian Series, no. 2 (New York: St. Vladimir's Seminary Press, 2001), p. 127. Cited in D. Richard Stuckwisch, "Justification and Deification in the Dialogue Between the Tübingen Theologians and Patriarch Jeremias II: A Research Report Submitted to Dr. Alan W. Borcherding In Partial Fulfillment of the Requirements for Sacred Theology Credit 'The Methodology of Systematic Theology'" (Fall 1993), revised and expanded for presentation to the faculty of Concordia Theological Seminary (Fort Wayne, IN: 1994), www.angelfire.com/ ny4/djw/lutherantheology.stuckwisch. html.

40. Ng, p. 2. Referencing D.L. Balás, "Divinization," in E. Ferguson, ed., *Encyclopedia of Early Christianity* (New York: Garland, 1997; 2nd ed.), vol. 1, p. 338.

41. Ng, p. 5; cf. William Ralph Inge, *Christian Mysticism* (London, 1899), p. 13.

42. B. Drewery, "Deification," in Peter Brooks, ed., *Christian Spirituality* (London: S.C.M. Press, 1975), pp. 54-55. Quoted in Ng, p. 8; see this chapter's n37 for Internet availability.

43. Athanasius, *Defense of the Nicene Definition*, in Schaff and Wace, vol. 4, p. 159.

44. Panayiotis Nellis, *Deification in Christ*, tr. N. Russell (New York: St. Vladimir's Seminary Press, 1987), pp. 121-139. Cited in Ng, p. 5.

45. Ng, p. 6, see this chapter's n30 for Internet availability.

46. "Theosis," *The Oxford Dictionary of Byzantium*, Alexander P. Kazhdan, et al., eds. (New York: Oxford University Press, 1991), p. 2069. Quoted in Stuckwisch, www.angelfire.com/ny4/djw/lutherantheology.stuckwisch.html.

47. Ng, p. 8; see this chapter's n30 for Internet availability.

48. For Roman Catholic views on this same subject, see Carmen Fragapane, "Called to be Children of God," www.orthodoxinfo.com/inquirers/frag_salv.htm; and Carl Olson, "Salvation by Christ," www.catholic.net/rcc/Periodicals/Faith/2001-6/anthropolgy.html.

49. Robert M. Bowman Jr., "Ye are Gods? Orthodox and Heretical Views on the Deification of Man," *Christian Research Journal* (Winter/Spring 1987), p. 18.

50. Cf. the following statements:

  • "[*Theosis*, deification] does not mean, as it may appear on the surface, that humanity shares in the essence of God. Human persons do not become God. Rather, because the work of Christ destroys the powers of evil, we are freed from those powers and able to come into fellowship with God....His redeemed creatures have been given the benefits and privileges of divinity through grace. The state of grace is seen as a state of communion with God, fellowship with the Trinity, a partaking of the divine" (Alan F. Johnson and Robert Webber, *What Christians Believe* [Grand Rapids, MI: Zondervan, 1993], p. 303).

  • We Christians have the promise of participating in the divine nature....Not only Eastern Orthodox but also Western theologians find solace in a sense of deification. Such restoration does not mean that we become God as the Father, Son and Holy Spirit are God. Our participation in the divine nature is in God's energies, not the essence, a participation through grace accepted in faith which includes being participants in Christ's sufferings" (F.W. Norris, "Deification: Consensual and Cogent," in *Scottish Journal of Theology* [1996], vol. 9, no. 4, p. 428).

  • "Deification (Greek *theosis*) is for Orthodoxy the goal of every Christian.... [Deification] is the whole human being, body and soul, who is transfigured in the Spirit into the likeness of the divine nature, and deification is the goal of every Christian" (Symeon Lash, "Deification," in Alan Richardson and John Bowden, eds., *The Westminster Dictionary of Christian Theology* [Philadelphia: Westminster Press, 1983], pp. 147-148).

51. *Catechism of the Catholic Church,* 1988, quoting *Athanasius,* www.usccb.org/cate chism/text/pt3sect1chpt3art2.htm. Pope Paul II himself positively referred to this subject in his May 27, 1998, General Audience titled "Spirit Enables Us to Share in Divine Nature": "The Holy Spirit's direct intervention in the Incarnation brings about the supreme grace, the 'grace of union,' in which human nature is united to the Person of the Word. This union is the source of every other grace, as St. Thomas explains" (Pope John Paul II, "Spirit Enables Us to Share in Divine Nature," May 27, 1998, www.stjo milton.org/resources/audience,htm#Spirit%20Enables%20Us%20to%20Share%20in%2 0Divine%20Nature, and at the Catholic Information Network, www.cin.org/jp2/ jp980527.html).

Roman Catholic deacon Keith Fournier commented on this issue in 2003: "The spiritual life is about an invitation to a song, a dance, an intimate, dynamic, growing, living, breathing, transforming relationship of love that has existed for all eternity in God. We are transformed by grace so that we become 'sons (and daughters) in the Son.' Many of the greatest of the early Church Fathers, such as Irenaeus and Athanasius, wrote eloquently of this 'participation' in the life of the Trinity through Jesus Christ. This participation of human beings in the very life of the Trinity through incorporation into Christ is often expressed in the famous patristic adage 'God became man that man may become God.' In the Eastern Christian tradition this exchange is referred to by the term 'deification' or 'theosis.' Understandably, without solid theological and spiritual grounding, it could be misunderstood. Perhaps, that is a part of the reason the terminology fell out of use in Western Christianity after the unfortunate 'divorce' that occurred within the One Church in 1054 A.D." (Keith A. Fournier, "The Trinity: Living In The Family Of God," *Catholic Online,* June 15, 2003, www.catholic.org/featured/head line.php?ID=258).

52. David Waltz is a regular poster to ZLMB. Before calling himself a Roman Catholic, Waltz stated: "I am a non-denominational Christian who is trying to determine which of the 28,000 plus denominations that call themselves Christian best represents Christianity in its highest form" (David Waltz, "Restoration," Nov. 1, 2000, Internet post at ZLMB).

53. David Waltz, "A New Look at Historic Christianity," *FARMS Review of Books,* vol. 12, no. 2, http://farms.byu.edu/display.php?table=review&id=361.

54. For example, in various posts at ZLMB, Waltz has presented deification quotes by early church fathers in support of the LDS doctrine of deification. He also has posted several statements by modern Catholic writers, whose remarks about being a partaker of the divine nature he interprets to mean that the LDS brand of deification can be accommodated (David Waltz, July 30, 2003, Internet post #1584 at ZLMB. Waltz cited G.H. Joyce, *The Catholic Doctrine of Grace* [London: 1920, pp. 34,35]; Matthias Joseph Scheeben, *The Mysteries of Christianity* [B. Herder Book Co.: St. Louis, n.d.], pp. 615,616,617,619; John Paul II, "Jesus, Son and Savior" [1996], General Audience of Sept, 2, 1987). None of these writers, however, were advancing the LDS deification.

55. David Waltz, "DeMura's Claim that Peterson Decontextualizes ECF," Oct. 24, 2000, Internet post #32 at ZLMB.

56. Daniel C. Peterson and Stephen D. Ricks, *Offenders for a Word* (SLC, UT: Aspen Books, 1992), p. 76.

57. Daniel Peterson, "DeMura's Claim that Peterson Decontextualizes ECF," Oct. 24, 2000, Internet post #18 at ZLMB.

58. Millet, *The Mormon Faith*, p. 175.

59. Barry Bickmore, "No, Really—Gods!" www.geocities.com/Athens/Parthenon/2671/realgod.html.

60. Waltz, "DeMura's Claim."

61. Pacumeni, "DeMura's Claim that Peterson Decontextualizes ECF," Oct. 25, 2000, Internet post #93 at ZLMB.

62. Irenaeus, Book III, chapter 19, in Roberts and Donaldson, vol. 1, p. 448. Irenaeus said, "He who was the Son of God became the Son of man, that man, having been taken into the Word, and receiving the adoption, might become the son of God. For by no other means could we have attained to incorruptibility and immortality, unless we had been united to incorruptibility and immortality." Irenaeus also explained, "[I]t was necessary, at first, that nature should be exhibited; then, after that, that what was mortal should be conquered and swallowed up by immortality, and the corruptible by incorruptibility, and that man should be made after the image and likeness of God, having received the knowledge of good and evil" (Book IV, in Roberts and Donaldson, vol. 1, p. 522).

63. "The concept of Deification was eventually articulated most precisely by Gregory Palamas in the fourteenth century….In his development of the doctrine of Deification, it was also necessary for Gregory to articulate and clarify a distinction between God's *essence* and His *energy*. By doing so, he was able to preserve the transcendence of God…while also supporting the participation of man with God in Christ. He showed that there is a real distinction in God between essence and energy; yet, both are uncreated. This distinction does not introduce any 'complexity' in God, since it is not a question of two essential realities; both the essence and the energy belong to the one God. But while the essence remains incommunicable (outside of the Godhead), there is a 'real and existential revelation of the divine life or *energy*' (Meyendorff, *Palamas*: p. 98).

"Gregory was able to make such a distinction, because Eastern theology identifies the source of the Godhead *hypostatically*, in the Person of the Father, instead of in the abstract 'divine Essence.' The essence and the energy of God each has its source in the concrete reality of Father, Son, and Spirit. Thus, God remains transcendent in His essence, even while man is deified in Christ through communion with the divine energy, which Gregory identifies with the grace of God" (Stuckwisch, www.angelfire.com/ny4/djw/lutherantheology.stuckwisch.html).

64. • *Option #1*—"When one considers the evidence that has been presented, the honest reader must ask how on earth could an 'Orthodox' Christian claim that a belief in human deification is not biblical. Informed Bible scholars today agree that the scriptures discussed above do support the concept of deification and the Early Church Fathers interpreted these same scriptures as evidence for this belief" (Kevin Graham, "Godlike: To Be or not to Be?," www.anti-mormonism-revealed.com/theosis.htm; cf. the remainder of the article for Graham's abuse of quotes from several early church fathers).

- *Option #2*—"[I]t is my considered judgment that the resemblances between the ancient Christian view and the Latter-day Saint view far outweigh the differences between them....One can extrapolate here, quite plausibly and on the basis of certain highly suggestive data, to an earlier stage of the doctrine of theosis. I believe—and, though I cannot perhaps prove it to the satisfaction of resolute and hostile skeptics, can adduce evidence to support my belief—that the earlier, relatively un-Hellenized Christians of the original church, and the Hebrews on whose foundation they built, held to a view of human deification much more close to that of the Latter-day Saints than was the teaching of Athanasius" (Peterson, Internet post #18 at ZLMB).

65. Richard John Neuhaus, "Is Mormonism Christian? A Respected Advocate for Inter-religious Cooperation Responds," 2000, www.irr.org/mit/neuhaus.html.

66. Neuhaus, www.irr.org/mit/neuhaus.html.

67. Merrill J. Bateman, "Christ Is the Reason," Jan 16, 2001, BYU devotional, http://speeches.byu.edu/htmlfiles/BatemanW01.html.

68. In 1992, David Knowlton noted, "Not surprisingly, Mormonism does focus tremendous attention on gender and sexuality. To become Gods—i.e., to attain exaltation—Mormon thought requires that man and woman be united through marriage" (David Knowlton, "On Mormon Masculinity," *Sunstone* [Aug. 1992], vol. 16, no. 2, p. 22).

69. Angel Abrea, "A Divine Nature and Destiny," June 15, 1999, BYU devotional, http://speeches.byu.edu/htmlfiles/AbreaSu99.html. Angel Abrea is a member of the First Quorum of the Seventy. Calfred B. Broderick, an LDS child development specialist, has noted that "the eternal preservation of reproductive sexuality is the central, distinguishing characteristic differentiating the exalted from the merely saved" (Calfred B. Broderick, "Three Philosophies of Sex, Plus One," *Dialogue: A Journal of Mormon Thought* [Autumn 1967], vol. 2, no. 3, p. 101).

70. Carter, in Ludlow, vol. 2, p. 553.

71. B.H. Roberts, *The Mormon Doctrine of Deity* (Bountiful, UT: Horizon Publishers; reprint, 1976, originally published in 1903), pp. 276-284.

72. George Q. Cannon, Oct. 31, 1880, in *JOD*, vol. 22, p. 125. Bruce McConkie said, "[E]ternal life consists of two things: (1) the continuation of the family unit in eternity, which means a continuation of the seeds or the everlasting begetting of children; and (2) the receipt of the fulness of the glory of the Father, which is all power in heaven and on earth" (Bruce R. McConkie, *The Millennial Messiah* [SLC: Deseret Book Co., 1982], p. 708).

    Cf. the following: "Joseph Smith explained that this continuation of 'the seeds' forever and ever, meant the power of procreation; in other words, the power to beget spirit children on the same principle as we were born to our Heavenly Parents, God the Eternal Father and our Eternal Mother. Therefore, a man cannot receive the highest exaltation without a woman, his wife, nor can a woman be exalted without her husband" (Milton R. Hunter, Apr. 4, 1949, in *CR*, p. 71).

Chapter 9: More Than One Wife

1. Gordon B. Hinckley, "Daughters of God," *Ensign*, Nov. 1991, p. 97, available at www.lds.org.

2. See Christopher Smith, "LDS Couple's Book Takes on Polygamy Shame," *Salt Lake Tribune*, July 15, 2002, www.sltrib.com (archives).

3. Mark Shaffer, "Teens Flee Polygamist Towns," *Arizona Republic*, Jan. 19, 2004, www.azcentral.com/families/articles/0120fam_polygamy.html.

4. Angie Welling, "Polygamy Ban Contested," *Deseret Morning News*, Jan. 13, 2004, www.deseretnews.com/dn/view/0,1249,585037355,00.html.

5. "Polygamy a factor in marriage debates," Mar. 29, 2004, www.religionwriters.com/public/tips/032904/032904b.shtml.

6. Jeff Jacoby, "Is Lawful Polygamy Next?" Jan. 16, 2004, www.townhall.com/columnists/jeffjacoby/jj20040116.shtml.

7. Melodie Moench Charles, "The Need for a New Mormon Heaven," *Dialogue: A Journal of Mormon Thought* (Fall 1988), vol. 21, no. 3, pp. 77-80.

8. Charles, pp. 79-80. Although Charles provided several references for her assertion, this aspect of LDS life is extremely difficult to document. It seems to be something that is felt more than taught; more of a mindset than a clearly articulated doctrinal position.

9. Robert L. Millet, "Joseph Smith and the New Testament," *Ensign*, Dec. 1986, p. 28, available at www.lds.org. Millet stated, "In a revelation recorded on 12 July 1843, the Lord explained that unless a marriage is sealed by the power of the holy priesthood, the marriage ends with death. If it is sealed, however, men and women might eventually qualify for eternal lives—the everlasting continuation of the family unit (see *D&C* 132:1-25)."

10. Charles, pp. 77-78.

11. Stephen E. Robinson, *Are Mormons Christian?* (SLC: Bookcraft. 1991), p. 92.

12. "[Polygamy] was not something the Prophet and others wanted to do; there is sufficient historical evidence that Joseph procrastinated the teaching of the principle to the generality of the Church for many years, until, according to several sources, he was instructed that if he did not do so he would be punished by God" (Robert Millet, *The Mormon Faith* [SLC: Shadow Mountain, 1998], p. 172).

13. Mary Elizabeth Rollins Lightner, "The Testimony of Mary Elizabeth Rollins Lightner," Apr. 14, 1905, stored at BYU Archives and Manuscripts, www.ldshistory.net/pc/merlbyu.htm. Lightner, who was sealed to Joseph Smith in 1842, stated, "An angel came to him and the last time he came with a drawn sword in his hand and told Joseph if he did not go into that principle, he would slay him." This story about a sword-wielding angel appears in many LDS sources (Joseph F. Smith, July 7, 1878, in *JOD*, vol. 20, pp. 28-29; and Lorenzo R. Snow, affidavit, quoted in "The Celestial Principle of Marriage," www.mormons.org.uk/celest.htm). For more information, see Todd Compton, *In Sacred Loneliness* (SLC: Signature Books, 1997), pp. 80-81; cf. Roger D. Launius and John E. Hallwas, *Kingdom on the Mississippi Revisited* (Urbana, IL: University of Illinois Press, 1996), p. 49.

14. "A Sketch in the Life of Nancy Naomi Tracy," n.d., p. 20. Quoted in George D. Smith, "Nauvoo Roots of Mormon Polygamy, 1841-46: A Preliminary Demographic Report," *Dialogue: A Journal of Mormon Thought* (Spring 1994), vol. 27, no. 1, p. 26.

15. Andrew Jenson, an assistant LDS church historian, said Alger was "one of the first plural wives sealed to the Prophet" (Andrew Jenson, "Plural Marriage," *HR*, May 1887, vol. 6,

nos. 3-5, p. 233; cf. John A. Widtsoe, *Joseph Smith—Seeker After Truth* [SLC: Deseret News, 1951], p. 237).

16. Compton, p. 34. After Emma's discovery, Fanny was forced to live with neighbors.

17. D&C CI:4 (1835 edition), p. 251. Of course, when the D&C was republished in 1876 (many years after polygamy had become a tenet of Mormonism), the 1835 denunciation of polygamy was expunged. It read as follows: "Inasmuch as this church of Christ has been reproached with the crime of fornication, and polygamy: we declare that we believe, that one man should have one wife; and one woman, but one husband, except in the case of death, when either is at liberty to marry again."

18. Richard S. Van Wagoner, *Mormon Polygamy: A History* (SLC: Signature Books, 1989), pp. 51-54, 59-60.

19. D&C 132:52.

20. Brigham Young, Feb. 4, 1851. Cited by Wilford Woodruff, in Scott G. Kenney, ed., *Wilford Woodruff's Journal* (Midvale, UT: Signature Books, 1983), under Feb. 4, 1851, vol. 4, p. 12.

21. U.S. Army officer John Gunnison observed that many LDS men had "a large number of wives" and that polygamy was "perfectly manifest to anyone residing long among them" (John W. Gunnison, *The Mormons or the Latter-day Saints, in the Valley of the Great Salt Lake* [London: Sampson, Low, Son, & Co., 1852], p. 67, www.olivercow dery.com/smithhome/1852GunB.htm#pg066a).

22. See Richard Abanes, *One Nation Under Gods: A History of the Mormon Church* (New York: Four Walls Eight Windows, 2002; paperback ed., 2003), pp. 281-328.

23. Abanes, pp. 311-328.

24. Shane LeGrande Whelan, *More Than One* (Bountiful, UT: Zion Publishers, 2001; rev. ed., 2002), p. 208. This aspect of *current* LDS teachings has been part of Mormon belief for many years, as evidenced by the words of well-known LDS apostle Charles W. Penrose: "In the case of a man marrying a wife in the everlasting covenant who dies while he continues in the flesh and marries another by the same divine law, each wife will come forth in her order and enter with him into his glory" (Charles W. Penrose, *Mormon Doctrine, Plain and Simple, or Leaves from the Tree of Life* [SLC: Juvenile Instructor Office, 1897], p. 66).

25. Bruce R. McConkie, *MD* (SLC: Bookcraft, 1958; rev. ed., 1966; 23rd printing, 1977), p. 238.

26. Joseph Fielding Smith, *Doctrines of Salvation* (SLC: Bookcraft, 1955), vol. 2, p. 67.

27. John J. Stewart, *Brigham Young and His Wives and the True Story of Plural Marriage* (SLC: Mercury Publishing Co., 1961), p. 41. Quoted in "The Gods of Mormonism," *Salt Lake City Messenger* (#87), Nov. 1994, www.utlm.org/newsletters/no87.htm.

28. Harold B. Lee, in *1974 Church Almanac* (SLC: Deseret News, 1974), p. 17.

29. Michael W. Hickenbotham, *Answering Challenging Mormon Questions* (Bountiful, UT: Horizon Publishers, 1995; 3rd printing, 1999), p. 61.

30. Gordon B. Hinckley, "What Are People Asking about Us?" *Ensign*, Nov. 1998, p. 70, available at www.lds.org.

31. William Clayton. Quoted in Jenson, p. 226.

32. Orson Pratt, Aug. 29, 1852, in *JOD*, vol. 1, p. 54.

33. William Clayton, in Robert C. Fillerup, comp., *William Clayton's Nauvoo Diaries and Personal Writings*, under Mar. 9, 1843, original in LDSCA, www.code-co.com/rcf/mhistdoc/clayton.htm.

34. Jan Shipps, "The Mormons in Politics: The First Hundred Years," Ph.D. diss., University of Colorado, 1965, p. 134. Cited in B. Carmon Hardy, *Solemn Covenant: The Mormon Polygamous Passage* (Urbana, IL: University of Illinois Press, 1992), p. 9.

35. Peter Wood, "Sex & Consequences," *The American Conservative*, July 28, 2003, www.amconmag.com/07_28_03/cover.html.

36. Wood, www.amconmag.com/07_28_03/cover.html.

37. Wood, www.amconmag.com/07_28_03/cover.html.

38. Fanny Stenhouse, *Tell It All* (Hartford, CT: A.D. Worthington and Co., 1875), pp. 468-469.

39. Stenhouse, p. 469.

40. Ann Eliza Young, *Wife Number 19* (Hartford, CT: Dustin, Gilman & Co., 1875), chapter 18, www.antimormon.8m.com/youngchp18.html.

41. Jay Deuel, "Brigham Young and Mormon Polygamy," www.cc.utah.edu/~jay/Brigham_Young/Brigham_Young.html; cf. Jeffery Ogden Johnson, "Determining and Defining 'Wife': The Brigham Young Households," *Dialogue: A Journal of Mormon Thought* (Fall 1987), vol. 20, no. 3, p. 64.

42. "You are sent out as shepherds to gather the sheep together; and remember that they are not your sheep: they belong to Him that sends you. Then do not make a choice of any of those sheep; do not make selections before they are brought home and put into the fold" (Heber C. Kimball, Aug. 28, 1852, in *JOD*, vol. 6, p. 256).

43. Heber C. Kimball. Quoted in Stanley P. Hirshon, *The Lion of the Lord* (New York: Alfred A. Knopf, 1969), pp. 129-130.

44. Ann Eliza Young, chapter 19, www.antimormon.8m.com/youngchp19.html.

45. LDS scholar and researcher Richard S. Van Wagoner has noted, "Pressures to live polygamously, however, were compelling to Mormon males desirous of advancement in church position. Apostle John Taylor was told by Joseph Smith to take a second wife, and when Taylor hesitated, Smith spelled out the consequences of failure to enter polygamy: 'Elder Taylor, have you concluded to enter into that principle and observe the counsel that you have received?' I told him I was thinking about it very seriously, when he replied, 'Unless that principle is observed and acted upon, you can proceed no further with the full fellowship of God.'...In 1875 Apostle Wilford Woodruff announced, 'We have many bishops and elders who have but one wife. They are abundantly qualified to enter the higher law and take more, but their wives will not let them. Any man who permits a woman to lead him and bind him down is but little account in the church and Kingdom of God'" (Van Wagoner, p. 97).

46. Ann Eliza Young, chapter 18, www.antimormon.8m.com/youngchp18.html. Two sets of Brigham's spouses were sisters (Clara and Lucy Decker and Mary and Lucy Bigelow),

while eight of his daughters shared husbands: Luna and Fanny were wed to George Thatcher; Mary and Caroline were given to Mark Croxall; Alice and Emily married Hiram Clawson; and Polly and Lovina were sealed to John D. Lee. Heber C. Kimball married five sets of sisters (Clarissa and Emily Cutler; Amanda and Anna Gheen; Harriet and Ellen Sanders; Hannah and Dorothy Moon; and Laura and Abigail Pitkin).

LDS leadership had no problem with near relatives marrying. Joseph Smith's own diary, under Oct. 26, 1843, records the sealing for eternity of John Bernhisel to his sister, Maria. Smith also sealed Bernhisel to four of his aunts and two cousins (Scott H. Faulring, ed., *An American Prophet's Record: The Diaries and Journals of Joseph Smith* [SLC: Signature Books,1987], p. 424).

Ann Eliza Young's recollections are further supported by many historical documents: "Polygamy introduces many curious cross-relationships, and intertwines that branches of the genealogical tree in a manner greatly to puzzle a mathematician, as well as to disgust the decent-minded. The marrying of two or more sisters is very common; one young Mormon merchant in Salt Lake City has three sisters....There are several cases of men marrying both mother (widow) and her daughter or daughters; taking the 'old woman' for the sake of getting the young ones" (Samuel Bowles, *Across the Continent: A Summer's Journey to the Rocky Mountains, the Mormons, and the Pacific States* [Springfield, MA: Samuel Bowles & Co., 1865], p. 123); "Many families, perhaps as many as 10% of the polygamous population, included two or more sisters as plural wives to one man" (Stanley S. Ivins, "Notes On Mormon Polygamy," quoted in D. Michael Quinn, *The New Mormon History* [SLC: Signature Books, 1992], p. 175).

To Brigham Young, incestuous marriages were no problem since all people were brothers and sisters born to Heavenly Father. He commented, "I believe in sisters marrying brothers, and brothers having their sisters for wives....This is something pertaining to our marriage relation. The whole world will think what an awful thing it is. What an awful thing it would be if the Mormons should just say we believe in marrying brothers and sisters" (Brigham Young, Oct. 8, 1854, in Fred C. Collier, ed., *The Teachings of President Brigham Young* [SLC: Collier's Publishing Co., 1987], vol. 3, pp. 362,368).

47. See J.W. Musser, "The New And Everlasting Covenant Of Marriage: An Interpretation Of Celestial Marriage, Plural Marriage, Polygamy," www.mormons.org. uk/New_Ever lasting_Covenant.htm.

48. Brigham Young, Aug. 19, 1866, in *JOD*, vol. 11, p. 269.

49. Young, in *JOD*, vol. 11, p. 268.

50. U.S. Congress, "Memorial Adopted by Citizens of Salt Lake City, Utah Territory," 41st Cong., 2nd Sess., Senate Misc. Document No. 12, Serial 1408, p. 1.

51. Kevinchill, "Official Doctrine???," Mar. 29, 2004, Internet post #2919 at ZLMB.

52. Wilford Woodruff, in Kenney, *Wilford Woodruff's Journal*, under Jan. 26, 1880, vol. 7, pp. 617, 621. This revelation was accepted as God's word by John Taylor and the Quorum of the Twelve. It stated, "And I say again wo[e] unto that Nation or House or people who seek to hinder my People from obeying the Patriarchal Law of Abraham which leadeth to a Celestial Glory...for whosoever doeth those things shall be damned Saith the Lord of Hosts." Ironically, this condemnation would eventually pertain to Woodruff himself.

53. Petition for Amnesty, Dec. 19, 1891. Reprinted in *Proceedings* (Washington, D.C.: Government Printing Office, 1904), vol. 1, p. 18.

54. "Now, sisters, do not say, 'I don't want a husband when I get up in the resurrection.' You do not know what you want....If in the resurrection you really want to be single and alone and live so forever and ever and be made servants, while others receive the higher order of intelligence and are bringing worlds into existence, you can have the privilege. They who will be exalted cannot perform all the labor, they must have servants and you can be servants to them" (Brigham Young, Aug. 31, 1873, in *JOD*, vol. 16, p. 167).

55. Brigham Young stated, "Why do we believe in and practice polygamy? Because the Lord introduced it to his servants in a revelation given to Joseph Smith, and the Lord's servants have always practiced it.... [T]his is the religion of Abraham, and, unless we do the works of Abraham, we are not Abraham's seed and heirs according to promise" (Brigham Young, July 6, 1862, in *JOD*, vol. 9, p. 322.

56. "[I]n a meeting of the First Presidency and Quorum of the Twelve, [John] Taylor related that Joseph Smith had once said to him, 'If we do not keep the same law that Our Heavenly Father has we cannot go with him....A man obeying a lower law is not qualified to preside over those who keep a higher law' " (Van Wagoner, p. 97. This citation is taken from the *Journals of Wilford Woodruff*, under Oct. 10, 1882).

57. N.B. Lundwall, comp., *Inspired Prophetic Warnings* (SLC: author, 1940), p. 117. Brigham Young gave this warning: "Now, where a man in this church says, 'I don't want but one wife, I will live my religion with one,' he will perhaps be saved in the Celestial kingdom; but when he gets there he will not find himself in possession of any wife at all. He has had a talent that he has hid up. He will come forward and say, 'Here is that which thou gavest me, I have not wasted it, and here is the one talent,' and he will not enjoy it but it will be taken and given to those who have improved the talents they received, and he will find himself without any wife, and he will remain single forever and ever" (Brigham Young, Aug. 31, 1873, in *JOD*, vol. 16, p. 166; cf. *Deseret News*, Sept. 17, 1873).

    Francis M. Lyman, president of the Quorum of the Twelve, remarked in 1883, "Celestial marriage is for the fulness of the glory of God. It is the crowning glory. a man has no right to one wife unless he is worthy of two....[T]here is no provision made for those who have had the chance & oppertunity [sic] and have disregarded that law. Men who disregard that law are in the same situation as if they broke any other law. they are transgressors" (Van Wagoner, p. 97).

58. Brigham Young. Quoted by Wilford Woodruff, in Kenney, *Wilford Woodruff's Journal*, under Aug. 31, 1873, vol. 7, p. 152.

59. H.R., letter to Editor [of the *Boston Bee*], reprinted in *T&S*, Mar. 15, 1843, vol. 4, no. 9, p. 143: "We are charged with advocating a plurality of wives....[T]his is as false as the many other ridiculous charges which are brought against us. No sect has a greater reverence for the laws of matrimony or the rights of private property; and we do what others do not, practice what we preach."

60. "To Our Readers," *MS&AD*, May 1837, vol. 3, no. 8, p. 511, www.centerplace.org/history/ma/v3n08.htm.

61. Ebenezer Robinson, letter to Jason W. Briggs, Jan. 28, 1880, LDSCA. On Dec. 29, 1873, Ebenezer and Angeline Robinson signed an affidavit saying that Hyrum Smith had come to their house in the fall of 1843 to teach them the doctrine of polygamy and that he had been wrong to oppose it.

62. Ebenezer Robinson, see previous note.

63. Historian George D. Smith related how Joseph resorted to this tactic during his marriage to 17-year-old Sarah Ann Whitney: "She disguised her relationship to the prophet by pretending to marry Joseph Corodon Kingsbury....Kingsbury wrote: 'I according to Pres. Joseph Smith & Council & others agreed to stand by Sarah Ann Whitney as though I was supposed to be her husband and [participated in] a pretended marriage for the purpose of...[b]ringing about the purposes of God in these last days...' Three weeks later, while in hiding, Joseph Smith wrote a revealing letter which he addressed to her parents...inviting them to bring their daughter to visit him 'just back of Brother Hyrums farm.' He advised Brother Whitney to 'come a little a head and nock [sic] at the south East corner of the house at the window.' He assured them, especially Sarah Ann, that 'it is the will of God that you should comfort me now.' He stressed the need for care 'to find out when Emma comes,' but 'when she is not here, there is the most perfect safty [sic].' The prophet warned them to 'burn this letter as soon as you read it'" (George D. Smith, "Nauvoo Roots of Mormon Polygamy, 1841-46: A Preliminary Demographic Report," *Dialogue: A Journal of Mormon Thought* [Spring 1994], vol. 27, no. 1, p. 27).

64. Van Wagoner, pp. 29-36, 98-100.

65. W. Wyl, *Mormon Portraits* (SLC: Tribune Printing & Publishing Co., 1886), p. 62. A reprint of this volume is at www.utlm.org/booklist/titles/up016_mormon portraits.htm.

66. *HC* (SLC: Deseret Book Co., 1976/1980), vol. 6, pp. 410-411.

67. George D. Smith, p. 9.

68. Compton, p. 15.

69. Compton, pp. 15-16; also see this chapter's n99, the year 1841.

70. Smith would sometimes only demand the wives of his followers as a test of their devotion to him. Then, after they offered up their spouse, he would tell them that they had passed their test and would not have to obey the request. Smith said to John Taylor, "'Brother John, I want Leonora.'" Taylor was stunned, "but after walking the floor all night, the obedient Elder said to Smith, 'If God wants Leonora He can have her.'" According to Wilford Woodruff, "That was all the prophet was after, to see where President Taylor stood in the matter, and said to him, Brother Taylor, I don't want your wife, I just wanted to know just where you stood" (Quotes of Joseph Smith, John Taylor, and Wilford Woodruff taken from Van Wagoner, p. 62; cf. Jedediah Grant, Feb. 19, 1854, in *JOD*, vol. 2, p. 14. Grant, Second Counselor to Brigham Young, said that Smith's "grand object in view" of asking for other men's wives, then relenting when they agreed to it, was "to try the people of God, to see what was in them").

71. Compton, pp. 20, 48-49.

72. Jedediah Grant. Quoted in T.B.H. Stenhouse, *The Rocky Mountain Saint* (New York: D. Appleton & Co., 1873; 1904 edition; published in SLC by Shepard Book Co.), p. 294.

73. Grant, in *JOD*, vol. 2, p. 14.

74. John D. Lee, *Mormonism Unveiled; Including The Remarkable Life And Confessions Of The Late Mormon Bishop John D. Lee* (St. Louis: N.D. Thompson and Co., 1877), p. 165, www.helpingmormons.org/Rare_Books.htm.

75. Lee, p. 165; cf. Ann Young, chapter 7, www.antimormon.8m.com/youngchp7.html.

76. C.F. Keil and F. Delitzsch, *Commentary on the Old Testament* (Peabody, MA: Hendrickson Publishers, 1996 edition), vol. 1, p. 73.

77. Walter A. Elwell, ed., *Baker Encyclopedia of the Bible* (Grand Rapids, MI: Baker Book House, 1988; 1995 edition), vol. 2, p. 1406.

78. "A virtuous woman [not *virtuous women*] is a crown to her husband" (Prov. 12:4); and "Who can find a virtuous woman [not *women*]? for her price is far above rubies. The heart of her husband doth safely trust in her [not *in them*]....Her husband [not *their husband*] is known in the gates, when he sitteth among the elders" (Prov. 31:10-11,23).

    According to *The International Standard Bible Encyclopedia*, polygamy (no matter who practiced it) contradicted the established Old Testament pattern for marriage, which was intended to give men and women equal status as co-creations of God: "[T]he Genesis dictum established monogamy as a working principle for mankind, and originally it was meant to signify the union of a male and a female who were counterparts to each other. The wife was in no way regarded as inferior to her husband, being considered in the first instance as specifically the 'essence of his essence'" (Geoffrey W. Bromiley, gen. ed., *The International Standard Bible Encyclopedia* [Grand Rapids, MI: William Eerdmans Publishing, 1986; updated edition, 1990], vol. 3, p. 901).

79. Bromiley, p. 901.

80. This particular belief is no longer widely held by Mormons. It has been relegated to the area of unsupportable speculation voiced by dead prophets and apostles.

81. Jedediah M. Grant, Aug. 7, 1853, in *JOD*, vol. 1, p. 346. Ann Young remembered being taught that Jesus Christ "was a practical polygamist; Mary and Martha, the sisters of Lazarus, were his plural wives, and Mary Magdalen was another. Also, the bridal feast at Cana of Galilee, where Jesus turned the water into wine, was on the occasion of one of his own marriages" (Ann Young, chapter 18, www.antimormon.8m.com/ youngchp 18.html).

82. Orson Hyde, Mar. 18, 1855, in *JOD*, vol. 2, p. 210.

83. "God the Father had a plurality of wives, one or more being in eternity, by whom He begat our spirits as well as the spirit of Jesus His Firstborn" (Orson Pratt, "Celestial Marriage," *The Seer*, Nov. 1853, vol. 1, no. 11, p. 172).

84. "For this cause shall a man leave his father and mother, and shall be joined unto his wife, and they two shall be one flesh....[L]et every one of you in particular so love his wife even as himself; and the wife see that she reverence her husband."

85. Contrary to these Bible verses, Heber C. Kimball taught that marriages would take place in the spirit world: "Supposing that I have a wife or a dozen of them....Suppose that I lose the whole of them before I go into the spirit world, but that I have been a good, faithful man all the days of my life, and lived my religion, and had favour with God, and was kind to them, do you think I will be destitute there [in the spirit world]? No, the Lord says there are more [women] there [in the spirit world] than there are here...."

"In the spirit world there is an increase of males and females, there are millions of them, and if I am faithful all the time, and continue right along with brother Brigham, we will go to brother Joseph [Smith] and say, 'Here we are brother Joseph'....He will say to us,...'Where are your wives?' 'They are back yonder; they would not follow us.' 'Never mind,' says Joseph, 'here are thousands, have all you want.' Perhaps some do not believe that, but I am just simple enough to believe it....I am looking for the day, and it is close at hand, when we will have a most heavenly time, one that will be romantic, one with all kinds of ups and downs, which is what I call romantic, for it will occupy in full all the time" (Heber C. Kimball, Feb. 1, 1857, in *JOD*, vol. 4, p. 209).

86. Stewart, p. 26.

87. *2001-2002 Church Almanac* (SLC: Deseret News, 2000), pp. 54-56.

88. Vern Anderson, "Absence of Polygamy In LDS Manual Stirs Controversy," *Salt Lake Tribune*, Apr. 5, 1998, p. C3.

89. Consider, for example, the following:

    • *Original Brigham Young Quote*—"Now let me say to the First Presidency, to the Apostles, to all the Bishops in Israel, and to every quorum, and especially to those who are presiding officers, Set that example before your *wives* and your children?" (Brigham Young, in John A. Widtsoe, ed., *Discourses of Brigham Young* [SLC: Deseret Book, 1966; reprint, 1977], p. 198), emphasis added.

    • *Excerpted Brigham Young Quote*—"Now let me say to the First Presidency, to the Apostles, to all the Bishops in Israel, and to every quorum, and especially to those who are presiding officers, Set that example before your [wife] and your children?" (*Brigham Young Manual*, pp. 164-165).

90. Ron Priddis. Quoted in Anderson.

91. Craig Manscill. Quoted in Anderson.

92. Merrill C. Oaks, Oct. 5, 1998, reprinted in "The Living Prophet: Our Source of Pure Doctrine," *Ensign*, Nov. 1998, p. 82, available at www.lds.org.

93. Quoted in Richard Packman, "Mormon Lying," www.home.teleport.com/~packham/lying.htm.

94. Daniel W. Bachman and Ronald K. Esplin, "Plural Marriage," in Daniel H. Ludlow, *Encyclopedia of Mormonism* (New York: Macmillan Publishing Co., 1992), vol. 3, p. 1095.

95. See Abanes, pp. 326-328.

96. Several aspects of the Manifesto indicate that it was not a revelation, but a political move:

    • It was written, rewritten, edited, and re-edited many times behind closed doors by various persons, including Mormon politicians, LDS apostles, and non-Mormon legal advisors. At the Reed Smoot hearings in 1904, George Reynolds said that he "'assisted to write it,' in collaboration with Charles W. Penrose and John R. Winder who 'transcribed the notes and changed the language slightly to adapt it for publication'" (D. Michael Quinn, "LDS Church Authority and New Plural Marriages, 1890-1904," *Dialogue: A Journal of Mormon Thought*, vol. 18, no. 1, pp. 11-12, www.lds-mormon.com/quinn_polygamy.shtml). Quinn also has noted, "John W. Woolley told his polygamist followers in the 1920s that 'Judge Zane [a non-Mormon] had as much to do with it [the Manifesto] as Wilford Woodruff except to sign it,' and Lorin C. Woolley told LDS Fundamentalists that Wilford Woodruff was not the author of the Manifesto, but that it was first written by Charles W. Penrose, Frank J. Cannon, and 'John H. White, the butcher,' revised by non-Mormon federal officials, and that Woodruff merely signed it" (also see *Proceedings*, vol. 2, pp. 51-52; and Thomas J. Rosser [missionary to England and Wales, quoted in John W. Pratt], letter dated Aug. 4, 1956, "The Manifesto of September 24, 1890," www.helping mormons.org/TLC_Manti/GospelDiscussionsFolder/PluralMarriage/PMManifesto Analysis.htm).

- It was addressed "To whom it may concern," a decidedly secular phrase that failed to hold the authority of a "Thus saith the Lord" declaration.

- The Manifesto "was not presented to the Church as a revelation either and was first issued on 25 September 1890 as a press release through the office of Utah's delegate in Congress, John T. Caine" (Richard S. Van Wagoner, Steven C. Walker, and Allen D. Roberts, "The 'Lectures on Faith': A Case Study in Decanonization," *Dialogue: A Journal of Mormon Thought* [Fall 1987], vol. 20, no. 3, p. 75).

- It was not signed by the First Presidency, but only by Wilford Woodruff.

- Woodruff worded the Manifesto to read, "I now publicly declare that *my advice* to the Latter-day Saints is to refrain from contracting any marriage forbidden by the law of the land" (emphasis added), which meant that the entire declaration was Woodruff's personal advice, rather than a command from God. Thus, a sort of theological loophole was given for disobedience.

- It was not voted on unanimously at any conference before being issued in September of 1890. Not until October did the general LDS membership receive an opportunity to vote on the new policy. But by that time the Manifesto was already binding on the Saints: "Although President Woodruff wrote in his diary on 25 September 1890 that he published the Manifesto after it was 'sustained by my Councilors and the 12 Apostles,' only three apostles approved it in manuscript, and half the Quorum was barely supportive when the apostles met on 30 September and 1 October 1890 to discuss the published document. Of the nine apostles present, two said that they were bewildered by the announcement (one referred to the 1886 and 1889 revelations that seemed to prohibit such a declaration), and of the seven apostles who announced their support, four specifically stated that they understood it to apply only to the United States" (Quinn, online www.ldsmormon.com/quinn_ polygamy .shtml).

97. In a 1911 telegram to Reed Smoot, LDS president Joseph F. Smith told Smoot that plural marriages had been solemnized in both Canada and Mexico (Joseph F. Smith, letter to Reed Smoot, Apr. 1, 1911, Reed Smoot Correspondence, LDSCA). However, in another letter written to Smoot by George Gibbs, it is communicated that Smith's inclusion of Canada in the telegram was a mistake (George Gibbs, letter to Reed Smoot, Apr. 12, 1911, Reed Smoot Correspondence, LDSCA). The certainty of this latter claim is questionable since no record exists of Smith correcting himself.

98. *Proceedings*, vol. 1, p. 129.

99. Not only did nineteenth-century Mormons disobey the law of the land regarding
     polygamy, but they did not even obey their own 1890 Manifesto. The very LDS men
     who validated the Manifesto and presented it to the church as a binding restriction,
     also violated it. Such less-than-admirable conduct can be traced all the way back to Joseph
     Smith Jr.:

     • *February 12, 1833:* "Sec 121. Bigamy consists in the having of two wives or two hus-
       bands at one and the same time, knowing that the former husband or wife is still
       alive. If any person or persons within this State, being married, or who shall here-
       after marry, do at any time marry any person or persons, the former husband or
       wife being alive, the person so offending shall, on conviction thereof, be punished
       by a fine, not exceeding one thousand dollars, and imprisoned in the penitentiary,
       not exceeding two years. It shall not be necessary to prove either of the said mar-
       riages by the register or certificate thereof, or other record evidence; but the same
       may be proved by such evidence as is admissible to prove a marriage in other cases,
       and when such second marriage shall have taken place without this state, cohabi-
       tation in this state after such second marriage shall be deemed the commission of
       the crime of bigamy, and the trial in such case may take place in the county where
       such cohabitation shall have occurred" (*Revised Laws of Illinois,* 1833, pp. 198-99).

     • *1832 or 1833:* Twenty-seven-year-old Joseph Smith *illegally* takes a second wife, in
       violation of Illinois law.

     • *1835:* Fanny moves into Joseph's home as his maidservant and adopted daughter—
       and secret wife. Moreover, contrary to Joseph's own private practices, the 1835 D&C
       is published and *falsely declares:* "Inasmuch as this church of Christ has been
       reproached with the crime of fornication, and polygamy: we declare that we believe,
       that one man should have one wife; and one woman, but one husband, except in
       the case of death, when either is at liberty to marry again" (D&C CI:4, 1835 edi-
       tion, p. 251).

     • *1835:* Smith (while in Ohio) begins to perform *illegal* marriages. For example, Smith
       violated Ohio law on November 23, 1835, by marrying Newel Knight to the *undi-
       vorced* Lydia G. Baily (Fawn Brodie, *No Man Knows My History* [New York: Vintage
       Books, 1995; orig. ed., Alfred A. Knopf, 1945], p. 183). D. Michael Quinn notes, "In
       addition to the bigamous character of this marriage, Smith had no license to per-
       form marriages in Ohio" (D. Michael Quinn, *The Mormon Hierarchy: Origins of Power*
       [SLC: Signature Books, 1994], p. 88). To justify the union, Smith used his theology:
       "'I have done it by the authority of the holy Priesthood and the Gentile law has no
       power to call me to an account for it. It is my religious priviledge *[sic]*'" (Joseph
       Smith. Quoted in Quinn, *Origins of Power,* p. 326 n32).

     • *1838 or 1839:* Smith *illegally* takes his third wife, Lucinda Pendleton.

     • *1841:* Smith *illegally* takes three more wives—Louisa Beaman; Zina Diantha
       Huntington; and Prescendia Lathrop Huntington Buell, while she is still married
       to Norman Buell (Brodie, p. 462). Smith also "marries" Clarissa Reed Hancock, the
       wife of Levi Hancock, while her legal husband is on a mission (Brodie, p. 464).

     • *1843:* Smith receives his revelation on plural marriage, but it is then kept secret for
       nearly ten years, being shared privately only with a select group of followers. He

illegally takes another wife, 19-year-old Emily Partridge, on Mar. 4, 1843. Four days later he *illegally* takes Emily's sister, Eliza, as a wife.

- *1843–1844:* Smith not only continues to perform *illegal* marriage ceremonies without a license, but does so for participants without proper licenses giving them civil permission to enter into marriage. This became a common practice since "Kirtland was full of converts who had left behind them spouses who could not be persuaded to join the church." Instead of obtaining licenses from the state, these couples received marriage certificates from Smith that were "according to the rules and regulations of the Church of the Latter-day Saints" (George D. Smith, "Mormon Plural Marriage," *Free Inquiry* (Summer 1992), vol. 12, no. 3, pp. 34-35). Moreover, Smith and other high-ranking LDS leaders continue to *illegally* acquire multiple wives (contrary to the Illinois law against bigamy).

- *1844 to 1846 or 1847:* Plural marriage, although still *illegal* in Illinois, is extended to a broader segment of the LDS community. Augusta Adams Cobb (1802–1886) is divorced by her husband, Henry Cobb (1798–1872) in 1846 on grounds of the *crime* of adultery with Brigham Young at Nauvoo. Augusta Cobb was baptized a Mormon in 1832 while living in Boston, but her husband did not convert. She then visited Nauvoo and upon her return to Boston in the fall of 1844 "told her husband that she loved Brigham and 'live or die, she was going to live with him.'" (Richard Van Wagoner, "Mormon Polyandry in Nauvoo," *Dialogue: A Journal of Mormon Thought* [Fall 1985], vol. 18, no. 3, p. 74). Augusta Cobb, as it turned out, had been *illegally* married to Young on Nov. 2, 1843.

- *1851:* In Utah, Brigham publicly admits his polygamous lifestyle.

- *1852:* Orson Pratt preaches the first public sermon on polygamy and Smith's 1843 revelation is revealed.

- *From 1852 into the 1870s:* Polygamy goes on virtually unchallenged in Utah.

- *1873:* George Q. Cannon, after being elected as a territorial representative, keeps his seat by *lying* to the House Committee on Elections. He flatly denies his relationship to four wives, going so far as to maintain that he is not cohabitating with any wives "in defiant or willful violation of the laws of Congress." Cannon even denies ever stressing the importance of polygamy as "paramount to all human laws," and claims that he never said he would obey polygamy "rather than the laws of any country" (House Misc. Doc. 49 [43-1], 1873, Serial 1617, 5).

- *1882:* The antipolygamy Edmunds Act is enacted by Congress. It called for heavy fines and imprisonment for those guilty of "*unlawful* cohabitation."

- *1883:* Faithful Mormon Rudger Clawson *illegally* marries Lydia Spencer.

- *1884:* Clawson and two other LDS are *convicted* under the Edmunds Act.

- *1885:* LDS president John Taylor and his two counselors, George Q. Cannon and Joseph F. Smith, go into hiding to avoid arrest for *illegal* cohabitation.

- *1885 to 1886:* Hundreds of prominent Mormons follow Taylor by disappearing into isolated parts of Utah or going on foreign missions. Their plural wives and children then *hinder law enforcement officials* as much as possible by giving false testimony, denying marital relationships, and refusing to answer questions posed by court authorities. Agnes W. Roskelley, for example, taught her children to tell strangers "that they didn't know what their name was; they didn't know where they lived; they didn't know who their dad or mother was" (Jesse Embry, *Mormon Polygamous Families* [SLC: University of Utah Press, 1987], p. 22).

- *1886:* Mormons establish polygamous communities in Mexico and Canada, where polygamy is also *illegal,* but where authorities did not interfere with the settlements.

- *1887:* 327 Mormons are *convicted* under antipolygamy laws. Virtually every prominent Mormon is in prison, just released from prison, or is a fugitive.

- *1888:* A plan is adopted whereby fugitive Mormons, in return for light sentences or fines, will give themselves up. But even after this deal is struck, high-ranking Mormons refuse to abide by U.S. laws, even after promising to do otherwise.

- *1889:* 334 Mormons are *convicted* under antipolygamy laws.

- *1890:* 1300 Mormons are *jailed* under antipolygamy laws.

100. Kenneth L. Cannon II, "After the Manifesto: Mormon Polygamy 1890-1906," in D. Michael Quinn, ed., *The New Mormon History* [SLC: Signature Books, 1992), p. 217 n38). Woodruff's encouragement was noted in the *Abraham H. Cannon Journal,* Oct. 24, 1894. The tradition in the Cannon family is that Smith performed the Abraham H. Cannon–Lillian Hamlin marriage on a pleasure cruise from Los Angeles to Catalina Island (see Hardy, pp. 216-222). Edna Smith (one of Joseph F. Smith's wives) stated that "Orson Smith," a local church leader in northern Utah, performed the ceremony (Carl A. Badger journal, Dec. 9, 1905). However, D. Michael Quinn has convincingly argued that "Orson Smith" was a code name for Joseph F. Smith and that Joseph F. Smith, when Second Counselor to the First Presidency in 1896, did indeed perform the wedding (D. Michael Quinn, "LDS Church Authority," www.ldsmormon.com/quinn_polygamy .shtml; cf. Quinn's nn301-303 from this same article).

101. Kenneth Cannon, p. 207.

102. Kenneth Cannon, p. 207.

103. Rulon C. Allred, *The Most Holy Principle* (Murray, UT: Gems Publishing Co., 1970-1975), vol. 4, p. 86.

104. Van Wagoner, p. 159. Anthony W. Ivins performed 29 of these marriages, which according to a Mar. 7, 1911, letter he wrote to his son, were done with the approval of the LDS church hierarchy. He stated, "You may depend upon. I have never performed a marriage ceremony without proper authority."

105. In 1902, for instance, Smith told Brigham Young Jr. that no plural marriages were "taking place to his knowledge in the Church either in the U.S. or any other country" and that no one had for years been "authorized to perform any such marriages" (Brigham Young Jr., *Journal History,* under June 5, 1902, New York Public Library). And at a 1903 meeting of apostles he said "he had not given his consent to anyone to solemnize plural marriages," nor did he "know of any such cases" (*Journal History,* under Nov. 19, 1903; cf. "John Henry Smith Diary," Nov. 19, 1903).

106. Smith, for example, could not remember making a speech at a Weber Stake Reunion in Ogden in 1903 (*Proceedings,* vol. 1, pp. 192-193). During this particular speech he

advocated polygamy and illegal cohabitation, even though earlier in his testimony he stated that he had never made any such statements.

107. *Proceedings,* vol. 1, pp. 145-147.

108. *Proceedings,* vol. 1, p. 127.

109. *Proceedings,* vol. 1, pp. 128, 335. Smith also described one meeting wherein he advocated polygamy as merely a "select gathering of a few persons," until documentation produced by the committee showed that in actuality it was a group of more than 50 high-ranking leaders of the church (*Proceedings,* vol. 1, 192-193.)

110. *Proceedings,* vol. 1, pp. 334-335. Smith's testimony on this point reads as follows:

    TAYLER: You say there is a State law forbidding unlawful cohabitation?

    SMITH: That is my understanding.

    TAYLER: And ever since that law was passed you have been violating it?

    SMITH: I think likely I have been practicing the same thing even before the law was passed.

    CHAIRMAN: ...you are violating the law?

    SMITH: The law of my State?

    CHAIRMAN: Yes.

    SMITH: Yes, sir.

    OVERMAN: Is there not a revelation published in the Book of Covenants here that you shall abide by the law of the State?

    SMITH: It includes both unlawful cohabitation and polygamy.

    OVERMAN: Is there not a revelation that you shall abide by the laws of the State and of the land?

    SMITH: Yes, sir.

    OVERMAN: If that is a revelation, are you not violating the laws of God?

    SMITH: I have admitted that, Mr. Senator, a great many times here.

111. Stanley S. Ivins, personal journal, under Nov. 19, 1944. Quoted in Cannon, p. 211. Ivins also noted, under Nov. 29, 1934, the concerns of one post-Manifesto plural wife regarding Smith's testimony: "I met K.K. Steffenson at lunch [about a month ago] and we got to talking about post-manifesto polygamy. His sister was a post-man wife of one of the— He said that she had refused to be married by anyone but Pres. Smith and he had married her in the Salt Lake Temple. When he later testified at the Smoot investigation that there had been no authorized post-manifesto plural marriages, she was upset and had her brother, K. K., go to see Pres. Smith about it. He told K.K. to tell his sister that her marriage was O.K., but he had had to say what he did in Washington to protect the Church" (see Van Wagoner, p. 174).

112. John Henry Smith excused his poor memory thus: "[I]t is a matter with which I have never charged myself in regard to dates. The date of my own birth has always been a little mixed in my own mind" (*Proceedings,* vol. 2, p. 285. John Henry Smith was born on Sept. 18, 1848.).

    Hyrum M. Smith (Joseph F. Smith's son) seriously blundered. He first stated adamantly that he had no memory at all of any discussions about polygamy at apostle meetings. But then he contradicted himself by assuring the committee that when the subject came up at meetings, the apostles were urged to stop the practice (*Proceedings*, vol. 1, pp. 510-511).

And then there was Mrs. Margaret Geddes, who swore that she was an unmarried mother, while at the same time declining to identify the father of her youngest child (*Proceedings*, vol. 2, p. 105). The Senate believed her, not being able to see into the future to 1912 when David Eccles, the richest man in the LDS church, died. Margaret Geddes filed suit as a plural wife for her share and her son's share of Eccles's estate, saying that her marriage to him was performed by one of the apostles—in 1898 (See "Scope and Content" of the David Eccles Papers, www.library.weber.edu/libabout/sandc.htm, located at Weber State University, Ogden, UT).

Exactly how many marriages like Geddes's took place may never be known because many of these polygamous unions were actually back-dated in church records to make it appear as if they had taken place before the Manifesto (Matthias Cowley, testimony before Quorum of the Twelve, 1911. Quoted in Samuel W. Taylor, *Rocky Mountain Empire* [Macmillan Publishing Co., Inc., 1978], p. 131).

Apostle Francis M. Lyman placed himself in perhaps the most comical light by first saying that although his continued cohabitation with plural wives was common knowledge in Utah, he still did not think Smoot was aware of it. However, Lyman soon found himself cornered by questions from Senator George Frisbie Hoar. The senator pointed out the absurdity of the entire Utah population knowing about Lyman's polygamy, while at the same time Reed Smoot—a fellow apostle—had somehow remained ignorant of it. Lyman answered: "I think it is accepted as a fact by Mr. Smoot, but I do not think he knows it," which prompted laughter from the committee members (*Proceedings*, vol. 1, p. 456).

113. *Proceedings*, vol. 2, pp. 284-285.

114. *Proceedings*, vol. 2, p. 3.

115. *Proceedings*, vol. 2, p. 44; cf. p. 45.

116. *Proceedings*, vol. 4, p. 13.

117. *Proceedings*, vol. 4, p. 14.

118. *Proceedings*, vol. 3, p. 204.

119. D. Michael Quinn, "Plural Marriages After The 1890 Manifesto," August 1991, available at www.ldshistory.net/pc/postman.htm.

120. Quinn, "Plural Marriages," www.ldshistory.net/pc/postman.htm.

121. D. Michael Quinn summarized these post-1890 statistics during a 1991 lecture: "All First Presidency members either allowed or authorized new plural marriages from 1890 to 1904, and a few as late as 1906 and 1907. One Church President married a plural wife, and three Counselors in the First Presidency performed marriages for men who had living wives already. A Presidency's secretary proposed polygamous marriage in 1903, and another Presidency's secretary performed a polygamous marriage in 1907. Of the sixteen men who served only as Apostles…eight of these sixteen men married post-Manifesto plural wives. Three of them who did not do so, performed plural marriages. Two of them who did not do either of the above, arranged for plural marriages....

"Now, looking at the men individually. Wilford Woodruff...personally approved 7 new plural marriages, to be performed in Mexico. He also approved polygamous ceremonies for a couple of Mexican residents as early as 1891. He delegated George Q. Cannon, his first counselor, to give approval for plural marriages from 1892 to 1898. That approval was in the form of written letters....Woodruff himself married a new Plural Wife in 1897....[Lorenzo Snow] cohabited with his youngest plural wife who went to Canada briefly, in 1896, to bear his last child. And in so doing, he violated the testimony that he had given publicly in 1891, that the Manifesto prohibited cohabitation with plural wives....[Joseph F. Smith] In 1896 as a counselor, he performed in the Salt Lake Temple a 'proxy plural marriage' for Abraham Cannon, which had been approved earlier by the First Presidency....Smith instructed Seymour B. Young of the First council of seventy, to perform two plural marriages in Mexico. And later that same year, second counselor Smith authorized Patriarch Alexander F. MacDonald to perform new plural marriages in Mexico for any Mexican residents who requested them.... George Q. Cannon was Presidency counselor and next in line to be Church President from 1899 to 1901. He personally authorized new plural marriages performed in Mexico, Canada, and the United States, from 1892 until his death in 1901. This included plural marriages performed for 3 of his sons and 3 of his nephews" (Quinn, "Plural Marriages," www.ldshistory.net/pc/postman.htm; cf. B. Carmen Hardy, *Solemn Covenant*, pp. 389-425, for a listing of post-1890 plural marriages).

122.   Hinckley has on numerous occasions demonstrated his willingness to seriously downplay any issues that might be construed as controversial (see Richard Abanes, "The PR Prophet," www.abanes.com/Hinckley.html).

123.   Gordon B. Hinckley, *Larry King Live*, Sept. 8, 1998, www.lds-mormon.com/lkl_00.shtml. In truth, the practice was not discontinued long after 1890, and it was not engaged in as a "very limited practice." Nevertheless, King dropped the issue and went on to discuss modern polygamy, which Hinckley condemned as illegal.

124.   Hinckley, "What Are People," available at www.lds.org.

Chapter 10: The "Christian" Question

1.   Stephen E. Robinson, "Are Mormons Christians?" *New Era*, May 1998, p. 41, available at www.lds.org.

2.   Bruce R. McConkie, *MD* (SLC: Bookcraft, 1958; rev. ed., 1966; 23rd printing, 1977), p. 513.

3.   Hartman Rector Jr., "Our Witness to the World," *Ensign*, July 1972, p. 64, available at www.lds.org.

4.   Boyd K. Packer, "The Peaceable Followers of Christ," *Ensign*, Apr. 1998, p. 62, available at www.lds.org.

5.   Jan Shipps. "Faith in Transition: Road to Salvation," *Online Newshour* (PBS), July 18, 1997, www.pbs.org/newshour/bb/religion/july-dec97/mormons_7-18.html.

6.   Jan Shipps, "Confronting the Mormon Question," www.beliefnet.com/story/25/story_2570_1.html. Shipps, along with her United Methodist denomination, parts company with other Protestant denominations, as she explains: "I was afraid that this turn toward conservatism might cause my church to join the Southern Baptists in charging that Mormonism is 'counterfeit Christianity.' Had United Methodism gone in that

direction, I would have been distressed, in part because such charges are mean-spirited and in part because they are simply wrong."

7. Shipps, "Confronting," www.beliefnet.com/story/25/story_2570_1.html.

8. See Associated Press, "Roman Catholics Rule on Mormons," July 19, 2001, available at www.rickross.com/reference/mormon/mormon48.html. "The Mormon Puzzle" (video produced by the Southern Baptist Convention, 1997), available at www.utlm .org/book list/titles/xv001_mormonpuzzle.htm. Lutheran Church Missouri Synod, "Are Mormons generally regarded as Christians, and how do their beliefs differ from those of the Missouri Synod?" (Q&A Internet site, www.lcms.org/cic/mormon.html); Gustav Niebuhr, "Adapting 'Mormon' to Emphasize Christianity," *New York Times,* Feb. 19, 2001, www.rickross.com/reference/mormon/mormon36.html; and David Van Biema, "Kingdom Come," *Time,* Aug. 4, 1997, p. 56, www.lds-mormon.com/time.shtml.

9. Gordon B. Hinckley, in *LDS Church News,* week ending June 20, 1998, p. 7, www.desnews .com/cn/(archives); and Gordon B. Hinckley, "We Look to Christ," Apr. 7, 2002, in *CR,* available at www.lds.org.

10. Bruce R. McConkie, "Our Relationship to the Lord," Mar. 2, 1982, BYU lecture, http://speeches.byu.edu/index.php?act-viewitem&id=602&tid=.

11. In the original, *ean tis aitēsēte me en tō onomati mou egō poiēsō.* Alfred Marshall, *The NASB-NIV Parallel New Testament in Greek and English* (Grand Rapids, MI: Zondervan, 1986), p. 313; cf. *The Apologist's Bible Commentary,* www.foranswer.org/ John/Jn14_14.htm. This reading does not appear in the King James Version of the Bible because the word "me" is not included in the Greek texts on which the KJV was based. However, the best and oldest manuscripts do have the word.

12. Dallin H. Oaks, "Apostasy and Restoration," *Ensign,* May 1995, p. 84, available at www.lds.org. Oaks stated: "[W]e believe in a Godhead of Father, Son, and Holy Ghost. However, we testify that these three members of the Godhead are three separate and distinct beings....In contrast, many Christians reject the idea of a tangible, personal God and a Godhead of three separate beings. They believe that God is a spirit and that the Godhead is only one God. In our view, these concepts are evidence of the falling away we call the Great Apostasy."

13. Oaks, available at www.lds.org.

14. Hoyt W. Brewster Jr., "I Have a Question," *Ensign,* July 1987, p. 65, available at www.lds.org.

15. •   *1838:* "[A]ll the priests who adhere to the sectarian religions of the day with all their followers, without one exception, receive their portion with the devil and his angels" (Joseph Smith, *EJ,* vol. 1, no. 4, p. 60, www.solomonspalding.com/docs/eldjur04 .htm). Smith made these charges specifically against those religious persons who had lent their support to Mormon critics.

    •   *1843:* "What is it that inspires professors of Christianity generally with a hope of salvation? It is that smooth, sophisticated influence of the devil, by which he deceives the whole world" (Joseph Smith, *HC* [SLC: Deseret Book Co., 1976/1980], Jan. 2, 1843, vol. 5, p. 218).

- *1854:* "[A]ll other churches are entirely destitute of all authority from God....Both the Catholics and Protestants are nothing less than the *'whore of Babylon'* whom the Lord denounces by the mouth of John the Revelator as having corrupted all the earth by their fornications and wickedness" (Orson Pratt, "Baptism for the Remission of Sins," Apr. 1854, *The Seer,* p. 255, reprinted in *The Seer* [SLC: Publishers Press, 1990]).

- *1855:* "The Gospel of modern Christendom shuts up the Lord, and stops all communication with Him. I want nothing to do with such a Gospel, I would rather prefer the Gospel of the dark ages, so called" (Wilford Woodruff, Feb. 25, 1855, in *JOD,* vol. 2, p. 196).

- *1857:* "The Christian world, I discovered, was like the captain and crew of a vessel on the ocean without a compass, and tossed to and fro whithersoever the wind listed to blow them. When the light came to me I saw that all the so-called Christian world was grovelling in darkness" (Brigham Young, July 26, 1857, in *JOD,* vol. 5, p. 73); "Christians—those poor, miserable priests brother Brigham was speaking about—some of them are the biggest whoremasters there are on the earth, and at the same time preaching righteousness to the children of men. The poor devils, they could not get up here and preach an oral discourse, to save themselves from hell; they are preaching their fathers' sermons—preaching sermons that were written a hundred years before they were born....You may get a Methodist priest to pour water on you, or sprinkle it on you, and baptize you face foremost, or lay you down the other way, and whatever mode you please, and you will be damned with your priest" (Heber C. Kimball, July 26, 1857, in *JOD,* vol. 5, pp. 89-90), "We may very properly say that the sectarian world do[es] not know anything correctly, so far as pertains to salvation...[T]hey cannot tell you so much as Balaam's ass told him. They are as ignorant as children" (Brigham Young, Sept. 13, 1857, in *JOD,* vol. 5, p. 229); "[A]re Christians ignorant? Yes, as ignorant of the things of God as the brute beast" (John Taylor, Nov. 1, 1857, in *JOD,* vol. 2, p. 25).

- *1858:* "We talk about Christianity, but it is a perfect pack of nonsense....[I]t is a sounding brass and a tinkling symbol; it is as corrupt as hell; and the Devil could not invent a better engine to spread his work than the Christianity of the nineteenth century" (John Taylor, Jan. 17, 1858, *JOD,* vol. 6, p. 167).

- *1860:* "[W]hen the god of this world is hoisted, the priest from the pulpit and the pious deacon and the people worship at its shrine....[T]he Christian world, so called, are heathens as to their knowledge of the salvation of God" (Brigham Young, Sept. 16, 1860, in *JOD,* vol. 8, p. 171); "With a regard to true theology, a more ignorant people never lived than the present so-called Christian world" (Brigham Young, Oct. 7, 1860, in *JOD,* vol. 8, p. 199).

- *1870:* "What does the Christian world know about God? Nothing....Why, so far as the things of God are concerned, they are the veriest fools; they know neither God nor the things of God" (John Taylor, May 6, 1870, in *JOD,* vol. 13, p. 225).

- *1891:* "What did he [Joseph] know about the creeds and organizations existing among the millions of Christians in Europe and America, thus to denounce them all without further ceremony....Joseph Smith, without any more knowledge of the religions of the world than what opportunities his attendance of the numerous revival meetings held in his immediate neighborhood had given him, denounced them all as false. (Andrew Jenson, Jan. 16, 1891, in Brian H. Stuy, ed., *Collected Discourses* [Burbank, CA: B.H.S. Publishing, 1988], vol. 2, p. 150).

- *1903:* "[O]rthodox Christian views of God are Pagan rather than Christian" (B.H. Roberts, *The Mormon Doctrine of Deity* [SLC: Horizon Publishers, 1982; original edition, 1903], p. 116).

- *1958:* "A perverted Christianity holds sway among the so-called Christians of apostate Christianity." "Evil spirits control much of the so-called religious worship in the world; for instance, the great creeds of Christendom were formulated so as to conform to their whispered promptings." "[A]ll the millions of apostate Christendom have abased themselves before the mythical throne of a mythical Christ....In large part the worship of apostate Christendom is performed in ignorance, as much so as was the worship of the Athenians who bowed before the Unknown God." "[The BOM] designated the Catholic Church as 'the mother of harlots' (1 Nephi 13:34; 14:15-17), a title which means that the protestant churches, the harlot daughters which broke off from the great and abominable church, would themselves be apostate churches" (McConkie, *MD*, pp. 132, 246, 269, 314-315).

16. "[D]eeply faithful Catholic and Protestant Christians continue to preach that Jesus Christ is the Redeemer of the world today among many peoples, both near and far. They enrich the moral and spiritual climate of the communities in which we all live, overcoming much of the moral and spiritual poverty that would exist in the world were they not proclaiming the Lordship of Jesus Christ" (Roger R. Keller, "Do I Know My Neighbor?" *Ensign*, Mar. 1991, p. 25, available at www.lds.org).

17. Hoyt W. Brewster Jr., "I Have a Question," *Ensign*, July 1987, p. 65, available at www.lds.org.

18. • *Traditional Christians worship a false God in vain:* "The belief that God has no body, parts, and passions is not a doctrine of Jesus Christ or a doctrine of the holy scriptures but is a doctrine of men, and to worship such a God is in vain. From the time when the Lord created man in his own image and likeness, men have created false gods to worship, such as golden calves, sculptured images, etc.; and billions through the centuries including the very elect have been deceived and misled" (Bernard P. Brockbank, "The Living Christ," *Ensign*, May 1977, p. 26, available at www.lds.org).

- *Traditional Christians follow the precepts of men:* "[Joseph] asked which of all the churches he should join. The Savior answered that he should join none of them, for they all taught for doctrine the precepts of men. And that is the reason for the thousand churches in the United States today—it is because they follow the precepts of men rather than the revelations" (LeGrand Richards, "The Things of God and Man," *Ensign*, Nov. 1977, p. 21, available at www.lds.org).

- *Traditional Christians do not know the real God:* "I thought of the many ways in which God's true nature is distorted in the teachings of so many Christian churches....Thank God—the *real* God—for the teachings of the restored gospel" (John A. Tvedtnes, "Children of the Most High," *Tambuli*, July 1984, p. 18, available at www.lds.org).

19. Kent P. Jackson, "Early Signs of the Apostasy," *Ensign,* Dec. 1984, p. 8, available at www.lds.org. Jackson is an assistant professor of ancient scripture at BYU.

20. "Our beliefs and actions may differ from those of others, but we, as good Christians, do not criticize other religions or their adherents" (Joseph B. Wirthlin, "Christians in Belief and Action," *Ensign,* Nov. 1996, p. 70, available at www.lds.org); "Elder Dallin H. Oaks, one of the Church's Twelve Apostles and a former Utah Supreme Court Justice, says members of The Church of Jesus Christ of Latter-day Saints are taught to respect other Christians, to declare their own belief but not to denigrate others" (LDS Church, "Christ in the Doctrine of the Church," 2003, available at www.lds.org).

21. "We do not diminish or tear down the faith others have in Christ, but seek only to share with them our additional knowledge of the Lamb, the Shepherd, the Holy One of Israel (see Ps. 71:22)—for their benefit and salvation" (Robert E. Wells, "Be a Friend, a Servant, a Son of the Savior," *Ensign,* Nov. 1982, p. 69, available at www.lds.org).

22. R. Lloyd Smith, "Sharing the Gospel with Sensitivity," *Ensign,* June 2002, p. 53, available at www.lds.org.

23. Cool59, "Building Rather Than Destroying," Dec. 2, 2003, Internet post #46 at ZLMB.

24. Rodney Turner, "Christ's Church in Ancient America," *Ensign,* Mar. 2000, p. 48, available at www.lds.org. Turner noted, "Spiritually and broadly speaking, it applies to the opposing powers of good and evil in the world: Nephi was shown that in the latter days there would be 'save two churches only; the one is the church of the Lamb of God, and the other is the church of the devil' (1 Ne. 14:10; compare 1 Ne. 22:22-23). In most instances in the Book of Mormon, the word *church* refers to the true church of God or Christ. False or apostate churches are clearly identified as such (see 1 Ne. 13:4-5; 2 Ne. 28:3-19)." The long history of this LDS belief can be seen in the following sources: the remarks made by Orson Hyde, n.d., in *JOD,* vol. 5, p. 139; George Q. Cannon, Apr. 6, 1884, in *JOD,* vol. 25, p. 127; and *MS&AD,* Jan. 1836, vol. 2, no. 4, p. 251.

25. LDS apostle B.H. Roberts noted, "I do not believe that Nephi here had reference to any one of the many divisions of Christendom. Nephi, in fact, recognized the existence of two churches only. One he styles, 'the church of the Lamb of God'; and the other he bluntly calls 'the church of the devil'" (B.H. Roberts, *New Witnesses for God* [SLC: The Deseret News, 1909], vol. 3, p. 263).

26. Roberts, p. 263, footnote "h." The most all-encompassing definition of the Devil's church, which included mainstream Christianity, was given by Bruce McConkie: "What is the church of the devil in our day, and where is the seat of her power?...The church of the devil is every evil and worldly organization on earth. It is all of the systems, both Christian and non-Christian, that have perverted the pure and perfect gospel; it is all of the governments and powers that run counter to the divine will; it is the societies and political parties and labor unions that sow strife and reap contention. It is communism; it is Islam; it is Buddhism; it is modern Christianity in all its parts. It is Germany under Hitler, Russia under Stalin, and Italy under Mussolini. It is the man of sin speaking in churches, orating in legislative halls, and commanding the armies of men. And its headquarters are everywhere—in Rome and Moscow, in Paris and London, in Teheran and Washington—everywhere that evil forces, either of church or state or society, can be influenced" (Bruce McConkie, *The Millennial Messiah* [SLC: Deseret Book Co., 1982], p. 55).

27. James E. Talmage, Oct. 19, 1928, in *CR*, p. 121.

28. McConkie, *MD*, p. 269.

29. LeGrand Richards, "Strange Creeds of Christendom," *Ensign*, Jan. 1973, p. 109, available at www.lds.org; Dallin H. Oaks, "Apostasy and Restoration," *Ensign*, May 1995, p. 84, available at www.lds.org; Hyde M. Merrill, "The Great Apostasy as Seen by Eusebius," *Ensign*, Nov. 1972, p. 34, available at www.lds.org; Jackson, "Early Signs of the Apostasy," available at www.lds.org.

30. Merrill, available at www.lds.org.

31. Stephen E. Robinson, "Warring against the Saints of God," *Ensign*, Jan. 1988, p. 34, available at www.lds.org. Clearly, Mormons do not view traditional Christianity as fitting into the Church of the lamb. Anthony W. Ivins, Juarez Stake President, stated the following in 1905: "[A]t the time the Book of Mormon was published to the world, the Church of the Lamb of God did not exist. It had not come into being in its organized form" (Anthony W. Ivins, Oct. 8, 1905, in *CR*, p. 55).

32. The LDS Topical Guide lists the following verses as alleged references to the Great Apostasy: Is. 24:5; 29:13; 60:2; Amos 8:1; Matt. 24:5,24; John 6:66; Acts 20:29; 1 Cor. 11:18; Gal. 1:6; 3:1; 2 Thes. 2:3; Gal. 3:1; 1 Tim. 1:6; 4:1; 2 Tim. 1:15; 2:18; 3:5; 4:4; Titus 1:16; James 4:1; 2 Pet. 2:1; 3:17; 1 Jn. 2:18; 4:1; Jude 1:4; Rev. 2:2; 13:7 ("Topical Guide," in *LDS Standard Works*, Quad, pp. 13-14).

33. Bruce R. McConkie, "Once or Twice in a Thousand Years," *Ensign*, Nov. 1975, p. 15, available at www.lds.org.

34. "Primary 5, 12: Important Ordinances Are Restored," p. 57, available at www.lds.org.

35. W.E. Vine, *Vine's Expository Dictionary of New Testament Words* (McLean, VA: MacDonald Publishing Co., no date), p. 85. This word is formed from *ek* ("out of") and *klésis* ("a calling").

36. Vine, p. 86.

37. The idea that God's "church" is one, visible, hierarchy-based organization developed after Christ throughout the several centuries immediately following his ascension and the death of his apostles. The birth and rise of Roman Catholicism actually originated in a postapostolic movement that in turn came from "a general weakening of the original spirit" of Christianity under Christ. This brought about "a tendency toward a legalistic conception and regulation of Christian life, as well as to a conception of the chuch which found its essence in external ordinances. And these ordinances, especially pertaining to the government of the church and the priesthood, continued to develop until they ended up in what is known as Roman Catholic Christianity" (J. Kostlin, "Church, The Christian," in Samuel MacCauley Jackson, ed.-in-chief, *The New Schaff-Herzog Encyclopedia of Religious Knowledge* (Grand Rapids, MI: Baker Book House, 1977), vol. 3, p. 79.

38. Kent P. Jackson, "I Have a Question," *Ensign*, Feb. 1995, p. 62, available at www.lds.org.

39. "Gospel Principles, Unit Five: The Church of Jesus Christ, 13: The Priesthood, What Is the Priesthood?," p. 81, available at www.lds.org.

40. "[P]riesthood authority was lost because the keys to use and pass along that authority had been held by the Apostles. Also lost was the continuing revelation that was

necessary to keep doctrine pure" ("The Best of Times," *New Era,* Apr. 2001, p. 8, available at www.lds.org).

41. "Gospel Principles," available at www.lds.org.

42. • *Non-LDS "Christian" baptism is invalid:* "When we are baptized by immersion *by one with the proper priesthood authority* and choose to follow our Savior, we then are in His kingdom and of His kingdom" (Robert D. Hales, "Special Witness: Of His Kingdom," *Friend,* Oct. 2002, p. 7, emphasis added, available at www.lds.org); "The storm of apostasy that had been prophesied swept over the earth. During the long spiritual darkness that followed, performing a baptism was as ineffective as flicking a light switch during a blackout" ("Power Restored," *New Era,* May 2003, p. 10, emphasis added, available at www.lds.org).

  • *Non-LDS "Christian" taking of sacrament is inappropriate:* "The ordinance of the Sacrament is administered by 'those having authority'—that is, by priesthood bearers" (Paul B. Pixton, in Daniel H. Ludlow, *Encyclopedia of Mormonism* [New York: Macmillan Publishing Co., 1992], vol. 3, p. 1244).

43. • *Non-LDS "Christian" new birth is false:* "Our second birth begins when we are baptized by water *by one holding the priesthood of God* and is completed when we are confirmed, and 'then cometh a remission of [our] sins by fire and by the Holy Ghost' " (James E. Faust, "Born Again," *Ensign,* May 2001, p. 54, available at www.lds.org).

  • *Non-LDS "Christians" have no gift of the Holy Ghost:* "The transcendent gift of the Holy Ghost, along with membership in The Church of Jesus Christ of Latter-day Saints, is bestowed by confirmation, by the laying on of hands *by those having priesthood authority*" (James E. Faust, "Born Again," *Ensign,* May 2001, p. 54, available at www.lds.org).

  • *Non-LDS "Christians" do not have forgiveness:* "It is one thing to repent. It is another to have our sins remitted or forgiven. The power to bring this about is found *in the Aaronic Priesthood*" (*Ensign,* May 1988, p. 46, available at www.lds.org); "We cannot overstate the importance of the Aaronic Priesthood in this. All of these vital steps pertaining to the remission of sins are performed through the saving ordinance of baptism and the renewing ordinance of the sacrament. Both of these ordinances are officiated *by holders of the Aaronic Priesthood under the direction of the bishopric*" (Dallin H. Oaks, *New Era,* May 1999, p. 6); "In order to receive forgiveness of sins and become clean, every one of us must personally repent and come unto Christ. Everyone who desires forgiveness of sin must be baptized *by one having authority*" ("Power Restored," *New Era,* May 2003, p. 10, available at www.lds.org).

44. "[F]rom its earliest days LDS Christians sought to distinguish themselves from Christians of other traditions. Other forms of Christianity, while bearing much truth and doing much good under the guidance of the Holy Spirit, are viewed as incomplete, lacking the authority of the priesthood of God, the temple ordinances, the comprehensive understanding of the Plan of Salvation, and the nonparadoxical understanding of the Godhead. Therefore, the designation 'saint' reflects attachment to the New Testament church, and also designates a difference from Catholic, Eastern Orthodox, and Protestant Christianity in the current dispensation" (Roger R. Keller, in Ludlow, vol. 1, p. 270). It is most interesting that this particular statement begins with an attempt to greatly soften

what early LDS leaders have repeatedly declared about modern Christianity (see this chapter's nn15, 18-19, 24-26, 28-30, 42-43).

45. This is my paraphrase of Smith's overall, general message.

46.

The Mormon Jesus	The Traditional Jesus
• A *literal* son (spirit-child) of a god (Elohim) and his wife.	• The uncreated, eternally existent, unique incarnation of God the Son.
• The elder brother of all spirits born in the pre-existence to Heavenly Father.	• The unique Son of God, with whom none can be compared.
• One of three gods overseeing this planet.	• The Second Person of the Holy Trinity.
• Atoned only for Adam's transgression, thereby providing the opportunity for us to obtain "eternal life" by our own efforts.	• Atoned for our personal sins, thereby securing "eternal life" for us, once we place our trust in his life, death, and resurrection.
• The *literal* spirit brother of Lucifer.	• No relation to Satan, who is an angelic being.
• Jesus' sacrificial death is not able to cleanse some people of *all* their sins.	• Jesus' sacrifice on the cross is able to cleanse every person of *all* their sins.
• There is no salvation without accepting Joseph Smith as a prophet of God.	• Jesus alone is the way, truth, and life. There is no need to recognize or follow a prophet.

47. Brockbank, available at www.lds.org.

48. Quoted in Herbert Toler, "Marching to A Different Drum," *Charisma* magazine, May 1996, p. 31.

49. Anthony M. Platt, "Born in the USA," *Los Angeles Times Book Review,* March 2, 1997, p. 8.

50. Boyd K. Packer, "The Peaceable Followers of Christ," *Ensign,* Apr. 1998, p. 62, available at www.lds.org.

51. Joseph B. Wirthlin, "Christians in Belief and Action," *Ensign,* Nov. 1996, p. 70, available at www.lds.org.

52. Although many supporters of religious freedom have claimed that such charges are false, my own in-depth research (which included listening to approximately 30 to 40 hours of David Koresh teaching tapes) revealed that such charges are indeed accurate. They also have been substantiated by the testimony of children released from the Branch Davidian compound. This is not to say that Federal authorities were justified in their handling of the Waco siege. Law enforcement officials failed miserably to bring the situation to a peaceful resolution.

53. Until the AIDS epidemic, this group also advocated and allowed adult–child sexual contact, free love, and child pornography (see resources online at www.exfamily.org/; www.watchman.org/profile/fampro.htm; and www.factnet.org/cults/children_of_god/experience_i.html?FACTNet).

54. See www.spilledcandy.com/ChristianWitches.htm; www.members.aol.com/Rawna Moon/moon.html; and www.crystalforest1.homestead.com/ChristianWitch.html.

55. James Thorner, "Christian Nudist Buys Camp with History of Segregation," *St. Petersburg Times,* Aug. 1, 2003, www.sptimes.com/2003/08/01/Pasco/Christian_nudist_ buys.shtml.

56. Daniel C. Peterson and Stephen D. Ricks, *Offenders for a Word* (Provo, UT: FARMS, 1998), p. 185.

57. Daniel C. Peterson, "Random Reflections of a Passing Scene," Aug. 8, 2003, lecture at the 2003 FAIR Conference, author's private notes.

58. Barry R. Bickmore, "Apostasy," www.fairlds.org/apol/morm201/m20106.html.

59. Robert M. Bowman Jr., *Orthodoxy and Heresy* (Grand Rapids, MI: Baker Book House, 1992), p. 116.

60. Bowman, p. 116, emphasis added.

61. Bowman's definition raises a thought-provoking question: *How perfectly must one understand theological concepts before one is saved?* It depends on *which* theological concept we're talking about. The truth regarding salvation, thankfully, is simple—simple enough that even the faith of a child is enough to save. One's simple understanding that someone named Jesus Christ died for one's sins is enough to save. Looking up to God and saying, "I'm sorry, I sinned, forgive me and save me," is enough to save. The Bible never asks us to become knowledgeable before we seek salvation. But a natural result of becoming saved is developing a thirst and hunger for understanding God's truth.

Few evangelical, Roman Catholic, Pentecostal, or Eastern Orthodox believers can articulate some of the finer points of Christian doctrine. The Trinity, for instance, is a belief that can usually be defined adequately and accurately only by theologians, pastors, apologists, and other Christians highly interested in doctrine. Others give it their best shot but often just end up articulating a form of modalism, albeit unintentionally. (Modalism is a heresy wherein the three Persons of the Godhead are reduced to a single Person who appears in different "modes" at different times. In this misunderstanding, the Father becomes the Son, who in turn becomes the Holy Ghost.)

Moreover, today's understanding of the Trinity did not even exist during the first few centuries of the church—although its component parts were embraced as early as the New Testament era (for example, the Father, Son, and Holy Ghost were all viewed as divine and worshiped). Surely, there existed Christians prior to the church councils that formally expressed the Trinity in creeds.

However persons today with an inadequate understanding of the Trinity can still be truly "Christian," just as Christ's Jewish followers were saved in the first century. How can this be? Simply put, such individuals do not (and did not) analyze their beliefs enough to *not* be saved. Most people are not equipped to slice and dice doctrine as finely as theologians, nor should they be expected to do so. To become a Christian, all we need to know is that Jesus loves us, that he died for our sins, and that we can rely on his power to save us—period. This, too, is what first-century Christians accepted. *Jesus was simply the Messiah to his followers.*

Only when believers started asking themselves questions like "*How* could Jesus be God if there exists only one God?" did church leaders gather together to find an answer (in church councils). These councils and their creeds also were needed to confront the many false doctrines that certain individuals and groups had begun to advocate. True believers in Christ knew that such individuals and groups were not faithfully representing what Jesus and his followers had taught, and for the sake of knowing what was true doctrine and what wasn't, they sought answers.

I have met several Mormons who believe little more than this very same thing. They have never really analyzed to any depth the ramifications of their own church's teachings about the Father, Son, and Holy Ghost; three in one; one in three; what *distinct* means as opposed to what *separate* means; or the term Godhead. These LDS friends of mine certainly believe in the BOM. But in the grand scheme of things, their belief in it matters very little since the actual text of the BOM does not diverge drastically from orthodox Christianity.

My LDS friends also accept living prophets and apostles. But again, this matters little. Countless Pentecostals who have a correct understanding of salvation uphold their own modern-day prophets *and* apostles. And many of these have delivered far more "thus saith the Lord" prophecies than any LDS leader in recent times.

Is this to say that all Mormons are saved—or that Mormonism as a religious belief system is Christian and leads to "eternal life"? No. What it means, as Bowman puts it, is, "Anyone who truly desires above all else to know the truth about God and his way of salvation can and will be saved" (Bowman, p. 26).

It is even more significant that most Mormons, like most Christians, do not tease out their beliefs and ideas enough to fully comprehend their ramifications. Particularly relevant to this issue is a 2003 survey by George Barna, which found that "only 9 percent of born-again Christians hold a biblical worldview" (WorldNet Daily.com, "Church Doesn't Think Like Jesus: Survey Shows Only 9% of Christians have Biblical Worldview," Dec. 3, 2003, www.worldnetdaily.com/news/article.asp?ARTICLE _ID=35926). This survey found that several major evangelical beliefs were not being held by mainstream Protestants: "For the purposes of the research, a biblical worldview was defined as believing that absolute moral truths exist; that such truth is defined by the Bible; and firm belief in six specific religious views. Those views were that Jesus Christ lived a sinless life; God is the all-powerful and all-knowing Creator of the universe and He still rules it today; salvation is a gift from God and cannot be earned; Satan is real; a Christian has a responsibility to share their faith in Christ with other people; and the Bible is accurate in all of its teachings. Only 7 percent of Protestants overall maintained a biblical worldview, according to the study. Of adults who attend mainline Protestant churches, only 2 percent shared those values. Among Catholics, less than one-half of 1 percent had a biblical worldview. The denominations that produced the highest proportions of adults with a biblical worldview were non-denominational Protestant churches, with 13 percent, Pentecostal churches, with 10 percent, and Baptist churches with 8 percent."

Would it be safe to say that all of these persons are not Christians? Of course not. At the same time, however, we must acknowledge several points that Bowman also notes (Bowman, pp. 24-25):1) Not everyone who calls Jesus their Lord is truly saved (Matthew 7:21); 2) belief in *a* Jesus does not necessarily mean belief in *the* Jesus (2 Corinthians 11:4); and 3) zealous and sincere persons are not necessarily correct in their religious views (Romans 10:2).

Additionally, there is a vast difference between someone not necessarily understanding a doctrine to its uttermost depths (or not thinking through a particular issue) and someone actively opposing a doctrine (for example, the Trinity). And although we might be able to make fairly accurate assessments about a person's salvation, we ourselves are making our judgments as flawed, fallible, sinful, and limited human beings. Reading the human heart is beyond our ability. We can make guesses, give opinions, voice concerns, and disagree. But in the end, God alone will decide.

62. Barry R. Bickmore, *Restoring the Ancient Church* (Ben Lomond, CA: FAIR, 1999), p. 28.

63. Robert L. Millet, *The Mormon Faith* (SLC: Shadow Mountain, 1998), p. 163.

64. Victor L. Ludlow, *Principles and Practices of the Restored Church* (SLC: Deseret Book, 1992), p. 513.

65. Victor L. Ludlow, p. 511.

66. Bickmore, *Restoring,* p. 25.

67. Bickmore, *Restoring,* pp. 27-28.

68. Bickmore, *Restoring,* p. 26.

69. Bickmore, *Restoring,* p. 25

70. Bickmore, *Restoring,* pp. 25-26.

71. Bickmore, *Restoring,* p. 27.

72. The same can be said for the other New Testament passages wherein either false teachers, false messiahs, false apostles and prophets, or false believers are mentioned. A number of Old Testament passages are also noted by Mormons, but in context these verses apply to the nation of Israel, not the church (see this chapter, n32).

73. Bickmore, *Restoring,* p. 25.

74. As for Paul's use of the term "all," Bible commentators see it as hyperbolic. It is an exaggeration "best understood as what [Newport] White calls 'the sweeping assertion of depression'" (R.V.G. Tasker, ed., *Tyndale New Testament Commentaries: The Pastoral Epistles* [Grand Rapids, MI: Eerdmans Publishing Co., 1957; 11th printing, 1980], vol. 14, p. 135).

75. Vine, p. 972.

76. Vine, p. 972.

77. Charles F. Pfeiffer and Everett F. Harrison, *The Wycliffe Bible Commentary* (Chicago: Moody Press, 1962), p. 1364.

78. Pfeiffer and Harrison, p. 1364.

79. Bickmore, *Restoring,* pp. 28-29.

80. It must be noted that in a private e-mail response to me, Bickmore was far less dogmatic in his assertions. He stated that he only *thought* that *maybe* Jude and John *may have* used the "Last time" for those days just prior to the great Apostasy (Barry Bickmore, private e-mail to Richard Abanes, "Question," Dec. 3, 2003).

81. Ezra Taft Benson, "Listen to a Prophet's Voice," *Ensign,* Jan. 1973, p. 57, available at www.lds.org.

82. LDS president Marion G. Romney warned of apostasy via a story about a man who doubted the policies of LDS president Heber J. Grant: "Then came the 'sixty-four dollar

question.' 'Do you believe that Heber J. Grant is a prophet of God?' His answer: 'I think he ought to keep his mouth shut about old age assistance.' Now I tell you that a man in his position is on the way to apostasy. He is forfeiting his chances for eternal life. So is everyone who cannot follow the living prophet of God" (Marion G. Romney, in *CR*, Apr. 6, 1953, p. 125; cf. Marion G. Romney, "Unity," *Ensign*, May 1983, p. 17, available at www.lds.org.

83. Smith may have foreseen this obvious argument. So in one revelation, he proclaimed that "there would never again be a collective falling away, only individual apostasy" (D&C 65:2) (Neal A. Maxwell, "From the Beginning," *Ensign*, Nov. 1993, p. 18, available at www.lds.org). Likewise, James E. Faust promised, "The dispensation of divine truth in which we now live, in distinction from previous dispensations, will not be destroyed by apostasy. This is in fulfillment of Daniel's prophecy that 'the God of heaven would set up a kingdom, which shall never be destroyed' nor 'left to other people' " (James E. Faust, "The Prophetic Voice," *Ensign*, May 1996, p. 4, available at www.lds.org). This prophecy from Daniel 2:44, however, applies not to 1820 and Joseph Smith, but to Christ and his establishment of the kingdom.

84. Bickmore, *Restoring*, p. 31.

85. Bickmore, *Restoring*, p. 31.

86. LDS author Richard L. Anderson writes, "Paul's central symbol of the apostasy is the man of sin or lawlessness sitting 'in the temple of God, shewing himself that he is God' (2 Thes. 2:4). Pounds of pages have been written about this being the Jerusalem temple, but that would be destroyed within two decades and would have no one sitting in it....

   "The real question is how Paul used the word temple in his writing. Almost always he used it figuratively—occasionally the body is a temple for God's Spirit, but usually the Church is the temple of God. The members ('ye,' older plural English for the plural Greek) are 'God's building' (1 Cor. 3:9), with Christ its foundation (1 Cor 3:11), or, in summary, 'the temple of God' (1 Cor. 3:16). Elsewhere Paul teaches about Christ as cornerstone, apostles as foundation, and members fitting into their places as a 'holy temple in the Lord' (Eph. 2:21). And in one of his last letters, Paul still spoke of 'the house of God, which is the church of the living God' (1 Tim. 3:15). Paul must define Paul, and his own words show that he was here referring to the Church" (Richard L. Anderson, *Understanding Paul* [SLC: Deseret Book, 1983], p. 86).

87. Bickmore, "Apostasy," www.fairlds.org/apol/morm201/m20106.html.

88. The Great Apostasy is summarized thus: "Rebellion within and persecution from without finally overcame the Church."

   • The Apostles were killed, and the perfect organization of the Church no longer existed on the earth.

   • The priesthood—the authority to act in God's name—was lost from the earth.

   • Various errors crept into Christian doctrine.

   • Creeds were formulated, which set in stone many of the errors that had crept in. Such mixing of human error with Scripture is "an 'abomination' to God."

   (Bickmore, "Apostasy," www.fairlds.org/apol/morm201/m20106.html.)

89. Bob Mims, "LDS Try to End Unauthorized Work for Jews," *Salt Lake Tribune*, May 2, 2001, www.sltrib.com (archives); and Associated Press, "Mormons meet with Jews over baptizing Holocaust victims," www.cnn.com/2002/US/West/12/10/baptizing.the.dead.ap/.

90. An excellent article detailing this passage is Luke P. Wilson, "Did Jesus Establish Baptism for The Dead?" 1996, www.irr.org/mit/baptdead.html (cf. www.equip.org/free/DM399.pdf).

Former Mormon Lane Thuett, who now works closely with Bill McKeever of Mormonism Research Ministries, has replied to this LDS doctrine as follows: "The Bible teaches that salvation is something which must be accepted 'today,' and in this life (2 Cor. 6:2; Luke 19:42; Heb. 4:7). After this life does not come a 'second chance' for salvation, but judgment (Heb. 9:27). The Apostle Paul taught that those who do not know God will get eternal punishment (2 Thess. 1:6-10). Obviously, after someone dies, they will know God, so if there was a second chance, then Paul was not teaching the true gospel. Jesus, Himself, also told about Lazarus and the rich man (Luke 16:19-31), an account that was obviously not a parable. He said that there is a chasm fixed between the righteous and the unrighteous—the righteous being those who believed in this life, the unrighteous being those who did not believe in this life. Obviously, as Christ informs us, those who were unrighteous in this life knew the truth once they got there. But Jesus tells us that they cannot cross from the unrighteous side to the righteous side. Their fate was fixed at death. If the LDS teachings about a 'second chance' salvation are true, then Jesus and Paul must have not been telling the truth.

"Even the Book of Mormon teaches that salvation is not possible after this life. Mosiah 2:38-39 teaches that if a man dies an enemy of God, then his fate is sealed, there is no second chance. Alma continuously taught this fact. In Alma 12:24, we read that 'this life' is the probationary state and the time to prepare to meet God. Not the next life. Alma 34:32-35 is adamant that if men do not accept salvation in 'this life,' then there is no hope for them in the next. 1 Nephi 10:21 also teaches that those who are wicked in this life do not get a second chance, but are cast off after death. The point is, that the LDS teachings concerning temple work for the dead contradict both the Bible and the Book of Mormon" (Lane Thuett, quoted in "Bill McKeever re Baptism for the Dead," Dec. 7, 2003, post to evangelical–LDS network).

In response to Thuett's essay, former Mormon Bob Witte wrote, "[W]hen I was a Mormon 'apologist' I would have countered Lane's response with the assertion that baptism on behalf of the dead is not so much for the commonly held 'second chance' scenario but is supporting more the idea of, 'one chance here, or one chance there.' To the LDS mind, 'the gospel' is only the laws and ordinances of Mormon doctrine. And of course, that gospel can only be delivered via their priesthood. Consequently, just the tiniest drop of mankind have sat through the Mormon missionary discussions (that is their 'one chance here'). So to the LDS mind, most 'missionary work' goes on after death (so the billions can have their 'one chance there' to accept Mormonism). However, baptism (and marriage) are earthly ordinances which can only be performed by mortals— thus the great emphasis on the temple work for the dead.

"Don't ever underestimate the emotional hold this can have on Mormons. We need to better deal with the straw man argument of 'what about the native on the Pacific island 1000 years ago who never heard of Jesus?' Get a good handle on the first couple of chapter of Romans. Don Richardson's 'Eternity In Their Hearts' was also helpful to me in this regard" (Bob Witte, "Bob Witte re Baptism of the Dead," Dec. 8, 2003, post to evangelical–LDS network; cf. Greg Koukl, "Is Baptism Necessary for Salvation?" www.str.org/free/commentaries/theology/isbaptis.htm).

91. Robert L. Millet, "I Have A Question," *Ensign*, Aug. 1987, p. 19, available at www.lds.org.

92. Helen Radkey, "The Mormon Church Attempts to Conceal Temple Records for Adolf Hitler," www.utlm.org/onlineresources/hitlertemplework.htm.

93. Jan Cienski, "Jews Urge Mormons to Curb Zeal," *National Post*, June 6, 2001, www.rick ross.com/reference/mormon/mormon43.html.

94. Erik Davis, "Database of the Dead," *Wired*, July 1999, www.wired.com/wired/archive/ 7.07/mormons_pr.html.

95. Mark Thiessen, "Jewish Group: Mormons Still Baptize Dead," *Guardian Unlimited*, April 10, 2004, www.guardian.co.uk/uslatest/story/0,1282,-3960698, 00.html.

96. Back in 1995, for instance, it was learned that Mormons baptized a veritable Who's Who of notable Jews, along with many Jews who had perished in Nazi concentration camps. The list of Jewish persons baptized into the church included Anne Frank, Sigmund Freud, David Ben-Gurion (Israel's first prime minister), and Ba'al Shem Tov, the eighteenth-century founder of Hasidic Judaism (Bob Mims, "LDS Try to End Unauthorized Work for Jews," *Salt Lake Tribune*, May 2, 2001, www.sltrib.com [archives]).

Aaron Breitbart, senior researcher for the Simon Wiesenthal Center, expressed sheer dismay: "These people were born Jews, they lived as Jews and many of them died because they were Jews....They would not have chosen to be baptized Mormons in life, and there is no reason they would want to be baptized by proxy in death" (Mims, www.sltrib.com [archives]). Only after "negotiations with Jewish officials" did the LDS Church remove "the names of 380,000 Holocaust victims from its database" (Bill Gladstone, "Jews press Mormon officials over posthumous baptisms," *Jewish Telegraphic Agency*, Dec. 13, 2002, www.jewishsf.com/bk021213/i50.shtml).

But then, new information came to light in 2002: "Ignoring church policy, some zealous followers have culled names from a wide variety of historical sources, including memorial books of Holocaust victims from Central and Eastern Europe" (Gladstone, www.jewishsf.com/bk021213/i50.shtml). Jewish names found in Mormon proxy baptism records include: Moses Maimonides, Menachem Begin, Albert Einstein, and Gilda Radner. " 'From their point of view, it's an article of faith, and from our point of view, it's a slap in the face,' said Rabbi Abraham Cooper, associate dean of the Simon Wiesenthal Center in Los Angeles" (Gladstone, www.jewishsf.com/bk021213/i50.shtml).

By late 2002, Jewish demands that all Jews be purged from LDS Church baptism records still had not been met (Peg McEntee, "Mormons Meet with Jews Over Baptizing Holocaust Victims," *Salt Lake Tribune*, Dec. 10, 2002, www.sltrib.com [archives]). Mormons were continuing to posthumously baptize "many deceased Jews, including thousands of Holocaust victims" (Gladstone, www.jewishsf.com/bk021213/i50.shtml)— despite a 1995 agreement signed by LDS officials to stop the practice: "Seven years after the church signed an agreement to do all it could to stop the practice, new evidence has emerged that the church's vast International Genealogical Index lists as many as 20,000 Shoah [holocaust] victims—and perhaps many more" (Gladstone, www.jew ishsf.com/bk021213/i50.shtml; cf. Julie Wiener, "Posthumous Baptisms Still An Issue," *The Jewish Week*, June 06, 2003, www.thejewishweek.com/news/newscontent.php3?art id=8043).

Meanwhile, however, LDS researchers were already prying into the death records of Orthodox Church members in Eastern Europe. The LDS church actually resorted to "paying an impoverished Russian archive US$0.10 a page for the names of dead people, to be used in its ritual" (Associated Press, "Russians fume at Mormon scheme to buy 'dead souls,'" *The [Moscow] Observer*, Monday, Nov. 24, 2003, p. 7, www.taipeitimes .com/News/world/archives/2003/11/24/2003077098; cf. Mark Thiessen, "Russian Orthodox Church concerned about proxy baptisms," *Salt Lake Tribune*, Dec. 6, 2003, www.sltrib.com [archives]). Nothing less than a furor erupted: "The Russian Orthodox Church has expressed its outrage at what it claims is a Mormon scheme to buy up the names of dead Russians in order to baptize '"dead souls"' in their faith....Father Igor Pchelintsov, spokesman for the local Orthodox Church, said: 'The teaching of the Mormons about the conversion of the dead contradicts reason and naturally causes concern among the faithful and creates a tense situation.'...Alexei Dvorkin, head of the Sectology Department of the Moscow St Tikhon Institute, said: '...At the beginning of this practice they were looking for their ancestors with the aim of baptizing them, but later they began to baptize everyone—Catholics, Muslims, Jewish, or Orthodox'" ("Russians Fume at Mormon Scheme to Buy 'Dead Souls,'" www.taipei times.com/ News/world/ archives/2003/11/24/2003077098; cf. Nick Paton Walsh, "Russians fume as Mormons 'buy souls,'" *The Guardian*, Nov. 23, 2003, www.guardian. co.uk/religion/Story/0,2763,1091340,00.html. Yevgeny Smirnov, LDS adviser to the Moscow region, sees no problem with his church's conduct. "Our church aims to create a database permitting people to look for their ancestors," he said. "Our ceremony is not rebaptism; it only gives the soul of the deceased person the freedom of choice to accept our belief or to reject it" ["Russians Fume at Mormon Scheme," www.taipei times.com/ News/world/archives/2003/11/24/2003077098]).

Then, in April 2004, it was discovered that Mormons were still posthumously baptizing Jewish Holocaust victims. This prompted the American Gathering of Jewish Holocaust Survivors (AGJHS) to begin considering legal action because the LDS Church had not upheld their end of the 1995 agreement (Ernest Michel. Quoted in Ian Urbina, "Rite for dead violates accord, group says," Dec. 22, 2003, *New York Times*, www.iht .com/articles/122369.html). Months earlier, however, Mormon officials had said that they had only agreed to remove the names originally found, but *never* agreed to "on a continual basis, go in and ferret out the Jewish names" (Ian Urbina, "Again, Jews Fault Mormons Over Posthumous Baptisms," *New York Times*, Dec. 21, 2003, www.rickross.com/reference/mormon/mormon135.html; and www.iht.com/articles/ 122369.html).

Ernest Michel, who helped negotiate the 1995 agreement on behalf of the AGJHS, argued in response, "'They put the names in there; they should have to take them out, and the agreement says as much,'" he said. "'Why should we have to do their job for them?'" (Urbina, www.rickross.com/reference/mormon/mormon135.html; and www.iht.com/ articles/122369.html). But in a Nov. 14, 2003, letter, LDS elder D. Todd Christofferson said that "the church did *not* agree to find and remove the names of all deceased Jews in its database of 400 million names. 'That would be an impossible undertaking,' Christofferson wrote" (Thiessen, www.guardian.co.uk/uslatest/story/0,1282,-39606 98,00.html).

97. Bill McKeever and Eric Johnson, *Mormonism 101* (Grand Rapids, MI: Baker Book House, 2000), p. 89.

98. Other Old Testament priesthood responsibilities included communicating God's law (Lev. 10:11; 2 Chron. 17:9); serving as judges (Deut. 17:9); and maintaining the nation's physical health (Lev. 13–15). These functions are listed in Richards, p. 504.

99. Richards, p. 464.

100. Richards, p. 468.

101. Bickmore, "Apostasy," www.fairlds.org/apol/morm201/m20106.html. Bickmore notes that "we would expect to find things in the Restored Church pertaining to the Mosaic dispensation, but not that of the New Testament Church."

102. Bickmore, "Apostasy," www.fairlds.org/apol/morm201/m20106.html.

103. Gordon B. Hinckley, "Words of the Prophet: 'Upon You My Fellow Servants,'" *New Era*, May 2002, p. 4, available at www.lds.org. The article declares that "in the exercise of our priesthood, we are acting in behalf of God our Eternal Father and Jesus Christ." *Gospel Principles* says that the LDS priesthood is "authority to act in the name of God to perform the sacred ordinances of the gospel....It is the power and authority by which those who are ordained to this power act in his name to do his work" (*Gospel Principles*, [SLC: LDSC, 1978; rev., 1979; Missionary Reference Library Edition, 1990], p. 73); cf. "The power and authority delegated by God to act in His name for the salvation of His children" (James E. Faust, *Ensign*, May 1997, p. 41, available at www.lds.org).

104. Angel Abrea, "A Divine Nature and Destiny," June 15, 1999, devotional address, http:// speeches.byu.edu/htmlfiles/AbreaSu99.html.

105. Bickmore, "Apostasy," www.fairlds.org/apol/morm201/m20106.html.

106. D. Guthrie and J.A. Motyer, eds., *The Eerdman's Bible Commentary* (Grand Rapids, MI: Eerdmans Publishing Co., 1989), p. 1241.

107. Guthrie and Motyer, p. 1203, emphasis added.

108. Guthrie and Motyer, p. 1203, emphasis added.

109. Bickmore, "Apostasy," www.fairlds.org/apol/morm201/m20106.html.

110. John J. O'Meara, tr., *Origen—On Prayer 28:9* (New York: Newman Press, 1954), p. 112 (This work is part of the *Ancient Christian Writers* series, vol. 19); as quoted in Bickmore, "Apostasy," www.fairlds.org/apol/morm201/m20106.html.

111. Spiros Zodhiates, gen. ed., *The Complete Word Study Dictionary* (Chattanooga, TN: AMG Publishers), p. 1365.

112. Kevin Graham, "Total Apostasy," Oct. 14, 2003, Internet post #883 at ZLMB.

113. Kevin Graham, "A Christian Responds," Oct. 15, 2003, Internet post #885 at ZLMB.

114. Peterson, "Random Reflections," author's private notes.

115. Peterson, "Random Reflections," author's private notes.

116. Gordon B. Hinckley, "Remarks at Pioneer Day Commemoration Concert," *Ensign*, Oct. 2001, p. 70, available at www.lds.org.

117. M. Russell Ballard, "Doctrine of Inclusion," *Ensign*, Nov. 2001, p. 35, available at www.lds.org. Ballard said, "Surely good neighbors should put forth every effort to understand each other and to be kind to one another regardless of religion, nationality, race, or culture....

"I have never heard the members of this Church urged to be anything but loving, kind, tolerant, and benevolent to our friends and neighbors of other faiths....[I]t has never been the policy of the Church that those who choose not to listen or to accept our message should be shunned or ignored. Indeed, the opposite is true. President Gordon B. Hinckley has repeatedly reminded us of this special obligation that we have as followers of the Lord Jesus Christ. I quote just one: 'Each of us is an individual. Each of us is different. There must be respect for those differences....We must work harder to build mutual respect, an attitude of forbearance, with tolerance one for another regardless of the doctrines and philosophies which we may espouse. Concerning these you and I may disagree. But we can do so with respect and civility' (*Teachings of Gordon B. Hinckley* [1997], 661, 665)....

"We must understand, however, that not everyone is going to accept our doctrine of the Restoration of the gospel of Jesus Christ. For the most part, our neighbors not of our faith are good, honorable people—every bit as good and honorable as we strive to be. They care about their families, just like we do. They want to make the world a better place, just like we do. They are kind and loving and generous and faithful, just like we seek to be....

"I now speak to all those who are not of our faith. If there are issues of concern, let us talk about them. We want to be helpful. Please understand, however, that our doctrines and teachings are set by the Lord, so sometimes we will have to agree to disagree with you, but we can do so without being disagreeable."

118. Marvin J. Ashton, "The Tongue Can Be a Sharp Sword," *Ensign*, May 1992, p. 18, available at www.lds.org. Ashton stated, "In the world today we are victims of many who use their tongues as sharp swords. The misuse of our tongues seems to add intrigue and destruction as the media and private persons indulge in this pastime. In the vernacular of the day, this destructive activity is called *bashing*. The dictionary reports that to bash is to strike with a heavy, crushing blow....

"We as members of the Church need to be reminded that the words 'Nay, speak no ill' are more than a phrase in a musical context but a recommended way of life. (See *Hymns*, no. 233.) We need to be reminded more than ever before that 'if there is anything virtuous, lovely, or of good report or praiseworthy, we seek after these things' (*AOF* 1:13.) If we follow that admonition, there is no time for the dastardly hobby of bashing instead of building....

"Some think the only way to get even, to get attention or advantage, or to win is to bash people. This kind of behavior is never appropriate. Oftentimes character and reputation and almost always self-esteem are destroyed under the hammer of this vicious practice. How far adrift we have allowed ourselves to go from the simple teaching 'If you can't say something good about someone or something, don't say anything' to where we now too often find ourselves involved in the bash business....

"It should come as no surprise that one of the adversary's tactics in the latter days is stirring up hatred among the children of men. He loves to see us criticize each other, make fun or take advantage of our neighbor's known flaws, and generally pick on each other. The Book of Mormon is clear from where all anger, malice, greed, and hate come....

"'The best and most clear indicator that we are progressing spiritually and coming unto Christ is the way we treat other people.'...Be one who nurtures and who builds. Be one who has an understanding and a forgiving heart, who looks for the best in people.

Leave people better than you found them. Be fair with your competitors, whether in business, athletics, or elsewhere. Don't get drawn into some of the parlance of our day and try to 'win' by intimidation or by undermining someone's character....

"If the adversary can influence us to pick on each other, to find fault, bash, and undermine, to judge or humiliate or taunt, half his battle is won. Why? Because though this sort of conduct may not equate with succumbing to grievous sin, it nevertheless neutralizes us spiritually. The Spirit of the Lord cannot dwell where there is bickering, judging, contention, or any kind of bashing....

"Once again may I emphasize the principle that when we truly become converted to Jesus Christ, committed to Him, an interesting thing happens: our attention turns to the welfare of our fellowman, and the way we treat others becomes increasingly filled with patience, kindness, a gentle acceptance, and a desire to play a positive role in their lives. This is the beginning of true conversion. Let us open our arms to each other, accept each other for who we are, assume everyone is doing the best he or she can, and look for ways to help leave quiet messages of love and encouragement instead of being destructive with bashing."

118. Roger Keller, Aug. 8, 2003, Q&A session at the 2003 FAIR Conference, author's private notes.

Appendix A: More on Polygamy

1. See *More Wives Than One* (Catherine Daynes, associate professor of history, Brigham Young University); *Mormon Polygamy: A History* (Richard Van Wagoner, clinical audiologist, BYU graduate); *Solemn Covenant* (B. Carmon Hardy, professor of history, California State University); and *In Sacred Loneliness* (Todd Compton, PhD, classics, University of California), to name but a few.

2. R.K. Harrison, "Polygamy," in Geoffrey W. Bromiley, gen. ed., *The International Standard Bible Encyclopedia* (Grand Rapids, MI: Eerdmans Publishing Co., 1986), vol. 3, p. 901.

3. D. Freeman, "Adultery," in Bromiley, vol. 1, p. 58.

4. Fordham quoting John A. Widtsoe, *Evidences and Reconciliations,* arranged by G. Homer Durham (SLC: Bookcraft, collector's ed. 4th printing, 1995), p. 390. Oddly, Fordham later notes as an aside, "Personally, I think the previously mentioned figure of 2%-4% is low, and that a more correct number of the total membership involved in plural marriage would be closer to 9%." One can only wonder, though, why Fordham would even bother to quote the 2%-4% figure, since he does not agree with it.

5. B. Carmon Hardy, *Solemn Covenant* (Urbana, IL: University of Illinois, 1992), p. 17.

6. Jeffrey Nichols, *Prostitution, Polygamy, and Power: Salt Lake City, 1847-1918* (Urbana, IL: University of Illinois Press, 2002), p. 17. Also see D. Michael Quinn, *Mormon Hierarchy: Extensions of Power* (SLC: Signature Books, 1997), p. 329; Richard Van Wagoner, *Mormon Polygamy: A History* (SLC: Signature Books, 1989), pp. 91-92; and Kathryn M. Daynes, *More Wives Than One* (Urbana, IL: University of Illinois, 2001), chapter 6.

7. Stanley S. Ivins, "Notes on Mormon Polygamy," in D. Michael Quinn, ed., *The New Mormon History* (SLC: Signature Books, 1992), pp. 170-171.

8. Fordham quoting Daniel H. Ludlow, ed., *Encyclopedia of Mormonism* (New York: Macmillan Publishing Company, 1992), "Brigham Young and His Twenty-One Wives" (photo caption), vol. 4, p. 1606.

9. Van Wagoner, p. 90.

10. Nichols, p. 17.

11. Daynes, pp. 191-192, emphasis added.

12. Van Wagoner, p. 96.

13. *Proceedings* (Washington, D.C.: Government Printing Office, 1904), vol. 1, p. 201.

14. Fordham, quoting *Brigham Young University Studies,* vol. 25, p. 97.

15. Van Wagoner, p. 90.

16. Compton, p. 199.

17. Melvin T. Smith, "Review of *The Autobiography of B. H. Roberts,*" *Utah Historical Quarterly,* www.signaturebooks.com/reviews/autobiog.htm.

18. Ann Eliza Web Young, *Wife Number 19* (Hartford, CT: Dustin, Gilman & Co., 1876), chapter 18, www.antimormon.8m.com/youngchp8.html.

19. Fanny Stenhouse, *Tell It All* (Hartford, CT: A.D. Worthington & Co., 1875), p. 522, www.antimormon.8m.com/fstenhousechp37.html.

20. Fordham, quoting Brigham H. Roberts, in Ben E. Rich, ed., *Character of the Mormon People: Scrapbook of Mormon Literature* (Chicago: Henry C. Etten & Co., 1913), vol. 1, p. 185.

21. Daynes, p. 128.

22. Eugene Campbell, *Establishing Zion* (SLC: Signature Books, 1988), p. 71.

23. Fordham, quoting Ludlow, vol. 3, p. 1094.

24. Ivins, p. 173.

25. See Ex. 20:8-11; 21:20,26-27; 23:9; Lev. 25:10, 39-43, 47-54.

26. David Waltz, "What About?" Apr. 4, 2004, Internet post at ZLMB.

27. Harrison, in G.W. Bromiley, vol. 3, p. 901.

28. Harrison, in G.W. Bromiley, vol. 3, p. 901.

29. *Polygamy merely mentioned:*

   • Sarai gave Hagar to Abram (Gen. 16:1-3)

   • Esau took his wives of the daughters of Canaan (Gen. 36:2)

   • Gideon had three score and ten sons and "many wives" (Judges 8:30)

   • "...and the lives of thy wives, and the lives of thy concubines" (2 Sam. 19:5, concerning David, king of Israel)

   • "...for he sent unto me for my wives" (1 Kings 20:7, concerning Ahab, king of Israel)

   • "Ashur the father of Tekoa had two wives" (1 Chron. 4:5)

   • "...for they had many wives and sons" (1 Chron. 7:4)

- Shaharaim had two wives (1 Chron. 8:8)
- "Reheboam...took eighteen wives, and threescore concubines" (2 Chron. 11:21)
- "Abijah...married fourteen wives" (2 Chron. 13:21)
- "Jehoiada took for him two wives" (2 Chron. 24:3)
- "If he take him another wife..." (Ex. 21:10—for more information on this second verse in Exodus, see previous discussion)

Polygamy only implied:

- "Hagar bare Abram a son" (Gen. 16:15)
- Jerubbaal had 70 sons (Judges 9:5)
- Jair, a judge in Israel, had 30 sons (Judges 10:3-4)
- Abdon, a Judge in Israel, had 40 sons (Judges 12:13-14)

Polygamy not even an issue:

- "God healed Abimelech, and his wife, and his maidservants" (Gen. 20:17). Regarding this verse, Fordham seems to think that God's healing of a pagan king's harem at the request of Abraham is somehow an endorsement of polygamy. But no such endorsement is actually present in the text.
- "Judah said unto Onan, go in unto thy brother's wife" (Gen. 38:8). This verse simply refers to Onan fulfilling the levirate marriage custom that called for a man to impregnate the wife of his *deceased* brother, if that brother had not had any children before dying.
- Moses married Zipporah, daughter of the priest of Midian (Ex. 2:21). This verse simply refers to Moses getting married. The related verse Fordham mentions—regarding the fact that Moses married an Ethiopian woman (Num. 12:1)—also is nothing but a reference to Moses getting married (see previous discussion). These two passages give no indication that Moses married the Ethiopian while Zipporah was still alive.

30. C.F. Keil and F. Delitzsch, *Commentary on the Old Testament* (Peabody, MA: Hendrickson Publishers, 1996), vol. 7, pp. 97-98.

31. "[T]he one-wife system not only degenerates the human family, both physically and intellectually, but it is entirely incompatible with philosophical notions of immortality; it is a lure to temptation, and has always proved a curse to a people" (John Taylor, *Millennial Star*, 1853, vol. 15, p. 227).

   "Monogamy, or restrictions by law to one wife, is no part of the economy of heaven among men. Such a system was commenced by the founders of the Roman empire.... Rome became the mistress of the world, and introduced this order of monogamy wherever her sway was acknowledged. Thus this monogamic order of marriage, so esteemed by modern Christians as a holy sacrament and divine institution, is nothing but a system established by a set of robbers....Why do we believe in and practice polygamy? Because the Lord introduced it to his servants in a revelation given to Joseph Smith, and the Lord's servants have always practised it. 'And is that religion popular in heaven?' it is the only popular religion there" (Brigham Young, *The Deseret News*, Aug. 6, 1862).

   "Those who are acquainted with the history [p.128] of the world are not ignorant that polygamy has always been the general rule and monogamy the exception. Since the founding of the Roman empire monogamy has prevailed more extensively than in times previous to that. The founders of that ancient empire were robbers and women stealers, and made laws favoring monogamy in consequence of the scarcity of women among them, and hence this monogamic system which now prevails throughout all Christendom, and which has been so fruitful a source of prostitution and whoredom throughout all the Christian monogamic cities of the Old and New World, until rottenness and decay are at the root of their institutions both national and religious. Polygamy did not have its origin with Joseph Smith, but it existed from the beginning" (Brigham Young, June 18, 1865, in *JOD*, vol. 11, p. 128).

"This law of monogamy, or the monogamic system, laid the foundation for prostitution and the evils and diseases of the most revolting nature and character under which modern Christendom groans" (Orson Pratt, Oct. 7, 1869, in *JOD*, vol. 13, p. 195).

"There might be circumstances and situations in which it would not be wisdom in the mind of God for His people to practice this principle, but so long as a people are guided by the Priesthood and revelations of God, there is no danger of evil arising therefrom. If we, as a people, had attempted to practice this principle without revelation, it is likely that we should have been led into grievous sins, and the condemnation of God would have rested upon us; but the Church waited until the proper time came, and then the people practiced it according to the mind and will of God, making a sacrifice of their own feelings in so doing. But the history of the world goes to prove that the practice of this principle, even by nations ignorant of the Gospel, has resulted in greater good to them than the practice of monogamy or the one-wife system in the so-called Christian nations....

"Where are the nations that have existed from time immemorial? They are not to be found in Christian monogamic Europe, but in Asia, among the polygamic races—China, Japan, Hindostan and the various races of that vast continent. Those nations, from the most remote times, practiced plural marriage handed down to them by their forefathers. Although they are looked upon by the nations of Europe as semi-civilized, you will not find among them woman prostituted, debased and degraded as she is through Christendom. She may be treated coldly and degraded, but among them, except where the Christian element prevails to a large extent, she is not debased and polluted, as she is among the so-called Christian nations. It is a fact worthy of note that the shortest-lived nations of which we have record have been monogamic.... [Rome] was a monogamic nation, and the numerous evils attending that system early laid the foundation for that ruin which eventually overtook her" (George Q. Cannon, in *JOD*, Oct. 9, 1869, vol. 13, p. 202).

32. Robert L. Millet and Richard L. Evans, "Review of Jon Krakauer's *Under the Banner of Heaven*," LDS Church Newsroom, available at www.lds.org. Millet and Evans write, "Thus plural marriage was a religious principle, not just a social experiment or a sexual aberration; this is the only valid and reasonable explanation as to why the practice was maintained in spite of decades of opposition and persecution. Latter-day Saints believed that plural marriages, when properly performed by authorized persons, were both legal and acceptable to God. Church leaders then and now are quick to observe, however, that monogamy is the rule and polygamy is the exception. Unauthorized practice of this principle is condemned in the Book of Mormon (Jacob 2:23-30, 34; 3:5), the Doctrine and Covenants (D&C 132:38-39), the sermons of Joseph Smith himself (*Teachings of*

454   Notes

the Prophet Joseph Smith, sel. Joseph Fielding Smith, Salt Lake City, Deseret, 1976, p. 324) and teachings of current Church leaders."

33. Brigham Young, June 18, 1865, in *JOD*, vol. 11, pp. 127-128.

Appendix B: Mormon Questions

1. To visit ZLMB, go to http://p080.ezboard.com/bpacumenispages.

2. I highly recommend ZLMB as a place to visit for those who want to interact with Mormons, learn about their beliefs, understand how they think, experience their take on life, or simply spend some online time with interesting people of faith.

3. It must be remembered that these are *very* brief replies. My hope is twofold: 1) that Mormons will at least understand evangelical thinking on various issues; 2) that evangelicals will have some brief answers to give Mormons who may be curious about those same topics.

4. See Robert Clouse, *The Meaning of the Millennium: Four Views;* Millard J. Erickson, *Contemporary Options in Eschatology;* Anthony A. Hoekema, *The Bible and the Future;* Oswald T. Allis, *Prophecy and the Church;* Gary DeMar, *Last Days Madness;* C. Marvin Pate, *Four Views on the Book of Revelation.*

5. See William Crockett, ed., *Four Views of Hell* (Grand Rapids, MI: Zondervan, 1992).

Appendix C: The Biblical Trinity

1. Walter A. Elwell, ed., *Evangelical Dictionary of Theology* (Grand Rapids, MI: Baker Book House, 1984; 1996 edition), p. 732; cf. Walter A. Elwell, ed., *Baker Encyclopedia of the Bible* (Grand Rapids, MI: Baker Book House, 1988; 1995 edition), vol. 2, p. 1485.

2. In *Christian Theology* (Grand Rapids, MI: Baker Book House, 1989), p. 329, Millard Erickson makes a particularly fascinating observation on a related passage: "According to Genesis 2:24, man and woman are to become one *(echad);* a union of two separate entities is entailed. It is significant that the same word is used of God in the *Shema.*...It seems that something is being affirmed here about the nature of God—he is an organism, that is, a unity of distinct parts."

3. Gleason Archer, *Encyclopedia of Bible Difficulties* (Grand Rapids: Zondervan, 1982), p. 359.

4. Concerning Jesus Christ, for example, he said that he would send his angels (Matthew 13:41), even though angels are commonly spoken of as God's angels (Luke 12:8-9; 15:10). Christ also forgave sins (Mark 2:5; Luke 5:20), even though God alone can forgive sins (Luke 5:21; Isaiah 43:25). He also said that he would judge humanity (Matthew 25:31-34), even though Scripture teaches that God will judge the world (Psalm 50:6; 98:9; Hebrews 12:23; James 4:12).

   Regarding the Holy Ghost, Luke 1:68,70 records Zacharias declaring: "Blessed be the Lord God of Israel;...[H]e spake by the mouth of his holy prophets." But then Paul stated: "Well spake the Holy Ghost by Esaias [Isaiah] the prophet unto our fathers" (Acts 28:25).

INDEXES

Bible Character Index
Person Index
Subject Index

Subject Index

OTHER BOOKS BY RICHARD ABANES

* **The Truth Behind the Da Vinci Code:**
  A Challenging Response to the Bestselling Novel

  "All descriptions of artwork, architecture, documents, and secret rituals in this novel are accurate." With these startling words, *The Da Vinci Code*—author Dan Brown's megaselling thriller—kicks you into high gear. After 454 nonstop pages, you've discovered a lot of shocking facts about history and Christianity...or have you?

  Award-winning investigative journalist Richard Abanes takes you down to the murky underpinnings of this multimillion-copy blockbuster that has confused so many readers. What do you really learn when the novel's assumptions are unearthed and scrutinized?

  - **The Code:** *Jesus was married to Mary Magdalene, whom he named leader of the church before his death.*
    The Truth: *This fantasy has no support even from the "Gnostic gospels" mentioned in the book, let alone from the historical data.*

  - **The Code:** *Since the year 1099, a supersecret society called "The Priory of Sion" has preserved knowledge of Jesus and Mary's descendants.*
    The Truth: *Today's "Priory of Sion" was founded in the early 1960s by a French con man who falsified documents to support the story of Jesus' "bloodline."*

  - **The Code:** *As a "Priory" leader and pagan goddess-worshipper, Leonardo da Vinci coded secret knowledge about Jesus and Mary into his paintings.*
    The Truth: *Da Vinci had no known ties to any secret societies. Any obscure images in his paintings likely reflect his personal creativity.*

  Probing, factual, and revealing, *The Truth Behind the Da Vinci Code* gives you the straightforward information you need to separate the facts from the fiction.

* **One Nation Under Gods: A History of the Mormon Church**

* **Harry Potter and the Bible: The Menace Behind the Magick**

* **Fantasy and Your Family: The Lord of the Rings, Harry Potter, and Magick in the Modern World**